Jennifer Westwood is a graduate of both Oxford and Cambridge. A specialist in Anglo-Saxon and Old Norse language and literature, she also belongs to the Folklore Society and the Viking Society. She has published several books for children drawing on myth and legend, including *Medieval Tales* (1967) and *Tales and Legends* (1971), and was a contributor to *The Faber Book of Northern Legends* edited by Kevin Crossley-Holland (1977).

JENNIFER WESTWOOD

Albion

A Guide to Legendary Britain

PALADIN
GRAFTON BOOKS
A Division of the Collins Publishing Group

LONDON GLASGOW
TORONTO SYDNEY AUCKLAND

Paladin
Grafton Books
A Division of the Collins Publishing Group
8 Grafton Street, London W1X 3LA

Published by Paladin Books 1987

First published in Great Britain by
Granada Publishing 1985

ISBN 0-586-08416-9

Printed in Great Britain by
St Edmundsbury Press Ltd, Bury St Edmunds, Suffolk

Set in Garamond

For Hodge and his master

Who would not treasure a fragment of Noah's Ark, a lock of Absalom's hair, Prester John's thumb-ring, Scheherezade's night-lamp, a glove of Caesar's or one of King Alfred's burnt cakes?

(Walter de la Mare,
Come Hither, 1923)

To save a mayd St George the Dragon slew –
A pretty tale, if all is told be true.
Most say there are no dragons, and 'tis sayd
There was no George, pray God there was a mayd.

('verses that I remember somewhere',
quoted by John Aubrey, *Remaines of
Gentilisme and Judaisme*, 1686–7)

Take yt on this condition,
Yt holds credyt by tradition.

(Francis Grose, *A Provincial
Glossary*, 1787)

Contents

Introduction

As junior fellow of his college, R. W. Revans was once obliged to find the evidence for settling two bets made in the senior common room:

> The first was as to whether so-and-so had ever been a fellow of King's College; my researches disclosed that he had in fact once been an assistant teacher in an elementary school in King's Road, Chelsea. The second was as to a remarkable dog owned by a long-defunct classical fellow of another college; the beast had been taught to speak Latin and conversed in the most agreeable fashion with any superior person who would open the conversation by enquiring after the animal's health. My researches showed that there was such a classical fellow, attended in his old age by a servant called Airedale, who had picked up a few tags of dog-latin which, for the price of half-a-pint of beer, he would recite.*

This anecdote, says Revans, demonstrates among other things the truth that 'simply talking about things, whether fellows of King's College or dogs that converse in Latin, may lead us into a willing self-deception'.

The garbling of fact in the interests of a good tale is just one of the ways in which legends and traditions come into being. Allied to it is rumour, springing from wrong assumptions, of which there is no better example, perhaps, than the Littlecote Scandal (p. 67). Here the legend followed almost immediately upon events, but sometimes memories have only slowly become occluded: hence stories which seem to be remnants of ancient mythology, such as that of Peg o'Nell (p. 392), or folk-memories of actual events, such

---

* R. W. Revans, *Action Learning* (London, 1980), p. 229.

as seem to underlie the legend of Stonehenge (p. 77). Then again there is what Christina Hole has called 'the universal itch to explain',* productive of stories to account for curious phenomena, as at Tewin (p. 154), for striking natural features such as The Wrekin (p. 322), or for place-names, for example Putney (p. 151). This last tale in particular illustrates the way in which stories of this sort come into being, not as naive explanations but as simple *jeux d'esprit* invented by storytellers.

It is easy to lose sight of the first storyteller and assume that a tale, like Topsy, just growed, especially if we fall victim to the delusion that all legends and traditions are ancient, and necessarily represent the quaint beliefs of rude forebears. As a matter of fact, many supposedly old tales are of comparatively recent invention – there are indeed visible periods of great activity in the manufacture of 'traditions', the late eighteenth to early nineteenth century, for example. But stories of such an origin are not to be lightly dismissed as bogus: legend-making is not something that took place only in the dim and distant past but a continuing process, and if it contains the right ingredients even a known fiction stands a fair chance of being accepted into oral tradition – such is the case of the 'Angel of Mons', a vision attested by many, though its history actually began with Arthur Machen's story 'The Bowmen'. And late or early, the motivations of the storytellers appear to be much the same, so that suddenly we see our supposedly naive forefathers as people as intelligent as ourselves, if less well-informed, creating stories for quite as sophisticated purposes.

To overcome the difficulties of accessibility which often make legends and traditions seem trivial and pointless, I have given them in rather full form and usually in the first recorded version; noted the fact if a tale conforms to a common pattern found elsewhere in Britain and sometimes abroad (a 'tale type'), and if it contains well-tried themes ('motifs'); taken stock of any visible pegs on which the story was hung, such as geographical features, place-names, monuments; as far as I am able explained matters of folklore and custom implicit in the tale and necessary to its understanding; and in the case of the more important legends discussed their repercussions and influence. By setting the stories in their context I

* Christina Hole, *English Folklore*, 2nd edn (London, 1944–5), p. xv.

hope to help the reader get better value from them, appreciating the skill with which generations of nameless storytellers attached a well-known tale to their own locality or, from nothing more than a rag, a bone and a hank of hair, concocted a new one.

The island of Albion, inhabited only by giants until Brutus renamed it Britain, is a storied land, but it is a fragile inheritance. '... the many good Bookes, and variety of Turnes of Affaires, have putt all the old Fables out of doors', wrote John Aubrey in the seventeenth century; 'and the divine art of Printing and Gunpowder have frighted away Robinn good-fellow and the Fayries.' Though we should not take this too much to heart – three centuries earlier, Chaucer says much the same thing, suggesting that fairies have always been, like fabulous monsters in the opinion of Sir Thomas Browne, 'Pieces of good and allowable invention unto the prudent spectator, but ... lookt on by vulgar eyes as literal truths' – Aubrey's point is an important one: that changing mental horizons reduce the hold on the imagination of certain sorts of story, leading sometimes to their loss. An essential precondition for the flourishing in oral tradition of some stories is, if not belief, then suspension of *dis*belief ('willing self-deception' as Revans calls it), which is why you will still find ghost stories alive and well in pubs, but are unlikely to hear tales of fairies. Similarly other traditions have fallen from grace because of changing physical conditions: street lighting and for all I know National Health spectacles have banished the bogey, and modern technology diminished the building feats of the Devil and his disciples. The anchors that once held many legends to their settings have been hoist so that they have drifted out of currency – locations like the Field of Forty Footsteps have been destroyed (p. 152) and 'proofs' of the truth of a tale swept away as so much lumber. Alas for the thighbone of Jack o' Legs, the Weston giant (p. 168).

With all this in mind, I have selected for this book of local legends and traditions not only famous and important tales but also lesser ones that have no life except in old records, often preferring one that seems to me to hold special interest to one that is better known. I have opted for variety and narrative content at the expense of comprehensiveness, and thus while I include several fully-fledged ghost stories, I exclude loose traditions of hauntings. By the same token, legendary witches find a place, but not, except by way of illustration, 'real' witches, witch-hunters and witch-trials. Because my concern is with the storytelling of the past, I have with rare exceptions limited my choice of tale to ones recorded before the end of the nineteenth century.

I have grouped the legends and traditions by region, both for the benefit of those who would like to visit the sites, and to bring out their special regional flavour. Where local government reorganization has cut across folklore boundaries – which tend to follow the geographical ones – I have not scrupled to ignore it, so that Herefordshire, for example, will be found in the Marches, but Worcestershire in the Heart of England. Wales, whose traditions are dominated by its unique national literature, I have treated as a unit; Scotland I have divided into two, reflecting the different imaginative temper of the English-speaking, Presbyterian Lowlands and the Gaelic Highlands. I ask the inhabitants of Orkney and Shetland to forgive me for numbering them among the 'Islands': in the entries themselves I have not ignored their distinctive Norse heritage. I hope that comparing regions will bring some surprises: most people, I think, will expect to find the greatest wealth of story in the Celtic areas, and may not be prepared for the rich diversity of, say, Yorkshire or Norfolk, whether this be a function of size or an accident of collecting.

Earlier this century a well-known zoologist pointed out that the recorded incidence of a species was directly related to the number of people studying it in the field. Certainly it looks as if the abundance of folklore in the Borders may have something to do with Sir Walter Scott and his activities as a purveyor of legend. How and by whom a tradition was recorded – whether a medieval chronicler or a poet, an antiquary, a diarist or a collector of folklore – clearly has a bearing on what construction we put on it, and to allow you to judge for yourself the quality of the record I have included notes on such men as Walter Map, Camden and Aubrey under Sources (p. 527).

For the rest, I hope that in attempting to unlock this storehouse of traditions having a local habitation I have not broken the butterfly on the wheel, but left you, in the words of Sir Philip Sidney, with 'A tale which holdeth children from play, and old men from the chimney corner.'

Acknowledgements

Though I take full responsibility for its mistakes, the credit for most of the spadework involved in this book goes to the many folklorists, historians, archaeologists and students of English and Welsh literature who have already worked the ground. First and foremost, I must record my obligation to the late Katharine Briggs, in particular to her books on fairy lore. Next, I would like to thank a number of scholars whose opinions I have merely summarized, notably A. D. H. Bivar, Rachel Bromwich, R. C. Cox, Dr Hilda Ellis Davidson, Ellen Ettlinger, L. V. Grinsell, Charles Kightly, F. J. North and Jacqueline Simpson. My use of their work is noted in the appropriate place. I am grateful to Mrs Bromwich and Cambridge University Press for permission to use the translation on p. 332; to V. Gordon Childe and W. R. Chambers Ltd for the extract on p. 283: to Carl Duerr for the chapter head on p. 527; to R. W. Revans and Blond & Briggs for the quotation on p. xi; and to the Estate of Lewis Thorpe and Penguin Books for the translations on pp. 348 and 363.

I have to thank the owners of a number of properties for time generously given: Peter Giffard of Chillington Hall; Neville Kemp, on behalf of R. Kemp of East Harling, owner of Oxfootstone Farm; N. Kerton of Higher Farm, Chilton Cantelo; Charles Legh of Adlington Hall; John McLeod of McLeod, of Dunvegan Castle; and Sir Seton Wills of Littlecote House. Others who have kindly given me local information are J. Leslie Allan of Melrose; Mr and Mrs J. Little of Welwyn Garden City (on Tewin); Mrs Mather of Kelso; Mrs Julia Moss of Oundle; Norman C. Reeves of Leominster; and John Stevens of Suffolk Herbs Limited, Little Cornard.

Sandra Unerman of the Folklore Society and Brigadier Peter Young of the Sealed Knot have given me the benefit of their advice, for which I here thank them. Special recognition is due to

Mr Arthur MacGregor of the Department of Antiquities, Ashmolean Museum, for his spirited and tireless search for Jack o' Legs.

A great many people have assisted me in their professional capacity: Mrs B. Atkinson, Burton Agnes Hall Preservation Trust Ltd; P. Bamford, Chester Library; F. H. P. Barker, Curator of Warwick Castle; Michael Boardman, Director of Leisure Services, Humberside County Council; Gavin Bowie, Hampshire County Museum Service; D. H. B. Chesshyre, Chester Herald; M. Farrer, Cambridge County Records Office; J. Foster, MoD: Lands; Margaret Fotheringham, East Midlands Tourist Board; Miss S. Gates, Central Reference Library, Lincoln; Colonel D. R. Gillies, C.A.D. Kineton; Richard Graves, Hereford & Worcester County Council; Nicholas Hall, Hampshire County Museum Service; H. A. Hanley, Buckinghamshire County Record Office; J. P. Haworth, National Trust; R. J. H. Hill, Hereford Library; Mrs P. W. Hind, Norfolk Naturalists Trust; Miss J. A. Holdworth, Ancient Monuments Administration, DoE; J. Hull, Oxford University Museum; Mrs I. D. M. Iles, Headmistress of Wroxall Abbey School; Berwyn Prys Jones, Translation Unit, Welsh Office; G. Kielsa, Snowdonia National Park; P. I. King, Northamptonshire Record Office; Mrs Lamb, Plymouth Central Library; Brian R. Lee, Director of Bisham Abbey National Sports Centre; K. McDade, Countryside Services, Hereford & Worcester; Mr Mackee, Wallace Collection; Dr Sue M. Margeson, Castle Museum, Norwich; Miss Matthews, Ipswich Public Library; Duncan Mirylees, Guildford Library; W. R. G. Moore, Central Museum, Northampton; Zoë Moore, Conservation and Land Division, Welsh Office; C. I. Morris, Gloucester Folk Museum; K. A. Odgers, Fitt Signs Ltd; Dr M. O'Sullivan, Staffordshire Records Office; D. R. Penrose, Agent for the Trustees of the Chatsworth Settlement; K. F. Raynor, City Health & Leisure Officer, Hereford; Miss A. E. Sandford, Museums Curator, Hereford; Howard J. Smith, Publications Unit, Birmingham City Museums and Art Gallery; R. G. Surridge, Islington Central Library; G. Swift, Director of Leisure, Wigan Metropolitan Borough Council; Ann Thackeray, National Portrait Gallery; J. Tubby, Norwich Brewery; David Viner, Corinium Museum, Cirencester; Peter Walne, Hertfordshire County Council Records Office; Rosemary Weinstein, Museum of London; Sister Winifred Wickens, Convent of the Holy Child, Mayfield;

J. F. Wilson, South Humberside Area Record Office; and Tim Wilson, National Trust.

Finally my thanks to the people who have been closely concerned with this book: to Richard Johnson, most patient of editors and cheerful through crisis; to Janet Bord, who generously spared time from her own books to read mine, and made many helpful suggestions; to Barbara Littlewood and Ann Wilson, who have combined professional advice with the stalwart support of old friends; and to Katie Fischel, who thought that she had come to type, but soon found herself cast in the role of universal factotum. This book owes her much.

As to what it owes to my husband, Brian Chandler – the dedication speaks for itself.

How to Use This Book

Sites are arranged alphabetically by region, mostly under their own names. Sites that no longer exist, however, or exist under other names, or are well-known only locally, are entered under the name of the place they are in and are best sought through the index.

Note that ancient monuments are listed under their own names followed by that of the civil parish, not the nearest place; and that place-names are often given in two different spellings, the old and the new. This is to help those who wish to follow up information in the National Monuments Register and old publications.

The maps preceding each region show the distribution of its sites. They should be used in conjunction with Ordnance Survey 1:50 000 maps. The sheet number at the head of each entry refers to the appropriate map, the four-figure grid reference accompanying it to the location of the site; four- and six-figure references within the entry pinpoint the story more precisely. I give six figures only when I judge them necessary, e.g. for sites marked only by generic names, such as 'Castle', on the map. Where a site is shown by name only on the OS 1:25 000 map, or where this is more helpful generally, I have said as much in the notes. OS 1:50 000 maps may be borrowed from your public library; OS 1:25 000 maps are normally not for loan, an exception being the Outdoor Leisure Series. Because most libraries' stocks of 1:25 000 maps are currently a mixed bag, I give sheet numbers only for the Outdoor Leisure and Pathfinder Series. The rule of thumb for finding which map you want in older series at this scale is to take the grid letters and the first and third figures of your four-figure reference, and look for that number.

Because *Albion* is a guide to legends rather than places, I have kept tourist information to a minimum. Times of opening are variable and subject to change, and except where the information is available only locally, I refer you to an appropriate publication. In the Notes:

AM = Ancient Monument (as defined by the Ancient Monuments Acts). Where these are accessible at 'any reasonable time' I have said so; otherwise consult the lists of historic monuments open to the public issued by the Historic Buildings & Monuments Commission for England (English Heritage), Cadw: Welsh Historic Monuments, and the Scottish Development Department.

NT, NTS = National Trust and National Trust for Scotland. Each issues an annual list of *Properties Open*, available from The National Trust, 36 Queen Anne's Gate, London SW1H 9AS, and The National Trust for Scotland, 5 Charlotte Square, Edinburgh EH2 4DU, as well as at NT/NTS shops. Properties not officially open to the public but accessible by custom can be found in the current *Properties of the National Trust* (or *National Trust for Scotland*).

HHC&G and M&G = *Historic Houses, Castles & Gardens* and *Museums & Galleries*, annually updated lists published by ABC Historic Publications and available from stationers. The former covers NT and NTS properties open to the public, as well as privately owned houses and castles.

Monuments and sites in civic ownership, including public parks, are normally readily accessible; many churches are now kept locked, but directions for getting the key are often posted in the porch. If this is not the case, enquire at the vicarage – visitors to the church are usually welcome. All other sites can be assumed to be on private land. Here consult the OS 1:25 000 Pathfinder Series: if public footpaths lead to or past the site, access is probably permitted by custom. Otherwise it is often worth asking locally for permission to visit. Please respect private property, not least because abuse of privilege can lead to the destruction of the site by justly indignant landowners.

I have often given legends and traditions in the exact words of my source. Sometimes I have thought it pedantic to 'translate' and only explained words of special difficulty. For the rest, if you go by the *sound* and not the *look* of the word, you will usually get the sense. The most important special letters used in the book are:

Þþ = *th* as in 'thing'   Ðð = *th* as in 'width'
Ȝ = *y* as in 'you'   ß = *ss*

Æ, æ = *a* as in 'Alfred' or *e* as in 'elf' (both spelled with æ in Old English). The name Æthelflæd under **Corfe Castle** (p. 60) should be pronounced with *e* to match 'Ethelred'.

I give detailed references only for specific arguments and opinions from modern writers. Authorities I refer to frequently may appear only as names and dates, for example 'Carew (1602)'. Who Carew was and what he wrote in 1602 is explained in Sources (pp. 527–37). I have also used the name-date system for a few nineteenth-century collectors. These will be found in the Bibliography (pp. 539–44). The dates that appear in the text after an author's name or the title of his book are intended to show when a tradition was current and so refer as near as possible to the time of writing. This will sometimes be a publication date; sometimes the date of a particular volume in a multi-volume work; sometimes the date of a letter or journal entry. Books which do not reappear either in Sources or the Bibliography can be assumed to have been published in their entirety in the year stated in the text, with a tolerance of one year to allow for the difference between title-page and registration date, a matter in which I have not thought it worth being consistent.

Albion

1

West Country

West Country

1 Athelney
2 Bath
3 Cadbury Castle
4 Cadbury Castle
5 Castle Dore
6 Chew Stoke
7 Childe's Tomb
8 Chilton Cantelo
9 Combe Sydenham Hall
10 Creech Hill
11 Dartmeet
12 Glastonbury
13 The Hurlers
14 Plymouth Hoe

15 Rillaton Barrow
16 St Just
17 Scilly Isles
18 Slaughter Bridge
19 Tavistock
20 Totnes
21 Trenrom Castle
22 Wistman's Wood
23 Zeal Monachorum

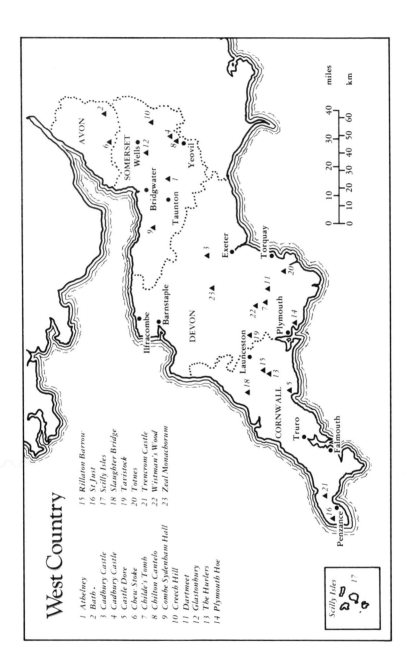

AVON

SOMERSET

Wells ●

Bridgwater ●

Taunton

Yeovil

Exeter ▲

Torquay ●

Barnstaple ●

DEVON

Ilfracombe ●

Launceston ▲

Plymouth ●

CORNWALL

Truro ●

Falmouth ●

Penzance

Scilly Isles

17

miles

km

0 10 20 30 40

0 10 20 30 40 50 60

In 878 A.D., the Anglo-Saxon Chronicle tells us, Danes of the
Great Army that had invaded England in 865 descended shortly
after Christmas on Wessex, taking the English by surprise, 'and
occupied the land of the West Saxons . . . and drove a great part of
the people across the sea, and conquered most of the others; and
people submitted to them, except King Alfred'. Alfred 'journeyed
in difficulties through the woods and fen-fastnesses with a small
force', perhaps only his bodyguard, falling back on Athelney, then
an island in the marshes. Here Asser takes up the tale. He had
heard from Alfred himself what hardships he had to face as a
homeless man in winter: 'He had nothing to live on except what he
could forage by frequent raids . . .'

   This picture of the first king of the English living like an outlaw
in the neighbourhood of Athelney is the background to the story
that everyone knows about him – 'How Alfred burnt the cakes'. It
happened one day that he had taken shelter in a herdsman's cottage
and was sitting by the fire, cleaning or mending his weapons, while
the herdsman's wife was baking loaves on the hearth. Suddenly she
saw the 'cakes' – they were probably barley bannocks – burning,
and fell to upbraiding the King:

   'Ca'sn thee mind the ke-aks, man, an doossen zee 'em burn?
   I'm boun thee's eat 'em vast enough az zoon az 'tiz the turn.'

The story comes from Asser's *Life of Alfred* written in 893 – the
original Latin here translated into English 'such as every housewife
in Somersetshire would understand'. Because it was thought to be
Asser's, the story of the cakes was long regarded as history, but it
is in fact an addition to Asser made in the sixteenth century by
Bishop Parker, who had found it in the twelfth-century *Annals of
St Neots*. These in turn got it from a Latin *Life* of St Neot,
composed in the late tenth or early eleventh century, and the story
seems to be an early folktale attached to Alfred's name a century
or so after his death when he was undergoing a wave of popularity
as *Engle hirde, Engle derling* ('shepherd of the English, darling of
the English').

   Not all versions of the story say that Alfred let the cakes burn, and we do not know what the point of the original tale was – did it show, not Alfred's preoccupation with his troubles, but the wretchedness of his estate, obliged to watch bread for his keep from a peasant? Or was it the old joke of a king hearing home truths from his subjects when he goes among them disguised – a theme popular in romances and traditional ballads, and attached to, among others, Charlemagne? Whatever its moral, Wiltshiremen thought enough of the tale to steal it and locate it at Brixton Deverill.

It was from Athelney in the spring of 878 A.D. that Alfred launched his counter-offensive against the Danes and won back his kingdom. He expressed his gratitude by building a royal monastery here, of which nothing now remains, but a tangible reminder of his connection with Athelney may be seen in the Ashmolean Museum, Oxford, in the shape of the Alfred Jewel. This was found about three hundred years ago at North Petherton, four miles from Athelney, and consists of a pear-shaped plate of rock crystal protecting the enamelled figure of a man believed to be Christ as Holy Wisdom or a personification of the sense of sight. The whole is encased in a gold band terminating in a boar's head, whose muzzle probably once held an ivory or wooden wand. Into the band are cut the words: AELFRED MEC HEHT GEWYRCAN, 'Alfred had me made', and the Jewel is thought to have been an *æstel*, one of the 'costly pointers' Alfred sent out with every copy of St Gregory's *Pastoral Care*, which he had translated into Old English for distribution among his bishops.

BATH, AVON   Sheet 172
(formerly SOMERSET)   ST 7564

> My grandsyre *Bladud* hight that found the *Bathes* by skill,
> A fethered King that practisde for to flye and soare:
> Whereby he felt the fall God wot against his will,
> And neuer went, roode, raignde nor spake, nor flew no more.

Thus Cordell in John Higgins's *Mirror for Magistrates* (1574). Bladud, her grandfather and the father of King Leir (see **Leicester**, p.236), was according to Geoffrey of Monmouth in the twelfth century the ancient British founder of Bath, who 'made hot Baths in it for the Benefit of the Publick'. He was, says Geoffrey,

... a very ingenious Man, and taught Necromancy in his

Kingdom, nor left off pursuing his Magical Operations, till he attempted to fly to the upper Region of the Air with Wings he had prepared, and fell down upon the Temple of *Apollo* in the City of *Trinovantum*,* where he was dashed to Pieces.

Geoffrey seems not to know another tradition concerning Bladud, that he was a leper who was cured of his disease by the medicinal mud in the hot springs at Bath. A tale no curiouser than his magical flight, which comes who knows whence? Perhaps from the classical legend of that other great artificer Daedalus (cf. **Wayland's Smithy**, p.278). It sounds as if the Roman spa of Aquae Sulis (Bath) so astonished the British that they chose to account for it as the work of a wizard, much like **Stonehenge** (p.77). It is perhaps worth noting that the Old English poem *The Ruin*, thought to be about Bath, describes it as *enta geweorc*, 'the work of giants'.

Roman Baths and Museum: Bath City Council. For times of opening, see *M&G*.

CADBURY CASTLE, CADBURY, DEVON

Sheet 192
SS 9105

Here you may see some fyve myle distant, to the south-east ... another down, called Dolbury-hill, between these two hills (you may be pleased to hear a pretty tale) that is said ... That a fiery dragon ... hath bynne often seene to flye between these hills, komming from the one to the other in the night season, whereby it is supposed ther is a great treasure hydd in each of them, and that the dragon is the trusty treasurer and sure keeper thereof ...

Thus Grose in his *Provincial Glossary* (1787) of the treasure supposed to lie in the hill-forts of Cadbury Castle (SS 913053) and Dolbury Hill (SS 972003). This was so great that a local rhyme boasted:

> If Cadburye-castle and Dolbury-hill dolven were,
> All England might ploughe with a golden sheere.

* Trinovantum – i.e. London (see **Guildhall**, p.133).

This is the rhyme as given by Grose, quoting Westcote's *View of Devonshire* (1630), but it was not the only version current by this date.

CADBURY CASTLE, SOUTH CADBURY, SOMERSET

Cadbury Castle is the best-known of the reputed sites of King Arthur's Camelot. It is, of course, not a castle in the Norman sense, but a hill-fort with four lines of bank and ditch defences, now partly overgrown by trees. As far as we know, the first person to identify it with Camelot was the antiquary John Leland in 1542. He wrote:

> At the very south end of the church of South-Cadbyri standeth Camallate, sometime a famous town or castle . . . The people can tell nothing there but that they have heard say that Arthur much resorted to Camalat.

Perhaps there *was* no local tradition, and Leland's own identification of the site was prompted by the names of Queen Camel (ST 5924) and West Camel (ST 5724), not far away. No matter. Camden swallowed it and in his *Britannia* (trans. Holland, 1610) says confidently: '*Camalet* a steepe hill, and hard to get up . . . The Inhabitants name it, King Arthurs Palace . . .'

In 1966–70, excavations were carried out here by the Camelot Research Committee to see if there were any truth in Leland's assertion. They discovered that the hill-fort had been constructed in the Iron Age, that the Romans had stormed it and evicted the survivors, and that during most of the Roman period it had lain empty. Then in the Arthurian years it was reoccupied. A large timber hall was built there, similar to the one at **Castle Dore** (p.10), and as at Castle Dore there was a great strengthening of the defences. Cadbury Castle was large, big enough to hold a thousand men, and was clearly the fortress of a person of importance. None of the other hill-forts reoccupied at this date can challenge it as a candidate for Camelot.

So were there local traditions that Leland was not told, or did he start something with his questions? A 'sleeping hero' tale may

King Arthur's Camelot: Cadbury Castle, South Cadbury, Somerset

have been attached to this earthwork since the sixteenth century, although in its earliest form Cadbury Castle is not mentioned, simply a hill near Glastonbury. Arthur, it is said, lies in the hollow hill or in a cavern closed by iron gates (in some versions golden ones). Sometimes they open, and then he can be seen inside. At the end of the last century, a party of antiquaries who visited the camp were asked by an old man of the neighbourhood if they had come to take out the king.

The tradition that Arthur was not dead, but would return, is mentioned by several medieval writers. Most of them attribute it to the Bretons – 'the Breton's lie' Robert Mannyng (1338) calls it – though Robert of Gloucester (*ca.* 1300) says that the Cornish also shared it. It was reported in the twelfth century that anyone who proclaimed in Armorica (Brittany) that Arthur had died like other men would be lucky not to be stoned to death. Likewise the chronicler Hermann of Tournai, writing in about 1146, tells us that in 1113 a party of nine French canons from Laon, after an adventure with a dragon at **Christchurch** (p.59), and a visit to 'Arthur's Oven', finally reached Bodmin, carrying with them the famous shrine of the Blessed Virgin that they had brought with them from France. A Cornishman with a withered arm kept vigil before this shrine, hoping for a cure, but got into an argument with one of the Canons' men about King Arthur. The Cornishman said he was still alive, but the servant did not believe him, 'whence a small tumult arose'. Others entered the fray and a brawl broke out in the church 'almost . . . to the shedding of blood'. The Cornishman did not get his cure.

As one would expect, the Welsh shared the Cornishmen's belief. In 1125 William of Malmesbury wrote that Arthur's grave was nowhere to be found, wherefore ancient ditties prophesied his return, while the person who continued Gaimar's *Estorie des Engles* (*ca*. 1150) says that in his day the Welsh threatened the Normans that they would finally win back their land with the help of King Arthur. Carried perhaps by Breton storytellers, the story of Arthur's survival spread far and wide: an Italian writer of *ca*. 1200 gives a model letter from a lecturer to his pupil, sarcastically telling him that he will graduate when Arthur comes to Britain, i.e. never.

Other leaders than Arthur have been expected back from the dead (see **Waltham Abbey**, p.162), but in his case the legend took three different forms. In the Arthurian romances of the twelfth century and later, he was borne to Avalon to be healed of his wounds, while from a Spanish writer, Julian del Castillo, in 1582, comes the statement that, according to common talk, King Arthur had been enchanted into a crow – a story that didn't escape Don Quixote. 'Have not your lordships read', says Don Quixote, 'the annals and histories of England, in which are recorded the renowned exploits of King Arthur . . . of whom there is an ancient tradition common in all that kingdom of Great Britain, that this king did not die, but by arts of enchantment, was transformed into a raven, and that in due course of time he will return to reign . . . for which cause it cannot be proved from that time to this, that any Englishman has ever killed a raven' (*Don Quixote*, 1605). This odd tale is indeed borne out by English tradition: in the eighteenth century, when a sportsman took a shot at a raven on Marazion Green, Cornwall, an old man rebuked him because the bird might be Arthur (see also **Tower of London**, p.158).

In many places, however, the legend of Arthur's survival follows the pattern of the 'sleeping hero' – the king or champion sleeps under a mountain or in a cave waiting to come to his country's aid in time of peril. In the fourteenth century this was told of Frederick

Barbarossa of Germany, who died in 1190 and was supposed to lie with six of his knights in a cavern under the Kyffhauserberg in Thuringia. Similar stories were told of Charlemagne, Henry the Fowler and the Emperor Henry V. Arthur himself was located in several places, not all of them in Britain. For example, Gervase of Tilbury, who visited Sicily in 1190, was told that the bishop of Catania's groom, searching for a runaway horse, entered a cleft in Mount Etna and there found Arthur lying wounded in a wonderful palace. In the nineteenth century, if not earlier, several caves in Wales were thought to house Arthur and his warriors, awaiting the day when they would come forth to recover their land; but the enemy English had him too – at Sewingshields, among other places (see under **Eildon Hills**, p.452). The legend of the sleeping king surrounded by his attendants goes back to classical times – the Roman historian Plutarch attaches it to an island near Britain, where, he says, the god Cronos was imprisoned and guarded by Briareus as he slept, surrounded by the deities who attended him.

In the nineteenth century there survived at Cadbury the idea that Arthur was the leader of the Wild Hunt, for an old track near the camp was called King Arthur's Lane and on wild winter nights he and his hounds could be heard rushing along it. The Wild Hunt, known in the Middle Ages to the peasantry of much of Europe, was in Welsh folk tradition led either by Arthur or by Gwyn ap Nudd, with whom he was often associated (see **Glastonbury**, p.21). In France, too, the Wild Hunt was known as 'la chasse Artu' from at least the twelfth century. Even if it was unknown at Cadbury in Leland's time, the tradition was itself a piece of genuine folklore and extremely old.

'Cadbury' is the name of several West Country hill-forts. Beware confusion not only with **Cadbury Castle, Devon**, (above) but also with the camp on Cadbury Hill, Congresbury (ST 443648), and Cadbury camp, Tickenham (ST 454725), both in Avon. 'Arthur's Oven' is by some identified with the King's Oven, a stone structure of uncertain date, perhaps the remains of a hut circle or pound, beside the highest stretch of the B3212 as it crosses Dartmoor. It was already well known as a landmark by 1240, and if it is the 'Arthur's Oven' the Canons saw, is one of the earliest recorded Arthurian sites. It is marked by name on OS 1:25 000 Outdoor Leisure Map 28, Dartmoor (North Sheet, SX 663803).

CASTLE DORE, ST SAMPSON, CORNWALL   Sheet 200
                                              SX 1054

Two or three miles inland from Fowey, reached by a track off the
B3269, is Castle Dore, an Iron Age hill-fort traditionally said to be
the court of King Mark in the tragic love story 'Tristan and Iseult'.
The connection of the area with the 'Tristan' legend is an early
one. The Anglo-Norman poet Beroul, telling the story in the
twelfth century, sets it near St Samson-in-Golant and says that
King Mark's palace was at 'Lancien', Lantyan or Lantyne, now a
farm a mile or two south of Lostwithiel (SX 1057). In the Middle
Ages, the manor of Lantyan-in-Golant included Castle Dore, so it
might have been the hill-fort itself that Beroul meant by 'Lancien'.

But King Mark's court is also located at the Mote of Mark, near
Rockcliffe, Dumfries & Galloway, while Tristan is believed to owe
his name to Drust, son of Talorc, a king of the Picts who reigned
in Scotland about 780 A.D. Moreover, a twelfth-century tradition
says that Tristan came from Lothian, and less than twenty miles
from the Mote of Mark is Trusty's Hill, 'Drust's' or 'Tristan's
Hill'.

The connection between this Pictish Tristan and the Tristan of
medieval legend is made in the Welsh *Triads*, where he appears as
Drystan, son of Tallwch, but is also said to be the lover of Essyllt,
wife of King March (Mark). Scholars believe that Drust was the
original hero of an episode in the Irish story 'The Wooing of
Emer', written down in the tenth century but probably in circulation during the ninth. The love story which forms the main plot
of 'Tristan and Iseult' came from another Irish tale, 'Diarmaid and
Grainne', which also existed already in the ninth century. Diarmaid
is the nephew of the chieftain Finn, and Grainne is Finn's young
wife. A magic spell causes her to fall in love with Diarmaid, and
she in turn places a spell on him which compels him to elope with
her. Finn pursues them into the forest, hunting them like animals,
despite which Diarmaid remains loyal to him, each night placing a
stone between himself and Grainne in bed. One day, when some
muddy water splashes Grainne's leg, she remarks that it is bolder
than Diarmaid. This breaks down his resistance and they become
lovers.

It tells us something about how a good story got about that it
seems to have been the Welsh who added this Irish tale to the

originally independent Pictish one of Drust, and perhaps also chose for the role of uncle the legendary King Mark of Cornwall, whose seat was at Tintagel (SX 0489), and who was celebrated in Welsh tradition as the hero (or rather victim) of a version of the classical story of King Midas and his ass's ears (see **Castellmarch**, p.335).

So far so good. But how did all this get to Castle Dore? Part of the answer is the Drustan Stone ('Long Stone', SX 112522) beside the A3082 leading down into Fowey. This is a monolith, now mounted on a pedestal and at present about seven feet (2 m) high, though it may once have been taller. It was found a little north of its present position and has had two or three changes of site: it was moved to this spot in 1971 from the crossroads opposite the lodge gates of Menabilly (SX 1051) once the home of Daphne du Maurier, who was to write her own version of the 'Tristan' story. It is still possible to make out faint signs of lettering on one face of the stone, traces of the Latin inscription DRUSTANUS HIC IACIT CUNO-MORI FILIUS, 'Here lies Drustanus, son of Cunomorus'. It evidently commemorates a chieftain or other notable person who died here, and is traditionally taken to mark the grave of the Tristan of legend. 'Cunomorus' is the Latin name of Cynfawr or Cynvawr, the historical ruler of Dumnonia, a British kingdom of which Cornwall was part, in the first half of the sixth century.

Excavation of Castle Dore carried out in 1935–6 suggested that, just as legend says, it was occupied in the Arthurian period. Located in a strategic position on a ridge down which an ancient track ran towards the sea, it was built in about the third century B.C. and used until the coming of the Romans, when it was abandoned. Like **Cadbury Castle, Somerset** (p.6), it was given a new lease of life as the stronghold of a Dark Age chieftain, who improved its defences and built a great timbered hall. This chieftain was almost certainly Cynfawr.

Now the *Life of St Paul Aurelian* (ninth century) says that Cynfawr was also called Mark; and in one of the Welsh *Triads* March or Mark is said to be, not the uncle, but the father of Tristan. Some Arthurian experts accept this as proving that Mark and Cynfawr were the same man, an historical person whose name in Latin may have been Marcus Cunomorus. According to this view, the fact that Tristan in the *Triads* is Mark/Cynfawr's son, not his nephew as in the romances, suggests that the story may at

Was this the gravestone of Tristan, lover of Iseult? The Tristan Stone, near Fowey, Cornwall

first have been one of rivalry between father and son over the father's second and younger wife (cf. the classical triangle of Theseus, Hippolytus and Phaedra).

Although this is very neat, and gives us both a real Mark and a real Tristan in the Arthurian period at Castle Dore, it does not explain the strong evidence for a northern Tristan. This can really only be accounted for by the assumption that the story of an originally Pictish hero was developed further in Wales; and that it was the gravestone at Fowey that drew the story south. The difficulty here is that of explaining what a Pictish royal name was doing in sixth-century Cornwall – unless Cynfawr himself knew the tale of an earlier Drust than the son of Talorc, and named his son after him.

Beroul's *Tristan and Iseult* has been translated by Alan Fedrick in Penguin Classics (Harmondsworth, 1970). Compulsory not to say compulsive reading for anyone interested in this site is *Castle Dor* (1962), a novel begun by Sir Arthur Quiller-Couch and finished by Daphne du Maurier, in which the tragic events of the Tristan legend are re-enacted here by another pair of star-crossed lovers in the nineteenth century.

CHEW STOKE, AVON
(formerly SOMERSET)

Although the church at Chew Stoke is now dedicated to St Andrew, it was once known as St Wigefort's and was the most important centre in this country of the cult of 'Maid Uncumber'.

St Wigefort, although entirely fictitious, still appears in the Roman martyrology as St Wilgefortis, said to have been the daughter of a king of Portugal. She had made a vow of virginity, and when her father wanted to marry her to the King of Sicily, prayed that she might be disfigured. Her prayers were answered and she grew a beard. The King of Sicily withdrew his offer, and her father, in a rage that his plans had been thwarted, had Wilgefortis crucified.

This outrageous story is based on a mistake. Wilgefortis is always represented as a bearded woman hanging on a cross, and her legend apparently grew out of a misunderstanding of one of the crucifixes showing Christ in a long robe, notably the Volto Santo of Lucca, of which copies were made and circulated throughout Europe. Although the Volto Santo was well known early in the Middle Ages ('by the Holy Face' was William Rufus's favourite blasphemy), the legend of Wilgefortis seems to belong almost to the eve of the Reformation. Her cult originated in the Netherlands and flourished, chiefly in England and Germany, in the fifteenth century.

At first she was mainly venerated as a saint who gave an easy death, without long suffering. For this reason she was known in southern Europe as Liberada, and in more northern lands as Kummernis, Comina or Ontcommene, names said to derive from German *öhne Kummer*, 'without anxiety'. In England these were taken to be something to do with 'encumbrance' and 'encumber' – 'In so moch that . . . women hath therfore chaunged her name and in stede of saynt wilgeforte call her saynt Vncumber bycause they rekone that . . . she wyll not fayle to vncomber theym of theyr housbondys' (thus Sir Thomas More). Among the altars dedicated to her was one at Old St Paul's – 'Poules' as Sir Thomas calls it in 1529, where 'women offer otys to saynt Wylgefort'.

> If ye cannot slepe, but slumber,
> Geve Otes unto Saynt Uncumber,

as it said in a sixteenth-century rhyme. But even Sir Thomas More failed satisfactorily to explain why oats were the price of freedom – a connection with *wild* oats is suggested. Whatever they symbolized, the oats offered to Uncumber expressed a real misery of the times – hers was not the only cult for getting rid of husbands (cf. **Winfarthing**, p.209).

CHILDE'S TOMB, LYDFORD, DEVON   Sheet 202
                                                SX 6270

Childe's Tomb is a stone cist on Dartmoor (SX 624703) to which has long been attached a curious tale. In his *Survey of Devon* (1605–30) Tristram Risdon writes:

> It is left us by Tradition that one *Childe* of *Plimstoke*, a Man of fair Possessions, having no Issue, ordained, by his Will, that wheresoever he should happen to be buried, to that Church his Lands should belong. It so fortuned, that he riding to hunt in the Forest of *Dartmore*, being in Pursuit of his Game, casually lost his Company, and his Way likewise. The Season then being so cold, and he so benummed therewith, as he was enforcd to kill his Horse, and embowelled him, to creep into his Belly to get Heat; which not able to preserve him, was there frozen to Death; and so found, was carried by *Tavistoke*-Men to be buried in the Church of that Abby; which was not so secretly done but the Inhabitants of *Plimstoke* had Knowledge thereof; which to prevent, they resorted to defend the Carriage of the Corps over the Bridge, where, they conceived Necessity compelled them to pass. But they were deceived by a Guile; for the *Tavistoke*-Men forthwith built a slight Bridge, and passed over at another Place without Resistance, buried the Body, and enjoyed the Lands; in Memory whereof the Bridge beareth the Name of *Guilebridge*, to this Day.

Later Risdon tells us that in the forest of Dartmoor were three remarkable things: Crocken Tor, where the Stannary court was held; **Wistman's Wood** (p.39); and Childe of Plymstock's tomb, 'whereon these verses were once to be read':

> *The fyrste that fyndes and bringes mee to my grave,*
> *The Priorie of* Plimstoke *they shall have.*

As Risdon says, the story is reminiscent of one told of Elsone, archbishop of Canterbury, who having spurned his predecessor Odo's tomb, was overtaken in the Alps by Odo's swift vengeance, being forced to try and warm his feet in his horse's carcass, yet at last dying of cold.

Dartmoor National Park. Use OS 1:25 000 Outdoor Leisure Map 28, Dartmoor (South Sheet).

CHILTON CANTELO, SOMERSET

Sheet 183
ST 5622

At Higher Farm, opposite the church, is a 'Screaming Skull' which according to a tradition current in the eighteenth century belonged to Theophilus Broome, who died in 1670 and asked that his head be kept at the farmhouse. In his *History and Antiquities of Somerset* (1791), John Collinson writes:

> At the north end of the transept is a stone with this inscription:- 'Here lyeth the body of Theophilus Brome ... who deceased the 18th of August 1670, aged 69. A man just in the actions of his life; true to his friends; forgave those that wronged him; and dyed in peace.' ...
> – N.B. There is a tradition in this parish, that the person here interred requested that his head might be taken off before his burial, and be preserved at the farm-house near the church, where a head, chop-fallen enough, is still shewn, which the tenants of the house have often endeavoured to commit to the bowels of the earth, but have been as often deterred by horrid noises, portentive of sad displeasure ...

A manuscript account of Brome's Head, apparently preserved at Higher Farm since 1829, contains statements from various parishioners confirming the tradition. 'Farmer Priddle and Edward Flooks', said Ann Dunman, 'remembered when the Scull was brought down stairs, and put in the Cupboard. Edward Flooks went to Yeovil, and bought a new Spade, and went to his Relation Mr. Clarke [the occupant of Higher Farm] who said "now Uncle Doctor, let us go and bury the Scull, when we have had a crust of

'Horrid noises portentive of sad displeasure' accompany attempts to move this 'Screaming Skull' at Higher Farm, Chilton Cantelo, Somerset

bread and cheese" he said no he would not; but after some time he went, but with an ill will, to bury it in the Churchyard. The Spade broke off at the first spit, and so they took it back again, he thought it presumptuous to attempt it, as the Man had begged that some part might be buried there and the rest in some other places.' Ann Dunman 'lived in the same House with Edward Flooks and had heard him say it several times'. She had also heard 'that Brome was a great Warrior, and begged that his Body might be laid in three Counties' – a theme also found in the lives of the saints (for example, St Oswald), and undoubtedly arising from the fact that their corpses were frequently dismembered for relics.

For another celebrated 'Screaming Skull', see **Burton Agnes Hall** (p.401).

Brome's Head may be seen by written appointment with the owners of Higher Farm, Mr and Mrs Kerton. His tomb is in St James's Church, beside the organ.

COMBE SYDENHAM HALL, MONKSILVER, SOMERSET

Sheet 181
ST 0737

In Spain Sir Francis Drake was known as *El Draco*, 'the Dragon', and was believed to be in league with the Devil. We might think this a matter of Spanish pride, had not the poet Lope de Vega in 1598 said that he had heard of Drake's commerce with the Devil from soldiers who had been in England as prisoners of war. Certainly in the same vein of superstition that makes us speak today of 'the luck of the Devil', there is an English tradition of transforming men whose rise to fame was, like Drake's, meteoric, into wizards – among them Cardinal Wolsey, Owen Glendower, Sir Walter Raleigh, and Cromwell.

There were several tales about 'Drake the Wizard' – 'all . . . of a wild and extravagant nature', says Mrs Bray (1832), who gives a variation on the famous story of the game of bowls. While Drake was playing kales (a sort of skittles) on Plymouth Hoe, he had news that a foreign fleet was sailing into the harbour, and after finishing his game, gave orders for a hatchet and a large block of timber to be brought. He chopped the wood up into smaller blocks and with some magic words threw them into the sea. As they touched the water, each of them became a fireship that sailed against the fleet and utterly destroyed it.

Another story told by Mrs Bray is that in Drake's day there was no fresh water in Plymouth, and the housewives had to go all the way to Plympton to wash their linen. Sir Francis decided to cure this, and one day called for his horse and rode off on to Dartmoor, where he hunted about for a spring. When he found one to his liking, he spoke a magic word and headed for home as fast as he could gallop, the spring following hard on his horse's heels all the way back. In fact Drake *did* bring water from Dartmoor to Plymouth, cutting an open leat or canal whose course may still be traced. This historical event has been recast in the light of the magical control of rivers exercised by such wizards as Michael Scot (and cf. the story of Llyn Lech Owen, under **Cardigan Bay**, p.332).

A tale that left a tangible memorial was one attached to Combe Sydenham Hall, home of the Sydenhams from the fourteenth century to 1730. Drake married the only surviving daughter of Sir George Sydenham, and the story goes that when he sailed off in the *Pelican* to circumnavigate the world, he was away so long that she despaired of seeing him again. After seven years she decided to remarry, but as the wedding party gathered in the church, one of the spirits that served Drake brought him the news in the Antipodes. At

once he took a cannon and fired it down into the sea, and so true
was his aim that the ball sped right through the globe and fell with
a bang between bride and groom as they reached the altar. 'It is
Drake's signal,' his lady exclaimed, 'I am still a wife', and calling
off the wedding went home to await his return.

This is a version of the widespread tale 'The Homecoming
Husband', at least as old as Homer, who tells it of Odysseus and
Penelope. 'Drake's cannon-ball' was for many years displayed at
Combe Sydenham (although apparently not in Mrs Bray's time)
and various traditions became attached to it: that it would roll in
times of national danger (probably from confusion with Drake's
Drum) and that, if taken away, it would return to the house of its
own accord, like 'self-returning' stones (cf. **Corngafallt**, p.336).

'Drake's cannon-ball', said by some to be a meteorite, though this is
uncertain, can once again be seen at Combe Sydenham Hall, south of
Watchet on the B3188, after a spell in the Somerset County Museum. For
times of opening, see *HHC&G*. Drake's Drum is kept at his home,
Buckland Abbey in Devon (Sheet 201, SX 4866), now run by the Plymouth
City Council as a museum. Opening times in *M&G*. The idea that the
Drum will summon Drake seems to date only from Henry Newbolt's
poem 'Drake's Drum', first published in the *St James's Gazette*, 1895. But
Robert Hunt (*Popular Romances of the West of England*, 1865) was told
by the former housekeeper of Buckland Abbey 'if the warrior hears the
drum . . . he rises and has a revel', and there was at about the same time
current in Devon a belief that the Drum had rolled of its own accord
before the Battle of Trafalgar.

CREECH HILL, SOMERSET   Sheet 183
                                                ST 6636

A farmer coming home late one night by way of Creech Hill saw a
figure lying in the road and went to its help. But as he reached it, it
shot up to more than human height and chased him all the way
home. His family ran out to help him and saw it bounding off up
the hill, shrieking with laughter.

It was a 'bullbeggar', a word for a bogey that goes back to the
sixteenth century, although the one in this story, collected in 1906,
probably only became attached to Creech Hill after the 1880s,

when two crossed bodies, supposed to be a Saxon and a Norman, were dug up during quarrying here. After this Creech Hill was held to be haunted by following footsteps and a black uncanny shape (cf. the Black Dog under **Bungay**, p.176).

Fiendish glee seems to be characteristic of this particular bogey – the similarly named galley-beggar of the two Stoweys used on dark winter nights to slide down the hill between Over and Nether Stowey (ST 1838 and ST 1939), sitting on a hurdle and hooting with merriment.

The Creech Hill bullbeggar is something between a bogle and a ghost, and its shooting up to an unnatural height belongs to the same tradition as that of the 'ghost' in Fletcher and Shirley's *The Night Walker* (1640, 1661):

> NURSE What's that that moves there . . .
>   That thing that walks.
> TOBY Would I had a Ladder to behold it . . .
>   I have no power to pray, it grows still longer,
>   'Tis Steeple high now, and it sayls away Nurse . . .
>   The Ghost three stories high, he has the Nurse sure,
>   He is boyling of her bones now, hark how she whistles.

The 'ghost' in the play is fortunately only one rogue standing on another's shoulders, but of course the imposture couldn't be expected to work – or make the audience laugh – if it hadn't been a common article of belief (cf. the spriggans of **Trencrom Castle**, p.37).

DARTMEET, DEVON

Sheet 180
SX 6772

Mrs Bray, writing to Robert Southey in 1832, describes the habits of the pisgies or pixies, the West Country fairies, of which the most notorious was 'pixy-leading': 'Many . . . are sent forth to lead poor travellers astray, to deceive them with those false lights called Will-o'-the-wisp, or to guide them a fine dance in trudging home through woods and waters, through bogs and quagmires, and every peril . . .'

A tragic story of a lad pixy-led on Dartmoor was attached to

Rowbrook Farm (SX 684725), near Dartmeet, a solitary farm on the side of the hill from which Sharp Tor rises. One winter evening, a lad who worked on the farm heard a voice calling from a distance, 'Jan Coo! Jan Coo!' He brought the other farmhands out into the yard to listen, but at first they could hear nothing but the rushing of the river. Then after a while they, too, heard it: 'Jan Coo! Jan Coo!' The next night they heard it again, and after that not a night passed but as soon as they sat down to supper the call came: 'Jan Coo! Jan Coo!' And every time, as soon as they answered, the voice fell silent and did not call again.

Towards the end of winter, as the lad and another hand were making their way home one night, they heard the voice coming from over the river, out of Langamarsh Pit. The boy shouted back, but this time the calls did not cease. Again came the cry, louder than before, and the boy started to run towards it, despite anything his companion could do, downhill towards the river. The other continued homeward, the voice still coming from Langamarsh Pit: 'Jan Coo! Jan Coo!' As he approached the farm, he heard it call again, and again as he neared the door: 'Jan Coo! Jan Coo!' Then it fell silent. The mysterious voice was never heard again, nor did the boy return. As no trace of him was found, it was commonly assumed that he had been 'led' by the pixies.

William Crossing, who tells the story in his *Tales of the Dartmoor Pixies* (1890), remarks that sceptics would say the voice was that of an owl, and that the boy had fallen into the river and been drowned, proving the truth of the rhyme:

> River of Dart, oh river of Dart,
> Every year thou claim'st a heart.

The contributor of this rhyme to *Notes & Queries*, 28 December 1850, writes:

> It is said that a year never passes without the drowning of one person, at least, in the Dart. The river has but few fords, and, like all mountain streams, it is liable to sudden risings, when the water comes down with great strength and violence . . . The moormen never say '*the* Dart,' but always 'Dart'. 'Dart came down last night – he is very full this morning.' The *cry* of the river is the name given to that louder sound which rises towards nightfall.

By other writers it is said that in certain conditions of the wind at Huccaby bridge (SX 659729) was heard a wailing cry followed by a fearful shriek locally regarded as the voice of the river demanding a victim.

Although Jan Coo's disappearance is in the story laid at the door of the pixies, the key to it is this traditional personification of the river and its 'cry'. The closest parallels to it are found in versions of a widespread story, 'The Hour has come, but not the Man', in which a voice from the river is heard to repeat this refrain until the arrival of its appointed victim (see **Conon House**, p.493).

Dartmoor National Park. Use OS 1:25 000 Outdoor Leisure Map 28, Dartmoor (South Sheet).

GLASTONBURY, SOMERSET

Sheet 182
ST 5039

In his *History of the Kings of Britain* (*ca.* 1136), Geoffrey of Monmouth says that King Arthur, 'mortally wounded' at his last battle of Camlann, was carried off to the Isle of Avalon to be healed of his wounds. Geoffrey probably got the name 'Avalon' from a French source, but was one of several medieval authors who connected it with the British word *aval*, meaning 'apple'. In Welsh texts the island is always called *ynys avallach*, taken by some both then and now to mean 'isle of apple trees', but another explanation of the name in medieval times was that it was the 'isle of Avallach', referring to the ruler of the island, who lived there with his daughters, including Morgan. Many modern scholars agree with this, saying that, whatever people later took it to mean, *avallach* was originally the same name as Aballac and Aballach, in early Welsh literature identified as the father of Modron, mother of the hero Owein. According to this view, the name was misinterpreted by Breton storytellers – Gerald of Wales (*ca.* 1216) and Gervase of Tilbury (*ca.* 1212) both seem to attribute to the Bretons rather than the Welsh the tale of how Arthur was taken to Avalon by Morgan le Fay – and in a sense the story was coming home, for the tale of an isle of nine enchantresses who cured the ills of those who sought them was attached by the classical geographer Pomponius Mela (fl. 40 A.D.) to the island of Sein, off the coast of

Armorica (later Brittany). At all events, the Bretons took the 'island of Avallach' of Welsh tradition to be a place-name, which they proceeded to confuse with Avaellon in Brittany, or the more famous Avallon in Burgundy, at the same time substituting for the Welsh goddess Modron their own water-spirit Morgan.

From the twelfth century onwards, this mythical isle, one of several Celtic Otherworld islands, was identified with Glastonbury. In early times Glastonbury was the next best thing to an island, the Tor, the present Abbey site and Wearyall Hill probably being almost entirely surrounded by water – Iron Age lake villages have been found on the road to Godney (ST 4842) and at Meare (ST 4541). There was a tradition that Christianity had reached it early, and it was associated with several Celtic saints. There was a Celtic monastic settlement on the summit of Glastonbury Tor, and when the Saxons arrived, they found on the present Abbey site what they called the 'Old Church', a structure of wattle and daub whose origins were already so dimmed by time that in the tenth century a tradition sprang up that it had been built by God himself (a tradition that led ultimately to Blake's 'Jerusalem' and the legend of Joseph of Arimathea and the Holy Thorn). To its ancient cemetery, which already contained the bones of St Patrick, St Indract and St Gildas, they added the remains of two kings, Edmund the Elder and Edmund Ironside. The Celtic conception of the Otherworld island had its origin in – or perhaps gave rise to – actual islands of the dead, and the island of Glastonbury, with its ancient cemetery, had all the qualifications.

People of Celtic stock used to call Glastonbury *Ineswitrin*, and that this was its original name was first mooted by Caradoc of Llancarvan, who in his *Life of St Gildas*, early in the twelfth century, says: 'Glastonia . . . that is, the glassy city, which took its name from *glass*, is a city that had its name originally in the British tongue.' He (or someone adding a note) later explains that this British name was 'Ynisgutrin', 'island of glass', which the English translated as 'Glastigberi'. In fact the reverse seems to be true: the original name which Caradoc latinizes as 'Glastonia' is thought to have contained the old Celtic and Gaulish word for woad, and to have meant 'the place where woad grew'. The Anglo-Saxons subsequently settling here called themselves *Glæstingas*, 'the people of Glastonia', and from this came *Glastinga ieg*, 'the island of the

Glastingas', the form of the name in the eighth century. On the mistaken assumption that it had something to do with glass, the British by the ninth century had translated the Old English name back into their own tongue as *Ineswitrin*, the Isle of Glass.

If this is so, Glastonbury was probably first connected with the Celtic Otherworld because of the pull of Arthurian legend. Some say the identification was helped along because there already existed in Welsh tradition a City of Glass. A poem known as 'The Spoils of Annwfn', probably pre-Conquest, describes an expedition led by Arthur to a city or fortress called by various names – it is Caer Siddi, 'the Fairy City', and also Caer Wydr, 'the City of Glass' – but evidently the same place as Annwfn, the Celtic Otherworld. The purpose of the raid was to carry off a magic cauldron tended by nine maidens. The resemblance of the City of Glass with its nine maidens to Avalon, which Geoffrey of Monmouth says in his *Life of Merlin* (*ca*. 1149) was the abode of nine sorceress-queens, could have led to their being identified by false logic. Stranger coincidences exist in legend and folklore, but it is also possible that Caer Wydr is not an ancient idea, and that it is and always was 'Glastonbury' (with OE *burh*, 'fort').

However this may be, Glastonbury Tor, in particular, came in Welsh tradition to be associated with Annwfn, and with Annwfn's lord, Gwyn ap Nudd, in later tradition the fairy king. Gwyn was king 'under the hill', associated in Wales with high places such as the hill-fort of Caer Drewyn near Corwen, whose name seems to come from *tref Wyn*, 'the homestead of Gwyn'. And it was on the eminence of Glastonbury Tor that he was encountered by Collen, the sixth-century wandering saint who gave his name to Llangollen. Collen had come to live as a hermit in a cell on the Tor, and one day overheard two men talking of Gwyn, who had his palace there. He rebuked them for speaking of devils, whereupon they warned him that Gwyn would not overlook such an insult, and would certainly send for him. Sure enough, a few days later, a messenger came to Collen's cell to invite him to visit Gwyn. Three times the saint refused, but at last agreed to go, though taking the precaution of hiding a flask of holy water under his cloak. He entered the hill by a secret door and found himself in a wonderful palace, where Gwyn sat in a golden chair. The king offered him food, but Collen refused it, no doubt because he knew that fairy

The fairy dwelling in the mound: Glastonbury Tor, Somerset

food was perilous (see **Orford Castle**, p.186). 'I do not eat the leaves of a tree,' he said, and after further boorish remarks sprinkled his holy water about him. King and palace vanished forthwith, and Collen found himself, like True Thomas (p.454), alone on the cold hillside.

In this story, from a *Life* of St Collen written in the sixteenth century, Gwyn is already the king of the fairy mound, as in eighteenth-century Welsh tradition, but in origin he was a god – the son of Nudd, the British god who as Nodens was honoured in a shrine at Lydney (SO 6012). He was early connected with Arthur, for example in the tale of the hunting of the great boar Twrch Trwyth (see **Corngafallt**, p.336) and has probably been drawn south along with Arthur because of Glastonbury Tor's hilltop site and the drifting together of different strands of lore about the Celtic Otherworld.

The identification of Glastonbury with Avalon led in about 1191 to the monks of Glastonbury making 'strenuous efforts' to find the grave of Arthur – which they duly did. 'It was the King himself who put them on to this,' remarks Gerald of Wales, meaning Henry II, and common sense may say that this was a monkish 'plant' on behalf of the King. Henry had trouble with the Welsh and might well have wanted to scotch the nationalistic rumours of Arthur's return to liberate Wales (see **Cadbury Castle, Somerset**, p.6), perhaps in the person of his grandson Arthur, son of

Constance of Brittany (where the legend of Arthur's survival had a stronghold).

To each according to his needs, however: there is enough room for doubt to enable those seeking an historical Arthur to believe he was buried here. At the same time, those who cherish the tradition of the Once and Future King can take comfort from the fact that the finding of Arthur's grave abated not one jot belief in his survival, reported as early as 1113, and still apparently held in the nineteenth century at Cadbury Castle. As the Black Book of Carmarthen says, 'concealed till Doomsday the grave of Arthur'.

Glastonbury Tor: NT. Well House Lane, off the A361 to Shepton Mallet, leads to both public paths up the hill. At Glastonbury Abbey itself, the site of Arthur's original grave is about fifty feet (15 m) from the south door of the Lady Chapel. The authenticity of the claim that it was Arthur's rests solely on the lead cross found in it, and the chances are that this was a forgery. The evidence is admirably laid out (though one may disagree with his conclusions) by Leslie Alcock in *Arthur's Britain* (Pelican, Harmondsworth, 1973; repr. 1975). Lydney Park, Gloucestershire, is open to the public – for times, see *HHC&G*. Besides the Roman temple-complex dedicated to Nodens, there are gardens and a museum.

THE HURLERS, LINKINHORNE, CORNWALL   Sheet 201
SX 2571

On Craddock Moor, near Minions, are three stone circles of thirteen, seventeen and nine surviving stones, which go by the name of 'The Hurlers'. Erected in the Bronze Age for purposes unknown, their name refers to a tradition mentioned by Camden (trans. Holland, 1610) that 'they had beene men sometime trans-formed into stones, for profaning the Lords Day, with hurling . . .'

Hurling matches, which were peculiar to Cornwall, were played between two teams, often two parishes, with forty to sixty men a side. It was a rough game, the object of which was to get the wooden ball when it was 'dealt' and carry it off to one's own goal, sometimes three or four miles distant. Robert Hunt in *Popular Romances of the West of England* (1865) says that until shortly before his own time it was commonly played on a Sunday after-noon. It was the distribution of The Hurlers that suggested the name – 'fixed in suche straglinge manner as those Countrye men doe in performinge that pastime *Hurlinge*' (Norden, 1584).

Dr James Yonge the Plymouth surgeon, writing in 1675, says of the Hurlers that 'they are now easily numbered, but the people have a story that they never could, till a man took many penny loaffes, and laying one on each hurler, did compute by the remainder what number they were'. The 'countless stones' tradition is attached to several megalithic sites in Britain – it is also mentioned in the sixteenth century for **Stonehenge** (p.77) and in the seventeenth for Stanton Drew. It is probably connected with the superstition attached by Nennius to the grave of Anir, 'son of Arthur the soldier', at Gamber Head, Llanwarne (Hereford & Worcester) – 'and men come to measure the tumulus, sometimes six feet in length, sometimes nine, sometimes twelve, sometimes fifteen. In what measure you should measure it in its turn, the second time you will not find it in the same measure, and I have tested it myself.'

The 'baker and loaves' story itself is reported for Stonehenge by Defoe in 1724, and in the nineteenth century for Little Kit's Coty (see **Kit's Coty House**, p.108), sometimes known as the Countless Stones.

AM (any reasonable time). Reached by a track off the minor road through Minions (SX 2671).

Turned to stone for hurling on Sunday: the Hurlers, Bodmin Moor,
Cornwall

PLYMOUTH HOE, DEVON

The story of 'Gogmagog's Leap', traditionally located at Plymouth Hoe, is first told by Geoffrey of Monmouth in about 1136. Geoffrey says that Brutus, the great-grandson of the hero Aeneas, came to Albion with his men, and because of its fruitfulness decided to settle here. He renamed the island Britain (supposed by Geoffrey to derive from 'Brutus') and drove the giants who inhabited it into the mountains of the west. One day when he and his followers were holding a festival at the port where they first landed, a party of giants attacked them. They fought back and killed all the giants except for one named Gogmagog who was twelve cubits high and could wield an uprooted oak as easily as a hazel wand. Him they kept alive to wrestle with Corineus, Duke of Cornwall, who, when Brutus was parcelling out the land of Britain amongst his followers, had chosen for his share the rocky land that came to be named after him, because he loved nothing so much as to wrestle with giants, and there were more of them in Cornwall than elsewhere. When the two opponents came to grips, Gogmagog hugged the Duke to him in so tight an embrace that three of his ribs were broken. Corineus was so enraged that he at once rushed to the nearest stretch of shore and hurled Gogmagog off the cliff to his death on the rocks below. The place at which this happened was thereafter known as Gogmagog's Leap.

'As for that rock, whence they say, this giant was cast down, it is now called the *Haw*', says Camden (trans. Holland, 1610) in his description of 'Plimmouth', although Weever in 1631 knew a different tradition in which Gogmagog fell 'from one of the rocks not farre from Dover'. However, there had been the figure of a giant cut into the chalk of the Hoe, evidently on the seaward slope just below the Citadel, at least since the closing years of the fifteenth century. The Plymouth Corporation audit book contains several entries concerning its maintenance, for example:

1541 It[em] P[ai]d to William Hawkyne, Baker, for cuttyng of
Gogmagog, the pycture of the Gyaunt at Hawe   8d

By 'cuttyng' is meant what in other entries is termed 'new cutting' or 'makyng clene', i.e. the periodic 'scouring' necessary to keep the outlines clear of weeds such as was carried out at other hill-figures, for example the White Horse at Uffington, Oxfordshire, often with some ceremony.

From this entry for 1541 it is clear that there was then only one figure, which was normally (though not here) referred to as 'the Gogmagog', as if this were the name for a particular type of giant. But by 1602, when Carew published his *Survey of Cornwall*, there were evidently two figures, which he describes as 'the pourtrayture of two men, the one bigger, the other lesser, with clubbes in their hands (whom they terme *Gog Magog*)'. Carew's statement is unsupported except by Westcote (1630), who may simply have copied him, but it is unlikely that Carew was mistaken – he lived at Antony House, on the other side of Plymouth Sound. It is possible that the second figure was cut for some special celebration. The last entry in the audit book concerning the Gogmagog is in 1566–7, and it is thought that, whether there was one figure or two, they ceased to be maintained round about Carew's time and were finally destroyed by the construction of the Citadel in the reign of Charles II.

There is no evidence that the turf-cut figure at Plymouth Hoe was an ancient one. From the Plymouth records one would guess that it came into being in the same wave of enthusiasm for Geoffrey's alternative history of Britain that led to the Elizabethan and early Jacobean plays of *Gorboduc, King Lear* and *Cymbeline* (and see **Guildhall**, p.133, and **Wandlebury Camp**, p.202). But where did Geoffrey get the story? There is no way of knowing how much of his work derives from an ancient book as he claimed, and how much he simply made up. The background to this tale is the tradition of the Trojan descent of the British – a claim made first for Charlemagne, King of the Franks, in the eighth century, and subsequently for the Saxons, Normans and Danes. After Geoffrey (and quite possibly because of him) all British history books up to the seventeenth century began with Brutus. As his name was held by false etymology to account for 'Britain', so 'Corineus' was invented to account for 'Cornwall' – perhaps by Geoffrey himself. The prevalence of giants in Cornwall was probably a genuine tradition that he had heard – Cornwall still has more giant stories than any other county – and one which probably arose because of its great number of megalithic monuments (see **Stonehenge**, p.77).

Behind the Leap itself may lie a tradition of 'giant's bones', such as Weever reports as displayed in the church of St Mary Aldermanbury (and see **Weston**, p.168). A nineteenth-century folklorist was told that, when the foundations of the Citadel at Plymouth were being dug, gigantic jaws and teeth were discovered that were identified as the bones of Gogmagog. Possibly similar finds in earlier times gave rise to the story of a giant's death which was by Geoffrey attached to the legend of Brutus because of his traditional landing-place at **Totnes** (p.36).

As for Gogmagog, two princes called Gog and Magog appear in the Bible, and there has been much argument as to whether English tradition at first contained two giants descended directly from them; or one giant called by their names rolled together; or a giant who originally had nothing to do with them at all. Geoffrey actually spells his giant's name *Goemagot*; the poet Layamon, writing about a hundred and fifty years later, calls him *Goemagog*, and it may be that an originally independent name has gradually been corrupted to *Gogmagog* because of the influence of the Bible. So who was Goemagot? We don't know. If Geoffrey got the name wrong, and it *did* originally have an -og- in it, he might have been the Gaulish/Irish culture god Ogmios, identified by the Celts with Hercules and often depicted with a club (see **Cerne Giant**, p.55).

Plymouth Citadel: AM (any reasonable time, at the discretion of the military). Antony House: NT. Times of opening also in *HHC&G*.

RILLATON BARROW, LINKINHORNE, CORNWALL

Whenever a hunter came near the Cheesewring (SX 258724) on Bodmin Moor, a druid who lived there received him seated on a rock later to be known as the Druid's Chair and offered him a drink out of a golden goblet. As many as fifty hunters might each approach and drink, and yet the goblet was never emptied. Once one of a party of hunters in Trewortha Marsh (SX 235759) swore he would drink the druid's cup dry, but though he rode to the rock and received it, and drank till he could drink no more, he failed to drain it. Angrily he threw the dregs in the druid's face and galloped off with the cup, but his horse plunged over the rocks and its rider broke his neck. He was buried on the spot, with the fateful goblet still clutched in his hand.

His supposed burial-place, Rillaton Barrow (SX 260719), north of **The Hurlers** (p.25), is a chambered round barrow covering a stone-lined grave. When it was opened in 1818, it was found indeed to contain a golden cup. 'A curious instance of the persistency of tradition', says the Rev. Sabine Baring-Gould (author of 'Onward, Christian soldiers'), who first tells the story in *A Book of the West: Cornwall* (1899). But although the story belongs to a widespread tale-type, 'Thefts from the Fairies' (cf. **Edenhall**, p.372), its location here is unsupported by any earlier author. Was it indeed a verified folk-memory, or a post-excavation 'tradition'? It looks very much like a revamp of a story told by Gervase of Tilbury (*ca.* 1212) about a mound in a certain forest-glade where, if a huntsman went alone and said 'I thirst', there immediately appeared a mysterious cup-bearer proffering a jewelled drinking-horn, which held a drink that dispelled all heat and weariness. One unprincipled hunter carried off the horn and presented it to the Earl of Gloucester, who promptly executed him as a thief, and subsequently gave the horn to Henry I. We should perhaps be cautious in accepting the Rillaton story as a genuine tradition, if only because Baring-Gould certainly knew Gervase's account, as well as its probable source in William of Newburgh (see **Willy Howe**, p.430) and was himself adept at embroidering on traditional material (in his *Old English Fairytales*, 1895).

Whether Baring-Gould had a hand in it or not, the story of the fairy cup may well have been attracted to Rillaton because of the Druid's Chair. These were fairly common in the West Country at the height of druid fever – Mrs Bray, for example, quotes her husband's journal for September 1802 concerning a rock on Pewtor, near Tavistock. 'From the form of it I could not hesitate to suppose that it was a Druidical seat of judgment,' he says, and goes on to compare it to a 'judgment seat' at Carnbrea.

The Rillaton Cup, which is an Early Bronze Age gold beaker, part of the furnishings of a grave, was lost sight of for many years, but eventually turned up again in the dressing-room of George V at Buckingham Palace, where it had found its way as treasure trove. It is now in the British Museum.

Duchy property. Reached by unmetalled road from Minions (SX 2671). The OS 1:25 000 map shows Trewortha Marsh by name; Rillaton Barrow appears simply as 'Tumulus' on both maps. The Rillaton Cup is currently displayed in the British Museum, Prehistoric and Romano-British Antiquities, Room 37.

ST JUST, CORNWALL   Sheet 180
                                                       SW 3631

The tin mines of Cornwall were inhabited by fairy miners called knockers from the sounds of their labour. They were thought to be the remnants of a people who inhabited Cornwall before the Celts and were neither good enough for Heaven nor bad enough for Hell (something frequently said of the fairies), or else the ghosts of Jews sent to the mines as penance for aiding and abetting the Crucifixion.

The belief in spirits of the mines is a widespread one – in Germany they are called kobolds – and in England and Wales goes back at least to the sixteenth century. 'Pioners or diggers for mettal, do affirme, that in many mines, there appeare straunge shapes and spirites, who are apparelled like vnto other laborers in the pit', says Lavater (*Of Ghostes and Spirites walking by Nyght*, 1572), and it is to this tradition that Hamlet refers when he calls his father's ghost 'old mole' and 'pioner'.

The knockers only worked rich lodes, and as Burton tells us in his *Anatomy of Melancholy* (1621): 'The mettall-men in some places account it good lucke, and a signe of treasure, and rich Ore when they see them' – a belief that lingered in Cornwall well into the nineteenth century. A tinner from Balleswidden Mine, near St Just, is reported as saying that he was hopeful about a particular lode 'because for every stroke of my pick, I heard three or four clicks from the knockers working ahead of me'.

Although the knockers could lead a miner to a good lode of tin, they were also to be feared, because, like other fairies, they could be vindictive if upset. William Bottrell in his *Traditions and Hearthside Stories of West Cornwall*, Second Series (1873) tells the story of Tom Trevorrow, a miner from St Just, who was working in the Ballowal Mine. One day Tom heard what he took to be the knockers and brusquely told them to be quiet and go away. He was immediately struck by a shower of small stones, but took no notice and continued working. After a while, he heard the knockers again, crying:

> 'Tom Trevorrow! Tom Trevorrow!
> Leave some of thy fuggan* for Bucca†
> Or bad luck to thee tomorrow.'

But Tom only cursed the knockers, and when they spoke again their voices had become angry:

> 'Tommy Trevorrow, Tommy Trevorrow!
> We'll send thee bad luck tomorrow,
> Thou old curmudgeon, to eat all thy fuggan
> And leave not a didjan‡ for Bucca.'

When Tom arrived at work next day, he found that a fall of rock had buried both his precious tools and the vein of ore he had been counting on for his next month's work. Misfortune seemed to dog him thereafter, and eventually he was forced to leave the mine and become a farm labourer.

SCILLY ISLES, CORNWALL   Sheet 203
                                             SV 9211

Perhaps the most romantic of Cornwall's Arthurian legends is that of what Tennyson calls 'the lost land of Lyonesse'. The tradition of a lost land between Land's End and the Scilly Isles is mentioned by Camden in his *Britannia* (trans. Holland, 1610). He points to a group of rocks about midway between Land's End and Scilly 'called in Cornish *Lethowsow*; by the English, *Seven-stones*' as evidence that Cornwall once extended further west. The Cornish, he says, called the area bounded by the rocks *Tregva*, 'a dwelling', and there were reports of windows 'and other stuff' being fished up there, and of the tops of houses being glimpsed beneath the waves. He goes on to tell how, when this land was drowned, a man called Trevilian (in Camden Trevelyan) managed to escape by leaping on his horse and galloping ahead of the waves. He describes

---

* fuggan - a traditional Cornish cake of barley-meal and pork fat; a pasty
† Bucca - another name for knocker, related to English 'Puck'
‡ didjan - a little piece

the arms of the Trevilians, said to commemorate this event, which bore the likeness of a horse issuing from the sea.

Camden got this material from Richard Carew, the Cornish antiquary, before Carew himself used it in his *Survey of Cornwall* (1602). The archaeological record suggests that this tradition of a lost land was based on observation. The Scillies are described by classical writers as one, or substantially one, large island as late as the fourth century A.D., and have visibly lost ground to the sea: in the Samson Flats (SV 8812) between Samson and Tresco, rows of stones appear at low tide which are evidently ancient field walls, and on St Martin's are the foundations of Iron Age huts whose floors are now below high-water mark. Moreover, in Carew's day St Michael's Mount was by the Cornish called '*Cara Cowze in Clowze*, that is, The hoar Rock in the Wood', and there were traditions of a drowned forest in the bay below the Mount. Robert Hunt (*Popular Romances of the West of England*, 1865) remembered going with other boys from his school in Penzance when the tide was out to see trees embedded in the sand and gathering leaves and beech-nuts from them.

The *written* record, however, indicates that the tradition of a drowned land spread to St Michael's Mount from Mont St Michel in Finistère through monastic records – the Cornish monastery was a daughter-house of the one in Brittany – and that the story draws heavily on the Breton tale of the drowning of Kêr-Is, a legendary city located in the Bay of Douarnenez. Kêr-Is was ruled by King Gradlon or Grallon, and was built on land reclaimed from the sea. One night, at the prompting of an enemy, the King's daughter Dahut stole from him the keys of the dykes and opened them. The whole of Kêr-Is was drowned, except Gradlon, warned by St Gwennolé. Dahut herself attempted to escape by throwing herself on the back of Gradlon's horse, but St Gwennolé struck her with his crozier so that she fell off into the sea.

The earliest reference to Kêr-Is comes from the *Histoire de Bretagne* of Pierre Le Baud (d. 1515), who says that it was drowned because of the sins of its people, and by 1680 a version of the tale was in print essentially like the nineteenth-century one above. Indeed, some form of the legend of the drowning of Kêr-Is seems to have been current since the twelfth century. Perhaps the coincidence of the two St Michael's Mounts, the evidence of ancient forests and the drowned city legend all contributed to the establishment off Cornwall of a lost land. There are, of course, many legends of lost lands off Western Europe, from the Atlantis of classical tradition to the Bottom Cantred in **Cardigan Bay** (p.332), and they are probably not so much folk-memories of actual inundations as 'explanations' of visible remains such as those on Scilly.

It was only from Carew's time onwards that the lost land was identified with the Lyonesse of Arthurian romance, an identification apparently based on a series of errors. In the earliest versions of the 'Tristan and Iseult' story, Tristan's native land is *Loenois*, the Old French name for Lothian in Scotland. Loenois was confused with Leonois in Brittany, perhaps by the wandering Breton storytellers who seem to have been responsible for spreading the Arthurian stories throughout Europe; then a neighbouring district in Brittany, Cornouaille, was taken to be Cornwall. When someone, perhaps Carew, in consequence of this looked for Tristan's kingdom of Lyonesse in Cornwall and could not find it, he assumed it to be the lost land of the St Michael's Mount tradition. Camden took the idea from Carew as we have seen, and coming as it did from two apparently reliable authorities, the story was accepted as gospel and endlessly repeated.

The Victorians embraced 'lost Lyonesse' with a sort of loony fervour. Davies Gilbert reports in *The Parochial History of Cornwall* (1838): 'The editor remembers a female relation of a former vicar of St Erth who, instructed by a dream, prepared decoctions of various herbs, and repairing to Land's End, poured them into the sea, with certain incantations, expecting to see the Lionesse country rise immediately out of the water . . .'

SLAUGHTER BRIDGE, CAMELFORD, CORNWALL

Sheet 200
SX 1085

A water-meadow near Slaughter Bridge, which crosses the River Camel about a mile above Camelford, is said to be the site of King Arthur's last battle, 'The strife of Camlann in which Arthur and Medraut perished', recorded in a possibly contemporary entry in the British Easter Annals for the year 539 A.D. That Camlann was fought near here is a tradition that goes back to Geoffrey of

Monmouth (*ca.* 1136), who says that the battle took place along the River Camel, though he does not tell us precisely where.

The antiquary Leland, writing in the sixteenth century, says in support of this story that 'pieces of armour, rings, and brass furniture for horses are sometimes digged up here by the country-men; and after so many ages, the tradition of a bloody victory in this place is still preserved'. Modern Arthurian experts think the armour better explained as the relics of a battle fought in 825 A.D. during the conquest of Cornwall by Egbert of Wessex. The tradition that Camlann was fought here is probably based on the assumption, very likely Geoffrey's, that 'Camlann' and 'Camel' are the same name. A stronger candidate for the site of this momentous battle is Birdoswald, Roman Camboglanna (see **Eildon Hills, p.452**).

Be this as it may, by Tudor times the Camelford area was not only firmly believed to be the site of Camlann but was challenging Glastonbury as the last resting-place of Arthur. Upstream on the bank of the Camel is King Arthur's Tomb (SX 109856), a flat stone slab about two feet by nine and a half (0.6 × 3 m) with a weathered Latin inscription, popularly believed to be Arthur's gravestone. Says Carew (1602), '. . . the old folks thereabouts will shew you a stone, bearing Arthur's name, though now depraved to Atry'. Unhappily, scholars nowadays read the still-legible inscription as: LATINI [H]IC IACIT FILIUS MAGARI, '[the monument of] Latinus. Here he lies, son of Magarus'.

This is not, in any case, the stone's original site. It was brought here in the eighteenth century, having previously served as a footbridge over a stream on the estate of Lord Falmouth. Prior to that it stood somewhere in the fields, a monument to Latinus, of whom we know only that, whoever he was (to quote the poet Aneirin) 'he was not Arthur'.

King Arthur's Tomb is marked as 'Inscribed Stone' on both the OS 1:50 000 and the OS 1:25 000 map.

TAVISTOCK, DEVON
Sheet 201
SX 4874

Belief in witches lingered in Devon, especially in country districts, long after 1736 when witchcraft ceased to be a capital offence. As late as 1924, when it was reported in *The Times* for 20 December, a man named Matthews, of Clyst St Lawrence (ST 0200), was sentenced at Cullompton Petty Sessions to a month's imprisonment for attacking a neighbour whom he believed had ill-wished his pig.

Tales about witches were common, and Mrs Bray, in a letter to Southey dated 1833, tells one current in her day about a witch at Tavistock whose little grandson used to get money from the local hunt by starting hares for them. He never failed to find one, but somehow it always got away, and eventually they became suspicious. They arranged to get the hunt off to a quicker start than usual and the hounds were hard on the heels of the hare when they heard the boy cry: 'Run, Granny, run; run for your life!' The hare dashed to the old woman's cottage and got in through a hole in the door, which the huntsmen tried to force open, but were unable to break down until the parson arrived to take off the witch's spell. They found no hare in the house, but only the old lady herself, scratched and bleeding, and still panting and out of breath as if she had run a long distance.

'WITCHES . . . often transform themselves into hares, and lead the hounds and huntsmen a long and fruitless chace', says Grose in his *Provincial Glossary* (1787), and goes on to relate that one of the witnesses at the trial of Julian Cox, at Taunton in 1663, said that one day when he was out hunting he started a hare near the accused's house and chased it until it hid under a bush. He managed to get hold of it, whereupon it turned into Julian Cox. Though he was terrified, he spoke to her and asked what she was doing there, but she was too out of breath to answer.

That wounds inflicted on a wer-animal would be reproduced on the shape-changer's body was an old tradition – it is mentioned by Gervase of Tilbury in the twelfth century.

TOTNES, DEVON   Sheet 202
                                                        SX 8060

The legend that Britain was founded by Brutus, a descendant of the Trojan hero Aeneas, is recounted under **Plymouth Hoe** (p.27). In Geoffrey of Monmouth's account of Brutus's arrival, he says that he came ashore at Totnes, and just as Plymouth Rock, Massachusetts, is held to be the spot where the Pilgrim Fathers first set foot on American soil, so now in Totnes is displayed the Brutus Stone, on which Brutus stepped as he alighted from his ship, exclaiming:

> 'Here I sit and here I rest,
> And this town shall be called Totnes.'

The folk-rhyme is one that was current in 1850 when it was contributed to *Notes & Queries* of 28 December. The Brutus Stone itself is a weathered granite boulder in Fore Street, now unfortunately reduced by about eighteen inches (45.7 cm) to make it flush with the pavement. It was known in the sixteenth century – in Hearne's *Curious Discourses* (1720) we find Joseph Holland writing in 1598 that Totnes is the oldest town in the country, and 'within that town is a great stone ... whereon the report is, that Brute reposed himself, when first he landed there'.

The stone is a long way from the river, and unless it has been moved was never a stepping-stone. One explanation of it is that it was originally called 'the Bruiter's stone' and was the place from which the town crier announced his 'bruit' or news. Another suggestion is that this is the stone mentioned in medieval law-suits as 'le Brodestone', 'the big stone'. Someone who knew his Geoffrey of Monmouth might easily make the jump from 'Brodestone' to 'Brutus Stone', and so give rise to the tale.

TRENCROM CASTLE, LUDGVAN, CORNWALL

Sheet 203
SW 5136

The cairns, cromlechs and ancient barrows of Cornwall were once haunted by spriggans, a race of fairies who traditionally guarded buried treasure. They were thought by some to be the ghosts of giants, hence perhaps their ability to change their size (but see **Creech Hill**, p.18).

On the summit of Trencrom Hill near Lelant have been found traces of hut-circles inside the small Iron Age hill-fort of Trencrom Castle (SW 518362). According to legend, giants once lived here who hid their treasure inside the hill. Robert Hunt (*Popular Romances of the West of England*, 1865) says that, one moonlight night 'not many years since', a man who thought he knew where the giants' gold was hidden went to the hill and began to dig. A great storm arose, and by the lightning's glare he saw swarms of spriggans coming out of the rocks. They looked 'as ugly as if they would eat him', and got bigger as they approached. Terrified, he ran off home, where he took to his bed, and for a long time after was unable to work.

Interference with ancient monuments, most frequently by treasure-hunters, was widely believed to provoke storms. 'Not many years sithence,' wrote Carew in 1602 of what seems to have been the Drustan Stone (see **Castle Dore**, p.10),

> . . . a gentleman, dwelling not far off, was persuaded . . . that treasure lay hidden under this stone: wherefore, in a fair moonshine night, thither with certain good fellows he hieth to dig it up . . . a pot of gold is the least of their expectation: but . . . in the midst of their toiling, the sky gathereth clouds, the moonlight is overcast with darkness, down falls a mighty shower, up riseth a blustering tempest, the thunder cracketh, the lightning flasheth: in conclusion, our money-seekers washed, instead of laden . . . and more afraid than hurt, are forced to abandon their enterprise, and seek shelter of the next house they could get into.

Similar magical storms blew up at **Long Meg and her Daughters** (p.381) and at Stanton Drew, where a violent thunderstorm followed the surveying of the stones by the Bath architect John Wood on 12 August 1740. The villagers immediately blamed this on his efforts. Earlier Westcote, in his *View of Devonshire* (1630), tells the story of a man who tried to break into Broken Barrow, near Challacombe, on Exmoor, but was so terrified by the sound of phantom horsemen that followed that he died soon after. Phantom horsemen have also been heard at the Iron Age hill-fort of Ruborough Camp, in Somerset.

NT, including the Bowl Rock beside the Lelant–Towednack road, supposed to have been thrown by one of the giants. Marked as 'Trencrom Castle' only on the OS 1:25 000 map. Stanton Drew Stone Circle: AM (any reasonable time on weekdays); Sheet 201, ST 6062. Broken Barrow is generally taken to be one of a group of three round barrows east of

Brockenbarrow Lane (Sheet 180, SS 666425). J. R. W. Coxhead in *The Devil in Devon* (1967), however, seems to identify it with Holwell Barrow (SS 673430). Brockenbarrow Lane is clearly marked (though not by name) on the OS 1:25 000 map, leading past Brockenbarrow Farm (SS 665418). Ruborough Camp is on Sheet 182, ST 2233.

WISTMAN'S WOOD, DARTMOOR, DEVON   Sheet 191
                                                    SX 6177

Up the valley of the West Dart from Two Bridges is Wistman's Wood (SX 6177), an ancient copse of stunted oaks traditionally said to have been planted by Isabella de Fortibus, Countess of Devon (see also **Great Wishford**, p.63). Certainly many of the trees, pedunculate oaks fantastically gnarled and draped with moss, are centuries old. Wistman's Wood and two other copses, Black Tor Beare and Piles Copse, are shown by historical records to have stood for hundreds of years, and it is thought that they may be the last survivors of the indigenous woodland of the Moor.

Not surprisingly, Wistman's Wood attracted legend. In the nineteenth century, it was reputed to be a haunt of the Wish Hounds, according to the Rev. Baring-Gould (*A Book of the West*, 1899), the local Dartmoor name for the Wild Hunt. The Wish Hounds are also related to the many Black Dogs that haunt Devon as well as other parts of the country (see **Bungay**, p.176) and were the inspiration for Sir Arthur Conan Doyle's *Hound of the Baskervilles*.

'Wish' and 'Wistman' seem to be connected. Mrs Bray's husband, much given to druids, was certain that 'Wistman' came from a (non-existent) Old English word *wissan*, 'to know' and that Wistman's Wood was a 'wood of wisemen', i.e. the sort of sacred grove where according to classical authors the druids worshipped. But 'Wistman', so-spelt at least since Risdon (*ca.* 1630), is thought locally to refer to the Devil, and it seems likely that both it and 'Wish' contain the dialect word 'whisht', meaning 'eerie', 'uncanny' – the wood being so named from its lonely situation, and strange and gloomy appearance.

The Wistman's Wood hounds may have been the pack that a Dartmoor farmer encountered one dark night as he was riding home from Widdecombe Fair. As Baring-Gould tells the story, he was going by way of Hamel Down, past a circle of standing stones,

Haunt of the Wish Hounds: Wistman's Wood, Dartmoor, Devon

when there swiftly and silently flew past him a pack of phantom
hounds urged on by a dark huntsman. The farmer called out to the
huntsman, demanding to know what sport he had had, and jestingly
asking for some of his game. 'Take that!' answered the huntsman,
tossing him a bundle as he passed. The farmer could not see what
was in the bundle until he got it home, when in the light of a
lantern he saw that it was the body of his own child.

The standing-stones on the farmer's route from Widdecombe
(SX 7176) over Hamel Down (SX 7080) may have been Grimspound (SX 701809), connected with Woden (see **Wansdyke**, p.83).
Woden often appears on the Continent as the leader of the Wild
Hunt, and as this story is also often told on the Continent, we
should perhaps be a little chary of accepting it as a local tradition –
though Baring-Gould says he heard it in the neighbourhood.
Whether he did or not, it was a stroke of storytelling genius to
locate it here, in the desolate setting of Dartmoor.

Dartmoor National Park. OS 1:25 000 Outdoor Leisure Map 28, Dartmoor (North Sheet) shows both Wistman's Wood, reached by public footpath from Two Bridges, and Black Tor Beare, Meldon (Black-a-tor-Copse, SX 5689). Piles Copse (SX 644622), in the parish of Harford, is on the other side (South Sheet) of the map.

ZEAL MONACHORUM, DEVON

Sheet 191
SS 7204

Associated with Zeal Monachorum is a tradition that perhaps more properly belongs to South Zeal (SX 6593), from the time of Henry III to the eighteenth century the seat of the Oxenham family, who are said to have possessed a hereditary death-warning in the form of a white bird. According to the version of the legend current in the nineteenth century (and told after a fashion by Charles Kingsley in *Westward Ho!*), the heiress Margaret Oxenham, 'Lady Margaret' as she is sometimes called, was about to marry Sir John of Roxamcowe, when on the morning of the wedding a white bird appeared, hovering over her. Later, as she stood before the altar of South Tawton church (SX 6594), her rejected lover, maddened with despair, rushed in and stabbed her. Ever since that time, a white bird has appeared just before the death of a member of the family.

The Oxenham Omen made its first appearance in a tract published in 1641 entitled 'A True Relation of an Apparition in the likenesse of a Bird with a white brest, that appeared hovering over the Death-Beds of some of the children of Mr. *James Oxenham, of Sale Monachorum, Devon, Gent.*'. The tract speaks of the death of John Oxenham, aged twenty-two, 'to whom two dayes before he yeelded up his soule to God, there appeared the likenesse of a bird with a white breast, hovering over him'. He died on 5 September 1635. Thomasine, wife of James Oxenham the younger, his brother; her sister Rebecca, aged eight; and Thomasine, daughter of James and Thomasine, a baby, died on 7, 9 and 15 September of the same year, all these deaths preceded by the apparition, '. . . and what is more,' says the tract, 'the said bird appeared to Grace, the Grandmother of the said John, over her death-bed . . . in the yeare of our Redemption, 1618'.

The tract has an engraved frontispiece divided into four compart-

ments, one to each death-bed. It repeats the names of the dead
(giving a different age for John) and also those of the witnesses to
the apparition. These witnesses were examined by the local minister
at the command of Joseph Hall, then bishop of Exeter, 'who
finding all their sayings to bee true and just, hath given approbation
for a Monument to bee erected in the Church for the perpetuall
memoriall of the fact, which was accordingly performed by the
care and labor of Edward Marshall Tomb-maker under St Dunstans
church in the west in Fleetstreet; of whom if any that doubt, may
receive ample satisfaction . . .'

The tombstone is next mentioned in a curious book called
Epistolae Ho-Elianae; or Familiar Letters by James Howell, pub-
lished in 1645, four years after the tract. In a letter addressed to a
'Mr E. D.', he writes:

> . . . I can tell you of a strange thing I saw lately here, and I
> believe 'tis true: As I pass'd by Saint Dunstans in Fleetstreet
> the last Saturday, I stepp'd into a Lapidary or Stone-cutters
> Shop, to treat with the Master for a Stone to be put upon my
> Fathers Tomb; And casting my eies up and down, I might
> spie a huge Marble with a large inscription upon't, which was
> thus, to my best remembrance . . .

Howell goes on to describe the inscription, which according to
him names the deceased as John Oxenham, his sister Mary, his
mother Elizabeth, and his son James 'who died a child in his
cradle', and mentions the apparition of the bird in its account of
each demise. He concludes: 'This Stone is to be sent to a Town
hard by Excester, wher this happen'd.'

Now we are told by the Lysonses in the sixth volume of their
Magna Britannia (1822) that the Oxenhams do not show up in the
parish register, church or churchyard of Zeal Monachorum. At
South Tawton, of those named in the tract, the parish register
mentions only Grace, who died 2 September 1618. Moreover in
the second volume of his *History of Devonshire*, published in 1793,
Polwhele says: 'The prodigy of the white bird . . . seems to be
little known at present to the common people at S. Tawton; nor
can I find anywhere a trace of the marble stone which Mr. Howell
saw in the lapidary's shop in London.'

The stone might never have reached Devon, but been lost in the

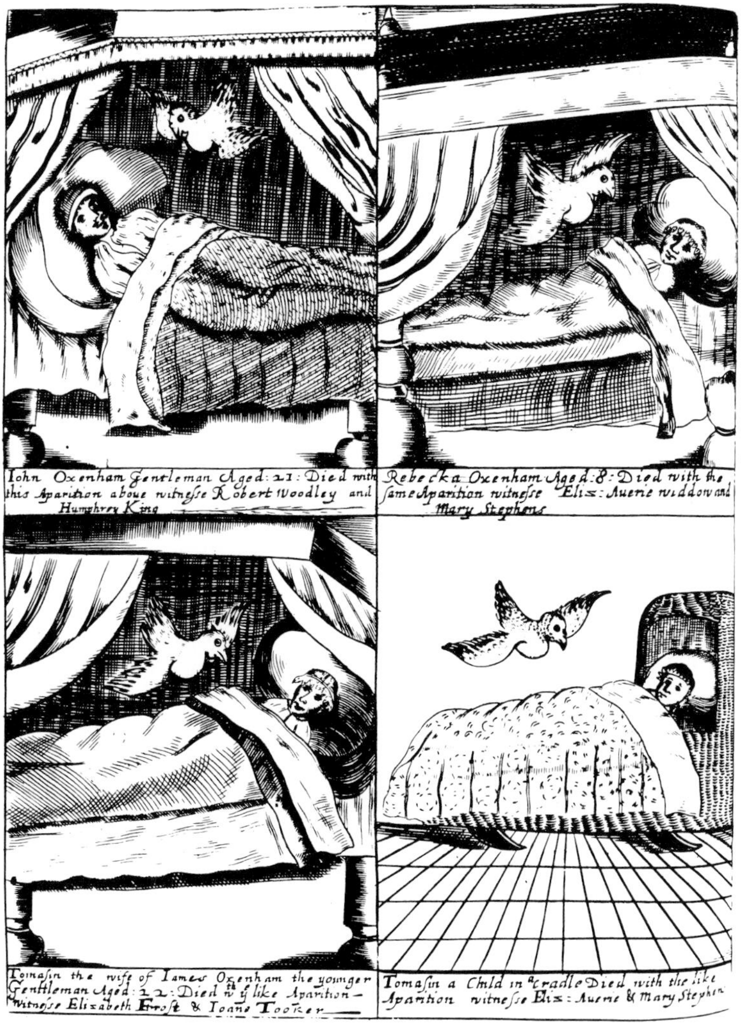
Iohn Oxenham Gentleman Aged: 21: Died with this Aparition aboue witnesse Robert Woodley and Humphrey King
Rebecka Oxenham Aged: 8: Died with the same Aparition witnesse Eliz: Auerie widdow and Mary Stephens
Tomasin the wife of Iames Oxenham the younger Gentleman Aged: 22: Died wth ye like Aparition witnesse Elizabeth Frost & Ioane Tooker
Tomasin a Child in a cradle Died with the like Aparition witnesse Eliz: Auerie & Mary Stephen

The Oxenham Omen: frontispiece of the seventeenth-century tract 'A True Relation of an Apparition in the likenesse of a Bird with a white brest, that appeared hovering over the Death-Beds of some of the children of Mr James Oxenham, of Sale Monachorum, Devon, Gent.' *British Library.*

Civil War or else the Great Fire of London: more likely it never existed. Howell's letter, although in most editions of his book dated 'July 3, 1632', is not dated in the first edition and was probably never meant to be sent – it is an 'imaginary' letter exploiting a sensational story for cash. Howell, historiographer royal to Charles II, was *ca.* 1642 confined to the Fleet Prison for political reasons for about eight years, and the antiquary Anthony Wood (1632–95) says that many of his letters were written there and published to relieve his wants. This would explain why he had to rely on his 'best remembrance' and so dismally failed, getting John, the first mentioned, right, the others all wrong (though he remembered the cradle). If he was the person who gave the letter a date, he got that wrong too: 1632 was before the deaths described by the tract.

How reliable is the tract? The strongest evidence against its being anything other than invention is Polwhele's statement that the story was 'little known . . . to the common people' and the fact that it is not mentioned by the Devonshire historian Westcote, who was living within a few miles of the scene whilst writing his *View of Devonshire* (1630). He was such a gossip it is inconceivable that he would not have repeated the tale had he heard it – and he *could* have known of Grace. Like the 'Strange and Terrible Wunder' (see **Bungay**, p.176), the 'True Relation' may have taken a single verifiable fact (Grace's death) as a peg on which to hang a story.

The story is itself based on a widespread tradition. According to Henderson's *Folk-Lore of the Northern Counties* (1879), 'the flying or hovering of birds around a house, and their resting on the windowsill or tapping against the pane, portends death'. Exactly this sort of portent is described in Deloney's *Thomas of Reading*, published between 1597 and 1600 (see **Colnbrook**, p.149), and in the eighteenth and nineteenth centuries it was often attached to particular families. The *Gentleman's Magazine* for November 1786 reports the strange apparition of a bird before the death of two successive generations of the Pearce family of Cranbrook, Kent, while the White Birds of Salisbury Plain that heralded the demise of the bishops of Salisbury were fairly reliably said to have been seen in 1885 and again in 1911. Whether invented by the author of the tract or no, the story of the white bird settled into a confirmed belief of the Oxenham family itself.

By the nineteenth century a new tenet had been added – that the bird was bound to appear for the death of a head of the family. It is supposed to have been seen by William Oxenham, who died in 1743, and to whom there is a monument in South Tawton church; and the Rev. Henry Nutcombe Oxenham, in the *Transactions of the Devonshire Association*, XIV (1882), writes:

> Shortly before the death of my late uncle, G. N. Oxenham, Esq., of 17 Earl's Terrace, Kensington, who was then the head of the family, this occurred: His only surviving daughter, now Mrs. Thomas Peter . . . and a friend of my aunt's, Miss Roberts, who happened to be staying in the house, but . . . had never heard of the family tradition, were sitting in the dining-room, immediately under his bedroom, about a week before his death, which took place on the 15th Dec., 1873, when their attention was roused by a shouting outside the window. On looking out they observed a white bird – which might have been a pigeon, but if so, was an unusually large one – perched on the thorntree outside the windows, and it remained there for several minutes, in spite of some workmen on the opposite side of the road throwing their hats at it, in the vain effort to drive it away. Miss Roberts mentioned this to my aunt at the time, though not of course attaching any special significance to it, and my aunt . . . repeated it to me soon after my uncle's death . . . but Mrs. Thomas Peter confirms in every particular the accuracy of this statement. Of the fact, therefore, there can be no reasonable doubt, whatever interpretation may be put upon it.

And what indeed do we make of it? The reality of a bird here seems unassailable, unless someone was romancing. Most will say coincidence: others may take the view that the tract was based on a genuine manifestation, or that it created a climate of belief in which such a manifestation was possible.

By far the most convincing account of birds as death-omens comes also from Devon. In his *History of Myddle* (1700–2), Richard Gough gives that rare thing, what seems to be a first-hand account of such an apparition, at the farm of Cayhowell. See *The History of Myddle*, ed. David Hey, Penguin (Harmondsworth, 1981), pp. 87–8.

2
Wessex

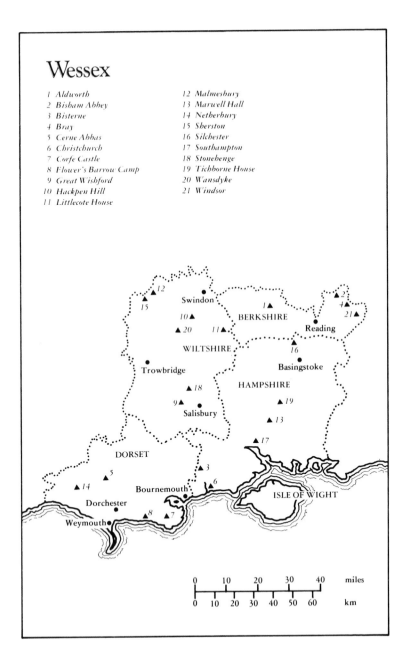

Wessex

▲ 12
15
Swindon
BERKSHIRE
1 ▲
2
4
21 ▲
Reading
10 ▲
▲ 20   11 ▲
WILTSHIRE
16
Basingstoke
Trowbridge
▲ 18
HAMPSHIRE
9 ▲
▲ 19
Salisbury
▲ 13
▲ 17
DORSET
▲ 3
▲ 5
6
▲ 14
Bournemouth
ISLE OF WIGHT
Dorchester
▲ 8 ▲ 7
Weymouth

| 0 | 10 | 20 | 30 | 40 | miles |
| 0 | 10 | 20 | 30 | 40 | 50 | 60 | km |

> The vulgar tradition is that four Johns were buried here, and
> they are described as follows:- John Long and John Strong,
> John Ever-afraid and John Never-afraid. They say that John
> Ever-afraid was afraid to be buried either in the church or out,
> and was consequently buried under the wall, where the arch
> appears on the outside by the south church door . . .

Such is the account in Gray's *History and Antiquities of Newbury*
(1839) of a tradition attached to four of the knights in Aldworth
church's rich collection of stone effigies. These at present consist
of three knights under canopies in the nave, two knights and a lady
under similar canopies in the south aisle, and two knights, one of
them accompanied by his wife, on table tombs under arcade arches
between the nave and the aisle. They are members of the de la
Beche family, beginning by the north door with what is probably
Sir Robert de la Beche, knighted by Edward I in *ca.* 1288. Most of
the monuments seem to have been made at around the same time
and presented to the church by one of the family in the mid
fourteenth century. They are known as the Aldworth Giants from
the huge size of some of them, especially Sir Philip, at whose feet
squats the little dwarf said in life to have always accompanied him
at Edward II's court in order to show off his stature.

Queen Elizabeth I once rode pillion here behind the Earl of
Leicester to see the knights, a visit recorded by Colonel Richard
Symonds, an officer in Charles I's army during the Civil War. On
2 May 1644 he jotted down in his notebook details of his own visit
to the church to make notes and drawings. Of all the effigies at
Aldworth (in his day popularly pronounced Alder), he believed
the one on the outside of the church to be the oldest, and says:

> The Comon people call this John Ever afraid
> & say farther that he gave his soul to the Diuel if
> euer he was buried either in church or churchyard
> So he was buried under the church*
> wall under an arch.

* church: Gray, followed by several authors, reads 'under the covering wall', but
the word in the MS is plainly 'church'.

The people call this statue John Strong.

'*The people call this statue John Strong.*'
Sketch by Col. Richard Symonds of one of the Aldworth Giants. BL Harley MS 965

Alas, John Ever-afraid is no more – the outside arch was blocked and his effigy destroyed or walled up sometime before 1798. Of the other giants, Symonds in his notebook (BL Harley MS 965) gives a sketch of what seems to be the effigy of Sir Philip de la Beche, with the caption: 'The people call this statue John Strong.'

Whether or not the Devil had dropped out of the story in local tradition by the time of Edward Gray, it is his presence that makes sense of it by explaining John Ever-afraid's fear. 'Neither within nor without' was a popular and widespread story which had earlier been told of Friar Bacon, the *doctor mirabilis* Roger Bacon (*ca.* 1214–91), who had been transformed by legend into a wizard. He sold himself to the Devil in return for knowledge on this same condition, but escaped by building a cell in the wall of the friary church, and living and dying there. Much the same tale was told in France of the sixteenth-century astrologer and prophet Michel de

Notredame – Nostradamus – who was buried in the sacristy wall. In Britain it is also related of the wizard Jack o' Kent at **Grosmont** (p.341), and of Piers Shonks of **Brent Pelham** (p.128) and the watchman of **Tolleshunt Knights** (p.157).

BISHAM ABBEY, BERKSHIRE

Sheet 175
SU 8484

Subsequent to the Dissolution of the Monasteries, Bisham Abbey was granted to Anne of Cleves by Edward VI, and in 1553 passed to Sir Philip Hoby, who between 1557 and 1561 built himself a mansion on the site. The Abbey has a celebrated ghost, Lady Elizabeth Hoby, whose splendid tomb can be seen in the parish church of All Saints. Here she appears in painted marble, in coronet, coif and ruff, with, lying at her knees, a child who died in infancy, apparently her only son by her second marriage, Francis or Thomas Russell. Facing her across a prayer-desk is her daughter, Anne Russell, and behind her are Elizabeth Russell and two Hoby daughters, Elizabeth and Anne, who like Francis died as children. Outside this group kneel her two surviving sons, Sir Edward and Sir Thomas Posthumus Hoby, born after his father's death.

This magnificent tomb cannot fail to have impressed all who saw it with the personality of the woman it commemorates and who herself ordered its execution. Just before her death at the age of eighty-one, she had written to the Garter King of Arms enquiring as to what was 'due to her calling' in the way of funeral rites, and the tomb was built in 1609 according to her instructions. She had already given the orders for the neighbouring monument to Sir Philip (d. 1558) and his half-brother, her husband Sir Thomas (d. 1566), herself composing their epitaphs in English, Latin and Greek.

One of four sisters celebrated for their learning, and a friend of Queen Elizabeth I, herself a scholar, she was capable and perhaps domineering. Edith Sitwell in her *English Eccentrics* (1933) says: 'During her lifetime, the appearance of Lady Hoby must have caused almost as much alarm as that of her ghost. She was, when living, a pest of outstanding quality.' This undoubtedly accounts for her legend. Because her young son William could not write without making blots, she beat him again and again, till at last she beat him to death. So great was her remorse for this unnatural act that, since her own death in 1609, she has continued to haunt the room where the tragedy happened, 'and as her apparition glides through the room it is always seen with a river passing close before her', in which she vainly attempts to wash the blood from her hands. This curious detail is reported in Chambers's *Book of Days* (1864); perhaps it was in an attempt to rationalize it that the current tradition arose that a ghostly basin floats before her as she walks.

The *Book of Days* also tells us: 'It is remarkable that about twenty years ago, in altering a window-shutter, a quantity of antique copy-books were discovered pushed into the rubble between the joists of the floor, and one of these books was so covered with blots, that it fully answered the description in the story.' Some accounts of the legend say that the copy-books bore the name in a childish hand of William Hoby: if so, they raise a problem. Lady Hoby was indeed troubled by the sons of her first marriage, especially the youngest, Thomas Posthumus, insomuch that she wrote to her brother-in-law, Lord Burleigh, asking how to deal with him. But there is no trace in her family of a William, and only her Russell son, Francis, died as an infant. Did the copy-books ever exist? Even if they did, one might suspect that the 'find' came first and the legend after (cf. **Rillaton Barrow**, p.29). Quite likely the whole story is a fairly late fabrication.

The ghost itself may have been suggested by the portrait of Lady Hoby, once attributed to Holbein, which still hangs in the Great Hall. She is shown with a very white face and wearing the mourning weeds of a baronet's widow, and it is in this sombre garb that she is supposed to haunt the Abbey. Indeed, one of its owners, Admiral Vansittart, tells a somewhat literary tale directly connected with the portrait. He and his brother had been sitting playing chess in the room where the portrait hung:

> We had finished playing, and my brother had gone up to bed. I stood for some time with my back to the wall, turning the day over in my mind. Minutes passed. I looked round. It was Dame Hoby. The frame on the wall was empty! Terrified, I fled from the room.

A curious feature of this ghost, according to Charles Harper in his

Haunted Houses (1907, rev. 1924), is that she appears like a photographic negative, the dark parts showing light, the light parts dark.

Bisham Abbey may be visited by appointment. Write to: The Director, The Sports Council, Bisham Abbey, Nr Marlow, Buckinghamshire.

BISTERNE, HAMPSHIRE

Sheet 195
SU 1401

Sr Moris Barkley the sonne of Sr John Barkley, of Beverston, beinge a man of great strength and courage, in his tyme there was bread in Hampshire neere Bistherne a devouring Dragon, who doing much mischief upon men and cattell and could not be destroyed but spoiled many in attempting it, making his den neere unto a Beacon. This Sr Moris Barkley armed himself and encountered with it and at length overcam and killed it but died himself soone after. This is the common saying even to this day in those parts of Hampshire, and the better to approve the same his children and posterity even to this present do beare for their Creast a Dragon standing before a burning beacon.

This story comes from a document from Berkeley Castle of a date earlier than 1618, and makes it clear that originally the tale of how Sir Maurice de Berkeley killed the Bisterne dragon was a 'charter myth' – one that sets out to explain how such-and-such a family came to own a particular piece of land, or to account for its coat-of-arms or how some custom had come about. In this case the story began as an explanation of the Berkeley badge, and was perhaps kept alive by a dragon's head over the main entrance to Bisterne Park.

A later version of the tale says that its hero set out for the fight equipped with a sword, a glass case and a jug of milk. He poured the milk into cans and hid inside the case, then while the dragon was lapping killed it. The source of this version, printed *ca.* 1925, says that the place where the dragon was slain was 'still' called Dragon Field. According to the version now current, Sir Maurice de Berkeley was accompanied by his two dogs, who both perished in the battle in Dragon Field.

The glass case may have entered the tale through confusion with medieval lore concerning the cockatrice, which could only be killed by reflecting its deadly glare back upon itself. The idea may indeed have come from Wherwell in the same county, where a cockatrice that lived under Wherwell Priory (SU 3940) was slain with a mirror (albeit by concussion) by a man named Green. The dragon's liking for milk was shared by the Lambton Worm of County Durham and the Laidley Worm of Spindlestone Heugh (see **Bamburgh Castle,** p.399), and by the dragons of **Deerhurst** (p.305) and **Mordiford,** Hereford & Worcester. The two dogs in the modern story may have been suggested by the statues of two dogs on the terrace of Bisterne Manor, but two faithful hounds also help in the dragon-slaying in the French medieval romance *The Dragon of Rhodes*, and dogs often accompany dragon-slayers on their tombs (see **Slingsby,** p.418).

Wherwell Priory, Sheet 185.

BRAY, BERKSHIRE   Sheet 175
                                                      SU 9079

'In good King Charles's golden days', begins that famous song 'The Vicar of Bray', written by an army officer in the time of George I, and it is in the reigns from Charles II to George I that he places the weathercock Vicar's inglorious career. But his was not the only version of this early eighteenth-century song, which also appeared under the title 'The Religious Turncoat' without any mention of Bray, and he has evidently updated it for his contemporaries.

The story comes from Fuller's *Worthies of England* (1662), where under the heading 'Barkshire' he says '. . . first we will despatch that sole proverb of this county, viz.

The Vicar of Bray will be vicar of Bray still.'

He continues:

The vivacious Vicar herof living under King Henry the Eighth, King Edward the Sixth, Queen Mary and Queen Elizabeth, was first a papist, then a protestant, then a papist, then a protestant again. He had seen some martyrs burnt (two miles off) at Windsor and found this fire too hot for his tender temper. This Vicar being taxed by one for being a Turn-coat ... 'Not so,' said he, 'for I always kept my principle, which is this, to live and die the Vicar of Bray.'

Fuller compares the Vicar's behaviour to that of opportunists 'now adayes', who though they cannot change the prevailing wind, contrive to set the sails of their mills in the right direction, so that 'wheresoever it bloweth, their grist shall certainly be grinded'. This, of course, is the message of the story which enabled eighteenth-century songwriters to adapt it to their own times, although its point was less dramatic than when it had been applied to the teething-troubles of the Reformation. Though Fuller does not name the Vicar of Bray, some identify him with Simon Alleyn, who became vicar there in 1551 and held the living through the reigns of Edward VI, Mary and Elizabeth.

CERNE GIANT, CERNE ABBAS, DORSET   Sheet 194
                                                          ST 6601

The celebrated Cerne Giant is, like the **Long Man of Wilmington** in Sussex (p.111), a gigantic human figure cut in outline in the turf of the hillside. He is 180 feet (55 m) high, and in his right hand wields a knobbed club 120 feet (36.5 m) long. Unmistakably priapic, his appearance has led many to suppose that he was a fertility god in ancient times. In support of this view, they point to the fact that right up to the nineteenth century there was dancing round the Maypole every first of May in the Iron Age banked enclosure known as The Trendle (OE *trendel*, 'circle') or Frying Pan, just above him (ST 667017). As late as the nineteenth century, too, it was believed that a barren woman could be cured by sitting on the Giant (a practice with parallels in France), although some said sexual intercourse needed to take place on the spot. A vicar of the same period put a stop to the 'scourings' that were held here every seven years, 'as', says Udal (*Dorsetshire Folk-Lore*, 1922), 'they tended to practical illustrations of the above superstitions'.

The earlier toleration by the Church of so obviously pagan a figure seems at first remarkable. It may be that the medieval abbey

The Cerne Giant: note The Trendle above him to the right

(ST 666015) was built so close to the giant as a way of exorcising its power or perhaps sanctifying it, in much the same way as a church was built near the stone circles of Stanton Drew, Somerset, and in Dorset itself within the henge monument of Knowlton Circles (SU 0210). This sort of re-use of a sacred site was at once an age-old practice – Bryn-celli-ddu, 'the dark grave-hill', on Anglesey, was deliberately built, shortly after 2000 B.C., on the site of an earlier henge monument – and in line with Pope Gregory the Great's advice to St Augustine in the sixth century to take over heathen temples and shrines, to encourage people to keep coming to their familiar places of worship. More than this, although the Church frequently fulminated against pagan practices (see **Windsor**, p.87), at a local level it knew when to let well alone, even to accommodate deep-seated superstitions. The Giant should probably be seen in the same light as a curious report in the Lanercost Chronicle that in 1268 the monks of Lanercost made a fertility figure of Priapus for the local people, whose cattle were diseased.

The foregoing of course assumes that the figure is an old one –

and this is not proven. There is no record of it prior to a letter by the county historian Hutchins in 1751. Although Camden (1586) tells us that St Augustine built Cerne Abbey after breaking the Saxon idol Heil (perhaps deduced from the *Helstone* that used to exist at Cerne), he does not mention the Giant; and a survey of Cerne in 1617 shows no sign of him, and no place-name connected with him – no 'Giant Hill' as today. Hutchins himself had heard that the Giant was 'a modern thing, cut out in Lord Holles's time' (1641–66); and indeed the first probable reference to him comes pat on this – in the 1670s John Gibbons wrote of a battle on Salisbury Plain won by 'the illustrious Stanenges and his Cerngick giants from King Divitiacus and his Belgae'.

However, most authorities agree that the silence of the Elizabethans is accidental and that Hutchins's information referred, not to a first cutting, but to the periodic scouring mentioned above. The Giant is consequently thought to be much older than the seventeenth century, although his actual origin is a matter of speculation. His proximity to the abbey prompted one traditional account of his beginnings – that he was made by the monks as a joke against their abbot. Another story in circulation in the eighteenth century was that the outline was that of a real giant who had devoured some sheep in Blackmoor (ST 6510) and then lay down to sleep off his feast. The enraged peasants caught him napping, killed him on the spot, and traced out his shape as a memorial.

The Dorsetshire novelist Thomas Hardy, in *The Dynasts* referring to 'Boney' – Napoleon Bonaparte, transformed into a bogey to frighten children with – writes: 'They say he lives upon human flesh, and has rashers of baby every morning for breakfast – for all the world like the Cernel Giant in olden times'. This may or may not have been a local tradition. It is in line with giant beliefs generally ('Fee, fi, fo, fum, I smell the blood of a British man', wrote Shakespeare in *King Lear*), but it does not accord with the beneficent character of the Cerne Giant that we can assume.

There have been several more or less informed guesses as to who he is. One conjecture is that he is the otherwise unknown 'Helith' mentioned by the chronicler Walter of Coventry in the thirteenth century; this has been connected with Camden's dubious 'Heil' and on a fancied resemblance between 'Helith/Heil' and the name of the Greek sun-god, Helios, has been constructed a cult of the sun, with attendant fertility rites, supposed to be centred on Cerne (cf. the Heel Stone, **Stonehenge**, p.77). This is mostly wishful thinking and false etymology.

Paradoxically, it was another trafficker in moonshine, the antiquary Stukeley, the man largely responsible for the 'druidification' of our megalithic monuments, who in 1764 led the way to a less romantic explanation of the Giant. He suggested that the figure represented the classical god/hero Hercules, whose emblem was a club. This is now the official view: the Giant is dated to the second century A.D. and the reign of the Emperor Commodus (180–93 A.D.), who believed that he was a reincarnation of Hercules and revived his cult. There is no archaeological evidence to dispute this theory and some to support it: the rather wooden figure of the giant has parallels in Romano-British art.

We should not think here of the simple strong-arm man of the tidy Graeco-Roman pantheon we were taught at school, but of Hercules as his worshippers, particularly his barbarian worshippers, saw him in the second century. Already in Ancient Greece Hercules was in some places an all-purpose god invoked for fertility, and when the Celts of Gaul encountered him they identified him as Ogmios, another strong man, a divine champion with a club, but also a culture-hero responsible for introducing the alphabet known as ogham. The Cerne Giant with his knobbly club might then be the British version of Ogmios, in whom some have seen the Gogmagog of **Plymouth Hoe** (p.27), the **Guildhall** (p.133), and **Wandlebury Camp** (p.202).

There is, however, another possibility. German soldiers in the Roman army, who perhaps knew nothing of Ogmios, identified Hercules and his club with their own thunder-god, at different times and in different places called Donar, Thunor and Thor. Now the Anglo-Saxons, while still living on the Continent, identified Thunor not with Hercules but with Jupiter – thus *dies Iovis*, 'Jupiter's Day' in the Roman week, became *Thunresdæg*, 'Thunor's Day', Thursday. The meeting-point of the two ideas is the Celtic god Taranis, worshipped by the Celts of the Rhineland, and linked on the one hand with the Roman Jupiter *tonitrator*, and on the other with the Germanic thunder-god Donar/Thunor/Thor: all their names are thought to contain the same element and to mean 'the thunderer'. Taranis was represented with a knobbly club, like Hercules/Ogmios, and also a wheel (see **Tilney All Saints**, p.198). All these gods – Donar, Thunor, Thor, Jupiter and Taranis, not to mention the Greek Zeus – are believed to go back to the same ancient European sky-god, associated with oak trees and lightning. The god's emblem was some heavy weapon meant to represent the thunder and lightning – the club, the hammer, in Greece the double-headed axe. He was invoked among other things for fertility, and the Maypole in The Trendle may in origin have been a surrogate for his sacred tree, an 'Oak of Thor', perhaps, such as the Anglo-Saxon missionary St Boniface felled with his own hand at Geismar.

NT. A path leads by way of the Abbey ruins to the Giant, but he is best viewed as a whole from the lay-by on the A352. Knowlton church and earthworks (Knowlton Circles): AM (any reasonable time). For the curious – the spiritual descendant of the monks of Lanercost was the Rev. John Johnson of **Cranbrook** (p.100), who in 1710 constructed a font in the church for total immersion in order to keep Baptists within his flock. Knowlton Circles, Sheet 195.

CHRISTCHURCH, DORSET
(formerly HAMPSHIRE)

Sheet 195
SZ 1593

Often told is the legend that the Carpenter of Nazareth himself laboured on the building of Christchurch cathedral, but how many remember now the Canons of Laon and the Christchurch Dragon? Yet this story was once so well known that in the fourteenth century it was even retold in far-off Iceland.

In 1112, the cathedral of Laon in France was destroyed by fire and funds had to be raised in order to rebuild. A party of canons was formed to take the cathedral's famous shrine of the Virgin Mary and other relics on a tour of northern France asking for donations. So successful was this that rebuilding began almost at once, but by 1113 money was running short again and a new fund-raising tour was planned. This time the Canons went to England, where they were well received everywhere except at Christchurch. Here the Dean bitterly resented their visit, for he found that the offerings of the rich merchants on which he had relied to finish the building of his own cathedral were being given instead to the shrine of the Virgin. He turned the Canons of Laon out into the rain with their shrine and their relics, but hardly had they left when there rose up out of the sea a five-headed dragon, spewing brimstone and fire. Those who had befriended the Canons the monster spared, but wrought utter havoc on the lands and livestock of the rest.

This jolly little story was told by a monk who signed himself *Hermann monachus*, usually identified as Hermann of Tournai (d. *ca.* 1147). It has a clear moral purpose, and need not cast doubt on his account of the Canons' visit to 'Arthur's Oven' (see **Cadbury Castle, Somerset**, p.6).

Apart from the priory church (SZ 152925) at Christchurch may still be seen, from roughly the period of the story, Christchurch Castle and Norman house (both AM).

CORFE CASTLE, DORSET
Sheet 195
SY 9681

On a knoll in a gap in the Purbeck Hills stand the ruins of Corfe Castle, of sinister reputation in history as in legend. Here in the dungeon King John once starved to death twenty-two French noblemen, and here the wretched Edward II was imprisoned before his murder at Berkeley.

But the castle already had a bad name, for on or near its site in Anglo-Saxon times was the royal manor of Corfe, where in 978 A.D. was murdered King Edward the Martyr. Still being reported in the nineteenth century as fact was the story that he had been hunting in the neighbourhood of Corfe, the residence of his stepmother Elfrida, and decided to visit her there. She came out to receive him and invited him to dismount, but, perhaps because he suspected her intentions, he refused, saying that he only had time for a draught of wine. Even as he drank it, he was stabbed in the back by an assassin whom Elfrida had hired for the crime which was to set her own son on the throne. Finding himself wounded, Edward spurred off on his horse, but soon collapsed and died from loss of blood. The pursuers sent after him by Elfrida easily traced him by the trail of blood and brought his body back to Corfe Castle, where it was thrown in a well. The local people later found it, led to the well, it was said, by a ray of light emanating from the body.

Now it is true that Edward was murdered at Corfe and his body subsequently interred hugger-mugger at nearby Wareham. 'In this year', says one version of the Anglo-Saxon Chronicle, 'King Edward was killed at the gap of Corfe on 18 March in the evening, and he was buried at Wareham without any royal honours.' It is also true that Ethelred, his half-brother, was implicated in the affair – Edward had come to visit him at Corfe, his mother's home, and there been set upon by a group of his retainers. But there is nothing to show that either Ethelred or his mother was directly involved, and that they quickly got rid of the body is no proof of their guilt, only that they knew what people would think.

And people *did* think – or were encouraged to do so. There had been strong opposition to Edward's succession after Edgar the Peaceful's death in 975 A.D.. Edgar had left two sons by two different women, both of them still alive – Æthelflæd, the mother of Edward, and Ælfthryth (Elfrida), mother of Ethelred. Æthelflæd had been set aside – she may never have been an official wife – but both children were regarded as legitimate, and both mothers wanted their sons to be king. The party of Edward (then about thirteen) argued that he was the eldest; the party of Ethelred (who may have been no more than six or seven) that Edward was unfit to rule. His violent behaviour had alienated many powerful men – even after he had become a saint and subject to whitewash, it was remembered that his outbursts of rage had terrified all who witnessed them.

Uncontrolled as Edward was, the great statesman St Dunstan put him on the throne, and there was naturally an outcry at his murder. A year after his death at Corfe, his body was removed from Wareham and buried with honour at Shaftesbury, in the nunnery church – an act evidently intended to reconcile Edward's supporters to Ethelred.

They had better have let him lie. Because he was a king who had died unjustly, he was swiftly transformed into a martyr, just as Edmund had been, with somewhat more justification (see **Hoxne**, p.182). Stories of miracles began to gather at his tomb, and thirty years later Ethelred was forced to declare him a saint – a political appointment, if you like, for while his cult was fervent enough, there is scarcely any doubt that it was deliberately fostered by his brother's enemies. As for the Elfrida of the story – although Queen

Ælfthryth was naturally one of the leaders of Ethelred's faction, no blame was attached to her until a hundred years after the event, when history was perhaps inevitably revamped in the light of the age-old tradition of the 'wicked stepmother'.

NT.

FLOWER'S BARROW CAMP,   Sheet 194
EAST LULWORTH, DORSET   SY 8680

Not far from East Lulworth, on the cliffs above Worbarrow Bay, is an Iron Age promontory fort known as Flower's Barrow (SY 863805). Hutchins, in his *History of Dorset* (1774), says that a spectral army was reported as having been seen one evening in December 1678 marching from Flower's Barrow over Grange Hill (Grange Heath, SZ 9083), making a 'great noise and clashing of arms'. As a result of this rumour, preparations for defence were

Where marched a Phantom Army: Flower's Barrow Camp, East Lulworth, Dorset

made. Other phantom armies have appeared at **Souther Fell** (p.389) and **Edge Hill** (p.266).

Ministry of Defence. Open to the public at week-ends.

GREAT WISHFORD, WILTSHIRE

Sheet 184
SU 0735

In 1640, the curate of Great Wishford, the Rev. Roger Powell, wrote on the flyleaf of the church's oldest register (1558–1640): 'There is in . . . our church . . . an ancient monument of stone of the ancestors of the Bonhams, and said to be that of Bonham and his wife that had seven children at one birth . . .' He goes on to quote the inscription on their memorial, a simple one in Latin that does no more than record the death-dates of Thomas Bonham, 'knight and benefactor of this church' (1473) and his wife Edith (1469), and ask a benediction on their souls.

We hear more of the 'seven children at one birth' from the antiquary John Aubrey, who visited Great Wishford in 1659 and in his *Natural History of Wiltshire* wrote:

This Mr Bonham's wife had two children at one birth, the first time, and he being troubled at it travelled and was absent seven yeares. After his return she was delivered of seven children at one birth. In this parish is a confident tradition that these seven children were all baptised at the font in this church, and that they were brought thither in a kind of chardger, which was dedicated to this church, and hung on two nailes, which are to be seen there yet, near the bellfree on the south side. Some old men are yet living, that doe remember the chardger. This tradition is entered into the register booke there, from whence I have taken this narrative.

In his note in the register, besides the stone in the floor of the church, the Rev. Powell describes two effigies 'said to be' those of Bonham and his wife: Aubrey does not mention them – a sound instinct because, whatever the locals thought, the figures are not those of the Bonhams, but are reliably dated to the previous century, *ca.* 1350.

The 'ancient monument of stone' can still be seen, though not in the place that Powell saw it: it was moved to the new north aisle when the church was enlarged and restored in 1864. Aubrey tells us that on the stone, above and below the inscription, were the figures in brass of Bonham and his wife, and their nine young children. The adult brasses were gone and the inscription worn away by the feet of worshippers already by the mid nineteenth century, but under the rectangular base on which the parents stood remain five of the nine children (the other four represented now, like the adults, only by indents). At the end of the fifteenth century it was unusual for children to have brasses of their own – they were normally shown in groups, girls under their mother, boys under their father. It was probably the oddity of the Bonham tomb that attracted the story of 'seven at one birth'.

The story itself, told as far afield as India, is a pious tale, intended to point out the folly of trying to dodge what Providence has ordained. The topographer Tristram Risdon had already (between 1605 and 1630) recorded it of Chulmleigh, Devon. Here the father had 'many Children', and, thinking himself 'too much blessed in that Kind', took himself off for seven years, only to be presented a year after his return with seven at one birth like the luckless Sir Thomas. Despairing of rearing them he took them in a basket to the river to drown them, but was met by the Countess of Devon, who asked him what he had. When he answered that he had whelps, she wanted to see them, and on discovering what the basket really held, took the babies home, and brought them up at her own expense. Later they were said to have become seven learned divines, and according to Thomas Westcote, Risdon's friend, writing in 1630, seven crosses near Tiverton were their memorials.

The basket of children sounds like the 'chardger' of children in the Great Wishford story, and perhaps one tradition influenced the other. But which came first is hard to say: judging by other stories accounting for the assorted lumber that was kept in old churches the 'chardger' may from the first have been one reason why the story was set here, both it and brasses being pointed out as 'proof'. Aubrey implies that it was not there in his day, but according to James Goulden, the schoolmaster of Great Wishford, in 1828: 'Three old persons of the parish ... declared to J. Goulden that they had seen the seive hung up in the church.' Was Aubrey mistaken? Were the 'chardger' and the seive the same object – a wickerwork affair like the Chulmleigh basket, a receptacle, perhaps, for the bread for church-ales such as is recorded for other churches?

Whatever the object was, it is as a sieve that it appears in current versions of the story, which are somewhat different from Aubrey's. By the time the Wiltshire historian Sir Richard Colt Hoare recounted the tradition at the beginning of the nineteenth century, it had acquired new features drawn from 'Homecoming Husband' stories, in which the husband is frequently a Crusader (see **Mab's Cross**, p.383), whence no doubt Colt Hoare's description of the effigy supposed to be Sir Thomas as being in pilgrim's dress.

The role of the spirit or saint in 'Homecoming Husband' stories (see **Combe Sydenham Hall**, p.16, and **Wroxall Abbey**, p.286) has been taken over by a witch perhaps partly suggested by a small figure kneeling at 'Sir Thomas's' head, now said to be the witch whispering in his ear.

Like similar legends elsewhere – and in Wiltshire it is also told of the mutilated effigies of two knights at Upton Scudamore (ST 8647) – the Great Wishford tale has merrily bowled along gathering up details from other stories and other places in the course of its career.

Upton Scudamore, Sheet 183. For information on Great Wishford I am indebted to Ellen Ettlinger's 'Seven Children at One Birth', *Folklore* 81, Winter 1970, pp. 268–75.

HACKPEN HILL, WILTSHIRE

Sheet 173
SU 1274

Like the Blackdown Hills, whose fairy fair was long ago recorded by Richard Bovet in his *Pandaemonium* (1684), Hackpen is a former haunt of the fairies. In 1645, the antiquary John Aubrey got from an old man called Ambrose Browne the tale of 'a hinde goeing upon Hack-pin with corne' who was led a dance by the fairies to the village, '& so was a shepherd of Winterbourne Basset'. The shepherd reported that the ground opened and he was taken into 'strange places' underground, where music was being played on viols and lutes. The shepherd got no good of his visit to the fairy mound, for 'never any afterwards enjoy themselves'.

The pixy-leading, the opening of the hillside, the fairy music, and the melancholy of people who have been with fairies are all part of long-established fairy tradition (cf. **Dartmeet**, p.19, and **Glastonbury**, p.21).

In the seventeenth century, the fairies could also be seen on the downs near Chippenham, if we are to believe Mr Hart, who seems to have been Aubrey's schoolmaster at the grammar school at Yatton Keynel (ST 8676). According to an account thought to have been written by Aubrey, Mr Hart in 1633/4 told his pupils that, coming over the downs at twilight and happening on a fairy ring, he saw a number of fairies going round and round, and singing 'and making all maner of small odd noyses'. When they saw him they pinched him all over 'and made a sorte of quick humming noyse all the time'. 'This relation I had of him myselfe,' says Aubrey, 'a few days after he was so tormented; but when I and my bedfellow Stump wente soon afterwards, at night time to the dances on the downes, we saw none of the elves or fairies.' The disappointment of Aubrey and Stump does not seem to have shattered their faith in Mr Hart's word – 'But indeede it is saide they seldom appeare to any persons who go to seeke for them'. Even if Mr Hart made the whole story up to amuse his pupils, most of what he said was standard fairy lore, and the 'odd small noyses' – the *sound* of the fairies – puts his tale in the same league as another fairy encounter recorded by Aubrey in his *Miscellanies*:

Anno. 1670, not far from *Cyrencester*, was an Apparition: Being demanded, whether a good Spirit, or a bad? returned no answer, but disappeared with a curious Perfume and most melodious Twang. Mr. *W. Lilly* believes it was a *Farie*.

The Ridgeway long-distance footpath crosses Hackpen Hill. Join the Overton Hill–Ogbourne St George stretch at Overton Hill (perhaps after visiting Avebury and the West Kennett Long Barrow). The stouthearted may like to continue to **Wayland's Smithy** (p.278) and Uffington White Horse. For detailed directions and distances, see Sean Jennett, *The Ridgeway Path* (HMSO for the Countryside Commission, 1976, 2nd imp. 1980).

LITTLECOTE HOUSE, WILTSHIRE

The exterior of Littlecote House is Elizabethan, but at one end are parts of an earlier building. The house was owned by the Darrell family from 1415 up to 1589, when it passed to the Pophams, a change of ownership traditionally associated with what Lord Macaulay described as 'a horrible and mysterious crime'. In the nineteenth century visitors to Littlecote would be shown a bed-curtain which apparently had had a small piece at the bottom cut out and sewn back in again, and this was offered as 'proof' of the following tale.

Late one night in 1575, a local midwife was called out by a mysterious stranger, who tied a blindfold over her eyes so that she could not see where they went. For an hour and a half she rode pillion behind him on his horse, until they entered a paved court, whence he led her into a house. They climbed a flight of stairs and entered a room, where the blindfold was removed. The midwife found herself in a bedchamber sumptuously furnished and occupied by a lady in labour and also a gentleman of 'haughty and ferocious' aspect. As soon as the lady's child was born – a son – this gentleman demanded it and threw it on the back of the fire. The midwife was then dismissed, but not before she had furtively snipped a piece off one of the bed-curtains; and although she was blindfolded again, she had the presence of mind to count the stairs as she left. A short distance from her own door, her guide swore her to secrecy, took off the blindfold, paid her in golden guineas, and departed. The midwife, in great unease, went next morning to a local magistrate and made a deposition of what she knew. A search was made, and on the strength of the number of stairs and the snippet of curtain, the house was identified as Littlecote, then the home of William Darrell, known as 'Wild Darrell' from the reckless life he led. Darrell was tried for murder at Salisbury, but bribed Sir John Popham, the judge, and got off scot free, only to die shortly after, as the result of a fall from his horse.

This is the story as told by Sir Walter Scott in his notes to *Rokeby* (1811). The place where Darrell broke his neck was still in his time known as 'Darrell's Stile'. Tradition subsequently added that the horse had been frightened by the phantom of a 'burning babe', and that the stile was thereafter haunted by Darrell with his phantom hounds (cf. **Combe Sydenham Hall**, p.16). It was also said that Littlecote itself was haunted by the child's mother, Darrell's sister, and that when the heir of Littlecote was about to die, Wild Darrell would drive up to the door with his coach and horses – said to have happened in 1831.

The legend was already known to Aubrey, who in his *Natural History of Wiltshire* (1656–91) speaks of Littlecote as 'Sir Thomas [sic.] Dayrell's, who was tryed for his life for burning a child'. In the notes on Sir John Popham (1531–1607) contained in the *Brief Lives*, he tells the story as it was known in his day:

> Sir . . . (John, I think) Dayrell, of Littlecote, in com. Wilts, having gott his ladie's waiting woman with child, when her travell came, sent a servant with a horse for a midwife, whom he was to bring hood-winked. She was brought, and layd the woman, but as soon as the child was borne, she sawe the knight take the child and murther it, and burnt it in the fire in the chamber. She having donne her business was extraordinarily rewarded for her paines, and sent blindfold away. This horrid action did much run in her mind, and she had a desire to discover it, but knew not where 'twas. She considered with herselfe the time that she was riding, and how many miles might be rode at that rate in that time, and that it must be some great person's house, for the roome was 12 foot high; and she could know the chamber if she sawe it. She went to a Justice of Peace, and search was made. The very chamber found. The knight was brought to his tryall; and to be short, this judge [i.e. Popham] had this noble howse, parke, and mannor, and (I thinke) more, for a bribe to save his life.

Just how much of either version is true? Certainly not the details – Sir John Popham was not made a judge until three years after Darrell's death in 1588/9; and Darrell died quietly in his own bed. From state papers Sir John seems to have had an unblemished career as Speaker of the House of Commons and finally Chief Justice, while Darrell was a local magistrate: yet both became subjects of legend. In Somerset it used to be said that Sir John came to much the same end as Darrell, having broken his neck whilst hunting in a small combe west of the Wellington Monument known as Wilscombe Bottom. There his horse stumbled and threw him into a deep pit said to be bottomless and to lead directly to Hell. Sir John was drowned, but because of his wife's prayers his ghost rises again at midnight every New Year's Eve and is advancing a cock's stride* a year towards her tomb at Wellington church.

How did these two men come to be cast as villains? In the nineteenth century, two pieces of evidence came to light which provide the foundation for the 'Littlecote Scandal'. One was a statement by a magistrate, Mr Bridges of Great Shefford (Berkshire), that he had taken down, on her death-bed, the deposition of a midwife, Mrs Barnes of Shefford, that she had once been called out by a message purporting to come from Lady Knyvett of Charlton House. After several hours on horseback, she found herself at a mansion she did not know, where she attended a lady in childbirth who was wearing a mask. Mrs Barnes does not mention herself being blindfolded, nor does she refer either to Littlecote or William Darrell. Most importantly in her account of what took place, the newborn child is not thrown on the fire but handed over to an elderly serving-woman. Mrs Barnes does, however, say that, as she was leaving, she was followed through the house and into the courtyard by a strong smell of burning.

The second piece of evidence was a letter discovered at Longleat, dated 2 January 1578/9, from Sir Henry Knyvett of Charlton to Sir John Thynne of Longleat, who had in his household a certain Mr Bonham. Mr Bonham's sister was William Darrell's mistress, and lived at Littlecote. The letter 'desires that Mr Bonham will inquire of his sister touching her usage at Will. Darrell's, the birth of her children, how many there were, and what became of them; for that the report of the murder of one of them was increasing foully, and will touch Will. Darrell to the quick.'

The rumours of murder, then, were contemporary, beginning perhaps with the idle gossip of the midwife. What happened next is unknown, but certainly Darrell sold the reversion of the Littlecote estate to Sir John in 1586, and Sir John took possession on Darrell's death. Did this circumstance lead to a slightly shady affair being rapidly inflated into something more sinister?

---

* A 'cock's stride', says the *Gentleman's Magazine* in 1759, is the measure of something tiny but perceptible:

> At New Year's tide,
> The days lengthen a cock's stride.

There are several similar stories – Sir Walter Scott knew a tale of the secret burning of an illegitimate child with its mother in Edinburgh's Canongate, while in his *Historical Memoirs* (1815) Sir Nathaniel Wraxall repeats an account he had had from Lady Hamilton (Lord Nelson's Emma) of how, in about 1743, an Irish physician resident in Rome was taken blindfold into the countryside in order to bleed to death a young noblewoman who had disgraced her family name. Wraxall also tells us of the Strasburg executioner, taken in about 1774 to an unknown castle to behead a lady, who was generally believed to have been Augusta Elizabeth, Princess of Tour and Taxis, in 1773 or 1774 separated from her husband and thereafter kept in close custody by her brother, the Prince of Württemberg.

Whether the Littlecote Scandal was only one of many such rumours or whether its celebrity gave rise to these later traditions, it bears more than a passing resemblance to the well-known tale 'Midwife to the Fairies' (see **Llandwrog**, p.345), and perhaps a real experience has been reshaped in the light of traditional beliefs. Certainly this reshaping has been at work on Will Darrell's name, bringing him into the sphere, as Wild Darrell, of both Wild Edric and the Wild Hunt (see **Clun Forest**, p.300, and **Peterborough**, p.187).

Littlecote or Littlecote House is open to the public. For times, see *HHC&G*. Wild Darrell's memorial is in Berkshire – on the north wall of Kintbury church (SU 3866) is a plaque bearing the inscription: 'In Memory Of Sir William Darrell, Of Littlecote in Wilts Knt, Who dyed without Issue, On the 1st of Oct. 1588'. Wellington Monument: NT. Another story attached to Sir John Popham was 'The Spanish Lady's Love', for which see **Adlington Hall** (p.291).

MALMESBURY ABBEY, WILTSHIRE
Sheet 173
ST 9387

St Adelme Abbot of Malmesburie . . .

This St gave a Bell to the Abbey, which when it was rung, had the power to make the *Thunder and Lightning* cease.

The Pope hearing of his Fame sent for him to preach at Rome: he had not above two daies warning to goe. Wherefore he conjured for a fleet spirit. up comes a spirit he askes how fleet. resp: as fleet as a bird in the aire. yt was not enough. Another as fleet as an arrowe out of a bow. not enough neither. a 3[r]d as swift as thought. This would doe. He commandes it to take the shape of a horse, and presently it was so: a blacke horse on which his great saddle and footcloth was putt. The first thing he thought on was St Pauls steeple Lead: he did kick it with his foot and asked where he was, and the spirit told him, etc. When he came to Rome the groome asked what he should give his horse quoth he a peck of live-coales. This from an old man at Malmesbury.

This story, recorded by Aubrey in the seventeenth century, represents the Anglo-Saxon saint Aldhelm (639–709 A.D.) as a magician, a not uncommon transformation for a scholar. The first notable Anglo-Saxon writer, Aldhelm was praised by King Alfred for his Old English verse (now lost), but was also renowned for learned Latin works which were widely read both here and on the Continent. It was undoubtedly on these that his reputation as a wizard was founded, as with those other great medieval magicians Roger Bacon and Michael Scot. Scot in particular was also credited with a magical flight to Rome in order to visit the Pope (see **Melrose Abbey**, p.475).

Quite what theological line the Popes took on such junketings is not, alas, on record.

MARWELL HALL, OWSLEBURY, HAMPSHIRE Sheet 185
SU 5021

Marwell Hall, near Winchester, is the scene of the tragic tale of the lost bride. The tradition is that, on her wedding-night, a beautiful young bride challenged her husband and wedding-guests to a game of hide-and-seek. She hid herself in an old oak chest, but the heavy lid shut her in, and though she was sought high and low, she was never found. Not, that is, till years later, when

> . . . an oak chest that had long lain hid,
> Was found in the castle, they raised the lid,
> And a skeleton form lay mouldering there,
>   In the bridal wreath of the lady fair.

So says a once-popular ballad, 'The Mistletoe Bough' by Thomas Haynes Bayley (pub. 1884), which sets the story on Christmas Eve when the house is decked with holly and mistletoe. The story of the tragic 'Mistletoe Bride' is located at several places other than Marwell Hall: at Bawdrip in Somerset; Brockdish Hall in Norfolk; **Minster Lovell Hall** in Oxfordshire (p.276); and in Hampshire both at Malshanger, near Basingstoke, and at Bramshill House, in the parish of Eversley, where Charles Kingsley was once the rector.

Marwell Hall's claim to be the setting was supported by a 'proof' – the very chest in which the bride had perished. Preserved at Upham (SU 5320) Rectory, the chest has now vanished, but the Mistletoe Bride haunts Marwell Hall, still, it is said, wearing her bridal clothes.

NETHERBURY, DORSET   Sheet 193
                                              SY 4799

In his *Dorsetshire Folk-Lore* (1922), Udal recounts a fine church-yard legend told him by an elderly lady in his family who had it from her great-aunt, which might mean that it was in circulation in the eighteenth century.

An old parish clerk and sexton of Netherby, the garden of whose cottage was divided from the churchyard only by a low wall, used to be annoyed night after night by a half-wit girl who would go to the church-porch and keep him awake by singing psalms. One moonlight night, he wrapped himself in a sheet and walked round to the porch where she was singing, thinking to frighten her. Things did not go as he had planned, for as he approached she looked round and said: 'Here's a soul coming! Whose soul be you? Be you my granfer's or granmer's, or – ' (naming someone recently buried there). Then, after a pause and looking round, she went on: 'H'm! souls *be* about tonight! For there's a black 'un, too, and he's trying to come up to the whit' 'un; and he's coming on so fast that if the whit' 'un don't take care the black 'un 'll catch 'en.'

The sexton, who had intended to frighten the girl but was now himself terrified, took to his heels, the girl clapping her hands and calling out after him: 'Run, whit' soul; black soul'll catch 'ee! Run, whit' soul; black soul'll catch 'ee!' several times with great fervour.

The sexton glanced over his shoulder and, sure enough, there was a dark figure close to his heels. He tore down the path and over the wall into his own garden, never stopping once till he was safe in his house. Such was the shock that he 'peeled' from head to foot and was ill a long time. The girl, need one add, was not disturbed again.

This is a version of an international tale known as 'Big 'Fraid and Little 'Fraid', a variant of which was used by Sir Walter Scott in his novel *The Bride of Lammermoor* (1819). In most English versions, the second ghost is real – as it is in the tale recorded in the *Denham Tracts* (1846–59) of Meg of Meldon in Northumberland, who seated herself on Meldon Bridge beside a man pretending to be her ghost. 'You've come to fley [frighten],' she said, 'and I've come to fley, let's baith fley thegither.' In the Netherbury legend, however, the 'ghost' is actually no more than the suggestible sexton's own shadow. In Cornwall in the nineteenth century was told a very similar tale of a strong-minded old lady from Raftra who turned the tables on a 'ghost' sent by her daughter to keep her from gallivanting out at night.

At Netherbury, the sexton would have been half-prepared to see a ghost by a custom attached to church porches noted by Aubrey in his *Remaines*:

> Mdm. ye sitting-up on Midsommer-eve in ye churche porch to see the Apparitions of those that should dye or be buried there, that yeare: mostly used by women: I have heard 'em tell strange stories of it.

The practice was still general in many parts of Ireland in 1880.

SHERSTON, WILTSHIRE
Sheet 173
ST 8585

> In the wall of the Church Porch on the outside, in a nich . . . is a little figure about 2 foote and a half high, ill done, which they call *Rattle Bone*, who, the tradition is, did much service against the Danes, when they infested this part of the countrey . . .
>
> *Mem.* The old woemen and children have these verses by tradition, *viz.*

'Fight well Rattlebone,
Thou shalt have Sherstone.'
  'What shall I with Sherston doe,
  Without I have all that belongs thereto?'
'Thou shalt have Wyck & Willesly,
Easton towne and Pinkeney.'

These are hamlets belonging to this parish. Their tradition is that the fight was in the ground called the Gaston. *Quaere*, what it signifies?

Such is the tradition recorded by Aubrey (1659–70) celebrating the hero Rattlebone. *Quaere*, what it signifies? Later it was said that Rattlebone fought at the Battle of Sherston between King Cnut and Edmund Ironside in 1016, and Edmund encouraged him with the promise of the manor of Sherston and its dependencies as listed in the rhyme – Wick (Wick Farm, ST 826849), Willesley (ST 8588), Easton Town (ST 8586) and Pinkney (ST 8686).

We learn more from an account printed by J. O. Halliwell in *Popular Rhymes and Nursery Tales of England* (1849) but written forty or fifty years previously:

When a schoolboy, I have often traced the intrenchments at Sherston Magna . . . and with other boys have gone in quest of a certain plant in the field where the battle was said to have been fought, which the inhabitants pretended dropt blood when gathered, and called *Danesblood* . . . supposed to have sprung from the blood of the Danes slain in that battle. Among other memorials, the statue of a brave warrior, vulgarly called Rattlebone, but whose real name I could never learn, is still standing upon a pedestal on the east side of the church-porch . . . where I saw it above fifty years ago: of whose bravery . . . many fabulous stories are told. One, in particular . . . built on the resemblance his shield bears to the shape of a tile-stone, which he is said to have placed over his stomach after it had been ripped up in battle, and by that means maintained the field . . .

The little figure on the church porch, from the fifteenth century, seems to be an ecclesiastic holding a book, not a warrior with his shield, much less Rattlebone with his tile. Inside the church is a wooden chest dating from the Middle Ages which is said to have been used to store Rattlebone's armour. It bears the initials 'R. B.', hence the tradition – did they also give Rattlebone his name?

As for the story, a similar one was attached to a monument in Overton Longueville church in what used to be Huntingdonshire. This is the effigy of a knight in armour, cross-legged, his feet resting on a lion, which Pinnock in his *History and Topography of Huntingdonshire* (1822) tells us was popularly supposed to be a Lord Longueville who, in battle against the Danes somewhere in the neighbourhood, was wounded in the abdomen so that his bowels fell out. Wrapping them round his left wrist, he went on fighting with his right hand, until he had killed the Danish king, whereafter he fell himself. A like feat of endurance is told of the Icelandic outlaw hero Gísli Súrsson in the early thirteenth-century *Gísla saga*.

For the belief that *Danesblood*, i.e. Danewort, sprang from the blood of the Danes, see **Bartlow Hills** (p.125).

Rattlebone can still be seen on the church porch and on the unique sign of Sherston's Rattlebone Inn.

SILCHESTER (CALLEVA) ROMAN TOWN, HAMPSHIRE

Sheet 175
SU 6362

And now remaineth nothing save the wals, which although they want their battlements, curtain, and coppe, yet they seeme to have been of a verie great height. For, the earth is so growne up with the rubble, that I could scarse with stouping low passe through an old posterne, which they call, *Onions Hole* ... There are heere daily digged up, bricks such as we call Britaine-bricks, and great store of Romane coine which they terme *Onions pennies*. For, they dreame that this Onion was a Giant, and dwelt in this citie.

Alas, no stories of the Giant Onion remain – he has been forgotten since Camden's day (1610). But we can still walk almost the complete circuit of the city walls of the Romano-British tribal capital of Calleva Atrebatum. Is Onion a last remnant of the Anglo-Saxon belief (or poetic convention) that Roman cities were the work of giants?

Roman city wall: AM. Access at any reasonable time. Parking by the church.

SOUTHAMPTON, HAMPSHIRE   Sheet 196
                                             SU 4212

Near Tangley is the site of a hill-fort (SU 326541) known as Bury Field or Berisbury camp, in the eighteenth century called Bevisbury; and on Ports Down (SU 6406), near Havant, was a long barrow that went by the name of Bevis's Grave. Bevis is the hero of a fourteenth-century romance, *Sir Bevis of Hamtoun*. He was the son of Sir Guy of Hampton (Southampton as it is today) and the daughter of the King of Scotland. After conniving with her lover at the murder of Sir Guy, Bevis's mother sent him to be sold as a slave in heathen lands. But there the Paynim king's daughter, Joisyan, fell in love with him and after various hair-raising adventures, including a dragon-fight, they escaped and returned to England. On the way they fell in with a giant, who after his defeat at Bevis's hands became his faithful companion. Bevis celebrated his homecoming to Hamtoun by boiling his mother's paramour into dog's meat in a great cauldron. His mother leapt to her death from the top of a high tower, and the people all hailed him as their deliverer. After many years and many adventures, Bevis and Joisyan, and Bevis's great horse, Arundel, all died within moments of each other.

The story of Bevis was based on an Anglo-Norman romance of the thirteenth century which shared some details with the story of Hamlet – including the letter which contains the bearer's own death-warrant. The tale remained popular for centuries:

> . . . mice and rats and such small deer,
> Have been Tom's food for seven long year

says Edgar in *King Lear*, well nigh quoting from the account of Bevis's imprisonment among the Paynims. First printed, as *Sir Bevis of Hampton, ca.* 1503, it was one of the stories John Bunyan knew as a child, and formed part of the chapbook collection of Samuel Pepys.

Some say that Bevis's Grave on Ports Down held Bevis and Joisyan, others that it was the grave of the giant Ascapard, who in some versions of the tale is killed by Bevis near Southampton and buried under a mound. It is said that Bevis's Grave was once opened and a skeleton of great size found, but this could have been either Ascapard or Bevis, who was in Sussex thought to be a giant (see **Arundel Castle**, p.98).

Over Southampton's medieval gateway, the Bar Gate, is a statue supposed to be that of Sir Bevis – in fact it is George III in Roman attire, put there in 1809. Similarly the Arundel Tower at the end of the north wall, in all probability named after Sir John Arundel, governor of the castle 1377–9, is given a touch of glamour by tradition – it is said to have been named after Bevis's horse, Arundel or Hirondelle, 'Swallow' – evidently a popular name for a hero's horse – cf. Hereward the Wake's Swallow at **Ely**, p.181.

Giant's Grave, Breamore, Sheet 184; Berisbury camp and Giant's Barrow, Overton, 185; Ports Down, 196. Berisbury camp is shown as Bevisbury on the OS 1:25 000 map.

STONEHENGE, AMESBURY, WILTSHIRE

Sheet 184
SU 1242

The 'noblest monument of Albion's isle', as Thomas Warton called it (1802), has borne the name 'Stonehenge' since the time of the Saxons. The Anglo-Norman poet Wace, writing in 1155, calls it the 'Hanging Stones' and Henry of Huntingdon in 1129–54 says it was given this name because the stones appear to float. Although this is said to be an optical illusion observable at Stonehenge and other stone circles, Henry's statement may be no more than an over-literal interpretation of the Anglo-Saxon name: the 'henge' comes from OE *hengen*, which meant 'hanging' and also 'gibbet', so that Stonehenge = 'stone gallows' – a name obviously given it from the shape of the great central trilithons.

Another name for Stonehenge that may go back to Saxon times is the 'Giants' Dance', the name used by Geoffrey of Monmouth (*ca.* 1136), the first author to give its legendary history. His story is that Aurelius Ambrosius, king of the Britons (wrongly believed by Geoffrey to have given his name to Amesbury) wanted to build a monument over the place where lay four hundred and sixty British

A. *Saxa que vocantur* Corselstones *pondere.12 tonnarum,*
altitudine.24 pedes, latitudine pedes.7. ambitu.10.
B. *Saxa que vocantur* Cronetts. *6.vel.7. tonnarum.*
C. *Locus cubi ossa humana effoduntur.*

The Giants' Dance: the stones of Stonehenge semi-humanized by
William Rogers, 1600

'Consuls and Princes' massacred at a feast through the treachery of Hengest's Saxons. He summoned the magician Merlin, who told him to send for the Giants' Dance from 'Killaraus', a mountain in Ireland. 'The Giants of old', said Merlin, 'brought them from the farthest Coasts of *Africa*, and placed them in *Ireland*, while they inhabited that Country.'

Aurelius sent his brother Uther Pendragon with an army of fifteen thousand men to fetch the stones, and they routed the Irish when they tried to resist the theft. But all their attempts to shift the stones proved to be of no avail until Merlin helped them, although not, it seems, by magic: '*Merlin* laughed at their vain Efforts, and then began his own Contrivances. At last when he had placed in Order the Engines that were necessary, he took down the Stones with an incredible Facility, and withal gave directions for carrying them to the Ships . . .' They were then ferried across the sea to Britain and re-erected exactly as they had been on Mount Killaraus, on the spot where the British nobles lay.

This story was repeated by umpteen medieval authors in roughly the same form, its main points being that the stones were dismantled and re-erected somewhere else; that it was moved by mechanical contrivances, not by magic; and that it was a funerary monument. Geoffrey's claim that the stones originally came from Africa may have been prompted by the Roman olive presses of North Africa, which are of trilithon shape and which up to the nineteenth century were believed to be prehistoric monuments. Mount Killaraus has not been identified, although some have suggested Kildare. The 'bluestones' which form part of Stonehenge have been shown conclusively to come from the Prescelly Hills in Pembrokeshire, a part of Wales thought to have been settled by peoples from Leinster from the third century onwards. This and the probable route of the bluestones from Wales up the River Severn may have been transformed in tradition into an Irish origin. The idea that Stonehenge was a funeral monument was not far from the mark: more than 300 barrows, mostly of the Bronze Age, exist in the immediate neighbourhood of Stonehenge, and in the Aubrey Holes and other holes near them were found fifty or sixty deposits of burnt human bones. At some time it seems to have been the focal point of a vast cemetery.

Much of Geoffrey's story could be his own work: the product

of observation, deduction and enthusiasm for Arthurian tradition. The coincidence of the supposed Irish origin of Stonehenge and the actual Welsh origin of the bluestones, however, can perhaps only be explained by the assumption that a tradition, not of its first building (Stonehenge I), but of the addition of the bluestones (Stonehenge II) and their subsequent dismantling and re-erection (Stonehenge III) was carefully handed down, at first orally, but later perhaps in writing. This is theoretically possible – Stonehenge II belongs to the Beaker culture, and it is thought that the Beaker people were the ones who introduced the ancestor of the British tongue into this country.

Geoffrey's story, fantastic though it may seem, is a lot closer to archaeology than the later traditions. In his unpublished *Monumenta Britannica* (*ca.* 1670), Aubrey says that 'one of the great stones that lies downe, on the west side, hath a cavity something resembling the print of a man's foot: concerning which the Shepherds and Countrey people have a Tradition (wch many of them doe steadfastly believe) that when Merlin conveyed these Stones from Ireland by Art Magick, the Devill hitt him in the heele with that stone, and so left the print there.' Aubrey's 'Heel Stone' is Stone 14 in the outer circle, not the present Heel Stone by the main road which bears a similar mark. The supernatural footprint left on a stone is such an ancient and widespread story (cf. **Corngafallt**, p.336, and **South Lopham**, p.192) as to leave little doubt that the Heel Stone's name means exactly what it says, and is not a corruption as many have supposed of 'Hele Stone', said to be connected with Greek *helios*, 'the sun', or with a (conjectured) Celtic expression meaning 'stone of the rising sun', or with OE *helan*, 'to hide' – the sun being hidden behind the (new) Hele Stone before it rises on the longest day of the year.

The connection of Merlin with Stonehenge was very probably made by the Arthur-minded Geoffrey or his source, 'a very ancient Book in the *British* Tongue' which he claims to have used, but which has never been traced and which was quite possibly imaginary. We see from other ancient monuments (cf. **Wansdyke**, p.83) that giants and Woden (alias Grim) were credited with the building of earthworks and megalithic monuments by the Anglo-Saxons, and that both were often replaced in medieval times by the Devil. Indeed, the Bath architect John Wood, writing in 1747, gives a story in which the Devil, not Merlin, transports Stonehenge to Salisbury Plain. Was this perhaps the natural development in local tradition, unaffected by Geoffrey, of the belief that giants had built Stonehenge? Certainly the name 'Giants' Dance' suggests this – early dances were usually ring-dances, and by his Latin expression *Chorea Gigantum* Geoffrey probably meant not 'Dancing Giants' but 'Giants' Ring'. Stonehenge may have been thought of as having been built by giants, much as in Norse mythology a giant built a *garðr*, a fenced sanctuary, for the gods and in the *Aeneid* the Cyclopses construct a wall round Elysium. In this case we can probably see in Geoffrey's statement that giants brought the stones from Africa a remnant of the story that went with the name.

A characteristically Germanic belief that has also to be taken into account is that giants were liable to be turned to stone if overtaken by the dawn. Although we have inherited from them only the prosaic name 'Stonehenge', did the Anglo-Saxons also perhaps think of it as a ring of petrified giants dancing hands on shoulders? A similar image seems to lie behind many stories of people turned to stone for dancing on a Sunday (see under **Haltadans**, p.505), and perhaps what we have here is a Germanic myth adapted to become a medieval moral legend. There is, as a matter of fact, a link between the petrified giants on the one hand and Sabbath-breaking dancers on the other in what used to be Prussia, where a circular stone formation, also known as the Giants' Dance, is said to be a group of giants turned to stone for dancing at the time for Mass.

Quite separate from Geoffrey's story is the tradition of the 'countless stones' (see **The Hurlers**, p.25), first mentioned by William Harrison in the 'Description of the Islande of Britayne' preceding Holinshed's *Chronicles* (1577) and subsequently included in Sir Philip Sidney's sonnet 'The Seven Wonders of England'. When King Charles II visited Stonehenge in 1651, his 'Arithmetike gave the lye to that fabulous tale that those stones cannot be told alike twice together', and Samuel Pepys, who came here on 11 June 1668, was also of the opinion that 'they are hard to tell, but yet may be told'. But that there *was* a problem is evident: the diarist John Evelyn in 1654 made their number ninety-five; the indomitable lady traveller Celia Fiennes in 1690 counted ninety-one; Daniel Defoe in 1724 said there were seventy-two; while

Stukeley the antiquary in 1740 wrote: 'Behold the solution of the mighty problem, the magical spell is broke, which has so long perplex'd the vulgar' – and reckoned them at a hundred and forty. Despite all these visitors who came to count and lived to tell the tale, there was a firmly held belief in both the eighteenth and nineteenth centuries that anyone who succeeded in numbering the stones would die.

AM. My account of the legends of Stonehenge is based on L. V. Grinsell's article, 'The Legendary History and Folklore of Stonehenge', *Folklore* 87, 1976:1, pp. 5–20.

TICHBORNE HOUSE, HAMPSHIRE

Sheet 185
SU 5630

In the days of Henry II, the lord of the manor of Tichborne was Sir Roger de Ticheburne, whose wife, Mabelle, was a pious and charitable woman. As she lay dying, she begged him for her sake to set aside as much land as would provide a dole of bread for the poor each Lady Day (25 March). He grudgingly replied that she could have as much land as she could walk around while a brand on the hearth continued burning, thinking that was no distance at all because she was too feeble. But Lady Mabelle was not daunted: though she could not walk, before the brand went out she had crawled round twenty-three acres, fields still said to be known as The Crawls. Then Lady Mabelle had herself carried back to bed and there, in the presence of her family, pronounced a curse on anyone who stopped the dole. The house would fall, she said, and the family come to an end for want of an heir, an event that would be foretold by a generation of seven sons followed by one of seven daughters.

The dole was religiously observed every Lady Day thereafter, until complaints from the magistrates about the vagabonds and gypsies it attracted to the district led in 1796 to it being discontinued. Thereupon Sir Henry Tichborne, the baronet of the day, had seven sons, and his eldest son had seven daughters. In 1803, when the house was being altered, part of the old fabric collapsed. Moreover, the family name was temporarily eclipsed when Sir Henry's third son, Edward, who to comply with the terms of a relative's will had changed his name to Doughty, unexpectedly became the ninth baronet in 1826.

After these disasters a modified dole was revived and has been unfailingly distributed on 25 March each year, even during the war, when rationing was in force. Instead of loaves, the dole now consists of flour distributed to all villagers of Tichborne, Cheriton and Lane End.

One may question whether Lady Mabelle's curse came before the calamities or after – family curses were extraordinarily popular in the eighteenth and nineteenth centuries. It is perhaps a late addition to the legend which belongs to the 'Lady Godiva' group of penitential tales. A similar tradition was attached to a piece of land called The Crawls at Bromfield in Shropshire, won as her portion by a girl who wanted to marry a poor man and whose father said her only dowry would be as much land as she could crawl round in a night. Such legends undoubtedly came about as explanations of bequests whose exact origin had been forgotten (as in many tales of people saved by bells, see **Ashby Folville**, p.215). But unlike many medieval bequests and endowments, the Tichborne Dole has not been swept away as no longer appropriate or convenient, and the original donor's intentions continue to be honoured by this ancient Catholic family.

The public are admitted to the open air service which accompanies the distribution of the dole. For details, consult the Southern Tourist Board, Town Hall Centre, Leigh Road, Eastleigh, Hampshire SO5 4DE, tel. (0703) 616027.

WANSDYKE, WILTSHIRE

Sheet 173
SU 0167–
ST 1966

The middest of this shire . . . is divided overthwart from East to West, with a Dike of wonderfull worke, cast up for many miles together in length: The people dwelling there about, call it *Wansdike*, which upon an errour generally received, they talke and tell to have been made by the divell upon a Wednesday. For in the Saxon tongue it is called, Wodenesdic that is to say, *the Ditch of Wooden or Mercurie* . . .

So Camden (trans. Holland, 1610) describes the great earthwork that runs from Andover in Hampshire all the way to Portishead, Avon. Camden was right in his conjecture about its name: thought to have been built in the sixth century A.D. as a defensive frontier, it has borne the same name since at least the tenth century, when it was called *Wodnes dīc*, 'Woden's Dyke', hence Wansdyke. It has been suggested that the Germanic god Woden (Norse Odin) had a cult centre above the Vale of Pewsey, where the earthwork runs, for nearby are places formerly known as *Wodnes beorh*, 'Woden's barrow', now Adam's Grave (SU 112634), near Alton Priors, and *Wodnes denu*, 'Woden's valley', in the bounds of West Overton (SU 1368). But it is also possible that these places simply took their names from the neighbouring Wansdyke.

Woden seems to have been the god the Anglo-Saxons most honoured – his name appears more often in English place-names than that of any other god – and he was deemed to be the ancestor of several lines of kings, including those of Wessex, the dynasty of Alfred. He is moreover the only one of their gods whose nickname they have passed on to us: that of Grim. A great many earthworks in southern England are known as Grim's Ditch or Grim's Dyke, in which 'Grim' seems to be related to OE *grīma*, 'mask', and to be used exactly as the Norsemen used the name 'Grimr' (from ON *gríma*, 'hood' or 'cowl') as a nickname for Odin, 'the Masked One', from his habit of going about in disguise.

In Norse myth Odin was the god of wisdom and magic, a characteristic he seems already to have had in earlier Germanic tradition: *Woden, id est furor*, 'Woden, that is frenzy', wrote Adam of Bremen in the twelfth century, referring probably to the battle-fury cultivated by Germanic warriors and reflected in the Norse sagas in accounts of berserks. Possibly drug-induced, it freed the dedicated warriors of his cult from inhibition and fear; its opposite was the 'war-fetter', a paralysis of the will which, according to the sagas, Odin could lay upon those who had lost his favour. His power to bind and loose seems to have been symbolized by the *valknut*, three interlinked triangles or rings, found on stones in Gotland, Sweden, associated with his cult.

It may well be a cult-centre of Woden that the Roman historian Tacitus is describing in his *Germania* (98 A.D.) when he speaks of the religious observances of the Semnones, who gathered at a set

time in a particular grove which no one might enter unless he were
bound with a cord. Their ritual began with a human sacrifice,
and later evidence suggests that Woden's rites were hanging and
stabbing. Odin in Norse mythology is 'the hanged one', the god of
the gallows, who hung for nine days and nine nights on 'a windy
tree' (the World Tree, Yggdrasill), a sacrifice 'myself to myself'. To
judge from early Scandinavian literature, kings and leaders went
through a symbolic version of this sacrifice in order to increase
their power, and the story of King Vikar demonstrates Odin's
unchancy character. For when Vikar went through his ritual death,
the calf's guts round his neck failed to break as intended, and the
reed with which he was touched was at the last moment transformed into a spear, so that his symbolic sacrifice became a sacrifice
indeed.

Although he was the war-god, Woden may, like Odin, have
been the god of mantic wisdom – Odin's sacrifice of himself to
himself was to win knowledge by passing through death (hence
Gandalf's progress from grey to white wizard in Tolkien's *Lord of
the Rings*). Wagner's robust valkyries, the War-father's hand-
maidens, are romantic descendants of something more sinister,
what the Anglo-Saxons called *wælcyrian*, 'corpse-choosers', not
choosers of the slain for the honour of entry into Valhalla, but
necromancers, last remnants, perhaps, of sacrificial priestesses.
Compare the 'Angel of Death' who throttled a slave-girl selected
to die with her master at a funeral among the Rus (Scandinavian
settlers in Russia), witnessed on his visit to the Volga in 922 A.D.
by the Arab traveller Ibn Fadlan.

It was perhaps the connection of Woden, via warfare, with the
unstable and the irrational, and thence by an easy step with magic,
that led to his name being linked by the Anglo-Saxons with
prehistoric earthworks and also other remains such as the Neolithic
flint mines of Grimes' Graves, Weeting, Norfolk, and the remains
of Bronze Age hut circles at Grimspound, Manaton, Devon. And
not only with *prehistoric* constructions – at Wansdyke, they gave
the god's name to an earthwork of the sixth century, perhaps their
own handiwork. To attribute such an earthwork to Woden in
historic times may have been purely a convention, just as in poetry
Roman cities such as Bath were referred to as *eald enta geweorc*,
'the ancient work of giants', though evidently not out of ignorance

Built by Woden, god of war and magic: the great earthwork of Wansdyke, Wiltshire

– in the seventh century St Cuthbert was given a guided tour of Carlisle by citizens who knew perfectly well that it was a Roman town.

This conventional aspect of the naming of earthworks argues against the suggestion that all these 'Grim' names represent OE *grīma* in its second sense of 'goblin, nightmare, spectre'. In the absence of evidence one way or the other, it is reasonable to assume that it is a question of scale – that *grīma*, 'goblin', lies behind, for example, Grimley, Worcestershire, which in 851 A.D. was *Grimanlea*, 'grove of the goblin', and is the ancestor of the Fairy Grim who in *The Life of Robin Goodfellow* (1628) cries like a 'skritch-owle' at sick men's windows:

> When candles burn both blue and dim,
> Old folkes will say, there's fairy Grim

– but that in the case of earthworks the reference is to something rather more stupendous. (It is easy to forget how much bigger the earthworks would have *looked* to the Anglo-Saxons than to us.)

That the Grim's Dykes are precisely analogous to Wansdyke and belong to the same widespread European tradition of giants as builders (cf. **Stonehenge**, p.77, and **Wade's Stone**, p.421), is suggested by the fact that in medieval times 'Grim' was supplanted as the builder by the Devil – indeed, some earthworks now carry both their names, for example, the many Grim's or Devil's Ditches of Oxfordshire. The Devil here is clearly not some minor diabolus but the Father of Lies, a direct replacement of the most powerful of pagan gods.

A certain unease if not a downright belief in the supernatural origin of such earthworks seems to have lingered late, at least in Buckinghamshire, where in 1910 it was reported that at Grim's Ditch, Bayman's Green Wood, there was once talk of filling in the ditch but 'the people were afraid to do it'.

Part Crown property, administered by the Historic Buildings & Monuments Commission for England. The A361 from Avebury to Devizes crosses the line of Wansdyke at SU 044664, at which point there is access to a footpath. Any reasonable time.

WINDSOR, BERKSHIRE

Sheet 175
SU 9676

> There is an old tale goes that Herne the hunter,
> Sometime a keeper here in Windsor Forest,
> Doth all the winter-time, at still midnight,
> Walk round about an oak, with great ragg'd horns,
> And there he blasts the tree, and takes the cattle,
> And makes milch-kine yield blood, and shakes a chain
> In a most hideous and dreadful manner.

These lines, spoken by Mistress Page in *The Merry Wives of Windsor* (1623), are the first evidence we have of the legend of Herne the hunter, who haunted Windsor park. The *Merry Wives* is thought to have been first performed at the Garter Feast at Windsor on the evening of 23 April 1597, and has many references to local people, places and things that would be familiar to its audience. Elsewhere Shakespeare makes use of widely held country beliefs concerning fairies, and though we have no earlier mention of

Herne, there is no reason to doubt that what Shakespeare tells us is a genuine tradition of his time.

The next account of Herne's legend comes from Samuel Ireland (the celebrated Shakespearean forger) in 1792: 'The story of this Herne, who was keeper in the forest in the time of Elizabeth runs thus:- That having committed some great offence, for which he feared to lose his situation and fall into disgrace, he was induced to hang himself on this tree [Herne's Oak]. The credulity of the times easily worked on the minds of the ignorant to suppose that his ghost should haunt the spot.' Setting it in the time of Elizabeth, Ireland makes the legend younger than does Shakespeare, who says that 'idle-headed eld . . . did deliver to our age, This tale . . .' But, like Shakespeare, Ireland takes it to be a ghost story of a common

'There is an old tale goes that Herne the hunter . . . Doth all the winter-time, at still midnight, Walk round about an oak': Herne's Oak, the Home Park, Windsor, from Samuel Ireland's Picturesque Views on the River Thames *(1792)*

kind in which the revenant, rattling his chains, haunts the scene of his crime or violent death (cf. **Tewin**, p.154).

Herne could have been a real person: Herne is a common enough medieval surname deriving from OE *hyrne*, 'a corner', and it may be that some hunting custom now lost lies behind the idea of the 'great ragg'd horns' – in *As You Like It* there is a scene in which a hunter is to be brought in triumph to the Duke with antlers on his head, to the accompaniment of a song:

> What shall he have that killed the deer?
> His leather skin and horns to wear.
>   Then sing him home . . .

There was, indeed, an attempt to identify Herne with a known person. The text of *The Merry Wives of Windsor* used above comes from the 1623 edition, but there had been an earlier pirate edition in 1602 in which Herne is called Horne. Alexander Pope thought that this pirate edition was Shakespeare's 'first imperfect sketch' of the play, a view which remained current until the end of the nineteenth century. On it was based the identification of our Herne with one 'Rychard Horne, yeoman', a poacher arraigned for hunting in the royal forests in the time of Henry VII. However, the 1602 pirate quarto is now regarded as an adaptation of the play made for use in the provinces and London, with the references to Windsor matters cut or changed as being unintelligible to other than a local audience. This being so, 'Herne' was probably changed to 'Horne' to underline the old joke of the cuckold's horns when Falstaff appears on the stage in antlers.

It seems likelier that Shakespeare's ghost was himself a rationalization of some older figure about whom memories had become confused. Was he perhaps a last remnant of a ceremonial that had its origin in Palaeolithic times? From the cavern of Trois-Frères, Ariège, France, come two rock-engravings which seem to show men in animal disguise: one, the 'Sorcerer', has antlers and the other seems to be dancing and playing a bowed instrument. It used to be said that these figures were magicians, but archaeologists today point out that the Upper Palaeolithic was a period of plenty when there was no stress on survival such as would lead to hunting magic, and that the animals most frequently drawn by Palaeolithic man were not those that his food debris shows he most often ate.

Yet these little figures were up to *something* – the same something, perhaps, that led the Mesolithic hunters of Star Carr, Yorkshire, to make head-dresses with antlers from the skulls of stags, and that from about 370 A.D. Christian writers begin to condemn. They speak of those who dress up as animals on the first of January, particularly the *cervulus*, or 'little deer', and in his *Penitentials* Theodore, Archbishop of Canterbury (668–90), says:

> If anyone at the kalends of January goes about as a stag or a bull, that is, making himself into a wild animal and dressing in the skin of a herd animal, and putting on the heads of beasts … penance for three years because this is devilish.

Theodore's law may or may not reflect English custom in the seventh century, but certainly this sounds like the English hobby-horse dances that in some places still survive. Most of these also took place around Christmastime, and while most involved horses, some horned animals appeared, especially in the Cotswolds, where the dancers carried 'the Broad', an imitation bull's head on a pole. Only in one dance that we know of did the performers disguise as deer, and this is the Abbots Bromley Horn Dance, thus described by Robert Plot in his *Natural History of Stafford-shire* (1686):

> At *Abbots*, or now rather *Pagets Bromley*, they had also within memory, a sort of sport, which they celebrated at *Christmas* (on *New-year*, and *Twelft-day*) call'd the *Hobby-horse dance*, from a person that carryed the image of a *horse* between his leggs, made of thin boards, and in his hand a *bow* and *arrow*, which passing through a *hole* in the *bow* … he made a *snapping* noise as he drew it to and fro, keeping time with the *Musick*: with this *Man* danced 6 others, carrying on their shoulders as many *Rain deers heads*, 3 of them painted *white*, and 3 *red* …

The Abbots Bromley Horn Dance – reminiscent of the Trois Frères man with a bow – is still performed today, though the hobby-horse is not quite as Plot describes and the horns have had several changes of colour. It is unique in Europe, but dances similar to the hobby-horse dances in general still take place, for example in Norway, at midwinter, often accompanied by a lot of noise from whips, horns and whistles. It may be that the antlered Herne who stalks round his oak 'all the winter-time' shaking his chain is a relic of the same tradition.

But there are other explanations. Herne is traced by some, both as to name and as to his 'great ragg'd horns', to the Celtic god Cernunnos, who is usually shown sitting crosslegged and wearing antlers. He appears on altars from Paris and Rheims, and in representations from Scotland and Ireland, but most spectacularly on the Gundestrup cauldron from Denmark (first century B.C.) where he is shown as 'lord of the animals', a figure that looks back to a similar seated god on a seal from Mohenjo-Daro in the Indus Valley civilization (*ca.* 2500 B.C.). On the Rheims altar he is pouring something out of a sack, variously said to be coins or acorns – that is, he may be represented as the deity of the oak, providing mast for the animals beneath him, a cow and a stag. The cult of Cernunnos was concerned with fecundity and he was also a god of the Underworld, two good reasons why, as Margaret Murray suggests, the image of the horned god may have been taken over by Christian artists to represent the Devil.

Herne also has features in common with the Wild Hunt (see **Peterborough**, p.187), but whether they are original or not is uncertain. What *is* certain is that this element seems to be increasing, partly because of the drift of folklore towards a few dominant patterns – just as many a former bogle is now a common or garden ghost, so many a wicked landowner is now a leader of the Wild Hunt – but partly, one suspects, because of the influence of Grimm's *Teutonic Mythology* (1835). Grimm thought, on evidence that now seems slight, that Herne was a Wild Huntsman, and so, it would seem, did Harrison Ainsworth, on whose account of Herne in *Windsor Castle* (1843) most Victorian and many later retellings of Herne's legend were based. As on the Continent a meeting with the Wild Huntsman was said to presage misfortune, so in this century it has been claimed that Herne's ghost appeared beneath his oak before the economic crisis of 1931, the abdication of Edward VIII in 1936, the outbreak of war in 1939 and the death of George VI in 1952. This 'tradition' began, some suggest, with Basil Hood's operetta *Merrie England* in 1902 but it is sufficiently in tune with genuine folklore to make it difficult to know what its beginnings were.

As to Herne's Oak – the tree traditionally held to be the one mentioned by Shakespeare – it has been pointed out that a 'foul oak' mentioned in a charter of 955 A.D. as being near Abingdon may be evidence that in Berkshire in ancient times there was an actual cult of the oak-tree, probably to do with the cult of the ancient European sky-god (see **Cerne Giant**, p.55). It may be so, and maybe Herne's Oak is the mast-yielding oak of Cernunnos. But not all famous oaks were once sacred. The Reformation Oak in Norfolk, north-east of Wymondham, traditionally the meeting-place of those involved in Kett's Rebellion in 1549, still demonstrates the advantages of a conspicuous tree as a rallying-point – as indeed Herne's Oak is used for a rendezvous in the *Merry Wives*.

In 1790, this ancient tree ceased to put forth new leaves and in the reign of George III it was cut down. Lady Ely enquired about this of the King himself, who told her that when he was a young man, he had been informed that a number of old oaks in Windsor park were unsightly and needed to come down. He gave orders for the felling of such trees, but was afterwards sorry that he had done so, for he found that among the rest what was left of Herne's Oak had also been destroyed. This must have been one of George's good days: when the fit was on him, he used to deny that the tree had been cut down. Despite the fact that the deed had been commemorated in the *Whitehall Evening Post* in an ode 'Upon Herne's Oak being cut down in the spring of 1796', the confusion sown by George led to a belief that Herne's Oak still stood – and so Queen Victoria believed. But Edward VII had the matter looked into, as the result of which Herne's Oak II was planted on 29 January 1906 on the site of its original, the tree mentioned in the *Merry Wives*, almost in the middle of the Home Park.

3
South-east

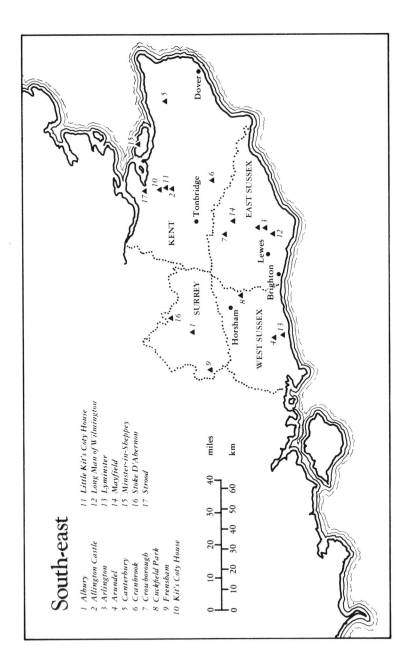

South-east

1 Albury
2 Allington Castle
3 Arlington
4 Arundel
5 Canterbury
6 Cranbrook
7 Crowborough
8 Cuckfield Park
9 Frensham
10 Kit's Coty House

11 Little Kit's Coty House
12 Long Man of Wilmington
13 Lyminster
14 Mayfield
15 Minster-in-Sheppey
16 Stoke D'Abernon
17 Strood

miles

km

0	10	20	30	40	
0	10	20	30	40	50	60

KENT

EAST SUSSEX

SURREY

WEST SUSSEX

Dover

●Tonbridge

Lewes
●

Brighton
●

Horsham
●

A mile or so east of Guildford, in a little glade, is a noted Surrey beauty spot known as 'Silent Pool' (TQ 061486). It is the upper and more picturesque of the Shireburn or Sherbourne Ponds, two deep pools formed by springs in the chalk at the foot of the Downs. Attached to it is a romantic tale of the time of the Crusades. When King John was ruling England, a village maiden named Emma went to bathe in Silent Pool. But the King was in the neighbourhood and spied her bathing there, and drove his horse into the water to reach her. To escape his clutches, she waded further and further in, until, out of her depth, she sank with a great cry. Her brother, who was nearby and heard her shriek, plunged into the Pool to save her, but could swim no more than she, and so they drowned together. It is said that if you come to Silent Pool at night you may see the ghost of Emma bathing or hear her despairing cry.

If so, it would be a remarkable thing, for this story is the invention of Martin Tupper (1810–89), who lived at Albury Park (TQ 0647), a Tudor mansion rebuilt by A. W. Pugin. Tupper – writer, inventor and antiquarian – is chiefly remembered now for his platitudinous verse, but it was in his totally unhistorical novel *Stephen Langton* (1858) that the story of Silent Pool first appeared – the role of King John perhaps suggested by the well-known tale of 'Matilda the Fair' (see **Little Dunmow**, p.142).

But let us not take all the glamour from Silent Pool. According to local tradition, the Pool is bottomless, perhaps a relic of an earlier belief that it was one of the entrances to the Underworld (cf. **Lyminster**, p.114). Some suppose it was once a sacred lake. Evidence of the common cult of wells and springs in this area is a wayside shrine with a pool fed by a spring, part of a Romano-Celtic site excavated by Tupper in 1839 and 1840 on Farley Heath (TQ 0544). Perhaps the springs at Silent Pool were also regarded as holy: certainly their water was prized in later times, for up to 1810 or 1811 a fair used to be held at Sherbourne on Palm Sunday during which those attending it would buy mugs of 'Roman water' from the springs.

Had Tupper heard of a 'White Lady' attached to the Pool or is it coincidence that there are 'ghosts' in other parts of England who may have begun life as water-spirits (see **Waddow Hall**, p.391)?

ALLINGTON CASTLE, KENT   Sheet 188
                                                     TQ 7457

This restored medieval castle in the northern part of Maidstone in 1492 became the residence of Sir Henry Wyatt, whose life was saved by a cat. Tradition says that, whilst a prisoner in the Tower in the reign of Richard III, he was kept alive by a cat who brought a pigeon to his window ledge each day. 'For this he would ever make much of cats, as other men will of their spaniels or hounds; and perhaps you shall not find his picture anywhere but, like Sir Christopher Hatton with his dog, with a cat behind him.' Sir Henry's son, Sir Thomas Wyatt, the poet, in 1526 brought back from Italy the brown pigeons still kept at the castle in memory of his father's deliverance.

The story of the cat is mentioned on a marble tablet on the north choir wall of the parish church at Boxley (TQ 7759). Erected in 1702, it reads (with more piety than punctuation):

> To the Memory of Sr HENRY WIAT of ALINGTON CASTLE Knight Banneret . . . who was imprisoned and tortured in the TOWER in the reign of KING RICHARD the third kept in the Dungeon where fed and preserved by a Cat.

Allington Castle, now owned by the Carmelite Order, is open to the public daily between 2 and 4 P.M.

ARLINGTON, EAST SUSSEX   Sheet 199
                                                     TQ 5407

Mrs Charlotte Latham, writing in 1878, says that the favourite Sussex fairytale of her youth was 'The Sweating Fairies'. This had already appeared in print in the *Literary Gazette* of 16 April 1825, and in 1854 the antiquary M. A. Lower published a dialect version which he had been told by William Fowington, an old countryman turned seventy. Will Fowington said that a brother of his wife's great-grandmother, Jeems [James] Meppom, was a farmer in a small way who used to thresh his own corn. His barn stood a good bit from the house, and the 'Pharisees' unbeknown to him used to come there by night and thresh out some wheat and 'wuts' for him, so that the heap of threshed corn was bigger in the morning than he had left it at night. He didn't know what to make of this, so one night he went out and laid up behind the straw-stack to see what was going on. For a long while nothing happened, and he was just giving up and going home when he heard an odd sort of sound. When he looked out of the straw, what should he see but two little men coming into the barn. They pulled off their jackets and began to thresh 'at de hem of a rate' with two little flails they had brought with them.

Mas' Meppom would ha' been froughten if dey had been bigger, but as dey was such tedious liddle fellers, he couldn't hardly help bustin' right out a-laffin' . . . At last dey got rader tired and left off to rest derselves, and one on 'em said, in a liddle squeakin' voice, as it might ha' bin a mouse a-talkin: 'I say, Puck, I tweat; do you tweat?'

At dat, Jeems couldn't contain hisself no-how, but set up a loud haw-haw; and jumpin' up from de strah hollered out: 'I'll tweat ye, ye liddle rascals! What bisness ha' you got in my barn?'

Well upon dis, de Pharisees picked up der frails and cut away right by him, and as dey passed by him he felt sich a queer pain in his head as if somebody had gi'en him a lamentable hard thump wud a hammer . . .

After lying unconscious in the barn all night, Jeems managed to stumble home and his wife sent for the doctor:

But bless ye, dat waunt no use; and old Jeems Meppom knowed it well enough. ''Tain't no use, sir,' he says, says he, to de doctor, 'de cuss of de Pharisees is upon me . . .'

And Mas' Meppom was right, for about a year afterwards he died, and Will could point to his grave in the churchyard.

In this dialect story of more than a hundred years ago, 'tweat' is a lisping, childish version of 'sweat', 'frails' are flails, 'hem' is a euphemism for Hell, and 'Pharisees' are of course fairies – the Sussex dialect had double plurals such as 'ghostses', hence 'fairies' became 'fairieses', and thence were confused with the Pharisees in the Bible.

Fairies were much about in Sussex generally. They used to dance at midnight on Midsummer Eve on Torberry or Tarberry Hill, where there was a hill-fort (TQ 781203), now almost destroyed, and a fairy funeral was once seen at Pulborough, on 'The Mount' – Park Mound, where are the remains of a Norman motte (TQ 037189). A story told of fairies at Beeding Hill (TQ 2109) can be found under **Hoghton** (p.378) and, as for Harrow Hill (TQ 0809), it was the last home of the fairies in England. This tradition came in 1934 from an old lady who had it from people 'before her time', and a similar one was used by Kipling in *Puck of Pook's Hill* (1906).

According to Will Fowington, Burlow Castle, an earthwork near Arlington, perhaps the site of a medieval castle, was a notorious haunt of the Pharisees and no one liked to go there after dark. To it he attaches a widespread fairytale, 'The Broken Peel' (see **Stowmarket**, p.193, and cf. **Osebury Rock**, p.277), which he tells as happening to his great-uncle's grandfather. 'The Sweating Fairies' itself was in the 1870s attached also to Washington (TQ 1212).

You may wonder why Jeems Meppom didn't want the fairies doing his threshing for him – the answer may lie in the old folk belief that fairies stole the 'foison', the nourishment, out of human food.

Harrow Hill, Park Mound and Torberry Hill, Sheet 197; Beeding Hill and Washington, Sheet 199.

ARUNDEL CASTLE, WEST SUSSEX   Sheet 197
                                                 TQ 0107

Arundel Castle is associated with Bevis of Hamtoun, a hero of medieval romance, and with his horse, Arundel, and his sword, Morglay. 'Hamtoun' is **Southampton** (p.76), but in Sussex tradition Bevis has been connected with Arundel because of his horse's name. The connection had been made already by the sixteenth century – Camden (1586) denies it, and one of his translators, Edmund Gibson (1695), comments: 'For that *Bevis* was founder of the Castle, is a current opinion handed down by tradition; and there is a tower in it still known by the name of *Bevis's tower*, which they say was his own apartment.'

The Sussex Bevis was a giant who could wade through the sea from Southampton to Cowes without getting his head wet. According to a tradition current in the nineteenth century, he gave the staff he used as he waded across to Bosham (SU 8003) as a keepsake. People pointed to a large pole kept in the church tower as 'proof' of the truth of this tale (cf. **Great Wishford**, p.63).

For many years Bevis served as warder to the Earls of Arundel, who built Bevis Tower for him to live in. When he felt his end was drawing near, he hurled his sword from the castle battlements, asking to be buried where it fell. It landed half a mile away, and there was made Bevis's Grave (a long barrow at TQ 693065 in Arundel Park, fairly recently destroyed). In the armoury of the castle is a sword nearly six feet long (5 ft 9 in/1.75 m) said to be the famous Morglay.

Arundel Castle is open to the public – for times, see *HHC&G*. The staff at Bosham church had been removed by the end of the nineteenth century, but not far away, on Telegraph Hill near Compton, is a long barrow sometimes known as Bevis's Thumb (SU 789155).

CANTERBURY CATHEDRAL, KENT

In the roof of Canterbury cathedral, over the site of Becket's tomb, is a gilt crescent traditionally taken to be the symbol of Islam and connected with the legend of the saint's parents.[*] The story goes that his father, Gilbert Becket, went on a crusade to the Holy Land and was there taken prisoner by a Saracen prince. His captor's daughter fell in love with him and helped him escape on the promise that, when he reached England again, he would send for her. But alas for her trust in the word of a Christian – safely in his own land, the faithless Gilbert forgot his promise. Years passed, and when she realized that he would never come, the Saracen maiden set out to find him. She knew only two words of English, her lover's name and the place where he lived, but by repeating

[*] So says Henry Bett in *English Legends* (1950), but I am unable to confirm it.

'Gilbert' and 'London', she managed to make her way to him, married him and became a Christian.

Gilbert and Mahaut, as the Saracen maiden was called, were said to have been buried in the graveyard of Old St Paul's. It is on record in the *Liber Albus*, the White Book of the City of London, compiled in 1419, that a ceremony by their graves often formed part of devotional visits to St Paul's by the London Corporation.

Their legend was accepted as fact by historians even as late as the nineteenth century, although the rescue from prison by the Saracen maid was a typical medieval fantasy (see **Southampton**, p.76). Similar in outline to the tale is a traditional ballad in several versions in which the hero's name is an echo of 'Becket' – 'Young Beichan', 'Lord Beichan', 'Young Bekie'. Legend and ballad probably come from one source, an early medieval tale known in several countries. Whatever its origin, the story of Becket's parents was already in circulation *ca.* 1300, not much more than a century after his death.

Note that the *Liber Albus* was compiled by John Carpenter, Common Clerk, and Richard Whitington, Mayor – the Dick Whittington of **Highgate Hill** (p.135).

CRANBROOK, KENT   Sheet 188
                                            TQ 7736

The Baker family once had large possessions in this neighbourhood, but in the reign of Edward VI, through extravagance and wild living, gradually lost all their lands until all that was left to them was one old house at Cranbrook. The last member of the family remaining when Queen Mary came to the throne was Sir Richard Baker, who had lived many years abroad as the result of a duel, but thought it was now safe to return because he, too, was a papist. He took up residence in the old mansion, where he lived alone except for one foreign servant. Very soon there were frightening tales of shrieks heard at night issuing from his house, of travellers being robbed in the district, or else of their being missed and never again heard of. Meantime it was noticed that Baker, who had returned to England poor, was little by little buying back his family lands.

At length Sir Richard began to pay court to a young lady who was known in that neighbourhood for the number of jewels she wore. He often pressed her to come and see his house, telling her that he had many curious things to show, and one day as she was passing she decided to take him at his word. She had with her a friend, a lady older than herself, who tried to dissuade her, but she would have none of this, and so they went to the door. When they knocked, they received no answer, but finding it unlocked they entered unbidden. At the head of the staircase in a cage there hung a parrot, who as they passed cried out:

> 'Peepoh, pretty lady, be not too bold,
> Or your red blood will soon run cold.'

But the young woman did not heed the warning, and on opening one of the doors found a room full of bodies, most of them women. Just then they heard a noise and looking out of the window saw Baker and his servant returning to the house with the body of another murdered woman. Nearly dead with fear, they hid under the staircase, but to their horror, as the murderers mounted the stairs, the dead woman's hand caught in the baluster, and with an oath Baker drew his sword and chopped it off. It fell into the lap of one of the ladies, and as soon as the murderers had passed by they made their escape, carrying with them the hand, which had a ring on one of its fingers.

On reaching home they told their story and displayed the ring. All the families who had lost relatives in mysterious circumstances were then told what had passed and agreed to ask Baker to a party at which constables would be concealed, ready to take him. He came unsuspecting, and when the young lady he had courted told him all that she had seen, pretending it was a dream, he replied that dreams were fables. 'But is this a fable?' she cried, producing the hand and the ring. At this the constables seized him, and he was found guilty and burnt, despite the Queen's efforts to save him.

This story was contributed to *Notes & Queries* in June 1850 by a correspondent who signed herself 'F.L.' She claimed to have come by the story as follows:

> I one day was looking over the different monuments in Cranbrook Church in Kent, when in the chancel my attention was arrested by one erected to the memory of Sir Richard

Baker. The gauntlet, gloves, helmet, and spurs were (as is often the case in monumental erections of Elizabethan date) suspended over the tomb. What chiefly attracted my attention was the colour of the gloves, which was red. The old woman who acted as my cicerone, seeing me look at them, said, 'Aye, miss, those are Bloody Baker's gloves; their red colour comes from the blood he shed.'

Her curiosity awakened, F.L. pressed her old guide to tell her the tale.

F.L.'s letter provoked indignant correspondence from other readers, who attacked the supposed historical basis of the legend, pointing out that Sir Richard, far from being notorious, was twice high-sheriff of Kent and in 1573 had the honour of entertaining Queen Elizabeth at Sissinghurst; that in Queen Mary's reign, his father, Sir John Baker, was still living; and that in the reign of Edward VI the family fortunes, so far from declining, were climbing very satisfactorily indeed. One, who knew Cranbrook, said there was no Baker monument there until 1736, and that the funeral achievements in the church hung over quite another tomb. The gloves, he said, were more brown than red, and he was quite sure there was no such local tradition. 'The story is wholly unknown in Cranbrook, and I do not believe that F.L. could have heard it there.'

What he himself had heard was a tradition concerning Sir John, Chancellor and Privy Counsellor to Henry VIII, Edward VI and Queen Mary, and remembered as a persecutor of Protestants, especially Anabaptists, of whom there were many thereabouts. It was said that he was only prevented from burning two at the stake by news of Queen Mary's death, which reached him at a place where three roads met, in 1852, as now, called Baker's Cross (TQ 7835). The correspondent suggests that it was he, not Sir Richard, who was called 'Bloody Baker', and that he came by the name just as Bloody Mary came by hers. Although he doesn't mention it, the parvise over the south porch of Cranbrook church was once known as 'Baker's Jail' from the belief that he had shut up Protestant prisoners there.

So perhaps Sir John, not Sir Richard, was the local villain. For the rest, if F.L. indeed made the whole thing up, she was not only a wonderful storyteller, but she was using traditional material. The germ of the story was undoubtedly the coincidence of the nickname 'Bloody Baker' with the gloves, whether red or not, hanging in Cranbrook church and suggestive of 'bloody hand' stories such as that told at **Stoke D'Abernon** (p.119) in nearby Surrey. The plot belongs to the same general type as Perrault's 'Bluebeard' (1698), but is usually held to be a version of the English folktale 'Mr Fox', recorded by Malone in his *Variorum Shakespeare* (1790). He got the story from a Mr Blakeway, who said he had heard it in childhood from a great-aunt of his. It seems to go back at least to the sixteenth century: when in 'Mr Fox' the lady recounts her 'dream', Mr Fox says at each stage, as a sort of refrain:

> 'It is not so, nor it was not so,
> And God forbid it should be so!'

which is thought to explain Benedick's 'Like the old tale, my Lord; it is not so, nor 'twas not so, but indeed, God forbid it should be so!' (*Much Ado About Nothing*, I.i).

However, 'Bloody Baker' has a talking bird, whereas 'Mr Fox' does not, and in this resembles 'The Robber Bridegroom' in Grimm's *Household Tales*. Did F.L. hear at Cranbrook a genuine version of 'Mr Fox', or some general tradition about Bloody Baker that led her by way of the gloves and 'bloody hand' stories to the severed hand in 'The Robber Bridegroom'? This she may well have known, as Grimm's *Tales* were first published in English (as *German Popular Stories*) in 1823–6.

'Bloody Baker' is sometimes attached to Sissinghurst Castle rather than Cranbrook, probably because it was built by Sir Richard.

The large marble pyramid at the west end of the north aisle of Cranbrook church was a new memorial erected in 1736 after the opening of the Baker family vault in the south aisle in 1725 had caused the collapse of a substantial part of aisle and nave. (A fragment of the monumental work of the vault, erected for Sir John, can today be seen on the right of the chancel arch.) The funeral achievements, including two gloves, now hanging on the south wall of the chancel, are replicas. The remains of Sir Richard Baker's home can still be seen at Sissinghurst Castle, where V. Sackville-West's celebrated garden is open to the public. NT. Times also in *HHC&G*.

CROWBOROUGH, EAST SUSSEX   Sheet 188
                                                TQ 5131

Crowborough is the happy possessor of England's oddest ghost.
Towards the end of the nineteenth century, a tradition was current
here that Jarvis Brook Road was haunted by a bag of soot, which
on certain nights would chase people. Once a blacksmith tried to
defy it, whereupon it pursued him all the way home.

Many a lane and road was once haunted by a bogey or a ghost
given to chasing people (cf. **Creech Hill**, p.18). And many a
country lane had an animal ghost, often a black one – most
frequently a Black Dog (see **Bungay**, p.176), but sometimes a
black sheep or calf, black pigs being especially frequent in the
byways of Wales. This tradition may help to explain why a bag of
soot.

But although some of these animal ghosts were undoubtedly
bizarre – for example, the headless duck that used to haunt a lane
from Stoak to Stanney in Cheshire – for comparable strangeness
we must turn to the transformations of the Hedley Kow (**Hedley
on the Hill**, p.405) and the spirit lore of the sixteenth and
seventeenth centuries. Samuel Harsnet in 1599 tells us that devils
who appeared to witches came in sundry shapes – 'of a brave
fellow like a wooer, of two little whelpes, that playing on the table,
ran into a dish of butter . . . and of an hay-stacke, promising them
bagges of gold . . .'

CUCKFIELD PARK, WEST SUSSEX   Sheet 198
                                                TQ 2924

Cuckfield Park is a much modernized Elizabethan manor house
approached by a great avenue of lime trees. It is the original of
Rookwood Hall in Harrison Ainsworth's novel *Rookwood* (1834),
though for the purposes of his story he locates that house in
Yorkshire. One of the lime trees at Cuckfield – prototype of 'the
fatal tree' in Ainsworth's novel, 'the last on the left hand before
you come to the clock-house' – was carefully preserved there in his
day because of a tradition that the shedding of a branch was a
portent of death in the family.

Other families had similar portents, though few were long-

The lime avenue where stood the 'fatal tree':
Cuckfield Park, West Sussex

established (for an exception, see **Brereton Hall**, p.298). A great many so-called 'family traditions' were the product of wishful thinking on the part of the newly rich in the eighteenth and nineteenth centuries, and the Cuckfield omen seems to be one of these – it was attached to the Sergisons, the collateral descendants (who also took his name) of Charles Sergison, a commissioner for the Royal Navy who bought the house in about 1690.

According to 'The Legend of the Lime-Tree' recited in *Rook-wood*, the tree sprang from a stake driven through the heart of a witch, but the Cuckfield tree belongs rather to the 'guardian tree' tradition, in which certain trees are closely associated with particular families (see **Dalhousie Castle**, p.443), and to matters of local belief. 'To dream that a tree is uprooted in your garden is regarded as a death-warning to the owner', said Mrs Latham, writing of West Sussex superstitions still current in 1868. The idea of a falling bough probably comes from superstitions attaching to the elm in many parts of the country, because of its habit of shedding branches without warning. Exactly parallel to the Cuckfield lime was the Prophet Elm of Credenhill Court (Hereford & Worcester), which warned the Eckleys of impending death.

FRENSHAM, SURREY   Sheet 186
                                       SU 8441

> In the vestry here, on the north side of the chancel, is an extraordinary great kettle, or caldron, which the inhabitants say, by tradition, was brought hither by the fairies, time out of mind, from Borough-hill, about a mile from hence. To this place, if any one went to borrow a yoke of oxen, money, &c, he might have it for a year, or longer, so he kept his word to return it. There is a cave, where some have fancied to hear musick. On this Borough-hill (in the tything of Cherte, in the parish of Frensham) is a great stone lying along, of the length of about six feet; they went to this stone, and knocked at it, and declared what they would borrow, and when they would repay, and a voice would answer, when they should come, and that they should find what they desir'd to borrow at that stone. This caldron, with the trivet, was borrow'd here after the manner aforesaid, but not return'd according to promise; and though the caldron was afterwards carried to the stone it could not be receiv'd, and ever since that time no borrowing there.

Thus the antiquary John Aubrey in his *Natural History and Antiquities of the County of Surrey*, published after his death in 1718–19. He was sceptical – he thought the cauldron belonged to the church and was used for church-ales and parish feasts. He was probably right: in medieval times, guilds, for example, were in the habit of keeping the utensils for their annual feast in the parish church, and these may have been lent out for other great occasions. We may be hearing a garbled version of this when, in *Remaines of Gentilisme and Judaisme* (1686–7), Aubrey speaks of the 'cavous place' at Borough Hill 'where people, against Weddings or &c bespoke Spitts, pewter, &c' – much as today one might borrow the WI teapot.

The idea of borrowing attached to the Frensham cauldron perhaps suggested the fairies through the widespread fairytale, 'The Borrowing Fairies', although in this it is the fairies who borrow and fail to return (cf. **Sandray**, p.515).

The precise whereabouts of Aubrey's 'Borough-hill' is unknown. The tithing of Churt is two miles (3.2 km) south of Frensham church, and on the common there are three conical hills known as The Devil's Jumps (SU 8639). In 1799, a correspondent writing in the *Gentleman's Magazine* reported that these hills – in his day called 'The Devil's Three Jumps' – were regarded locally with awe, and that formerly, on Whit Tuesday, the country people used to gather to dance and make merry on the easternmost and highest. This might have been Borough Hill. Alternatively, the story might have begun as an explanation of Kettlebury Hill in the parish of Elsted (SU 9043).

Today the fairies have been supplanted by a witch, probably because of the association of witches and cauldrons. This one was called Mother Ludlam, and she lived in Mother Ludlam's Hole, a cave in the grounds of Moor Park (SU 8646), which had become an object of curiosity by 1782, when the Hon. John Byng was in the area, and disregarding his landlord's advice 'that Mother Ludlam's Cave was not worth seeing', took himself there by chaise:

> Leaving our chaise at the mill, a short walk brought us thro' the wood to Mother Ludlam's Hole; a great cavity in a sandy rock, thro' which runs a little stream; it is paved, has several stone benches in it, and is by much the best place I ever saw for a cold collation on a summer's day: never was place more adapted for quiet meditation . . . Mother Ludlam is reported to have been a witch of benevolent temper, who benefited, instead of injuring, her poor neighbours.

According to tradition, she would lend them anything they asked – they would find whatever they had bespoken on their doorsteps when they got home. But what was borrowed had to be returned within two days, and when a man who had borrowed her cauldron failed to bring it back in the time allotted, Mother Ludlam refused to take it back at all and vanished from the neighbourhood.

This is clearly the same story as Aubrey's, but the cave is not the same cave. Through Mother Ludlam's Hole flows the water from

St Mary's Well (SU 871459), which once supplied Waverley Abbey (SU 8645) with water. Aubrey mentions this well, but does not connect it with the cauldron: he had heard a (mistaken) tradition that the spring was originally called Ludwell. According to another tradition, a hermit once lived in a cave by this spring, and taken together these probably explain how the cave came to be known as Mother *Lud*lam's Hole.

Moor Park, once the home of Sir William Temple and his wife, Dorothy Osborne (of the *Letters*), is now an adult education centre. Mother Ludlam's Hole is near the drive. The cauldron, which some say is medieval, others sixteenth-century, is kept in Frensham church.

KIT'S COTY HOUSE and LITTLE KIT'S COTY HOUSE, KENT

Sheet 188
TQ 7460

In this battaile were slaine the generalls of both sides, *Catigern* the Britane, and *Horsa* the Saxon: Of whome the one, burned at Horsted not farre from hence, gaue name to the place: and *Catigern* honored with a stately and solemne funerall is thought to have beene enterred neere unto *Ailesford* where under the side of a hill I saw foure huge rude, hard stones erected, two for the sides, one transversall in the midest betweene them, and the hugest of all piled and laied over them in manner of the British monument which is called *Stone-heng* but not so artificially with mortis and tenents. Verily the unskilfull common people terme it at this day, of the same *Catigern, Keiths* or *Kits Coty house*.

So Camden in his *Britannia* (trans. Holland, 1610) introduces us to the legends of Horsted and Kit's Coty House, and with them two of the chief players in the traditional account of the Anglo-Saxon settlement of Britain.

The story known to the Anglo-Saxon historian Bede, who finished his great *History of the English Church and People* in 731 A.D., was that during the time of the Emperors Martian and Valentinian III, the beginning of whose joint reign he placed in 449 A.D., three warships of Angles or Saxons came to Britain at the invitation of a British 'tyrant' called Vortigern, and were granted

The tomb of Catigern: Kit's Coty House, Aylesford, Kent

land in the eastern part of the island, in return for defending it against the Picts and Scots. But after they had repelled the invaders, they sent back news of their success to their continental brethren, adding that the country was fertile and the Britons cowardly. More boatloads soon arrived, and these also received land for their services. It was not long before their numbers were so great they were able to blackmail Vortigern, threatening to ally themselves with the Picts unless their demands were met. 'Nor were they slow to carry out their threats', and this was the beginning of the Anglo-Saxon domination of Britain.

'Their first chieftains are said to have been Hengest and Horsa', continues Bede. 'The latter was subsequently killed in battle against the Britons, and was buried in east Kent, where a monument bearing his name still stands.' Bede may here be reporting the folklore of his day. The outline of his story comes from Gildas's *Ruin of Britain* (*ca*. 540 A.D.), but Gildas mentions no names and these – Vortigern, Hengest, Horsa – Bede has himself supplied, possibly from old traditions handed down in verse. Such traditions were also available to the writer of the Anglo-Saxon Chronicle, who adds to Bede's account the names of the battles fought by Hengest and Horsa in Kent, and the information that Horsa was killed in battle against Vortigern at *Agæles threp*, traditionally Aylesford.

Hereafter Hengest and his son Æsc 'took the kingdom', and this has down the ages been taken to mean that Hengest was the founder of the kingdom of Kent. But the kings of Kent do not seem to have thought so – they called themselves Oiscingas, implying that they traced their descent from Oisc, an archaic name which the Chronicle tried to make sense of by rendering as Æsc, or 'Ash'. Probably what we have here are two separate traditions – one of the historical founder of the Oiscing dynasty, and one of the mythical founder of Kent – which someone has later attempted to reconcile.

For Hengest, and by the same token, Horsa, do not appear to have been real men. Their names mean 'Stallion' and 'Horse', perhaps referring to clan totems, and they could well personify either the federate Germanic troops known from archaeology to have been stationed in Britain as part of the Roman army from the fourth century A.D., or Germanic mercenaries invited to Britain in continuance of this policy in the fifth century by Celtic leaders, as the story says.

They may even have been gods, like the twin founders of many cities and dynasties – Romulus and Remus in Rome, Ibor and Agio among the Langobards, Ambri and Assi among the Vandals – all thought to be manifestations of a cult known in ancient Sparta as that of the Dioscuroi, the Divine Twins, Castor and Polydeuces. When this divine pair appeared in person, they rode white horses – hence possibly the names Hengest and Horsa. Certainly the Divine Twins seem to have been known to Germanic peoples – Tacitus tells us of a tribe living in the region of Breslau who worshipped such a pair, whom he equates with Castor and Polydeuces, under the name of the Alcis.

Men or gods, Hengest and Horsa were long remembered. Horsa's monument in east Kent mentioned by Bede was in later ages identified with a 'flint-heap' at Horsted, as the result of a piece of folk- or more likely antiquarian etymology, which interpreted the name as 'Horsa's Place' (whereas like other Horsteds and Horsteads it seems to mean 'stud-farm'). The connection of Vortigern's son Catigern with the megalithic burial chamber of Kit's Coty House (TQ 745608) seems first to have been made by Lambard in his *Perambulation of Kent* (1570) in an attempt to explain 'Citscotehouse' in terms of 'history'. A later tradition that probably grew out of this is mentioned by Hercules Ayleway in 1722 – that Kit's Coty House and Little Kit's Coty House (TQ 744604) were raised over rival kings of Kent killed in battle against each other.

Little Kit's Coty House, demolished *ca.* 1690, is also known as the 'Countless Stones' (see **The Hurlers**, p.25), a name it probably got after being reduced to its present jumble. A legend of Hengest is also attached to Tonge Castle (TQ 9364) – see **Caistor** (p.222).

AM (any reasonable time). Kit's Coty House is reached by a track beginning just where the road from Burham (the Pilgrim's Way) joins the minor road leading off the A229 to Aylesford. Little Kit's Coty House is further down the Aylesford road on the left. The old Ministry of Works notices call the monuments Kit's Coty and Little Kit's Coty, because 'coty' and 'house' mean the same (cf. dovecot). The OS is content to follow tradition. Who Kit was, nobody knows, though some have said a local shepherd.

THE LONG MAN OF WILMINGTON, EAST SUSSEX

Sheet 199
TQ 5403

Cut in the turf of the steep north face of Windover Hill is the gigantic figure of the Long Man of Wilmington, about 230 feet (70 m) in length and holding in either hand a staff as long as himself. The Long Man, in the past known also as the Lone and the Lanky Man, was given his present appearance in 1874, by which time he had become overgrown and visible only in certain lights or after snow. The then Duke of Devonshire paid for his restoration and had him outlined in bricks as he is today. The figure is now maintained by the Sussex Archaeological Trust.

Nothing is known of the Long Man's history. The earliest account of him comes from 1779, at which time he was thought to be holding a rake and a scythe. There is a tradition that he once wore a hat, although this possibly arose from confusion with a local rhyme recorded in the first half of the nineteenth century:

When Firle Hill and Long Man has a cap,
We a A'ston gets a drap

– A'ston being Alciston. As in weather-rhymes up and down the country, the 'cap' is cloud-cover – 'Vch hille hade a hatte, a myst-hakel* huge', as it says in *Sir Gawain and the Green Knight*.

If he really did once have a 'hat' – and an illustration produced for an archaeological journal in 1851 shows what might be the last faint traces of a helmet neck-guard – the Long Man may be identical with the naked warrior in a horned helmet, carrying two spears, engraved on a belt-buckle found in a seventh-century Anglo-Saxon grave at Finglesham, Kent. This figure and others like it on Scandinavian helmets are connected with the cult of the war-god, and probably represent either him or his followers. The tips of the Long Man's spears and his helmet might have been grassed over when Sussex became Christian.

In an article in *Folklore* 90 (1979), Jacqueline Simpson pointed out that the Long Man at the time of Domesday Book lay in a Hundred named *Wandelmestrei*, thought possibly to contain the name Wændel, and the OE words *helm* and *treo(w)*, which could be taken to mean 'The tree of the helmeted Wændel'. Now there is another place named after a Wændel, which seems also to have had a giant – **Wandlebury Camp** (p.202) in Cambridgeshire. It may be that here we have, in the one place the name, in the other the figure, of a lost Anglo-Saxon god of war.

Other suggestions are that the Long Man is in fact the 'Fighting Man' which served as the badge of King Harold II Godwinsson, last of the Anglo-Saxon kings (see **Waltham Abbey**, p.162), or that he was cut as a landmark by the monks of the Benedictine priory of Wilmington, much as the monks of Monks Risborough, Buckinghamshire, are thought to have cut the Whiteleaf Cross. But a giant is not the most obvious landmark for a monk to cut, and it is more likely that the priory came after the Long Man and was founded close to him as a sort of exorcism (cf. **Cerne Giant**, p.55).

Of the many identifications offered for the Long Man – St Paul, Muhammad, a Roman soldier, a Saxon haymaker – one of the most interesting is the suggestion of Alfred Watkins in *The Old Straight Track* (1925) that he was a ley-man or dodman, a prehistoric

* myst-hakel = a cloak of mist

Wargod, dodman or giant? The Long Man of Wilmington, East Sussex

surveyor with his two sighting staves. But there is no evidence that the figure is quite so ancient: he is most likely to be, if not Anglo-Saxon, from the Celtic Iron Age, between about 700 B.C. and the Roman Conquest.

Perhaps we should rest content with local tradition, which says that the Long Man was a giant and this is a memorial to him. There are various accounts of how he died: most say that there were once two giants who lived on Windover Hill and Firle Beacon (TQ 485059) and that they quarrelled. They began to hurl stones at each other, and the Windover giant was killed, the present figure being the outline of his body where he fell. Some say that he is buried in the long barrow on the crest of the hill now known as Hunter's Burgh (TQ 550037). Also to be seen on Windover Hill are the marks left by the stones the giants threw – actually the depressions left by flint-mines.

The Long Man is reached by a signposted footpath leading off the minor road from Wilmington to Litlington. Firle Beacon, Sheet 198.

LYMINSTER, WEST SUSSEX

Near Lyminster church is a deep pool (TQ 023049) fed by an underground spring so powerful that though a stream flows out of the pool it never dries up, even in the hottest weather. The pool is about thirty feet (9 m) deep, but used to be thought bottomless – the story goes that the villagers once took the six bellropes from the church tower and tied them end to end, but still they did not touch the bottom.

This pool is known as the Knucker Hole, and in it once lived the Lyminster Knucker, a fearsome dragon who for years ravaged the countryside for many miles around, carrying off cattle and men,

Home of a man-eating dragon:
the Knucker Hole, Lyminster, West Sussex

and devouring them in the marsh-fastnesses of the Arun valley. At last the King of Sussex offered his daughter's hand to anyone who could kill the Knucker, and a passing knight errant undertook the task, killed the monster and married the princess. Being now a married man, he gave up errantry to settle at Lyminster, where he later died. His grave can still be seen in the churchyard there.

This is the gist of the tale as told in the nineteenth century. In later accounts, its hero is not a knight but a local man who overcomes the dragon by low cunning. In the *Sussex County Magazine* in 1929 appeared a version of the story told by a hedger from nearby Toddington. The hero of this was Jim Puttock, 'a young chap from Wick'. When the Mayor of Arundel offered a large reward to anyone who would kill the Knucker, Jim came forward for the job. He began by making 'the biggest pudden that was ever seen' and carting it to just beyond the Arundel bridge, where the Knucker was lying with his head 'just below Bill Dawes's' and his tail tearing up the trees in Batworth Park:

And . . . he sings out, affable-like, 'How do, Man?'
  'How do, Dragon,' says Jim.
  'What you got there?' says Dragon, sniffing.
  'Pudden,' says Jim.
  'Pudden?' says Dragon. 'What be that?'
  'Just you try,' says Jim.
And he didn't want no more telling – pudden, horses, tug, they was gone in a blink . . .
  ''Tweren't bad,' says Knucker, licking his lips.
  'Like another?' says Jim.
  'Shouldn't mind,' says he.
  'Right,' says Jim. 'Bring 'ee one 'sarternoon.' But he knew better 'n that, surelye.

Like the stones in 'The Wolf and the Seven Little Kids', the pudden weighs heavy on the Knucker, so that he can't stand up. And while he is thus immobilized, Jim hits him on the head with an axe. This comic version, too, ends with Jim's grave being pointed out as proof of the tale.

The gravestone shown as Jim's, and earlier the knight's, is indeed a medieval tombstone, with a weathered design of a cross over a herringbone pattern, said to represent the knight's sword laid across the Knucker's ribs. The stone used to lie in the churchyard, as the story says, but is now inside the church to protect it from further wear and tear.

Although the Knucker in these tales is a dragon, he was originally a water-monster. Several other Sussex ponds – some of them likewise bottomless – once shared the same name, thought to come from OE *nicor*, used in the Anglo-Saxon epic poem *Beowulf* (early eighth century) both of monsters living in the sea and of the creatures in the desolate mere – 'No man so wise that knows its bottom' – where also dwelt the ogre Grendel and his mother. Setting out with a few companions, Beowulf goes by narrow paths through an uninhabited land of beetling crags and pools that are *nicorhūsa*, the homes of monsters. He comes to a dismal wood, its trees all coated with rime, on the edge of a cliff: below it lies the mere. Sea-dragons are swimming in its waters and on the ledges of the cliff bask other monsters (*nicras*). In those unplumbed depths, Beowulf finds a vaulted place in which is not water but air, the home of Grendel's mother, one of 'Cain's kin' – the ettins, evil spirits and giants who are the enemies of God, and might properly be thought of as inhabiting the Bottomless Pit.

A far cry from Jim to Beowulf, perhaps, but clearly the idea of a bottomless pool, inhabited by a monster and (in some places) connected with Hell, has been around a very long time. At Pershore, Hereford & Worcester, in 1263 was a pond called *Nikerpoll*, 'Knucker's Pool', while on the boundaries of Ham in Wiltshire and Crediton in Devon were ponds that may have been specifically connected with the Beowulf-story, *Grendles mere* (931 A.D.) and *Grendeles pytt* (739 A.D.).

MAYFIELD, EAST SUSSEX

Sheet 188
TQ 5827

The most celebrated of the many tales of the Devil in Sussex is that of his encounter with St Dunstan at Mayfield. Although Dunstan (909–88 A.D.) was successively abbot of Glastonbury, bishop of Worcester, bishop of London and archbishop of Canterbury, the greatest churchman and also statesman of his day, he still liked to pursue the crafts he had practised as a hermit early in his career. These included metalwork, and tradition says that he had a smithy of his own in the grounds of Mayfield Palace, the favourite country seat of the archbishops of Canterbury.

One day, as he was making a chalice, the Devil came to him disguised as a beautiful young woman, in order to tempt him. But Dunstan knew very well whom he was dealing with and worked steadily at his forge, while she sidled nearer and nearer. The moment she came within reach, he snatched his pincers from the fire and seized her by the nose. With a loud shriek the Devil assumed his own shape, but still Dunstan held on stoutly, and dragged him by his nose round and round the smithy. At last, when both were tired, he opened the pincers. The Devil fled at once to Tunbridge Wells, in Kent, to cool his burning nose in the chalybeate springs, giving them the reddish tinge they have to this day.

'A story at least as trite as it's true', R. H. Barham calls it, but it has been loved for centuries. Its ultimate source is Eadmer's *Life of St Dunstan* written *ca.* 1120, but it has been much embroidered in the course of time – in one version the young woman before turning back into the Devil goes through a series of transformations something like the one by which the hero is disenchanted in the old ballad of 'Tam Lin'. Indeed the story is still putting forth new variations – a tradition that Tongdean (TQ 2807) is the place where the *tongs* fell off the Devil's nose as he flew away was first recorded in 1965.

Walter Gale, a Sussex schoolmaster, tells us that in 1749 could be seen at Mayfield a pair of pincers which the inhabitants said were the very ones Dunstan used to 'lead the Devil by the nose'. These are perhaps the same tongs found with other metalwork during the restoration of the Old Palace during the 1860s and still preserved at Mayfield. Let us disregard sceptics who say they were not made before the thirteenth century.

The Old Palace is now occupied by the Convent of the Holy Child and a public school for girls attached to the convent. Visitors are welcome, except to parts in use by the school. The church, formerly the Great Hall, is open all day. Apart from the tongs, displayed in the Front Hall, may be seen the well-house covering St Dunstan's Well, probably the spring which Eadmer tells us St Dunstan caused to flow by striking the ground with his staff. Here, too, is the so-called 'St Dunstan's anvil'.

MINSTER-IN-SHEPPEY, KENT   Sheet 178
                                               TQ 9573

In the old monastic church (OE *mynster*) which gives Minster-in-Sheppey its name is a canopied tomb with the effigy of a knight. He lies on one side with his helmet under his head, his legs crossed, and at his feet a page. Behind him, the head of a horse is rising from the waves. This is Sir Robert de Shurland, who died *ca.* 1310 and was Lord Warden of the Cinque Ports under Edward I.

The topographer Hasted (1782), writing of this tomb, says:

> The figure of the horse's head ... has given rise to a tale, which has been reported among the common people for many years, *viz.* That sir Robert having upon some disgust at a priest, buried him alive, swam on his horse two miles through the sea to the King, who was then on ship-board near this island, and having obtained his pardon, swam back again to the shore, where being told, his horse had performed this by magic art, he cut off his head. About a twelvemonth after which, riding a hunting near the same place, the horse he was then upon stumbled, and threw him upon the scull of his former horse, by which he was so much bruised, that it caused his death: in memory of which, the figure of a horse's head was placed by him on his tomb.

Hasted was undoubtedly correct in thinking that the horse's head came first, the story after. Some attributed it, he says, to Sir Robert's having received a grant of liberties for his manor of Sheppey that included 'wreck of the sea' – a privilege which entitled him to claim all flotsam he could touch with the point of his lance by riding a horse into the surf at ebb-tide. The same piece of heraldry possibly lies behind the story of Trevilian (see **Scilly Isles**, p.32).

Known since at least the seventeenth century, Sir Robert's story is today most often met with in the version of R. H. Barham in his *Ingoldsby Legends* (1840). According to this, after swimming back to the shore on his horse, Grey Dolphin, Sir Robert met a witch, who prophesied that the horse would be his death. To defeat the prophecy, he cut off Grey Dolphin's head, then some months afterwards, walking on the beach, kicked what he took to be a stone but was the skull of the horse. It was shattered by the blow,

*The horse fated to slay his master commemorated in stone:
the tomb of Sir Robert de Shurland, Minster-in-Sheppey, Kent*

a splinter pierced his foot, and he died a month later. A number of
legends turn upon the unexpected fulfilment of a prophecy in this
way – a story very like this one comes from **Penhesgyn** (p.355).

STOKE D'ABERNON, SURREY

Sheet 178
TQ 1259

A contributor to *Notes & Queries* in 1850 relates a story told him
in explanation of the 'bloody hand' on a monument in Stoke
D'Abernon church. Two young brothers of the family of Vincent
were out shooting on Fairmile Common (TQ 1261) a couple of
miles away. They had put up several birds but were unable to get a
single shot, and the elder swore with an oath that he would fire at
whatever they next met with. They had not gone much further
when the miller of a nearby mill (which was still standing in 1850)
passed them with some remark. Jokingly, the younger brother
reminded the elder of his oath, and he straightway fired at the
miller, who fell dead upon the spot. The money and influence of
the Vincents shielded their heir from pursuit, and he continued to

live in hiding on the estate, but died some years later, still racked with remorse. To commemorate his rash deed and his untimely death, the 'bloody hand' was placed upon the monument.

This story undoubtedly had its origin in the arms of the Vincents, successors in the female line through five families to the D'Abernons, first lords of the manor here. These included the Red Hand of Ulster, the badge of baronetcy, which has in several places given rise to 'bloody hand' legends (see **Aston Hall**, p.261; and cf. **Cranbrook**, p.100). This being so, it cannot be older than 1620, the year in which Sir Francis Vincent became First Baronet. The 'bloody hand' can be seen on various shields carrying the Vincent arms in the Norbury Chapel, and also on the Elizabethan pulpit, to which Sir Francis added his arms after being made a baronet. It does not, however, appear on the splendid Vincent monument as the story seems to imply.

Stoke D'Abernon church has many treasures apart from the painted effigies of the Vincent family – notably England's oldest brass, that of Sir John D'Abernon, dating from 1277. For this reason it is normally kept locked, but is open to visitors at week-ends, thanks to the good offices of voluntary Church Guides.

STROOD, KENT
Sheet 178
TQ 7369

It was once proverbial that the men of Kent had tails, and even now the inhabitants of Strood are sometimes called 'Kentish long-tails', a tradition that goes back to a story current at least as early as the fifteenth century. According to this, the townspeople of Strood took the part of Henry II in his quarrel with Becket, and cut off the tail of the Archbishop's mule as he was passing through the town. For this, he condemned their descendants to be born with tails and 'afterward', says Polydore Vergil (*ca.* 1470–*ca.*1555), 'afterward (by the will of God) it so happened that every one that came of that kindred of men which played that naughty prank were born with tails . . .'

The story has a historical basis. 'They have attacked my servants, they have cut off my sumpter mule's tail, they have carried off the casks of wine that was the King's own gift,' complained Becket, arguing with his murderers in Canterbury Cathedral and referring to insults he had been offered in the preceding week. The docking of his sumpter-mule's tail undoubtedly led to the 'tailed men' legend being attached to St Thomas – but it was not a new story: similar tales were told of St Augustine and the men of Dorset, St Egwin and the blacksmiths of Alcester, and St Boniface and the Frisians.

In his *English Votaries* (1551), 'Bilious Bale' claims that it was on account of such stories that 'an englysh man now can not trauayle in an other lande by waye of merchaundise or anye other honest occupyenge, but it is most contumeliously throwne in his tethe, that all Englyshe men haue tayles'. This 'infamye of tails' had reached the Germans already by the fourteenth century, when they mocked the English mystic Margery Kempe as 'English sterte' – 'sterte' being OE *steort*, 'rump or tail', the same word as in 'redstart'.

Stories of tailed men die hard – remember Lord Montboddo, the eccentric eighteenth-century English nobleman who believed that men were descended from monkeys and were born with tails instantly severed by watchful midwives.

4

London and the
Home Counties

London and the Home Counties

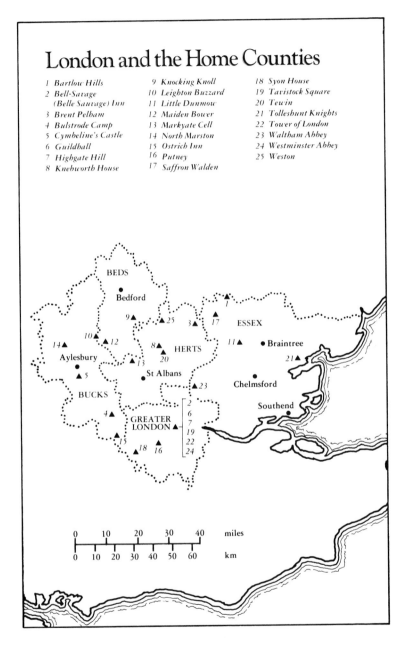

1 Bartlow Hills
2 Bell-Savage
   (Belle Sauvage) Inn
3 Brent Pelham
4 Bulstrode Camp
5 Cymbeline's Castle
6 Guildhall
7 Highgate Hill
8 Knebworth House

9 Knocking Knoll
10 Leighton Buzzard
11 Little Dunmow
12 Maiden Bower
13 Markyate Cell
14 North Marston
15 Ostrich Inn
16 Putney
17 Saffron Walden

18 Syon House
19 Tavistock Square
20 Tewin
21 Tolleshunt Knights
22 Tower of London
23 Waltham Abbey
24 Westminster Abbey
25 Weston

BEDS

● Bedford

9 ▲   ▲ 25   3 ▲   ▲   ▲ 17   ESSEX
                              1

10 ▲   ▲ 12   11 ▲   ● Braintree
14 ▲   8 ▲   HERTS   21 ▲
Aylesbury   ▲ 13   20

● 5   ● St Albans   Chelmsford ●

BUCKS   ▲ 23   Southend ●

                          ⎡ 2
4 ▲   6
GREATER   7
LONDON ▲   19
                           22
▲ 15   ▲ 18 ▲   24 ⎦
        16

0   10   20   30   40   miles

0   10 20 30 40 50 60   km

On 18 October 1016, one of the decisive battles of English history was fought at *Assandun* between King Edmund Ironside and the Danish invader Cnut. The English were defeated, and Cnut effectively won the kingdom by his victory. On this day and at this place, says the Anglo-Saxon Chronicle, fell the great Anglo-Scandinavian leader Ulfkell Snilling of East Anglia and 'all the flower of the English nation'.

The site of *Assandun* was traditionally identified as Ashdon (TL 5842), and Cnut was said to have built the church there over the graves of the English in remorse, and to have buried his own dead under the round barrows known as the Bartlow Hills. The battle site has now been identified as Ashingdon in south-east Essex, and the barrows almost certainly predate the Viking Age, but the 'foure little hils or *Burries*' as Camden calls them in the *Britannia* of 1610 have a more potent claim to be the tombs of Danes than mere facts of history or archaeology:

> The country people say that they were reared after a field there fought against the Danes. For, *Dane-wort* which with bloud-red berries, commeth up heere plenteously, they still call by no other name than *Danes-bloud*, of the number of Danes that there were slaine, verily beleeving that it blometh from their bloud.

The same tradition was recorded by Aubrey (1656–85) of 'Danes-blood' growing at Slaughterford in Wiltshire, while Gatton in Surrey, he says, was 'renowned for a great slaughter committed on the plundering Danes by the women', a tradition confirmed in the eyes of the inhabitants by the abundance of Danewort thereabouts.

Danewort is the dwarf elder (*Sambucus ebulus*), still locally called by that name in Berkshire, and known in Suffolk and Somerset as Dane Weed, while in Northern Ireland Aubrey's 'Danesblood' still survives. Of many traditions of flowers growing from men's blood – compare the poppies of Flanders – this is perhaps the most interesting. The dwarf elder's Old English name, *wealwyrt*, walwort, meant 'foreigner plant', and could imply a foreign origin (cf. *wealh hnutu*, walnut, 'foreign nut'), but the

The 'Battle hills': copper engraving of the Bartlow Hills, Essex, 1776

OED takes the view that it was always connected with the shedding of foreign blood. Certainly *wealh*, 'foreigner', is the same word that gave us 'Welsh', and perhaps the Welsh have been replaced by the Danes as the archetypal enemy.

There is no trace of the name 'Danewort' until William Turner uses it in his *Herbal* in 1538. In 1640 the botanist Parkinson explained: 'It is supposed it tooke the name Danewort from the strong purging quality it hath many times bringing them that use it unto a fluxe, which then we say they are troubled with the Danes.'

The 'danes' is sometimes assumed from this to be an entirely separate word meaning diarrhoea, and it has been suggested that the connection between Danewort and Danes was a conclusion leapt to by Camden in the 1607 *Britannia*, where the name 'Danes-bloud' first appears. But in fact walwort, dwarf elder, had already been associated with the Danes for at least a century. In his account of the Danish conquest of Mercia, the historian John Rous of Warwick (d.1491) says that in villages where the people were slaughtered by the Danes, one could see the herb *ebulus* still growing luxuriantly from the *ebullition* of their blood. Whether this etymological fancy lay behind walwort's reputation; whether it was because of the plant's appearance – in September its stems and leaves turn red, and when ripe its fruit gives off a purple juice; whether someone observed that the dwarf elder grew particularly well in churchyards (where it was perhaps planted like other herbs for greater efficacy); or whether, since it likes disturbed ground, it really did flourish on battlefields and around tumuli, we shall probably never know. But certainly Camden is likely to have encouraged the spread of the tradition when he related it of the Bartlow Hills.

BELL-SAVAGE (BELLE SAUVAGE) INN, LUDGATE HILL, LONDON

Sheet 177
TQ 3181

The Bell-Savage Inn first appears on record in 1452 as Savage's Inn, otherwise called the Bell on the Hoop. The two names, the first evidently that of its proprietor, the second taken from its sign, a bell perched on a hoop, were later run together as Bell-Savage. At some stage the spelling of the name seems to have been affected by (or did it give rise to?) the tradition that in 1616–17 the Red Indian princess Pocahontas was a guest here, hence Belle Sauvage, 'the Beautiful Savage'. In the eighteenth century this was one of London's great coaching inns, but in 1873 it was demolished and a printing works built in its place. This in turn was destroyed in 1940, when it was bombed, and in 1967 the site was made into a garden.

Before there were permanent theatres in London, plays used to be performed in the courtyards of certain inns, of which the Bell-Savage was one. In Shakespeare's time the equivalent of Music Hall also took place here. In *Love's Labour's Lost*, when Moth is trying to prove how simple is a certain piece of arithmetic, he says, 'The dancing horse will tell you', believed to be an allusion to the famous Banks's Horse. His name was Marocco or Morocco, and he had been trained by his owner, a Scotsman named Banks, to perform such tricks as counting the numbers on dice, picking up and taking a glove to any member of the audience described by his master, and to dance 'the Canaries'. In 1595 this wonderful beast was exhibited at the Bell-Savage, as we know from a pamphlet, 'Maroccus Exstaticus: or Bankes Bay Horse in a Traunce; . . . a merry dialogue between Bankes and his Beast . . . intituled to Mine Host of the Belsauage and all his honest guests'.

Whatever they thought of Banks's Horse at the Bell-Savage, in Scotland in 1596 they believed it to be animated by a spirit, and when Banks tried to use this idea as a publicity stunt in France he created a scare of diabolic possession, which he only managed to pass off by having the horse bow to a man in the crowd with a cross on his hat. It was perhaps because of this incident that a rumour later spread that Banks and his horse had been burnt at Rome by the order of the Pope. This rumour may have helped attach to the Bell-Savage another tale of diablerie, recorded by the puritanical William Prynne in his *Histrio-mastix* (1633) concerning,

> . . . the visible apparition of the Devill on the Stage at the *Belsavage Playhouse, in Queene* Elizabeths *dayes, (to the great amazement both of the Actors and Spectators) whiles they were prophanely playing the History of* Faustus (the truth of which I have heard from many now alive, who well remember it,) *there being some distracted with that fearfull sight* . . .

The play was, of course, Marlowe's *Tragicall History of Dr Faustus* (*ca.* 1588) in which, when Faustus sets out to 'trie the vttermost Magicke can performe', he conjures by means of a Latin spell which he recites on stage. This evidently shocked Elizabethan audiences, and already by 1604 there had sprung up the tradition that the Devil himself had responded to Faustus's summons. Another, undated, version of the story sets it at Exeter, where 'as a certain nomber of Devels kept everie one his circle there, and as Faustus was busie in his magicall invocations, on a sudden they were all dasht . . . for they were all perswaded, there was one devell too many amongst them . . .'

The site of the Bell-Savage is on the north side of Ludgate Hill at the beginning of Seacoal Lane.

BRENT PELHAM, HERTFORDSHIRE   Sheet 167
TL 4330

In a deep recess in the north wall of the nave of St Mary's church is a tomb purporting to be that of an eleventh-century lord of the manor named Piers Shonks. The black marble slab covering the tomb is elaborately carved with the winged symbols of the Four Evangelists (angel, lion, eagle and bull) at the four corners, and at the top an angel bearing Shonks's soul to Heaven. In the centre, the staff of a tall cross is thrust into the jaws of a coiled dragon.

In his *History of Hertfordshire* (1728), the county historian Nathaniel Salmon concludes his account of Shonks and his tomb with

> ... the Relation given me by an old Farmer in the Parish, who valued himself for being born in the Air that Shonk breathed.
>
> He saith, Shonk was a Giant that dwelt in this Parish, who fought with a Giant of *Barkway*, named Cadmus, and worsted him; upon which *Barkway* hath paid a Quit-Rent to *Pelham* ever since.

This land-ownership legend arose from circumstances of historical record: a family named Shank (with an *a*) held property in Brent Pelham in the fourteenth century, including what Weever in his *Ancient Funerall Monuments* (1631) described as 'an ancient decaied House, well moated . . . called, O Piers Shoonkes'. The house was about a mile to the south-east of Brent Pelham church, and a moated barn known as Shonks Barn still stood here in Salmon's day. One member of the family, Peter Shank, was granted another manor, in the parish of Barkway (TL 3835), by Richard FitzAlan, Earl of Arundel. This Peter is evidently our Piers.

A different story, well known at the end of the nineteenth century, was that under the roots of a yew tree that used to stand at the boundary of Great Pepsells and Little Pepsells fields was the lair of a dragon. It terrorized the district round about until one day Piers Shonks, the lord of the manor, determined to destroy it. Clad in full armour and carrying his sword and spear, he set out for the dragon's lair, accompanied by an attendant and three dogs so fleet of foot they were thought to be winged. After a fierce battle with the dragon, Shonks thrust his spear down its throat and thus destroyed it. But now the Evil One made his appearance, seeking vengeance for the death of his servant, and vowed he would have Shonks body and soul, were he buried within the church or without. But Shonks outwitted the Devil, for as he lay dying he called for his bow and shot an arrow that struck the north wall of the nave. There his tomb was built and there he rests, neither within the church nor without.

Although Weever seems not to have known it, this story was already in existence in his day. On the wall behind Piers Shonks's tomb is a Latin inscription followed by:

O PIERS SHONKS

WHO DIED ANNO 1086

and then an English translation:

> Nothing of Cadmus nor St George, those names
> Of great renown, survives them but their fames:
> Time was so sharp set as to make no Bones
> Of theirs, nor of their monumental Stones.
> But Shonks one serpent kills, to'ther defies,
> And in this wall as in a fortress lies.

Salmon suggests that the verses were written by a former vicar of Brent Pelham, Raphael Keen, who died in 1614, after nearly seventy-six years in the parish. The main part of Shonks's tomb is datable on stylistic grounds to the thirteenth century, but the brick base on which it rests and the arch above it seem to be Tudor work, so it is likely that Keen himself had it restored at the same time as adding the inscription. He must have known a tradition, subsequently lost, about the date of Shonks's death, unless he invented it. Either way it is too early to fit the tomb or the fourteenth-century date of Peter Shank.

Keen's verses show that he knew both the dragon-slaying and the wall-burial stories, so the two must have come together before the mid sixteenth century. The first part of the story 'explains' the tomb: the Devil, traditionally symbolized as a dragon, has here as elsewhere (see **Little Cornard**, p. 185), become a dragon indeed; the shaft of the cross has become a spear; and the symbols of the Four Evangelists have been transmogrified into Piers's helper and his hounds. The situation of the tomb attracted the 'neither within nor without' legend to give an end to the story (see also **Aldworth**, p.49, **Grosmont**, p.341 and **Tolleshunt Knights**, p.157). If Piers

Shonks is the same as Peter Shank – and the giant legend makes this reasonably certain – then the 'explanation' of the tomb and its identification as Piers Shonks's must have taken place between the fourteenth and the sixteenth centuries. Who is actually in the tomb, and whether the dragon-slaying was originally told of him, we are never likely to know.

Support is said to have been given to the tradition that Piers Shonks was a giant in 1861 when the tomb was opened and unusually large bones were found – but this is a common claim (cf. **Southampton**, p.76, and **Weston**, p.168).

BULSTRODE CAMP, BULSTRODE PARK, Sheet 176
GERRARD'S CROSS, BUCKINGHAMSHIRE SU 9988

Bulstrode Camp (SU 995880), oval in shape, and originally defended by two ditched outer banks, is the largest hill-fort in Buckinghamshire. Excavations in 1926 failed to date the site, but a curious legend is attached to it. It is said that at the Norman Conquest, William the Conqueror gave the manor of the Shobbington family in Buckinghamshire to one of his followers, who came with armed men to take possession. The Saxon lord of the manor entrenched himself and his men behind the earthwork and put up a stiff resistance. Finally, as he had no horses, he mounted his party on bulls and routed the Normans. When William heard of this, he sent for the stout-hearted thane, and Shobbington and his seven sons be*strode* their *bulls* and went to court. William was so delighted that he allowed him to keep the estate, and conferred on him and his heirs for ever the name of 'Bulstrode'.

Recorded in M. A. Lower's *English Surnames* (3rd edn, 1849), the story is a piece of popular etymology explaining the name 'Bulstrode', and the arms of the Bulstrode family, which include a bull in canting allusion to the name, actually believed to consist of OE *bula* + *strōd*, 'bull-marsh'. Whatever the truth of the tale, the antiquity of the Bulstrodes was a matter of family pride commemorated in a rhyme given in Murray's *Handbook for Travellers in Berks, Bucks, & Oxfordshire* (1860):

> When William conquer'd English ground,
> Bulstrode had per annum three hundred pound.

CYMBELINE'S CASTLE, GREAT KIMBLE, BUCKINGHAMSHIRE

Great Kimble is said to have got its name from the British king Cunobelin, whom the Romans called Cunobelinus and Shakespeare Cymbeline. This may be popular etymology; more likely it is an antiquarian invention based on early spellings of 'Kimble'. A tenth-century reference to Great Kimble contains the word *Cynebellinga* which looks something like 'Cunobelin', but is in fact thought to contain OE *cyne* 'royal' and *bell(e)*, probably 'hill', the hill being called 'royal' either because a royal burial or other event was connected with it, or because it was prominent.

Near Great Kimble, commanding the prehistoric track of the Icknield Way, is a small motte-and-bailey earthwork known as Cymbeline's Castle (SP 833064), of which it is nowadays said that if you run round it seven times the Devil will appear. According to a tradition reported by the county historian Lipscomb (1847), Cymbeline's Mount, as it was then known, was built by Cunobelin as his hold, but this is undoubtedly a guess on the strength of Great Kimble's name and the celebrity of Shakespeare's play *Cymbeline*, written between 1606 and 1611, and based, as far as the Roman bits go, on the confused account in Holinshed's *Chronicles* (1577).

Though the connection between Shakespeare's play and historical fact is slight, he was right in making Cymbeline central to the affairs of his day. Cunobelin was king of the Catuvellauni of Hertfordshire and the surrounding district, and from about 10 A.D. ruler also of the Trinovantes of Essex. Effectively the suzerain of south-east Britain, he built himself a new capital, Camulodunon, 'the fortress of Camulos' (the war-god), at what is now Colchester. A client-king of the Romans, his death was indirectly a cause of the Roman invasion.

Cunobelin was a great man who impressed himself on the popular imagination – his figure seems to lie behind both Coel, the eponymous founder of Colchester in medieval if not earlier tradition (see **Sarn Helen**, p.355) and Old King Cole of the nursery rhyme, though the honours here are shared with a Reading clothier, Thomas Cole, who under the name 'Old Cole' was famous for his wealth (see **Ostrich Inn**, p.149), and with *Coel Hen Guotepauc*, 'Old Cole the Splendid' (for whom see **Coylton**, p.437).

Cymbeline's Castle is to the right of the public footpath through Chequers park beginning opposite the cottages next to Ellesborough church (SP 836067). This footpath, clearly marked on the OS 1:25 000 map, Pathfinder Series, Sheet SP 80/90 (Chesham and Wendover), joins up with the Ridgeway Path.

GUILDHALL, LONDON

Sheet 177
TQ 3281

In another version of the story of the founding of Britain by the Trojan leader Brutus (see **Plymouth Hoe**, p.27), Brutus captures two giants, Gog and Magog, and makes them porters of his palace at Troynovant (New Troy, i.e. London). This version seems to be connected with the Guildhall in the City of London, which has housed the effigies of a pair of giants for at least three centuries. The giants are at present called Gog and Magog, but in Tudor times they were known as Gogmagog and Corineus. They were paraded in a pageant to welcome Philip of Spain on his marriage to Mary in 1554, and in 1558, when Elizabeth I passed in procession from the Tower of London to Westminster, 'Gogmagog the Albion' and 'Corineus the Briton' saluted her from the Temple Bar.

Giants have appeared in civic processions in London for more than five centuries – in 1415 a pair of them welcomed Henry V home after Agincourt – and those at the Guildhall were long a popular feature of the Lord Mayor's show, between whiles being stationed at either end of a balcony inside the Hall. But prior to 1554 they seem to have been called Samson and Hercules, names that were perhaps supplanted by Gogmagog and Corineus in Tudor times when interest in the legends of Albion was at its height (see **Wandlebury Camp**, p.202). Subsequently, because of confusion about Gogmagog's name, they came (quite without official cognizance) to be called Gog and Magog, as in the Bible.

Bishop Hall in 1597 speaks of the 'crab-tree porter of the Guildhall gates' with his 'frightful beetle', so either he knew the story of Gog and Magog serving as porters, or perhaps at one time the giants actually stood at the doors of the Guildhall, i.e. were atlantes (male figures used as supporting columns) like the pair holding up the porch of Samson and Hercules House in Tombland, Norwich (built ?1657). The Guildhall legend *might* have arisen

*Corineus and Gogmagog: figures carved by Captain
Richard Saunders in 1708 and destroyed in the London Blitz*

from this circumstance; equally, the placing of the giants might have been in response to the legend.

On the whole the tradition of the porters seems to be an embroidery of Geoffrey of Monmouth's story of Gogmagog and Corineus, invented to explain the presence of the figures at the Guildhall and given wide currency by children's books such as *The History of the Trojan Wars and Troy's Destruction*, published in 1735.

The idea of civic giants as the symbols of power and authority of a city came in the first place from the Continent – a notable example there is the Bremen 'Roland', a stone statue in the marketplace erected on the spot where in 1366 an earlier wooden effigy had been destroyed by fire. The Continental giants are believed to descend from a statue of the Emperor Otto II made about 980 A.D. and placed in the Stadthaus at Magdeburg as a palladium.

Today the Guildhall giants stand on pedestals in the west gallery. These statues, 9 ft 3 in (2.82 m) high, replaced an older and even larger pair, 14 ft 6 in (4.42 m) high, destroyed in the Blitz in 1940. The earlier giants were themselves carved by a Captain Richard Saunders in 1708 to replace a still older pair destroyed in the Great

Fire of London. Captain Saunders's figures were gaudily coloured, with hands and faces gory from battle. The costumes of the giants probably have not changed much since Tudor times – the present Gog is still armed with a morningstar, perhaps the 'frightful beetle' mentioned by Bishop Hall.

The Guildhall is open to visitors Mon.–Fri. 10–5.

HIGHGATE HILL, LONDON

Sheet 177
TQ 2987

One of the most famous English fairytales is 'Dick Whittington and his Cat'. The story goes that Dick Whittington was a poor boy who lived in the time of Edward III. He made his way to London to seek his fortune, having heard that its streets were paved with gold, but found nothing better than work as a scullion in the house of a rich merchant, Mr Fitzwarren. There Dick suffered from the ill-humour of the cook, and also from the mice that plagued his attic until for one penny he bought a cat. This was his only possession, and when Mr Fitzwarren had a ship ready to sail and asked his servants if they wanted a stake in the voyage, Dick had nothing to venture except the cat. The ship sailed away and came at last to the coast of Barbary, where the captain heard that the King's palace was overrun with rats. He brought Dick's cat to the palace, and it soon despatched the rats, whereupon the grateful King bought the ship's entire cargo for a great sum of money, and the cat for ten times as much again.

Dick, meantime, was once more being persecuted by the cook and made up his mind to run away. He got as far as Holloway, and sat down on a stone to rest. There he heard the bells of Bow church ringing, and they seemed to say:

> Turn again, Whittington,
> Lord Mayor of London.

Dick *did* turn back, and, not long after that, Mr Fitzwarren's ship returned with the news that Dick was a wealthy man. He married Alice Fitzwarren, his master's daughter, and rose to be, not once, but thrice Lord Mayor of London.

The tale of a poor boy whose fortune is made by a cat is found in twenty-six different countries. In the fifteenth century it was told of a merchant in Genoa, but perhaps its most famous version is 'Puss in Boots'. In England it attached itself to a real person, Sir Richard Whittington, a mercer in the reign of Henry V who lent large sums of money to the King to pay for his wars in France. Sir Richard was indeed thrice Lord Mayor of London, in 1397–8, 1406–7 and 1419–20. But his was not a rags-to-riches story: he was the son of a well-to-do Gloucestershire squire and inherited a respectable fortune. His 'Alice' was the daughter of Sir Ovo Fitzwaryn of Dorset, but he died childless in 1423, leaving substantial legacies to various charities.

The cat was probably first attached to Dick in the reign of Queen Elizabeth I; the story certainly had its present form by the seventeenth century. There are allusions to it from about 1600 onwards, and a licence to publish *The History of Sir Richard Whittington* was granted to one Thomas Pavier in 1604. The story is sometimes connected, whether as cause or effect, with a limestone bas-relief found in a house in Gloucester in 1862. Some accounts say the house belonged to the Whittingtons, others that it belonged to the Berkeley family in the fifteenth century – the Berkeley connection being that Richard Whittington's mother was the widow of Sir Thomas Berkeley of Coberley Manor when she married Sir William Whittington of Pauntley Court. The Whittingtons indeed had a town house in Gloucester in the fifteenth century, next to St Nicholas's Church in Westgate Street, almost opposite the present Gloucester Folk Museum, but it disappeared in the 1530s. In any case, the bas-relief was not found on this site but another some way further up Westgate Street where it came to light in the foundations of a cabinet-maker and upholsterer's house. Not even the cat is certain – some interpret the creature as a lamb – and the carving probably has no original connection with the story, but was simply hailed as Dick and the cat upon discovery, much as 'giant's bones' were identified as Gogmagog at **Plymouth Hoe** (p.27).

Though Coberley Manor is traditionally said to have been Dick Whittington's birthplace (from the idea that his mother's Whittington marriage came first), Dick's story has now become associated chiefly with London. In one of the earliest versions of

Is this Dick Whittington? Bas-relief of a boy holding what some take to be a cat, found in a house in Westgate Street, Gloucester, and now in Gloucester Folk Museum

'Whittington and his Cat', Dick rests at 'Bun Hill', perhaps Bunhill Fields, but in later chapbooks he stops at Holloway, hence his long association with the Whittington Stone on Highgate Hill. The original was not a milestone as is assumed in some versions of the story and almost all pantomimes (one way London, one way Gloucester), but the remains of a wayside cross which stood in front of a piece of ground (between Macdonald Road and Salisbury Close) known as the Lazarcot or Lazarette Field, from the Lazar House or hospital for lepers erected there in 1473. In 1795, the original Whittington Stone was sawn in half and removed by an Islington parish officer to be used as paving stone. The inhabitants of Islington protested, and another stone was placed in its stead. This second stone has been removed, replaced, restored, and re-sited, but is today still only about forty feet from its original position, though now enclosed by railings and surmounted by the figure of a cat.

Whittington's Cat was commissioned in 1964 from Jonathan Kennedy and Tony Southwell. The bas-relief of the boy with the 'cat' is still preserved in Gloucester Folk Museum – for times, see *M&G* – but because its origins are so uncertain it is no longer on display. However, because it is generally agreed to be 'Renaissance' and might just be some seventeenth-century stonemason's idea of Dick and his cat, I give its picture.

KNEBWORTH HOUSE, HERTFORDSHIRE   Sheet 166
TL 2520

One of Britain's most famous death-warnings is the 'Radiant Boy', now said to appear to members of the Lytton family at Knebworth House. His most celebrated manifestation was when he appeared to Lord Castlereagh some years before he ended his life, on 12 August 1822, by cutting his throat.

Sir Walter Scott had heard Castlereagh speak of the Radiant Boy 'at one of his wife's supper parties in Paris in 1815', and seven years later wrote in a letter to Lady Abercorn:

> I remember his once telling seriously and with great minuteness the particulars of an apparition which he thought he had seen. It was a naked child, which he saw slip out of the grate of a bedroom while he looked at the decaying fire. It increased at every step it advanced towards him, and again diminished in size till it went into the fireplace and disappeared. I could not tell what to make of so wild a story told by a man whose habits were equally remote from quizzing or inventing a mere tale of wonder. The truth is now plain that the vision had been the creation of a temporary access of his constitutional infirmity.

Lockhart, who had often heard his father-in-law tell the story, adds to this that with its increase in size the naked child 'assumed the appearance of a ghastly giant, pale as death, with a bleeding wound on the brow, and eyes glaring with rage and despair'. The sequence of events made a deep impression on Scott, who in his journal on 1 November 1826 wrote: 'He is gone . . . I shall always tremble when any friend of mine becomes visionary.'

One wonders whether Scott's frequent retellings of the story helped put it into general circulation – for Lady Abercorn had written from Florence in 1822, 'I never heard of his having named it to any one else ...' Certainly the Radiant Boy was in the nineteenth century much aired, and a curious tale arose that 'Cutthroat Castlereagh' had himself appeared on the island of Stromboli at the moment of his death.

As for the Radiant Boy, was he perhaps something more than a figment of Castlereagh's tormented imagination? Chillingham Castle also had one 'till lately', according to Murray in 1873, and so did Corby Castle, on the Eden, near Carlisle, though he would not appear for P. Fraser Tytler, the historian, who after staying there overnight on 8 November 1840 wrote to his sister:

> I have come away without seeing the radiant boy of Corby. This was extraordinary, for I had to walk to my bedroom every night through a long dark gallery of which you could not see the termination, with old warriors frowning down on me, and the moon streaming in through the Gothic window at the end – circumstance which one would have thought any well-conditioned ghost would have profited by.

The Rev. Sabine Baring-Gould in his *Yorkshire Oddities* (1874) mentions a boy with a shining face who had been seen in certain houses in Lincolnshire and elsewhere, and of whom he had received an account from an old Yorkshire farmer who was nicknamed 'John Mealyface':

> John M. was riding one night to Thirsk, when he suddenly saw pass him a radiant Boy on a white horse. There was no sound of footfall as he drew nigh. Old John was first aware of the approach of the mysterious rider by seeing the shadow of himself and his horse flung before him on the high road. Thinking there might be a carriage with lamps, he was not unduly alarmed till by the shortening of the shadow he knew that the light must be near him, and then he was surprised to hear no sound. He thereupon turned in his saddle, and at the same moment the Radiant Boy passed him. He was a child of about eleven, with a fresh bright face. 'Had he any clothes on, and if so what were they like?' I asked; but John took no

notice of particulars. The boy rode on till he came to a gate which led into a field; he stooped as if to open the gate, rode through, and all was instantly dark.

Though one suspects that the expression 'radiant Boy' was Baring-Gould's and not the farmer's, John Mealyface's account, with its lack of 'particulars', sounds sufficiently genuine. Although like the others it post-dates Scott, it may be that what Castlereagh saw was, if not a 'real' ghost, at least a hallucination in a traditional mould.

It must be said that the atmosphere at Knebworth was right for phantasms. Though the present mansion, in the 'Gothick' taste, is romantic enough, it was evidently the old house, dating from 1563 and largely pulled down in 1811 or 1812, that inspired the tradition. The novelist Edward Bulwer-Lytton, author of *The Last Days of Pompeii* (1834), who was to inherit Knebworth from his mother, was allowed as a boy to roam 'that old, half-feudal pile', and in a letter wrote:

> I remember especially a long narrow gallery adjoining the great drawing-room (and hung with faded and grim portraits) which terminated in rooms that were called, 'haunted'. They were of great antiquity, covered with gloomy tapestry, and containing huge chimney-pieces with rude reliefs set in oak frames grotesquely carved. In another room adjoining these . . . was a curious trap-door that gave access to a chamber beneath it – if chamber it can be called, which had neither doors nor windows [this was known as Hell-hole] . . . How could I help writing romances when I had walked, trembling at my own footstep, through that long gallery, with its ghostly portraits, mused in those tapestry chambers, and peeped, with bristling hair, into the shadowy abysses of Hell-hole.

The 'haunted rooms' were among those demolished, but were still in 1883 remembered with mingled pride and awe by a few aged inhabitants of Knebworth village. The old house was also 'truth-fully described' in a ghost-story invented there one Christmastime in about 1800 by a Miss James, one of the guests. They had asked the gatekeeper and other villagers about 'the ghost', but no one knew anything other than that there *was* one, so each member of the party set about writing its history. Miss James's story was entitled 'Jenny Spinner; or, the Ghost of Knebworth House', about an apparition whose spinning-wheel was often heard, and who seems to have got her name from Arkwright's Spinning Jenny.

With memories of such a house still current, and with the habit of fantasy deliberately cultivated in it, it would not be surprising if Castlereagh saw, rather than for the purposes of dinner-party conversation *said* he saw, the ghastly apparition of the Radiant Boy.

Knebworth House and Park are open to the public – for times see *HHC&G*. On Saturdays and Sundays, May to September, British Rail run special excursions to Knebworth from King's Cross.

KNOCKING KNOLL, SHILLINGTON, BEDFORDSHIRE

Sheet 166
TL 1330

Just to the east of Pegsdon Common Farm is Knocking Knoll (TL 133309), the remains of a round barrow. At certain times, it is said, one can hear an old man knocking to be let out. A more elaborate version of the legend that appeared in the *Hertfordshire Illustrated Review* in 1894 says that a British chieftain is buried here with his treasure chest, and from time to time knocks thrice on it to make sure it is still there. The hill is sometimes referred to locally as 'Money Knoll'. The 'hidden treasure' story is a common one which has perhaps been grafted on to an earlier tale that set out to explain why the hill is so called. Actually the name seems to come from an ancient British word that survives in modern Welsh as *cnycyn*, 'bump, small hillock'.

LEIGHTON BUZZARD, BEDFORDSHIRE

Sheet 165
SP 9225

On a pillar in All Saints' Church is a little sketch – a graffito – probably drawn in the fifteenth century by someone guarding the church's precious relic of the cloak of St Hugh. Tradition says that it represents the mythical Simon and Nell, makers of the first Simnel Cake. They are supposed to have quarrelled as to whether to have for dinner a boiled pudding or a baked pie. Neither would yield, so first they boiled the mix, then baked it, and called the result 'simnel' (Sim + Nell).

In fact the word 'simnel' seems to be related to 'semolina', and in the Middle Ages to have denoted a specially fine kind of flour. From the dictionary of John de Garlande in the thirteenth century we learn that the name was also used of certain cakes exposed for sale in the windows of hucksters.

These cakes may have had a religious significance.

> I'll to thee a simnel bring,
> 'Gainst thou go a-mothering;
> So that, when she blesses thee,
> Half that blessing thou'lt give me

wrote the poet Herrick at the beginning of the seventeenth century, and it appears that in his time it was the custom at Gloucester for young people to take simnels to their mothers on Mid-Lent or Mothering Sunday (cf. the Whirlin' Cakes of **Leverington**, p.185).

It was in the nineteenth century still the custom at Bury in Lancashire to make Simnel Cakes for Mid-Lent Sunday, while at Shrewsbury they were made during Lent and Easter, and also at Christmas. They were raised cakes with a pastry crust made of fine flour and water, and coloured with saffron. Inside was a rich fruit cake. They were tied up in a cloth and boiled for several hours, after which they were brushed with egg and baked. This resulted in a crust as hard as wood, the subject of several jokes as to surprising uses for simnels.

LITTLE DUNMOW, ESSEX
Sheet 167
TG 6521

Of the former Priory Church of Little Dunmow only the Lady Chapel survives (now the parish church). On the left facing the altar are two tombs, one supporting alabaster effigies of Walter FitzWalter (d.1431) and his wife Elizabeth, the other with an effigy of Joan Devereux (d.1409), Walter's mother. But Joan has been forgotten – legend says that this is the tomb of Matilda the Fair or Robin Hood's Maid Marian.

The story of Matilda the Fair, the subject of one of Drayton's *Heroicall Epistles* (1598), is told by Weever in his *Ancient Funerall Monuments* (1631) thus:

About the yeare 1213, saith the booke of *Dunmow*, there arose a great discord betwixt king *Iohn* and his Barons, because of *Matilda* surnamed the faire, daughter of *Robert Fitz-water*, whom the King vnlawfully loued, but could not obtaine her, nor her fathers consent thereunto. Whereupon, and for other like causes, ensued warre through the whole Realme. The king banished the said *Fitz-water* amongst other, and caused his Castle, called *Baynard*, and other his houses to be spoiled. Which being done, he sent a messenger vnto *Matilda* the faire, about his old Suit in Loue . . . And because she would not agree to his wicked motion, the messenger poisoned a boiled or potched Egge, against she was hungrie, and gaue it vnto her, wherof she died, the yeare 1213.

This story was reproduced as history into the nineteenth century. Meantime, in his play *The Downfall of Robert Earl of Huntingdon* (1601), the Elizabethan playwright Anthony Munday had made the outlaw Robin Hood the Earl of Huntingdon, not a yeoman as he had been in earlier ballads, and identified his bride Matilda (otherwise Maid Marian) as Matilda FitzWalter, probably because a FitzWalter had in real life married an earl of Huntingdon's daughter. The sequel to the play, *The Death of Robert Earl of Huntingdon*, written with Henry Chettle (d. ?1607), embroidered the earlier tale of the death of Matilda, giving rise to a story told in the nineteenth century that, after Robin Hood died, Matilda/Marian took refuge at Dunmow Priory. King John sent Robert de Medewe to her with what seemed to be a token of his love – a bracelet – which Robert unwittingly gave to her, not knowing it was poisoned. Matilda was no longer young, but she was still beautiful, and he fell in love with her, and turned back on his road to London to see her again. It was night when he reached the priory, and from the church came the sound of a funeral dirge. When he entered, he found Matilda lying lifeless on a flower-decked bier, for the bracelet had eaten its way to the bone and poisoned her. Robert flung himself on the bier, cursing himself, and never returned to Court but became a monk.

Little Dunmow is also famous for the custom of the Flitch – see Christina Hole, *British Folk Customs* (Paladin, London, 1977).

MAIDEN BOWER, HOUGHTON REGIS, BEDFORDSHIRE

The Maiden Bower (SP 996225) is a small Iron Age plateau fort built over a Neolithic causewayed camp. During the middle Iron Age it was the scene of a fierce battle resulting in a slaughter, but its legend concerns its making, not its violent past. According to a story recorded in 1904, a queen cut a bull's hide into strips, and joining them end to end, arranged them in a circle on the ground. The king then ordered his troops to follow her pattern, and dig the rampart and ditch we see today. A parallel tale is told of *Lled Croen yr Ych*, 'the Width of the Ox-hide' in the parish of Llanbrynmair, Powys, which is thought to be the retaining circle of a round barrow. A tradition from the nineteenth century says that this was the grave of a long-horned ox who died of grief at being parted from his mate. When he died, he was skinned and his hide stretched on the ground and surrounded by a circle of stones. Both these stories seem to be garbled versions of the 'oxhide' tale found at **Caistor** (p.222), and told in antiquity of the founding of Carthage.

The Maiden Bower is off the A5, about a hundred yards up the road to Sewell, on the left.

MARKYATE CELL, HERTFORDSHIRE

The best-known of Hertfordshire's many treasure legends is that of the old house of Markyate Cell:

> Near the Cell there is a Well.
> Near the Well there is a Tree.
> And under the Tree the Treasure be.

On this site from the twelfth century up to the Reformation stood the priory of St Trinity-in-the-Wood, which thereafter fell into the hands of Humphrey Bourchier, third Baron Berners, who, says Leland (*ca.* 1506–52), 'on the est side of it did much coste in translating of the priorie into a maner-place; but . . . left it nothing endid'. 'Endid' or not, the house was subsequently bought from

Henry VIII by George Ferrers, in whose family it continued until the mid seventeenth century. It is supposedly to one of the Ferrers that the treasure-legend is attached – their most notorious member, known to thousands from the Margaret Lockwood film (1945) as 'The Wicked Lady'.

The Wicked Lady was Lady Catherine Ferrers, said to have lived at Markyate in the eighteenth century, and to have been in the habit of stealing out at night to lead a double life as a highwayman. Wearing men's clothes and a mask, and riding a black horse with white stockings that could gallop like the wind, she was the terror of travellers along the Holyhead Road. Eventually she was shot at a place called No Man's Land, and made her way home, mortally wounded. She was found lying dead outside a door leading by a secret staircase to the room where she used to put on her highwayman clothes.

This story is reported in *History of Hertfordshire* (1879–81) by Cussans, who writes:

> The doorway was built up, and so remained for certainly a hundred and fifty years. The late Mr. Adey, who pulled down a large portion of the old building after the fire of 1840, determined to reopen the doorway, but there was not one of the local labourers who could be induced to undertake the work, and Mr. Adey was obliged to send to London to get men to do it. On opening the doorway, a narrow stone staircase was found. At the top was a stout oak door, which was broken down, but it afterwards appeared that it might have been opened by pressing a concealed spring. Nothing was found in the room but innumerable bats ... During the last fire, in 1840, many of the labourers, who were assisting in checking it, positively asserted that they saw Lady Ferrers swinging herself on a branch of a large sycamore, standing near the house. Mr. Adey was away from home at the time; but before his return, so impressed were the men with the reality of the apparition, that they took upon themselves to saw the branch off, and were greatly surprised that they were not handsomely rewarded, by the owner, for such zeal.

Cussans adds that the story of the 'Wicked Lady Ferrers' was 'in this present year of 1878' religiously believed by most of the inhabitants of Markyate Street. Certainly people thought that the destruction of Markyate Cell by fire in 1840 was her work. Tradition said, moreover, that the Markyate treasure lay under the sycamore tree on which the Wicked Lady swung, though it does not make it clear whether it was thought to be her loot.

But was there really a Wicked Lady? If indeed there was – and this is a singular legend that well deserves to be true – then she was probably not a Ferrers: she is a century too late. As Cussans points out, the story hinges on a coincidence of names, and the Wicked Lady may owe both name and reputation to the Earl of Ferrers, 'The Wicked Lord Ferrers', hanged in 1760 at Tyburn Tree.

If the Wicked Lady is a figment, she doesn't know it. She is still said to ride the roads at night from St Albans as far as Kimpton, and from Markyate Cell almost to Dunstable. She also used to be a familiar sight about the house. Augustus Hare (1894) writes: 'She constantly haunts the place. Mr Adey, who lives there now, meets her on the stairs, and wishes her "Goodnight". Once, seeing her with her arms stretched out in the doorway, he called out to his wife, who was outside, "Now we've caught her!" and they rushed upon her from both sides, but caught – nothing!'

The Wicked Lady is, of course, far from being the only ghost who comes back to revisit the scene of her crimes.

Markyate Cell, rebuilt on a smaller scale after its destruction by fire in 1840, is fairly well screened from the road, but there is a good view of it from behind the church. It is not open to the public. Markyate Street is now plain Markyate (TL 0616). The film *The Wicked Lady* was remade by Michael Winner in 1983. It will be interesting to see whether it has as much influence as the Margaret Lockwood–James Mason version in keeping the story alive.

NORTH MARSTON, BUCKINGHAMSHIRE   Sheet 165
SP 7722

The rector of North Marston from 1290 to 1314 was Sir John Schorne or Shorne, popularly revered as a saint, although he was never canonized. He appears to have been born at some time in the thirteenth century at the village of Shorne in Kent, but nothing else is known of him. Bishop Latimer (*ca.* 1485–1555) in one of his sermons speaks scathingly of 'the popish pilgrimage, which we were wont to use in times past, in running hither and thither to Master John Shorn, or to Our Lady of Walsingham'. At North Marston, as at Walsingham, there was a chalybeate spring believed to have healing properties: it was said to have burst from the ground when Sir John struck it with his staff, a 'miracle' often accredited to saints. A well was built round the spring and pilgrims paid to drink from a gold cup chained to the wall. It had the reputation of healing 'scorbutic and cutaneous diseases, ague and gout', and a glass of water drunk at night would cure a cold by the morning. The offerings of the pilgrims were so abundant that, at the Reformation, when pilgrimages ceased, Eton College, which had a claim on part of the revenue, was said to have lost an income of £500 a year. In North Marston itself some of the proceeds are said to have gone into the building of the chancel of the very fine parish church.

Above the church vestry is a priest's room with a fireplace and also a small window overlooking the chancel, so that it was perhaps used by priests watching over Sir John Schorne's shrine. This was probably at the end of the south aisle – the niche at floor level there is thought once to have held the saint's bones. These were removed to the Lincoln, formerly the Schorne, Chantry in St George's Chapel, Windsor, in 1478, but the holy well remained on the pilgrim circuit right up to the Reformation. After the pilgrimages had ceased, the water from the well was used only for watering cattle – its taste, like that of the water from many chalybeate springs, was evidently pretty disgusting. But perhaps its mineral content declined in the course of time – at any rate, in 1835 the spring became the regular source of water for the village.

The spring has never failed and is still there, not far from the church, and still called 'Schorne's Well', although now covered by hatches and accessed by a pump. A tantalizing snippet of legend is all that otherwise remains of this once celebrated saint. Browne Willis, quoted by the Buckinghamshire historian Lipscomb (1847), says that inscribed on the wall of the well was the rhyme:

> Sir John Shorne
> Gentleman born
> Conjured the Devil into a boot.

One of the commissioners sent out during the Dissolution of the Monasteries (1536–9) reported back to Thomas Cromwell: 'At Merston Master John Schorn stondith blessing a bote, whereunto they do say he conveyed the devill', and Lipscomb says that Sir John used to be represented in the windows of the chancel with a boot under his arm, 'into which he was squeezing a little puppet in the likeness of Satan'. Some think that the window between the priest's room and the chancel once contained the mechanical figure of a devil in a boot, the original, perhaps, of the Jack in the Box. Certainly such contrivances were not unknown in medieval churches – in Llandderfel church, Gwynedd, can still be seen the wooden horse of its patron, St Derfel, said to have been one of King Arthur's warriors: pilgrims to his shrine up to the Reformation used to be edified by a wooden image of the saint himself whose head, arms and eyes all moved mechanically.

Such things were destroyed at the Reformation – the image of St Derfel was burnt at Smithfield along with a priest who refused to deny that it had caused miracles – and the whys and wherefores of Sir John's story are lost, but in its heyday it may have been something like the Norse tales of 'The Master Smith' and 'The Lad and the Deil', in which the Devil is tricked into a steel purse and a nut.

The boot became Sir John's attribute – like St Anthony's pig or St Lawrence's gridiron – and he can still be seen with it on fifteenth-century rood-screens at Suffield, Gateley and Cawston, all in Norfolk: a saint who could deal with the ague would have been a good friend to marshmen.

Many houses in the village centre were destroyed by fire in 1700, and it is much better to approach the church on foot rather than in a car. Park at the Bell Inn and follow the lane past Holden's Shop. Ignore the first left turn, but bear left past Yeoman Cottage (formerly the Armed Yeoman public house) to the church. Inside the church a picture-guide is on sale. For the well, on leaving the church, turn right down Schorne Lane, then left, and it is in front of you. At Winslow (SP 7627), the next village to North Marston, there is a pub that goes under the sign of The Devil in the Boot, formerly simply The Boot.

OSTRICH INN, COLNBROOK, Sheet 176
BUCKINGHAMSHIRE TQ 0277

The Ostrich Inn at Colnbrook goes back to 1106, and it is said that King John paused here to recruit his strength on his way to sign Magna Carta. A more sinister tradition is that in medieval times the inn was run by a couple called Jarman who used to murder rich travellers in their beds by precipitating them through a trapdoor into a cauldron of boiling ale. They used to account for the disappearance of their visitors by saying they had left very early in the morning before anyone was up, but they were found out when the horse of their sixtieth victim got loose and was recognized. This last victim was a wealthy Reading clothier, Thomas Cole, who on journeys to London always dined 'at the signe of the Crane' at Colnbrook, and was in the habit of giving the hostess there his money to look after. When Cole's horse was found wandering in the village, a search was made for him, and his body discovered in a nearby stream. Seeing that the game was up, Jarman attempted to flee, but was overtaken by justice, and he and his wife were both hanged in Windsor Forest.

'And some say, that the riuer whereinto *Cole* was cast, did euer since carry the name of *Cole*, being called, The riuer of *Cole*, and the towne of Colebrooke.' As a matter of fact, up to the seventeenth century, the name was always spelled without an *n* (which it only acquired later from the name of the River Colne). But the first part of the name seems to be not 'Cole' but an old personal name *Cola*, i.e. it is 'Cola's brook'.

The story comes from Thomas Deloney's novel *The pleasant Historie of Thomas of Reading*, written between 1597 and 1600. It is one of several tales celebrating the great merchants of England, of which 'Dick Whittington and his Cat' is the best-known example. Deloney had been a weaver, and *Thomas of Reading* exalts the clothiers' trade – its heroes are six clothiers known as 'the six worthie yeomen of the West', of whom Thomas became the most famous. At the same time, the story is probably based on a local tradition which Deloney picked up in the course of his life as a wandering artisan, roaming from town to town and keeping tavern company. Another tale we owe largely to him is that of the ballad 'The Spanish Lady's Love' (see **Adlington Hall**, p.291) and he also produced a popular ballad of Fair Rosamond (see **Woodstock**, p.283).

Deloney's Chapter 11, describing the murder, is a masterpiece of melodrama. Thomas arrives at the Crane, where Jarman and his wife resolve to make away with him. 'With that the scritch owle cried piteously, and anone after the night rauen sate, croking hard by his window' – omens of death which he disregards. The murderers wait until he has gone to bed,

> ... and when they had listned at his chamber doore, they heard the man sound asleepe. All is safe, quoth they, and downe into the kitchin they goe, their seruants being all in bedde, and pulling out the yron pins, downe fel the bed, and the man dropt out in to the boyling caldron. He being dead, they betwixt them cast his body into the riuer, his clothes they hid away, and made all things as it should be ...

The story was deservedly popular in the seventeenth century as a chapbook (Pepys had a copy) and Cole's name became proverbial for wealth – he was familiarly known as 'Old Cole' and may be the 'Old King Cole' of the nursery rhyme (but see **Cymbeline's Castle**, p.132). In Deloney's story 'Iarman' is landlord of the Crane, without doubt the inn at Colnbrook now known as the Ostrich. At the turn of the last century the falling floor no longer existed (if it ever had), but the landlord still showed visitors the room where the murder took place, and old women and schoolchildren could still give an account of the crime that tallied almost exactly with Deloney. Possibly Deloney actually picked the story up at Colnbrook, where it continued little changed, or more likely the form of the story has been fixed by his novel.

The story of course bears a resemblance to that of Sweeney Todd, usually traced back to an early-nineteenth-century French source. Both probably embody a persistent fantasy about landlords. In *Thomas of Reading*, the clothiers' wives are gossiping about the murder, of which they have heard wildly varying reports (including that it was made known by a talking horse – cf. **Bell-Savage Inn**, p.127):

> No neighbour, it was not at London, said another: I hear say twas comming from London, at a place called Colebrooke, and it is reported for truth, that the Inholder [innkeeper] made pies of him, and penny pasties, yea, and made his owne seruant eate a piece of him.

Let not this deter you from the gargantuan Elizabethan meals served at the Ostrich Inn today. You will be following in august footsteps: the present building dates from the early sixteenth century and 'Queen Elizabeth slept here' in 1558 on one of her progresses.

PUTNEY, LONDON

Sheet 176
TQ 2375

> According to vulgar tradition, the churches of Putney and Fulham were built by two sisters, who had but one hammer between them, which they interchanged by throwing it cross the river, on a word agreed between them; those on the Surrey side made use of the word, put it nigh!; those on the opposite shore, heave it full home; whence the churches, and from them the villages, were called Putnigh and Fullhome, since corrupted to Putney and Fulham.

This curious tale, from Grose's *Provincial Glossary* (1787), is a cheerful variation of one commonly told of giants (see **Wade's Stone**, p.421), and from this we can safely assume that the sisters were giantesses.

SAFFRON WALDEN, ESSEX

Sheet 154
TL 5438

'So called of the great plentie of Saffron growing in the fields round about the Towne', says Weever in his *Ancient Funerall Monuments* (1631). Hakluyt (d.1616) had earlier reported that, when he visited the town, he was told a tradition that the saffron had first been brought to England from the Levant by a pilgrim in the reign of Edward III. He smuggled it home in a hollowed-out staff, 'for if he had been taken, by the law of the country from whence it came, he had died for the fact'. Saffron was expensive – hence the romantic account of its origins. The hollow staff also figures in the tale of how silkworm eggs were first smuggled out of China into the West.

SYON HOUSE, ISLEWORTH, LONDON
(formerly MIDDLESEX)

Sheet 176
TQ 1776

> The Nun of *Sion*, with the Frier of *Shean*,
> Went under water to play the Quean

says a rhyme in James Howell's *Lexicon Tetraglotton* (1659–60) referring to the tradition that there was an underground passage between the convent of Syon and the friary of Sheen at Richmond, in Surrey.

This unedifying, and for that reason undoubtedly highly popular, piece of folklore was also current in the nineteenth century in Leicestershire, where steps were supposed to have been found leading down into a subterranean passage connecting a nunnery that once stood in the neighbourhood of the Humber Stone with Leicester Abbey. This was if anything more libellous than the tradition about Syon and Sheen, as there seems never to have been such a convent. It is food for thought that a goodly proportion of English fantasy life, especially in solidly Puritan areas such as the Fens, has been spent on the sexual congress of monks and nuns. Subterranean passages are, of course, ten a penny.

The Brigittine convent, founded by Henry V in 1415 and moved to Isleworth in 1431, was built on the site of the present Syon House. Both Syon House and Syon Park Gardens are open to the public – for times, see *HHC&G*. At Richmond, the site of the house of Franciscan Observant Friars, founded by Henry VII at roughly the same time as he rebuilt the old Sheen Palace as Richmond Palace (1499), was on the site now partly occupied by Old Friars, Old Palace Yard, off Richmond Green.

TAVISTOCK SQUARE, BLOOMSBURY,
LONDON

Sheet 176
TQ 3082

Before it was built over at the end of the eighteenth century, the area behind University College London was known as Southampton Fields, and before that, Long Fields. Here, so it is said, at the time of the Monmouth Rebellion (1685), a duel took place between two brothers whose footsteps were left imprinted for ever on the ground.

A letter dated 1778 was published in the *Gentleman's Magazine* in 1804 describing a visit to 'the Brothers' Steps' and recounting their legend:

> They are situate in the field about half a mile from Montague House, in a North direction; and the prevailing tradition concerning them is, that two brothers quarrelled about a worthless woman, and . . . they decided it by a duel. The print of their feet is near three inches in depth, and remains totally barren . . . Their number I did not reckon, but suppose they may be about ninety. A bank on which the first fell, who was mortally wounded and died on the spot, retains the form of his agonising posture by the curse of barrenness, while the grass grows round it. A friend of mine showed me these steps in the year 1760, when he could trace them back by old people to the year 1686; but it was generally supposed to have happened in the early part of the reign of Charles II. There are people now living who well remember their being ploughed up, and barley sown, to deface them; but all was labour in vain; for the prints returned in a short time to their original form. There is one thing I nearly forgot to mention: that a place on the bank is still to be seen, where, tradition says, the wretched woman sat to see the combat.

It is not clear from the letter whether its writer had heard how many Brothers' Steps there were supposed to be, but by the early nineteenth century their number was fixed at forty (in the Middle East the traditional number for 'a lot', hence, for example, 'Ali Baba and the Forty Thieves'). The story was popularized as 'The Field of the Forty Footsteps' by the Misses Porter in their *Coming Out* (1828) and produced as a melodrama at Tottenham Street Theatre. 'Since the above was written, they have been enclosed from public view, or nearly built over', says the person who sent the letter to the *Gentleman's Magazine*, yet visits to see them evidently continued: the poet Southey in his *Commonplace Book* (1849–51) tells how a labourer took him to a spot 'about three-quarters of a mile north of Montague house and five hundred yards east of Tottenham Court Road' and showed him the same three sights – the footsteps, the mark of the body and the place on the bank. 'The steps are the size of a large human foot', he writes, 'about three inches deep, and lie nearly from north-east to south-west. We counted only twenty-six; but we were not exact in counting.' The place where one or other of the brothers had fallen was still in his time bare of grass.

This barren patch and the bank on which the woman sat are now gone, but it is said that the Brothers' Steps themselves can still be seen in the south-west corner of Tavistock Square Gardens, near the tree planted in 1953 in honour of Mahatma Gandhi. I am happy to report that there *are* bare patches there which could be taken for footprints.

That the prints of the feet or fallen bodies of persons enacting some tragedy could be permanently burnt into the ground was once a common fancy. In his *Diary* for 10 July 1696, Abraham de la Pryme writes:

> The ingenious Mr. Lee told us that he was present at the siege of Colchester, and that he saw the two loyal and couragious gentlemen, S^r Ch[arles] Lucas, and Sr George Lile, executed there, when the rebells took the town. He says that they were both brought bound into the castle-yard, and ... stood expecting the fatal bullets, which accordingly came and killed them both stark dead in a minnit, who, falling backward, lay there a good while before that they were taken up and buried. But, from that time to this, 'tis observed that no grass will grow where these two brave men fell, but that there is to this day the exact figure on the ground in hay time that they fell in ...

Such prints were the record of strong passions – burnt into grass by sheer wickedness as at **Kington** (p.309) or into stone by holy rage as at **Smithills Hall** (p.388). Like stories of the prints left by magical animals (see **Corngafallt**, p.336, and **South Lopham**, p.192), such traditions seem to go back to a very ancient layer of belief indeed, that of the 'divine footprint' left by the culture hero or god.

TEWIN, HERTFORDSHIRE

Sheet 166
TL 2714

In the beautifully situated churchyard of St Peter's Church is the tomb of Lady Anne Grimston of Gorhambury, who died on 22 November 1713. The story goes that she did not believe in the

Proof of the truth of the resurrection: the tomb of
Lady Anne Grimston, Tewin, Hertfordshire

resurrection of the body and as she was dying scornfully declared: 'If, indeed, there is a Life hereafter trees will rend asunder my tomb.' Seven trees, ash and sycamore, *did* force their way through her tomb, as a lesson to the unbelieving.

Although most versions of the story specify seven trees, there are now three, perhaps four, their trunks grown together. They do not 'rend asunder' the tomb, but their roots have grown under it and tilted it slightly, and on one side the original railings are embedded in their trunks. Neither the trees nor the legend are mentioned by the Hertfordshire historian Nathaniel Salmon (1728), but in 1843 John Steel, the curate of Tewin, felt obliged to deplore it as superstitious nonsense.

A similar legend is attached to the Fig Tree Tomb at Watford, but the idea of the split tomb may have been an importation. In the churchyard of Holy Trinity, Hanover, is a tomb not unlike the Tewin one, in which was buried the Gräfin Henriette von Rüling, a friend of Frederick the Great, who died in 1782. The tomb bears the inscription 'This tomb must not be opened through all eternity', popularly interpreted as a defiance of the dogma of the resurrection of the body. The iron cover of this tomb was similarly riven by trees and much the same legend attached to it as at Tewin.

Also in the parish of Tewin is the grave of Walter Clibbon or Clibborn, a piemaker of Wareside in the eighteenth century who had turned footpad. 'On Saterday the 28th of December 1782 about 6 clock in the evening was Shott Dead Old Walter Clibbon, And one of his sons Taken . . .' wrote the Hertfordshire farmer John Carrington in his *Diary* (1797–1810). Clibbon at this time lived at Babb's Green near Ware (TL 3916) 'and used to go a Robing with his sons as they grew upp as footpads every winter season, for he kept them at home for that purpose . . .' They had committed many robberies and one murder, but met their just deserts when, 'robed in smock frocks with there faces blacked', they lurked in a wood in Oakenvalley Bottom near Bull's Green to waylay farmers coming home from Hertford market. The first they stopped was the younger Whittenbury from Datchworth, who went straight to his uncle, Benjamin Whittenbury of Queen Hoo Hall. Calling his man, George North, to bring a gun, and summoning his son Thomas, Benjamin 'took his stick & Dogg' and went to Oakenvalley Bottom to take a look. Luck was not with the footpads – they immediately set on Whittenbury and his two companions in the belief that they, too, were farmers. In the tussle that followed, George North, on Benjamin's command, shot the elder Clibbon, '& killd the old Roogue on the Spott'. One son ran away, the other was taken and hanged. The following Monday the 'corroner' and jury met, 'and they found he met his death as he deserved & they buried him by the road side where he was dead'. The aftermath of this nicely illustrates eighteenth-century social distinctions: the hapless George North was tried for the murder of Clibbon, albeit acquitted, whereas Benjamin Whittenbury got an inscribed silver cup from the Lord Lieutenant.

So much is history. A stout stake was erected by the place where Clibbon fell, probably simply as a marker, but the tradition has sprung up that it was driven through the old man to stop him 'walking'. In this connection we should note that the custom of burying suicides and other undesirables at crossroads, often with a stake driven through their hearts, was practised in England as late as 1823, when an Act of Parliament was passed ordering parishes to set aside a piece of unconsecrated ground for this purpose. It was rushed through Parliament at the request of George IV, whose coach had been delayed during such a burial at the junction of Hobart Place and Grosvenor Place by crowds who had come to see the spectacle. The burial in this way of a celebrated murderer who was also a suicide is described by Thomas de Quincey in his essay 'On Murder Considered as One of the Fine Arts' (1827).

Tewin church can be reached either by road or by the footpath (not the bridleway) to the left of the Rose and Crown. Lady Anne's tomb is at the east end of the church. The date on her tomb is clearly 1713, as Salmon says, though Cussans, in his *History of Hertfordshire* (1874–8), followed by several modern authors, gives 1710. Clibbon's Post stands about a third of a mile (0.5 km) along on the right-hand side of the road from Bull's Green to Bramfield. The original stake was renewed in 1880 by Abel Henry Smith, MP, of Woodhall Park, then again in 1927 by the East Herts Archaeological Society. A notable example of a crossroads burial is the Boy's (or Gypsy's) Grave on the B1506 from Newmarket to Bury, at the Chippenham–Moulton crossroads (Sheet 154, TL 6463). The boy is said to have hung himself on a nearby tree after losing his sheep, and his grave is still tended, it is thought, by roadmen or gypsies. Certainly someone leaves flowers on it.

TOLLESHUNT KNIGHTS, ESSEX
Sheet 168
TL 9115

In the parish of Tolleshunt Knights in the nineteenth century was an uncultivated field and at some distance from it an old manor house which was known as Barn Hall. Legend said that the hall was intended to have been built on the field, but the Devil destroyed in the night what had been done in the day. A knight with two dogs was sent to watch the site, and when the Devil came fought and conquered him. But the Devil snatched a beam from the building, and hurling it through the darkness exclaimed:

> 'Whereso'er this beam shall fall,
> There shall stand Barn Hall.'

He further swore that he would have the knight at his death whether he was buried in the church or out, but the knight outwitted him by having himself buried in the wall.

Such is the legend of Barn Hall (Barn Hall Farm is at TL 929148) as told by W. E. A. Axon in *Stray Chapters in Literature, Folk-*

Lore, and Archaeology (1888). Tales like this one are most often told of churches, but for another secular building, see **Callaly Castle** (p.403). The 'neither within nor without' story is likewise found in other places (cf. **Aldworth**, p.49; **Brent Pelham**, p.128; and **Grosmont**, p.341).

An interesting variant of the Barn Hall legend speaks of a watchman instead of the knight, accompanied by his three spey bitches. When the Devil cried out, 'Who's there?' the man answered, 'God and myself and my three spey bitches', and the Devil was powerless to do him harm. On the following night the Devil again asked 'Who's there?' and got the same answer. But on the third night, when the Devil said 'Who's there?', the watchman answered, 'Myself and my three spey bitches and God', and by putting himself before God lost his invulnerability. The Devil tore out his heart but his friends buried it in the church wall, neither in nor out, as in the previous version.

The story embodies an old superstition mentioned by Aubrey in his *Remaines* (1686–7):

> I believe all over England, a spaied bitch is accounted wholesome in a House; that is to say, they have a strong beliefe that it keeps away evill spirits from haunting of a House; *e.g.* amongst many other instances, at Cranborn in Dorset about 1686, a house was haunted, and two Tenants successively went away . . . for that reason: a third came and brought his spaied bitch, and was never troubled.

TOWER OF LONDON, LONDON

Sheet 177
TQ 3380

In the fourteenth-century *Mabinogion* is told the story of how Bendigeidfran, Bran the Blessed, king of Britain, invaded Ireland at the head of the hosts of the Island of the Mighty. Bran himself, too big to sail in a ship, waded through the sea and laid himself across the Shannon as a bridge for his men to cross over. At the battle which followed, the Irish put to good use a magic cauldron, given them earlier by Bran (see **Bedd Branwen**, p.327) which had the power to raise the dead to life. At last only seven of Bran's host were left, with Bran himself wounded to death by a poisoned spear

Was Bran's head buried on the White Mount a talisman such as this? Romano-British cult head from Caerwent, now in Newport Museum and Art Gallery

that had pierced his foot. He commanded his followers to cut off his head and take it to 'the White Hill' in London, where it was to be buried with its face towards France.

The seven companions bore the head back to Britain and set out for London, stopping on the way first at Harlech, where they spent seven years listening to the three magic birds of Rhiannon, oblivious of the passing of time; and again at Gwales (the island of Grasholm, off the Pembrokeshire coast), where they lingered eighty years until a forbidden door was opened and they remembered their task. All this time, the head of Bran stayed uncorrupt, and as good company in death as he had been in life. Eventually they came to London, and buried the head in the White Hill as they had been commanded. While it was buried there, no invasion from across the sea came to this island. The Welsh *Triads* add that it was King Arthur who destroyed this protection: 'And Arthur disclosed the head of Bran the Blessed from the White Hill, since he did not desire that this Island should be guarded by anyone's strength but his own.'

The White Hill of the story is usually identified with Tower

Hill, on which in the Conqueror's reign was built the great stone keep later known as the White Tower. This is thought to have got its name from the fact that in the thirteenth century the exterior was whitewashed, but the Welsh tradition of the White Hill is older than this – a poet of the twelfth to early thirteenth century also refers to it as 'the white eminence of London'. The word 'white' in its Welsh name can mean 'holy', and it is possible that the Conqueror chose the site because it already had powerful associations. Quite apart from the story of Bran's head, there existed a tradition that Brutus, the founder of Troynovant (New Troy or London – see **Guildhall**, p.133) was buried here.

Other cities also had legendary palladiums – magic talismans to keep them safe from attack – the most famous being the *Salvatio Romae*, built by Vergil (in medieval legend a magician rather than a poet) to protect Rome. That the dead might act as such guardians is also seen in Camden's (1610) account of the British king Vortimer, buried in Lincoln against his will: 'For hee was in a full and assured hope perswaded, that if hee were enterred in the sea shore, his verie ghost was able to protect the Britans from the Saxons, as writeth *Ninius* . . . ' (Did William the Conqueror have this in mind? See **Waltham Abbey**, p.162.)

The story of Bran's head may have some connection with the custom of keeping ravens on Tower Hill, although this is thought to have been introduced by Charles II. The name 'Bran' is believed by some to mean 'crow' or 'raven', and, like the head of Bran, the ravens' presence is said to keep the country safe from invasion. The raven had other curious lore attached to it: in Cornwall and perhaps other parts of the country it was thought unlucky to kill a raven, because it might be a reincarnation of King Arthur (see **Cadbury Castle, Somerset**, p.6).

The keeping of the head as a talisman is probably an echo of a British cult of the head. Classical writers describe the Celts as head-hunters who kept the heads of their fallen enemies as trophies, and dramatic evidence of a cult of the head comes from a shrine found at Roquepertuse (Bouches-du-Rhône, France), dating from the third or fourth century B.C., whose portal was carved with niches for human skulls, some of them still *in situ*. Stone heads, perhaps of guardian deities, are also characteristic of Celtic sculpture both in Britain and Ireland, while the decapitation of enemies is a recurrent theme in ancient Irish literature – Cu Chulainn arrives at Emain Macha: 'A single chariot warrior is here . . . and terribly he comes. He has in the chariot the bloody heads of his enemies.'

Specially valued heads would be given special treatment. 'They embalm in cedar oil the heads of the most distinguished enemies, and preserve them carefully in a chest and display them with pride to strangers saying that for this head one of their ancestors, or his father, or the man himself refused the offer of a large sum of money' (Diodorus Siculus, writing in the first century B.C.). These severed heads were not simply trophies – the head was thought to house the soul and that of a distinguished enemy brought his distinction and his prowess with it. It had a sort of divinity and was probably regarded as a talisman.

This Celtic cult of the head is held to explain several curious traditions – broken-down relics of an ancient belief. One is the speaking head of Bran, perfectly preserved and a protection for the land. Another is the brazen head made by Friar Bacon – Roger Bacon transformed in legend into a wizard – that obscurely said 'Time is', 'Time was', 'Time is passed', before bursting into flames. (This one appeared in R. Greene's *Friar Bacon and Friar Bungay* in 1594, but there are others in medieval tales.) Here, too, ultimately belong Britain's many 'Screaming Skulls' (see **Burton Agnes Hall**, p.401, and **Chilton Cantelo**, p.15).

The gigantic Bran himself is thought to be a primitive, perhaps pre-Celtic god later grafted on to British tradition. With his wounded foot, he is possibly the original of the Fisher King in the Grail legend (see **Dinas Bran**, p.338), and his story gave rise to (or perhaps explained) an old proverb still remembered in the eighteenth century, when it was included by Francis Grose in his *Provincial Glossary* (1787): 'He that will be a head let him be a bridge.'

AM. Times of opening also in *HHC&G*.

WALTHAM ABBEY, ESSEX

'This Abby was founded by a King of England, who of all other raigned least and lost most,' as it says in Weever's *Ancient Funerall Monuments* (1631). 'For within the compasse of a yeare, hee lost both his life and his kingdome, at one cast, and both of them to a Stranger . . .' On the other hand he won a curious form of immortality denied to any other English king, for Weever is speaking of Harold II Godwinsson, Harold of England, who had ties with Waltham Abbey and prayed for victory here in 1066, before marching to meet the Norman invader William.

Here in the churchyard, at the east end of the church, a flat slab marks the site of the High Altar, behind which Harold is said to have been interred after that fateful encounter at Hastings in 1066. In the reign of Elizabeth I, a gardener of Sir Edward Denny digging near this spot discovered a large stone coffin which from its location was assumed to contain the corpse of the King. On being opened, its contents fell to dust.

But was it Harold? Although William of Malmesbury (*ca.* 1090–1143) says that Harold was buried here, the contemporary Norman chronicler William of Poitiers says that the Conqueror jeeringly committed Harold's body to the care of William Malet for burial on the seashore, to 'guard the land and sea'. This is quite likely to be true – William certainly would not want Harold to become a martyr and focus for rebellion as Edward the Martyr had been (see **Corfe Castle**, p.60). The two stories can be reconciled if we assume that William later decided to conciliate the English by having Harold's body moved to his favourite abbey of Waltham.

However, there was a third and more potent tradition about the death of Harold, which clearly demonstrates how right William was to be wary. William of Poitiers says that the king was hard to identify, and this, together with the confusion over his burial place, fuelled a belief that he was still alive. Contemporary records – William of Poitiers, one version of the Anglo-Saxon Chronicle, the Bayeux Tapestry – are in no doubt that Harold was slain at the Battle of Hastings – *Harold interfectus est*. But the Icelandic tale of Heming Ásláksson, written in the thirteenth century, relates the aftermath of the battle as follows.

The night after Harold had fallen, a peasant and his wife drove their cart to the battlefield to strip the dead. They saw a bright light shining above the great heaps of corpses and decided that there must be a holy man among them. As they were clearing away the bodies on the spot where they saw the light, a man's arm came up out of the corpses, on it a great gold ring. The peasant took hold of the arm and asked whether its owner were still alive. 'I am alive,' came the answer. The woman said: 'I believe this is the King.'

They unearthed him and took him home with them. Next day, Heming Ásláksson, a Norwegian formerly in Harold's service, came to see him. Heming offered to raise an army to win back the kingdom, but Harold said he knew that many of the English had already sworn fealty to William and he would not be the cause of their breaking their oaths. 'I wish now to follow the example of King Olaf Tryggvason,' he said; a hermitage should be built for him at Canterbury, so he could watch William when he went to church.

Three years later, William heard the bells ringing all over Canterbury, and asked the cause. Heming answered, 'I understand that a monk has died, whose name was Harold.'

'Harold who?' asked the King.

'Godwinsson,' answered Heming.

'Who has been seeing to him?' said the King.

'I have,' responded Heming.

'If so, you are a dead man,' said the King. 'But let me see the body.' Heming led him to the cell where the hermit's body lay. It was naked and everyone recognized Harold. After that, William had Harold's body clothed in royal attire and buried with the greatest honour.

This story is based on a strong English tradition. Gerald of Wales, writing *ca.* 1191, says that the Saxons cherished a belief that Harold was alive and reports the rumour that a hermit, deeply scarred and blinded in his left eye, long dwelt in a cell near the abbey of St John at Chester. Some said he was visited there by Henry I, who had a long conversation with him, and on his death-bed declared himself satisfied that it was indeed Harold.

The *Life of Harold*, written perhaps about 1216, a century and a half after the events it describes, also says that Harold ended his days at Chester, but after many years abroad as a pilgrim, followed on his return to England by ten years in a cave near Dover as an anchorite – thus, like the tale of Heming, connecting him with Kent if not with Canterbury. The *Life* says further that Edith Swan-neck, Harold's concubine, was asked to identify his body among the slain, but even she who knew him so well chose the wrong man. For in the reign of Henry II, when Harold's brother Gurth, then of great age, was asked by the Abbot of Waltham whether the remains they had were indeed the King's, he replied, 'You may have some countryman, but you have not Harold.'

English society at the time of Harold's death was actually Anglo-Scandinavian: this makes it less surprising that the story of Harold's survival was told not only in the tale of Heming but in two Icelandic sagas, and that the pilgrimage in the *Life of Harold* seems to have been borrowed from another survival story – the one to which Harold himself refers – that of the Norwegian king Olaf Tryggvason.

The 'official' version of Olaf's death is that, having been defeated in the sea-battle of Svold in 999 or 1000 A.D., he leapt overboard from his great ship, the Long Serpent, and was drowned. But even this flamboyant and dramatic ending (he was wearing a scarlet cloak) was not enough for the storytellers: a legend later sprang up that he had cast off his coat of mail under the water, swum beneath the enemy ships, and been taken aboard a Wendish cutter. Thereafter he went to the Holy Land, where he lived many years as a monk. Belief in Olaf's survival must have followed immediately on his death – it is referred to by his friend and godson Hallfredar the Troublesome Poet already in the early eleventh century, although Hallfredar did not believe it – and the Holy Land tradition is mentioned in a *Life of Olaf* written in Iceland *ca.* 1200.

Curiously enough, that Harold in real life should have modelled himself on Olaf is not impossible. *The Longer Saga of Olaf Tryggvason* tells how Edward the Confessor, because of the friendship between his father, Ethelred the Unready, and Olaf – Olaf was Ethelred's godson – used to read Olaf's story to his court every year on Easter Day from a book which Olaf himself had sent him from Jerusalem. One year, after the reading, Edward announced that news had come from Syria that Olaf was dead – thirty-six years after his official death at Svold.

Perhaps there was just such a book at Edward's court, wherever it came from. But the dovetailing of the two survival traditions belongs to fiction. Rejection of the news of the death of famous men (and indeed women – Anastasia) is a widespread phenomenon and survival stories have sprung up, sometimes about commoners, but mostly about kings – Richard II, Alexander I of Russia, who reigned as late as 1801–25 and was also believed to have ended as a hermit, James IV of Scotland, Sebastian of Portugal, 'the Hidden King'. Some were expected to return, and were subjects of an internationally known tale 'The Return of the Warrior', told of 'sleeping heroes' such as Arthur (see **Cadbury Castle**, **Somerset**, p.6) and Holger Danske, sleeping under Kronborg Castle (Shakespeare's Elsinore) until the hour of Denmark's greatest danger, when he will return.

A rumour that Harold, too, was expected to return and defeat the Normans is mentioned by several nineteenth-century authors, and in itself seems likely enough, though it cannot be traced to early sources. What these *do* say is that his life was uncannily prolonged – one Scandinavian and two English writers report that he was supposed to have lived to the reign of Henry I, while the twelfth-century chronicler Ralph of Coggeshall says there was a belief that he survived to the time of Henry II (making him about a hundred and sixty-eight).

The strength of belief in survival stories in the Middle Ages can be judged from the case of Baldwin IX, Count of Flanders, who had been made Emperor of Constantinople in 1204 when the Crusaders sacked the city, but was killed within the year. Some two decades later, a *hermit* of great stature appeared, claiming to be Baldwin, and quickly gathered a huge mob of enthusiastic supporters, from which Joanna, Baldwin's daughter and successor, barely escaped with her life. The hermit was then summoned before Lewis VIII of France, who after interviewing him declared him an impostor. He was duly hanged, but only after fierce fighting, for many people believed him to be divine (they used to drink the water he washed in). Still people refused to accept Joanna and waited for Baldwin's return: the myth had proved stronger than the reality.

Waltham Abbey Gatehouse and Entrance to Cloisters, and Harold's (or Stoney) Bridge: AM (any reasonable time). The Hermitage, near the ruined church of St John at Chester, is reputed to have been the cell where Harold spent his last days. It may indeed have been used as an anchorite's cell, but appears to date only from the fourteenth century. Rudyard Kipling gives a different but moving account of Harold's survival in *Rewards and Fairies* (1910), in the story 'The Tree of Justice'. For the extraordinary case of the Pseudo-Baldwin, see Norman Cohn, *The Pursuit of the Millennium* (London, 1957).

WESTMINSTER ABBEY, LONDON   Sheet 176
TQ 2979

It is said that Henry IV died in the Jerusalem chamber of Westminster Abbey in unexpected fulfilment of a prophecy that he would die in Jerusalem. In *Henry the Fourth, Part 2*, Shakespeare makes the King ask if the chamber where he first collapsed had any special name. When Warwick replies, '''Tis call'd Jerusalem, my noble lord', Henry exclaims:

> 'Laud be to God! Even there my life must end.
> It hath been prophesied to me, many years,
> I should not die but in Jerusalem,
> Which vainly I suppos'd the Holy Land.
> But bear me to that chamber; there I'll lie;
> In that Jerusalem shall Harry die.'

A parallel story was told in medieval times of Gerbert – Pope Sylvester II (d. 1003) – who was said to have learned magic while among the Mohammedans in Spain and to have owned a brazen head which answered questions (see **Torbarrow Hill**, p.320). On one occasion the head told him that he would not die before he had celebrated Mass in Jerusalem – a prophecy unexpectedly fulfilled when he died whilst celebrating Mass in the church of Santa Croce in Gerusalemme, in Rome.

In *The Bruce* by the Scottish poet John Barbour (*ca.* 1320–95) we read how Edward I, expecting to die in the 'burgh' of Jerusalem, died at Burgh-on-the-Sands, near Carlisle, and there are many non-Jerusalem versions. Shakespeare's Richard III, in a fey moment contemplating the Earl of Richmond's rising star, recalls the start he gave when he heard at Exeter from the Mayor that the castle was called 'Rougemont', because 'a bard of Ireland' had foretold that he would not live long after seeing Richmond.

Ancestral, perhaps, to all such tales are classical legends of the mistaken understanding of an oracle. Pausanias in his *Guide to Greece* (*ca.* 150 A.D.) tells us how Epaminondas was warned by the Delphic oracle to avoid *pelagos*, which he took to mean 'sea' and so refrained from embarking on a vessel. In the event he was killed in battle in Arcadia at an oakwood called Pelagos. The same idea of Fate fulfilling itself despite all precautions underlies the many tales of people killed by a dead creature's tooth or fang (see **Minster-in-Sheppey**, p.118, and **Penhesgyn**, p.355).

The Jerusalem Chamber is shown to visitors, when it is not in use, as part of a comprehensive tour of the Abbey and its treasures. It probably got its name from its original tapestries. Henry is said to have been laid in front of the fire and there to have died, having fallen sick during a devotional visit to the Abbey on the eve of departure for the Holy Land (1413). While in the Abbey, see the Coronation Chair with the Stone of Scone (see **Scone Palace**, p.517).

Where a prophecy was unexpectedly fulfilled: the Jerusalem Chamber, Westminster Abbey, London

WESTON, HERTFORDSHIRE

Just inside the gate of Weston churchyard are two stones fourteen feet (4.3 m) apart, said to mark the grave of Jack o' Legs, the Weston giant. The earliest account of Jack was written by Nathaniel Salmon in his *History of Hertfordshire* (1728):

> This Giant, called *Jack of Legs*, as Fame goes, lived in a Wood here, was a great Robber, but a generous one, for he plundered the Rich to feed the Poor. He took Bread from the *Baldock* bakers frequently, who taking him at an Advantage, put out his Eyes, and after hanged him upon a Knoll in *Baldock Field*. He made them at his Exit but one single Request, which they granted: That he might have his Bow put into his Hand, and where-ever his Arrow fell he should be buried, which happened to be in *Weston* Church-yard.

Later, the stories of other legendary robbers were attached to him. Jack's Hill (TL 2329) near Gravely was supposed to be where he spied out rich travellers, and 'Jack's Cave', filled in in the nineteenth century, was where he hid his loot. Some said that he was the founder of Weston church, having asked that those who had benefited by his generosity should build a chapel there for the salvation of his soul.

Salmon thought that Jack's deeds were based on the real feats of arms, 'told by Nursery Fires, till they were thus happily improved', of Richard de Clare, Earl of Pembroke, nicknamed 'Strongbow' from his exploits. Strongbow was lord of the manor of Weston, and although he was banished to Ireland for siding with Stephen against Matilda, his family regained their lands here in the reign of Henry II. A lingering memory of the name 'Strongbow' might have suggested the story of Jack's firing his bow on his deathbed, although this is a common story, told also of another Hertfordshire hero, Piers Shonks of **Brent Pelham** (p.128; and cf. **Tilney All Saints**, p.198, and **Arundel Castle**, p.98).

'It is not improbable', Salmon comments of the stones held to mark Jack's grave, 'that they belonged to two several Graves . . .', and indeed they have every appearance of being two footstones. Be that as it may, on their account Weston churchyard became a place of pilgrimage for the curious. Moreover, the parish clerks of Weston would for a tip exhibit what they claimed was Jack's thigh-bone, a very long bone which used to be kept in the parish chest. One of the visitors to the churchyard was John Tradescant – whether the Elder or the Younger is not clear, though the Elder was at one time gardener at Hatfield. Salmon says that he bought the thigh-bone from the parish clerk of the day and it became one of the 'rarities' displayed in the celebrated 'Tradescant's Ark' at Lambeth, which after the younger Tradescant's death in 1662 eventually became the nucleus of the Ashmolean Museum. Alas, on Oxford shines the light of reason. In *The Ashmolean Museum* (1870), J. H. Parker writes:

> About the end of the last, and the early part of the present century . . . one of the curiosities shewn, which was especially attractive to the more ignorant of the visitors, was the Leg-bone of an Elephant, which was exhibited and labelled as the Thigh-bone of a Giant; and it was stated that this bone was bought of the Clerk of the Parish of Baldock . . . On the appointment of Mr. John Shute Duncan as Keeper of the Museum, one of his first acts was to have the label erased from the bone, which is now in the Anatomical Department of the New Museum.

Even this meagre distinction has now been denied. The bone, which got not so much as a mention in the catalogue of Tradescant's 'rarities' made in 1656, and had but a brief moment of glory as (so it is thought) No. 109 in the Ashmolean Museum Catalogue of 1836, 'The femur or thigh bone of an Elephant', has now disappeared.

5

East Anglia and the Fens

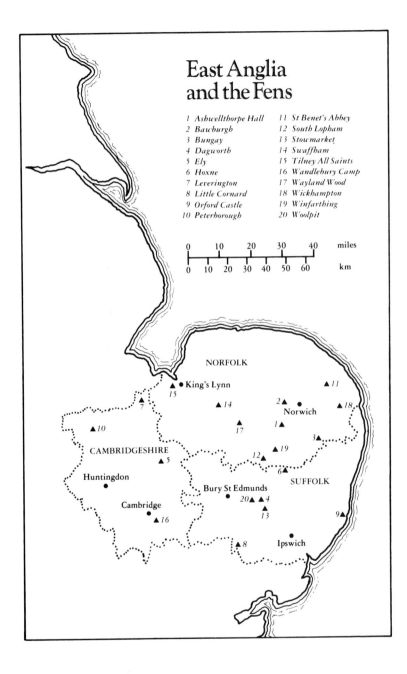

East Anglia
and the Fens

1 Ashwellthorpe Hall
2 Bawburgh
3 Bungay
4 Dagworth
5 Ely
6 Hoxne
7 Leverington
8 Little Cornard
9 Orford Castle
10 Peterborough

11 St Benet's Abbey
12 South Lopham
13 Stowmarket
14 Swaffham
15 Tilney All Saints
16 Wandlebury Camp
17 Wayland Wood
18 Wickhampton
19 Winfarthing
20 Woolpit

0	10	20	30	40	miles

0	10	20	30	40	50	60	km

NORFOLK

▲ ● King's Lynn
▲ 15

▲ 11

▲ 14

2 ▲
Norwich ●

▲ 18

1 ▲

▲ 17

3 ▲

▲ 10

CAMBRIDGESHIRE

▲ 5

12 ▲   ▲ 19

6 ▲

Huntingdon ●

Bury St Edmunds ●
20 ▲   ▲ 4

SUFFOLK

Cambridge ●
▲ 16

13

9 ▲

▲ 8

Ipswich ●

ASHWELLTHORPE HALL, NORFOLK

Sheet 144
TM 1597

Sir Thomas Knyvett of Ashwellthorpe Hall, who died in 1616, was celebrated for his hospitality and good nature. According to the old ballad of 'The Ashwellthorpe Miracle', printed by Blomefield in 1769, a marvel occurred at the Hall in Sir Thomas's time 'the tradition of which', says Murray's *Handbook* for 1870, 'has not quite passed away'. One Christmas-time a stranger presented himself at the door, and after showing the company an acorn set it down in the middle of the hall. Immediately an oak tree sprang up, which very soon had filled the hall with its branches and borne acorns. When these duly fell, two stalwart men came in and cut it down, but no one could move it. The stranger said he would demonstrate how feeble they were:

> Two goslings young and green,
> They then came whewting in,

and carried the tree out of the door, leaving behind not so much as a chip from its felling.

Murray wonders if the story is to be explained 'by the glamour of a magic lanthorn', but its source lies in traditions of the legerdemain worked by *tregetours*, the illusionists often mentioned in medieval romance, who, says Chaucer in his 'Franklin's Tale'

> . . . withinne an halle large,
> Have maad come in a water and a barge,
> And in the halle rowen up and doun.
> Somtyme hath semed come a grym leoun;
> And somtyme floures sprynge as in a mede;
> Somtyme a vyne, and grapes white and rede . . .

Such tricks were being performed in real life in the sixteenth century, to judge from Aubrey's *Remaines* (1686–7):

I have heard my grandfather Lyte say, that old father Davis told him, he saw such a thing donne in a Gentlemans hall at Christmas, at or neer Durseley in Gloucestershire, about the middle of King Henry the eight's reigne. Edmund Wyld, Esq. saies, that it is credibly reported, that one showed the new King of France, in anno 1689, or 1690, this trick, sc. to make the apparition of an Oake, &c. in a hall, as described by Chaucer, and no conjuration.

And certainly we hear from the *Gentleman's Magazine* in 1731 that on 15 February a well-known mountebank called Faux for the benefit of the Algerian ambassador and his party 'raised up an apple tree, which bore ripe apples in less than a minute's time, which most of the company tasted of', while in the 1880s the 'cunning man' Nicholas Johnson, of Devauden in Monmouthshire, would (to his wife's annoyance) make a small oak tree grow in the middle of his kitchen, and when the acorns fell produce a sow and her litter to eat them. One can still watch this trick being performed in India, where it is done by means of a series of mango trees, at different stages of development, growing in identical earthenware pots, deftly substituted one for another.

The present Tudor-style Hall (TM 150978), built in 1831 and 1845 on the moated site of the ancient seat of the Knyvetts and incorporating part of the earlier house, is now an hotel run by The Disabled Drivers' Association. It is open to non-residents.

BAWBURGH (pron. BABER), NORFOLK   Sheet 144
TG 1508

St Walstan, the saint of agricultural workers and sick animals, is traditionally said to have been born at Bawburgh in 965 A.D. The son of a king of East Anglia, at the age of twelve he renounced his heritage and went to work as a farmhand at Taverham, near Norwich (TG 1613). Because of his holiness, the farmer would have made him his heir, but Walstan would accept only the calves of a certain cow, for he had been told by an angel that they would bear him to his grave. One day when he was mowing a meadow, the angel came again to warn him of the approach of death. He went on mowing until the end was at hand, then, calling his master and fellow labourers, asked them to lay him on a cart, yoke his two oxen to it and let them have their heads. When he was dead, they did as he had bidden them and yoked up the oxen, who immediately made their way to Costessey Wood (TG 1711). When they were obliged to cross deep water in the wood (perhaps a ford across the Wensum), the wheels passed over as if it had been dry land, and it was long believed that their traces could still be seen on the surface of the water. Twice on their journey the oxen stopped to rest, and in each place a spring burst forth from the ground. They stopped for a third time at Bawburgh, and there the saint was buried and a church built over his body.

Walstan's legend is preserved in two *Lives*, Latin and English, the Latin one written on a vellum-covered wooden triptych that used to hang over his shrine. The English one, written in verse in the late fifteenth century, is especially full of folklore themes. In medieval saints' lives generally, animals often determine the burial place of the saint, perhaps a dim memory of the reading of omens in pagan times. The spring that bursts forth from the saint's grave or where his body has rested is likewise a frequently recurring blend of Christian symbolism and the ancient Celtic cult of rivers and springs (see **Waddow Hall**, p.391).

The water of the second miraculous spring in this story, known as St Walstan's Well and still to be seen on a farm below Bawburgh church (TG 153087), became famous for the cure of sick animals and was at one time sold in the streets of Norwich. Though dates are given for Walstan's birth and death (1016), he seems to be mythical – the Christianized version, perhaps, of the deity to whom the spring was once sacred (cf. Lady's Well, **Woolpit**, p.210), or some old agricultural god. Certainly Walstan was connected with fertility: 'Bilious Bale' in his *English Votaries* (1551) says that Walstan was firmly believed to restore the lost genitals of both men and animals ('I thynke ye haue seldome redde the lyke'), and that he 'became after the maner of Priapus the God of their Feldes in Northfolke ... al mowers and sythe folowers sekynge hym ones in ye yeare'. His was a spring festival moreover, held on 30 May and not wholly unlike the Royal Norfolk Show today, the 'mowers and sythe folowers' bringing their animals with them to be blest.

St Walstan's Well is marked (as St Waltan's Well) on the OS 1:25 000 map. His shrine was on the north side of the parish church. There was a hermitage on or beside Bawburgh bridge, and the hermit would conduct pilgrims seeking cures from the bridge to the church, sprinkling them with hyssop and holy water. The church was almost totally rebuilt in the early fourteenth century out of their offerings, but after the shrine had been swept away by the Reformation became ruinous and forsaken. It was repaired again at the Revision in 1633, and has subsequently been heavily restored. St Walstan is represented, sometimes with his two oxen but more often with a scythe, on several Norfolk roodscreens: Barnham Broom (TG 0807), Litcham (TF 8817), Ludham (TG 3818), North Burlingham (St Andrew's; TG 3610), Sparham (TG 0719) and, on a chest said to have been made up with panels from a roodscreen, Denton (TM 2788). At Barnham Broom, Denton, Litcham and Ludham you will also see St Edmund the Martyr (see **Hoxne**, p.182). On Ludham, see also under **St Benet's Abbey** (p.191). Litcham, Sheet 132; Taverham, Costessey, Ludham, North Burlingham and Sparham, 133; Bawburgh and Barnham Broom, 144; Denton, 156.

BUNGAY, SUFFOLK

Sheet 156
TM 3389

A spectral black dog haunts many parts of the country – in Lancashire called 'Trash' or 'Skriker', and on the Isle of Man, where he haunted Peel Castle, known as the Mauthe Doog. In Norfolk he is called Shuck, Old Shuck or the Shuck Dog, and in Suffolk Shock, his name perhaps coming from OE *scucca*, a demon. He usually appears as a black shaggy dog of enormous size, with eyes like saucers that glow in the dark, but sometimes he is invisible, his presence only detected from the blast of his hot breath and his padding footsteps.

Black Dogs were in some places thought to be the ghosts of the unquiet dead. The wicked Lady Howard in Devon was so transformed, and the *Gentleman's Magazine* for 1731 included an account of a dark grey dog which appeared several times between December 1729 and December 1730 to a Scottish farmer, William Sutor, and finally revealed itself to be the ghost of David Sutor, compelled to wear that shape for having murdered a man more than thirty-five years previously with the aid of a dog. He directed William to a certain bush under which were buried his victim's bones, requesting him to give them Christian burial. Once this was done, his spirit could rest.

By the time these traditions were recorded, some confusion between originally distinct sorts of manifestation may have set in, for in some tales Shuck or Shock seems more like the shape-changing bogeys the Picktree Brag and the Hedley Kow (see

*The claw-marks of the Black Dog on the north door
of Blythburgh church, Suffolk*

Hedley on the Hill, p.405). Now and then he takes the form of a calf, and on one occasion at least appeared with 'a donkey's head and a smooth, velvet hide'. One dark night in the 1860s, Goodman Kemp of Woodbridge rushed into the Melton Horse and Groom and asked for a shotgun to shoot the shock that hung on the toll-bar gate. Emboldened by the company that turned out with him to see it, he tried to seize the shock, but it snapped fiercely at his hand and vanished, leaving its toothmarks on his thumb to his dying day.

Note that the shock hung on the toll-gate: Black Dogs commonly haunted lanes, footpaths, bridges, crossroads and gateways – all points of transition, from ancient times held to be weak spots in the fabric dividing the mortal world from the supernatural. One of the Norfolk Shuck's favourite runs was from Overstrand (TG

2440) to Runton (TG 1842), where, said a nineteenth-century tale, a man called Finch from Neatishead once met him as he was walking along the road after dark. Thinking the dog was Dick Allard's, which had snapped at him a couple of times, he said to himself he would get his own back: 'You will not turn out of the road for me, and I will not turn out of the road for you.' Along came the dog, up the middle of the road, and Finch aimed a kick at him, but his foot went through as if through paper. Shuck here is a phantom, and Black Dogs generally are thought to be connected with the packs of spectral hounds – the Gabriel Ratchets or Dandy Dogs – that accompany the Wild Hunt (see **Peterborough**, p.187). Perhaps they were originally psychopomps – escorts of the dead on their journey to the Underworld. Certainly they sometimes act as 'fetches', appearing as portents of death and disaster, as one did at Wicken in Cambridgeshire.

This would explain a certain ambivalence of attitude towards Black Dogs, which in some places are disposed to be friendly, acting as guardians and guides to lonely travellers – unless this is British sentiment at work on old tradition. For while in Suffolk Shuck is usually harmless if let well alone, in Norfolk none can set eyes on him and live, again a characteristic of the Wild Hunt (see **Clun Forest**, p.300). And it is in this demonic character that he first appears in print, in an old tract by Abraham Fleming (d.1607) entitled 'A straunge and terrible Wunder wrought very late in the parish Church of Bongay . . .' On Sunday, 4 August 1577, between nine and ten in the morning, when most people were at church, there broke over Bungay 'a great tempest . . . the like whereof hath been seldome seene', with cracks of thunder that made the church 'as it were quake and stagger'. Hard upon this there appeared what to the congregation seemed to be a great black dog ('an horrible shaped thing'). 'This black dog . . . runing all along down the body of the church with great swiftnesse, and incredible haste, among the people . . . passed between two persons, as they were kneeling upon their knees, and . . . wrung the necks of them bothe at one instant clene backward . . .' Passing another man in the congregation, the dog 'gave him such a gripe on the back, that therewith all he was presently drawen togither and shrunk up, as it were a peece of lether scorched in a hot fire; or as the mouth of a purse or bag, drawen togither with a string'. This one 'dyed not';

nor did the church clerk, who was outside cleaning the gutter when a violent clap of thunder knocked him off his perch. The Black Dog appeared to him whilst he was still 'all amased', but did him no further harm. In proof that the dog was not a hallucination, says Fleming, 'there are remaining in the stones of the church, and likewise in the church dore which are mervelously renten and torn, ye marks as it were of his clawes or talans'.

The Black Dog visited Blythburgh on the same day, where 'placing himself uppon a maine balk or beam . . . sodainly he gave a swinge down through ye church', killing two men and a boy, and burning someone's hand. Both here and at Bungay his activities sound suspiciously like the effects of ball lightning, the 'purplish nebecula', perhaps, which Aubrey tells us entered the church at Loughton, Cheshire, during a tempest in about 1649, 'killing many'. And indeed, if we look in Holinshed's *Chronicles* (1577), we find the events at Bungay narrated without mention of the Black Dog. Fleming's timing is slightly different from Holinshed's, and so is his list of casualties, while the way in which he speaks of the man shrunk up like 'a peece of lether' as believed to be 'yet alive' suggests that he had a local informant. To this informant we could owe the Black Dog: in other words, Fleming might be telling us what the people of Bungay thought of the event which to Holinshed and the outside world was simply 'a strange and terrible tempest'.

But it has to be said that Bungay's apparition is not unique. A pamphlet entitled 'The Wonders of this Windie Winter' had already appeared in 1613, telling how, one Sunday at Great Chart in Kent, during a tempest, when the people were at evening prayer, there 'broake into the Church a most ugly shape of the ayer like unto a broadeyd bul'. This apparition struck the minister's left arm, leaving it blackened and paralysed, and in the stampede that ensued a miller was killed. After that, the bull vanished, taking with it part of the wall. All this, it is implied, came about because people *would* talk in church. Even setting aside bulls and Black Dogs, are we really to believe that ball lightning entered all these churches, or are we dealing with a good tale going the rounds?

Whatever the truth of the matter, Bungay's Black Dog can still be seen near the Butter Cross (TM 337897) in the shape of a weather-vane. This surmounts a lamp-standard erected in 1933 on the site of the old town pump, and an inscription concludes:

All down the church in midst of fire
The hellish monster flew;
And passing onwards to the quire
He many people slew.

The Black Dog also appears on a carved wooden Dole Cupboard in St Mary's Church, dated 1675, but thought to be nineteenth-century. The marks of his 'talans', alas, are harder to find.

St Mary's Church is now redundant. For access, see notice in church porch. Marks said to have been left by the Black Dog *can* still be seen at Blythburgh. Overstrand and Runton, Sheet 133.

DAGWORTH, SUFFOLK   Sheet 155
                                        TM 0461

The chronicler Ralph of Coggeshall, writing at the turn of the twelfth century, tells the story of a fairy child named Malekin who haunted Dagworth Castle. She used to talk to its inhabitants, speaking to the servants 'according to the idiom of the region', i.e. in broad Suffolk, but using Latin to the priest, with whom she discussed the Scriptures. She said that she was a human child stolen from a cornfield by fairies while her mother was working. She had lived with the fairies for seven years, and after another seven would be free to return to her own world. Meantime she could be heard and felt, but not seen – the only person who *had* seen her was a servant-girl who used to put out food for her and with whom she had become friends. This girl often asked Malekin to make herself visible, and she finally agreed, but only after the other had promised neither to touch nor try to detain her. The girl said afterwards that Malekin was like a tiny child and was dressed in a white linen tunic.

Of all the stories of fairy changelings in Britain this is the strangest, with Malekin something between a fairy (small and invisible), a ghost (attached to a particular place), and a traditional Brownie (living in relationship with humans and eating their food). Her evident dependence on human food may be explained by the belief that to eat fairy food would mean perpetual captivity in

fairyland (cf. **Glastonbury**, p.21), much as Persephone was condemned to spend four (some said six) months of the year in the
Underworld by eating a few pomegranate seeds.

ELY, CAMBRIDGESHIRE

Sheet 143
TL 5380

Fenland's most famous hero is the outlaw Hereward the Wake
(meaning 'wary'). The real Hereward held lands in Warwickshire
and Lincolnshire at the time of Edward the Confessor, left England
some time after 1062, and later reappeared to plunder the Abbey of
Peterborough (1070) and hold the Isle of Ely against the Normans
(1071). From these sparse facts has grown the legend of Hereward,
son of Leofric, Earl of Mercia (or Leofric of Bourne, Lincolnshire).
In his youth he kept wild company, and when he was fourteen his
father persuaded King Edward to make him an outlaw. He was
brought back to England by the news that the Normans had seized
his father's estates, and he became the leader of a band of Saxon
nobles who were still holding out against the Conquest from the
great Abbey at Ely.

William the Conqueror led his army to Ely, then an island in the
Fens, and was three times foiled by Hereward in the attempt to
build a causeway across the marshes. The third time, while William
was encamped at Brandon, Hereward rode there on his horse, a
noble beast called Swallow, on the way meeting a potter, who
agreed to exchange clothes with him and lend him his wares. In
this disguise Hereward got into William's camp and overheard his
plans (as according to legend King Alfred disguised himself as a
harper to enter the camp of the Danes). When William built his
third causeway, and proceeded to send his soldiers along it to
attack Ely, Hereward's men, hidden in the reeds, set fire to the
vegetation. The Normans were engulfed by the flames, and those
who tried to escape were either drowned in the marsh or picked
off by English arrows.

But now the monks of Ely grew tired of the siege and let the
Normans in by a secret path. Hereward escaped with a handful of
men and was soon leading a new resistance. Eventually William
made peace with him, but he still had other enemies. One day a
chaplain, whom he had asked to keep watch while he slept,

betrayed him and sixteen Normans broke into the house. Though he slew fifteen of his attackers with his lance or his famous sword Brainbiter, and the sixteenth with his shield, he fell at last when four more knights entered and stabbed him in the back with their spears.

Hereward was already well known in the Fens by 1070 – the Anglo-Saxon Chronicle (at this time being written at Peterborough) says simply that among those at the sack of Peterborough were 'Hereward and his crew'. Like Edric Wilde (see **Clun Forest**, p.300), it was as a resistance leader that he first became famous, but soon frankly fabulous stories were attracted to his name. Within eighty years of the real Hereward's death, the Hereward of legend was in full cry, in the *Estorie des Engles* of Geoffrey Gaimar (fl. ?1140) and the *Gesta Herewardii Saxonis* ('Deeds of Hereward the Saxon'). The author of the *Gesta*, writing no more than fifty years after William's assault on Ely, tells us on the one hand that he remembers seeing fishermen dredging Norman skeletons, still in their rusty armour, out of the fen; on the other, that Hereward once slew a Cornish giant.

Songs were being sung about Hereward in taverns a hundred years after his death; and in the thirteenth century people still visited a ruined wooden castle in the Fens which was known as Hereward's Castle. But later he was supplanted by another outlaw-hero, Robin Hood, as a symbol of resistance to oppression.

HOXNE (pron. HOXEN), SUFFOLK

Sheet 156
TM 1777

On the road leading from Hoxne to Cross Street is Goldbrook Bridge. The story goes that when King Edmund of the East Angles was fleeing from the Danes he hid under the bridge, but was betrayed by a newly married couple returning home in the evening, who by the light of the moon saw his gilt spurs reflected in the water. The King laid a curse on couples who crossed the bridge thereafter, on the way to their wedding. 'A superstitious regard is paid to this sentence even to this day; as not one will pass over the bridge in their way to the parish church on that occasion.' When Edmund Gillingwater wrote this, in his *Historical Account of*

The wolf guarding St Edmund's head:
bench-end from Hadleigh church, Suffolk

Lowestoft (ca. 1790), the bridge was known as 'Gold-Bridge' from the spurs, but now it is usually said that the stream itself took its name from this incident, and in the nineteenth century it was claimed that the King's bright armour could still sometimes be seen glimmering through the water.

History has nothing to say of Goldbrook Bridge. King Edmund, killed in battle against the Danes in 870 in defence of his kingdom, had by the time of the Anglo-Saxon scholar Ælfric (*ca.* 955–1020) been transformed into a Christian martyr. In Ælfric's account, which he says came ultimately from an eyewitness, Edmund's own sword-bearer, the King was defeated at *Hægelisdun*, traditionally identified with Hoxne, and offered his life if he would renounce his faith. When he refused, he was tied to a tree and shot full of spears 'like a hedgehog's bristles'. Then the Danes cut off his head and hid it in thick brambles in a wood, so that it could not be buried. When they had gone, the local people searched for the head, calling out to keep track of each other in the woods, 'Where are you now, friend?' Then the head answered 'Here! Here! Here!', and every time they called, so the head answered, until they found it. When they got to the bramble-thicket, there lay a grey wolf with the head between his paws, guarding it from the other wild animals. He allowed them to carry it back to Hoxne, following them as if he had been tame, and when he had seen it to safety returned to the woods.

This story is commemorated among other places at Hadleigh in Suffolk (TM 0242), where a fourteenth-century bench-end in the south chapel of the parish church shows the wolf holding Edmund's head. At Hoxne itself, in a field on your left as you go towards Cross Street, is a monument (TM 183766) marking the site of what was traditionally said to be the tree of Edmund's martyrdom, an oak that 'fell by its own weight', August 1843.

The legend of St Edmund and the wolf is depicted in carvings on the north door of Wells Cathedral, Somerset, and in a Victorian carving on a beam in the parish church of Greensted-juxta-Ongar, Essex, where St Edmund's bier rested on its return to Bury St Edmund's (formerly St Edmundsbury, 'St Edmund's town') from London where it had been taken for safety from Vikings. A carving of the wolf, with the head below it, also appears in a fifteenth-century insertion in the front of Moyses' Hall, in the Cornhill, Bury. This is now a museum – for times of opening, see *M&G*. The immense popularity of Edmund as a royal saint, and the prestige of his shrine at Bury, are attested by many representations of him in churches up and down the country. Scenes from his life can be seen on roof bosses in Norwich cathedral, and he is portrayed (usually identified by an arrow or arrows) on a score of roodscreens – for examples in Norfolk, see under **Bawburgh** (p.174). There are perhaps a dozen wall-paintings of Edmund's martyrdom, including a fine fifteenth-century one in the church of SS Peter and Paul, Pickering, North Yorkshire; in Suffolk there is one at Troston (TL 8972). Still in Suffolk, the martyrdom also appears on a misericorde at Norton (TL 9565). The most famous representation of Edmund, however, is on the Wilton Diptych in the National Gallery, London. Bury St Edmunds, Hadleigh, Norton and Troston, Sheet 155.

LEVERINGTON, CAMBRIDGESHIRE   Sheet 143
                                                                TF 4411

Up to the middle of the last century, Whirlin', Whirling or

Whirlwind cakes were made in Leverington for sale at the village feast, and the day on which it was held was called Whirling Sunday. According to a tradition recorded in *Fenland Notes & Queries* I (1891), the custom was to commemorate an old lady in Leverington who was making some cakes for the feast one Mid Lent Sunday when the Devil appeared and whisked her off over the church steeple in a whirlwind.

The custom, though not the story, was known in 1789, and this curious little tale, with its hint of punishment for Sabbath-breaking and its overtones of the fairy eddy (see **Duffus Castle**, p.495), was perhaps invented to account for something whose origins had been forgotten. Whirling Sunday is Passion Sunday, the fifth in Lent, which was formerly known as Care, Carle, Carline or Carling Sunday. In Scotland a family feast was often held on that day, at which a spiced cake called a Car Cake was customarily eaten. It is not much of a step from Carline/Carling to Whirlin'/Whirling, and thence to Whirlwind and the old lady in the tale.

LITTLE CORNARD, SUFFOLK

Sheet 155
TL 9039

According to a fifteenth-century chronicle now in Canterbury Cathedral, a battle between two fire-breathing dragons took place on the afternoon of Friday, 25 September 1449, near the village of Little Cornard. One of the dragons was black and lived on Kedington Hill (TL 8938), while the other, which was 'reddish and spotted', came from Ballingdon Hill (TL 8640) on the Essex side of the border. After a fight that lasted an hour, the Essex dragon won, and both combatants returned to their own hills. The site of this battle, a marshy field next to the Stour between Little and Great Cornard, was known locally as Sharpfight Meadow. It is now called Shalford Meadow, and is said also to have been the place where Boadicea and her Iceni decimated the Ninth Legion from Colchester.

Like a curious business at Bures, astride the Essex/Suffolk border (TL 9034), also in the fifteenth century, this story looks as if it may have commemorated some skirmish between rival villages, unless both dragon fights were inspired by the thirteenth-century wall painting of a dragon in nearby Wissington (Wiston, TL 9533) church. In Scriptural language the dragon is the Devil, and, placed as it is above the north or Devil's door, the identity of the Wissington dragon is in no doubt.

ORFORD CASTLE, SUFFOLK   Sheet 169
                                                        TM 4194

The chronicler Ralph of Coggeshall reports that in the reign of Henry II some fishermen caught in their nets a 'wild man' whom they brought to Bartholomew de Glanville, the castellan of Orford Castle, as a curiosity. He was completely naked and had the appearance of a man. The hair of his head seemed torn and rubbed, but he had a bushy beard and was shaggy about the breast. He ate whatever food he was given, but preferred raw fish to cooked, and this he would squeeze in his hands until all the moisture was out. He would not or could not speak, even when they hung him up by his feet and tortured him. He always went to bed as soon as the sun had set, and stayed there until it rose again.

For a long time he was guarded day and night, lest he escape back to the sea. Once they took him to the sea-gate and let him go, having first placed a triple row of nets between him and the open sea. But he broke through the nets and swam out to sea, now diving into the depths, now lifting himself above the waves and showing himself to those on shore, as if mocking them. After he had played in the sea a long time, he swam back of his own accord and stayed with them at Orford another two months. But he was less carefully guarded now, and eventually slipped secretly back to the sea, never to return. They could not decide if he were man or fish, or else an evil spirit which had possessed the body of a drowned sailor.

'A tradition of this monster, known as "the wild man of Orford", still exists in the village', says Murray's East Anglian *Handbook* (1870), but this may well be quoted directly from Grose, *Antiquities of England and Wales* (1773–87). Whether this local tradition stemmed from Ralph's chronicle or was a genuine folk-memory is impossible now to say.

We actually know the name of another twelfth-century merman, Nicholas Pipe, but he, alas, lived in Mediterranean waters.

Orford Castle (TM 420500), commissioned by Henry II and completed in 1173, served as a royal castle for 170 years, often in the care of a royal constable. Later it changed hands several times, eventually being granted by Edward III to Robert of Ufford in perpetuity. The only surviving part is the keep: AM.

PETERBOROUGH, CAMBRIDGESHIRE (formerly HUNTINGDONSHIRE)

Sheet 142
TL 1998

The version of the Anglo-Saxon Chronicle kept up at Peterborough Abbey, under the year 1127, speaks bitterly of Henry of Poitou, a rapacious abbot who 'did nothing good there and left nothing good there', having been appointed to the post only because he was a relation of Henry II. His coming to the see, says the chronicler, was heralded by a portent:

> Let it not be thought remarkable, when we tell the truth, because it was fully known over all the country, that as soon as he came there . . . then soon afterwards many people saw and heard many hunters hunting. The hunters were black and big and loathsome, and their hounds all black and wide-eyed and loathsome, and they rode on black horses and black goats. This was seen in the very deer-park in the town of Peterborough, and in all the woods that there were between this town and Stamford, and the monks heard the horns blow that they were blowing at night. Trustworthy people noticed them at night, and said that it seemed to them there might well be about twenty or thirty hornblowers. This was seen and heard from the time he came there all Lent up to Easter.

Aubrey, writing in the seventeenth century, tells of a similar portent:

> Moreover it is credibly told of many honest men, that fiue miles from *Blonsdon* in *Wiltshire*, a crie of houndes was heard in the ayre, the self same day that the first Earthquake was, and the noyse was so great that was made, that they seemed three or four score couple, whereat diuerse toke their Grey-houndes, thinking some gentlemen had bin hunting in the chase, and thoughte to course: yet some of those that went out of their houses, seeing nothing below abrode, loked

vpwards to the skyes, and there espyed in the ayre fiue or sixe
houndes perfectlye to be diserned . . .

Packs of spectral hounds are said to have been seen in full cry all
over Britain – in the North they are generally known as the Gabriel
Hounds, in Devon the Yeth (Heath) or Wisht Hounds, in Cornwall
Dando and his Dogs or the Devil and his Dandy Dogs, in Wales
the Cwm Annwn, the Hounds of Hell. Sometimes they are said,
like the Norfolk Shuck (see **Bungay**, p.176), to be great black
hounds with fiery eyes – often eyes as big as saucers, like the
'wide-eyed' Peterborough hounds. Generally, however, they are
not seen, only heard passing overhead on cloudy or stormy nights.
In this form they may be identical with the mysterious Seven
Whistlers, of which Jabez Allies (1846) writes:

> . . . I have been informed by Mr. John Pressdee of Worcester,
> that the country people used to talk a good deal about the
> 'Seven Whistlers' when he was a boy, and that he frequently
> heard his late grandfather, John Pressdee, who lived at Cuck-
> old's Knoll, in Suckley, say that he oftentimes, at night, when
> he happened to be upon the hill by his house, heard six out of
> the 'Seven Whistlers' pass over his head, but that no more
> than six of them were ever heard by him, or by any one else
> to whistle at one time, and that should the seven whistle
> together the world would be at an end.

Certainly the hounds are everywhere supposed to be portents of
death and disaster, and a belated traveller hearing them would fling
himself face downward on the ground to avoid seeing them (cf. the
precautions taken by the miner and his daughter, **Clun Forest**,
p.300). Henderson (*Folk-Lore of the Northern Counties*, 1879)
tells us:

> Sometimes they appear to hang over a house, and then death
> or calamity are sure to visit it. A Yorkshire friend informs me
> that when a child was burned to death in Sheffield, a few years
> ago, the neighbours immediately called to mind how the
> Gabriel hounds had passed above the house not long before.

The northern name Gabriel Hounds or Gabble Retchets (dogs)
had nothing to do with the Angel Gabriel but contained an old

word for 'corpse', explained by the traditions concerning them. Sometimes it is the Devil who leads them, hunting lost souls, while in Devon the hounds were themselves thought to be the souls of unbaptized children. According to Henderson, in the neighbourhood of Leeds the Gabble Retchets were likewise thought to be the souls of infants who had died before baptism, doomed for ever to flit round their parents' homes.

These packs of spectral hounds with their huntsmen are manifestations of the Wild Hunt, which in Germany, too, included the souls of unbaptized babies in the train of 'Frau Bertha', who sometimes accompanied the Wild Huntsman, and which in the Franche Comté was believed to be King Herod pursuing the Holy Innocents. The Wild Huntsman everywhere was a demonic figure, who would throw unsuspecting peasants their share of 'game' with horrific consequences (see **Wistman's Wood**, p.39). This savage and tricky being is generally thought to be an aspect of Woden, a god who was characterized by his duplicity (see **Wansdyke**, p.83), as in parts of Germany and Scandinavia the Wild Hunt was known as 'Woden's Hunt'.

The visitation of the Wild Hunt at Peterborough was not its only appearance in Britain in the twelfth century. Walter Map, writing *ca.* 1190, tells the story of King Herla, whom he knew as its leader (see **Hereford**, p.306), and later adds:

The nocturnal companies and squadrons, too, which were called of Herlethingus, were sufficiently well-known appearances in England down to the time of Henry II, our present lord. They were troops engaged in endless wandering, in an aimless round, keeping an awestruck silence, and in them many persons were seen alive who were known to have died. This household of Herlethingus was last seen in the marches of Wales and Hereford in the first year of the reign of Henry II, about noonday: they travelled as we do, with carts and sumpter horses, pack-saddles and panniers, hawks and hounds, and a concourse of men and women. Those who saw them first raised the whole country against them with horns and shouts, and . . . because they were unable to wring a word from them by addressing them, made ready to extort an answer with their weapons. They, however, rose up into the air and vanished on a sudden.

The expression Map uses to describe the Wild Hunt, the *familia Herlethingi*, 'the household of Herlethingus', is believed to be the result of a misunderstanding. It appears to contain the word 'thing' in its Old English sense of 'troop, assembly', and in itself to mean 'the troop of Herle'. Some trace 'Herle' back to Herian, a name of Woden/Odin as lord of the troops of warriors (ON *herjar*) who thronged Valhalla. However this may be, it is one of several similar names for the leader of the Hunt, called by Ordericus Vitalis (writing 1123–41) the *familia Herlechini*, 'the household of Herlechinus', just as later in some parts of France it was *la Mesnie Herlequin* (whence eventually the figure of Harlequin, who first appeared on the Paris stage towards the end of the sixteenth century). Peter of Blois, archdeacon of Bath and London (*ca.* 1135–1204) calls it *milites Herlewini*, 'the troop of Herlewin', while in the fourteenth-century poem *Mum and the Sothsegger* an unruly rabble is called *Hurlewaynis kynne*, 'the kindred of Hurlewain'.

As the old name was corrupted and its meaning lost, leadership of the Hunt was transferred to real or imaginary leaders of the past – Gervase of Tilbury (writing *ca.* 1212) calls the Hunt *familia Arturi*, 'the household of Arthur', and later in some places in France it was known as *la Chasse Artus* or 'Arthur's hunt'. In Denmark its leader was the celebrated King Waldemar, hero of many tales, or else King Christian II. In nineteenth-century England the demonic huntsman might be any one of a number of local heroes or villains, usually of the landowning class – often a hunting squire such as Dando and his Dogs, condemned to hunt for evermore for hunting on a Sunday (cf. Mallt y Nos under **Llowes**, p.349), or someone who had otherwise achieved fame or notoriety, for example Sir Francis Drake and 'Wild Darrell' (see **Combe Sydenham Hall**, p.16, and **Littlecote House**, p.67). Though the ancient Herlething was forgotten under that name, beliefs connected with it long survived not only in traditions such as these concerning spectral huntsmen and their hounds, but probably also that of the sinister 'hell waine' listed by Reginald Scot in his *Discovery of Witchcraft* (1584) among common apparitions. Belief in the hell wain as the wagon in which were borne the souls of the dead survived late in Wales and the West Country, and seems to underlie the many reports of phantom coaches with headless horses from East Anglia and elsewhere.

ST BENET'S ABBEY, HORNING, NORFOLK   Sheet 134
                                              TG 3815

> Then passeth *Thirn** neare the decaied great Abbay called
> Saint *Benet in the Holme*: which *Knut* the *Dane* built, and the
> monkes afterward so strengthned with most strong wals and
> bulwarks, that it seemed rather a Castle than a Cloister. In so
> much, that William the *Conquerour* could not winne it by
> assault, untill a monke betraied it into his hands upon this
> condition, that himselfe might be made Abbot thereof. Which
> was done accordingly: but forthwith, this new Abbot for
> beeing a traitour, (as the inhabitants make report) was hanged
> up by the kings commandement, and so justly punished for
> this treason.

This story, told by Camden in his *Britannia* (trans. Holland, 1610),
is not the only tale attached to the ruined abbey of St Benet's
Hulme or St Bene't-at-Holme. A fearful winged dragon is said
once to have terrorized the people of nearby Ludham (TG 3813),
which when its lair was blocked with a stone went roaring off
along the causeway to St Benet's and vanished into the vaults. The
tradition probably had its origin in the carvings over the west gate
of the abbey, now inside a mill built into the ruins in the eighteenth
century and itself long derelict. Seen from inside the ruins, above
the left of the gate is a man with a sword, and on the right, a lion,
both 'much defaced thro' time', as Blomefield puts it in his
History of Norfolk (1739). 'This ... I take to be figures much
misrepresented', he says, perhaps alluding to the tale. The man is
clearer than Blomefield would have us believe, but the lion *does*
look somewhat like a griffin.

The same figures, only plainer, can be seen on the restored St Ethelbert's
Gate, one of two gates leading into the Cathedral Close, Norwich. St
Benet's Abbey, painted so often by the Norwich School, is best seen from
the river, if possible. By car or on foot it is reached by a cart-track used as
a public path, off the minor road leading from Ludham to Johnson's
Street.

* River Thurne (TG 3915)

SOUTH LOPHAM, NORFOLK   Sheet 144
                                 TM 0481

'This Town is remarkable among the Country People for three WONDERS,' says Blomefield in the first volume of his *History of Norfolk* (1739). The first was the Selfgrown Stile, a stile formed naturally by a tree.

> The Second is, the *Ox-Foot Stone*, which lies in a Meadow so called; it is a large Stone of the Pebble kind, on which is the fair Impression of an Oxe's Foot, which seems to be natural, the Fable of it is, that in a great Dearth (No-body knows when) there came a Cow constantly to that Place, which suffered herself to be milked (as long as the Dearth lasted) by the poor People, but when that decreased she struck her Foot against that Stone, which made the Impression, and immediately disappeared.

The Selfgrown Stile is long vanished, but the third wonder, Lopham Ford, where the Little Ouse and the Waveney rise within a few yards of each other, can still be seen – or at least the muddy sources can, the ford itself having disappeared under the B1113. As for the Oxfoot Stone, it is a slab of sandstone about three feet by two (1 x 0.68 m), and six to nine inches (15–23 cm) in depth. It bears a shallow impression resembling the hoofprint of a cow, in all probability left by a fossil. In 1815 it apparently lay in an acre of land known as the 'Oxfootpiece' but was later moved and used as a roadside mounting block. It was moved again for safety in recent times to its present position to the right of the door of Oxfootstone Farm.

The story of the magic cow is told in many parts of the country, but usually she disappears because a malevolent witch milks her dry by milking her into a sieve (cf. **Guy's Cliffe**, p.269, and **Mitchell's Fold**, p.314).

The Oxfoot Stone may be seen over the garden wall of Oxfootstone Farm (TG 053809), in Brickkiln Lane leading off the A1066 to Low Common. The farm is shown by name on the OS 1:25 000 map. The site of Lopham Ford is marked on the 1:50 000 map (TM 039790), but only the source of the Waveney is easily accessible.

STOWMARKET, SUFFOLK

The Stowmarket area was formerly a particular haunt of fairies, locally called 'feriers' or 'ferishers'. Perhaps the most remarkable thing in the accounts of them printed in 1844 by the Rev. A. G. H. Hollingsworth, as an appendix to his *History of Stowmarket*, is that they were most of them sandy-coloured. They never appeared as long as anyone was about, and as soon as they saw anybody they vanished away. In the houses, after they had fled, sparks of fire as bright as stars used to appear under the feet of the persons who disturbed them.

A man who lived 'at the cottages in the hop-ground on the Bury road' was coming home one night, '20 years since', and was crossing a meadow when he saw, not far from three ash trees and by bright moonlight, perhaps a dozen fairies, the biggest about three feet high and the smallest like dolls. Their dresses sparkled as if with spangles, 'like the girls at shows at Stow Fair', but they themselves seemed light and shadowy.

> I passed on, saying, the Lord have mercy on me, but them must be the fairies, and being alone then on the path over the field could see them as plain as I do you. I looked after them when I got over the style, and they were there, just the same moving round and round. I ran home and called three women to come back with me and see them. But when we got to the place they were all gone. I could not make out any particular things about their faces. I might be 40 yards from them, and I did not like to stop and stare at them. I was quite sober at the time.

A curiously vivid story came from an old lady of nearly eighty – which puts the events she relates back to around 1760. Her mother was lying in bed with her husband and a baby a few weeks old at her side (the old lady couldn't remember if it was herself or her sister). She woke during the night in a dimmish light and missed the child. Frightened that the 'feriers' had taken it, she jumped out of bed, 'and there sure enough a number of the little sandy things had got the baby at the foot of the bed and were undressing it'. They fled through a hole in the floor, shrieking with laughter, and when the mother picked up her child she found that they had laid all the pins head to head as they took them out of its clothes. For months afterwards she slept with the baby between herself and her husband, its nightclothes pinned to the sheets and pillow. The same old lady had heard of a woman who actually had her child stolen and a changeling, 'a poor thing', left in its place. She was kind to it, however, and every morning when she got up found a small piece of money in her pocket.

In nearby Onehouse (TM 0259) there was a house that about a hundred years before was regularly visited by ferishers. The man who lived in the house used to keep it very clean and tidy, as the fairies couldn't abide dirt, and by way of return they would cut and bring in faggots, and fill his oven with dry wood every night. They also left a shilling under the leg of a chair. One fairy often came and warned him never to tell of their visits, or shilling, wood and ferishers would never come again. Unfortunately he did tell of his good luck, and it left him for ever (cf. **Willy Howe**, p.430). The fairy who had spoken to him wore yellow satin shoes and a long green coat with a golden belt, and had sandy hair and complexion.

From the same parish came a version of the widespread story 'The Fairy Peel'. A man was ploughing in a field when a fairy, 'quite small and sandy-coloured', came to him and asked him to mend his peel (a flat iron with a handle for taking bread out of an oven). If he did so, said the fairy, he should have a hot cake. The ploughman soon made a new handle for the peel, and shortly after a smoking hot cake appeared in the furrow near him. (For the superstitions behind this story, see **Osebury Rock**, p.277.)

Another common tale located at Onehouse was 'The Fairy Midwife':

> A fairy man came to a woman in the parish and asked her to attend his wife at her lying in, she did so and went to fairy land, and afterwards came home none the worse for her trip. But one Thursday at the market in Stowe, she saw the fairy man in a butcher's shop helping himself to some beef. On this she goes up and spoke to him. Whereupon much surprised, he bids her say nothing about it, and inquires with which eye she could see him, for when in fairy land he had rubbed one of her eyes with some ointment. On pointing to the gifted eye, he blew into it, and from that time she could never see a fairy again.

A Welsh version of this story, with the same theme of the 'gifted eye', was told at **Llandwrog** (p.345).

The fairy beliefs current around Stowmarket in the eighteenth century were already old. The ferishers who chopped the wood are perhaps none other than the Portunes described by Gervase of Tilbury in the twelfth century – 'a secret and unknown generation' of diminutive stature, with the wrinkled faces of old men, who haunted farmhouses where they would labour by night in domestic drudgery. Of the snatching away of babies by the fairies, we have a first-person account from a Gloucester man, R. Willis, in his little devotional book *Mount Tabor, or Private Exercises of a Penitential Sinner* (1639), where under the heading 'Upon an extraordinary accident which befell me in my swadling cloaths' he writes:

> Such an accident (by relation of others,) befell me within a few daies after my birth, whilst my mother lay in of me being her second child, when I was taken from her side, and by my suddain and fierce crying recovered again, being found sticking between the bed-stead and the wall: and if I had not cryed in that manner as I did, our gossips had a conceit that I had been quite carried away by the Fairies they know not whither, and some elfe or changeling (as they call it) laid in my room.

SWAFFHAM, NORFOLK

Sheet 144
TF 8109

The clergy stalls in Swaffham parish church are nineteenth-century, but incorporate the remains of some medieval wood-carving: on each side of the south stall stands a man with a pack on his back, and below him is a chained and muzzled dog; on each side of the north stall is the effigy of a man in a shop, with below him a woman looking over a shop door. These once formed part of the family pews of John Chapman, benefactor and churchwarden of the church during its rebuilding (*ca.* 1462), and are traditionally said to represent him and his wife. The carvings are a rebus on the name 'Chapman', meaning 'merchant', and represent the merchant in his simplest form – as a pedlar with his pack or as a shopkeeper. Consequently, although John Chapman was a man in a fair way of business, who paid for the new north aisle of Swaffham church and gave it other generous gifts, he came to be remembered as 'The Pedlar of Swaffham', the hero of an old tale.

Constant tradition says that there lived in former times, in Soffham, *alias* Sopham, in Norfolk, a certain pedlar, who dreamed that if he went to London bridge, and stood there, he should hear very joyfull newse, which he at first sleighted, but afterwards, his dream being dubled and trebled upon him, he resolv'd to try the issue of it, and accordingly went to London, and stood on the bridge there two or three days, looking about him, but heard nothing, that might yield him any

*The Pedlar of Swaffham: bench-end, clergy stalls,
St Peter and Paul's Church, Swaffham, Norfolk*

comfort. At last it happen'd that a shopkeeper there, hard by, haveing noted his fruitless standing, seeing that he neither sold any wares, nor asked any almes, went to him, and most earnestly begged to know what he wanted there, or what his business was; to which the pedlar honestly answer'd, that he had dream'd that if he came to London, and stood upon the bridge, he should hear good newse; at which the shopkeeper laught heartily, asking him if he was such a fool to take a jorney on such a silly errand, adding, 'I'll tell thee, country fellow, last night I dream'd that I was at Sopham, in Norfolk, a place utterly unknown to me, where, methought behind a pedlar's house, in a certain orchard, and under a great oak tree, if I digged, I should find a vast treasure! Now think you,' says he, 'that I am such a fool to take such a long jorney upon me at the instigation of a silly dream? No, no, I'm wiser. Therefore, good fellow, learn witt of me, and get you home, and mind your business.' The pedlar observeing his words, what he sayd he had dream'd, and knowing that they concenterd in him, glad of such joyfull newse, went speedily home, and digged, and found a prodigious great treasure, with which he grew exceeding rich; and Soffham church, being for the most part fal'n down, he set on workmen, and re-edifyd it most sumptuously, at his own charges; and to this day there is his statue therein, cut in stone, with his pack at his back, and his dogg at his heels . . .

This is the tale as recounted by Abraham de la Pryme in his *Diary* for 10 November 1699, and I give it because the Yorkshire diarist was a better storyteller by far than the Garter King of Arms, Sir William Dugdale, responsible for the earliest version. Sent in a letter to Sir Roger Twisden dated 29 January 1652/3 and included by him in his *Remembrances*, this has a slightly different ending: 'After a Time it happen'd that one, who came to his House and beholding the Pot, observed an Inscription upon it, which being in *Latin*, he Interpreted it, that under that there was an other twice as good.' Blomefield in the third volume of his *History of Norfolk* (1769) adds the note: 'The common Tradition is, it was in English Rhyme, viz.

> Where this stood,
> Is another as good.

Or as some will have it,

> Under me doth lye,
> Another much Richer than I.'

One pot or two, the story of 'The Pedlar of Swaffham' is the earliest known English version of the tale 'The Treasure at Home', found all over central Europe, from Denmark to Sicily, and appearing in several Oriental collections of stories, including the *Arabian Nights*. In Britain it was set, among other places, at Upsall Castle in North Yorkshire, while Dundonald Castle, Strathclyde, was supposed to have been founded by one Din Donald, who like the Swaffham pedlar was directed by a dream to go and stand on London Bridge, where he would hear 'joyfull newse'.

Fragments of medieval stained glass in the windows of the north aisle of SS Peter and Paul, Swaffham, may be the remains of representations of John Chapman and his family, mentioned by both Dugdale and de la Pryme. In the nave, a pedlar and his dog also appear as poppyheads on the ends of the two front pews, made in the nineteenth century. The Pedlar of Swaffham can also be seen on the town sign, carved in oak in 1925 by Harry Carter, son of Sir Howard Carter, a leader of the expedition which discovered the tomb of Tutankhamun in 1922.

TILNEY ALL SAINTS, NORFOLK   Sheet 131
                                             TF 5617

In the churchyard of Tilney All Saints is a stone nearly eight feet (2.7 m) long that is said to be the gravestone of Tom Hickathrift, the hero of the Marshland. According to local report in the 1960s, Tom hurled the stone from a riverbank three miles away, saying that he wished to be buried where it fell. Bouncing off the roof of Tilney church, it fell in the churchyard, where it lies to this day (cf. **Brent Pelham**, p.128). The stone was in the seventeenth century said to have carved on it a cross within a circle, popularly believed to be a representation of the weapon with which Tom once slew a giant.

The story goes that Tom was born in the reign of William the Conqueror and that by the age of ten he was already six feet tall. He was a dullard at school and inordinately lazy, sitting idly by the fire, eating as much as would feed five men, while his poor widowed mother worked to support them both. But Tom early gave proof of great strength and his fame began to grow. He went to work for a Wisbech brewer, and it was his job to make deliveries from King's Lynn to Wisbech, a journey of twenty miles skirting the Smeeth, the great common belonging to 'the seven towns of the Marshland' – Walpole St Peter, Walsoken, West Walton, Terrington, Clenchwarden, Emnett and Tilney. Now the Smeeth had to be avoided because it was the preserve of a giant who had

Tom Hickathrift and the Giant of the Smeeth:
seventeenth-century pargeting on the Sun Inn, Saffron Walden

been terrorizing the district for many years. After going the long
way round for several weeks, Tom thought he would halve his
journey by cutting straight across, but hardly had he set foot on
the common than the giant came roaring out and challenged him to
battle. From his cave the giant fetched a club as big as a mill-post,
but Tom, undaunted, took up an axle and a cart-wheel to serve
instead of sword and shield. Though the contest was hard, Tom's
prodigious strength in the end prevailed and he struck the giant's
head off. Venturing into the cave, he there found gold and silver
enough to make him rich for life.

The stories of how Tom gave proof of his strength and how he
overcame the giant of the Smeeth are probably the earliest traditions
about him, appearing in a chapbook of *ca.* 1660 – one of the 'small
merry' books collected by Samuel Pepys and now in the Pepys
Library, Magdalene College, Cambridge. Chapbooks of the eighteenth century and later children's books also told how he conquered a Kentish giant, how he got married and was knighted, and
how Tom the Tinker became his boon companion until he was
slain by a lion.

Tom's early history is that of 'The Unpromising Hero', the
lubberly lad who sits by the fire until some great occasion gives
him his chance to shine. An example is the Russian folk-hero Ilya
Muromets, and our Anglo-Saxon ancestors seem to have told such
a tale about Offa I of Angeln (for whom see **Offa's Dyke**, p.316).
Was 'Hickifric', as Dugdale calls him, an Anglo-Saxon hero or
god, as some have suggested? Or did the beginnings of his tale lie
in some ancient wrangle over grazing rights on the common,
famous for its verdure? (Someone once told James I that anyone
leaving a stick overnight on the Smeeth would be hard put to it to
find it next morning, the grass grew so quickly; to which the King
dryly replied that he knew many a field in Scotland where a horse
left overnight would similarly next day have vanished.) At any
rate, Sir William Dugdale seems to have known nothing of the
giant, and nor did Weever, who in his *Ancient Funerall Monuments*
(1631) tells the local tradition thus:

> In the Churchyard is a ridg'd Altar, Tombe or Sepulchre of a
> wondrous antique fashion, vpon which an Axell-tree and a
> cart-wheele are insculped; Vnder this Funerall Monument, the
> Towne-dwellers say that one *Hikifricke* lies interred; of whom

(as it hath gone by tradition from Father to the Sonne) they thus likewise report: How that vpon a time (no man knowes how long since) there happened a great quarrell betwixt the Lord of this land or ground, and the Inhabitants of the foresaid seuen villages, about the meere-markes, limits, or bondaries of this fruitfull feeding place; the matter came to a battell or skirmish, in which the said Inhabitants being not able to resist the Landlord and his forces, began to giue backe; *Hikifricke*, driuing his carte along, and perceiuing that his neighbours were fainthearted, and ready to take flight, he shooke the Axell-tree from the cart, which he vsed instead of a sword, and tooke one of the cart-wheeles which he held as a buckler; with these weapons (in a furious rage, you must imagine) he set vpon the Common aduersaries, or aduersaries of the Common, encouraged his neighbours to go forward, and fight valiantly in defence of their liberties; who being animated by his manly prowesse, they tooke heart to grasse, as the prouerbe is, insomuch that they chased the Landlord and his companie, to the vtmost verge of the said Common; which from that time they haue quietly enjoyed to this very day.

This story, as Weever remarks, is something like the tale told by Hector Boece in his *Chronicle of Scotland* (1526) of Hay of Errol, who in a battle with the Danes in 942 beat stragglers from the Scottish army back into line with a plough-beam. Whatever may be true of Errol, some have seen in Hickathrift a memory of representations of the Celtic thunder-god Taranis, whose symbols were a club and a wheel (see **Cerne Giant**, p.55). Such is the ragbag of folk-memory that all these things may have played their part in the legend – a dispute over common rights, the story of Hay of Errol, and attempts to 'explain' unintelligible Celtic images.

Whatever his origins, several monuments still testify locally to Hickathrift's popularity. In the churchyard of Tilney All Saints, as well as his grave at the south-east corner of the church (the long slab in three pieces), can be seen two of the three surviving 'Hickathrift's candlesticks', actually the uprights of old memorial crosses. On one of them are five indentations, said to be the marks of his fingers and thumb. The third 'candlestick' is in the vicarage garden at Terrington St John (TF 5315), immediately outside the north door of the church. Besides these memorials, there is at Walpole

St Peter (TF 5016), in a corner of the chancel wall of the church, a stone figure said to be that of Tom, locally supposed to have beaten the Devil at football in the churchyard. He can also be seen on the seventeenth-century pargeting of the Sun Inn, Saffron Walden: NT (not open to the public). The Smeeth still exists but today is mainly down to orchard and cereals, not pasture.

WANDLEBURY CAMP, STAPLEFORD, CAMBRIDGESHIRE

Sheet 154
TL 4953

> Neare unto *Cambridge* on the South-East side, there appeare aloft certaine high hilles, the Students call them *Gogmagog-Hilles*: *Henry of Huntingdon* tearmed them *AmoeniΒima montana de Balsham*, that is, *The most pleasant mountaines of Balsham* . . . On the top of these hilles, I saw a fort intrenched, and the same very large, strengthned with a threefold rampire . . . *Gervase of Tilbury* seemeth to call it *Vandelbiria* . . . Touching the Martiall spectre, or sprite that walked heere, which he added to the rest, because it is but a meere toyish and fantasticall devise of the doting vulgar sort, I willing overpasse it. For it is not my purpose, to tell pleasant tales, and tickle eares.

This is Camden in his *Britannia* (trans. Holland, 1610), and his chilliness towards the tale of the 'Martiall spectre' is a pity, for it is a good one. After mentioning Wandlebury Camp, the Iron Age hill-fort on the Gogmagogs, and discussing its name, which he mistakenly derived from 'Vandal', Gervase (*ca.* 1212) goes on to say:

> There is a very ancient tradition, attested by popular report, that if a warrior enters this level space at dead of night, when the moon is shining, and cries 'Knight to Knight come forth!' immediately he will be confronted by a warrior, armed for fight, who, charging horse to horse, either dismounts his adversary or is dismounted. But I should add that the warrior must enter the enclosure alone, although his companions may look on from outside.

This tradition, he says, was put to the test by a knight called Osbert Fitzhugh, who had heard of it while staying at Cambridge

Castle. He and his squire rode up to Wandlebury Camp, and while the squire remained outside the rampart, Osbert entered the enclosure alone. He issued the challenge, 'and in response a knight or what looked like a knight, came forth to meet him . . .' Osbert boldly encountered his adversary, and in the course of the fight succeeded in unhorsing him, and casting him on the ground. He seized the bridle of the horse to lead it off as spoils, and at this the phantom knight leapt to his feet, hurled his spear so that it pierced Osbert's thigh, and vanished. Osbert led the horse from the camp and entrusted it to his squire. Of uncommon beauty and vigour, it was tall and fierce of eye, and both it and all its trappings were as black as night. They tethered it in the courtyard of Cambridge Castle, and roused the people from sleep to hear Osbert's adventure. And just as well they did: 'At cockcrow, the horse, prancing, snorting and pawing the earth, suddenly burst the reins that held it . . . fled, vanished, and none could trace it.' But though the horse

'Knight to Knight, come forth!'
Wandlebury Camp, Stapleford, Cambridgeshire

had gone, a proof remained of the truth of their tale, for every year on that same night Osbert's wound would open and bleed anew – sure sign of its supernatural origin.

Though Camden dismissed this story, if Gervase was indeed right in thinking it a local tradition, it may be that genuine folk belief underlies the many tales of encounters with supernatural knights – usually guardians of fords or springs – found in medieval romances.

Attempts have been made to connect this story with the turf-cut figure of a giant that was visible here in the eighteenth century. The Cambridgeshire antiquary William Cole writes: 'When I was a boy about 1724 I remember my Father or Mother, as it happened that I went with one or the other of them to Cambridge, the Road from Baberham [Babraham] there lying through the Camp ... always used to stop to show me the figure of the Giant carved in the Turf; concerning whom there were many traditions now worn away.' What were the 'many traditions'? One, perhaps, was the mistaken idea derived from Gervase that Vandals had had a hand in the building of Wandlebury, a 'tradition' that gave rise to the spelling 'Vandlebury', recorded from 1808, and the hypothesis that Vandal prisoners serving in the Roman army cut the giant *ca.* 300 A.D.. This is unsupported by etymology – the name means 'Wændel's fort' – and there is no solid evidence that the figure of the giant was an old one. Gervase does not mention such a giant, and nor does Camden, and nor indeed, in his *Orthoepia Gallica, or Fruits for the French* (1593) does Eliot, although having said that the hills were made by 'Atlas, cousin-germane to Gogmagog', he takes the trouble to tell us that we can see an image of Gogmagog's rival Corineus at the London **Guildhall** (p.133).

Camden's silence is the most potent – for he had been there. One wonders if the cutting of the giant could even have been *prompted* by his visit and the subsequent appearance of the *Britannia*, the first Latin edition of which was published in 1586? The earliest reference to the giant we have comes from *Mundus alter et idem* (1605), by Joseph Hall, a Cambridge graduate; and in 1640 John Layer describes it as 'a high and mighty figure of a giant which the scholars of Cambridge cut upon the turf'. Note that Camden also attributed the name of the '*Gogmagog-Hilles*', which first appears in Saxton's *Atlas of England and Wales* (1576), to students. Whether Camden played any part in it or not, possibly both name and giant belong to the sixteenth-century revival of interest in the legends of Albion that produced *King Lear* and *Cymbeline* (see **Leicester**, p.236, and **Cymbeline's Castle**, p.132). Few British hill-figures are in fact ancient: the giant at Wandlebury could well have been made by Cambridge students in the same spirit as the Marlborough White Horse, cut in 1804 by a party of boys from Mr Greasley's Academy. They might have had in mind the already existing turf-cut Gogmagog at **Plymouth Hoe** (p.27), and also the tradition mentioned in *Mandeville's Travels* (first English translation ?1496) that Alexander the Great imprisoned the Ten Tribes of Israel, personified as Gog and Magog, in mountains near the Caspian Sea.

The waters have been muddied by the archaeologist T. C. Lethbridge, who claimed to have discovered during excavations at Wandlebury in 1955–6 the outlines of three figures, one of them an earth goddess. He believed that the figures were ancient, and that they were once visited for the performance of fertility rites. Certainly games were held in the Gogmagogs, for in 1574 the University authorities ordained that 'no scholar of what degree soever he be' should attend them; and it is true that similar games or 'pastimes' were held near hill-figures acknowledged as ancient, the Uffington White Horse and the **Cerne Giant** (p.55). But the antiquarian idea that the pastimes were the remnants of ancient rituals connected with the figures is mostly speculation. The link between them may eventually prove to be no more than their *location*: sites easily found because visible over a wide area were commonly chosen for gatherings – natural hills and barrows were often used as meeting-places for the Anglo-Saxon hundreds, and an obvious parallel is the celebrated Cotswold Games.

Lethbridge's methods were unacceptable to most archaeologists, and his conclusions doubtful on several grounds, but even if we cannot quite believe in his 'buried gods' there is a possibility that there *was* an ancient hill-figure, which perhaps only in the sixteenth century got the name 'Gogmagog', by this time evidently used generically to denote the figure of a giant. There is place-name evidence that the **Long Man of Wilmington** (p.111) was in Anglo-Saxon times known as 'the helmeted Wændel', the same personal name that underlies the name of Wandlebury Camp, and it may be that in both places was commemorated some long-forgotten hero or god.

Cambridge Preservation Society (any time). The printing of the name of the Cambridgeshire hills as 'Gog Magog Hills' by the Ordnance Survey reflects the confusion that has arisen as to whether British legend knows one giant, Gogmagog, or two, Gog and Magog – on this subject, see under **Guildhall** (p.133). Gervase's story of the Black Knight was the chief source of the 'Host's Tale' in the third Canto of Sir Walter Scott's *Marmion*.

WAYLAND WOOD, NR WATTON, NORFOLK   Sheet 144
TF 9299

Associated with Wayland Wood is the story known as 'The Babes in the Wood' or 'The Children in the Wood', the subject of an old English ballad sung to the tune of 'Rogero'. A small brother and sister are left by their dying parents to the care of their uncle, but in order to steal their inheritance he hires two ruffians to take them into a wood and murder them. One of the ruffians cannot bring himself to carry out the dreadful deed, and when he fails to persuade the other to let the children go, kills him instead. He leaves the Babes deep in the wood, promising to come back with food, but he does not return. At last the Babes die of hunger in each other's arms, and a robin covers them with leaves. The murder comes to light when the ruffian is about to be hanged for another crime and confesses the whole story; but the Wicked Uncle has already met his just deserts and perished in debtor's prison.

The first printed text of the ballad was registered at Stationers' Hall on 15 October 1595 as 'The Norfolk Gent. His Will and Testament and howe he commytted the keeping of his children to his owne brother, whoe delte most wickedly with them and howe God plagued him for it'. The publisher was Thomas Millington of Norwich, and soon after publication the story was associated with Wayland Wood, which was corrupted to 'The Wailing Wood' and is so marked on old maps. Nearby Griston Old Hall (TF 9398) was identified as the house of the Wicked Uncle and people living in 1879 remembered seeing carvings there representing the story. Griston Old Hall was wholly or partly rebuilt by Thomas May in

1597, two years after the ballad's first appearance, and he may have added the carvings during rebuilding.

The plot of 'The Babes in the Wood' is roughly the same as that of the second of *Two Lamentable Tragedies* by R. Yarrington (1601), a melodrama about 'a young child murthered in a wood by two ruffins with the consent of his unkle'. The ballad version may have been located in Norfolk because of an incident in the history of the de Greys, who bought Griston Old Hall in 1541. Thomas de Grey, a ward of Queen Elizabeth I, was married in infancy, orphaned when he was seven, and died at the age of eleven during or after a visit to his stepmother. The cry of foul play was raised and the blame laid at the door not of the stepmother but the boy's uncle, Robert de Grey, who succeeded to his nephew's property and promptly tried to rob his young widow of her dowry. A legal battle ensued in which Robert was only partly successful. Imprisoned many times in Norwich and London for Recusancy, Robert died in 1601 deeply in debt to the Crown.

To this germ were added the folktale motifs of the compassionate ruffian and the brother and sister lost in a wood (as in 'Hansel and Gretel'). The various printings of the ballad do not differ from one another very much, but the prose chapbook versions, which continued to be printed into the nineteenth century, contain greater variations. In the original ballad, the little girl is called Jane but none of the other characters are given names, whereas in eighteenth-century chapbooks everyone in the story is identified, the ruffians rejoicing in the names Rawbones and Woudkill. Similarly, the robin of the original became the troop of robins familiar now from pantomime.

Addison wrote in the *Spectator*: 'The old ballad of the *Children in the Wood* is one of the darling songs of the common people, and has been the delight of most Englishmen in some part of their age.' Although condemned in 1802 by the educator Sarah Trimmer as 'absolutely unfit for the perusal of children', the Babes' pathetic story remained popular, and when in August 1879 the great oak under which they were supposed to have died was struck by lightning and demolished, people came from miles around for souvenirs.

Wayland Wood was acquired in 1975 by the Norfolk Naturalists Trust.

No dogs are allowed and prior permission to enter is needed. Write to: The Norfolk Naturalists Trust, 72 The Close, Norwich.

WICKHAMPTON, NORFOLK   Sheet 134
                                          TG 4205

In the chancel of the parish church, against the north wall, are two late-thirteenth-century altar tombs bearing the recumbent figures of Sir William Gerbrygge (De Gerbridge) and his wife. According to a correspondent of *Notes & Queries* in 1855, their hands, folded in prayer, once enclosed heart-shaped pieces of stone which were pointed out as 'proof' of a tale used to terrify children into good behaviour:

> When a child, having had an infantine quarrel with my brother, we were taken by our nurse to see these figures; and were informed that they were two brothers named Hampton, who had quarrelled, and fought, and *torn each other's hearts out* . . . Divine vengeance turned their bodies to stone; and, with their hearts in their hands, they were placed in the church as a monument of their wickedness. The parish, too, which had been the scene of their unnatural conflict, had its name changed; and, from that time, bore the name of Wicked-Hampton, since contracted into Wickhampton. The shields of arms over the tombs were those with which the brothers fought; and the actual locality of the combat is marked by a piece of flint masonry, let into the side of a ditch. This, I have since ascertained, is the boundary of Halvergate and Wickhampton . . . I always gave the nurse the credit of having invented the story, until, a few years ago, I happened to be in the church, inspecting it, when a nurse-maid took the opportunity of the doors being open to enter with her charge, and recounted the tale, to the no small horror of a little girl and boy who accompanied her, and, by the evidence of their countenances, gave implicit credence to it.

All the elderly people of the parish were acquainted with the legend, and added that the brothers had quarrelled over the boundary between the two parishes belonging to them, and that just as one had received the name of Wicked-Hampton, so the other had been called Hell-fire-gate, later corrupted to Halvergate (TG 4206).

Both effigies are described in *Notes & Queries* as holding their pieces of stone 'till very recently', a statement echoed by John Glyde in his *Norfolk Garland* (1872) as 'until the last few years'. But either the original statement was never meant to imply that the knight had lost his heart as well as the lady, whose hands are missing, or it has been replaced – for it is certainly there, a cushion of stone the size and shape of a sheep's heart. Only by a great stretch of the imagination could the two figures ever have been taken for brothers – the lady sports a fine and unmistakably female head-dress – but compare 'Shakespeare on a Deer' at **Charlecote Park** (p.264).

As well as its tombs, Wickhampton church contains three splendid fourteenth-century wall-paintings, including one of 'The Three Living and the Three Dead', a medieval moral fable against the vanity of earthly desires. Three kings in the pride of life meet three corpses, who convey the message 'As we are, so shall you be.'

WINFARTHING, NORFOLK

Sheet 144
TM 1085

In Winfarthing, a little Village in Norfolke, there was a certeyne Swerd, called the Good Swerd of Winfarthyng, this Swerd was counted so precious a Relique, and of so great Virtue, that there was a solemne Pilgrimage used unto it, wyth large Giftes and Offringes, with Vow makings, Crouchinges, & Kissinges: This Swerd was visited far and near, for many & sundry Purposes, but specialy for thinges that were lost, and for horses that were eyther stolen or else rune astray, it helped also unto the Shortening of a married Mans Life, if that the Wyfe which was weary of her Husband, would set a Candle before that Swerd every Sunday for the Space of a whole Yeare, no Sunday excepted, for then all was vain, whatsoever was done before.

I have many Times heard when I was a Child, of diverse ancient Men and Wemen, that this Swerd was the Swerd of a certayne Theif, which took Sanctuary in that Church-Yard, and afterwards through the Negligence of the Watchmen escaped, and left his Swerd behind him, which being found, and laid up in a certaine old Chest, was afterward through the Suttilty of the Parson and the Clerk of the same Parish, made a precious Relique, full of Vertue, able to do much, but specially to enrich the Box*, and make fat the Parson's Pouch.

Such is the account given by Thomas Becon in his *Reliques of Rome* (1563) of the Good Sword of Winfarthing, one of the many objects of pilgrimage swept away by the Reformation. The anti-clerical explanation of the sword was perhaps invented after its real identity had been forgotten. It used to be housed in a chapel at the end of the south aisle of the parish church, and may originally have been shown as the sword of the 'Good Thief', to whom chapels were occasionally consecrated. Another way of getting shot of an unwanted husband in the Middle Ages, for those who could not make the pilgrimage to Winfarthing, was to offer 'otys' at 'Poules' to St Uncumber (see **Chew Stoke**, p.13).

WOOLPIT, SUFFOLK
Sheet 155
TL 9762

Wulpet is a Mercat towne, and soundeth asmuch as, *The Woolues pit*, if we may beleeue *Nubrigensis*, who hath told as prety and formall a tale of this place, as is that fable called the TRVE NARRATION of *Lucian*: namely, how two little boies (forsooth) of a greene colour ... after they had made along journey by passages under the ground, from out of another world from the *Antipodes* and Saint *Martins* land, came up heere: of whom if you would know more, repaire to the authour himselfe, where you shall find such matters as will make you laugh your fill, if you have a laughing spleene.

Thus Camden in his *Britannia* (trans. Holland, 1610), though as capable as the next man of swallowing moonshine if colourably dressed up with false etymology, balks at the 'prety and formall' tale of 'The Green Children'.

Repairing to the author – not indeed '*Nubrigensis*', but Ralph of

* poor-box

Coggeshall, writing at the monastery of Coggeshall in Essex in about 1210 – we hear that at St Mary's of the Wolf-pits within living memory were found, near the mouth of one of the pits, a boy and a girl whose skins were green. Their speech was unintelligible to the villagers who found them, so they took them to the house of Sir Richard de Calne, the local landowner. The children cried and refused all food until they happened to see some freshly cut beans being brought into the house, when they indicated by signs that they would like some. After they had been shown how to open the pods, they ate the beans avidly, and for a long time would touch no other food. The boy, who was always listless, soon died, but the girl, by contrast, throve, and as she became accustomed to other food gradually lost her greenness. She lived for many years in Sir Richard's household, but was rather wanton ('as I have frequently heard from him and his family').

When asked about her people, she said they lived in a twilight land where the sun never shone, and were all green like herself. Asked how she came to this country, she said she and her brother were following their flocks when they came to a cavern, where they heard a sound of bells. The sound led them through the cavern to another exit, and as they emerged into the light of day, they were overcome by the brightness and lay senseless for a long time. Terrified by the noise made by those who found them, they attempted to escape, but could not find the cavern again before being caught.

To this story, '*Nubrigensis*' – William of Newburgh, a monastery in Yorkshire – adds further details. He sets it in the reign of King Stephen and says that the children appeared at harvest-time; that they both learned to speak English; and that the girl married a man from Lynn. She said their country was called St Martin's Land and its people were Christians. The sun did not rise there, but from it they could see a bright country divided from their own by a broad river. William does not say where he got the tale, but it looks as if he traded stories with Ralph, who had collected this locally. Either William preserved several details that Ralph had chosen not to use, or he did some embroidery on his own account, recognizing the tale's similarity to others that he knew. For behind this seemingly factual account lie memories of the Celtic Otherworld, which might be reached through a cavern and where enchanting music was heard, and of the fairies, who traditionally wore green.

Woolpit (OE *wulfpytt*) was clearly distinguished by its pits for trapping wolves, and that one of these prosaic holes in the ground should have become the subject of so mysterious a legend is perhaps not remarkable. The starting-point of the story may have lain in the fact that in medieval times pilgrimages were made to Our Lady of Woolpit, the waters of whose well – Lady's Well, in a meadow behind the church (TL 976626) – had a reputation for curing diseases of the eye. If the well was sacred also in pagan times, as seems to have been the case at the more famous Walsingham, perhaps the 'The Green Children' is the remnant of a tradition attached to it.

6
English Shires

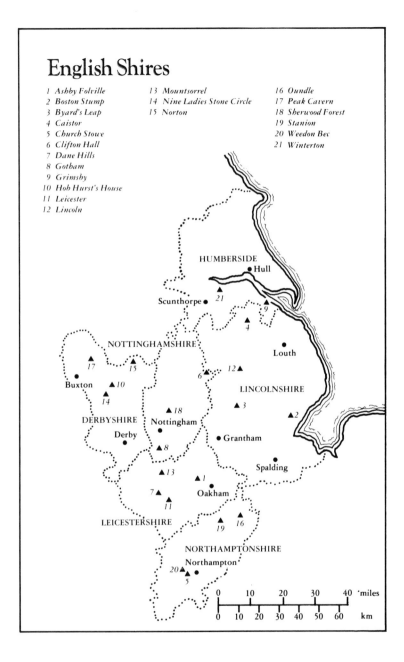

English Shires

1 Ashby Folville
2 Boston Stump
3 Byard's Leap
4 Caistor
5 Church Stowe
6 Clifton Hall
7 Dane Hills
8 Gotham
9 Grimsby
10 Hob Hurst's House
11 Leicester
12 Lincoln

13 Mountsorrel
14 Nine Ladies Stone Circle
15 Norton

16 Oundle
17 Peak Cavern
18 Sherwood Forest
19 Stanion
20 Weedon Bec
21 Winterton

HUMBERSIDE

● Hull

Scunthorpe ● ▲ 21

▲
9 ▲

▲
4

NOTTINGHAMSHIRE

▲
17

▲
15

Louth ●

▲
6

12 ▲

LINCOLNSHIRE

Buxton ●

▲ 10

▲
14

▲ 3

▲ 2

DERBYSHIRE

▲ 18

Nottingham ●

Derby ●

▲ 8

● Grantham

Spalding ●

▲ 13

▲ 1

7 ▲

Oakham ●

11

LEICESTERSHIRE

▲
19

▲
16

NORTHAMPTONSHIRE

Northampton ●

20 ▲ ●
5

0   10   20   30   40 ´miles

0   10   20   30   40   50   60   km

Up to the early nineteenth century, the floor of Ashby Folville church used to be strewn with hay or rushes according to season, from the first Sunday in August up to Christmas-time. The hay for this was grown on a piece of land marked out by three large stones in a field called 'The Bartlemews', between Ashby Pastures (SK 7013) and Thorpe Thrussels (SK 726130). It was said that two ladies who had been overtaken by darkness and lost their way followed the sound of the church bells to safety. On the spot where they first heard the bells, they dropped a handkerchief, and there next day it was found. They left the produce of that piece of land yearly to the church thereafter, to commemorate their escape. However, when this story was recorded in the nineteenth century, the land had 'recently' been sold and part of the money used to mend the church windows.

The hay- or rush-strewing at Ashby Folville was a vestige of the once widespread custom of 'rush-bearing', normally the chief event of the annual festival of a church's patron saint, when the rushes to cover the floor for the coming year would be brought into the church in ceremonial procession. 'The Bartlemews' from which the hay came for this event may well have been left to the church for this express purpose by a medieval bequest.

The story 'explaining' the custom is a common one, however, used in many places to account for benefactions whose real origins had been forgotten. At Wingrave, near Aylesbury, the bringing-in of fresh hay on the Sunday following 29 June was similarly explained by the tale of a man who had lost his way and been guided by the sound of bells. The same tale is often used – and perhaps this is where it began – to account for curfews and the ringing of special bells, such as those which used to be rung at Newark, in Nottinghamshire, for an hour on six successive nights in October and November. This was known as 'Ringing for Gofer' because, so the story went, a merchant called Gofer lost in Sherwood Forest had been guided home by the Newark bells, and in gratitude for his deliverance, had left a bequest to provide for the ringing of bells ever after on the dark winter nights.

Similar stories were told at Curdworth in Warwickshire, and at Barton-upon-Humber and Stamford Bridge, both Humberside. At

Burgh le Marsh in Lincolnshire, where the tolling of a bell once prevented a shipwreck, the grateful skipper gave the church a piece of land thenceforth known as 'Bell String Acre', because its rent was to be spent on keeping the bell-ropes in order. Such stories are half-fact, half-fiction – for actual bequests of this sort are known, for example at Berwick St John in Wiltshire, where in 1735 provision was made for the church bells to be rung on winter nights to guide travellers on the Downs.

The usefulness of bells as guides in an England once heavily wooded is shown by a true account of some Vikings who only found the monastery they had come to sack when by an unfortunate coincidence the monks started to ring its bells. Much the same tale was attached to Brinkburn Priory in Northumberland, which is hidden in a cleft between the wooded banks of the Coquet. The priory fell prey to a band of Scottish moss-troopers when, thinking the danger past, the monks prematurely rang the thanksgiving bells.

For rush-bearing generally, and churches where the custom still survives, see Christina Hole, *British Folk Customs* (Paladin, London, 1977). Thorpe Thrussels is marked on the OS 1:25 000 map.

BOSTON STUMP, LINCOLNSHIRE

Sheet 131
TF 3244

> Boston, Boston, Boston!
> Thou hast naught to boast on,
> But a Grand Sluice, and a high steeple;
> A proud conceited ignorant people,
> And a coast where souls are lost on.

So, according to Wheeler's *History of the Fens* (1868), said a visitor whose expectations were disappointed at the opening of the Grand Sluice on 15 October 1766. But if he thought nothing of the Sluice, can he really have failed to be impressed by the 'high steeple' – the famous Boston Stump, 272 feet (83 m) high, and a landmark for many miles? The tower of the medieval parish church of St Botolph's, it can be seen across the Wash and 'As high as Boston Stump' has become proverbial.

Built on woolpacks: Boston Stump, Lincolnshire

The Stump, which was completed in 1470, was commonly believed to have been built on woolpacks, a tradition connected with many bridges as well as towers. Leland, in 1538, describing the bridge at Wadebridge in Cornwall, says it was built about eighty years before his time, and that as the site was sandy the builder 'almost despaired to perform the bridge until such time as he laid packs of wool for foundation'. In 1617, Fynes Moryson in his *Itinerary* gives the same tradition of London Bridge, of which Donald Lupton says in *London and the Countrey carbonadoed* (1632), 'his arches out-face the water, and like judges in the parliament, are placed upon wool-sacks'.

Aubrey in his *Remaines* (1686–7) gives the rational man's explanation for such legends:

> The tradition at Salisbury is, that Our Ladies-church there was built upon Wool-packs; but I doe beleive, that was a Figurative expression, as if one should say, that Paules church at London were built upon Coale: because the Found for the building is raised by a tax out of ye Coales that are brought from Newcastle; so I presume, that when Salisbury church was building, there was a Tax layd upon the woolsacks; Wiltshire being the greatest Wooll countrey in England.

While there is no doubt that the most important factor in English medieval commerce was the wool trade, which reached its highest peak in the fifteenth century, whether or not these structures were specifically funded by a tax on wool is another question. Probably the allusion was a general one, as in the iconographic tradition remarked on by the Hon. John Byng in his diary for 26 June 1784, where he notes that at Northleach church in Gloucestershire 'there are many old brasses . . . to the memory of wealthy clothiers, all standing on a sheep & woolpack; for this place formerly flourish'd by the wool trade, now quite lost'. That much of the prosperity arising from wool found its way into good works (of which bridgebuilding was reckoned one) is confirmed by the tale of Sir Thomas Barton, a merchant of the Staple, who at the end of the fifteenth century rebuilt the church at Holme in Nottinghamshire. On his house was inscribed:

> I thank God and ever shall,
> It is the sheepe that payed for all.

Boston Stump is open daily (except Sundays) in summer, on Wednesdays and Saturdays in winter, and by arrangement with the vicar of St Botolph's Church. Sir Thomas Barton's tomb is in Holme church, near Newark-on-Trent (SK 8059).

BYARD'S LEAP, CRANWELL & BYARD'S LEAP, LINCOLNSHIRE

Sheet 130
TF 9849

On the great Roman road from Leicester to Lincoln, once known as Ermine Street and now more prosaically as the B6403, just at the point where it is crossed by the Sleaford–Newark road (A17), stands the once almost solitary farmhouse of Byard's Leap Farm. Formerly extra-parochial, it became in Victoria's reign a parish in its own right, now combined with Cranwell.

> Close by the entrance gateway to this farm-house, on the road side, is a block of stone, such as not uncommonly may be seen near old houses of the kind, forming two steps, from which a rider mounted his horse. This stone is inscribed with the words 'Byard's Leap' . . . It is situated in the midst of what was once a lonely tract of high land, almost a waste, extending for many miles, and called Ancaster Heath . . . The pedestrian who follows the footpath which runs along the Eastern side of the great Roman highway, will observe, at a distance of some fifty yards northwards from the farmhouse of Byard's Leap, and near a pond by the roadside, four very large iron horse shoes, embedded in the soil. If he measures the distance of these shoes from the pond he will find that it is twenty paces, or sixty feet, and sixty feet was the length of Byard's Leap . . .
>
> Opposite the farm of 'Byard's Leap', is a plantation . . . Within that wood, inhabiting, as it is said, a cave, but more likely a deserted quarry . . . there lived the pest and terror of the country side in the person of an old woman, known far and wide as . . . the witch.

This description of Byard's or Bayard's Leap, written by the Rev. J. Conway Walter, comes from *Bygone Lincolnshire*, edited by William Andrews (1891). The story behind the name had already been told many times with many variations. As the Rev. Walter himself tells it, the people of the neighbourhood decided to 'get shut' of the witch and the shepherd at the farm was elected to do it. He was to lead the farmhorses out to drink at the pond opposite the hag's den, and to throw a stone in the water as the horses drank. Whichever horse raised its head first, he was to mount and call the old witch to get up behind him. When she had done so, he was to stab her with the two-edged knife he had brought with him for the purpose, at which hopefully she would fall off and be drowned. At the appointed time the shepherd carried out his instructions, and the first horse that raised its head was a blind one called Bayard – a very great piece of luck, as no horse that could see would let itself come in contact with the witch. The shepherd mounted Bayard and called to the old woman, who replied, 'Wait till I've buckled my shoes and suckled my cubs, and I'll be with you.' At length she came and mounted the horse, and he plunged the knife in her breast. In her agony she clutched Bayard's back with her long sharp claws and he made one wild sudden bound that landed him a full sixty feet from the spot. The witch as predicted fell off his back into the pond and was drowned.

According to an earlier account that appeared in *Notes & Queries*, 25 December 1852, the hero was a knight who was riding past when the witch who haunted the place sprang up behind him on the back of Bayard, his horse, who in terror made three great jumps, afterwards marked by three stones about thirty yards apart. In this version the witch resembles the traditional lane-haunting ghost who leaps up behind horsemen to throttle them (see **Kington**, p.309), while in the first her response is patently that of a bogey. This is particularly clear from an alternative version of her reply:

'I must suckle my cubs,
I must buckle my shoes,
And then I will give you your supper.'

which has a long last line on which the bogey jumps out (cf. **Obtrusch Tumulus**, p.416).

The *Notes & Queries* version of the legend raises the question of what was to be seen at Byard's Leap – three stones or four horseshoes? In fact neither account quite agrees with what the Rev. Walter had heard from the owner of Byard's Leap in his day, a Colonel Reeve, who said that in his father's time 'Bayard's jump was denoted by eight holes in the ground, but at length they got worn out; and finding this to be the case, he [Colonel Reeve] himself had the present large horse-shoes made and put into large blocks of stone, to prevent their being easily removed'.

'The holes said to have been made by the horse's feet,' remarks *White's Directory of Lincolnshire* for 1856, 'are supposed to be nothing more than the boundaries of four parishes.' Whatever they may originally have been, from Addy's *Household Tales* (1895) we learn that the footprints were customarily kept clean after the manner of the annual scourings of the Uffington White Horse.

Addy implies in his notes to the story that Byard himself was white, evidently because he had been told that many white horses were blind. But Byard's colour would have been *bay*, for his name is a form of *bayard*, originally an adjective meaning 'bay-coloured', thence 'a bayard', a bay-coloured horse. The Rev. Walter thought that Byard's name was 'doubtless derived from the celebrated French warrior, Peter Bayard' – the Chevalier Bayard (?1476–1524), the knight *sans peur et sans reproche* – inexplicably ignoring perhaps the most famous horse of medieval romance, Bayard, the wonderful dun-coloured horse given by Charlemagne to the French hero Renaud de Montauban, who could magically lengthen his back in order to carry Renaud and his brothers, the Four Sons of Aymon, all at the same time.

The story of Renaud and his horse Bayard was told in a twelfth-century *chanson de geste* and remained popular throughout the Middle Ages. A French prose version was translated by Caxton in *ca.* 1489 as *The right pleasant and goodly Historie of the Foure Sonnes of Aimon*, and in Queen Elizabeth's reign the story was turned into a play. Renaud himself became the hero Rinaldo of Italian poetry, and in Belgium effigies of the Four Sons were once a regular part of civic processions. Renaud was associated with several places in Belgium, Germany and France, especially the Ardennes, where in the village of Château-Renaud, near Mont-hermé, visitors were shown a high rock supposed to be the site of Renaud's castle Montfort, where could be seen the ruins of 'Bayard's Stable'. One of Bayard's hoofprints – and this brings us close to our story – could be seen in the Forest of Soignes, near Brabant, another on a rock in Dinant.

As a result of the tremendous popularity of this tale, 'Bayard' came to be a mock-heroic name for a horse. Whether as a development of this, or because there was actually a story to that effect, from the early fourteenth century onwards '*Blind* Bayard' begins to appear in proverbial sayings as typifying recklessness. The connection between Bayard and blindness is already there in Chaucer's *Troilus and Criseyde*, where we hear of Troilus's cock-sure conviction that he will never be caught by love. 'O blynde world, O blynde entencioun!' Chaucer exclaims. 'This Troilus is clomben on the stair, And litel weneth that he moot descenden'. He is like 'proud Bayard' who 'gynneth for to skippe Out of the weye ... Til he a lasshe have of the longe whippe', a timely reminder: 'Though I praunce al byforn ... yet am I but an hors'.

'Bayard the blinde stede ... He goth there no man will him bidde' (Gower, 1393); 'Bee bolde vpon it lyke blynde bayarde' (Sir Thomas More, 1532); 'As ... boldly as blind bayard rusheth into battle' (*ca.* 1630) – this is how our Lincolnshire Byard comes to be blind. The apparently simple tradition of Byard's Leap amply illustrates the richness of English folklore, which can draw into one tale a 'prodigious leap' story (see **The Soldier's Leap**, p.521), a traditional jumping-out bogey in the shape of a witch, the proverbial Blind Bayard, and behind him still perhaps the shadowy figure of the magical Bayard of romance.

Today Byard's Leap is marked by two sets of four horseshoes, about fifty yards apart, raised on legs like trivets above the ground. If the 'large blocks of stone' are there, they are not visible. Because the line of the road has been altered, the horseshoes are now on a species of island between the present B6403 and the original road, in front of a garage and café.

CAISTOR, LINCOLNSHIRE

Sheet 113
TA 1101

This day I went with some other company to Castor. I expected to have found it (that is so famous in both the Roman and Saxon historys) to be some great and large town, but when I got there I was deceived, it being but a little place, yet mighty famous for its great markits and fairs ... It was here that Hengist begg'd so much ground of King Vortigern as he was able to encompass with an ox-hide, who, not well understanding his meaning, granted him his request, thinking that he meant no more than he could cover with an ox-hide. But Hengist cut it all into small thongs, and by that means encompast in round about a great compass of land, and built an exceeding strong castle upon part thereof, part of whose ruins I took notice of, it being a wall five or six yards thick. But, when Christianity came, they pull'd the castle down, and built the church in the place where it stood, of the stone that it was built off.

'This day' was 19 June 1695 and the visitor to Caistor the diarist Abraham de la Pryme. As its name implies, Caistor was a Roman station (*castra*), 'an ancient Castle', says Camden, who also knew the tale, '. . . called . . . in the old English Saxons tongue . . . *Thong-caster*, . . . aptly named . . . of an hide cut into pieces'.

Actually the Old English name was *Tunnaceaster*, from which 'Thong-caster' seems to have evolved under the influence of a legend attached to several places called Tong – notably Tonge, near Sittingbourne, Kent, Tong in Shropshire, and the Kyle of Tongue, Caithness (now Highland). The story is a piece of folk-etymology, a fanciful 'explanation' of these names, all in fact from ON *tunga*, 'a strip of land'.

Although one might have assumed that the story spread to other Tongs from Tonge Castle in Kent, Hengest's traditional stamping ground (see **Kit's Coty House**, p.108), it seems to have been set in Lincolnshire from almost its first appearance. In the twelfth century Geoffrey of Monmouth says that, after the Saxons had helped Vortigern defeat the Picts 'beyond *Humber*', Vortigern 'gave their general *Hengist* large Possessions of Land in *Lindesia*', i.e. Lindsey. Later in the same chapter he tells the ox-hide story, saying that with the thong Hengest 'encompassed a rocky Place' and there built his castle, 'afterwards called in the *British* Tongue *Kaercorrei*, in the *Saxon Thancastre*, that is *Thong-Castle*.' Whether or not he meant to imply that Thong Castle was in Lincolnshire, that is what later writers assumed.

But whether the legend was first attached to Caistor or Tonge, it did not originate there. The story of the grant of as much land as a bull's hide would cover is widespread and ancient, and was told, among others by Vergil, of the founding of Carthage: when Dido fled from Tyre, and landed on the coast of Africa, she bought from the inhabitants as much ground as could be encompassed by a bull's hide. This she proceeded to cut into strips, with which she enclosed the area on which the citadel of Carthage was built. The citadel was thereafter called Byrsa (Greek for 'a hide') in memory of the exploit – and this, too, seems to be popular etymology, for 'Byrsa' is likely to be a misinterpretation of something like the Hebrew name Bozrah, meaning 'fortification'.

Jacob Grimm thought that the story reflected the same traditional practices as the Anglo-Saxon unit of land measurement, the hide.

This varied from time to time and place to place, but in seventh-century Wessex was about forty acres (16 ha). In fact this 'hide' and animal 'hide' seem to be unconnected: the first, OE *hīd*, is thought to be derived from OE *hīwan*, 'a household', and to have meant as much land as would support one family – which is why the amount changes; while the second, OE *hyd*, is the same word as Latin *cutis*. 'As well,' observed J. U. Powell, writing on this tradition in *Folklore* in 1933:

> As well might we connect 'ham' in the sense of a meadow, which is often found in place-names, with 'ham' meaning the hinder part of a pig, because the waiters in the Vauxhall Gardens were, according to the wits of the time, supposed to be able to carve a ham into slices thin enough to cover an acre.

But stories similar to that of 'Thong-caster' are known as far afield as Nepal, and it is a matter of record that when the Methodist missionary to China, Samuel Pollard (1864–1915), began to preach in the Miao villages, he bought a site at Stone Gateway 'as much as a cowhide would enclose after it had been cut into narrow strips'. So although such traditions have nothing to do with the Anglo-Saxon 'hide', they may well be a last memory of a world-wide prehistoric practice, echoed in a slightly different form in the legend attached to **Maiden Bower** (p.144).

The supposed ruin of Hengest's castle viewed by Abraham de la Pryme can still be seen – it is the Roman bastion south of the church (TA 116012). A curious tenure custom, the Caistor Gad-Whip ceremony, observed until about the middle of the last century, is described by Christina Hole in *British Folk Customs* (Paladin, London, 1977). The gad-whip had a very long thong, and the ceremony may be somehow connected with the 'Thong-caster' legend, though it is not as ancient – it is mentioned by neither Camden nor Blount.

CHURCH STOWE, NORTHAMPTONSHIRE   Sheet 152
SP 6357

Church Stowe used to be referred to as 'Stowe-Nine-Churches', possibly because in the time of Henry VII there were nine advowsons attached to the manor. But tradition said it arose when the Lord of the manor, who wanted to build a church in what was then Stowe, chose a hill-top site and set his craftsmen to work. Nine times they laid the foundations, but nine times next morning could find no trace of their previous day's endeavours. Trenches, materials, tools – all were gone. After a search, they were discovered on the spot where the present church now stands, and a man was set to watch at night to see who it was who was moving the stones. Next morning he reported seeing 'summat bigger nor a hog', and after this the attempt was abandoned, and the present church built on the site indicated to them by this supernatural means.

This story, recounted in Sternberg's *Dialect and Folklore of Northamptonshire* (1851), has many parallels, sometimes attached to buildings such as castles (cf. **Callaly Castle**, p.403), but most often to churches. Significantly Stowe church stands on a mound and is dedicated to St Michael. Many British churches stand on hill-top sites, whether natural eminences (as at St Michael's Mount, Cornwall) or artificial mounds, sometimes ancient barrows (as at Cheriton, Hampshire, and Fimber, Yorkshire). To many of these hill-top churches is attached the story of the 'disputed site', told in Leicestershire at Breedon on the Hill (SK 4022), where the church stands within the ramparts of an Iron Age fort, and in North-amptonshire itself at Great Brington (SP 6664), where the church stands on a hill, and Great Oxenden (SP 7383) where the whole village is on high ground.

'I remember', wrote Aubrey in the seventeenth century, 'my honoured friend Sr W. Dugdale, told me his Remarque, viz. that most churches dedicated to St Michael either stood on high ground, or els had a very high Tower or steeple', and conversely the most frequent hill-top dedication is to St Michael – who threw Lucifer out of Heaven and might be regarded as the natural saint to oppose the Devil in high places. Moreover, we are told in the *South English Legendary* (thirteenth century) that after the Fallen Angels had been routed from Heaven, the less sinful among them were allowed to haunt the earth, dwelling in woods and on high hills, and known to men as 'elves'. From this it has been surmised that earlier Celtic hill-top shrines were subsequently 'christianized' by the building of churches (Aubrey refers us to St Jerome, who 'speakes . . . of their building their Christian Churches where their old Ethnick ones were') and that the motif of the disputed site of a church symbolizes the conflict of interests between pagan and

Nine times moved from its site by 'summat bigger nor a hog': the parish church of Church Stowe or 'Stowe-Nine-Churches', Northamptonshire

Christian. Some have even suggested that it is a memory of night-time raids by pagans to prevent the desecration of their holy places, but the legend at Stowe runs counter to this, for the supposedly sacred site finally chosen *is* the hill-top site.

The 'summat bigger nor a hog' may be a garbled version of a tradition in which the new site is chosen by pigs. A sow suckling her piglets showed St Brannoc where to build his church at Braunton, Devon, after attempts to build on a site he had himself chosen had been frustrated. Similarly, at Winwick, Cheshire, a pig moved the stones of the new church to the spot where St Oswald of Northumbria had been killed in 642 A.D.. It is supposed to have cried 'We-ee-wick!', hence Winwick, but the original reason for the tale being attached to Winwick is a pig sculpted on the church tower just above the west entrance.

At Burnley, in Lancashire, St Peter's Church was similarly supposed to have been built in Godly Lane, but pigs moved it to the present site. Again a pig is represented on the church, on the south side of the steeple, and also on the font. A sow and her farrow, otherwise unexplained, appear on bosses and bench-ends in West Country churches, such as Broad Clyst, Sampford Courtney, Spreyton and Ugborough, all in Devon. Some say that in iconography as in legend still lingers a trace of the boar sacred to the Indo-European peoples, including the Scandinavians and the Celts. A more prosaic explanation is that the sow and her farrow descend from a tradition of the founding of Rome.

CLIFTON HALL, NORTH CLIFTON, NOTTINGHAMSHIRE

Sheet 121
SK 8272

In his *Miscellanies* (1696), Aubrey writes: ''Tis commonly reported, that before an Heir of the *Cliftons*, of *Clifton* in *Nottinghamshire*, dies, that a Sturgeon is taken in the River *Trent* by that place.' From the fact that he makes no further comment, we must suppose that this was a well-known tradition in his day, giving this family death-omen, unlike most, a respectable longevity (cf. **Brereton Hall**, p.298).

The present Clifton Hall, a recently restored Georgian mansion, is now part of Trent Polytechnic and open to the public by appointment only. Applications to The Assistant Director (Administration), Trent Polytechnic, Burton Street, Nottingham.

DANE HILLS, LEICESTERSHIRE

Sheet 140
SK 5604

Now swallowed up by the suburban sprawl of the city of Leicester is a series of low hills known as the Dane Hills and formerly wasteland. On the side of one of these mounds, there was once a cave cut out of the sandstone, about ten or twelve feet (3–4 m) across, subsequently filled with soil. It was known as Black Annis's Bower, and Black Annis herself was said to have been a savage hag with great teeth and long nails who devoured human victims.

According to verses by an 'ingenious young poet', one Lieutenant John Heyrick, quoted in Nichols's *History of Leicestershire* (1804), Black Annis's features were a livid blue, and the blood of children and lambs stained the floor of her cavern, which she had scooped from the rock with her claws.

Later she was known as 'Black Anna'. A contributor to the *Leicester Chronicle* in 1874 wrote:

Little children who went to run on the Dane Hills, were

If Black Annis was ever a goddess, was she something like this?
Carved figure outside All Saints Church, Braunston,
Leicestershire (formerly Rutland)

assured that she (Black Anna) lay in wait there, to snatch them
away to her 'bower'; and that many like themselves she had
'scratched to death with her claws, sucked their blood, and
hung up their skins to dry'.

Black Anna was also believed at this time to be in the habit of
crouching in an old oak that grew in a cleft over her cave, ready to
spring out on passers-by. At the end of the nineteenth century, her
name appears as 'Cat Anna', and she is said to be a witch who lived
in the cellars under Leicester Castle. An underground passage was
supposed to lead from the castle to the Dane Hills, along which
Cat Anna ran.

Who was Black Annis or Anna? In a curious book called
Naology (1846), the Rev. John Dudley connected her name with
the Celtic goddess Anu, in Irish tradition often confused with
Danu, the mother of the Tuatha de Danann, in Welsh the 'Children
of Don'. Her devouring of children, Dudley suggested, was an
echo of cannibalistic rites conducted in these hills by the ancient
Britons, but any connection is likely to be more indirect and to be
part of the development of the goddess into an ogress.

The Celtic mother-goddess – represented among others by Anu
or Danu, the Morrighan, and the quasi-historical Medhbh – was
goddess both of sexuality and of war. Her terrifying aspect seems
to have led to her becoming in later lore a hag – for example the
Blue Hag of the Highlands, the *Cailleach Bheur*, whom Black
Annis with her livid face resembles. That such Celtic mother-
goddesses were once worshipped in this area is attested by what
seems to be a carving of a fertility goddess standing just outside
Braunston church (SK 8306).

Support for Dudley's idea may possibly also come from an old
custom that used to be practised in the Dane Hills – the Easter
Monday Drag Hunt. A dead cat soaked in aniseed used to be
dragged from Black Annis's Bower Close through the city to the
house of the Mayor, where a reception followed. Great numbers of
people used to assemble in the Dane Hills to watch this event. The
Hunt gradually dwindled away after about 1767, though an Easter
Monday Fair continued to be held in the Hills for some years to
come.

The first mention of the Drag Hunt in the town records comes from 1668, although it is then described as very old. But can we rely on this statement? Most towns like to think that their ceremonies are ancient. Before we too fervently embrace the idea of continuity with the Celtic past, we should perhaps look again at a suggestion made by 'Mr Burton' and quoted by Nichols that Black Annis was Agnes Scott, commemorated in a window and a brass in Swithland church (SK 5413). 'This *Agnes Scott*, as I guess, was an Anchoress; and the word *Antrix* in this epitaph [on the brass] coined from *antrum*, a cave, wherein she lived; and certainly (as I have been credibly informed) there is a cave near Leicester . . . at this day called Black Agnes's Bower.' And if we are prepared to take seriously the notion of a connection between 'Anu' and 'Annis', then we should also ponder the possibility of one between 'Cat Anna' and the Drag Hunt cat, 'Annis' and 'aniseed', and not neglect the fact that among the mayors of Leicester mentioned by Nichols is one named Annis. We can assume coincidence, but it is more likely, perhaps, that anchoress, cat hunt and mayor have all played their part in the evolution of the legend. It is worthy of note that public sports in high places – in themselves seemingly part of an ancient tradition – elsewhere may have come first and legends followed (cf. **Wandlebury Camp**, p.202).

The Dane Hills are two miles (3 km) from the city centre, on the right as you leave Leicester by King Richard's Road and Glenfield Road.

GOTHAM, NOTTINGHAMSHIRE   Sheet 129
                                             SK 5330

> Three wise men of Gotham
> Went to sea in a bowl;
> And if the bowl had been stronger,
> My song would have been longer

runs a rhyme in J. O. Halliwell's *Popular Rhymes & Nursery Tales of England* (1849). In Halliwell's day some claimed that the Gothamites came from near Pevensey, but traditionally the village of 'numskulls' or fools is Gotham in Nottinghamshire.

'*As wise as a man of* Gotham', explains John Ray in his *Compleat Collection of English Proverbs* (4th edn, 1768), 'passeth for the

Periphrasis of a fool, and an hundred fopperies are feigned and fathered on the town's-folk . . .' The traditional explanation of their reputation for folly is that the infamous King John, on his way to Nottingham (no doubt to conspire with the Sheriff), attempted to pass through fields belonging to the village. Afraid that this would establish a right of way, the villagers forcibly prevented him, and when he later sent some of his men to punish them, hit on the plan of pretending to be mad and so not responsible for their actions. When the King's officers arrived, they found some of the villagers trying to drown an eel in a pailful of water, others rolling cheeses down a hill so that they would take themselves to Nottingham market, and yet others standing hand in hand around a bush with a cuckoo in it, hoping to pen the bird and so capture Spring.

The tradition of the Wise Men of Gotham goes back at least to late medieval times. They are referred to in the Townely (sometimes called the Wakefield) Mystery Plays and later, in the reign of Henry VIII, appeared *The Merie Tales of the Mad Men of Gotham*, attributed (wrongly) to Andrew Boorde (*ca.* 1490–1549).

'Numskull' tales are told in other lands, and the stories of Gotham attached to other English villages. At Houghton Regis in Bedfordshire they used to hold a black cat out of the window to see if it was snowing, and the cuckoo was penned in **Borrowdale** (p.370) as well as at Zennor in Cornwall and Madeley, Shropshire. The story 'The Moonrakers' has been attached to Wiltshiremen at least since the days of Francis Grose, who entered it thus in his *Provincial Glossary* (1787):

Wiltshire moon-rakers Some Wiltshire rusticks, as the story goes, seeing the figure of the moon in a pond, attempted to take it out.

Today it is associated particularly with Bishops Cannings.

The underlying reason for all these stories seems to have been inter-village rivalry – they are on a par with traditional jibing rhymes such as:

> Cheshire bred,
> Strong i' the arm and weak i' the head

or:

Halton, Rudby, Entrepen,
Far more rogues than honest men!

Sometimes Gothamite stories are told 'straight' – the numskulls really *are* numskulls – but very often, as in the tale of King John, there is a twist showing that they were not after all so stupid. Such turns to traditional follies were very likely added by 'numskull' villages themselves, defending their reputations.

At Gotham proper, the adventure of 'The Pent Cuckoo' was locally remembered. In Chambers's *Book of Days* (1864) we read that on an eminence about a mile south of the village there still stood a bush known as the 'Cuckoo Bush', planted on the site of the one in the story. This is still commemorated in the name of Cuckoo Bush Farm (SK 533288).

GRIMSBY, HUMBERSIDE (formerly LINCOLNSHIRE)

Sheet 113
TA 2709

The ancient town seal of Grimsby, thought to be at least as old as the reign of Edward I, has three figures on it: a man with a drawn sword and shield, and, on either side of him, two smaller representations of a man and a woman, over each of their heads a crown. The figures are labelled 'Gryem', 'Habloc' and 'Goldebvrgh', and the seal commemorates the traditional founding of Grimsby by a Danish fisherman named Grim.

Grim had been ordered by the usurper Godard to drown the true heir to the Danish throne, a boy named Havelok, but instead escaped with him to England. When he was of an age to work, Havelok found employment as a scullion to the Earl of Lincoln. There he soon became famous for his prowess at sports, and when this came to the ears of Earl Godrich of Cornwall, the regent of England, he decided to marry off his ward, Goldborough, heiress to the kingdom, to the base-born scullion so that his own son could be king.

Goldborough and Havelok were forced into marriage upon pain of death, and Goldborough resented this degradation bitterly until one night she saw a light shining from her husband's mouth as he lay asleep. She saw, too, a cross on his shoulder, which the voice of an angel explained was the mark of a king, prophesying that

*Grim, Havelok and Goldborough on the old seal of Grimsby,
now in the South Humberside Record Office, Grimsby*

Havelok would rule both England and Denmark. Grim's fishermen
sons were prevailed upon to take Havelok and Goldborough to
Denmark, where they were befriended by Earl Ubbe, who, when
he discovered that Havelok was the true heir to the throne, led the
overthrow of Godard and invaded England. There they defeated
Godrich and burnt him to death, and Havelok, as Goldborough's
husband, became king. They lived happily thereafter, he ruling the
two kingdoms for sixty years, she bearing him fifteen children.

This story is told in *The Lay of Havelok*, a poem which survives
in a copy of the fourteenth century but was probably composed
before 1300. The story itself was known earlier than this, for it is
also told in two Anglo-French versions of the twelfth century,
Gaimar's *L'Estorie des Engles* and *Le Lai d'Havelok*. Scholars have
suggested that 'Havelok' is the Celtic name Abloc, sometimes used
as a substitute for ON *Ólafr* and OE *Anlaf*. In the French versions
of the story, the hero is called *Cuaran*, a Celtic word meaning
'sock' or 'sandal of untanned leather'. Hence Havelok has been

identified with the famous Ólafr 'Cuaran' – Ólafr Sihtricsson – one of the Northern alliance defeated by King Athelstan at the Battle of Brunanburh (937 A.D.). But the adventures of Havelok and Ólafr 'Cuaran' bear no resemblance – the connection is only in name.

The north and east of England from the Tees to Watling Street was settled by descendants of the Viking armies of the ninth century. Within this 'Danelaw', as it was called, in Yorkshire and around the 'Five Boroughs' – Derby, Nottingham, Leicester, Lincoln and Stamford – Scandinavian law and customs prevailed. Here one would expect the names if not the stories of Scandinavian heroes to survive, and this is what happened at Scarborough, supposed to have been founded by Ðorgils Skarði – Ðorgils 'Hare-lip' of the Icelandic *Kormáks saga*, who appears in the page of Robert Mannyng of Brunne as a British giant called Scardyng.

But if Havelok's name commemorates a real man, his adventures are purely imaginary, those of a stock hero of romance. The light that issues from his mouth belongs to the same tradition as the flames that played round the head of the sleeping infant Servius Tullius in classical legend. The birth-mark that reveals him as a king is also a familiar motif.

Legendary or not, local traditions of Havelok were strong. Robert Mannyng, who in 1338 completed a translation of the *Chronicle* of Peter Langtoft, adds to it the note:

> Men sais in Lyncoln castelle ligges ʒit a stone,
> Þat Havelok kast wele forbi euerilkone.
> & ʒit þe chapelle standes þer he weddid his wife,
> Goldburgh þe kynges douhter . . .

This stone was evidently the one which according to *Le Lai d'Havelok* was cast down by Havelok from the tower of the monastery at Lincoln on townsmen who were attacking him. A similar tradition existed at Grimsby in the time of Gervase Holles, who in the 1630s notes 'that Havelocke did sometymes reside in Grimsby, may be gathered from a great blew Boundry-stone, lying at yᵉ East ende of Briggowgate, which retaines yᵉ name of *Havelocke's-Stone* to this day.'

The matrix of the seal of Grimsby (see illustration) is preserved at the

South Humberside Record Office, Town Hall, Grimsby, where it may be seen upon request. A mosaic depicting the seal also decorates the wall of Grimsby Central Library. The Havelock Stone, which used to stand in Wellowgate, on the boundary between the parish of Grimsby and the hamlet of Wellow, is now in the grounds of the Welholme Galleries, Welholme Road, Grimsby, a museum administered by Grimsby Borough Council. For opening hours, see *M&G*.

HOB HURST'S HOUSE, BEELEY, DERBYSHIRE   Sheet 119
SK 2869

Hob Hurst's House is a Bronze Age round barrow (SK 287692) surrounded by an unusually high bank and ditch (1600–1000 B.C.). When the cairn was excavated in 1853, at the centre was found a stone-lined grave or cist in which a body had been cremated. But, like **Wayland's Smithy** (p.278), the barrow was remembered not as a tomb but as a dwelling – the house of the bogey or boggart Hob Hurst, also known as Hob Thurst and Hob Thrush (see **Obtrusch Tumulus**, p.416).

From Dore (SK 3081), now part of Sheffield, but originally on the boundary between Derbyshire and Yorkshire (it is OE *dōr*, 'door' or 'pass', i.e. between Mercia and Northumbria) comes a tale of Hob Thrush recorded in 1895 by S. O. Addy in his *Household Tales*:

> Once upon a time there was a poor shoemaker who could not earn enough to keep himself and his family. This grieved him very much, but one morning when he came downstairs he found a piece of leather which he had cut out already made into a pair of shoes, which were beautifully finished. He sold these shoes the same day, and with the money he bought as much leather as would make two pairs of shoes. The next morning he found that this leather too had been made into shoes, but he did not know who had done it. In this way his stock of shoes kept always getting bigger. He very much wished to know who had made the shoes, so he told his wife he would stay up all night and watch, and then he found Hob Thrust at work upon the leather. As soon as Hob Thrust had finished a pair of shoes the shoemaker took them and put them into a cupboard. Immediately after that Hob Thrust finished another pair, which the shoemaker also took up and

put away. Then he made first one pair of shoes and then another so fast that the little shop was soon filled with them, and as there was no more room in the house the shoemaker threw the shoes out of the window as fast as Hob Thrust could make them.

As Addy points out, the first part of the tale is identical with 'The Elves', one of Grimm's *Kinder- und Hausmärchen* (Household Tales). But the Derbyshire version may have been in circulation before the Brothers Grimm were translated into English, 1823–6, because, Addy says, it had given rise to a traditional retort in the Sheffield area, if a man boasted of the number of knives he could make in a day: 'Ah, tha can mak 'em faster than Hob Thrust can throw shoes out o' t' window.'

Use OS 1:25 000 Outdoor Leisure Map 24, The White Peak (East Sheet). Hob Hurst's House stands on the south-west edge of Brampton East Moor, south of a track from Chatsworth to Upper Loads. AM, but on land owned and occupied by The Trustees of the Chatsworth Settlement. No public right of way; permission to visit, together with a recommended route, should be sought from The Trustees of the Chatsworth Settlement, Estate Office, Derbyshire Estates, Edensor, Bakewell, Derbyshire DE4 1PJ. Note that there is no 'house' to be seen as at **Kit's Coty House** (p.108), but little more than the remains of the barrow and its bank.

LEICESTER, LEICESTERSHIRE   Sheet 140
                                               SK 5804

After this unhappy Fate of *Bladud, Leir* his Son was advanced to the Throne, and nobly governed his Country sixty Years. He built upon the River *Sore* a City called in the *British* tongue *Kaerleir*, in the *Saxon Leircestre*. He was without Male Issue, but had three Daughters whose Names were *Gonorilla, Regan,* and *Cordeilla*, of whom he was doatingly fond, but especially of his youngest *Cordeilla*.

So begins Geoffrey of Monmouth's story of Leir, the legendary founder of Leicester, which was to lead in time to Shakespeare's masterpiece *King Lear*. As Geoffrey tells it, when he was very old, Leir wished to discover which of his daughters loved him best in order to give her the largest share of his kingdom. Gonerilla and Regan both swear that they love him more than their lives, Cordeilla simply that she loves him more than anyone else in the world. When he presses for more than this, she gives the riddling answer: 'You are worth just as much as you possess, and that is the measure of my love for you.' She means that she loves him according to his deserts – and these are great – but he believes that she values him only for his possessions and grows angry. He marries the two elder girls to the Dukes of Cornwall and Albany, agreeing that after his death they shall share the kingdom, but Cordeilla, when the King of the Franks, having heard of her beauty, asks for her in marriage, he despatches her to France without a dowry.

In a few years, just as in *King Lear*, Gonerilla and Regan contrive to strip the old king of all his followers, and he begins to wonder if he would not be better off with his youngest daughter. Half suspecting that she will do nothing for him, because of his treatment of her, he makes his way to France, where he is given a loving welcome. Cordeilla's husband, the King of the Franks, supplies him with an army, with which he reconquers Britain and resumes his reign. But three years after this he dies, likewise the King of the Franks, and Cordeilla inherits:

> . . . so that *Cordeilla* now obtaining the Government of the Kingdom, buried her Father in a certain Vault, which she ordered to be made for him under the River *Sore* in *Leicester*. The Subterraneous Place where he was buried, had been built to the Honour of the God *Janus*. And here all the Workmen of the City, upon the anniversary Solemnity of that Festival, used to begin their yearly Labours.

Cordeilla ruled the kingdom for five years, but then her sisters' sons rebelled against her and cast her into prison, where she took her own life.

Geoffrey's *History* was widely known both in England and on the Continent, and this story was retold in early chronicles again and again. Nearer Shakespeare's time, it appears among other places in the chronicles of Fabian and Holinshed, in Spenser's *Faerie Queene* and in William Warner's *Albion's England*. Shakespeare himself drew chiefly on *The True Chronicle Historie of*

King Leir and his Three Daughters . . ., a play published in 1605, 'As it hath bene divers and sundry times lately acted', probably in 1594 and possibly earlier. This interest in the story in Tudor times was part of the fashion for the legendary history of Britain that produced *Locrine* and *Gorbuduc, Cymbeline* and the rest, and which sprang from the 'Tudor myth', promulgated by this dynasty ever since Henry VII appointed a commission to trace the Tudors' British ancestry, to bolster his claim to the throne.

So much for where Geoffrey's story went to; but where did it come from? There is no trace of it before he tells it, *ca.* 1136. But although the tale does not appear in Welsh literature as one might expect, the name 'Leir' itself seems to be that of the Celtic Llyr, father of Branwen and Bendigeidfran (see **Bedd Branwen**, p.327 and **Tower of London**, p.158). His connection with Leicester is doubtful and may be a fancy of Geoffrey's own, based on false etymology – the name 'Leicester' is in fact thought to contain an old river-name, Latin *Legra*, in Old English perhaps *Ligor* or *Legor*. The pivot of the tale was very likely the tradition Geoffrey knew about the underground chamber dedicated to Janus – probably part of Leicester's Roman remains. Supposed entrances to this chamber were still being pointed out when the Rev. John Nichols was writing his *History of Leicestershire* (1795–1815), and a cave in New Park was said to be the place where King Lear hid from his enemies.

If the reasons why the story was attached to Leicester are obscure, the plot itself clearly belongs to a class of tale well-known in European and Indian tradition concerning filial ingratitude. The Lear-story exists in at least twenty-six variants, in twenty-five of which the 'love-test' is that of 'The Goose-Girl at the Well', one of Grimm's *Kinder- und Hausmärchen* or 'Household Tales'. In this the princess replies to her father's question that she loves him like salt, which he takes to mean that she holds him cheap, whereas what she is saying is that he is vital to her very existence. Geoffrey or his predecessor may have known the story in this form but altered it to make more of the human relationship, or simply to conceal the fact that what was being told was not history but folktale.

A curious footnote to the story of Leir – and one that may have been known to Shakespeare – was 'the Annesley case', involving a wealthy Kentish courtier and 'gentleman pensioner' of Elizabeth I, Brian Annesley, and his three daughters. The two eldest of these three, Grace and Christian, had titled husbands; the youngest, Cordell, was unmarried and lived at home. Christian plays no part in events, but in October 1603 Grace tried to get her father judged a lunatic, on the grounds that he was 'altogether unfit to govern himself or his estate'. Cordell, who had taken control of his affairs, prevented Grace's husband from entering the house to make an inventory of the old man's chattels, and wrote protesting to Robert Cecil, who had intervened in the case, that for his services to the Crown her father 'deserved a better agnomination, than at his last gasp to be recorded and registered a Lunatic . . .' She appears to have won the day, for when Brian Annesley died in July 1604 and left most of the property to Cordell, though Grace and her husband disputed the will, it was on 3 December upheld by the Prerogative Court. Legend has now and then affected the *reporting* of real events (see **Aston Hall**, p.261 and **Littlecote House**, p.67), but this seems to be a case where life paralleled legend, perhaps coincidentally – the story of Leir is after all about basic human motives – but perhaps as an acting out of the parts predicated for the characters by Cordell's name.

LINCOLN, LINCOLNSHIRE

Sheet 121
SK 9771

> They take the Christians to be the cause of every disaster of the State, of every misfortune of the people. If the Tiber reaches the wall, if the Nile does not reach the fields, if the sky does not move or if the earth does, if there is a famine or if there is a plague, the cry is at once, 'The Christians to the lions!'

This is the early Christian Father Tertullian writing of the Romans, who exploited as their scapegoats the Christians and the hatred they inspired as a minority deviant from the social norm. When the Christians became the majority, their scapegoats were the Jews, a choice apparently sanctioned by their religion – had not the Jews rejected Christ? The Jews, too, were blamed for natural disasters – one of which was the Black Death. Believed to smear the doorposts

and lintels of houses with poisonous matter, the Jews were massacred by mobs or judicially burnt at the stake for 'plague-
spreading' in Switzerland, Burgundy and Provence. Among other
charges against them – and one the Romans in their day had
levelled against the Christians – was ritual murder.

It is perhaps no coincidence that in England this first rears its
head in the Anglo-Saxon Chronicle for the year 1137. The Chronicle has been summing up the calamities of Stephen's reign –
nineteen years when 'they said openly that Christ and his saints
were asleep'. The chronicler paints a picture of robber-barons in
their castles, their torture chambers full, their outlying villages
forced to pay for protection or burn, the land laid waste by their
ceaseless strife. 'Then corn was dear, and meat and butter and
cheese . . . Wretched people died of starvation . . . There had never
been till then greater misery in the country . . .'

And right here on cue enters the scapegoat:

> In his [King Stephen's] time, the Jews of Norwich bought a
> Christian child before Easter and tortured him with all the
> torture that our Lord was tortured with; and on Good Friday
> hanged him on a cross . . . and then buried him. They expected
> it would be concealed, but our Lord made it plain that he was
> a holy martyr, and the monks took him and buried him with
> ceremony in the monastery . . . and he is called St William.

The legend of St William seems to have had its origin in the
discovery in 1144, in a wood at Thorpe (TG 2609), outside
Norwich, of the mutilated body of a boy. Not until five years after
the event was it first alleged that he was the victim of ritual murder
by the Jews. Whoever started the rumour, it was fostered by
William Thurbe, bishop of Norwich 1146–72, and Thomas of
Monmouth, a Benedictine monk of the Priory at Norwich, who in
1172–3 wrote a *Life* of the 'saint' with circumstantial details of his
'martyrdom'.

As a stunt to pull pilgrims it was successful, which may well be
why the Jews of Gloucester were accused of murdering a child in
1160, those of Bury St Edmunds in 1181, the Jews of Norwich
again in 1235 and 1240. But the most famous child-murder of them
all was undoubtedly that of 'Little St Hugh' of Lincoln, recorded

under the year 1255 in the Annals of Waverley and by Matthew Paris, both of them contemporary with the event.

Matthew tells us that the Jews of Lincoln stole a boy of eight or nine years old, whose name was Hugh, whom on 27 August they scourged and crucified. When the child's mother went looking for him and was told he had last been seen playing with some Jewish children, she entered a certain Jew's house and discovered the body in a *puteus*, variously translated as a well or cesspit. She roused the citizens, who forced an entry and carried the body away, and the King's Justiciary, John de Lexington, who happened to be in Lincoln at the time, had the Jew, one Copin, seized and examined. Copin confessed to the deed and said it was his people's custom thus to sacrifice a child each year. The boy was buried in Lincoln cathedral, venerated as a saint and there performed miracles (though his cult was not recognized).

This is not entirely fantasy: the body of a boy who had been missing for three weeks evidently *was* found in a cesspool where he may have fallen while playing, and the 'murder' blamed on the Jews. The *Liber de Antiquis Legibus* or 'Book of Ancient Laws', a chronicle of London originally compiled in about 1274, says that on St Cecilia's Day (22 November) ninety-two Jews were brought from Lincoln to Westminster, accused of murdering a male Christian child. They were all committed to the Tower of London, and eighteen, who had attempted to insist on the right of a foreigner to be tried by a mixed jury, were summarily 'the same day drawn, and, after the hour of dinner . . . hanged'. There is little question but that here we are seeing the cruel distortion by myth of reality (cf. **Littlecote House**, p.67).

Probably the oldest report of ritual murder by the Jews is from the pre-Christian writer Democritus who alleged that every seven years the Jews captured a stranger and cut him to pieces in the temple. The idea recurred in the twelfth century, in the case of William of Norwich, when Theobald of Canterbury, a Jewish convert, explained that the Jews were required to sacrifice a Christian child annually at Easter. At about the same time there appears the popular idea that the murders were for the purpose of collecting blood, and that Jewish ritual required Christian blood at Passover – an idea that ignored Jewish religious taboos and foisted on them notions derived from witchcraft, for human blood was well known to be employed in witches' ritual and sorcery (as late as the eighteenth century, on 13 July 1784, two women in Hamburg were broken on the wheel for having murdered a *Jew* in order to get his blood for this purpose).

'A Jew is as full of idolatry and sorcery as nine cows have hair on their backs,' said Martin Luther, and in Matthew's account of the death of Hugh we hear that they disembowelled the corpse 'for what purpose is unknown; but it was said it was to practice sorcery'. Mockery of Christian rites, blood-collecting for witchcraft – whatever the purpose, the charge of child-murder was one the Jew could fear whenever a child's body was found. Although several popes – Innocent IV, Gregory X, Nicholas V, among others – forbade their clergy to countenance the myth, it was almost always from the clergy that such charges came, because they stood directly to profit.

A parallel tale to the legend of Little St Hugh, which possibly helped the distortion of fact in the direction of myth, since a version of it, the 'Miracle of the Virgin', had already been current for thirty or forty years, is used by Chaucer as his 'Prioress's Tale'. One of many, this story tells of a choir-boy or school-boy murdered by the Jews, who is sought for and found by his mother, a poor widow (another turn of the screw) and borne to the nearest abbey. There on his bier the dead child begins to sing the hymn to the Virgin 'O alma redemptoris mater'. '"My throte is kut unto my nekke boon," seyde this child. "I sholde have dyed, ye, longe tyme agon."' But he must sing in honour of the Virgin until someone removes a grain she has laid on his tongue. When this is done, he dies.

This, like Matthew's legend, contains precisely the right mix of sadism and sentiment to appeal to the medieval mind. Probably the search for the dead child by its mother, as much as the anti-Semitism, kept the story of Little St Hugh alive: at any rate it became first an Anglo-French ballad, and later an English ballad, collected from oral tradition in the eighteenth century, called 'Sir Hugh, or, The Jew's Daughter':

> Four and twenty bonny boys
>   Were playing at the ba,
> And by it came him sweet Sir Hugh,
>   And he playd oer them a'.

He kicked the ba with his right foot,
  And catchd it wi his knee,
And throuch-and-thro the Jew's window
  He gard the bonny ba flee . . .

'Throw down the ba, ye Jew's daughter,
  Throw down the ba to me!'
'Never a bit,' says the Jew's daughter,
  'Till up to me come ye.'

And so the scene is set for murder.

Charges of child-murder were still being made against the Jews in the last century – as at Neuhoven, near Düsseldorf, in 1834, when the murder of a child of six provoked the destruction of two Jewish houses and a synagogue. Old legends die hard; and as we in our generation have seen, old prejudices die even harder.

The imaginative visitor to Lincoln may set the scene of the crime at any one of three early medieval houses: the Jew's House and Jews' Court in The Strait, and Aaron the Jew's House up Steep Hill. They are thought to be the oldest dwelling houses still in use (though not as habitations) in Britain. Little St Hugh is not to be confused with Hugh of Lincoln, canonized in 1220, whom Ruskin called 'the most beautiful sacerdotal figure known to me in history'. This is the man who, visiting Fécamp, after the abbot refused to part with the precious relic of the Magdalene's arm-bone, tried to bite a lump off it with his teeth, while the agitated monks cried, 'O, O, proh nefas' – 'For shame, for shame!' Anyone who can still agree with Ruskin after reading this (and see also **Woodstock**, p.283) may like to know that, though St Hugh's shrine in the Angel Choir was dismantled at the Reformation, his funeral is recorded in the rose window in the south transept known as the Bishop's Eye. For a story about the Bishop's Eye and its partner, the Dean's Eye, in the north transept, see **Roslin Chapel** (p.482).

MOUNTSORREL, LEICESTERSHIRE

Sheet 129
SK 5815

About Mountsorrel, or Mountstrill . . . the country-people have a story of a giant or devil, named Bell, who once, in a merry vein, took three prodigious leaps, which they thus describe. At a place, thence after called Mountsorril [sic.], he mounted his sorrel horse, and leaped a mile, to a place, from it since name Oneleap, now corrupted to Wanlip; thence, he leaped another mile, to a village called Burst-all, from the bursting both of himself, his girts, and his horse; the third leap was also a mile, but the violence of the exertion and shock killed him, and he was there buried, and the place has ever since been denominated Bell's-grave, or Bell-grave.

This story is given by Francis Grose in his *Provincial Glossary* (1787) as background to a proverb apparently current in his time, 'He leaps like the belle giant, or devil of Mountsorril'. The events of the legend were also commemorated in a rhyme which appeared in *Notes & Queries* (1852):

> Mountsorrel he mounted at,
> Rodely he rode by,
> Onelep he leaped o'er,
> At Birstall he burst his gall,
> At Belgrave he was buried at.

The legend is onomastic, that is, it sets out to explain certain names – Mountsorrel, Wanlip (SK 6010), Birstall (SK 5909) and Belgrave (SK 5907) – to which the rhyme adds Rothley (SK 5812). It is interesting, if for nothing else, then for showing how far back goes the Leicestershire pronunciation of 'one' as 'wan'.

As to its age, Grose got the tale from the Stamford antiquary Francis Peck, also writing in the eighteenth century. It certainly cannot go further back than the time of Domesday Book, in which Belgrave appears as *Medegrave*. It is at bottom one of many British stories of prodigious leaps (cf. **Byard's Leap**, p.218, and **The Soldier's Leap**, p.521).

Birstall and Belgrave, Sheet 140.

NINE LADIES STONE CIRCLE, STANTON, DERBYSHIRE

Sheet 119
SK 2463

The Nine Ladies is the name of a small stone circle of nine blocks of gritstone, the tallest of which now stands only 3ft 3in (1 m) above ground level. West-southwest of the circle is a solitary standing-stone known as the King Stone, now leaning, but probably originally erect. The Nine Ladies are nowadays said to be women petrified for dancing on the Sabbath (as at Stanton Drew, see under **Haltadans**, p.505), the King Stone apparently playing the role of the fiddler or piper.

Although the name 'the Nine Ladies' has been in use at least since 1848, the legend may be new – it is not mentioned, for instance, in J. Percy Heathcote's *Birchover, Its Prehistoric and Druidical Remains* (rev. edn, 1934), though he generally notes such things. What he does say is that the Nine Stones on Harthill Moor (SK 225626), not far from Robin Hood's Stride, were sometimes by writers called 'the Grey Ladies' because of a tradition that they danced at midnight. But he found not much local evidence for such a belief – 'There is little of this tradition now and it is more than probable that early guide book writers invented it.'

Very likely the Nine Ladies and the Grey Ladies both started with a name – a simple personification – and only later acquired a

The Nine Stones of Harthill Moor, also known as the Grey Ladies
and believed to dance at midnight

tale. Although there (probably) *are* nine stones in the Nine Ladies circle, the word 'nine' in names such as this often bears no relation to the actual number of stones but is a convention. There are Nine Stones at Altarnun, Cornwall, Belstone, Devon, Durris, Kincardineshire (now Grampians), Whittingehame, Lothian, and Winterborne Abbas, Dorset. There are also, in Cornwall, several groups of Nine Maidens – at Boskednan in the parish of Madron, at St Buryan, and at Stithians (all stone circles), and St Columb Major (a stone row).

Because some stone circles with 'nine' in their name are traditionally said to be dancers petrified for breaking the Sabbath, and because the Nine Stones on Belstone Common were in the mid nineteenth century said to dance every day at midday, it has been surmised that the name contained not 'nine' but 'none', the ninth hour of the day in ecclesiastical reckoning, when the service called 'Nones' was performed. When Nones was shifted from three in the afternoon to midday, the word 'none' came to mean midday – our noon.

This explanation does not cover the fact that antiquities other than standing-stones have names including 'Nine' – for example, Nine Barrows, Priddy, Somerset, and Ninebarrow Down, near Corfe. Elsewhere we find 'Seven' in similar situations, as at the Seven Barrows on Lambourn Down, in Berkshire, where actually there are more than forty. Probably what we have in all these cases is simply number superstition. 'I hope good luck lies in odd numbers!' said Falstaff, and this belief pervades Western tradition, from the Seven Wonders of the World and the occult powers of the seventh son of a seventh son, to the fiddlers three Old King Cole called for and the nine lives of the cat. Note that if one walks *three* times round the *Nine* Stanes or Deil's Stanes, Urquhart, Grampian, at midnight, the Devil will appear.

AM (any reasonable time). A description is included in the DoE guide *Arbor Low* by D. Thompson (HMSO, 1963). Both the Nine Ladies and the Nine Stones are in the Peak District National Park. Use OS 1:25 000 Outdoor Leisure Map 24, The White Peak (East Sheet). Signposted from Birchover is a path to the Nine Ladies which leads directly to the site from a disused quarry on the Birchover–Stanton Lees road. The path will take you past a group of cairns, in the centre of the largest of which you will see a stone cist left exposed by the excavator, which contained the cremated bones of a boy. Such a cist may lie behind the description of Branwen's tomb at **Bedd Branwen** (p.327). The Nine Stones (marked simply 'Stone Circle' on the map) are reached by a path off the Alport–Elton road, from which they can be seen opposite a farm.

NORTON, DERBYSHIRE
Sheet 110
(now in SHEFFIELD, SOUTH YORKSHIRE)
SK 3582

Like neighbouring Dore, Norton has been swallowed up by Sheffield and is now officially in South Yorkshire. I am leaving it where it historically belongs, because here and at Dore the collector S. O. Addy collected some of the finest Derbyshire traditions for his *Household Tales*.

Among these, published in 1895, was a 'droll' told at and set in Norton – 'Nicorbore and his Money':

> There was once a silly man called Nicorbore, who lived as a servant in a gentleman's family. One day a sixpence was given to him. He took the coin and buried it in the garden under a gooseberry-bush, 'for,' said he to himself, 'the sixpence will grow bigger.' Another servant who had watched Nicorbore burying the sixpence put a shilling in its place. The next day when Nicorbore went to look at his sixpence he found it had grown into a shilling. 'I think thou hast grown a bit,' he said, 'but I think thou'lt grow a bit bigger yet.' When he went to look under the gooseberry-bush again he found a half-crown instead of a shilling. 'I think thou'lt grow bigger yet,' he said, and buried the half-crown again. The next time he found that the half-crown had grown into a five-shilling piece. So he buried the five-shilling piece under the gooseberry-bush again; but the next time he went to look it had grown into a four-shilling piece. Nicorbore could not understand this, but he buried the coin as before, and soon afterwards he found it had grown into a shilling, then into a sixpence, and lastly into a threepenny piece. Then he said to the threepenny piece 'I'll put thee in my pocket, or thou'lt grow away altogether.'

Among other tales told of Nicorbore was that he once drowned a litter of pigs because they had prick ears, thinking that they were hounds, whose ears should droop. Although some storytellers spoke of him as an actual person who had been a servant in Norton at 'The Oaks' (Oakes Park, SK 3682), Addy thought his name came from OE *nicor*, meaning a water-monster (for whom see **Lyminster**, p.114). If so, his character has changed, for the stories told of him are typical 'numskull' tales like those told of the Wise Men of **Gotham** (p.230).

OUNDLE, NORTHAMPTONSHIRE   Sheet 141
                                                   TL 0388

> When I was a School-Boy at *Oundle*, in *Northamptonshire*; about the *Scots* coming into *England*, I heard a Well, in one *Dobs*'s Yard, drum like any Drum beating a March. I heard it at a distance: Then I went and put my Head into the Mouth of the Well, and heard it distinctly, and no Body in the Well. It lasted several Days and Nights, so as all the Country-People came to hear it. And so it drumm'd on several Changes of Times.
>
> When King *Charles* the Second died, I went to the *Oundle* Carrier, at the *Ram*-Inn in *Smithfield*; who told me their Well had drumm'd and many People came to hear it. And I heard, it drumm'd once since.

So Richard Baxter in his *Certainty of the Worlds of Spirits* (1691) describes the Oundle Drumming Well, once famous, now vanished.

A few years later, the Rev. John Morton wrote in his *Natural History of Northamptonshire* (1712) that the beats were regularly spaced and that 'The noise or sound at first is less loud, becomes louder by degrees, and then abates'. The cause was judged by a contributor to the *Northampton Mercury* on 11 June 1744 to be 'Explosions of the Air entering the Water at the Bottom of the Well', weak or non-existent when the well was low, but loud enough to be heard in a wet season.

According to the same source, drummings earlier in the century had been held to portend, on 18 January 1700/1, the death of James II the following September, and on 4 June 1701, 7 December 1702 and 4 June 1704, events of the War of the Spanish Succession, including the Battle of Höchstädt, when it 'beat a glorious Point of

War for ten days together'. The well was heard again, 'having been silent for many years', on 20 April 1752, 22 May 1758 and 7 June 1765, the last recorded drumming.

Other springs audibly pulsate, of course. It was partly the loudness of the Oundle well, but more particularly the *sporadic* nature of its outbursts that marked it as a portent – many intermittent springs were held to be prophetic. Such for example was the Gypsey Race in Cleveland in the twelfth century (see under **Willy Howe**, p.430), and in Warkworth's *Chronicle* we hear of springs that in the thirteenth year of Edward IV suddenly began to run and were taken as omens. Presaging a 'gret hote somere', when 'unyversalle feveres' were rife and 'in feld in harvist tyme men fylle downe sodanly', their message was reinforced by 'a voyce cryenge in the heyre, betwyx Laicetere and Bambury, uppon Dunmothe, and in dyverse othere places, herde a long tyme cryinge, Bowes! Bowes! which was herde of xl. menne; and some menne saw that he that cryed so was a hedles manne . . .'

The Drumming Well is still commemorated by the name of Drumming Well Lane, connecting Milton Road and West Street. 'Dunmothe', i.e. Dunsmore, Sheet 140.

PEAK CAVERN, DERBYSHIRE
Sheet 110
SK 1482

> There are in *High Peake* wonders three,
> A deepe hole, Cave and Den . . .

as it says in a verse given by Camden in his *Britannia* (trans. Holland, 1610). The 'Cave' was Peak Cavern, of which he tells us:

> Neere unto this *Burgh* there standeth upon the top of an hill an old Castle sometimes belonging to the *Peverels*, called *The Castle in the Peake* . . . Under which, there is a caue or hole within the ground, called, saving your reverence, *The Devils Arse*, that gapeth with a wide mouth and hath in it many turnings and retyring roomes: wherein, for sooth, *Gervase of Tilbury*, whether for want of knowing the truth, or upon a delight hee had in fabling, hath written, that a Shepheard saw a verie wide and large Country with riverets and brookes

running here and there through it, and huge pooles of dead and standing waters. Notwithstanding, by reason of these and such like fables, this *Hole* is reckoned for one of the wonders of England . . .

The entrance to the Otherworld Kingdom: Peak Cavern,
Derbyshire, in a nineteenth-century engraving

Gervase's story was a tale he had got from Robert, Prior of Kenilworth (*ca.* 1160–80), who was born in this neighbourhood. It was to the effect that, one winter day, a swineherd in the employ of William Peveril, who then owned the castle (SK 1582), missed a sow about to farrow, and after searching to no avail concluded that she must have wandered into the cave. As the remarkable wind that habitually eddied round it was not then blowing, he decided to risk going into this place of evil reputation rather than risk his master's ire (as well he might – William was in 1155 exiled for having poisoned Ranulf, Earl of Chester). After the swineherd had gone a long way in, he began to see light and emerged into a wide and cultivated plain, where reapers were gathering in the harvest. He caught sight of his sow, safely delivered of her litter, under an overhanging thorn, and after being dismissed kindly by the lord of that country returned with her the same way he had come. On emerging into Derbyshire, he found it was still winter there.

Similar tales were current elsewhere at this time, both in England and Wales – the story recalls the account of the Green Children of **Woolpit** (p.210) and the tale of Elidyr from the **Vale of Neath** (p.363). All three legends probably stem from Celtic notions of the Otherworld kingdom.

Peak District National Park. Use OS 1:25 000 Outdoor Leisure Map 24, The White Peak (East Sheet). Peveril Castle: AM.

SHERWOOD FOREST, NOTTINGHAMSHIRE

Sheet 120
SK 5850–
6477

> Lythe and listin, gentilmen,
> That be of frebore blode;
> I shall you tel of a gode yeman,
> His name was Robyn Hode.

Tales of Robin Hood have been in circulation at least since the high Middle Ages, probably in the form of ballads – '. . . I can [know] rymes of Robyn Hood and Randolf, erle of Chestre', says Sloth in *Piers Plowman* in about 1380.

The common tradition is that he was captain of a band of

outlaws who had their abode in the Forest of Sherwood and lived by hunting the deer and robbing rich travellers, often to help the poor. Robin's lieutenant was a hulking fellow known as Little John, and among his company were Friar Tuck, William Scadlock (Will Scarlet), and Much the Miller's Son. With them in the greenwood lived Robin's wife or mistress Maid Marian (for whose reputed tomb see **Little Dunmow**, p.142).

Some said that Robin was born at Locksley in Nottinghamshire, and having wasted his inheritance was forced to lead the life of an outlaw. When in his old age he felt infirmity coming upon him, he went to Kirklees Priory in Yorkshire, to seek the help of the prioress, his aunt. But she betrayed him by opening a vein and allowing him to bleed to death. According to a tradition that first appears in the eighteenth century, when Robin realized what she had done, he summoned up his last strength and blew a great blast on his horn which brought Little John from the forest. Robin begged him to give him his bow, and fired an arrow through the window, saying that where it struck the ground, there should he be buried. A stone in **Kirklees Park** (p.413) is said to mark the spot.

A series of ballads about Robin Hood, apparently from the later fourteenth century, was printed as *A Lytell Geste of Robyn Hood* by Wynkyn de Worde in about 1495. In the *Lytell Geste* he is associated, not with Richard I as commonly, certainly since Sir Walter Scott's *Ivanhoe*, but with Edward II, and it is said that in the household expenses of this king a certain 'Robyn Hode' is mentioned, as a 'vadlet' or porter of the chamber, between April and November 1324.

Was there a real Robin Hood? Since the days of Grimm it has often been said that he is a mythological personage, 'Robin of the Wood', connected with the Green Man image found in churches. His presence in the May Day revels up and down the country has been cited in support of this view, but Robin figured generally in plays and pageants – in the fifteenth century Sir John Paston kept a servant whose business it was 'to pleye Seint Jorge and Robin Hod and the Shryf of Notyngham' (though how he could play *both* the last must remain a mystery).

Robin seems to have been adopted into the May Games only in the fifteenth century, when he was identified as one of the pastoral pair Robin and Marion, celebrated in French songs and poems of the thirteenth century, and in a play by Adam de la Halle (*ca.* 1280), which in the fourteenth century was annually performed at Angers at Whitsuntide. Maid Marian does not appear in the early Robin Hood tales, and it looks as if she came from France, first in the Whitsuntide play, passing thence into the May Games, and finally in the sixteenth century into the legend.

Probably a stock character of the May Games, whether the French Robin or another, has taken on the identity of an historical outlaw to become the romantic hero of the greenwood. Note that in *Piers Plowman* Robin's name is coupled with that of Ranulf, Earl of Chester, a real, not fictitious, person. Robin's great popularity, attested by place- and monument-names – Robin Hood's Bay in Yorkshire (from 1544), Robin Hood's Butts in no fewer than six counties: Cleveland, Dorset, Shropshire, Somerset, Staffordshire and North Yorkshire – need not reflect, as earlier scholars claimed, his origins as a solar hero or else as the Green Man and the subject of a fertility cult, but simply the fact that he was an anti-authoritarian figure.

In the earliest forms of his legend he is an outlaw, living in the woods of Barnsdale, in the West Riding of Yorkshire, a little south of Pontefract – only from the seventeenth century has the setting been mainly in Nottinghamshire. In the early tales, too, he is a yeoman, the best that ever bare bow, and not a nobleman as later. He is not a Saxon rebel fighting the Normans (as in *Ivanhoe*) but a common or garden bandit, robbing the rich, to be sure – but that is common sense, and of giving to the poor we hear nothing. Just as later ages loved tales of highwaymen – Dick Turpin – and outlaws – Billy the Kid – so medieval audiences loved Robin, a man who, reprehensible as his actions might be, could be seen to cock a snook at the propertied classes. Although from the first he is said to have been devoted to the Virgin, only later had he grafted on to him high social ideals, perhaps to make him more suitable for children.

But though a transformation had been worked on him, he was no cardboard figure, but a living hero still in people's imaginations into the nineteenth century; a correspondent of the *Gentleman's Magazine* in 1852 reported hearing some twenty years before from 'an honest and intelligent Yorkshireman' of Robin's life in the greenwood: 'The only thing Robin could not stand was a cold thaw.'

At Edwinstone, near Mansfield, is the Robin Hood Visitor Centre and Country Park (SK 6267). The Park, which consists of 450 acres (182 ha) of Sherwood Forest and includes the Major Oak, associated with Robin Hood, is open all the year from dawn to dusk. For the very variable opening times of the Visitor Centre, see *Your Guide to the English Shires* (updated annually) from the East Midlands Tourist Board, Exchequergate, Lincoln. Tel. Lincoln (0522) 31521. St Anne's Well, once to the north of Nottingham and in the bounds of Sherwood, was known as Robin Hood's Well already in the sixteenth century. Barnsdale Forest has now dwindled to a small wood north-west of Doncaster, but the Barnsdale Robin is still commemorated at Robin Hood's Well, so named by 1622, on the east side of the Great North Road (A1) about a mile south of its junction with the A639. This was one of the best-known halting-places on the road, up to the nineteenth century supporting two inns. Interestingly enough, it is still a lay-by frequented by truckers. The Well, with a cover designed by Vanbrugh for the Earl of Carlisle, is plainly visible from both carriageways. Little John's reputed grave can be seen in the churchyard at Hathersage, Derbyshire. No one interested in Robin Hood's legend should miss J. C. Holt's *Robin Hood* (London, 1982).

STANION, NORTHAMPTONSHIRE

Sheet 141
SP 9186

In St Peter's Church is preserved a six-foot bone known as the Dun Cow's Rib. The story told of it is that of the fairy cow who is milked into a sieve, but unlike her more resolute sisters of **Mitchell's Fold** (p.314) and **South Lopham** (p.192) this poor creature became exhausted and died.

The 'rib' was perhaps one of a pair of whalebones, once in fashion for arches, and has been covered all over with visitors' initials. But no matter – praise is due to Stanion for holding fast to the Dun Cow's memorial when elsewhere such relics have been tidied away.

Another Dun Cow's Rib used to be displayed over the door of an old farmhouse in the township of Whittingham in Kirkham parish, Lancashire. The farmhouse, known to Harland and Wilkinson (1873) as 'the Old Rib' but also as Dun Cow Rib Farm or Moor House, was photographed for the *Victoria County History of Lancashire* in 1912, but has since been demolished. See also **Guy's Cliffe**, p.269.

WEEDON BEC, NORTHAMPTONSHIRE

> . . . Weedon, where 'tis said,
> Saint Werburg, princely born, a most religious maid,
> From these peculiar fields, by prayer the wild geese drove.

Thus Drayton in his *Poly-olbion* (1612) refers to the legend of St Werburg (d. *ca.* 700), traditionally said to be the daughter of King Wulfhere of Mercia, who after his death became a nun at Ely under St Etheldreda. Later Werburg herself perhaps became Abbess, but her uncle King Ethelred summoned her home and gave her charge of several nunneries, founded or refounded by her, including Hanbury in Staffordshire, Threckingham in Lincolnshire, and Weedon.

Once when the wild geese were playing havoc with the cornfields there, Werburg sent her steward Alnoth to summon them to the grange and there bade them begone. But the geese continued to hover around Weedon until St Werburg by a miracle restored to life one of their number who had been killed and eaten. Thereupon they took flight and wild geese have never been seen in Weedon again.

This story was first told by Goscelin of Saint-Bertin, who from 1080 on moved from monastery to monastery round England, writing *Lives* of the local saints, his *Life* of Werburg being occasioned by her translation at Chester in 1095. He took the story of the geese from a *Life* he had written earlier, of the Flemish saint Amalburga. In Normandy the same tale was told of St Opportune, except that the birds were ducks, and the one restored to life had some leg-bones missing – why ducks waddle to this day.

WINTERTON, HUMBERSIDE
(formerly LINCOLNSHIRE)

They have a tradition at Winterton that there was formerly one Mr. Lacy, that lived there and was a very rich man, who, being grown very aged, gave all that he had away unto his three sons, upon condition that one should keep him one week, and another another. But it happened within a little while that they were all weary of him, after that they had got what they had, and regarded him no more than a dog. The old man percieveing how he was sleighted, went to an attorny to see if his skill could not afford him any help in his troubles. The attorny told him that no law in the land could help him nor yield him any comfort, but there was one thing onely which would certainly do, which, if he would perform, he would reveal to him. At which the poor old man was exceeding glad and desired him for God's sake to reveal the same, for he was almost pined and starved to dead, and he would most willingly do it rather than live as he did. 'Well,' says the lawyer, 'you have been a great friend of mine in my need, and I will now be one to you in your need. I will lend you a strong box with a strong lock on it, in which shall be contained 1000 *l*.; you shall on such a day pretend to have fetched it out of such a close, where it shall be supposed that you hid, and carry it into one of your son's houses, and make it your business every week, while you are sojourning with such or such a son, to be always counting of the money, and ratleing it about, and you shall see that, for the love of it, they'll soon love you again, and make very much of you, and maintain you joyfully, willingly, and plentifully, unto your dying day.['] The old man having thank'd the lawyer for this good advice and kind proffer, received within a few days the aforesayd box full of money, and having so managed it as above, his graceless sons soon fell in love with him again, and made mighty much of him, and percieving that their love to him continued stedfast and firm, he one day took it out of the house and carry'd it to the lawyer, thanking him exceedingly for the lent thereof. But when he got to his sons he made them believe that [he] had hidden it again, and that he would give it him of them whome he loved best when he dyd. This made them all so observant of him that he lived the rest of his days in great peace, plenty, and happiness amongst them, and dyed full of years. But a while before he dyd he u[p]braded them for their former ingratitude, told them the whole history of the box, and forgave them.

This fine tale, told in his *Diary* for 16 October 1696 by Abraham de la Pryme, was attached to an old Winterton family, numbers of whom appeared in the parish register. Perhaps there *was* such an incident – human nature does not change – but the story goes back at least to medieval times and is often told in connection with the tradition of the Holy Maul (see **Bargates**, p.292).

7
Heart of England

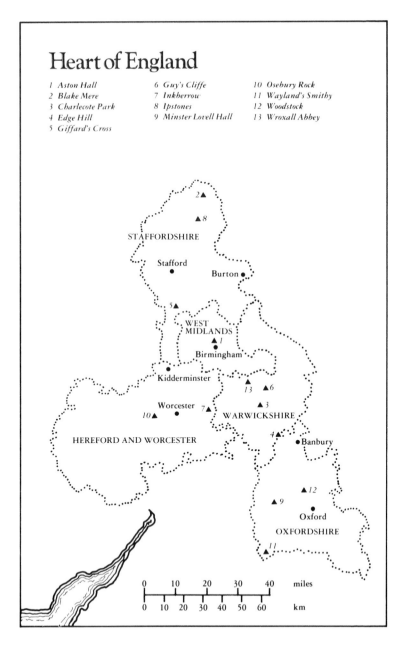

Heart of England

1 *Aston Hall*
2 *Blake Mere*
3 *Charlecote Park*
4 *Edge Hill*
5 *Giffard's Cross*

6 *Guy's Cliffe*
7 *Inkberrow*
8 *Ipstones*
9 *Minster Lovell Hall*

10 *Osebury Rock*
11 *Wayland's Smithy*
12 *Woodstock*
13 *Wroxall Abbey*

2 ▲

▲ 8

STAFFORDSHIRE

Stafford
●

Burton ●

5 ▲

WEST
MIDLANDS

▲ 1

Birmingham
●

Kidderminster
●

13 ▲   ▲ 6

Worcester   7 ▲
●   ▲ 3

10 ▲   WARWICKSHIRE

HEREFORD AND WORCESTER

4 ▲
● Banbury

▲ 12

▲ 9

Oxford
●

OXFORDSHIRE

11 ▲

0	10	20	30	40	miles

0	10	20	30	40	50	60	km

Aston Hall, now in the heart of Birmingham, is a fine Jacobean house built between 1618 and 1635 by Sir Thomas Holte. He had previously lived at Duddeston Hall, where, so said tradition, he had murdered his cook by running him through with a spit and burying him under the floor of the cellar where he fell. But murder will out – and it was commonly believed that for this deed he was forced to bear the 'bloody hand' in his arms. So much local credence had the tale that when in 1850 Duddeston Hall was razed to the ground, speculation was rife 'among persons who from their position in society might be supposed to be better informed' as to whether the cook's skeleton would be found under the cellar floor.

Alas, not – 'the bloody hand' (still to be seen in his arms in Aston church) is no more than the Red Hand of Ulster, the source of many gory tales (cf. 'Bloody Baker', **Cranbrook**, p.100). To the story of the Holte murder, recorded in *Notes & Queries* in 1850 hard upon the destruction of Duddeston Hall, was added a tradition (printed in 1856 in the same periodical) about a window in Aston church containing the Holte arms: 'and there . . . the hand has been painted *minus* one finger; and to explain this I was told that one of the Holtes was compelled to place the bloody hand in his arms, and transmit the same to his descendants, who were allowed *to take one finger off* for each generation until, all the fingers and thumbs being *deducted*, it might at length be dispensed with altogether.'

The interesting thing is that the story began in Sir Thomas's lifetime – in 1606 he successfully sued one of his neighbours for having said that he had split his cook's head with a cleaver. Damages were reduced, however, after an appeal on the grounds that the defendant never actually claimed that the cook had been killed. Here, as at **Littlecote House** (p.67), we seem to see local rumour hardening into 'fact', thence passing into legend. One reason for the spread of the story may be that Sir Thomas was a Royalist, who entertained Charles I on his way to Edgehill, whereas the people of Birmingham were notorious Parliamentarians – in 1643 Aston Hall was stormed, twelve people killed and the rest taken prisoner. It seems as if propaganda may well underlie the tale.

Forced to bear the 'bloody hand' for murdering his cook:
Sir Thomas Holte (1571–1654) of Aston Hall,
West Midlands, painted in the early eighteenth-century

Duddeston Hall was in the middle of the eighteenth century converted into a tavern and pleasure gardens called 'Vauxhall' – hence the present district of Vauxhall with Duddeston Manor Road and Duddeston Station. Aston Hall itself remained in the possession of the descendants of Sir Thomas Holte until the early nineteenth century, then in 1864 became the property of Birmingham Corporation. Now a branch of Birmingham Museums and Art Gallery, it is open to the public – for times, see *HHC&G*. A portrait of Sir Thomas, painted in about 1710 but based on a lost portrait of *ca.* 1600, hangs in the Vestibule.

BLAKE MERE, NR LEEK, STAFFORDSHIRE   Sheet 119
SJ 0461

In his *Natural History of Stafford-shire* (1686), Dr Robert Plot turns a sceptical eye on 'the Black Mere of Morridge', in the Moorlands, a district of noisome 'Boggs' and peat-cuttings filled with stagnant water from which 'contagious vapors' came:

> . . . yet are not these neither so bad as some have fancyed the *water* is of the *black-Meer* of *Morridge*, which I take to be nothing more than such as those in the *peat-pits*; though it be confidently reported that no *Cattle* will drink of it, no *bird* light on it, or fly over it; all which are as false as that it is *bottomlesse*; it being found upon measure scarce four *yards* in the deepest place, my *Horse* also drinking when I was there as freely as I ever saw Him at any other place, and the *fowle* so far from declining to fly over it, that I spake with several that had seen *Geese* upon it; so that I take this to be as good as the rest, notwithstanding the vulgar disrepute it lyes under.

But the pool – now known as Blake Mere, just off the Buxton road (SJ 040613) refused easily to yield up the evil reputation it had borne since at least the days of Alexander Neckam (1157–1217). Also known as 'Mermaid's Pool', it was throughout the nineteenth century believed to have a mermaid lurking in it, waiting to draw travellers to their deaths. It was said that she had once warned workmen that if the waters were let out, they 'would drown all Leek and Leek-Frith' – about as likely a tale as that Llyn y Fan Fach, in Dyfed, could overwhelm Brecon.

But common sense is not required of folktales, and traditions such as these go a long way back. Lake Avernus (Lago Averno near Pozzuoli) was in ancient times generally thought to be one of the entrances to the Underworld and never visited by birds – 'Avernus' being derived from Greek *a-ornos*, 'birdless'.

Peak District National Park. Use OS 1:25 000 Outdoor Leisure Map 24, The White Peak (West Sheet). The Black Mere mermaid is still commemorated by the Mermaid Inn (SJ 036606), previously Blackmere House, probably a drover's inn on Morridge (roughly SJ 0365–SJ 0254).

CHARLECOTE PARK, WARWICKSHIRE   Sheet 151
                                                                   SP 2656

It is not to be wondered at that in the county of his birth Shakespeare should be remembered in local legend. He is said, for example, to have taken part in a drinking-match at the Falcon in Bidford (SP 1051) and slept off its effects under a crab-apple tree beside the Stratford road. This tradition was already long known in Warwickshire by the end of the eighteenth century and 'Shakespeare's Crab-tree' was pointed out until it was felled in 1824.

The most famous story about him, however, is the one attached to Charlecote Park, about four miles (7 km) out of Stratford. Charlecote had been the home of the Lucy family since 1247, and the present house was built in 1558. Shakespeare, the story goes, was caught poaching deer in Charlecote Park and haled before Sir Thomas Lucy. He promptly took his revenge by making a ballad about him and nailing it on his gate. This provoked Sir Thomas even further, and Shakespeare was forced to leave his home in Stratford and seek his fortune in London.

Shakespeare died in 1616 and by the end of the century the poaching story was in full swing. That the 'bitter ballad' had been nailed to the gate of Charlecote Park was a tradition preserved by the antiquary Oldys (d. 1761), who for good measure quotes its first stanza:

> A parliemente member, a justice of peace,
> At home a poor scare-crowe, at London an asse,
> If lowsie is Lucy, as some volke miscalle it,
> Then Lucy is lowsie whatever befall it:
>> He thinks himself greate,
>> Yet an asse in his state

We allowe by his ears but with asses to mate.
If Lucy is lowsie, as some volke miscalle it,
Sing lowsie Lucy, whatever befall it.

(The play on 'lowsie' and 'Lucy' reflects local pronunciation of 'Lucy' at the time.) These lines were all that could be remembered of the ballad by an old man from Turbich, Worcestershire, who died in 1703 and who had often heard the poaching story from old people in Stratford.

But another contender for Shakespeare's ballad is given by the diarist John Byng, who in 1781 quotes from an old manuscript an account of how, in about 1690, the Cambridge Professor of Greek heard an old woman at a Stratford inn sing the following:

Sir Thomas was too covetous
 To covet so much deer;
When horns enough upon his head
 Most plainly did appear.

Had not his worship one deer left,
 What then he had a wife
Took pains enough to find him horns
 Shou'd hold him during life.

The Professor gave her a new gown for her efforts – she would have got ten guineas if she could have remembered the rest.

Along with the poaching story went a traditional belief that Justice Shallow in *Henry IV* and *The Merry Wives of Windsor* was a caricature of Sir Thomas, and scholars have argued over this for the best part of two centuries. Thomas de Quincey said roundly 'the tale is fabulous and rotten to its core', and by others we are told that there were no deer at Charlecote Park in Shakespeare's time, that Oldys's fragment comes from a ballad (which still survives) written in the time of Charles II, that Byng's version was the work of the redoubtable Shakespearean forger William Chetwood, and that Shallow was actually modelled on a notoriously rapacious Surrey justice, William Gardiner.

Whether or no, the Lucys themselves seem to have believed the poaching story, if not quite in its usual form. In his *Visits to Remarkable Places* (1840), William Howitt reports Mrs Lucy of Charlecote as telling him that it was untrue that Shakespeare had been caught poaching at Charlecote – in reality it had been at the old Park at Fulbrook, where Fulbrook Castle once stood.

Howitt was also told by persons in the neighbourhood that a lead statue in the park of 'Diana with a Stag' was 'Shakespeare on a Deer'. Such was the grip of tradition that they had convinced themselves, despite appearances to the contrary, such as Diana's womanly form, that this was our national poet making his escape.

NT. Times of opening also in *HHC&G*. Whatever the case in Shakespeare's time, the park now supports herds of red and fallow deer. 'Diana with a Stag', shown on a map of 1791 at the end of the lime avenue, disappeared early in the nineteenth century. Sir Thomas Lucy's likeness in alabaster can be seen in the Lucy Chapel, Charlecote church. 'Shakespeare's Crab-tree' is shown on Sheet 54 of the original OS 1 in map, published in 1831, from surveys done in 1811–15.

EDGE HILL, WARWICKSHIRE
Sheet 151
SP 3747

Perhaps the most dramatic story arising from the English Civil War is that of the phantom army seen after the Battle of Edgehill in 1642:

> ... between twelve and one of the clock in the morning was heard by some sheepherds, and other countrey-men, and travellers, first the sound of drummes afar off, and the noyse of souldiers, as it were, giving out their last groanes; at which they were much amazed, and amazed stood still, till it seemed, by the neerenesse of the noyse to approach them; at which too much affrighted, they sought to withdraw as fast as possibly they could; but then, on the sudden ... appeared in the ayre the same incorporeall souldiers that made those clamours, and immediately, with Ensignes display'd, Drummes beating, Musquets going off, Cannons Discharged, horses neyghing, which also to these men were visible, the alarum or entrance to this game of death was strucke up ... and so pell mell to it they went ...

After about three hours' fighting, the soldiers in the King's colours fled, but those of Parliament 'stayed a good space triumphing ...

then, with all their Drummes, Trumpets, Ordnance, and Souldiers, vanished . . .' The spectators at once hurried to Keinton and knocked up the Justice of the Peace and also the parson, and told them upon oath what they had seen. The next night, a Sunday, which was Christmas night, they too went to Edge Hill, with other 'substantiall Inhabitants', and saw the same apparition. It appeared again the following Saturday and Sunday nights, and the week-end after that, and news of it reached the King, Charles I, at his headquarters at Oxford. He sent six 'Gentlemen of credit', who the next Saturday night also witnessed the phenomenon – 'and so on Sunday'. They recognized some of the slain.

'What this doth portend, God only knoweth, and time perhaps will discover,' says the pamphleteer who recorded these events in 'A Great Wonder in Heaven' published soon after, in January 1643. But he thought it was a sign of God's wrath against the land for the civil wars 'which He in his good time finish' – and this should warn us not to accept the phantom army too readily as a genuine manifestation. A good deal of propaganda was published in pamphlets for either side during the Civil War, including much that should have strained credulity – for example, that Prince Rupert's beloved dog Boy was his familiar. Though it favours neither side, but is a general warning, the Edgehill story may have started in the same way.

Fiction or not, it would have been readily accepted, as phantom armies had a long tradition behind them, especially at the sites of battles. The Greek historian Pausanias says that at Marathon 'every night you may hear horses neighing and men fighting', though he does not say that anything was seen. Such spectres were also known to the Romans and Jews – they appeared during the Maccabees wars and before the fall of Jerusalem to Titus. In the Middle Ages they were reported in various places, and in more recent times one manifested itself on **Souther Fell** (p.389). Walter Map's account of the 'nocturnal companies and squadrons' of the Herlethingus suggests that, in European tradition at least, there was a strong connection between spectral armies and the Wild Hunt (see **Hereford**, p.306, and **Peterborough**, p.187).

Although watch has been kept on Edge Hill from time to time, there have been no more appearances, though some local people have claimed to hear the sounds of the battle on its anniversary, 23 October.

The site of the Battle of Edgehill (SP 3549) is owned by the Ministry of Defence and is within the boundary of the Army Central Ammunition Depot, Kineton. Visits can sometimes be arranged for recognized groups by applying in writing to The Commandant, C.A.D. Kineton, Temple Herdewyke, Leamington Spa, Warwickshire. (Because of rebuilding, no visits will be possible before 1987.) The battlefield can be seen below one from the high ridge of Edge Hill.

GIFFARD'S CROSS, CHILLINGTON HALL, STAFFORDSHIRE

Sheet 127
SJ 8807

About a mile from Chillington Hall (SJ 8606), in the garden of the lodge at the entrance gates to the oak avenue, stands an old and weathered cross (SJ 881076) said to be the original Giffard's Cross. In Harrison Ainsworth's *Boscobel* (1872), Father Huddleston tells its story.

'That is called Giffard's Cross,' said Father Huddleston, 'and it was set up in old times by Sir John Giffard. Sir John, who was excessively fond of the chase, kept a collection of wild beasts, amongst them a very beautiful, but very fierce panther, which he valued more than all the rest. One day, it chanced that this savage animal slipped out of its cage, and escaped into the park. Made aware of what had happened by the cries of his terrified household, Sir John snatched up an arbalist, and rushed out into the park, accompanied by his eldest son. He easily ascertained the direction taken by the panther, for the beast had been seen to skirt the avenue . . . Sir John and his son ran as swiftly as they could, and were still speeding on, when they beheld a young woman and a child coming along the road. At the same moment, they discovered the panther couched amid the fern, evidently waiting for his prey. Sir John and his son had halted, and though the distance was almost too great, the old knight prepared to launch a bolt at the beast. But while he was adjusting his cross-bow, his son remarked that he was out of breath, and fearing he might miss his aim from this cause, called out to him in French, '*Prenez haleine, tirez fort!*' ['Take breath, pull strong'] . . . Just as the panther was about to spring, the bolt flew, and was lodged in the animal's brain. On the spot where the mortally wounded beast rolled on the ground, this memorial was placed. Thence-forward, also, Sir John Giffard adopted as his motto the words of counsel addressed to him by his son.'

Ainsworth had visited Chillington Hall and also had access to local records, so, as at **Cuckfield Park** (p.104), his fictional account is probably based on local tradition. It is in any case Ainsworth's story that is told today. The legend either explains or is confirmed by the two Giffard crests: Sir John Giffard, who succeeded to Chillington on the death of his father in 1486, was in 1513 granted a panther's head as a crest, and in 1523 a demi-archer 'in his hands a bow and arrow, drawn to the head or'.

Chillington Hall, rebuilt in about 1785, still belongs to the Giffard family and is open to the public – for times, see *HHC&G*. The Giffard motto and crests are carved over the fireplace in the Saloon. The tomb of Sir John Giffard (d. 1556) is in the chancel of Brewood church (SJ 8808).

GUY'S CLIFFE, WARWICKSHIRE

Sheet 151
SP 2966

Under this hill, hard by the river *Avon* standeth *Guy-cliffe*, others call it *Gib-cliffe*, the dwelling house at this day of Sir *Thomas Beau-foe* ... Heere, as the report goes, that valiant knight and noble Worthy so much celebrated, Sir *Guy of Warwick*, after he had born the brunt of sundry troubles, and atchieved many painful exploits, built a Chappell, led an Eremits life, and in the end was buried.

Such is Camden's description of Guy's Cliffe in his *Britannia* (trans. Holland, 1610). Wiser men, he continues, think that the place took its name from Guy Beauchamp, Earl of Warwick, and that 'St Margaret's Chapel' at Guy's Cliffe was built by Richard Beauchamp, who erected there a 'mighty and giantlike statue' of Earl Guy. It was this Guy, Fuller tells us in his *Worthies* (1662), to whom the saying 'He is the black Bear of Arden' referred, being used of someone who was an object of terror. The allusion was partly to the Warwick crest, the bear and ragged staff, partly to the character of Guy, '*Grim* of Person and *Surly* of resolution'.

Already by Camden's time, the historical Guy of Warwick and

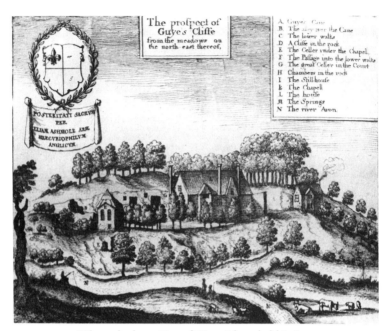

POSTERITATI SACRVM
PER.
ELIAM ASHMOLE ARM.
MERCVRIOPHILVM
ANGLICVM.

Where the hero Guy of Warwick ended his days:
'The prospect of Guy's Cliffe', showing the chapel and cave,
from Sir William Dugdale's Antiquities of Warwickshire *(1656)*

the legendary 'Sir Guy' were thoroughly confused. Numbered
among the Nine Worthies along with King Arthur, Sir Guy was
said to have lived in Saxon times, in the reign of King Athelstan,
and like Dick Whittington was a poor boy who made good – the
son of a steward, who, by his great feats of arms, proved himself
worthy of the Earl of Warwick's daughter Felice (later Phyllis).
Not long after their marriage, he set off for the Holy Land,
returning after many adventures to find the Danes encamped
outside Winchester. He undertook to fight in single combat against
the Danish champion, the giant Colbrand, and killed him. Another
celebrated feat was his ridding Dunsmore Heath (SP 4272) near
Dunchurch of the terrifying Dun Cow, a fairy cow milked dry in
traditional fashion and by human greed transformed into a monster.

After his return from the Holy Land, Guy decided to end his
days as a hermit and took up his abode in a lonely cell in the

Forest of Arden. He begged for food every day at Warwick Castle and was given it by his wife, who did not recognize him. Just before he died, however, he made himself known by means of a ring (as in the story at **Wroxall Abbey**, p.286). Two weeks after his death, Felice or Phyllis also died, and they were buried together in one grave.

This 'romauns of prys', as Chaucer calls it, originated in French around 1200. Early in the reign of Elizabeth I appeared the first printed version in English, *The Booke of the Most Victoryous Prince Guy of Warwick*, subsequently turned into a ballad and then a chapbook, and remaining popular right up to the nineteenth century. Its historical basis is slight – it is undoubtedly set in Athelstan's reign only because of his victory over the Danes at *Brunanburh* in 937 A.D. It has been suggested, however, that 'Guy' is a Norman attempt at the Old English name Wigod, and that the original Guy may have been Wigod of Wallingford, Edward the Confessor's cupbearer, who had some connection regarding land with the sheriff of Warwick.

However that may be, most of the story is legendary. The return of the husband unrecognized by his wife, his life as a hermit, and recognition by means of a ring all appear in the tale of a hero called Guido in the *Gesta Romanorum*, and it may be that he and Guy are one. The Dun Cow was attached to the story comparatively late – she is first mentioned in 1579 by a Dr Caius, who in 1552 had been shown her relics at Warwick and Coventry, and in the chapel at Guy's Cliffe had seen a rib over six feet (1.83 m) long and nine inches (23 cm) round purporting to be hers (cf. **Stanion**, p.254, and **Wade's Stone**, p.421). Subsequently the Dun Cow was said to have begun her career as the blameless White Cow of **Mitchell's Fold** (p.314).

Relics of Guy himself also helped keep the story alive. The diarist John Evelyn in 1654 visited Warwick Castle and was shown, among other things, Guy's sword and cooking-pot. Meantime *Kibbeclive* or *Gibbeclive*, as it was known until the fifteenth century, had been transformed under the influence of the legend to 'Guy's Cliffe', the chapel to 'Guy's Chapel', and the statue to Guy himself. A cave in the sandstone of Guy's Cliffe to the east of the chapel (which the historian John Rous, who was chaplain there to 1491, tells us sheltered a Saxon hermit) replaced the Forest of

The 'mighty and giantlike statue' of Earl Guy seen by Camden,
Guy's Cliffe Chapel, Warwickshire

Arden cell and became 'Sir Guy's Grot'. Eventually there was even a 'Guy's Leap' – though the person who leapt from it was Phyllis, who jumped to her death thence when Guy died.

Guy's Chapel and Cave are in the grounds of Guy's Cliffe House – not the two-storeyed house that Sir William Dugdale knew (see illus.), but its Georgian replacement, built soon after 1757, and itself a ruin by 1966. Inside the (possibly) thirteenth-century chapel, carved out of the rock against which it is built, still stands the 'mighty and giantlike statue' which Camden saw. A figure in armour nearly nine feet (2.74 m) high, it is somewhat more timeworn than even in Dugdale's day. Above and below the rocky ledge on which house and chapel stand are caves and rock-cut chambers. Guy's Cave housed a hermit in 1334, but it is doubtful if one was there in Saxon times. The 'reliques' seen by John Evelyn are still displayed at Warwick Castle – Guy's Sword in the Armoury, Guy's Cooking Pot, about six hundred years old and made of bell metal, in the

Great Hall. Also in the Armoury is a silver and bronze statuette of Sir Guy killing the Dun Cow by Emile Jeannest (1854). The Castle is open to the public – for times see *HHC&G*. Both 'Guy of Warwick' and 'The Dun Cow' were popular inn signs, and at Swainsthorpe in Norfolk the Dun Cow still carries a board with the following inscription:

> Walk in Gentlemen,
> I Trust You'll Find
> The Dun Cow's Milk
> Is To Your Mind.

Dunsmore Heath, Sheet 140.

INKBERROW, HEREFORD & WORCESTER (formerly WORCESTERSHIRE)

Sheet 150
SP 0157

Long ago, the church at Inkberrow was pulled down and rebuilt on a new site, which happened to be near a fairy dwelling. The fairies objected to this, and tried to hinder the move by returning the building materials each night to their former position. It was labour in vain – the builders had their way. But for many a day afterwards, it was said, from time to time was heard the following lament:

> Neither sleep, neither lie,
> For Inkbro's ting tangs hang so nigh.

(This is the rhyme as recorded by Jabez Allies in 1852 – later writers give other words.)

The story is one of countless church-siting traditions, in which attempts to build a church are persistently hindered by some supernatural power (cf. **Church Stowe**, p.224). But this form of the tale is very nearly unique in Britain. In 1940, the folklorist Ruth Tongue collected a story set on Exmoor of a fairy family who wanted to move out of earshot of the 'Withypool ding-dongs'; otherwise the closest parallels come from Scandinavia. When Lagga Kirk in Upland was built, a giant driven out of his hillock by the sound of its bells told a passing peasant, 'I must go away now, because of this kling-klang.'

The Devil was likewise unnerved by the sound of bells and we find the reason for this in Caxton's *Golden Legend* (?1483):

It is said, the evill spirytes that ben in the regyon of thayre*, doubte moche when they here the belles rongen: and this is the cause why the belles ben rongen whan it thondreth, and whan grete tempeste and outrages of wether happen, to the ende that the feindes and wycked spirytes should be abashed and flee, and cease of the movynge of tempeste.

IPSTONES, STAFFORDSHIRE

Sheet 119
SK 0249

Anno 165– At —— in the *Moorlands* in *Staffordshire*, lived a poor old Man, who had been a long time Lame. One *Sunday* in the Afternoon he being alone, one knock'd at his Door: he bade him open it and come in. The Stranger desired a Cup of Beer; the Lame Man desired him to take a Dish and draw some, for he was not able to do it himself. The Stranger asked the poor Old Man how long he had been ill? The poor Man told him. Said the Stranger I can cure you. Take two or three Balm Leaves steeped in your Beer for a Fortnight, or three Weeks, and you will be restored to your Health; but constantly and zealously serve God. The poor Man did so, and became perfectly well. This Stranger was in a Purple-shag Gown, such as was not seen or known in those Parts. And no Body in the Street (after Even Song) did see any one in such a colour'd Habit. Dr. *Gilbert Sheldon*, (since Arch-Bishop of *Canterbury*) was then in the *Moorlands* and justified the Truth of this, to *Elias Ashmole* Esq; from whom I had this Account . . .

Thus Aubrey in his *Miscellanies* records the appearance somewhere near Ipstones, in the Moorlands, of the Wandering Jew. The earliest mention of this mysterious figure comes from Matthew Paris (*ca.* 1200–59), who says that in 1228 an archbishop from Armenia visited St Albans (where Matthew was a monk) and in conversation was asked if he had heard anything of a certain Joseph, supposed to have been present at the Crucifixion and to be still alive. To which an interpreter in the archbishop's retinue replied that the archbishop had indeed often talked to this Joseph at his own table.

* thayre = the air

Joseph's story was that, when Jesus was being dragged from the hall of Pontius Pilate to be crucified, the porter at the gate, a man named Cartaphilus, struck Him on the back with his hand and said mockingly, 'Go quicker, Jesus, go quicker. Why do you loiter?' Jesus, looking back, replied, 'I am going, and you will wait till I return.' Cartaphilus was still waiting – for he had afterwards been baptized and received the name of Joseph. As Joseph he had often been seen both in Armenia and other countries.

Other medieval accounts of the Wandering Jew repeat much the same story, then he disappears until the sixteenth century. In 1505 we hear of him in Bohemia, and in 1547 Paul van Eitzen (1522–98), Bishop of Schleswig, was reported to have met him in Hamburg. He told the Bishop that formerly he had been a shoemaker named Ahasverus, who had hurried Jesus on, much as in Matthew's account. The Bishop said that the Jew, who dined at his table, ate and drank sparingly, was never seen to laugh, spoke the language of every land he came to, and was so knowledgeable on ancient history it was impossible not to believe his tale.

The Wandering Jew was reported in 1575 in Madrid, in 1599 in Vienna, in Lübeck in 1601 or 1603, and shortly after this in Moscow. In 1604 he appeared in Paris, in 1633 again in Hamburg, and in 1640 in Brussels, calling himself Isaac Laquedem. In 1642 he visited Leipzig and in 1658 Stamford in Lincolnshire. Peck's continuation of his *Survey of Stanford* to 1660 includes an eyewitness account from Samuel Wallis of Stamford of his visitation. It is much the same story as Aubrey's – an old man in a purple coat came to Wallis's door asking for a cup of small beer, and cured Wallis of consumption, using bloodwort and red sage. Whether these sixteenth- and seventeenth-century reports are fictions or refer to impostors is difficult to say. Certainly a young man was put on trial at Toledo in 1547 for claiming to be the Wandering Jew, and at the end of the seventeenth or beginning of the eighteenth century a charlatan posing as the Jew visited England, Denmark and Sweden, where he disappeared. Other impostors or madmen believing themselves to be the Jew are reported in England in the early nineteenth century, and from our own times comes a case of what looks like genuine self-deception – a stockbroker on Wall Street in the 1940s who used to read up on his past in New York Public Library and whose visiting cards were inscribed, 'T. W. Jew'.

The Wandering Jew has been explained as a personification of the Jewish race, whose homelessness the Church interpreted as a punishment for rejecting the Messiah – a tradition that underlies Cornish beliefs concerning the knockers (see **St Just**, p.31). The curse of deathlessness for impiety also links the Wandering Jew to certain of the Wild Huntsmen (for example, Moll Walbee, **Llowes**, p.349), hence in Northern France in the nineteenth century, when a violent storm broke overhead, peasants would still say '*C'est le Juif-errant qui passe*'. But as an image of the outcast of God, he is even more closely linked to that other deathless exile, the Flying Dutchman.

MINSTER LOVELL HALL, OXFORDSHIRE   Sheet 164
SP 3211

> The Cat, the Rat and Lovel the Dog
> They all ruled England under the Hog

said the anti-Yorkists. The Hog is of course Richard III, and 'Lovel the Dog' was his childhood friend and minister Francis Lovel, who after Richard's death escaped to Flanders, where he espoused the cause of Lambert Simnel. In May 1487, he marched on York, expecting help from Richard's supporters, but was defeated at Stamford Bridge. In his *History of Henry VII* (1622), Francis Bacon writes:

> Of the Lord Lovel there went a report, that he fled and swam over the Trent on horseback, but could not recover the farther side by reason of the steepness of the bank, and was drowned in the river. But another report leaves him not there, but that he lived long after it in a cave or vault.

Refusal to accept the death of a leader is a common phenomenon (see **Cadbury Castle, Somerset**, p.6, and **Waltham Abbey**, p.162), and it is not surprising to hear such a rumour about Lovel, or in the nineteenth century encounter the tale that he came home to Minster Lovell and lived there in a secret room, his whereabouts known only to one servant, who kept the key. When this servant fell ill and died, Lord Lovel was left to starve. This story is said to have received confirmation when workmen broke into a secret room at Minster Lovell and found the body of a man sitting at a table, with an open book before him and a dog at his feet. They saw this scene for a few moments only before the air rushed in and the bodies crumbled to dust.

This 'confirmation' stems from an eighteenth-century report that workmen at Minster Lovell nearly a hundred years before had found a man's body in a secret room. There, too, were the remains of several barrels and jars, from which it was surmised that he had come to the end of his stores and so had perished. The source of this report was John Manners, third Duke of Rutland, who related it in the hearing of the Clerk of the House of Commons, William Cowper, on 8 May 1728. Because its authority seemed unquestionable, it was very widely believed, people assuming that the body was Lovel's.

But was the report true? If not – and it is unconfirmed – the Duke may have been doing no more than repeating a rumour designed to 'authenticate' the old tale. Note the likeness of this story, especially in its later form, to one told by the diarist Abraham de la Pryme in 1697 of Thornton Abbey (now Humberside):

> There is a current story that about one hundred years ago, as one was pulling down some of these old buildings, they discover'd a little hollow room, which was a monk's cell, with the exact figure of a monk in all his cloaths, set before a little table, with an old parchment book before, and a pen and ink and paper, all which fell to ashes when they were shaked and touched.

This story was repeated by the antiquary Stukeley and may have been well known. Whatever the truth of the matter, one macabre tale has attracted another – also told of Minster Lovell Hall is 'The Mistletoe Bride', for which see **Marwell Hall** (p.71).

The picturesque ruins of Minster Lovell Hall, built in the fifteenth century, are close by the church, overlooking the river Windrush. AM.

OSEBURY ROCK, LULSLEY, HEREFORD & WORCESTER (formerly WORCESTERSHIRE)

Sheet 150
SO 7455

Osebury or Rosebury Rock, a headland bordering on the Teme near Lulsley, was traditionally said to be a favourite haunt of the fairies. They had a cave there, which was still shown in Jabez Allies's day (1846), and he tells us: 'There . . . is a saying in the neighbourhood, that if woman should break her peel . . . and should leave it for a little while at the fairies cave in Osebury Rock, it would be mended for her' (cf. **Frensham**, p.106, and **Wayland's Smithy**, p.278).

Allies tells the story of how once, as a man and boy were ploughing in a nearby field, they heard an outcry in the copse on the steep face of the rock. On going to see what was the matter, they found a fairy crying that he had lost his pick. The ploughman found it for him, at which the fairy said, if they went to a certain corner of the field they had been ploughing, they would get their reward. When they looked, they found bread, cheese and cider, which the ploughman ate, but which the boy was too terrified to touch.

This is a version of a widespread story known as 'The Cake in the Furrow', usually interpreted as a relic of the practice of making offerings of food and drink in the fields at the start of the year's ploughing. The offering was sometimes put in the furrow or thrown on to the field. In Scotland this was called 'streeking the plough' and was the equivalent of the English Plough Monday festival. How offerings *to* supernatural beings came to be thought of as gifts *from* them is unexplained – but certainly fairies were widely believed often to give such gifts. 'Fairies are particularly fond of making cakes,' says Grose in his *Provincial Glossary* (1787), 'in the doing of which they are said to be very noisy.' He continues:

> In Ireland, they frequently lay bannocks, a kind of oaten cakes, in the way of travellers over the mountains; and if they do not accept of the intended favour, and eat the bannock, or at least take it up, they seldom escape a hearty beating, or something worse.

The ploughman at Osebury who accepted the bread and cheese evidently knew more about fairies than the frightened boy.

WAYLAND'S SMITHY, OXFORDSHIRE   Sheet 174
(formerly BERKSHIRE)   SU 2888

A local tradition that goes back at least a thousand years is that of

Wayland Smith, who had his smithy in the megalithic chamber tomb on the Ridgeway, not far from the Uffington White Horse. In his *Letter to Dr Mead concerning Antiquities in Berkshire* (1738), the antiquary Francis Wise reports:

> At this place lived formerly an invisible Smith, and if a traveller's Horse had lost a Shoe upon the road, he had no more to do than to bring the Horse to this place with a piece of money, and leaving both there for some little time, he might come again and find the money gone, but the Horse new shod.

This tradition was still very much alive in the nineteenth century. 'The village children', wrote Sir Walter Scott's friend, Mrs Hughes, who lived at Uffington, 'religiously believe the old legend of the visionary Smith; and often visit the spot to hear the clink of his hammer.' Sir Walter used the tradition in his novel *Kenilworth* (1821), making his smith human; but in Kipling's *Puck of Pook's Hill* (1906) he is a dethroned god forced to make his living as a blacksmith after the coming of Christianity. This is sometimes repeated as part of the legend, but is Kipling's own guess – Wayland was never a god, but a giant or elf.

Wayland or Weland as the Anglo-Saxons called him is the Norse Völundr, a smith of supernatural skill who was captured by a king called Niđuđr and lamed so he could not escape. Set to work by his captor, he enticed the king's two young sons to his forge, killed them and made cups from their skulls which he then sent to the king. When the king's daughter came to him, asking him to mend her ring – one that had been taken from Völundr – he drugged and then raped her, and escaped by magic through the air, taunting King Niđuđr as he flew overhead.

This tale of savage vengeance is told in an Old Norse poem written down in the thirteenth century, but in England the story was known several centuries earlier. Incidents from it are referred to in the Old English poem *Deor*, which survives in a manuscript from the second half of the tenth century, and Weland and Widia, his son by the princess, are mentioned in the fragmentary heroic poem *Waldere*, written down *ca.* 1000. Earlier still is the Frank's Casket, a carved whalebone box, now in the British Museum,

Smith of the Gods: Wayland in his smithy.
The Frank's Casket, eighth century, British Museum

thought to have been made in Northumbria in the eighth century. One of the scenes carved on it is generally agreed to be from the story of Völundr – a smith stands by his anvil, one leg bent as if lame, in his left hand what looks like a pair of tongs gripping a human head. He holds out a cup to two women, one of them perhaps the princess. Next to this group is a man and four birds, two of which he has by the neck. We are told in the Old Norse *Saga of Thiðrek* (thirteenth century) that Völundr escaped from captivity on wings made by his brother Egil, and some scholars believe that this is Egil collecting feathers, while what looks like a pair of wings appears in a similar scene carved on a Viking Age picture-stone from Gotland in Sweden. However, others believe that in the saga wings have replaced the magical flight of the earlier form of the story in imitation of those made by the Labyrinth-builder Daedalus to escape with Icarus from Crete.

The megalithic tomb on the Ridgeway, built over a smaller barrow *ca.* 3600 B.C. and itself formerly covered by a mound, had been exposed and rifled already by Saxon times. Known to Wise and earlier writers simply as 'Wayland Smith', to others as 'Wayland Smith's Cave', its name goes back at least to the ninth century, when in a Berkshire charter of 855 A.D. it is referred to as *Welandes smiððe*. Some writers have made what seems an obvious connection between the mysterious smith and the great White Horse at Uffington (SU 3086), but it is not certain that such a link would have existed in the Anglo-Saxon mind. The Anglo-Saxons do not seem to have been in the habit of shoeing horses much before the eleventh century, and Weland's name to them meant something more than a blacksmith – 'that famous and wise goldsmith Weland', King Alfred calls him, and it is jewels and jewelled cups he makes in Old Norse legend and in Geoffrey of Monmouth's *Life of Merlin* (soon after 1148). But Weland was pre-eminently a swordsmith and armourer – he made Beowulf's mailcoat and was remembered for his swords not only in Old English poetry but also in French medieval *chansons de geste* and the twelfth-century chronicle of the Counts of Angoulesme.

In both Norse and English tradition, Weland is 'of the race of elves', but perhaps, since elves were bigger than men, they were not clearly distinguished from giants. For wonderful swords, as well as edifices of stone, were traditionally *enta geweorc*, 'the work of giants', like Weland's father, Wade (see **Wade's Stone**, p.421). A similar ambiguity hangs over other famous Germanic smiths – Alberich in the German *Nibelung* legend, Regin in Old Norse, both variously described as dwarves or giants. They, like Weland, and indeed like elves, were connected with the 'hollow hills' and belong to the widespread Germanic tradition of 'the Craftsman in the Mound' – magical smiths who live in hills or caves or stone burial chambers also abound in the later folklore of Denmark, Belgium and North Germany.

The calling of smith has long been associated with magic and secrecy. In his *Prehistoric Communities of the British Isles* (2nd edn, 1947), V. Gordon Childe tells us that a group of smiths lived and worked in a limestone cave excavated by a branch of the Heathery Burn near Stanhope in County Durham. Various tools of their trade were found, as well as some of their products, and evidence of their wealth. Yet they lived apart from the community in a dank and narrow cave. A skeleton found near the hearth might show that they were buried where they had lived. 'But broken

human skulls near by remind us that in barbarous societies metallur-
gical science is still bound up with mystic rites for which human
blood may well have been required.' The isolation from the rest of
society of the uncanny and dangerous smith may once have been
the norm – people at different times in many parts of the world
have been accustomed to leave money or goods at a certain spot as
barter for objects collected later from unseen makers. That this
happened at more than one place in Britain, probably in the
transitional phase between Bronze and Iron Ages, is suggested by
many tales of objects mended or borrowed at fairy mounds (see
Frensham, p.106; **Osebury Rock**, p.277). Curiously enough, when
Wayland's Smithy was excavated in 1921, two iron currency bars
of Iron Age date were found buried there, as if in offering.

This is the only hint we have that there was ever a real smith at
Wayland's Smithy, and we shall probably never know if we are
dealing with the *memory* of a hidden smith, or a *tradition* arising
from memories of such men – 'the Craftsman in the Mound' – or a
specific *legend* based on that tradition. And specific legend there is.
Weland, like the Greek and Roman smiths Hephaestos and Vulcan,
was lame, and if we pursue this thought we find in the Greek
scholiast on Apollonius Rhodius a tale possibly current in the first
century B.C., that among Vulcan's favoured haunts were the
volcanic islands near Sicily that include Vulcano, and that 'it was
formerly said that, whoever chose to carry there a piece of
unwrought iron, and at the same time deposit the value of the
labour, would, on presenting himself there on the following morning, find it made into a sword, or whatever other object he had
desired'.

The resemblance of Weland to Vulcan, while it might go back to
a shared Indo-European tradition, is perhaps more likely to be the
result of borrowing from classical legend, possibly by Goths
serving in the Roman army. Such borrowing would also account
for Weland's escape, like Daedalus, on wings. But these things are
never simple, and if a connection was indeed made between Weland
and Daedalus by Germanic mercenaries in Roman times, another
legendary reason for calling a tomb 'Wayland's Smithy' appears.
The sort of stone maze elsewhere in Scandinavia called Trojeburg
and Trojenborg, 'Troy Castle' (cf. English Troy Towns), was in
Iceland known as *Völundarhús*, 'Wayland's House', and in a
fourteenth-century Icelandic manuscript, under a picture of the

Labyrinth, we find the caption *Völundarhús, id est domus Daedali*
('Wayland's House, that is, the house of Daedalus'). Could *this*
perhaps have been why the megalithic tomb, already laid bare in
Anglo-Saxon times, was associated with Wayland – because with
its three stone chambers it suggested a labyrinth?

AM (any reasonable time). By far the best way to see it is as part of a walk
along the Ridgeway Path. It is on the stretch between Ogbourne St
George and Uffington Castle – see Sean Jennett, *The Ridgeway Path*
(HMSO for the Countryside Commission, 1976; 2nd imp. 1980). For
maximum drama, try to see it at dawn – but remember to take a torch for
inside the tomb. The starting point for any account of Wayland is Dr
Hilda Ellis Davidson's article 'Weland the Smith', *Folklore* 69, September
1958, pp. 145–59.

WOODSTOCK, OXFORDSHIRE

Sheet 161
SP 4416

Rosamond the faire daughter of Walter, Lord Clifford, Concubine to Henry the 2. (poysoned by Q. Elianor as some
thought) died at Wodstock, where K. Henry had made for her
an house of a wonderfull working, so that no man or woman
might come to her, but if hee were instructed by the king . . .
This house after some was named *Labyrinthus*, or *Dedalus*
worke, which was thought to be an house wrought like vnto a
knotte in a garden, called a Maze, but it was commonly sayde
that lastly the Queene came to her by a clewe of thredde, or
silke, and so dealt with her, that shee liued not long after . . .

Such is the story of Fair Rosamond, mistress of Henry II, as told
by John Stow in his *Annales of England* (1592). It was a favourite
tale, told by many generations of writers with much variation as to
details. The jealousy of Henry's queen, the formidable Eleanor,
first appears in the fourteenth century; the 'clewe of thredde' (no
doubt borrowed from the story of Theseus and the Minotaur) at
the beginning of the sixteenth. The ballad 'On the Death of Faire
Rosamond' by Thomas Deloney (1607) made popular a version in
which Queen Eleanor, entering the maze, offers Rosamond the
choice of sword or cup – and she chooses the poison.

The maze itself was part of the story from its first appearance, in the *Polychronicon* of Ranulph Higden (trans. Trevisa, 1387). 'Rosamond's Bower', as it came to be called, suggests an arbour at the heart of a garden maze, but early writers thought of it as a building – 'a chambre of wonder craft, wonderliche i-made by Dedalus werke', says Higden, while the poet Drayton in *Englands Heroicall Epistles* (1597) speaks of subterranean vaults arched and walled with brick and stone.

These early accounts indeed make one wonder if the tale was at least in part a reworking of that of King Locrine and Estrildis, told by Geoffrey of Monmouth (*ca.* 1136). Locrine, the son of Brutus (see **Plymouth Hoe**, p.27), ordered a cave to be dug underneath Troy Novant – in other words London – in which to conceal his mistress Estrildis from Gwendolen, his wife, and more particularly from Gwendolen's powerful father, Corineus. There she was hidden for seven years, in the care of servants, and there he visited her without anyone being the wiser. In her hiding-place, Estrildis bore him a daughter, Habren, in Latin Sabrina. As soon as Corineus was dead, Locrine seized his chance to set Gwendolen aside and make Estrildis queen, but Gwendolen raised an army and he was killed in battle. Gwendolen now took over the kingdom and, learning the secret of the cave, had Estrildis and her daughter drowned in the river which has since then borne Sabrina's name and been called the Severn.

But though this British legend of the beautiful girl hidden in an underground chamber from the jealousy of a queen may have contributed to the story of Rosamond, there may well have been some reality behind the tale of the labyrinth. Despite Camden's assertion (1610) that its 'many inexplicable windings, backward and forward' were 'no where to be seene at this day', the ruins of what was supposed to be 'Rosamond's Bower' were up to the eighteenth century shown in the grounds of the old royal palace at Woodstock. 'Just by the Pool at Woodstock', writes Thomas Hearne in 1719, 'are seen the Foundations of a large Building, which, I believe, was the very same Building that was contrived for Rosamund.' Just what it was we shall never know – together with the remains of the palace it was destroyed when the Duchess of Marlborough built Blenheim.

The powerful image of the maze is now so much part of the tale that it scarcely matters what it was – perhaps no more than a house built by Henry for his mistress inside the palace grounds. For whatever the status of the bower, Rosamond herself, Henry's *Rosa mundi* or 'Rose of the World', was a real person, probably, as tradition asserts, the daughter of Walter de Clifford, son of Richard Fitzponce, who on acquiring Clifford Castle on the Wye by marriage assumed 'Clifford' as his family name.

Rosamond was not poisoned by Eleanor, but retired of her own accord to Godstow nunnery near Oxford, where she lived for a number of years, dying there in about 1176. Henry was generous to Godstow on her account, and perhaps because of this the nuns cherished her memory. When Hugh of Lincoln visited Godstow in 1191 he saw before the High Altar a carved tomb draped with hangings of silk. Asking who was buried there, and expecting to be told some saint, or at least a king, he was horrified to hear that the tomb was Rosamond's and ordered it destroyed. Rosamond was reburied in the Chapter House, and Higden tells us that on the new tomb was the epitaph:

> Hic jacet in tumba rosa mundi, non rosa munda.
> Non redolet, sed olet, quae redolere solet

which Trevisa translates as 'Here lieth in tomb the rose of the world, not a clean rose; it smelleth not sweet, but it stinketh, that was wont to smell full sweet.' A later generation was less spiteful – the antiquary Leland records that when, at the Dissolution of the Monasteries, the tomb was opened, 'A very swete smell came out of it'.

For whatever St Hugh's thoughts on the matter, popular sympathies had remained with Rosamond, not Eleanor. The shrine-like tomb might have gone, but people continued to visit Godstow to see a stone to which was attached the following odd little legend. When exhorted to repentance, Rosamond replied that she was confident of salvation. How would they know, the nuns asked? Pointing to a tree then covered in leaves, she said that if she were saved, the tree would turn to stone. At her death this duly occurred. Although by Hearne's time the stone had vanished, at Lower Wolvercote could still be seen 'Rosamond's Tree', on the site of the original tree.

Not to be outdone, the people of Woodstock also showed a 'Rosamond's Stone', but this one, Hearne tells us, was displayed 'for no other reason but to get Money'. It was not their only attraction, however:

On the North West side of the Remains of the old Mannour
House ... is a Pool, that is commonly called *Rosamund's
Pool*, or *Rosamund's Well*, being the same in which she used
to bath herself ...

The appeal of her legend seems not to have diminished with time.
In the early nineteenth century, in Buckinghamshire, local tradition
still maintained that Henry had built her a retreat in or near
Kingswood, and a century ago her footsteps and the silken rustling
of her skirts could be heard at Creslow Manor, perhaps because it
once belonged to a cadet branch of the Cliffords.

Of Rosamond as a person we know next to nothing, but if
indeed it is true that 'by their fruits ye shall know them', we
should perhaps remark that the two men whom tradition claims as
Rosamond's sons, William Longsword, Earl of Salisbury, and
Geoffrey, Archbishop of York, behaved rather better towards
Henry than his sons by Eleanor. As for Rosamond's beauty, it is
commemorated by a rose, *Rosa gallica versicolor*, crimson striped
with pink and white – apt to the 'young, brisk, airy Lady' that
Hearne imagined her.

The site of the old palace at Woodstock is in the grounds of Blenheim
Palace, and is marked by a pillar east of the Grand Bridge on the north
side of the lake. Here, too, is 'Fair Rosamond's Well' (SP 437166).
Blenheim Palace is open to the public – for times see *HHC&G*. *Rosa
gallica versicolor* is available from several rose specialists – I can recommend
Peter Beales Roses, Intwood Nurseries, Swardeston, Norwich NR14 8EA.
It is easy to grow, though subject to mildew – no doubt the blighting
influence of St Hugh.

WROXALL ABBEY, WARWICKSHIRE   Sheet 139
                                             SP 2270

In the twelfth century, the lord of the manor of Wroxall was a
certain Hugh de Hatton, who went as a Crusader to the Holy
Land and was there taken prisoner. He lay in prison seven years,
but then remembering that his parish church was dedicated to St
Leonard, besought the saint for his help. St Leonard appeared and
commanded Hugh to go home and at his church found a house of
Benedictine nuns. Hugh took this for a dream, but St Leonard

again appeared and repeated his command, and Hugh vowed he would carry it out:

> Which Vow was no sooner made than that he became miraculously carryed thence, with his Fetters, and set in *Wroxhall* woods, not far distant from his own house; yet knew not where he was, untill a Shepherd of his own, passing through those thickets, accidentally found him; and after some communication (though he was at first not a little affrighted, in respect he saw a person so overgrown with hair) discovered all unto him. Whereupon his Lady and Children, having advertisement, came forthwith to him, but believed not that he was her husband, till he shewed her a piece of a Ring, that had been broken betwixt them . . .

This, in the words of Sir William Dugdale, Garter King of Arms and author of *The Antiquities of Warwickshire* (1656), is the story of the foundation of Wroxall Abbey. It is first mentioned in a fifteenth-century cartulary of the priory – and we should perhaps pay heed to the fact that the fifteenth century was a fertile breeding ground of charter legends.

The Abbey church (now the parish church) is indeed dedicated to St Leonard of Limousin, hence probably the tale, for he is the patron saint of prisoners, customarily shown carrying fetters, and perhaps having had them hung up in his honour in churches –

> . . . *Leonerd* of the prisoners doth, the bandes a sunder pull,
> And breakes the prison doores and chaines, wherwith his Church is full

as Barnabe Googe tells us in *The Popish Kingdome* (1570). The story is a version of a widespread tale, 'The Homecoming Husband', of which the most famous example, perhaps, is the return of Odysseus to Penelope. This variant, in which the husband is identified by a broken ring, is in England often told of Crusaders (cf. **Mab's Cross**, p.383). At Wolverley, Worcestershire (SO 8279), the very fetters worn by Sir John Attwood are said to have hung over his tomb for years, just as those of the Crusader Leonard de Reresby according to tradition hung in St Leonard's Church, Thrybergh, South Yorkshire.

Another legend attached to Wroxall Abbey is 'Snow in Summer', for which see **St Bees** (p.387).

The ruins of Wroxall Abbey (correctly marked 'priory' on the map) lie within the grounds of Wroxall Abbey School. These may be visited on Open Days under the National Gardens Scheme – for details, see *Gardens of England & Wales Open to the Public*, published annually and available from The National Gardens Scheme, 57 Lower Belgrave Street, London SW1, and from stationers. Wolverley, Sheet 138.

8
The Marches

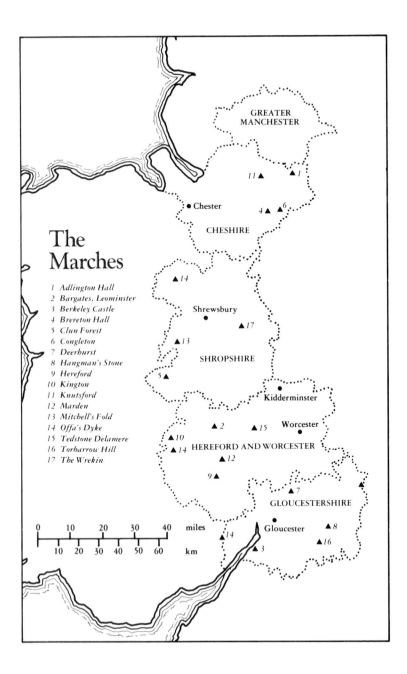

The Marches

1 Adlington Hall
2 Bargates, Leominster
3 Berkeley Castle
4 Brereton Hall
5 Clun Forest
6 Congleton
7 Deerhurst
8 Hangman's Stone
9 Hereford
10 Kington
11 Knutsford
12 Marden
13 Mitchell's Fold
14 Offa's Dyke
15 Tedstone Delamere
16 Torbarrow Hill
17 The Wrekin

GREATER MANCHESTER

● Chester

CHESHIRE

SHROPSHIRE

Shrewsbury ●

Kidderminster ●

Worcester ●

HEREFORD AND WORCESTER

GLOUCESTERSHIRE

Gloucester ●

0   10   20   30   40   miles
10 20 30 40 50 60   km

> Will you heare a Spanish Lady
>   how she wooed an Englishman . . .

begins the beautiful old ballad known as 'The Spanish Lady's
Love'. The 'Englishman' in the story is evidently a companion of
the Earl of Essex on the Cadiz Expedition (June–August 1596),
which defeated the Spanish fleet and held the city for a fortnight.
The 'Spanish Lady' is one of the prisoners, who falls in love with
her captor, and, when the order comes to leave Cadiz, begs him to
take her with him to England.

But the Englishman is evasive. It would disgrace her, he says, to
travel in company with soldiers like a camp-follower: then she will
disguise herself as his page. He has no money to pay for the
voyage: she will pay for it herself, with her 'chaines and Iewels'.
The voyage is hazardous: should she fear storms, she asks, when
she is ready to lay down her life for him? He is forced at last to
come to the point:

> 'Courteous Lady be contented
>   here comes all that breeds the strife,
> I in *England* haue already
>   a sweet woman to my wife.'

The Spanish Lady gallantly begs his pardon and gives him gifts to
take home with him:

> 'Commend me to thy louing Lady
>   beare to her this chaine of gold,
> And these bracelets for a token,
>   grieuing that I was so bold.'

As for herself, she will enter a nunnery and spend the rest of her
life in prayer for her Englishman and his lady.

This affecting tale has been popular since the beginning of the
seventeenth century. As 'The Spanish Ladies Loue to an English
Gentleman' it was entered in the Stationers' Register on 11 June
1603 and came from the pen of the silk-weaver Thomas Deloney.
By 1616 it was already well-enough known to be quoted in a
Jacobean comedy, *Cupid's Whirligig*, by Edward Sharpham and in

1633 it was parodied in William Rowley's *A Match at Midnight*. More recently a version of it was sung by Laurence Olivier in the film *Fire Over England* (1937).

How far the story was Deloney's own invention and how far a current tale is doubtful. Certainly here as elsewhere (see **Ostrich Inn**, p.149, and **Woodstock**, p.283) he is drawing on popular tradition – his Spanish Lady is fired not simply by romantic love but by an ardent desire for an English husband. For English *wives* were proverbially fortunate – as the Dutchman Emanuel van Meteren said in the sixteenth century, 'England is the paradise of married women'.

Whoever started it, the story passed into the nation's repertoire of popular legends and became attached to several different people – Sir John Popham of **Littlecote House** (p.67), Sir Richard Levison of Trentham, Staffordshire, and Sir John Bolle of Thorpe Hall, Lincolnshire. In Cheshire it was told of Sir Uryan Legh of Adlington, knighted by Essex at the taking of Cadiz, and later (1613) to become High Sheriff of Cheshire. It is said that the gold necklace sent to Sir Uryan's wife by the Spanish Lady was long treasured in the Legh family. The present owner of Adlington Hall, Charles Legh, writes: 'My grandmother always said that the gold chain was here when she inherited the Hall in 1896, but was subsequently stolen!'

At Adlington Hall, in the drawing-room, still hangs a portrait of Sir Uryan with a gold chain round his neck. It hangs to his waist, and his right hand rests on it, one loop being twisted round his thumb, as if drawing attention to it. Painted in about 1610, this portrait may well have kept the legend alive, even if it did not prompt its attachment to Sir Uryan.

Adlington Hall, five miles (8 km) north of Macclesfield off the A523, is open to the public. For times, see *HHC&G*. The timber buildings on its north and east sides are mostly from the sixteenth century, the period of the tale.

BARGATES, LEOMINSTER, HEREFORD & WORCESTER (formerly HEREFORDSHIRE)

Sheet 149
SO 4959

In the Bargates are four small almshouses founded by a charitable widow in 1736 and subsequently rebuilt. The dedication stone reads: 'This hospital was erected by Hester Clark and endowed at her death with 20 pounds per annum, to four decayed widows.'* Local tradition says that Hester Clark fell on hard times herself and became an inmate of her own almshouses, a legend that is attached – whether cause or effect is uncertain – to a curious effigy. In the central gable of the almshouses is the wooden figure of a man, probably from the original building. Wearing nothing but a cocked hat and a loincloth, he carries in his hand an axe or hatchet, which has now lost its head. Under him is the following verse:

> He that gives away all
> before he is Dead,
> Let em take this Hatchet
> and knock him on ye head.

The rhyme and the tradition behind it are much older than Hester Clark – a case of an existing tradition being taken over by a local personality. In a twelfth-century Latin story we read how an old man, after surrendering his property to his daughter's husband, was then (like Lear) treated worse and worse until at last he was driven out of the house. He contrived to secure better treatment by pretending he had in a chest a sum of money laid by, partly to be spent for the good of his soul, but partly to be disposed of as he chose. When he was on the point of death, his family hastened to open the box, but found in it nothing but a mallet, on which, in English, was inscribed:

> Wyht suylc a betel be he smyten,
> That al the werld hyt mote wyten,
> That gyfht his sone al his thing,
> And goht hymself a beggyn.

('With such a beetle [i.e. club or mallet] may he be smitten, so that all the world know it, that gives his son all his goods and himself goes a-begging.') There is another early English version of this rhyme, suggesting that the tradition was English and not Latin, and that it was well known. The story seems to have stayed in

---

* This is the inscription as given by Mrs Leather in her *Folk-Lore of Herefordshire* (1912). It is differently reported by other authorities. Was she mistaken or has it changed? Mr Norman C. Reeves of Leominster tells me that today it reads 'Hester Clark widow' and that the word 'decayed' appears to have been erased.

circulation for many centuries – it is told, without the mallet or the rhyme, by the seventeenth-century diarist Abraham de la Pryme of a man at **Winterton** (p.255), and in 1862 the Scottish collector J. F. Campbell heard it, in Gaelic, with both.

German scholars of the nineteenth century tell us that on the front of a house at Osnabrück and on the city gates of several towns in Silesia and Saxony, there used to hang mallets accompanied by verses almost identical with the Bargates rhyme. Grimm believed that these mallets were actually the hammer-symbol of Donar/ Thunor/Thor, the Germanic thunder-god, which had once been suspended or represented at the entrances to heathen temples, and with the coming of Christianity found a place on churches and gates to cities as dedicatory symbols of good luck. Later, when their significance was totally forgotten, a legend sprang up to account for them.

But even if the 'betel' began life as the hammer of Thor, why was it explained in just this way? The answer seems to be, because mallets were already associated with hitting old people on the head. There was a persistent tradition going back to at least classical times that certain nations killed off their aged. The Elder Pliny, for example, reports (77 A.D.) that when old people among the Hyperboreans were tired of living, they flung themselves off a high rock into the sea, after feasting with their kinsfolk. Much the same tradition is found in nineteenth-century Sweden where there were local reports of *ättestupor* or 'family cliffs' over which old people had thrown themselves in former times.

This Swedish tradition seems to be confirmed by the fourteenth-century Icelandic *Gautreks saga*, in which an eccentric family of misers are in the habit of flinging themselves off the *Ætternistapi* or 'Family Cliff' – 'And then they can go to Odin, while their children are spared all the trouble and expense of having to take care of them . . .' But *Gautreks saga* is fiction, and though it was written by a man of antiquarian interests, is not wholly to be trusted as a record of genuine custom. As for the *ättestupor*, though they are numerous, it is possible that they descend, name and all, from the *Ætternistapi*, for *Gautreks saga* was widely popular in printed form from the seventeenth century on.

So though the indications are that the elderly were sacrificed off cliffs in pagan Northern Europe (the Hyperboreans were thought to live beyond the North Pole), we cannot be sure it ever happened.

There is a slightly stronger case for the custom of clubbing the old to death. In Sweden it was said that if an old person were too weak to travel to the 'family cliff' to throw himself off, his kinsman would save him from the disgrace of a 'straw-death', i.e. dying in his bed, by beating him to death with the 'family club'. One such club was in the nineteenth century still preserved at a farmhouse in East Gotland. The hatchet at Leominster, the 'betel' in the Latin story, and the 'family club' are curiously echoed by the antiquary Aubrey in his *Remaines of Judaisme and Gentilisme* (1686–7), where he notes as an 'old Countrie Story':

> The Holy-mawle, w^ch (they fancy) hung behind the Church dore, wch when the father was seaventie the sonne might fetch, to knock his father in the head, as effœte, & of no more use.

It is said by Henry Bett in *English Myths and Traditions* (1952) that the tradition of the Holy Maul survived in the remoter parts of Shropshire and in Staffordshire until quite recent times.

The practice of hitting the old on the head once they had become 'effœte' is reported from several times and places. The Latin geographer Pomponius Mela (fl. 40 A.D.) tells us that in Sardinia there was a law which allowed sons to kill their fathers with a cudgel when they got old, and in the North such a custom is said to have survived very late, especially around the Baltic. From Prussia comes the tale that a Count Schulenberg once rescued an old man who was being bludgeoned to death by his sons at a place called Jammerholz or 'Woeful Wood'. The old man lived another twenty years as his hall-porter – so much for being 'of no more use'. Similarly, a Countess of Mansfeld in the fourteenth century saved an old man from being done to death on Luneberg Heath, while our own king George II, returning from hunting in the Göhrde Walde, saved a peasant from death at the hands of his grandson, who had already dug his grave.

Were it not for these apparently historical instances, one might think it no more than a tale, an 'old Countrie Story', for most reports of the killing of the old set it in the distant past or faraway places, among the Hyperboreans or (in the medieval *Queste del Graal*) the outlandish 'men of Wales'. But it seems to be something more than travellers' tales of Blemmyae and Sciapods – a remnant of ancient custom. Whether or not the actual *practice* survived into

'Let em take this Hatchet and knock him on ye head':
effigy on the Bargates Almshouses, Leominster

recorded times, the report of it has been kept alive partly for its shock-value (cf. the long-lived tradition of the ritual murder of children by Jews under **Lincoln**, p.239) and partly, one suspects, for a certain sadistic pleasure in the telling akin to that derived from tales of child-eating ogres, for many centuries used to scare little children witless.

BERKELEY CASTLE, GLOUCESTERSHIRE Sheet 162
ST 6898

Berkeley Castle had a sinister reputation even before the murder there in 1327 of Edward II. William of Malmesbury (*ca.* 1090–1143) in his chronicle under the year 1065 tells the story of 'The Witch of Berkeley':

There resided at Berkeley a woman addicted to witchcraft . . . and skilled in ancient augury . . . On a certain day . . . a jack-daw, which was a very great favourite, chattered a little more loudly than usual. On hearing which the woman's . . . countenance grew pale, and deeply groaning, 'This day,' said she, 'my plough has completed its last furrow; to-day I shall hear of, and suffer, some dreadful calamity.'

Even as she spoke, a messenger arrived who told her that her son and his whole family had met with death by accident. She sent for her remaining children, who were a monk and a nun, and to them confessed her witchcraft. She told them that, though they could not help her soul, they might yet save her body by sewing up her corpse in the skin of a stag and laying it on its back in a stone coffin. This they were to fasten with three iron chains. If she lay secure for three nights, on the fourth day they should bury her, though she feared that the earth might refuse to receive her.

They carried out her instructions, but all was in vain, for on the first two nights, the devils burst open the door of the church, though it had been bolted, and broke asunder two of the chains:

On the third night, about cock-crow, the whole monastery seemed to be overthrown from its very foundation, by the clamour of the approaching enemy. One devil, more terrible . . . than the rest, and of loftier stature, broke the gates to shivers . . . He proceeded . . . towards the coffin, and calling on the woman by name, commanded her to rise. She replying that she could not on account of the chains: 'You shall be loosed,' said he . . . and directly he broke the chain . . . as though it had been flax. He also beat down the cover of the coffin with his foot, and taking her by the hand, before them all, he dragged her out of the church. At the doors appeared a black horse, proudly neighing, with iron hooks projecting over his whole back; on which the wretched creature was placed, and, immediately . . . vanished from the eyes of the beholders; her pitiable cries, however . . . were heard for nearly the space of four miles.

This story is made up of medieval stock-in-trade: Charles Martel was similarly carried off by devils at his death, and the demonic black horse is reminiscent of the one that appeared at **Wandlebury**

Camp (p.202). It is none the less horrifying and clearly comes from the age of belief – the great demon is nothing like the Devil of later folklore, often a gullible buffoon.

The 'Witch of Berkeley' seems not to have survived in local tradition unless it is to be connected with what John Smith of Nibley (1567–1640), steward of Berkeley Hundred, tells us in notes he made about Berkeley Castle concerning a monstrous toad. Out of a well-like dungeon in the Keep, 'as tradition tells', in the reign of Henry VII, was drawn a toad 'of an incredible bignes, which in the deepe dry dust in the bottome thereof, had doubtlesse lived ... divers hundred of yeares'. He himself had seen, nearly half a century before, the 'portraicture' of this toad on the door of the great hall, 'in bredth ... more then a foot, neere 16. inches, and in length more', and been assured by 'divers aged persons' it was the exact size of the real toad. Since he first saw it, it had been 'outworne with time', but in the eighteenth century a stuffed animal skin in the hall was being pointed out by the old wives of Berkeley as the toad. Toads were, of course, numbered among the familiars of witches.

Berkeley Castle, still lived in by the Berkeley family, is open to the public. For times, see *HHC&G*.

BRERETON HALL, CHESHIRE

Sheet 118
SJ 7865

> A wonder it is that I shall tell you, and yet no other than I haue heard verified upon the credit of many credible persons, and commonlie beleeved: That before any heire of this house of the *Breretons* dieth, there bee seene in a poole adjoining, bodies of trees swimming for certaine daies together.

So says Camden in his *Britannia* (trans. Holland, 1610). Among the many family death-warnings in this country, the Brereton omen is distinguished by its long history and its celebration by famous authors. Sir Philip Sidney places it second only to Stonehenge in his sonnet 'The Seven Wonders of England' (*ca.* 1581), and Michael Drayton includes it in the *Poly-olbion* (1612). In the nineteenth century it was to inspire 'The Vassal's Lament for the Fallen Tree' by Felicia Hemans – a name now little known, but 'The Boy Stood on the Burning Deck' is hers.

Why such a superstition should be attached to this 'poole' is unknown, but possibly it was because it had a forbidding appearance: Drayton calls it 'that black ominous Mere . . . of neighbours, *Black-mere* nam'd, of strangers, Breretons-Lake'. As for the tradition itself, there was once a widespread belief that trees gave warning of death. It may have been this that Shakespeare had in mind when in *Richard III* he wrote:

> 'Tis thought the king is dead; we will not stay –
> The bay trees in our country are all wither'd.

Certainly, Lupton, in his *Thousand Notable Things* (1579) reports: 'If a fyre tree be touched, wythered, or burned with lyghtning: it sygnifies, that the maister or mistresse therof shall shortly dye', and it was still commonly held in West Sussex in the 1860s that to dream of a tree being uprooted in your garden was a forewarning of your death. Sometimes particular trees acted as family death-warnings, often by the shedding of a branch (as at **Cuckfield Park**, p.104; **Dalhousie Castle**, p.443), and this may take us back to the ancient notion of a 'guardian tree'.

I am uncertain quite where on the map to locate this legend. Drayton's Blackmere or Brereton's Lake, first mentioned, as *Brerton Mere*, in 1445, is, according to J. McNeal Dodgson in *The Place-Names of Cheshire*, Pt 2 (1970), identical with Brereton Pool (SJ 7765). However, in *Knutsford, Its Traditions and History* (1859), Henry Green attaches the tale to 'Bagmere', once an extensive lake, which was drained and brought into cultivation in the eighteenth century, and now survives only as the moated site of Bag Mere (SJ 7964). The similarity between 'Blackmere' and 'Bagmere' might lead one to suppose that the two were identical, and this is indeed what Egerton Leigh in his *Ballads and Legends of Cheshire* (1867) tells us when he speaks of the Mere as being known by the three names 'Brereton's lake', 'Blackmere' and 'Bagmere'. But McNeal Dodgson does not connect Blackmere ('black pool') and Bag Mere ('bog pool'), and nor apparently did Camden, who begins his piece on Brereton by saying that the 'Dan . . . flowing out of the *Poole* called *Bagmere* passeth by *Brereton*.' He then goes on to speak of the house and the tradition attached to the 'poole adjoining', as if 'the Poole called Bagmere' and the 'poole adjoining' were quite distinct. It does not seem possible from the map today that Brereton Pool and Bag Mere were part of the same lake before draining, so has the tradition been transferred from Blackmere to Bag Mere because of the similarity of name, or was Drayton mistaken in equating Brereton's Lake and Blackmere? The map-makers are no help: the pictorial map of Cheshire in *Poly-olbion* shows only Brereton's Lake, other early maps up to and including Burdett (1777) only Bag Mere. All we can do is visit both.

CLUN FOREST, SHROPSHIRE   Sheet 137
                                              SO 2186

> Clunton and Clunbury,
> Clungunford and Clun,
> Are the quietest places
> Under the sun,

says one version of a folk-rhyme recorded in the nineteenth century. Quiet enough, certainly, for the peace-loving fairies, for Clun Forest is the setting of one of England's oldest fairytales, the story of Edric Wild and his fairy wife.

Walter Map, writing in the twelfth century, says that Edric Wild (in Latin *sylvaticus*, the forest-man or the savage) was 'so named from his bodily activity and his rollicking talk and deeds'. He was lord of the manor of Ledbury North, and a man of great prowess. Once when he was returning late from hunting through wild country, uncertain of his path, and accompanied only by a page,

> he . . . came upon a large building at the edge of the forest . . . and when he was near it, seeing a light inside, he looked in and saw a great dance of numbers of noble ladies. They were most comely to look upon, and finely clad in fair habits of linen . . . and were greater and taller than our women . . . They were circling with airy motion . . . and from their subdued voices singing . . . a delicate sound came to his ears; but their words he could not understand.

One of them seemed to him fairer than the rest, and seized with a sudden and uncontrollable passion for her, he rushed inside the house, snatched her up and carried her off. For three days and three nights she spoke not a word, but on the fourth day she acknowledged him as her husband and said he would prosper henceforth 'until you reproach me either with the sisters from whom you snatched me, or the place or wood or anything thereabout, from which I come: but from that day you will fall away from happiness, and when I am gone you will fail . . .'

He swore to be faithful to her and they were married. News of these events came to the ears of William the Bastard, newly on the English throne, and he sent for the pair to see if what he had heard were true. They brought to London with them many witnesses, and depositions from those who could not come, and he was convinced of the truth of their story. 'A great proof of her fairy nature was the great beauty of the woman, the like of which had never been seen or heard of . . .'

Satisfied, William sent them home again, but trouble was to follow:

> It happened later, after the lapse of many years, that Edric, coming back from hunting about the third hour of the night and not finding her, called her and bade her be summoned, and because she was slow to come said, with an angry look: 'Was it your sisters that kept you so long?' The rest of his abuse was addressed to the air, for when her sisters were named she vanished.

At once repentant, Edric sought the spot where he had first found her, but though he called her day and night, she never returned, and he shortly after died of grief. He left an heir, Alnod, son of the fairy wife, who later presented the manor of Ledbury to the bishops of Hereford, in whose possession it continued into Map's own day.

The story of the fairy wife lost by the breaking of a condition she had imposed is widespread and ancient – one form of it is the classical legend of Cupid and Psyche, although here the supernatural partner is the husband. The proof of Edric's wife's fairy nature was her beauty, and it has been suggested that outstandingly beautiful women were once nicknamed 'fairy' or 'fay', and later explained as actual fairies. At all events, fairies were in the Middle Ages reckoned among the ancestors of several noble families, notably the Counts of Poitou, descended from the fairy Melusine, who after her husband broke the vital condition – that he should never see her naked – continued to haunt the ramparts of the Castle of Lusignan as a family death-warning. Several other great families actually altered their pedigrees to include her as an ancestress – the ruling house of Luxembourg, for example – and indeed Map may have retold this story of Edric and his fairy wife as a compliment to his patron, Henry II, who himself numbered Melusine among his forebears.

Map knew another story of a fairy wife, caught by Gwestin Gwestiniog when she came out of **Llangorse Lake** (p.346) to dance in the moonlight. In later Welsh folklore, too, the fairy wife usually has her home in a lake, as at Llyn-y-Fan-Fach in Dyfed. Melusine herself was a water spirit, and the reason why she and other fairy wives acquiesced in their marriages by capture is given by Paracelsus in his *Book of nymphs, sylphs, pigmies and salamanders and of other spirits* (1566), where he says that of the elementals it is the nymphs or undines of the water element who most resemble men, whom they wish to marry in order to gain immortal souls (a theme that reappears in Hans Andersen's 'Little Mermaid').

The story of Edric Wild and his fairy wife is a notable example of how traditional tales can become attached to historical persons very shortly after their lifetime. Walter Map was writing *ca.* 1180, and we first hear of Edric in 1067, when, according to the version of the Anglo-Saxon Chronicle kept at Worcester, 'Edric the Wild and the Welsh rose in revolt and attacked the garrison at Hereford and inflicted heavy losses on them.' He held Shropshire against the Conqueror for three years, but made peace with him in 1070, and in 1072, when William launched an expedition against Scotland, Edric accompanied him.

What happened to him in the end is uncertain. According to the Domesday Book, he owned manors all over Herefordshire and Shropshire, and even into Wales, though his main holdings were concentrated in the hills of south-west Shropshire – the Long Mynd, Stiperstones, Clun Forest area – and around Wigmore in Herefordshire. By 1087, when the Domesday Book was compiled, every one of these properties was in Norman hands, notably those of Ralph Mortimer of Wigmore, and the fifteenth-century chronicler of the Mortimer family tells us that Sir Ralph 'by the power of his sword and of fortune' won Edric's lands after besieging him in Wigmore castle and handing him over in chains to the King, who condemned him to perpetual imprisonment. This may be a garbled account of a rebellion of 1075 led by Roger, Earl of Hereford. Edric might have joined this revolt and tried to hold Wigmore for Roger, but been brought down by his fall. Equally, the story may have been invented as a cover for pure piracy and to show a Norman Mortimer triumphing over an English hero.

Like that other leader of the English resistance, Hereward the Wake (see **Ely**, p.181), Edric Wild became the focus for many floating traditions. In the nineteenth century, he was still remembered as the leader of the Fairy Rade (see **Hereford**, p.306), appearing as a portent of war, riding over the hills in the direction of the enemy's country. This tradition came from a miner's daughter from Rorrington (SJ 3000), on the edge of Edric's lands, who said that her father had seen them heading south in Napoleon's time, and that she and her father had both seen them riding northwards at Minsterley (SJ 3705) in 1853 or 1854, just before the outbreak of the Crimean War. Edric, called 'Wild Edric' in Shropshire tradition, was mounted on a white horse at the head of the band, and rode with his wife, Lady Godda, beside him. The girl watched them out of sight over the hills to the north.

The account was given 'some years ago' to the girl's mistress, who repeated it to Charlotte Burne. But Miss Burne adds cautiously (1883): 'I never succeeded in getting a second version of this curious story, and the woman who told it could not be traced.' We might well be chary of accepting at face value some of the features of her tale, which includes details of Saxon costume which sound as if they have been added on for 'authenticity'. As to the name 'Lady Godda', in Germany the leader of the Wild Hunt was sometimes Frau Gauden or Gode, condemned to hunt for evermore because in life she had declared 'The chase is better than Heaven!' The Welsh told this same story of *Mallt y Nos*, 'Matilda of the Night' (see **Llowes**, p.349), but should we believe in a Lady Godda handed down in English tradition from early times, or in one conscientiously got up in Old English by someone who had read Jacob Grimm's account of Frau Gauden, published in 1835 (though to be fair not in English till 1883)?

For the rest, the story has the authentic ring of English folklore – Edric and his wife wear green, the traditional fairy colour, and the miner bids his daughter cover her face, all but the eyes, and on no account to speak as the cavalcade passes, lest she go mad, and these are precautions commonly taken when meeting the Wild Hunt, or the related phantom coaches, or Black Dogs. Indeed, in the nineteenth century, the ghost of Wild Edric was said to haunt the hills round Church Stretton (SO 4953) in the form of a huge

black dog with fiery eyes, much like the Norfolk Shuck (see
Bungay, p.176).

Edric's manor of Ledbury North is now Lydbury North (SO 3585), near
Bishop's Castle.

CONGLETON, CHESHIRE   Sheet 118
                                                          SJ 8663

> Congleton rare, Congleton rare,
> Sold the Bible to pay for a bear

says a traditional Cheshire folk-rhyme printed in the *Saturday
Review*, 27 April 1889. Bear-baiting, like bull-baiting and cock-
fighting, was a popular feature of Wakes Week in several places
right up to the nineteenth century, and the story goes that when
the town bear died just before the Congleton Wakes in 1662, the
citizens gave the money set aside for a new Bible for the church to
the bearward instead, to buy the town a new bear.

Egerton Leigh (in his *Ballads and Legends of Cheshire*, 1867)
gives the Congleton tradition not as a rhyme but a proverb –
'Congleton Town where they sold the Bible to buy a Bear'. In his
time the Congleton people used to claim that they had only
swapped the *old* Bible for a bear, having already bought a new one.
But Leigh illustrates Congleton's sense of priorities with extracts
from the town accounts:

	£	s	d
1589. Paid the Trafford's man the bearward	0	4	4
1601. Gave to the bearward at the great cock-fight	0	6	8
1613. Fetching the bears at the wakes, 3. 6d.; ditto			
two more bears, 1s.; bearward, 15s.	0	19	6

whereas a certain Mr Carr in 1599 only got five shillings for
preaching four sermons.

One might well believe the Congleton tradition to be literally
true, were it not that the very same story and a similar rhyme are
attached to Clifton-upon-Dunsmore, Warwickshire.

DEERHURST, GLOUCESTERSHIRE   Sheet 150
                                                    SO 8729

> There goes a story, that a serpent of a prodigious bigness was
> a great grievance to all the country about Deerhurst, by
> poisoning the inhabitants, and killing their cattle. The inhabi-
> tants petitioned the king, and a proclamation was issued out,
> that whosoever should kill the serpent, should enjoy an estate
> on Walton hill in this parish, which then belonged to the
> crown. One John Smith, a labourer, undertook it, and suc-
> ceeded; for finding the serpent lying in the sun, with his scales
> ruffled up, he struck between the scales with his ax, and struck
> off his head.

Thus Sir Robert Atkyns, in *The Ancient and Present State of
Glocestershire* (1712), tells the story of the Deerhurst dragon.
Samuel Rudder, who in his *New History of Gloucestershire* (1779)
repeats the tale almost word for word, adds (without telling us
where he got it) the detail that John Smith put out milk for the
'serpent', which it drank and so fell asleep. Whether he had heard
this locally or whether it came from some other tale is unknown –
dragons fond of milk are also reported at **Bisterne** (p.53); Lambton
Castle, County Durham; Mordiford, Hereford & Worcester; and
Sexhow, North Yorkshire. The Deerhurst monster is a 'serpent' –
we assume 'dragon' from similar tales and from the description –
and in countries as far apart as Sweden and India snakes have been
thought to be fond of milk.

Deerhurst's dragon legend may have been prompted, and has
been kept alive, by the ferocious animal heads carved in stone in its
Anglo-Saxon church. One or all of these are said to be the
Deerhurst Dragon. The story probably originated as a tenure
legend, invented to explain the ownership of the estate on 'Walton
hill' (SO 8928) which in Atkyns's day still belonged to a family
named Smith. Moreover, 'Mr Lane, who married a widow of that
family, has the ax in his possession' (cf. the **Sockburn** falchion,
p.419).

The Priory church at Deerhurst is one of the two finest Anglo-Saxon
churches in Britain. One of the animal heads can be seen over its outer
doorway, the others are inside. Just up the lane from the church is Odda's

Chapel (SO 869298) built in 1056 by the lord of the manor, Earl Odda, a friend of Edward the Confessor – its dedication stone is now in the Ashmolean Museum, Oxford. Odda's Chapel: AM (any reasonable time).

HANGMAN'S STONE, PRESTON, NR CIRENCESTER, GLOUCESTERSHIRE

Sheet 163
SP 0400

> . . . at the distance of two miles from the town, but in this parish, there stands an antient, rude stone, about four feet high, lately painted and mark'd as a mile stone. This is vulgarly called *Hangman's Stone*, because, it is said, a fellow resting a sheep thereon, (which he had stolen, and tied its legs together for the convenience of carrying it) was there strangled, by the animal's getting its legs round his neck in struggling.

Samuel Rudder, who tells this story in his *New History of Gloucestershire* (1799), thought that the original name of the stone might have been 'Hereman-stone' (from OE *here-man*, 'a soldier') and that it was 'an antient monument for some military person' possibly connected with nearby Ermine Street.

In fact the stone probably got its name from the story – the same tale of a sheep-thief strangled by his sheep is told on the Blackdown Hills and in Allendale, and was attached to another 'Hangman's Stone' near Northleach (SP 1114).

In the *Journal of the Gloucestershire Society for Industrial Archaeology* for 1983, J. Hartland of the Cirencester Archaeological and Historical Society turnpike study group reports that 'this stone has not been seen for some 40 years'. About two miles out of Cirencester on the Cricklade road, it was re-used as a milestone when the road was turnpiked in 1758.

HEREFORD, HEREFORD & WORCESTER (formerly HEREFORDSHIRE)

Sheet 149
SO 5139

Into the River Wye at or near Hereford vanished King Herla and his Rade, one of the earliest appearances of the Wild Hunt. Our account of Herla comes from a medieval book of gossip, *De Nugis Curialium* or 'Courtiers' Trifles', written *ca.* 1190 by the Herefordshire-born Walter Map. 'One of the most ancient of the British kings', as Map calls him, Herla was once visited at his court by a pigmy riding on a goat. The mannikin told him he was lord of many kings, and that he wished to be a guest at Herla's wedding. 'Let this be a lasting agreement between us, that I shall first attend your wedding and you mine on the same day a year hence.' With that, he vanished from sight, but on the King's wedding day returned with a host of followers and his own pavilions for them to sit in. Out of the pavilions darted his servants, bearing food served on gold plate and wine in vessels each carved from a single gem. Herla's own servants sat idle, while the pigmies went to and fro, their garments and jewels making them shine like lights. During the feast, their king came to where Herla sat and reminded him of his agreement, then, without waiting for a reply, departed 'about cock-crow'.

A year later he called on Herla to fulfil his promise, and led the King and his men into a cave in a cliff. After an interval of darkness they came, in light which seemed to proceed not from sun or moon but a myriad lamps, to a great palace. Here was celebrated in its turn the pigmy king's wedding, after which Herla and his companions took their leave, laden with gifts of horses, dogs and hawks, and hunting gear. 'The pigmy escorted them as far as the place where darkness began, and then presented the king with a small bloodhound to carry, strictly enjoining him that on no account must any of his train dismount until that dog leapt from the arms of his bearer . . .' When they came once more to the light of day, they met an old shepherd whom Herla asked for news of the Queen. He gazed at him with astonishment, and said he could hardly understand his speech, as he himself was a Saxon. The only queen of that name of whom he had heard was a queen of the ancient Britons, the wife of King Herla, 'and he, the old story says, disappeared in company with a pigmy at this very cliff, and was never seen on earth again, and it is now two hundred year since the Saxons took possession of this kingdom.'

The King, who thought he had made a stay of but three days, could scarce sit his horse for amazement. Some of his company, forgetting the pigmy's orders, dismounted before the dog had alighted, and in a moment fell into dust. Whereupon the King . . . warned the rest under pain of a like death not to touch the earth before the alighting of the dog. The dog has not yet alighted.

And the story says that this King Herla still holds on his mad course with his band in eternal wanderings, without stop or stay. Many assert that they have often seen the band: but recently, it is said, in the first year of the coronation of our King Henry, it ceased to visit our land in force as before. In that year it was seen by many Welshmen to plunge into the Wye, the river of Hereford. From that hour the phantom journeying has ceased . . .

The pigmy king who visited Herla was clearly a fairy – Oberon, the fairy king, is the size of a three-year-old child in the medieval romance *Huon of Bordeaux*, and not much bigger, perhaps, was the child-fairy Malekin of **Dagworth** (p.183). The fairy or Otherworld kingdom entered through a cave appears in other early fairytales (cf. **Woolpit**, p.210), while the shining of the fairies like lights and their vanishing at cock-crow are recurrent themes of later folklore.

Herla's story unites two different traditions: first, the supernatural lapse of time in fairyland, found all over the world, especially in the Celtic lands, although best known, perhaps, from Washington Irving's 'Rip van Winkle' (1819–20). The second tradition is that of the Wild Hunt, which drifts naturally towards fairytales because of the idea of a hunt riding in procession – the fairy knights and ladies of human or more than human size met with in Celtic legend and medieval romance are often engaged thus in the 'Fairy Rade'.

And just as the home of the fairies was often 'under the hill', so on the Continent the Wild Hunt used to emerge from a hill or mound. The Hunt was composed of dead souls, and it is thought that the fairies, too, descended in part from the dead in their burial mounds. One hill supposed to be the home of the Wild Hunt was the Hörsellberg in Thuringia – which was also the Venusberg of the Tannhäuser legend, entered through a cave leading to a brilliantly lit underground kingdom, a place of feasting and delight. Though we think of 'Tannhäuser' as German, its beginnings were very probably Celtic, embodying Celtic beliefs about the Otherworld. It was undoubtedly because the fairyland in the Herla story, too, was felt by medieval listeners to be Celtic, that Herla is called a British king. But the clue of thread weaves round and round – his name is not Celtic, but belongs to the Wild Hunt (see **Peterborough**, p.187).

KINGTON, HEREFORD & WORCESTER   Sheet 148
(formerly HEREFORDSHIRE)   SO 3057

The most troublesome ghost in Herefordshire in the nineteenth century was Black Vaughan of Hergest Court (SO 283554), usually identified as Sir Thomas Vaughan, who died at the Battle of Banbury in 1469 and whose effigy can be seen in Kington church.

He was so wicked that he could not rest after death, but came back 'stronger and stronger all the while', until at last he grew so bold that he would appear in broad daylight. He used to upset wagons of hay and leap on to the crupper behind farmers' wives riding to market. He would take the form of a fly to torment the horses, and to cap his mad career came into Kington church in the form of a bull. Finally people grew so afraid of him that 'they got twelve parsons, with twelve candles, to wait in the church to try and read him down into a silver snuff-box'. So said the old man who told Mrs Leather the tale, duly recorded in her *Folk-Lore of Herefordshire* (1912). The story continues very much like the one told at Hyssington in Powys of 'The Flayed Bull of Bagbury'. The parsons began to 'read', but one by one their candles went out, except for the parson of Kington's. He was braver than the rest, 'though to tell the truth, he was nearly blind and not a pertickler sober man'. He read and read and read, and Black Vaughan felt himself going down and down and down, until the snuff-box was nearly shut. Then the parson said: 'Vaughan, where will thou be laid?' and he answered, 'Anywhere, anywhere, but not in the Red Sea!' So they shut him up in the snuff-box, and buried him for a thousand years at the bottom of Hergest Pool. 'But the time is nearly up!'

An oak tree near Hergest was pointed out as the spot where Black Vaughan used to stand – the grass never grew there again and his two footprints were plain to see upon the ground. A man from Kington told Mrs Leather he had seen 'Vaughan's footmarks' as a boy, but by her time they had vanished. As, indeed, had the oak, felled some years before by a man who thereafter went mad.

Reading a ghost down, i.e. making it dwindle by reading at it without cease from the Bible or Prayer Book, was the traditional method of laying a ghost in the Marches. The ghost's request not to be thrown into the Red Sea also appears in other stories. Usually, like Brer Rabbit and the Briar Patch, this is exactly where

Black Vaughan and Gethin the Terrible: effigies of Sir Thomas Vaughan and his wife, St Mary's Church, Kington, Hereford & Worcester

he *is* thrown. But unlike Brer Rabbit, the ghost is not up to tricks – the Red Sea really is the last place he wants to be. Why this should be so is not clear, but one suggestion (made in 1812, so such stories must go back to at least the eighteenth century) is that it stems from the Book of Tobit, where the Evil Spirit is said to fly to the utmost parts of Egypt and be bound there.

That a ghost might leap up behind one on one's horse was a common fear in the district – to be reckoned with in neighbouring Shropshire were the horrible Man-Monkey near Woodseaves (SJ 6931), and Madam Pigott, who haunted the lanes between Chetwynd and Edgmond (SJ 7321–7219). The dobies of the West Riding and the buckies of Lowland Scotland, too, would leap up behind riders and attempt to garrotte them.

As for Black Vaughan's footprints, burnt by his evil passions into the grass, they have a parallel in the 'Brothers' Steps' of **Tavistock Square** (p.152). The same belief is expressed in a proverb current in the eighteenth century: 'Where the Great Turk's horse once treads, the grass will never grow.'

See also **Offa's Dyke** (p.316). Beside Sir Thomas Vaughan, on his altar tomb in the south chapel of St Mary's Church, lies his wife Ellen, who was popularly known as 'Gethin the Terrible', because she avenged her brother's death by shooting his murderer at an archery contest.

KNUTSFORD, CHESHIRE

Knutsford, best known for its sanding custom, said like its name to commemorate King Cnut (ON *Knútr*), who after fording the river shook the sand from his shoes as a wedding passed by, is also the possessor of a fine churchyard legend.

An old woman was once buried in the Old Churchyard with a bag of nuts under her head, as she herself had requested. Once buried, however, she found them uncomfortable and turned over in her grave. But this side was just as bad as the other one had been, so she got out of her coffin, and sat on her tombstone, shivering, poor soul, and cracked and ate the nuts, scattering the shells all round. When the bag was empty, she shook it out and put it under her head, and with this for a pillow was at last at rest. But one nut had been missed and fallen out of the bag, and this one took root on her grave, growing in time to a hazel tree. 'I have myself plucked a leaf from one of its branches,' wrote the local historian Henry Green, in his *Knutsford, Its Traditions and History* (1859), but although the tree was looked on with wonder, it had already in his time been reduced to a 'shattered stem' by being raided by truants for its nuts.

Why was the old woman buried with a bag of nuts, traditionally associated with marriage and childbirth? The story might be an echo of one of the *Hundred Mery Tales* (1526), in which a man who dearly loved nuts asked his executors to bury him with a bagful, and someone later seen with such a bag was mistaken for his ghost. A version of this, in which a man goes to the churchyard to get the bag of nuts that lies under his mother's head, survived at Calver in Derbyshire into the nineteenth century and was included by S. O. Addy in his *Household Tales* (1895).

Originally a wedding-custom, sanding is now practised only on Royal May Day, despite its name any convenient day in May or June. Write to or ring North West Tourist Board, The Last Drop Village, Bromley Cross, Bolton, Lancashire BL7 9PZ. Tel. (0204) 591511.

MARDEN, HEREFORD & WORCESTER   Sheet 149
(formerly HEREFORDSHIRE)   SO 5147

Current in Mrs E. M. Leather's day and included in her *Folk-Lore of Herefordshire* (1912) was the tradition that Marden church in former times stood close to the river, and that by some mischance one of its bells had been allowed to fall into it. It was immediately seized by a mermaid who carried it to the bottom and held it fast, so that any number of horses could not move it. According to some, the people of Marden were told by a wise man how to recover it; others said that the bell itself gave instructions from the bottom of the river. At any rate, a team of white freemartins (heifers) was to be attached to the bell with yokes made of yew wood and bands of 'wittern', and it was to be drawn up in silence.

The instructions were followed and the bell hoisted to the bank, with the mermaid asleep inside it. But in his excitement, one of the drivers called out:

> 'In spite of all the devils in hell,
> Now we'll land Marden's great bell.'

This woke the mermaid, who darted back into the water again, taking the bell with her, and crying:

> 'If it had not been
> For your wittern bands
> And your yew tree pin,
> I'd have had your twelve free-martins in.'

The bell has never been recovered, and may still be heard ringing at the bottom of a deep pool in the river, in answer to the bells of the church.

Similar stories of lost bells were also told of Rostherne Mere and Combermere in Cheshire, and in Shropshire of Colemere, Shomere, and Berth Pool at Baschurch, though of these only Rostherne Mere also had a mermaid. The necessity for silence whilst seeking treasure is a common belief, whilst the white freemartins are an echo of oxen whose unblemished whiteness is the condition for recovering lost bells at Bosham and (in garbled form) Alfoldean, both in West Sussex, and at Oxenford, Surrey.

The Marden bell-legend was told to Mrs Leather by Mr Galliers of King's Pyon and 'completed from other oral versions'. Had it not been first recorded so long after the event, one might have thought it a case of verified folk-memory, for in 1848, in clearing out a pond at Marden, an ancient bronze bell was actually discovered. It lay under the mud and rubbish of centuries, and is of a Celtic type, rectangular, still with a loop by which it was suspended but its clapper gone. It may have had some association with St Ethelbert, king of the East Angles, murdered by Offa of Mercia in 794 A.D. (see **Offa's Dyke**, p.316). His body is traditionally said to have been buried by the River Lugg at Marden and only later translated to Hereford, to become the focus of a powerful cult – another proof of the English devotion to royal martyrs (cf. **Corfe Castle**, p.60 and **Hoxne**, p.182). The pond in which the Marden bell was found is very near the church, said to stand on the site of Ethelbert's grave. Legend tells us that when his body was lifted out of this grave, a miraculous spring gushed forth. Once resorted to for cures, it has now been dry for many years.

The Marden bell-legend incorporates the old folk-belief that 'wittern' or 'witty', i.e. rowan, was potent against witchcraft. In the mid nineteenth century in Herefordshire a piece of rowan would be placed above every cottage door and pigcot on May morning, and in Mrs Leather's time the saying was still current that 'the withy is the tree on which the devil hanged his mother'. The use of rowan in the yokes of oxen, as in the story, is mentioned earlier by Aubrey in his *Natural History and Antiquities of Surrey*, where, speaking of the 'whitty' tree, he says:

In Herefordshire they are not uncommon; and they used, when I was a boy, to make pinnes for the yoakes of their oxen of them, believing it had vertue to preserve them from being forespoken, as they call it; and they used to plant one by their dwellinghouse, believing it to preserve from witches and evill eyes.

The Marden bell can still be seen in Hereford City Museum, Broad Street, Hereford. For times of opening, see *M&G*. St Ethelbert's Well is behind the font in Marden church.

MITCHELL'S FOLD, CHIRBURY, SHROPSHIRE

> In times gone by, before anyone now living can remember, there was once a dreadful famine all about this country, and the people had like to be clemmed.* There were many more living in this part then, than what there are now, and times were very bad indeed. And all they had to depend upon was, that there used to come a fairy cow upon the hill, up at Mitchell's Fold, night and morning, to be milked. A beautiful pure white cow she was, and no matter how many came there to milk her, there was always enough for all, so long as every one that came only took one pailful. It was in this way: if any one was to milk her dry, she would go away and never come again; but so long as every one took only a pailful apiece, she never would be dry ... Well, and at last there came an old witch, Mitchell her name was. A bad old woman she was, and did a deal of harm, and had a spite against everybody. And she brought a riddle, and milked the cow into that, and of course the poor thing couldn't fill it. And the old woman milked her, and milked her, and at last she milked her dry, and the cow was never seen there again, not after.

This is the story of 'The White Cow of Mitchell's Fold' as given by Charlotte Burne in her *Shropshire Folk-Lore* (1883). Held to account for the name of the partly dismantled stone circle on Corndon Hill, the legend was well known locally in Miss Burne's time, and is a version of a widespread tale of a fairy cow who gives her milk freely in time of famine until someone abuses her gift. At Audlem in Cheshire (SJ 6644) the tale is told to account for a huge bone displayed in the tower of Doddington Park and said to be that of the fairy cow, who died of grief when she failed to fill the witch's sieve. At **South Lopham** (p.192), the cow stamped in anger and left her hoofprint forever on a stone. *Y Fuwch Laethwen* ('The Milk-white Milch Cow') appeared in the Vale of Towy (Tywi), and *Y Fuwch Frech* ('The Freckled Cow') pastured on Mynydd Hiraethog, Clwyd. Indeed, The Freckled Cow, like the cow of Mitchell's Fold, was associated with a stone circle, or the retaining circle of a cairn, destroyed between 1860 and 1870, near Clocaenog.

* clemmed – starved

Embedded in the legend is a piece of popular lore: milking cows dry or milking them until the blood came was one of the charges in real life levelled at witches.

According to Miss Burne's informant, the Mitchell's Fold witch got her deserts by being turned into stone, with other stones round her to keep her in – and hence the name. In sober truth it is more likely to be descriptive (cf. **Stonehenge**, p.77), coming from OE *micel*, *mycel*, meaning 'big', 'large'. By the seventeenth century, however, it was thought to be a personal name: in *ca*.1690 the Welsh antiquary Edward Llwyd writes it as 'Medgel's Fold'. In a letter written in 1752 to his brother, Dr A. C. Ducarel, James Ducarel reports:

> I must tell you that the country people have many legends, fables, and traditions concerning *Medgley's Fold*, where they say a great personage, I believe a Giant, use[d] to milk his cows ...

Cattle-owning giants are known elsewhere in England (cf. **Wade's Stone**, p.421) and the idea of a stone circle as the fold or pound of a supernatural being is embodied in the name of the prehistoric enclosure of Grimspound, Manaton, Devon (see under **Wansdyke**, p.83). Perhaps to a simple tradition of a giant's fold was later added the story of the fairy cow, but if so it had already happened by the mid eighteenth century. For in November 1753, William Stukeley noted of *'Midgel's Fold'* the same tale that Camden's translator Gough was thirty years later to add to the *Britannia*:

> On the north side of *Cornden* hill ... is a circle of stones called *Madges Pinfold*, or *Milking fold*, from the vulgar tradition of a cow that gave milk there enough for all honest people that wanted, till some wicked person or witch milked her into a sieve; from which time she disappeared ...

Either Gough had not heard it all or between 1753 and 1883 the legend was still growing – Charles Harteshorne in his *Salopia Antiqua* (1841) tells us that the fairy cow afterwards wandered off to Dunsmore Heath where she became the famous Dun Cow killed by Guy of Warwick (see **Guy's Cliffe**, p.269).

'There used to be more stones than there are now,' said Miss Burne's informant, 'but they have been taken away at one time or

The wicked witch of Mitchell's Fold milking the fairy cow: north capital,
Holy Trinity Church, Middleton-in-Chirbury, Shropshire

another. There was a farmer lived by there, and he blew up some
of them and took away the pieces to put round his horsepond, but
he never did no good after.' Though misfortune was commonly
believed to overtake those who meddled with ancient stones, this
has not deterred the vandals. Mitchell's Fold today has only fifteen
visible stones, but may once have had double this number.

AM (any reasonable time). The story of the fairy cow can be seen on a
capital in Middleton-in-Chirbury church (SO 2999), carved by the vicar,
the Rev. W. Brewster, in 1879.

OFFA'S DYKE, KINGTON to KNIGHTON,   Sheet 148
HEREFORD & WORCESTER   SO 2956
(formerly HEREFORDSHIRE)

> Taffy was a Welshman,
> Taffy was a thief . . .

and it was partly to prevent Taffy running off with his cattle and
sheep that Offa, king of Mercia 757–96 A.D., undertook the
building of the great earthwork that bears his name. A bank

generally ditched on the Welsh-facing, westward side, it runs (with some gaps where there were natural barriers) for 169 miles (270.4 km) from Prestatyn in Clwyd to Sedbury on the Severn estuary, just east of the River Wye. The alignment was chosen to prevent the Welsh raiding to the east, and was set out to give as wide a view westward as possible. It is unlikely that the whole length was manned, and it was largely a formal frontier which must have been agreed with the Welsh, who evidently gained some concessions – place-names along the border show that several Anglian settlements were given up to them. After more than a thousand years, with only minor modifications, the dyke remains the boundary between England and Wales, a lasting monument to the name of Offa.

For the curious fact is that earthworks in Britain are generally reckoned to be the work of Woden or the Devil – yet here, despite the scale of the undertaking, which might well have suggested supernatural power, the real builder was remembered in the name, in Welsh *Clawdd Offa*, in English Offa's Dyke. (Though the English name is recorded only from the thirteenth century, as *Offedik*, this almost certainly goes back to Old English *Offan dīc*.) Offa was remembered both because of the impact of this great work and because he was a powerful king who impressed himself on his contemporaries. For a third of a century he was overlord of the Southern English, and was the only ruler in Western Europe who could presume to treat as an equal with the Emperor Charlemagne.

More than that, he carried about him the charisma of legend. He was the namesake and descendant of the semi-legendary Offa of Angeln (the Anglian homeland in Schleswig), of whom many tales survived into both English and Danish tradition. Like the original Hamlet, he was an 'unpromising hero', the lubberly boy who eventually shows his worth. There was also a well-known story about his wife, of which more later. This Offa, says *Widsith*, an Anglo-Saxon poem of which the kernel goes back to the fourth century, drew between his own people and the *Myrgingas* a boundary *bi Fifeldor*, along the Eider, and this frontier was observed by the Angles and Swabians ever after. We can scarcely doubt that Offa of Mercia, greatest of the Anglian kingdoms in England, had this tradition in mind when he drew his own boundary from sea to sea against the Welsh.

But this associating of himself with the traditions of the Continental Angles was to prove a two-edged sword. In the Anglo-Saxon epic *Beowulf* (perhaps eighth century), we hear that Offa of Angeln had a queen called Thryth, who seems to have been the subject of a tale much like *The Taming of the Shrew*, in which a haughty princess, perilous to her wooers, eventually became a model wife. Now the wife of Offa of Mercia happened to be called Cynethryth, and with two Offas and two ladies whose name was 'Thryth', the inevitable happened: the old legends of Offa the First were transferred to his descendant, Offa the Second.

In the *Lives of the Two Offas*, a Latin work written in about 1200 by a monk of St Albans, we learn that a beautiful but wicked girl, a kinswoman of Charlemagne, was because of some crime cast adrift in an open boat without a rudder or sail. She drifted to the shores of this country and was led before King Offa of Mercia. Her name was Drida (=Thryth) she said, and her banishment had been secured by certain men whose offers of marriage she had spurned. Offa was deceived by her beauty and married her, and from that time on she was called Quendrida, 'id est regina Drida' (OE *cwēn* = queen). But once married she showed her true colours and embarked on a series of plots and assassinations, including an attempt on the life of the King and the murder of Ethelbert of East Anglia, her daughter's suitor, at Offa's palace at Sutton Walls (see also **Marden**, p.312). But retribution finally overtook her – after many years, she was set on by robbers and thrown into a well, where she drowned. It was, says the monkish author, in thanksgiving for this release that Offa founded the abbey of St Albans.

The monk who wrote this story seems to have known more than one version of it, and may have been drawing on a tradition of his day, or repeating a tale invented at St Albans. For, like the legend of St Kenelm, a king of Mercia supposed to have been murdered by his wicked sister Quendryth (=Quendrida), it is a libel on 'Quendrida', and the monks of St Albans had a motive for this – they wished to clear their founder, Offa, of the murder of Ethelbert and so foisted it on to his wife. But whether they were encouraging a misconception that already existed, or spreading a slander of their own, they could not have done it but for the legend of the wicked Thryth. The coincidence of Thryth–Cynethryth–Quendryth in the stories of Offa I and II, and St Kenelm, is not as great

The notorious Drida cast adrift in her boat, BL MS Cotton Nero D.1

as it sounds. Almost half the women in the Mercian royal family had names that included 'thryth', so it is easy to see how such confusion arose. Indeed, such was the power of the old legend of the wicked queen somewhere in the pedigree of the Mercians, that even Offa's daughter, Eadburg, acquired a reputation for evil, though she had quite a different name.

The Offa's Dyke Path, opened in 1971, runs from Prestatyn to near Chepstow. The stretch between Kington and Knighton takes you past one of the best lengths of the earthwork, on Rushock Hill (SO 2959). An additional reason for starting at Kington is that you can walk past Hergest Court (for story see **Kington**, p.309), not to be confused with Hergest Croft (SO 284567) and its splendid gardens (times of opening in *HHC&G*). These houses are marked by name on the OS 1:25 000 map.

TEDSTONE DELAMERE, HEREFORD & WORCESTER (formerly HEREFORDSHIRE)

Sheet 149
SO 6958

In the bed of the Sapey brook between Tedstone Delamere and Upper Sapey (SO 6863) are blocks of stone with marks like horseshoes on them. The Herefordshire historian Duncumb, writing in 1812, gives a 'traditional account' of their origin, which he says in his time was 'still implicitly credited by the common people'. A mare and her colt were stolen in the night from a neighbouring farmer, some centuries before, and the farmer's daughter prayed that she and the servants might recover them by following their footprints. The trail was easy to follow until the footprints reached the brook, when they suddenly vanished. Suspecting that the thief had led the horses down the stream, the girl looked at the bed of the brook, and there plain to see in the solid rock were the horses' hoofmarks. Following them, they found the thief and the horses, some say in a spot called 'the Witchery Hole', others at 'the Hoar Stone'.

'Many pretended vestiges of the mare and colt are still pointed out in the channel of the brook by the credulous peasantry,' says Duncumb, 'and many more have been cut away by the felon chissel to deck the simple mantel-piece of the rustic naturalist.' But enough of the prints must have been left to keep the tradition alive to the end of the century, when was recorded the belief that the Hoar Stone was the robber, petrified for his crimes (cf. **Carreg Leidr**, p.335).

In a later version of the story, the hoofprints were those of a mare and colt that brought St Catherine Audley to Ledbury (SO 7138). 'Blessed Catherine of Ledbury' was a local saint who was miraculously guided to Ledbury by bells that rang without hands – Wordsworth retells the legend in a sonnet (1835).

TORBARROW HILL (TAR BARROWS),   Sheet 163
CIRENCESTER, GLOUCESTERSHIRE   SP 0202

Two men digging a gravel-pit at the foot of this hill, having sunk four yards deep, discovered an entrance into the hill, where they found several rooms with their furniture, which being touched, crumbled to dust. In one of them were several images and urns, some with ashes, others full of coins, with Latin inscriptions on them. Entering another, they were surprized at seeing the figure of a man in armour, having a truncheon in its hand, and a light, in a glass like a lamp, burning before it. At their first approach, the image made an effort to strike, so at the second step, but with greater force; but at the third it struck a violent blow, which broke the glass to pieces, and extinguished the light. Having a lanthorn, they had just time to observe, that on the left hand (I suppose of the figure) lay two heads embalmed, with long beards, and the skin looking like parchment, when hearing a hollow noise like a groan, they hastily quitted those dark appartments, and immediately the earth fell in, and buried all the curiosities.

Such is the account given by Samuel Rudder in his *New History of Gloucestershire* (1779) of a mysterious cavern found inside Torbarrow Hill. His source was a paper printed by William Budden in 1685 and the tale sounds like a highly coloured description of a barrow-breaking – from the Middle Ages on, tumuli were often rifled – and may be a treasure-seeker's version of 'the one that got away'.

The dramatic details are taken not from imagination, however, but from medieval tradition. The automaton treasure-guardian, the everlasting flame and the speaking head are found in tales about Gerbert, Pope Sylvester II, who because of his knowledge of mechanics and mathematics was remembered as a great magician. One story tells how there was in Rome an eternal flame before which stood the statue of an archer with an arrow aimed at the fire. An inscription on the statue read, 'If anyone touches me, I shall shoot.' One day someone touched the statue, it fired its arrow, and put out the fire, which could not be rekindled. In another tale, Gerbert and his servant find a cavern underground filled with treasure. In the passages stood golden knights, who as soon as anyone touched the treasure brandished their weapons. In the cavern was a chamber lit by a carbuncle, opposite which there stood the statue of a child with a bow in his hand. When Gerbert's servant pocketed a little knife, the golden knights set up a clamour and the statue of the boy let fly an arrow and put out the carbuncle. Gerbert and his man were unable to find their way out of the cave until the servant had given back the knife. In a third story Gerbert (like Roger Bacon) makes a magic head which speaks and foretells the future.

All three stories were subsequently told of the Roman poet Vergil – in later tradition transformed into a magician – and were widely known. They may derive from reports of the wonderful automata at the Byzantine court, and from pseudo-scientific beliefs concerning *asbestos*, whose name means something like 'unquench-able' and from this was wrongly assumed to be a mineral which, once lit, could never be extinguished. Camden in his *Britannia* (trans. Holland, 1610) also mentions a belief that the ancients possessed the art of dissolving gold into an oil that would burn in sepulchres untended for many ages.

Elements of these medieval stories eventually found their way into popular legend. The sleeping knights who guarded the treasure of Craig y Ddinas in Mid Glamorgan, for example, have much in common with Gerbert's golden warriors.

What Rudder refers to as Torbarrow Hill is the site of two burial mounds on Whiteway Farm (SP 031025) shown on Isaac Taylor's map of 1777 as 'Tar Barrows or Tarbury'. The main barrow had been opened about a dozen years before and nothing found but a small coin and a large square stone. Excavation in 1935 exposed what may have been this slab, but produced no other results.

THE WREKIN, SHROPSHIRE   Sheet 127
                                                      SJ 6308

Perhaps the best-known story in Shropshire is the one that describes the origin of the Wrekin. As Miss Burne tells it in 1883, there was once a wicked old giant in Wales who for some reason had a spite against the people of Shrewsbury. He made up his mind to dam the Severn and cause a flood that would drown the whole town, and accordingly off he set, carrying a spadeful of earth. He tramped mile after mile, trying to find the way, until at last he met a cobbler carrying a sack of old boots and shoes on his back, which he was taking from Shrewsbury home to Wellington to mend. The giant called out to him. 'I say,' he said, 'how far is it to Shrewsbury?' The cobbler asked him why he wanted to know, and the stupid giant told him. The cobbler saw it would never do to let him reach the town. 'Eh!' he said, 'you'll never get to Shrewsbury, not to-day, *nor* to-morrow. Why, look at me! *I'm* just come from Shrewsbury, and I've had time to wear out all these old boots and shoes on the road since I started.' And he showed him his sack. The giant couldn't carry his load any further, so he dropped it where he stood, and scraped his boots on the spade, and went off home again to Wales. And where he dropped his load, there stands the Wrekin, and where he scraped his boots is the little hill called The Ercall (SJ 645097).

'It is a story current among all classes, and told with many variations,' says Miss Burne. It was in circulation in the first half of her century, and is probably much older. The 'lying cobbler' tale occurs elsewhere – in neighbouring Herefordshire it is told of Robin Hood's Butts (Pyon Hill and Butthouse Knap) near Canon Pyon (SP 4549), and of the tumulus known as 'the Devil's Shovelful' at Shobdon (SO 3932). Here the vengeful person with the spade is the Devil, who seems often to have replaced the giant in 'giant as builder' stories – of the Wrekin legend, an elderly lady told Charlotte Burne: 'They generally call it the devil nowadays, but the older people say it was a giant.'

9
Wales

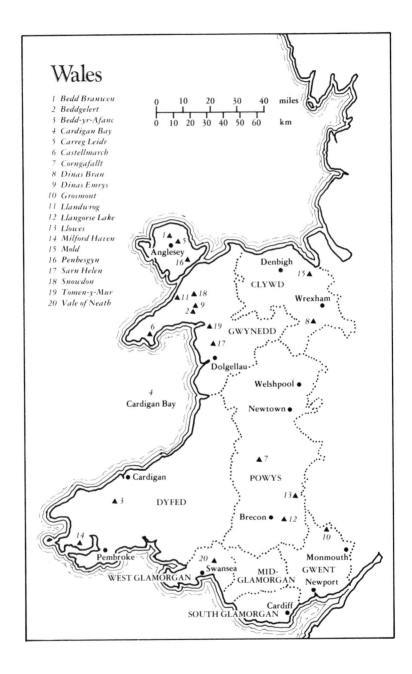

Wales

1 *Bedd Branwen*
2 *Beddgelert*
3 *Bedd-yr-Afanc*
4 *Cardigan Bay*
5 *Carreg Leidr*
6 *Castellmarch*
7 *Corngafallt*
8 *Dinas Bran*
9 *Dinas Emrys*
10 *Grosmont*
11 *Llandwrog*
12 *Llangorse Lake*
13 *Llowes*
14 *Milford Haven*
15 *Mold*
16 *Penhesgyn*
17 *Sarn Helen*
18 *Snowdon*
19 *Tomen-y-Mur*
20 *Vale of Neath*

0   10   20   30   40   miles

0 10 20 30 40 50 60   km

1 ▲ ▲ 5
Anglesey
16 ▲

Denbigh ●

15 ▲

CLYWD

11 ▲ ▲ 18
▲ 9
2 ▲

Wrexham ●

6 ▲

▲ 19

GWYNEDD

8 ▲ ▲

▲ 17

Dolgellau ●

Welshpool ●

Newtown ●

4
Cardigan Bay

▲ 7

POWYS

● Cardigan

13 ▲ ▲

▲ 3   DYFED

Brecon ● ▲ 12

14
▲

10 ▲

Pembroke ●

20 ▲

Monmouth

Swansea ●

MID-

GWENT

WEST GLAMORGAN

GLAMORGAN

Newport ●

Cardiff ●

SOUTH GLAMORGAN

Close to the River Alaw near Llanbabo is a ruined cairn (SH 361850) said to be the grave of Branwen, daughter of Llyr, whose unhappy history is told in the *Mabinogion*. Bran, king of the Island of the Mighty, was sitting with his brother Manawydan on the rock of Harlech, looking over the sea, when they saw the ships of the king of Ireland heading their way. He had come to ask for the hand of their sister, Branwen, and the wedding-feast took place at the royal court of Aberffraw (SH 3568), during which a quarrel broke out that ended with Bran giving the Irish king, in order to appease him, his greatest treasure, a cauldron that restored the dead to life.

For a year Branwen was held in high honour at the Irish court, but after that she was made to suffer for the outrage at the wedding-feast by being forced to serve as a cook in the kitchen. This she endured for three years, but meantime trained a starling to carry a message to her brother Bran. The starling found him at Caer Seint in Arfon (see **Sarn Helen**, p.355) and in response to her appeal the hosts of Britain invaded Ireland, Bran, too big for a ship, striding through the waves and laying himself down as a bridge for his men to cross the Shannon. In the battle that followed, the Irish put the cauldron to use, restoring the slain to fight another day. Bran himself was mortally wounded in the foot by a poisoned spear, and ordered his followers once he was dead to cut off his head and bear it back to London, to 'the White Mount', where they were to bury it with its face towards France.

They bore the head back to Britain, Branwen with them:

> And they came to land at Aber Alaw in Talebolion. And then they sat down and rested them. Then she looked on Ireland and the Island of the Mighty, what she might see of them. 'Alas, Son of God,' said she, 'woe is me that ever I was born: two good islands have been laid waste because of me!' And she heaved a great sigh, and with that broke her heart. And a four-sided grave was made for her, and she was buried there on the bank of the Alaw.

Branwen's grave on the banks of the Alaw has been identified with the Llanbabo cairn since the 1722 edition of Camden's *Britannia*,

largely in the absence of other candidates. In fact excavations of
the site in 1813 and 1967–8 showed that this was the tomb not of
one person but many. The mound, now rather low and inconspicu-
ous, stands in the centre of a slight natural rise in a bend of the
Alaw. When it was raised this was an open meadow, full of
buttercups, and nearby were woods of oak, hazel and alder. Here a
cairn ring was built round a standing-stone which had already been
there for some time, and had had offerings buried at its foot, unless
these were made when the cairn was constructed, by way of
rededication. After the cairn had been built, the whole was covered
by a mound, probably never very high, the stone at the centre
always visible. The barrow dates from about 1400 B.C. and was
built to house the cremated remains of members of a Bronze Age
family or community; probably no more than a generation later, it
was opened and another batch of cremations simultaneously
interred. When the barrow was dug into in 1813, a funerary pot
was found enclosed in a small cist – a stone box – and the 1967–8
excavations uncovered a similar but five-sided cist.

Some take the 'four-sided grave' of the *Mabinogion* to refer to
such a cist, or to one of the large cists used at various periods to
receive the bodies of the dead, such as one made of thin upright
slabs of stone which was dug into the top of a barrow (SH 354806)
at Treiorwerth, near Bodedern, in Roman or even early Christian
times. It is perhaps not a point worth refining – 'four-sided grave'
might mean no more than the ordinary rectangular grave for a
single body in use in the Bronze Age as today.

Not all local storytellers seem to have known that Branwen's
grave was on the bank of the Alaw. In his *Ten Days' Tour through
the Isle of Anglesea* (1802), the Rev. John Skinner reports of the
Bodowyr burial chamber near Llandidan (SJ 462681):

> . . . there is a tradition amongst the Welsh that this rude
> memorial was erected over the grave of a British princess
> named Bronwen who flourished in the year of the world
> 3105 !!!!

As for Branwen or Bronwen herself, there is not much to suggest
that she is a figure of great antiquity, but her brothers Bran and
Manawydan were believed to be sister's sons of Beli Mawr, 'Beli
the Great', an ancestor-god from whom several of the royal
dynasties of Wales claimed their descent. Bran played a part in the

evolution of the High History of the Grail (see **Dinas Bran**, p.338), and his head became a national palladium (see **Tower of London**, p.158).

Bodowyr burial chamber: AM (any reasonable time).

BEDDGELERT, GWYNEDD Sheet 115
(formerly CAERNARVONSHIRE) SH 5948

Llewellyn the Great had a hound named Gelert, who one day stubbornly refused to go hunting with his master. When Llewellyn returned from the chase, the dog bounded joyfully to meet him, his muzzle smeared with blood, and on entering the house Llewellyn found his son's cradle overturned, the bed coverings bloody and no baby to be seen. He at once concluded that the hound had killed the child, and plunged his sword into Gelert's side. Hardly had he done so, when he heard a wail, and found the baby under the cradle, safe and sound. Nearby was a huge grey wolf, lying dead and mangled. It now became tragically plain that Gelert had killed the wolf and saved the child, only to die at the hands of his master. Smitten with remorse, Llewellyn raised a tomb over the faithful hound and this was known thereafter as Beddgelert or 'Gelert's Grave'.

This sad tale is now traditional in the village of Beddgelert at the foot of Snowdon, where Llewellyn the Great had a house. The village is believed to have got its name from a greyhound given to Llewellyn in 1205 by his father-in-law, King John. The story of the hound slain in hasty error was only attached to Llewellyn's dog in 1793–4 by a local innkeeper, who combined the two traditions. The new story was then popularized in a ballad by the Hon. William Spencer, known to have visited the innkeeper some time before 1800, when his poem was published.

But although it has only been attached to Gelert since the eighteenth century, the legend itself is extremely old. It was told in India of a mongoose who saved a brahmin's son from a snake, and as a moral tale illustrating the folly of hasty action, appeared in a third-century-A.D. collection of tales in Sanskrit known as the *Panchatantra* or 'Five Books'. This was subsequently translated into Persian, and thence, in the eighth century, into Arabic, and so found its way into the *Book of Sindibad*. The *Book of Sindibad* (which later became part of the *Arabian Nights* – Sindibad is Sinbad the Sailor) reached Europe as a collection of tales entitled *The Seven Sages of Rome*, and there is a Welsh version of this in the Red Book of Hergest which dates from the fourteenth century.

The mongoose, an animal unknown to the Arabs, had by this time become first a weasel, then a dog. The snake remained a snake, and as such appears in the Red Book. In Welsh folklore, however, the snake is replaced by a wolf, presumably because this was thought a more likely adversary.

The literary route followed by the story to Europe – where it is known in virtually every country – is the same as that taken by another famous tale 'The Treasure at Home', of which the classic English version is 'The Pedlar of Swaffham' (see **Swaffham**, p.195). But not everyone agrees that this is how it got to Beddgelert – some think it may have reached the West in oral tradition, as a similar tale was told in the second century A.D. by the Greek author Pausanias, in which a child is saved, as in Wales, from a wolf, by a snake, after whom was named the city of Ophiteia or 'Snake Town'. It may be that the story originated in an actual event – there is an account purporting to be fact of a mongoose killed in India in about 1920 as the result of the same sort of hasty error.

Snowdonia National Park. 'Gelert's Grave' (SH 590477) at Beddgelert is modern, but stands on a mound *ca.* 260 feet (79.25 m) in diameter, which some say is a burial mound. The Royal Commission on Ancient and Historical Monuments (1960), however, judge it to be a natural formation.

BEDD-YR-AFANC, BRYNBERIAN, DYFED   Sheet 145
(formerly PEMBROKESHIRE)   SN 1035

Just off the B4329 from Cardigan to Haverfordwest, across the moor from the village of Brynberian, is a Neolithic gallery grave (marked 'long cairn' on the map, SN 108346), dating from about 1500 B.C. This is the Bedd-yr-Afanc or 'Monster's Grave', also known as Crug-yr-Afanc, 'Monster's Mound'. The *afanc* is said to have been caught in a pool near Brynberian bridge and buried up here on the mountainside.

We are not told how the *afanc* was captured, but the antiquary

Edward Llwyd, writing in 1693, tells a similar tale of one caught in a pool called Llyn yr Afanc above Bettws-y-Coed on the River Conwy. A maiden enticed him out of the water and while he slept with his head on her knees and one claw on her breast, they bound him with chains. When he woke, he cast off the chains in fury and rushed back down to the lake, tearing the girl's breast off in the process. Then two oxen were hitched to a chain and they dragged the *afanc* out of his pool and up to Llyn Cwm Ffynnon Las, where he was left. This procedure is much the same as the prescribed method for catching a unicorn, but the creature was clearly some sort of a water monster.

According to tradition, an *afanc* used to live in the 'Bearded Lake', Llyn Barfog, Gwynedd (SN 6598). The story is attached to Hu Gadarn, 'Hu the Mighty', who, say the Welsh *Triads*, 'first taught the Cymry how to plough' and led them to the island of Britain. In his time, 'Llyn Llion' burst its banks, drowning all save one man and one woman, from whom Britain was peopled again. It was Hu Gadarn's two great horned oxen that dragged the *afanc* out of the lake on to dry land so that it could not happen again. Llyn Barfog was one of several lakes identified with 'Llyn Llion', and in the nineteenth century it was still believed to be dangerous to let out its waters – this had indeed been tried within living memory, and heavy and prolonged rains followed.

The *afanc* in the 'Llyn Llion' story was evidently responsible for the flood, though we are not told how – nor yet what exactly the *afanc* was. A beaver, suggested Llwyd; a crocodile, said someone else, but these are scarcely big enough to cause such disasters. Evidently the name was remembered but not the creature – could it perhaps have been the sort of water-dwelling ogre the Anglo-Saxons had, like Grendel's mother in *Beowulf* (see **Lyminster**, p.114)? For in the *Mabinogion*, it is *humanoid* – living in a cave and lurking behind a pillar at the entrance to cast its poisoned spear at all comers, until it is killed by Peredur.

Pembrokeshire Coast National Park. Llyn Barfog, Sheet 135.

CARDIGAN BAY, DYFED

Below the waters of Cardigan Bay lies Cantre'r Gwaelod, 'the Bottom Cantred', according to legend overwhelmed by the sea. It was a fertile land, forty miles in length and twenty in breadth, stretching from the Teifi to Bardsey Island (SJ 1221). In it were sixteen fine cities, and it was protected from the sea by a dyke and sluices. But when Gwyddno Garanhir ('Longshanks') was lord of the cantred, the keeper of the dyke was a certain Seithenhin, a drunkard, who one night in his cups left open the sluice-gates. The sea came rushing in and few of the inhabitants escaped. When the sea is still and the water clear, the buildings of Cantre'r Gwaelod can still be seen, and the faint music of its church bells heard floating up from the depths.

This is the story of Cantre'r Gwaelod as it is now told, but it probably only began to take this form in the mid seventeenth century, after the antiquary Robert Vaughan of Hengwrt connected it with Sarn Badrig, a submerged pebble ridge running for some miles out into Cardigan Bay north of Barmouth (SH 6115). Sarn Badrig is a natural formation, but Vaughan believed it to be man-made – 'a stone wall made as a fence against the sea'. Thereafter, in the course of the eighteenth and nineteenth centuries, were added the ideas that it was through drunkenness that the dyke was breached, that Seithenhin was its keeper, and that the sound of the bells of the lost cantred can still be heard (this last being an almost inevitable theme of 'sunken city' traditions).

Certainly in its oldest known form the legend was rather different. From the Black Book of Carmarthen, from about the mid thirteenth century, comes a Welsh poem containing these verses:

> Stand forth, Seithenhin,
> and look upon the fury of the sea;
> it has covered Maes Gwyddneu.

> Accursed be the maiden
> who released it after the feast;
> the fountain-cupbearer of the raging sea . . .

The cry of Margaret from the back of the bay horse;
it was the mighty and generous God who did it;
usual after excess is want . . .

The grave of Seithenhin the presumptuous,
between Kaer Kenedir and the shore;
how magnificent a lord.

Here Seithenhin, not Gwyddno, appears to be the ruler of Cantre'r Gwaelod, a tradition also recorded in the twelfth-century *Bonedd y Saint*, 'Genealogies of the Saints'. And it is not he but the maiden Mererid (Margaret), the 'fountain-cupbearer', who is responsible for the flood. Gwyddno is mentioned only in so far as he has given his name to Maes Gwyddneu, 'the Plain of Gwyddno', generally assumed to be another name for the Bottom Cantred.

The story evidently began as, or has been influenced by, a tale of an overflowing fountain like the one told of Llyn Llech Owen (SN 5615). A man named Owen living on Mynydd Mawr had a well covered by a large flagstone. This he was always careful to replace, but one day after watering his horse he forgot. As he rode away, he looked back, and saw that the well had burst and the water was pouring out. He rode back and galloped round the flood, and it was the horse's track round the water that stopped its outpouring. Had Owen not ridden round it thus, it would have drowned the whole district. In memory of this event, the lake formed by the flood was called Llyn Llech Owen, or 'the Lake of Owen's Flag'. This undoubtedly goes back to the same Celtic tradition as the Irish 'Death of Eochaid man Mairid', in which Eochaid's daughter, charged with guarding a magic well, one day fails to replace its cover, with the result that it overflows and forms Lough Neagh. The differences between the modern and the earlier form of the Cardigan Bay legend can be accounted for as misunderstandings of the poem in the Black Book, and adaptation towards the usual pattern of sunken city stories, in which the city is overwhelmed because of evil living. Traditions of such cities are found along the coasts of north-west Europe, and in its medieval form the legend seems to have been affected by the biblical stories of Noah's Flood and the destruction of Sodom and Gomorrah. The Black Book poem represents a half-way stage – the inundation *is* a punishment, but for presumption, a favourite cause of tragedy in Welsh literature (and cf. the story of Remius Sylvius under **Llangorse Lake**, p.346).

The story of Cantre'r Gwaelod is undoubtedly related to the Breton legend of the drowning of Kêr-Is ('the Bottom Fortress'). Known from the sixteenth century, this is thought to have influenced the legend of Tresilian told in the **Scilly Isles** (p.32); and it has itself (in the nineteenth century) been affected by the Black Book poem. Although the comings and goings between these stories can no longer be clearly traced, it is likely that the Welsh and Breton tales both go back to the same tradition – some have said an account of a real flood that took place somewhere in the Celtic world in the sixth century, the period with which Gwyddno and the characters in the Kêr-Is tale are all associated. This was then localized at various places, in Wales becoming attached to Gwyddno, originally a hero of the Men of the North, whose kingdom tradition located in Cardigan Bay as early as the ninth century.

Whenever the connection between Cardigan Bay and Gwyddno was first made, it was enshrined in local place-names. Borth was once Porth Wydno, 'Gwyddno's Harbour', and at the end of the natural causeway of Sarn Cynvelyn, of which more later, was a group of rocks known as Caer Wyddno, 'Gwyddno's Fortress'. These place-names suggest how the Bottom Cantred came to be located in Cardigan Bay. In the bay are three *sarnau* or 'causeways' – Sarn Badrig, which runs out from the coast between Harlech and Barmouth; Sarn y Bwch, running out from Aberdysini; and Sarn Cynvelyn ('Cymbeline's Causeway' – see **Cymbeline's Castle**, p.132), running out between Borth and Aberystwyth. Geologists believe these causeways to be wholly natural, the shingle and boulder ridges that once lay between the river-beds of a land surface subsequently submerged. Moreover, at low tides at various times, the remains of a submerged forest have been revealed between Borth and Ynyslas (SN 6092). So there is indeed a sunken land in Cardigan Bay, its submergence the result of a slow rise in sea level thought to have lasted beyond Neolithic times but to have ended before the Iron Age. The story of Cantre'r Gwaelod *might* be a memory of this change handed down to the Iron Age Celts: more likely it comes from observation – i.e. is an 'explanation' of the submerged forest and the *sarnau*. Gerald of Wales, for example, noted tree-trunks exposed by the storm in the winter of 1171–2 at

Newgale in St Bride's Bay (SM 8422), and the straight lines of the *sarnau* underwater seen from high ground would readily suggest dykes. The similar tale of the drowning of Llys Helig, 'the Court of Helig', for its evil life, seems to be based on similar 'ruins' in Conwy Bay.

A cantred or cantref, a hundred, was a territorial unit that varied from place to place, but for the purposes of this story can be reckoned at about a third of the former county of Cardiganshire. The story of Cantre'r Gwaelod was burlesqued by Thomas Love Peacock in his novel *The Misfortunes of Elphin* (1829). A visible memorial of the legend is the medieval church of St Tanwg, at Llandanwg (SH 5728), Gwynedd, said to have served Cantre'r Gwaelod in its heyday. The little low church, whose churchyard is fast disappearing under the sand, is set in NT property – access from the public car park at Llandanwg. I am indebted for information on the legend of Cantre'r Gwaelod to Rachel Bromwich's essay 'Cantre'r Gwaelod and Kêr-Is', in *The Early Cultures of North-West Europe* (H.M. Chadwick Memorial Studies), ed. Cyril Fox and Bruce Dickins (Cambridge, 1950), pp. 217–41; and to F. J. North's *Sunken Cities* (Cardiff, 1957).

CARREG LEIDR, LLANDYFRYDOG, GWYNEDD (ANGLESEY)

Sheet 114
SH 4484

South of Llandyfrydog is a standing stone (SH 446843) that resembles a man with a pack on his back and is known as Carreg Leidr or Carreg y Lleidr, 'the Robber's Stone'. 'The country people report that a thief who had stolen some books from a neighbouring church was in this place turned into stone with the sack containing his theft laying over his shoulder', as the Rev. John Skinner says in his *Ten Days' Tour through the Isle of Anglesea* (1802). Later in the century it was said that, every Christmas Eve, the stone moved three times round the field it stood in when it heard the clock strike twelve. A similar tradition attaches to many stones.

CASTELLMARCH, ABERSOCH, GWYNEDD (formerly CAERNARVONSHIRE)

Sheet 123
SH 3129

Castellmarch or 'Mark's Castle' is a seventeenth-century mansion

north of Abersoch, so-called in the belief that it stood on the site
of the castle of King Mark, the husband of Iseult (see **Castle Dore**,
p.10). The Welsh form of Mark is March, and *march* is also
Welsh for 'horse'. This led to the following story being told of
Castellmarch.

One of Arthur's warriors, whose name was March Amheirchion,
was Lord of Castellmarch in Lleyn. He had horse's ears, and used
to kill every barber that came to shave his beard for fear that he
would be unable to keep the terrible secret. On the spot where he
buried their bodies, there grew a clump of reeds, one of which
someone cut to make a pipe. But when he tried to play it, the only
tune that it would play was 'March Amheirchion has horse's ears'.
March would have killed the man, had he not discovered for
himself that the pipe would play nothing else, and when he heard
where the reed had been cut, made no further effort to hide the
murders or his ears.

This story goes back to at least the seventeenth century – when
it was published in the 1860 volume of *Brython*, it was attributed
to 'Edward Llwyd, 1693' and evidently came from one of the great
Welsh antiquary's letters. It was still current at Castellmarch at the
end of the nineteenth century, though it took the folklorist Sir
John Rhys a fortnight to extract it from an old blacksmith there, as
'he would never have thought of repeating such nonsense'.

Nonsense or not, it was a popular tale found also in Cornwall
and Brittany, and in Ireland told of a king named Labraid Lorc.
More than that, it is, of course, the same tale as the ancient Greek
story 'King Midas has ass's ears'.

CORNGAFALLT, POWYS
(formerly BRECKNOCKSHIRE)

Sheet 147
SN 9464

There is another wonderful thing in the region which is called
Buelt. There is in that place a heap of stones, and one stone
superposed on the pile with the footprint of a dog on it. When
he hunted the boar Troynt, Cabal, who was the dog of Arthur
the soldier, impressed his footprint on the stone and Arthur
afterwards collected a pile of stones under the stone, whereon
was the footprint of his dog, and it is called Carn Cabal. And
men come and carry the stone in their hands for the space of a

day and a night, and on the morrow it is found upon its pile.

Thus Nennius *ca.* 800 A.D. tells of one of the Marvels of Wales. Buelt was the south-central district whose name has been preserved in Builth Wells, and Carn Cabal, later Carn Cafall, 'Cabal's Cairn', is traditionally identified with one of a group of cairns on the hill now known as Corngafallt.

The hunting of the great boar Twrch Trwyth (Nennius's Troynt) is related at length in 'Culhwch and Olwen', written in its present form probably as early as 1100. Culhwch wishes to marry Olwen, daughter of Ysbaddaden Chief Giant. But Ysbaddaden is destined to live only so long as his daughter remains unwed, so he has all her suitors killed. The only way to win Olwen's hand is to offer to perform any tasks her father demands, and this Culhwch undertakes to do. Among other things, he must gather the marvellous horses, huntsmen and hounds who alone can catch the magic boar, Twrch Trwyth, for as Ysbaddaden explains, 'There is no comb and shears in the world wherewith my hair may be dressed, so exceeding stiff it is, save the comb and shears that are between the two ears of Twrch Trwyth . . .'

The tasks are *meant* to be impossible, but, with the help of Arthur and his men, Culhwch sets out to achieve them. The hunting of Twrch Trwyth and his seven piglets begins in Ireland, but soon moves across to Wales. Landing at Porth-clais (SM 7423), just below St David's in Dyfed, they go by way of Prescelly Top (Foel Cwm-cerwyn, SN 0931) across Towy (Tywi), through the valleys of the rivers Loughor and Amman (SS 6007, SN 6513), and the parish of Bettws (SN 6511), to Ynys Pen Llwch or 'Pool's End Isle', below Pontardawe (SN 7204). In this great pursuit all the piglets have been killed, and Twrch Trwyth goes on alone to the mouth of the Severn. Here, in the waters below the meeting of the Severn and the Wye, a great battle takes place. The *razor* and shears are seized (some confusion here), but Twrch Trwyth himself escapes to Cornwall, where at length the comb is won, and the boar driven into the sea, never to return.

Although Cabal is with Arthur at the hunting of Twrch Trwyth, *Carn* Cabal is not mentioned, and indeed the chase goes nowhere near Corngafallt. Best, perhaps, not to set too much store by Nennius, for as Camden says, 'stuffed hee hath that little booke with many a pretty lie'. Certainly, 'self-returning stone' or not (a tradition that survived, for example, at the Rollright Stones, in Oxfordshire), the curious will be hard put to it to find the footprint. We do not know precisely what *sort* of footprint to look for – was Cabal indeed a dog or was he, as his name (Latin *caballus*) implies, a horse? Arthur's horse (in Welsh *march Arthur*) certainly left his hoofprint on a hill above the A493, on a rock known as Carn March Arthur (SN 651982), when Arthur came here to kill an *afanc* that lived in Llyn Barfog (see **Bedd-yr-Afanc**, p.330).

We may not be able to find Cabal's footprint, but we can still see what is traditionally held to be a monument to King Arthur's sons, killed in the hunting of Twrch Trwyth – the Ty-newydd standing-stones, also known as Cerrig Meibion Arthur, 'The Stones of the Sons of Arthur', in the parish of Mynachlog-Ddu, Dyfed (SN 118310). Carn March Arthur, Sheet 135; Cerrig Meibion Arthur, Sheet 145.

DINAS BRAN, LLANGOLLEN, CLYWD (formerly DENBIGHSHIRE)

Sheet 117
SJ 2243

On a high round hill above the Vale of Llangollen, marked 'Castell' on the map (SJ 222431), is a hill-fort with Iron Age ramparts enclosing the remains of a medieval castle. The name it bears, Dinas Bran or 'Bran's stronghold', is thought to refer to 'Bran the Blessed', hero of a tale in the *Mabinogion* (see **Tower of London**, p.158). If so, then Dinas Bran is the strongest candidate we have for the most mysterious place in Arthurian legend, the Castle of the Grail.

The lame Fisher King of the Grail Castle, whose maiming is linked to the blight of the land – the 'Waste Land' theme – seems an echo of Bran, wounded in the foot in a conflict that leaves Wales and Ireland blasted (see **Bedd Branwen**, p.327). Moreover, one early version of the Grail story actually calls the Fisher King Bron; and although the Castle of the Grail is usually named Corbenic, Malory (d. 1471) calls it Corbin – an old French word for raven or crow. It must be more than chance that this is also the meaning of 'Bran', and that Dinas Bran was to the Hon. John Byng in 1794 known as 'Crow Castle'.

Just as in the Grail stories of 'Perceval' (twelfth century) and 'Peredur' (fourteenth) the hero comes to a river or lake, sees the

Corbin, the Grail Castle: Dinas Bran, Clwyd

Fisher King or his servants fishing and is invited by him to his nearby castle, so, in the mid-thirteenth-century romance of the Norman outlaw Fulk Fitzwarren, does Fulk come by the same route to a Castle of Wonders, known as 'Chastiel Bran' and located somewhere in the Welsh Marches. Was this Dinas Bran? It is evocative enough to be the home of the Grail, its castle, a ruin since *ca.* 1282, desolate and mysterious on its eminence.

For another story attached to Dinas Bran, see the next entry.

DINAS EMRYS, BEDDGELERT, GWYNEDD (formerly CAERNARVONSHIRE)

Sheet 115
SH 6049

Dinas Emrys is a small hill-fort in the valley of Nant Gwynant, north-east of Beddgelert. Its name means 'Fort of Ambrose' and of it Nennius, writing *ca.* 800 A.D., tells the following tale.

After the British tyrant Vortigern's policy of settling Saxons in Britain had so tragically misfired (see **Kit's Coty House**, p.108), he tried to build a stronghold in Snowdonia, but three times, in the night, the building materials mysteriously vanished. He consulted his magicians, who told him he would only succeed if he sprinkled the foundations with the blood of a boy born without a father. Such a boy was found and when he was brought to the King, told him that beneath a certain stone was a pool, which was undermining his foundations. In the pool they would find a tent containing two dragons, one red, the other white. Everything turned out as the boy had said, and when the dragons were uncovered they began to fight. First the white one seemed to be winning, but then the red one drove him out of the tent. The boy said the tent was Britain, the white dragon the Saxons, and the red the Welsh, who in the fullness of time would reconquer their lands. Vortigern himself must give up his citadel to the boy, whose name was Emrys or 'Ambrose' and who, it is implied, was that same Ambrosius Aurelianus whom tradition claims launched the counter-attack against the Saxons which King Arthur led.

When Geoffrey of Monmouth retold this story in the twelfth century, he changed the boy's name to Merlin, and said he was discovered at Carmarthen, where he was born of the union of an incubus and a nun. Ambrosius becomes a separate character, and nothing is said of his taking over the fortress. It was partly due to the popularity of Geoffrey's story that the Red Dragon became the emblem of Wales.

The story of the birth of Emrys belongs to an ancient Celtic pattern found in both Irish and Welsh legend – that of the 'Wonderchild' born of a human mother and Otherworld father. The story of the begetting of Arthur by Uther Pendragon when magically disguised is another version of the same tale.

The need to sprinkle the foundations with the blood of a child is a memory of foundation-sacrifice, once widely practised – and, indeed, there were attempts by workmen to sacrifice children under Dutch and German dykes as late as 1717. The disappearance of the building materials every night foreshadows a common folktale 'A Disputed Site for a Church', in which the Devil, witches, fairies or unspecified supernatural forces undo at night the work done by day, forcing the builders to change the site. In Wales in the nineteenth and early twentieth centuries this story was told of many churches including those of Corwn and Denbigh in Clwyd; Llangranog and Llanfihangel Genau'r-glyn (Llandre) in Dyfed; Llangan in South Glamorgan; and Aberdaron, Llanbedr and Ffestiniog in Gwynedd.

Curiously enough, Nennius's wonder tale has some foundation in fact. Archaeology has shown that, though Dinas Emrys was built in the pre-Roman Iron Age, it was re-occupied in the second half of the fifth century, i.e. about the time of the real Ambrosius if he ever existed. Moreover, excavations in the 1950s discovered, in a natural hollow south of the remains of a tower (probably twelfth century), an artificial pool, probably constructed in the first or second century as a cistern for a small settlement. A roughly circular platform of stone was later built on the north-west edge of the pool, resting partly on peat which had been formed after it silted up. The platform appears to belong to the post-Roman occupation of the site, so the covered pool was probably a reality in the time of which Nennius writes, certainly at the time *at* which he wrote. The 'Wonderchild' story, therefore, may well have been told of the site in order to account for the hidden pool.

Although Nennius's Emrys is commemorated in the name of the place, it is Geoffrey's Merlin who appears in its later folklore. A tradition recorded in 1861 says that Merlin left a treasure here that can only be found by the person he intended it for, a youth with blue eyes and yellow hair. This probably springs from a common belief in Snowdonia that treasures in caves belong to the Goidels or Irishmen, who will eventually find them. A 'right heir' story is similarly attached to **Dinas Bran** (p.338) where the finder of the treasure will be a boy followed by a light-eyed dog, such as were said to see the wind.

Snowdonia National Park. Use OS 1:25 000 Outdoor Leisure Map 17, Snowdonia National Park (Snowdon).

GROSMONT, GWENT (formerly MONMOUTHSHIRE)

Sheet 161
SO 4024

Several features of the landscape on both sides of the Welsh border are traditionally said to be the work of Jack o' Kent, a famous wizard. The cleft in the west side of the Skirrid (SO 3318), for example, riven by a landslip, was in 1903 accounted for by a Kentchurch woman as having been caused by Jack when he jumped off the Sugar Loaf (SO 2718) on to it – 'and there's his heel mark to this day'. In the Wye Valley in the early part of this century it was said that 'he were always a-flinging stones' and that they could never thereafter be shifted – among the testimonials to his strength are Harold's Stones, just south of Trelleck (Tryleg, SO 4905), of which more later.

The handiwork of the magician Jack o'Kent:
Harold's Stones, Trelleck, Gwent

Said to have lived on the Welsh border either at Grosmont or Kentchurch in Herefordshire (SO 4125), Jack o' Kent has been famous for several centuries. He must already have been well known by 1595 when he appears in the play *John a Kent and John a Cumber* by Anthony Munday. There are half a dozen candidates for a historical Jack o'Kent, ranging from Owen Glendower to the fifteenth-century Welsh poet Sion Cent. One of the most likely is the learned astrologer Dr John Kent Caerleon, who lived in the fifteenth century and wrote a book on witchcraft.

Like the great medieval scholar Roger Bacon, the real Jack, John or Sion was transformed into a magician-hero. He sold his soul to the Devil as a boy in exchange for the power to do whatever he set his hand to, and to be able to summon the Devil's aid. He got the Devil to build a bridge across the Monnow between Grosmont and Kentchurch, by the same trick the old woman used at Devil's Bridge (Pontarfynach), Dyfed (see **Kirkby Lonsdale**, p.379), and another story of how he outwitted the 'old 'un' was 'The Mowing Contest'. Jack and the Devil agreed to have a match at mowing hay, but Jack got up during the night and stuck the Devil's half of the meadow with harrow tines, so that he had to keep stopping to whet his scythe, muttering the while 'Bur-dock, Jack! Bur-dock, Jack!', thinking the tines were burdocks, and so Jack won.

It was said at Trelleck, which gets its name (thought to mean 'the three stones') from three standing-stones just south of the village, that the Devil once challenged Jack to a throwing match on Trelleck Beacon (SO 5105). Jack threw first, the Devil threw further, but Jack threw further still, and the Devil ran off defeated. The stones remain as proof of the truth of the tale – although their name, 'Harold's Stones', preserves another tradition, that they commemorate a battle fought by Harold of England here.

Of the many trials of strength and cunning between the Devil and Jack, the most famous is 'The Tops and the Butts', an international tale, told, like 'The Mowing Contest', in several places. One day Jack took the Devil into a field of wheat that was just springing up and asked him, 'Which will you have, the tops or the butts?' There was not much top to be seen, so the Devil said he'd have the butts or bottoms. But at harvest time, Jack got the wheat and the Devil only the straw. So next year, the Devil chose tops, but this time the field had been sown with turnip seed, and all he got at harvest was the greens.

Jack even managed to outwit the Devil at his death – for the terms of his contract were the same as Piers Shonks's of **Brent Pelham** (p.128), and, nearer at hand, of a fourteenth-century vicar of Treimeirchion, Flintshire (now Clwyd), and like them he had himself buried in the church wall, some say at Grosmont, others at Kentchurch or Skenfrith. An old lady at Wigmore in 1908 remembered her mother telling her how at Jack's funeral a voice was heard to say:

> 'False David Sir Ivan
> False alive, false dead.'

She supposed 'David Sir Ivan' to be the Welsh name for 'Jacky Kent' – 'Sir Ivan' sounds like Sion, the Welsh for John.

Though these stories were all recorded in the nineteenth and twentieth centuries, some of the traditions about Jack o' Kent have a long history. According to a tale collected in Grosmont in 1908, Jack had magic horses which galloped through the air at great speed. He once set out at dawn from Kentchurch to take a mincepie to the King, and reached London in time for breakfast, while the pie was still hot, despite having been delayed when his garter got hooked in the weathercock as he flew over the church. This sort of magical speed was a common attribute of magicians, and a similar tale was once told of St Aldhelm of **Malmesbury Abbey** (p.70).

Though Jack o' Kent often outwitted the Devil, he was not taken to be entirely on the side of the angels. At the turn of the century, a room at Kentchurch Court (SO 4225) was still being shown as his bedroom and it was said that on stormy nights his ghost had been seen issuing from a recess. He was also used as an ogre to frighten children – 'You be careful, or Jackie Kent will get you!'

An old cross on the north side of Grosmont churchyard is said to mark Jack o' Kent's grave. In the church, in the south-east corner of the nave, is an effigy supposed to be of Jack, though probably that of a knight, perhaps one of the lords of Grosmont Castle (SO 4025): AM (any reasonable time). The bridge built by the Devil is the stone bridge at the foot of Cupid's Hill. The tradition that Harold's Stones commemorate a battle is recorded on a sundial dating from 1689 in Trelleck church. Trelleck, Sheet 162.

LLANDWROG, GWYNEDD
(formerly CAERNARVONSHIRE)

Attached to a farm in the nineteenth century known as Garth Dorwen, near Llandwrog, is a fairy-tale that deserves more than a fleeting mention as an outstanding example of the widespread tale 'Midwife to the Fairies'. Published in his *Celtic Folklore* in 1901 it had been told to the folklorist Sir John Rhys in 1882 by William Thomas Solomon, a gardener at Glynllifon (SH 4555).

An old man and his wife lived at Garth Dorwen long ago who went to Caernarfon to hire a servant at the Fair. They hired a girl with yellow hair standing a little apart from the rest, who duly came to her place at the appointed time. The spinning in those days was done after supper on the long winter nights, and the girl, Eilian, would go out into the meadow to spin by the light of the moon. Here the Tylwyth Teg, the fairies, used to come to her to sing and to dance. But one day in spring she ran off with the Tylwyth Teg and no more was heard of her. The field where she was last seen was in Mr Solomon's day still known as Eilian's Field, and the meadow where she spun as Maid's Meadow.

Now the old woman at Garth Dorwen helped women in childbed, and some time after this, a gentleman on horseback came to the door one night when the moon was full, to fetch her to his lady. The old woman rode pillion behind him and they came to Rhos-y-Cowrt. In the centre of the *rhos* (moor) was what appeared to be an old fortification – this went by the name of Bryn y Pibion. Here they entered a large cave and came into a room – and it was the finest place the old woman had seen in her life – where the wife lay in bed. When the baby was born, and she had dressed it by the fire, the husband gave her ointment to anoint its eyes, warning her not to get it in her own. But one of her eyes happening to itch, she rubbed it, with the finger she had used to anoint the baby's eyes. At once she saw with that eye that the fine chamber was a cave, the bed a ring of stones lined with rushes and withered bracken, and the gentleman's wife none other than her servant girl Eilian; yet with the other eye, she still saw the grandest place that ever she had seen.

Not long afterwards, the old woman went to Caernarfon market, and there saw the husband. 'How is Eilian?' she said. 'She is pretty

well, thank you,' he answered, 'but with what eye do you see me?'
'With this one,' she replied, and at once he took a bulrush and put
it out.

Solomon heard this story from his mother, who had it in her
turn from an old woman living at Garth Dorwen some years
before, putting the tradition well back into the eighteenth century.
However, the story of the magic ointment and the 'seeing eye' was
in circulation well before this – indeed, at **Littlecote House** (p.67)
in the seventeenth century 'Midwife to the Fairies' seems to have
influenced actual events. In Wales a similar tale was also told at
Swydd Ffynnon, Cardiganshire.

Often in these stories, the fairy husband is seen stealing meat,
fondly supposing himself invisible (cf. **Stowmarket**, p.193). Other
Welsh markets attended by fairies were to be found at Aberdaron
and **Milford Haven** (p.352).

Garth Dorwen is marked (as Garth-dorwen) on the OS 1:25 000 map.

LLANGORSE LAKE (LLYN SYFADDAN),   Sheet 161
POWYS   SO 1226
(formerly BRECKNOCKSHIRE)

Writing of Llyn Syfaddan or Llangorse Lake in his *Britannia*
(trans. Holland, 1610), the antiquary William Camden tells us:

> It hath beene a currant speech of long continuance among the
> neighbours there about, that where now the *Meere* is, there
> was in times past a City, which being swallowed up in an
> earth quake, resigned up the place unto the waters.

The drowned city story of Camden's day may have been the
forerunner of one that came from an old man of Hay and was
printed by Edward Davies in his *Mythology and Rites of the British
Druids* (1809). This tells how Llyn Syfaddan was once the site of a
great and wicked city drowned for its sins, a widespread tale going
back at least to classical times, with the Greek legend of Philemon
and Baucis, and the Roman tradition that the palace of Remius
Sylvius, who had constructed machines to imitate thunder and
lightning and set himself up as the equal of Jupiter, was because of
this impiety struck by a thunderbolt and drowned by the Alban

'Where now the Meere *is, there was in times past a City':*
Llangorse Lake, Powys

lake, beneath whose waters it could still be seen.

Rather different is a second story told of Llyn Syfaddan, that a beautiful lady, the heiress of all the land now covered by the lake, was courted by a young man, whom she could not accept because of his poverty. In his despair, the young man murdered a carrier bearing a large sum of money, and for fear of discovery, buried him on the spot. When he told the lady what he had done, she refused to marry him until he returned to the grave at night to appease the ghost said now to be troubling the place. There at the grave 'he heard at midnight a voice cry aloud, "Is there no vengeance for innocent blood?" and another voice answer, "Not until the ninth generation."' He told the lady what he had heard but she said scornfully, 'Before that time we shall be rotten in our graves, therefore we will enjoy ourselves while we may.' The pair married, and years afterwards, when they were old, invited all their descendants to a feast, at the height of which they were swallowed by a terrible earthquake and covered over by the lake. Although similar vengeance stories were told of Kenfig Pool, Porthcawl, Glamorgan; Bala Lake, Gwynedd; and Llynclys, Shropshire, these are all believed to have been influenced by the Llyn Syfaddan legend, circulating in written form by about 1700.

At Llyn Syfaddan, the inundation story might just be a folk-memory of an actual occurrence. Lake-dwellers are believed to have lived on a crannog at the north end of the lake (SO 129269) – an artificial stockaded island such as was built, especially in the lochs of Scotland and Ireland, in the early Iron Age, and in some places inhabited up to medieval times. The drowning of such lake dwellings during a climatic change known to have taken place about 500 B.C. might account for this and similar legends. But it is much more likely that the story is the result of observation (cf. **Scilly Isles**, p.32), attached to Llyn Syfaddan because signs of former habitation had been seen.

Certainly the lake has long had a reputation for strangeness. In the twelfth century Walter Map knew it as the home of a Lady of the Lake while Gerald of Wales in the same century informs us:

> The local inhabitants will assure you that the lake has many miraculous properties. As I have already told you, it sometimes turns bright green, and in our days it has been known to become scarlet, not all over, but as if blood were flowing along certain currents and eddies. What is more, those who live there sometimes observe it to be completely covered with buildings or rich pasture-lands, or adorned with gardens and orchards . . .

The redness can be accounted for naturally – as Leland puts it, 'after a great reyne Lleueney [Llyfni] cummeth out of the montaynes with such a rage that he bringethe the color of the dark redde sand with hym, and ys sene by the color wher he violently passeth thorough the mere'. But what were the mysterious orchards? Floating islands as perhaps were the Green Islands of the Sea (see **Milford Haven**, p.352)? Or the beginnings of the tradition of the lost city?

Brecon Beacons National Park. A story very like 'Philemon and Baucis' was in the nineteenth century told of Semer Water, North Yorkshire.

LLOWES, POWYS
(formerly RADNORSHIRE)

Until recently there stood in the churchyard at Llowes a large, flat, upright stone with a wheel-cross carved on one side, and on the other a Latin cross. The carving has been dated to the eleventh century, but the stone itself is probably a pre-Christian standing-stone. The 'christianization' of the standing-stone would follow Church practice in other places. In the seventh-century *Life* of St Samson of Dol we are told that when the saint was in Cornwall he came upon a group of people worshipping 'an abominable image'. After converting them by a miracle, he commemorated the event by cutting a cross on the hitherto pagan stone.

Theophilus Jones, whose *History of the County of Brecknock* was published in 1805, had heard that the cross was a memorial to a local anchorite called Wechlen, but he also knew a popular tradition, still current in the later nineteenth century, that this was Moll Walbee's stone. Moll Walbee was a giantess who built Hay Castle (SO 229423) in a night, the stone either falling from her apron as she was passing Llowes, or else being felt in her shoe and hurled angrily across the Wye from Hay.

Moll was a real person – Matilda de St Valery, who like the Queen was Matilda or Maud, and became known in Welsh as Malld Walbri. She was the wife of William de Braose, a baron in the reign of King John, who built Colwyn Castle (SO 1054) and Painscastle (SO 167461), in Welsh called Castell Paen but also referred to (in Latin) as *Castrum Matildis*, 'Castle Maud', perhaps because Maud, whom Camden (trans. Holland, 1610) calls 'a very shrewd, stout, and malapert stomack-full' woman, had defended it successfully against the Welsh in 1195.

The Welsh had much to remember against William de Braose and not surprisingly he became the subject of legend. On Monday, 28 March 1870, the Rev. Francis Kilvert wrote in his diary concerning the 'Normandy kings' – the Norman barons of the Marches:

> The one who lived at Painscastle was a giant. This giant carried off to Painscastle 'screaming and noising' Miss Phillips of the Screen Farm near Erwood whom he found disporting herself with her lover Arthur on or at Bychllyn Pool. Arthur sent for

Hurled from Hay by a giantess: Moll Walbee's stone. Celtic cross of St Meilig, now in Llowes church, Powys

help to old Radnor Castle and Cefn y Blaen. At Cefn y Blaen there were then 40 men each 7 feet high. The giant on the other hand sent for succour to Court Evan Gwynne where there was an 'army', also to Hay Castle and Lord Clifford of Clifford Castle. While these hostile forces were converging upon Painscastle, a woman in the castle favoured the girl's escape and dressed her in man's clothes to this end. Arthur, watching for her outside and not knowing of the disguise, seeing what he thought was a man and one of his enemies coming out of the castle shot his lover dead with an arrow. Arthur then furious stormed the castle with a battle axe: took it and killed the giant.

Maud herself gave rise to several tales which became more and more fantastic with the course of time. At first she played the role of archetypal local tyrant. A fifteenth-century story in Welsh tells how Malld Walbri commanded Madog, a dispossessed chieftain, to shoot an apple from his youngest son's head. This he accomplished without hurting the child, but later his cousin, Y Rhingyll Du ('The Black Sergeant'), seized Malld and *her* son and hanged them in her own tower. The shooting of the apple is, of course, the William Tell legend, first attached to the Swiss hero at some time between the late thirteenth and late fifteenth centuries. When the story was first told of Malld is unknown, but her end in it is an echo of the death of the real Maud, connected with the great scandal of the reign of King John – the murder of his nephew, Arthur of Brittany.

Soon after 1207, William de Braose fell from favour – because of his debts, said the King, but this does not explain why he particularly hounded Maud. Roger of Wendover, writing in the early thirteenth century, knew a story that accounted for this. In March 1208, he tells us, John sent a messenger to de Braose demanding hostages for his good behaviour. Before he could speak, Maud took the reply out of William's mouth and said she would not trust hostages to John because of his murder of Arthur. When John was told this, he was furious, as well he might be, for though gossip was rife concerning Arthur's end, no one knew for certain what had happened – except possibly de Braose, the man who had captured Arthur and handed him over to the King.

Evidently he knew too much and by the same token so did Maud. Moreover Maud had shown a disposition to talk and this would explain why John, though content to exile de Braose, cast Maud and her son into prison, probably at Windsor, though some said **Corfe** (p.60). Wherever it was, they never re-emerged, and it was commonly said that they had starved to death. Tradition avers that they were only given a sheaf of wheat and a piece of raw bacon to live on, and that when after eleven days the door of their dungeon was opened, both of them were dead, Maud having half-devoured the cheeks of her son. Whatever the true details, the

story of Maud's death crops up in every chronicle of the period –
it was the sensation of the time.

The horror of Maud's death, plus her notoriety amongst the
Welsh, may have led to her being cast as leader of the Wild Hunt
(cf. **Littlecote House**, p.67). She seems to be identical with another
Matilda or Maud, in Welsh tradition *Mallt y Nos*, 'Matilda of the
Night', who, when rebuked for her love of hunting, tartly replied
that if there were no hunting in Heaven, to Heaven she would not
go. For this impiety she was condemned to join the Cwn Annwn,
the Hounds of Hell, and course with them through the air on
stormy nights – the story which is in Germany told of 'Frau
Goden' (see **Clun Forest**, p.300).

Moll Walbee's stone (Carreg Mawd Walbi) is now inside Llowes church,
where it was placed in 1956 for safekeeping. In the church at Hay-on-Wye
is an effigy reputed to be hers, but probably that of a monk. The site of
Hay Castle is on the OS 1:25 000 map. For more about Moll Walbee, see
H. R. Ellis Davidson's article 'Folklore and Man's Past', *Folklore* 74,
Winter 1963, pp. 62–79, to which I am indebted.

MILFORD HAVEN (ABERDAUGLEDDYF),   Sheet 157
DYFED   SM 8504
(formerly PEMBROKESHIRE)

Somewhere off Milford Haven lie the Green Islands of the Sea, the
invisible country of the fairies. Wirt Sikes, the United States Consul
for Wales, who in his *British Goblins* (1880) collected many Welsh
fairy traditions, says that traces of belief in the Green Islands were
still to be found in Pembrokeshire and southern Carmarthenshire
in his day:

> There are sailors on that romantic coast who still talk of the
> green meadows of enchantment lying in the Irish channel to
> the west of Pembrokeshire. Sometimes they are visible to the
> eyes of mortals for a brief space, when they suddenly vanish.
> There are traditions of sailors who, in the early part of the
> present century, actually went ashore on the fairy islands, not
> knowing that they were such, until they returned to their
> boats, when they were filled with awe at seeing the islands
> disappear from their sight . . . simply vanishing suddenly.

Earlier, in *Cambrian Superstitions* (1831), William Howell had reported that the fairies inhabiting the Green Islands were believed to have regularly attended the markets at Milford Haven and Laugharne (Lacharn, SN 3010). They made their purchases without speaking, laying down the right money without having to ask, and departing in silence. Sometimes they were invisible, but they were often seen by the sharpsighted. The Milford Haven folk could plainly see the Green Islands a short distance out from land, and it was thought that the fairies went back and forth through a subterranean gallery at the bottom of the sea.

The Green Islands are an echo of the ancient Celtic Otherworld island – Avalon, Tir Nan Og, the mysterious Hy Breasil – but may also have some foundation in reality. They could well have been floating islands such as the one reported in the *Pembroke County Guardian* for 1 November 1896 as having been seen some years before by a Captain John Evans. When passing Grassholme Island (SM 5909), in what he had always known as deep water, he was surprised to see to windward of him a large tract of land covered with a green meadow. It was not *above* water, but a few feet *below* it, so that the grass was stirred by the ripple. Captain Evans had heard old people say there was a floating island off there that unexpectedly came and went. Similar islands, of matted vegetation or peat, are known in inland waters elsewhere, for example on Llyn y Dywarchen, Snowdonia, on Redes Mere, Capesthorne, Cheshire, and on Derwent Water, near Lodore.

For Llyn y Dywarchen, see OS 1:25 000 Outdoor Leisure Map 18, Snowdonia National Park (Bala), SH 763420. Wordsworth has left a description of the Derwent Water floating island in his *Guide through the District of the Lakes* (5th edn, 1835). Capesthorne Hall, in whose grounds Redes Mere lies, is open to the public – for times, see *HHC&G*.

MOLD (YR WYDDGRUG), CLWYD (formerly FLINTSHIRE)

Sheet 117
SJ 2364

Near Mold was once a tumulus known as Bryn-yr-ellylon, 'the hill of the fairies'. When it was being cleared in 1833, workmen came on the skeleton of a tall man laid out at full length and wearing a collar or cape of gold. A local vicar wrote to the Society of

'A coat of gold which shone like the sun': gold cape from Mold, Clwyd, ca. 1400 B.C., British Museum

Antiquaries soon afterwards vouching for the fact that, some time before, an old woman returning late at night to Mold had seen a figure 'of unusual size, clothed in a coat of gold which shone like the sun', crossing the road towards the spot where the collar was found.

'There had been no spectre, of course,' writes Henry Bett in his *English Myths and Traditions* (1953), 'but the popular memory had retained the detail of the golden armour for a millenium and a half.' This is, 'of course', pretty fair bunkum. Since the evidence for the ghost comes from after the collar was found, we cannot assume this to be a classic example of anything other than that common phenomenon, the post-excavation tradition. Nineteenth-century clergymen were, like anyone else, subject to wishful thinking (cf. **Rillaton Barrow**, p.29).

The cape from Mold, made of embossed sheet gold in the early Bronze Age, *ca.* 1400 B.C., was broken up on discovery and its fragments dispersed. Luckily, some were acquired by the British Museum and reconstructed, and can now be seen in Prehistoric and Romano-British Antiquities, Room 35.

PENHESGYN, NR PENMYNYDD, GWYNEDD   Sheet 114
(ANGLESEY)   SH 5374

Of old it was prophesied that a viper would come to Penhesgyn and kill the heir, who was therefore sent to England to cheat his fate. When the viper appeared at Penhesgyn, a pit was dug in a field and covered with a brass vessel, which, gleaming in the sun, attracted the serpent so that it could be caught and killed. The heir returned, was shown the dead viper, and kicked it in contempt. But its fang pierced his foot and poisoned him, so that he died as was foretold.

This story, current around Penmynydd in the 1860s, is one of several Welsh legends concerning vipers. Here the viper is the villain of the piece in a tale told at many times, in many places, of a prophecy unexpectedly fulfilled by a dead creature's bite (cf. **Minster-in-Sheppey**, p.118). Another Welsh version of the story involves a kind of dragon called a *carrog*, supposed to have given its name to Dol-y-Carrog in the Vale of Conwy.

SARN HELEN, GWYNEDD   Sheet 124
(formerly MERIONETHSHIRE)   SH 7229

> And not farre from hence, neere unto a little village called *Fastineog*, there is a street or *Port-way* paved with stone, that passeth through these cumbersome and in a manner, unpassable mountaines. Which, considering that the Britans name it *Sarn Helen*, that is, *Helen's street*, it is not to bee thought, but that *Helena* mother to *Constantine* the Great, who did many such like famous workes throughout the Roman Empire, laied the same with stone.

Thus Camden in his *Britannia* (trans. Holland, 1610) accounts for the great Roman road that still runs below the fort at **Tomen-y-Mur** (p.360) where met the southward routes from Kanovium (Caerhun, SH 7770) and Segontium (Caernarfon, SH 4762). Other Roman roads in Wales are called by the same name, but this is the only one that lies in the territory of the Helen or Elen of legend.

This is Elen of the Legions, Elen of the Hosts, whose story is told in the *Mabinogion*. In 'The Dream of Macsen Wledig' ('Lord Macsen'), we learn that, once upon a time, when the Roman

Emperor Macsen was out hunting, he lay down to sleep in the heat
of noon and dreamt that he sailed to a distant island. Crossing to
its furthest shore, he found himself among mountains, and looking
down could see another island, and a great castle at a river-mouth.
He went down to the castle and entered, and was greeted by a girl,
the daughter of its owner. He sat beside her in her golden chair,
and just as he had his arms around her, was woken by the noise of
the hunt.

Macsen now found himself so in love with the girl that 'nothing
could be got from him save sleep'. He so neglected his empire that
at length his counsellors advised him to send messengers to look
for the castle. After a year of fruitless search they came to Britain,
and when they reached its western heights, they saw Anglesey
opposite and a castle at the mouth of the Seint. In the castle they
found the girl and told her of Macsen's dream. But she was
sceptical. 'I doubt not what you tell me,' she said, 'nor on the
other hand do I overmuch believe it.' She will not go to Rome to
marry Macsen – if he loves her, let him come to her.

So Macsen returned to Arfon and married the girl, who as her
morning-gift asked for three strongholds to be built, at Arfon
(Caernarfon), Caer Llion (Caerleon) and Caer Fyrddin
(Carmarthen):

> Thereafter Elen thought to make high roads from one strong-
> hold to another across the island of Britain. And the roads
> were made. And for that reason they are called the Roads of
> Elen of the Hosts . . .

But seven years later, a usurper arose in Rome, and Macsen
returned there with his legions. Elen's brothers with their warriors
went too, and it was the Britons who retook the city for Macsen,
after which some went home, while others remained abroad and
founded Brittany.

The story compresses into one man's lifetime historical events
that were spread over several decades. Macsen is better known as
Magnus Maximus, a soldier born in Spain, who served in the
Roman army in Britain in the second half of the fourth century.
Early in 383 A.D., disgruntled with the rule of the Emperor Gratian,
Maximus' legionaries proclaimed him emperor and he immediately
invaded Gaul, taking with him his own legion and what native

auxiliaries he could muster. He met and killed Gratian, and subsequently marched on Rome, but was himself defeated and decapitated at Aquila in 388.

Maximus, who had marched away with his legion, was remembered as the man who had stripped Britain of its defences, leaving it a prey to Picts, Scots and Saxons. In fact the closing phase of the Roman withdrawal from Britain did not take place until the 420s, and it was as the aftermath of this that many Britons fled to Armorica, thereafter called Brittany. But although history has been reshuffled in the interests of a good tale, Macsen's traditional association with this area is not wholly unfounded. The great castle at the mouth of the river Seint should probably be taken to be not Caernarfon Castle but Roman Segontium, which began life *ca.* 78 A.D. as an earth-and-timber fort, but was subsequently rebuilt in stone. While to Roman eyes it was never much more than an auxiliary fort of the regional fortress at Chester, the British writer Nennius (*ca.* 800 A.D.) looks back on '*Caer Segeint*' as one of the twenty-eight cities of Britain. In 383 A.D., when Maximus invaded Gaul, Segontium was evacuated, leaving only a small garrison behind. In 390, this garrison also left, and locals may well have remembered the end of Segontium as the work of Maximus.

As for how Helen or Elen came into the story – Constantine the Great was another home-grown emperor, elected in 306 A.D. by the legions stationed at York, and it was undoubtedly this fact that led to his being conflated in legend with Maximus. Helena's transformation from Constantine's mother to Maximus' wife was probably helped along by the fact that her husband, the Emperor Constantius Chlorus, had a name not unlike his son's, and was also active in Britain. Although coins minted in her name show that Helena was known in Roman Britain, there is no reason to suppose that she ever set foot here. Her official history can be found in any dictionary of saints – for of course she is the great St Helena, the finder of the True Cross. For our purpose, it is enough to know that she came not from Britain but from what is now Turkey, that she was not a princess but humbly born, and that she was accredited with finding the True Cross by St Ambrose about sixty years after her death.

Whether or not Helena was especially honoured by the early British Christians because of her connection with this land, by

Norman times a desire for this most powerful saint to actually *be* British had created a tradition that she was born at Colchester in Essex, the daughter of King Coel (see **Cymbeline's Castle**, p.132). The Colchester legend and 'The Dream of Macsen Wledig' are founded on the belief that a Roman married the British heiress and thus won the kingdom. Perhaps what we have here is a wish-revised version (pandering to British pride) of a tradition recorded on the Pillar of Eliseg in Clwyd that the British tyrant Vortigern married Maximus' daughter Sevira. A political marriage of this sort might have made sense in the Britain of the fifth century – certainly Vortigern appears to have tried to continue Roman policies and may have represented himself as the inheritor of the mantle of Rome. But kings in search of prestigious ancestors often chose them from the ranks of famous heroes, and this may have no more reality than the claim that the kingdom of Kent was founded by Hengest and Horsa (see **Kit's Coty House**, p.108). That Vortigern is also said by Nennius to have married Hengest's daughter Rowena should warn us perhaps not to place too much faith in his marriages. Though winning the kingdom by marrying the old king's daughter may well once have been the custom in ancient societies, it has also long been fossilized in legend as a way of explaining shifts of power.

'The Dream of Macsen Wledig' dates from the fourteenth century, the Colchester tradition from the twelfth. It may be that Helena made a special impact on the Britons, so that they eventually credited her with building the Roman roads. But the likelihood is that someone misinterpreted or misheard, or simply had the fancy to 'explain' the Welsh term *sarn hoelen*, 'paved causeway', describing the Roman roads, and thus drew Colchester's Helen into an originally separate tale about the hero Macsen. For in the Middle Ages, with its thirst for relics, everyone wanted a share in the story of the finding of the True Cross. In York, so Camden tells us, under the now demolished church of St Helen-on-the-Wall, was found the tomb of Constantius Chlorus, with the 'eternal flame' supposed to be manufactured by the ancients still burning in it, while 'Matthew of Westminster' tells us that, when Edward I captured Caernarfon, he found the remains of 'that great prince, the father of the noble emperor Constantine', now (1283) identified with Maximus. It is probably not by chance that in that year the

Welsh gave up to Edward a 'large portion of the cross of the Lord, which, in the language of the Welch, is called Croizneth'.

Snowdonia National Park. Sarn Helen runs through the centre of the Park, linking Caerhun and Tomen-y-Mur, leaving it at Pennal, where it crosses the Dyfi. The exact line of the road is doubtful, and a better guide at the moment than the Ordnance Survey, for those who would like to set foot on Sarn Helen themselves, is E. G. Bowen and C. A. Gresham, *The History of Merioneth*, Merioneth Historical and Record Society (1967), vol. I, pp. 249–50. This will direct you to a fine stretch of road beginning at SH 727318, between the cottage of Pen y Stryd and Capel Pen y Stryd, over Fridd Glap (SH 724334) to east of Bryn Llefrith (SH 722337). Segontium Roman Fort (SH 4862): AM. Opening times also in *M&G*. The Pillar of Eliseg, Llanysilio-yn-Ial, Clwyd (SJ 203445): AM (any reasonable time). A guide pamphlet is available from Valle Crucis Abbey nearby. 'Croizneth' or the Cross Neyt was *ca.* 1352 given to St George's Chapel, Windsor. In 1548 the back of it, made of gold, was sold by the Chapter. What happened to the rest is unknown, but representations of it can be seen in the Chapel on roof-bosses and in the angelic choir around the east window. Segontium, Sheet 115; Pillar of Eliseg, 117.

SNOWDON (YR WYDDFA), GWYNEDD (formerly CAERNARVONSHIRE)

Sheet 115
SH 6154

> Ar y drum oer dramaur,
> Yno gorwedd Ricca Gawr

('On the ridge cold and vast, There the Giant Ricca lies'), wrote the poet Rhys Goch Eryri, a native of the parish of Beddgelert said to have died in 1420. The grave of which he speaks was a cairn on the summit of Snowdon known in the nineteenth century as *Carnedd y Cawr*, 'the Giant's Cairn', until it was removed to make way for an hotel.

The Giant Ricca is better known as Rhita, whom Geoffrey of Monmouth in the twelfth century says was the giant of Mount Arvaius, in other words, Snowdon. He had made himself a cloak out of the beards of kings he had slain, and sent a message to King Arthur, telling him to send *his* beard. Since Arthur was more famous than the other kings, he said, he would sew it higher on the cloak than all the rest. But if Arthur refused, then Rhita challenged him to a single combat on Snowdon, the winner to take both the cloak and the beard of the man he had beaten. Arthur accepted the challenge, killed Rhita and won the wonderful cloak.

Snowdonia National Park. Use OS 1:25 000 Outdoor Leisure Map 17, Snowdonia National Park (Snowdon). A modern cairn marking the highest point of Snowdon is on or near the site, SH 610543.

TOMEN-Y-MUR, MAENTWROG, GWYNEDD   Sheet 124
(formerly MERIONETHSHIRE)   SH 7038

In a natural setting of wild beauty is the remote Roman fort of Tomen-y-Mur, built by Agricola in about 78 A.D. Originally an earth-and-timber fort, it was later reduced in size and given a stone wall. It was only occupied until about 140 A.D., but the site was later recognized as a strategic one by the Normans – the large circular motte in the middle of one of the ramparts was probably the work in 1096 of William Rufus. The Roman stone has long since been robbed to build the field-walls of the neighbourhood, but the earthworks themselves are well preserved and still impressive.

To this site was attached, whether in the Dark or the Middle Ages, what is perhaps the most poignant story in the *Mabinogion*. Math, lord of Gwynedd, a magician who 'might not live save while his two feet were in the fold of a maiden's lap', needs a new foot-bearer, and his nephew Gwydion suggests his sister Aranrhod. To test her virginity, Math has her step over a magic wand, and with that step she drops a boy with yellow hair who becomes a child of the sea and for that reason is called Dylan Eil Ton, 'Dylan son of Wave'. Only Gwydion notices that as she makes for the door she also drops 'a small something'. This 'something' he catches up, wraps in silk and places in a chest at the foot of his bed. One day he hears a cry from the chest and finds another child, whom he rears at court until he is four years old. Then he takes the boy to his mother at her castle but she will have nothing to do with him, and refuses to give him a name.

Gwydion, whom the story sometimes calls the boy's uncle, sometimes his father (i.e. like the hero Sigurd he is the child of incest), tricks her into giving him the name of Lleu Llaw Gyffes,

'Bright one of the Skilful Hand', and brings him up at Dinas Dinlle (SH 4356). Now Aranrhod swears that Lleu will never carry arms unless she herself grants them – which she will never do. But again Gwydion tricks her, and at last she lays on the boy the doom that he will never wed a mortal woman. Then Math and Gwydion take 'the flowers of the oak, and the flowers of the broom, and the flowers of the meadowsweet' and from them conjure a woman, the most beautiful ever seen, and they give her the name of Blodeuedd, the Welsh for 'Flowers'.

Lleu takes Blodeuedd to his court at Mur Castell (Tomen-y-Mur), and all goes well for a time. But one day when he is away visiting Math, Blodeuedd sees Gronw Bebyr, lord of Penllyn, riding past the court and offers him hospitality. The pair of them fall in love and plot together to kill Lleu when he returns. As with many heroes – the Greek Achilles, the biblical Samson – it is difficult to kill Lleu. He can only be slain under certain conditions: neither within a house nor without; neither on foot nor on horseback; and the weapon to be a poisoned spear that has been a year in the making. So now Blodeuedd, like Delilah, inveigles Lleu into telling her the conditions and how to fulfil them. A year later, when Gronw has made the poisoned spear, she prepares a bath for Lleu on the banks of the Cynfal (SH 7041), with a thatched roof overhead (neither within nor without), and by the tub places a goat. Lleu sets one foot on the tub, the other on the goat (neither on foot nor on horseback), and at that moment, Gronw rises up from behind a hill and casts the spear at him. It pierces Lleu in the side and with a dreadful shriek he rises into the air in the form of an eagle and is seen no more.

But while Gronw and Blodeuedd set up house at Mur Castell, Gwydion scours the woods and mountains of North Wales, and at last finds Lleu in the Nantlle valley (NP 5053) below Snowdon, perched in a tree. By his magic he returns him to his human form again and they set out together in pursuit of their revenge. Seeing them coming from the heights of Mur Castell, Blodeuedd flees with her maidens from the court across the Cynfal. But looking over their shoulders in fear as they go, the maidens stumble backwards into a lake and are all drowned. Blodeuedd herself is caught by Gwydion at the edge of the lake and by his magic is turned into an owl. Her punishment is to be hated by all other birds, so that she can only come out at night. But her name will not be lost – it shall henceforth be Blodeuwedd. Blodeuwedd is still 'owl' in Welsh, the storyteller says – and 'Flower-face' is no bad name for an owl.

As for Gronw, he is made to stand where Lleu had stood, while Lleu casts at him with the spear. But 'since it was through a woman's wiles I did to thee that which I did', he asks to be allowed to set a rock between them. Yet when Lleu hurls the spear, it passes clean through the rock and breaks Gronw's back – and there to this day (says the story) on the banks of the Cynfal stands Llech Ronw, 'Gronw's Stone', with the hole right through it. And still up on the moors, above Ffestiniog, is a little lake called Llyn y Morynion or 'the Maidens' Lake'.

The story is the age-old one of breach of hospitality (another version is the theft of Helen of Troy). Today one might well take the view that Math and Gwydion got what they asked for by playing at God, and feel some sympathy for Blodeuedd. But Gronw's shuffling excuse (so like Adam's) reminds us that the tale was aimed at an audience bred in the anti-feminist tradition of the Church. And though there is not much prettier than an owl, traditionally it was the most abhorred of birds, mobbed by the others and the subject of a tale referred to in *Hamlet* (IV.v.42–3), 'The Owl was Baker's Daughter', in which when Christ asked for bread, the baker's daughter took care he should not be given too much, and for her lack of charity was turned into an owl. In the Middle Ages, too, the owl was proverbial for fouling its own nest, and this may have been in the storyteller's mind, though the owl-legend was probably first caught up into the tale of the adulterous Blodeuedd for the sake of the play on her name, Blodeuedd/Blodeuwedd. The original ending of her legend is perhaps hinted at in a tradition preserved by the Welsh poet Antony Powel (d. 1618), that she was not turned into a bird but buried under a 'cairn' – the rock of Craig-y-Ddinas in Mid-Glamorgan.

Snowdonia National Park. Use OS 1:25 000 Outdoor Leisure Maps 18, Snowdonia National Park (Bala) and 19, Snowdonia National Park (Harlech). The Nanttle valley appears on Map 17 (Snowdon) of the same series. Footpaths lead to 'Llyn y Morynion' (Llyn Morynion, SH 7342) and past what is hopefully the site of Llech Ronw, now commemorated in the name Llech-Goronwy (SH 716403). This farm is about half a mile from the Cynfal, but Berwyn Prys Jones of the Welsh Office Translation Unit suggests that the original farmhouse may have been nearer the river bank. 'Mur Castell' in the story probably refers specifically to the Norman motte, Castell Tomen-y-Mur (SH 706387). The site as a whole (on private property and at present inaccessible) is reached by a minor road off the A470 south of Ffestiniog. Following this road, you will pass on your right the only known amphitheatre in Roman Britain attached to an auxiliary fort. It may have been a cockpit – Blodeuedd was evidently not the only one to get bored, for all the beauty of its setting, at Tomen-y-Mur. The hill-fort of Dinas Dinlle is marked on OS 1:50 000 map, Sheet 123, as is 'Caer Arianrhod' (with an *i*), a reef of stones (SH 4254) traditionally taken to be the ruined castle of Aranrhod. Craig-y-Ddinas, Sheet 160, SN 9108. 'Mobbing the owl' became a moral emblem and is portrayed in wood, for example, on a misericorde in Norwich cathedral.

VALE OF NEATH (CWM NEDD), WEST GLAMORGAN (formerly GLAMORGAN)

Sheet 170
SN 8303

In the nineteenth century, the Vale of Neath was held to be a haunt of the fairies. Craig-y-Ddinas (SN 9108) was one of their strongholds and on this rock was held the court of the last fairies in Wales. When Wirt Sikes was writing *British Goblins* (1880), there were still men alive who remembered the fairies coming there, though they were no longer seen, having been driven out by the Methodists.

The tradition of fairies in this area goes a long way back. In his *Journey through Wales*, written *ca.* 1191, Gerald of Wales tells the following story, set around Neath and Swansea:

> Somewhat before our own time an odd thing happened in these parts. The priest Elidyr always maintained that it was he who was the person concerned. When he was a young innocent only twelve years old and learning to read, he ran away one day and hid under the hollow bank of some river or other, for he had had more than enough of the harsh discipline ... meted out by his teacher ... Two days passed and there he still lay hidden, with nothing at all to eat. Then two tiny men appeared, no bigger than pigmies. 'If you will come away with us,' they said, 'we will take you to a land where all is playtime and pleasure.' The boy agreed to go ...

They led him through an underground tunnel to a beautiful land of meadows and rivers, where, however, the days were rather dark, because the sun did not shine, and the nights pitch-black, for there was neither moon nor stars.

The people there were very tiny, but perfectly formed, fair in complexion, the men with flowing hair. They had horses about as big as greyhounds, and never ate meat or fish, but lived on junkets. More than anything in the world they hated lies. Elidyr was brought before their king, who handed him over to his son, a child like himself, and they would play together with a golden ball. Elidyr used often to return to the upper world to see his mother, and was never hindered. But one day she asked him to bring back some of the fairies' gold, and he stole the golden ball. He ran home with it to his mother by his usual route, hotly pursued by two of the pigmies. Rushing in, he tripped over the threshold, and as he fell the ball slipped from his hand. The little men at his heels snatched it up and ran off, showing him their contempt for his behaviour. The boy got to his feet, red with shame at what he had done, and set out back along the road he usually took, 'down the path to the river'. But when he came to where the passage had been, he could not find the entrance, and though he searched for nearly a year along the overhanging banks of the river, he never found it again.

The boy later became a priest, and whenever David Fitzgerald, bishop of St David's (d. 1176), asked him about what happened, he would burst into tears. He could still remember the language of the fairies, and the Bishop told Gerald of Wales (who was his nephew) that it sounded like Greek. Because of the legend of Brutus (see **Plymouth Hoe**, p.27), Gerald concluded from this that it was early Welsh – one is reminded of the Welsh-speaking demons who tormented St Guthlac in the Fens.

If Elidyr was lying to cover his truancy, he was spinning a traditional yarn which he could expect to be believed. The underground land of the fairies is found in other early fairytales in Britain (cf. **Woolpit**, p.210), as well as in Ireland, where the fairies inhabit the *sidh* or fairy mound – the tumulus or barrow – suggesting that fairies owe at least a part of their origin to a cult of the dead. For different, although connected, concepts of fairyland in Wales, see **Milford Haven** (p.352).

Craig-y-Ddinas, Sheet 160.

10
North-west

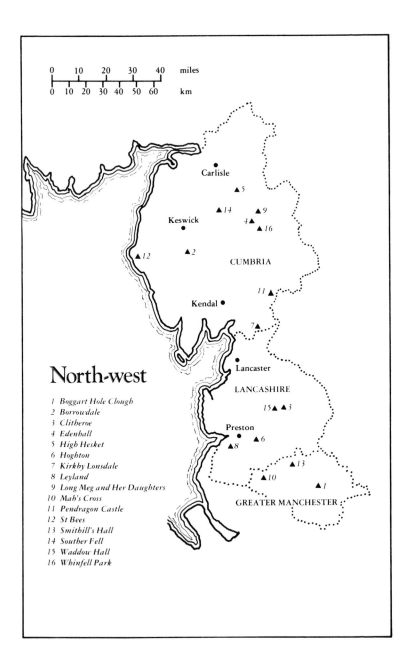

0 10 20 30 40 miles
0 10 20 30 40 50 60 km

● Carlisle

▲ 5

▲ 14   ▲ 9

● Keswick   4 ▲
                 ▲ 16

▲ 12   ▲ 2

CUMBRIA

11 ▲

● Kendal

7 ▲

● Lancaster

LANCASHIRE

15 ▲ ▲ 3

● Preston   ▲ 6

▲ 8

▲ 13

▲ 10   ▲ 1

GREATER MANCHESTER

North-west

1 *Boggart Hole Clough*
2 *Borrowdale*
3 *Clitheroe*
4 *Edenhall*
5 *High Hesket*
6 *Hoghton*
7 *Kirkby Lonsdale*
8 *Leyland*
9 *Long Meg and Her Daughters*
10 *Mab's Cross*
11 *Pendragon Castle*
12 *St Bees*
13 *Smithill's Hall*
14 *Souther Fell*
15 *Waddow Hall*
16 *Whinfell Park*

On the left hand, reader, as thou goest towards Manchester, ascending from Blackley, is a rather deep valley, green swarded, and embowered in plantations and woods . . . Here, at the time Plant was speaking of, stood a very ancient house, built partly of old fashioned bricks, and partly of a timber frame, filled with raddlings and daub . . . It was a lone and desolate-looking house indeed; misty and fearful, even at noon-day. It was known as 'Boggart-ho'' or 'Fyrin-ho''; and the gorge in which it was situated, was, and still is known as 'Boggart' or 'Fyrin-ho' Kloof', 'the glen of the hall of the spirits'.

Such is Samuel Bamford's description of what is now Boggart Hole Clough in his *Passages in the Life of a Radical* (1844). The house called 'Boggart-ho'' ('Boggart Hall') seems also to be the one meant by Crofton Croker in a story he gave to Roby for *Traditions of Lancashire* (1829). This was the well-known 'Aye, we're flitting' (see **Obtrusch Tumulus**, p.416), now often told of Boggart Hole Clough, although there is nothing to suggest that it was known to the local people before Roby's *Traditions* appeared. Probably Roby needed a boggart-story to go with the name of the Clough and Croker supplied one – he had already told it in his own *Fairy Legends* (1825) of an Irish *Cluricaune*. For the tale in *Traditions* is no more than a worked-up version of a Yorkshire tale contributed to the *Literary Gazette*, 16 April 1825, by a reader who had just seen the *Fairy Legends* and recognized the *Cluricaune* story as one that was also told in the neighbourhood of his native village. 'Indeed I am acquainted with the identical farm-house where the mischievous goblin . . . dislodged by its pranks a farmer and his family.'

This farmer was George Gilbertson, whose household was persistently disturbed by the boggart clattering about as if in heavy clogs. The most notable feature of the account is the game the children used to play, posting a shoe-horn through a knot-hole in the boarding under the stairs, whence it would be fired straight back at the head of the child concerned. This they called 'laking wit Boggart', 'playing with the boggart'. This and other details are repeated almost verbatim by Croker in the tale he gave Roby – indeed, though the farmer is now called George Cheetham, his neighbour is still John Marshall as in the *Literary Gazette*. So though Croker says the tale was attached to the old farm-house in Boggart Hole Clough and was told him by 'a very worthy old lady', there is some room for doubt. Certainly Croker had seen the *Gazette* story because he included it as a Yorkshire tale in a second edition of *Fairy Legends* (1826).

Truer to local tradition, perhaps, is the story Bamford tells, as coming from 'Plant' (so-called by Bamford because of his interest in herbs) whom he met in prison. Plant, 'a firm believer in ghosts, witches, and hobgoblins', told him of an encounter he had had whilst gathering 'Saint John's Fearn Seed' near the Boggart Hall. A lad called Bangle, who was lovelorn, went to Limping Billy of Radcliffe Bridge, the local seer, for advice, and Limping Billy told him his only hope of winning the girl was to get some fernseed 'and if he but secured three grains of that, he might bring to him whatever he wished, that walked, flew, or swam'. Bangle enlisted the help of Plant and 'Chirrup' (a bird-catcher) and at midnight on St John's Eve they met at the Clough, where the 'fearn' (bracken) was growing thick among the oaks and hazels, and proceeded as far as the Fyrin-ho'.

> The first word spoken was, 'What hast thou?'
> 'Mine is breawn an' roof [brown and rough]' said Plant, exhibiting a brown earthen dish. 'What has thou?' . . .
> 'Mine is breet [bright] enough,' said Chirrup, shewing a pewter platter . . . 'What has thou?'
>
> > 'Teed [tied] wi' web an' woof,
> > Mine is deep enough,'
>
> said Bangle, displaying a musty, dun skull, with the cap sawn off above the eyes, and left flapping like a lid . . .

When they got to the right spot, they held their vessels one above the other under the 'fearn', the skull bottommost, with its lid open, and Plant said:

> > 'Good Saint John, this seed we crave,
> > We have dared; shall we have?'

To which a voice responded:

> 'Now the moon is downward starting,
> Moon and stars are all departing;
> Quick, quick; shake, shake;
> He whose heart shall soonest break,
> Let him take.'

Suddenly they saw a hooded figure standing near, darkness 'came down like a swoop', and the 'fearn' was shaken. There followed dramatic events, culminating in a vision of beautiful children and women singing. The men stood terrified, until Bangle broke the spell by saying, 'God bless 'em'. There came an almighty crash, as if all the trees in the Clough were being torn up by the roots, and from the thickets terrible forms appeared. The men ran as if sped on the wind, losing one another, and for all of them it turned out badly: Plant lay unconscious for three days; Chirrup went mad; and though Bangle made his charm and summoned the girl, he

Scene of magic and mystery: Boggart Hole Clough, Blackley,
Greater Manchester (photo taken at the beginning of this century)

died three months later. Plant himself, Bamford says, after getting out of prison, left his wife and since then had not been heard of.

Underneath the romantic trappings of the story, we seem to see genuine country magic, with its special ceremonial. In nineteenth-century Lincolnshire, too, the way to gather fernseed was to hold two pewter platters one above the other under the ferns. The 'seed' was supposed to go through the top platter and be caught on the one underneath. Fernseed was believed to be invisible – not surprising since fern has spores – except at midnight on St John's Eve (Midsummer Night), when it ripened. In Lincolnshire gathering fernseed was an infallible charm for summoning the Devil – was this the hooded figure Plant and company saw, and not the Fyrin-ho' boggart? – but a more general belief was that if you wore it in your shoe, you would become invisible. The gathering for this purpose too was traditionally attended by danger. In his *Pandaemonium* (1684), Richard Bovet says:

> I remember I was told of one who went to gether it, and the spirits whisk't by his ears like bullets, and sometimes struck his hat and other parts of his body; in fine, although he apprehended he had gotten a quantity of it, and secured it in papers, and a box besides, when he came home he found all empty.

BORROWDALE, CUMBRIA   Sheet 90
(formerly WESTMORLAND)   NY 2514

The Borrowdale folk once took it into their heads to build a wall across the dale to keep the cuckoo in, and make spring last forever. When the 'gowk', as you would expect, flew over the barricade, one of the dalesmen cried, 'By gow! If we'd nobbut laid another line o' stanes atop, we'd a copped 'im.'

This is supposed to be why the dialect word 'gowk' for a cuckoo also means 'a fool'. The 'Pent Cuckoo' story was already 'an old commonplace joke' when Clarke published his *Survey of the Lakes* in 1789. Behind it lies not only the old tradition of the village of fools (see **Gotham**, p.230), but centuries-old superstitions about the cuckoo. Aristotle, for example, denies the belief current in his day that cuckoos in winter turned into hawks – which did not prevent its still being held into this century in Cheshire, where a field at Great Budworth was once pointed out to an ornithologist as the place where the change occurred.

Implicit in the 'Pent Cuckoo' and in the following Cornish tale is the idea that the bird was the bringer – not just the herald – of spring. One bitter cold April, a farmer invited some friends to come in and sit by his fire, on to which he threw a hollow log. Out flew a cuckoo, and at once the weather changed, becoming warm and seasonal. This was in Cornwall said to be the origin of Towednack Cuckoo Feast, held thereafter every year on the Sunday nearest 28 April, to commemorate the day the cuckoo brought the spring.

CLITHEROE, LANCASHIRE
Sheet 103
SD 7441

A poor tailor once sold his soul to the Devil, to be collected in seven years' time, in exchange for three magic wishes. But he unthinkingly wished for a collop of bacon, and wished his wife away, and then wished her back again, and wasted his wishes. So when the seven years were up and the Devil returned, the tailor tricked him into granting him another wish. This done – 'Then,' said the tailor, 'I wish that you were riding back to Hell on yonder dun horse and never able to plague me again.' The Devil went off with a roar, fixed to the back of the horse, and the tailor lived happily to a good old age. When he died, one of his relations bought his house and set up as an innkeeper under the sign of 'The Dule upo' Dun'.

The story was, some say, attached to a black-and-white timbered inn on the road from Clitheroe to Gisburn, near the village of Chatburn (SD 7644). Others claim it was between Clitheroe and Waddington, and this is the neighbourhood in which William Dobson places it in his *Rambles by the Ribble* (1864) when he speaks in the same breath of 'Waddow wood, Brungerley, where were the old hypping stones, Clitheroe wood, and the site of "Dule upo' Dun".' Wherever it was, the sign showed the Devil on a scraggy dun horse departing at full gallop from a door where stood 'a small hilarious tailor'. This sign hung over the door 'till lately', according to Harland and Wilkinson (1873), and seems to

have been still there when Roby was writing the second series of
Traditions of Lancashire (1831).

EDENHALL, CUMBRIA   Sheet 90
(formerly CUMBERLAND)   NY 5632

In the Victoria and Albert Museum is a glass beaker with a flaring
rim, painted in red, blue, green and white enamels, and gilded.
Made in Syria about the middle of the thirteenth century, it was
quite possibly brought home to England by a returning Crusader.
Astonishingly for a glass of this age, it is in perfect condition,
because for centuries it has been protected by a leather case made
specially for it, probably in the fourteenth century. Now celebrated
as the 'Luck of Edenhall', it was clearly always a cherished object,
and although its early history is unknown, it is likely that it was an
heirloom that came into the possession of the Musgrave family of
Edenhall during the Middle Ages.

The story of the Luck begins with the first appearance in print,
in 1729, of a version made by James Ralph of 'The Drinking

*The Luck of Edenhall:
thirteenth-century
Syrian glass beaker now
in the Victoria and
Albert Museum*

Match. A new Ballad in Imitation of Chevy Chace. By a Person of Quality' (1722). The 'Person of Quality' turned out to be Philip, first Duke of Wharton, who thus celebrated a colossal drunk engaged in with his Musgrave cousin at Edenhall, probably in September 1721. It was later said that the Duke insisted on drinking healths out of the precious glass, and that either he threw it into the air or let it fall, and only the presence of mind of the butler saved its history from ending right there.

However that may be – and this tradition did not go on record until 1849 – when James Ralph produced *his* version of the ballad, he changed the opening lines from:

> God prosper long our Lord the King
> And also Edenhall

to:

> God prosper long from being broke
> The Luck of Eden Hall.

More than half a century later, an account of the origin of the 'Luck' appeared, in the *Gentleman's Magazine* for August 1791. Its author, probably a relative of the Cumberland Musgraves, writes:

Tradition . . . says, that a party of Fairies were drinking and making merry round a well near the Hall, called St Cuthbert's well; but, being interrupted by the intrusion of some curious people, they were frightened, and made a hasty retreat, and left the cup in question: one of the last screaming out,

> If this cup should break or fall,
> Farewell the Luck of Edenhall.

This was the basis of several later romanticized accounts of the Luck, culminating in Longfellow's translation of a German ballad of 1834 in which it is imagined as being broken at a feast, with disastrous consequences:

> In storms the foe with fire and sword;
> He in the night had scaled the wall,
> Slain by the sword lies the youthful Lord,
> But holds in his hand the crystal tall,
> The shattered Luck of Edenhall.

In fact the Luck was well looked after: in the eighteenth century, when the family 'or other curious people' wanted to drink out of it, a napkin was held underneath in case of accident – a practice springing from, or giving rise to, the story about the butler. At all events, the glass remained in the possession of the Musgrave family until 1926, when it was loaned to the Victoria and Albert. Although in one sense the luck of Edenhall ran out in 1934, when the house was demolished, its other Luck survived and was acquired by the Museum outright in 1958.

The leather case of the Luck, said to be its second, bears the sacred monogram IHS, suggesting that this glass, like others that have survived in Church treasuries and elsewhere on the Continent, was once used as a memorial cup or chalice. But was it always a Christian cup? E. S. Hartland in *The Science of Fairytales* (1891) argued that 'fairy cups' such as the Luck of Edenhall and the Ballafletcher Cup from the Isle of Man were originally 'sacrificial vessels dedicated to the old pagan worship of the house-spirits'. He pointed out that Cumbria and the Isle of Man were areas settled by Norsemen, and that in the sagas we several times hear of the *hamingja*, a female guardian spirit of the house who could be passed on by the head of the house at his death as his 'luck', usually to another member of the family. The vessel connected with the worship of this hereditary guardian spirit might, Hartland suggests, come to be regarded as the family 'luck' in its concrete sense.

An attractive theory, but not in fact borne out by the Edenhall beaker's history. To support his idea that such fairy cups, like some ancient monuments, were later christianized, Hartland mentions several chalices in Sweden said to have been given to churches by priests who had been offered drink in them by Berg-women, i.e. trolls. This takes us back to an ancient legend concerning fairy cups (see **Willy Howe**, p.430), from which it seems likely that, far from being pagan cups that were christianized, these were vessels whose medieval religious use was after the Reformation forgotten or suppressed in order to save them from the iconoclasts, the traditional folklore of the fairy cup later being invoked to explain them. Moreover, the OED tells us that 'luck' in its concrete sense of talisman only dates from James Ralph's ballad – that it was in fact the tale of the Luck of Edenhall that added it to the language.

At least four other families in Cumbria also had their Lucks, undoubtedly by way of imitation. The most important of these is the Luck of Muncaster, a fifteenth-century glass bowl preserved at Muncaster Castle (SD 1096) near Ravenglass, which is said to have been presented to Sir John Pennington of Muncaster by Henry VI. An inscription in Muncaster church which tells us that 'Holie Kinge Harrye gave Sir John a brauce wrkyd glass cuppe . . . whyles the familie shold kepe hit unbrecken they shold gretely thryve' is generally admitted to be the work of another Sir John Pennington, first Lord Muncaster (d.1813), in emulation of his distant kinsmen, the Musgraves.

The Luck of Edenhall may be seen at the Victoria and Albert Museum, London; the Luck of Muncaster at Muncaster Castle. There is also the Luck of Workington, an agate cup said to be the gift of Mary Queen of Scots to Sir Henry Curwen of Workington Hall, now at Belle Isle, Bowness-on-Windermere. Muncaster Castle and Belle Isle are open to the public – for times see *HHC&G*. Muncaster Castle, Sheet 96.

HIGH HESKET, CUMBRIA
(formerly CUMBERLAND)

Sheet 86
NY 4744

Near the church of High Hesket there was once a lake known in the time of William Rufus as *Tarn Wadalyne*. 'It covers about one hundred acres of land, and breeds some of the finest carp in the kingdom,' wrote the county historian Hutchinson in 1794. But carp notwithstanding, in the 1850s it was drained and turned into pasture land, breaking a powerful link with the past.

For Tarn Wadling, as it was latterly called, was in the Middle Ages associated with King Arthur, who had his court at Carlisle. It is mentioned in romances of the late fourteenth and early fifteenth centuries, one of them telling how, in performance of a vow, Sir Gawain watches all night by the Tarn, evidently a place where adventures could be expected. But the most celebrated story of Gawain at Tarn Wadling is told in 'The Marriage of Sir Gawain', a ballad which Bishop Percy found in a seventeenth-century manuscript and reprinted in his *Reliques*. The ballad is fragmentary, and the Bishop pieced it out with 'Gothic' embellishments – a damsel in distress, a boon, a giant, a castle ringed about with spells.

Fortunately the story can be reconstructed from the fragments themselves helped out by other versions – for much the same tale was told by Gower as 'The Tale of Florent' in his *Confessio Amantis* and by Chaucer as 'The Wife of Bath's Tale', as well as in a (probably) fifteenth-century romance called *The Weddynge of Sir Gawen and Dame Ragnell.*

The story goes that, when Arthur was holding court at 'merry Carlile', some days after Christmas he was riding through Inglewood when he was encountered at Tarn Wadling by a 'bold barron' with a great club. The baron barred his way and challenged him to single combat or else to pay a ransom by answering the riddle: what is it women most desire? Arthur declines combat and chooses the riddle, returning to Carlisle to ask his court what they think the solution is. None of their answers seems quite right but, such as they are, he rides back with them on New Year's Day to keep the tryst at Tarn Wadling. On a desolate moor on his journey, he meets a lady as ugly as sin sitting between an oak and a green holly. She offers to help him in his plight and he promises her his 'cozen' Gawain for her husband if she can tell him the answer. This she agrees to do, and when he finds the baron waiting for him at Tarn Wadling, Arthur is able to say that what women most desire is to have their own will.

Arthur returns to Carlisle, and in the spring leads his knights out to fetch the ugly lady. Without mentioning the bargain he has made, he tells them that one of them must be her husband – to which they react with alarm.

> Then some tooke vp their hawkes in hast,
> And some tooke vp their hounds,
> And some swore they wold not marry her
> For citty nor for towne.

Gawain, however, celebrated in medieval romance for his courtesy, says he will take her – whereupon she is transformed into a most beautiful woman. There is still one snag – she can be beautiful by day or by night, but not both. Which would Gawain prefer? By night, he says, when they are together in bed. 'Alas! then I must hyde my selfe,' she says, for it will humiliate her to have to appear ugly at court. 'Gentle' Gawain leaves the choice to her, and this act of courtesy and compassion breaks the magic spell under which she and the baron, her brother, have laboured and which was cast on them by their wicked stepmother – he to challenge passers-by and ask his riddle, she to remain ugly until some man could be found to marry her and give her her own way.

This tale of the Loathly Lady is believed to go back to early Irish stories in which the test for kingship seems to be willingness to kiss or lie with a hag who by that act is transformed into a beautiful woman – the Sovereignty of Ireland. Early added to this tale were the choice of beauty by day or night, and the riddle on which the hero's life depends, and in this form the story entered a cycle of tales about the northern hero Gawain, the Sovereignty carried over as domestic 'maisterie'.

The story was perhaps from the first set in this district, for Gower's Florent is captured in the Marches, while in *Dame Ragnell* the setting is specifically named as the Forest of Inglewood. Whether this romance grew out of the ballad or the other way about, the ballad's even more precise location of the tale at Tarn Wadling probably arose because the lake already had an uncanny reputation. Gervase of Tilbury, writing *ca.* 1212, tells of a valley beside a public road and surrounded by a forest running from near Carlisle to Penrith, where at one o'clock every day was heard a mysterious ringing of bells. The natives of the region called the valley *Laikibrait*, thought to be Old French for 'the lake that cries'. This is virtually certainly Tarn Wadling – which lay beside a Roman road running through Inglewood – for in the reign of Edward I we hear of 'the lake of Terwathelan which is called Laykebrayt'.

But why should Tarn Wadling be called 'the lake that cries'? The simple view is that in Gervase's day there must have existed a story like the one told of the Tarn in the nineteenth century, that a witch who was refused alms in a certain village drowned it in revenge. This story was told in many places to account for lakes, often with the detail that the bells of the church could still be heard. But this explanation depends on the assumption that the name '*Laikibrait*' and Gervase's bells refer to the same tradition – that 'the lake that cries' was so-called *because* of the ringing of bells – which is not what he says. Had Gervase not mentioned bells, we might have assumed that *Laikibrait* got its name because when it froze it gave out 'a horrible groaning sound' such as Gerald of Wales reports of **Llangorse Lake** (p.346).

Another reason for locating the story at Tarn Wadling may have been because, to the north-east of the lake, on an eminence adjoining Aiketgate (NY 4846), was an ancient castle known to Leland in the sixteenth century as 'Castle Lewin'. Hutchinson, however, in the eighteenth, writes: 'It is called, by the neighbouring inhabitants, *Castle Hewin*, and the neighbouring tenants pay to the Lord of the manor, a yearly rent, which is called Castle Hewin rent.' He continues: 'Tradition reports it to have been one of the fortresses and strongholds of King Ewaine', i.e. Owain of Strathclyde (king *ca.* 920–37), remembered at Penrith in the sixteenth century as the giant Sir Hugh Cesario. It may well have been the old custom of Castle Hewin rent and traditions in this neighbourhood of Ewaine that suggested the 'bold barron' with his great club exacting toll of passers-by at Tarn Wadling.

For the identification of Tarn Wadling with *Laikibrait*, see R. C. Cox, 'Tarn Wadling and Gervase of Tilbury's "Laikibrait"', *Folklore* 85, Spring 1974, pp.128–30.

HOGHTON, LANCASHIRE

Sheet 102
SD 6125

Two poachers at Hoghton were catching rabbits by putting sacks over the mouths of what they thought rabbit-holes but which were fairies' homes. Thinking they had caught several rabbits, the pair of them slung the sacks over their shoulders and were just making off when they heard a small voice from one of the sacks call:

'Dick, wheer art ta?'

To which a voice from the other sack replied:

'In a sack,
On a back,
Riding up Hoghton Brow!'

The poachers were so frightened that they dropped the sacks and bolted. Next morning they found them by the roadside, neatly folded.

The story is told of Hoghton Brow by James Bowker in his

Goblin Tales of Lancashire (1883), but had earlier in the century been told of 'Barley Brow', also in Lancashire, and of Beeding Hill, West Sussex.

KIRKBY LONSDALE, CUMBRIA
(formerly WESTMORLAND)

Sheet 97
SD 6178

Of the many evidences of the Devil and his works in the former county of Westmorland, perhaps the finest is the bridge he built at Kirkby Lonsdale over the rocky gorge of the Lune. Tradition says that an old woman's cow strayed over the water and by evening when she went to look for it the river was in spate. Suddenly the Devil appeared and offered to build her a bridge by the morning in

The Devil's Bridge: fifteenth-century bridge
at Kirkby Lonsdale, Cumbria

return for the first living thing to cross. To this the old woman agreed, and when at dawn she returned, the bridge was built and the Devil expecting his price. He thought it would be the old woman, crossing the bridge to fetch her cow, but she set down a little dog she had hidden under her cloak. She threw a bun on the bridge, the dog at once chased the bun and fulfilled the contract. With a great howl of rage – for the dog was no use to him, having no soul – the Devil vanished, leaving his collar behind, which he had taken off while he was at work.

The Devil's Neck-Collar can still be seen, looking downstream, on the right bank between the old fifteenth-century bridge and the new. So, too, can his fingermarks, left on the coping stone of the second recess on the right going towards Casterton.

'The Dog on the Bridge' is an international folktale told also of Devil's Bridge (Pontarfynach) in Dyfed, the lowest of three spanning the narrow gorge of the river Mynach below Bryn Garv. It was in the nineteenth century likewise told of bridges over the Reuss in Switzerland and the Main in Germany (though here with a cock not a dog). The story was made popular by Longfellow, who included the Swiss Devil's Bridge tale in the *Golden Legend*, written after a tour of Europe in 1826. Longfellow may have been influenced by the Kirkby Lonsdale tradition, current in the eighteenth century, when it was recorded by the Rev. John Hutton in his *Tour to Ingleborough* (1780).

The bridge is in Bridge Brow, a continuation of Main Street.

LEYLAND, LANCASHIRE
Sheet 102
SD 5421

In his *Popular Rhymes and Nursery Tales of England* (1849), James Orchard Halliwell reports a local tradition current sixty years before his time that, on the day the builders finished Leyland church, it was mysteriously shifted during the night to another spot. Entering the church next day, the villagers saw a marble tablet on the wall which read:

> Here thou shalt be,
> And here thou shalt stand,
> And thou shalt be called
> The church of Ley-land.

The church stands in the original centre of the village; the town has now grown towards the north. It was probably to explain the oddity of its situation that the 'disputed site' legend was first told. Similar stories are attached to other churches in Lancashire, for example Newchurch in Rossendale, and St Chad's, Rochdale (now Greater Manchester).

LONG MEG AND HER DAUGHTERS, HUNSONBY, CUMBRIA (formerly CUMBERLAND)

Sheet 91
NY 5737

Here, at one of Britain's largest prehistoric stone circles, current folklore says that a local witch and her coven were of old turned into stone. Long Meg herself is a single narrow sandstone shaft, twelve feet (3.6 m) high, standing just outside the ring formed by her Daughters – fewer than in 1634, when three Norwich soldiers spoke of seeing 'Stony Meg and her 77 daughters as hard-hearted as herself'.

Camden is the first to mention the circle (or rather oval) by name, using a description sent to him in about 1600 by Reginald Bainbrigg, 'Scholemaister of Applebie', who wrote:

> Besides litle Salkeld, not far frome Crawdundailewaith, wher the Romaines have fought some great Battle, ther standes certaine monuments or pyramides of stone, placed ther equal distance one frome an other in modum coronae [in the manner of a crown]. They are commonlie called meg with hir daughters. They are huge great stones, long meg standes above the ground in sight, xv fote long and thre fathome about.

Though some say Long Meg was Meg of Meldon, an early-seventeenth-century witch, she is more likely to have got her name from the saying 'As long as Meg of Westminster', of which Fuller in his *Worthies* (1662) tells us:

> This is applyed to persons very tall, especially if they have

Hop-pole-heighth wanting *breadth* proportionable thereunto. That such a *gyant woman* ever was in *Westminster*, cannot be proved by any good witness, (I pass not for a late *lying Pamphlet*) though some in proof thereof produce her Gravestone on the *south-side* of the *Cloistures*, which (I confess) is as long an large and entire *Marble*, as ever I beheld.

The 'late *lying Pamphlet*' was the tract *The Life of Long Meg of Westminster* (1635) which tells of the giantess supposed from the size of the gravestone to be buried there, but Fuller, who is of the opinion that no woman would ever have been buried in a monks' graveyard, suggests that the stone actually marks a mass grave of monks who died in a year of plague. He has his own notion of Meg's identity:

If there be any truth in the Proverb, it rather relateth to a great Gun, lying in the Tower, commonly call'd *long Megg*, and in troublesome times . . . brought to Westminster . . .

However that may be, several legends sprang up accounting for Long Meg as a victim of petrifaction. Celia Fiennes, who passed this way in 1698, wrote afterwards:

A mile from Peroth [Penrith] in a low bottom a moorish place stands Great Mag and her Sisters, the story is that these soliciting her to an unlawfull love by an enchantment are turned with her into stone . . .

One would like to know more of this 'unlawfull love', but Stukeley (1743) says no more than that '*long Meg and her daughters*' were 'believed to have been human, turn'd into stones', and the county historian Hutchinson (1793) that they were witches thus petrified.

Besides the petrifaction legend, there was a tradition that these were 'countless stones'. So the redoubtable Celia tells us, 'they affirme they cannot be counted twice alike as is the story of Stonidge' (**Stonehenge**, p.77). It was also believed to be dangerous to interfere with the stones – in the nineteenth century it was said that if you broke a piece off Meg she would bleed, and that when Colonel Lacy, who enlarged Lacy's Caves (NY 5638) on the river Eden, tried to blast the circle away, such a tempest arose that his workmen fled in fear. Storms were similarly said to spring up at the desecration of barrows and other ancient monuments (cf. **Trencrom Castle**, p.37).

Lacy's Caves, Sheet 90.

MAB'S CROSS, WIGAN, GTR MANCHESTER (formerly LANCASHIRE)

Sheet 108
SD 5805

At the top of Standishgate, one of the old entrances to the town, stands a ruined stone cross to which is attached the following tale:

Sir William Bradshaghe ... was A great traueller and A Souldyer and married To Mabell daughter and Sole heire of Hugh Noris de Haghe and Blackrode [Haigh and Blackrod] ... of this Mabel is a story by tradition of undouted verity that in Sr William Bradshage's absence (beinge 10 yeares away in the wares) she married a welch k^t Sr William retorninge from the wares came in a Palmers habit amongst the Poore to haghe. Who when she saw & congetringe [conjecturing] that he favoured her former husband wept, for which the k^t chasticed her at wich Sr William went and made him selfe Knawne to his Tennants in wch space the k^t fled, but neare to Newton Parke Sr William ouertooke him and slue him. The said Dame Mabell was enioyned by her confessor to doe Pennances by going onest [once] euery week barefout and bare legg'd to a Crosse ner Wigan from the haghe wilest she liued & is called Mabb + to this day ...

Such is the story told in the genealogical roll of the Bradshaighs of Haigh Hall (SD 6008), drawn up in 1647 and reproduced (in black letter) by Sir Walter Scott in the introduction to *The Betrothed* (1825). Scott, who had heard the story early in life from Lady Balcarres of Haigh, not only uses the plot in *The Betrothed*, one of his 'Tales of the Crusaders', but also mentions it in a note to the 1829 edition of *Waverley*, commenting on its likeness to a fifteenth-century German ballad, 'The Noble Moringer', and remarking that many such incidents must have taken place during the Crusades because of the difficulty of getting news.

Roby (1829) and Harland and Wilkinson (1873) say that Sir

William was 'in the holy wars' instead of 'the wares' and then proceed to explain that he was never a Crusader – was indeed not born until about 1280, ten years after the last Crusade. The genealogical roll itself dates events to the reign of Edward II, and if there is any truth in the tradition, Sir William was perhaps a prisoner of the Scots during the disastrous invasion of Scotland that ended in 1314 at Bannockburn.

Based on historical events or not, the story bears the stamp of a widespread version of 'The Homecoming Husband' in which the husband, disguised as a pilgrim, identifies himself by means of a ring. This story is told in the medieval romance of *King Horn*, written in about 1225, and also figures in the legend of Guy of Warwick (see **Guy's Cliffe**, p.269). In local tradition it is often told of returning Crusaders (see **Wroxall Abbey**, p.286).

Sir William, who is said to have been outlawed for a year and a day for the murder of the Welsh knight, was himself murdered in an affray on Monday, 16 August 1333. He was buried in Wigan parish church, where Lady Mabel in 1338 founded the Bradshaigh chantry. Here their effigies can still be seen, he in his armour, she in a long robe and veil. The figures were already in the nineteenth century badly mutilated, and that of Lady Mabel was entirely recut, while Sir William's was copied by the sculptor John Gibson (1790–1866). The original, totally defaced effigy is next to the renovated pair.

Mab's Cross is still in Standishgate, but opposite its original site in front of 138 Wigan Lane. It was moved in 1922. Haigh Hall (the present house is nineteenth-century) descended in the female line from the Bradshaighs to the Lindsays, Earls of Crawford and Balcarres, and is now owned by Wigan Metropolitan Borough. Its park is a public open space. The name 'Bradshaigh', I am told, is pronounced 'Bradshaw', being a telescoped version of Bradshaw of Haigh.

PENDRAGON CASTLE, MALLERSTANG, CUMBRIA (formerly WESTMORLAND)

Sheet 91
NY 7802

> *Let* Uter-Pendragon *do what he can,*
> *The River* Eden *will run as it ran.*

Above the river Eden in the valley of Mallerstang stands Pendragon Castle, 'which', says Camden, 'hath nothing left unto it unconsumed by time, besides the bare name, and an heape of stones'. This was 1586 (trans. Holland, 1610). But he must have been talking to the wrong people, for in 1662 Fuller in his *Worthies* gives the 'proverb' quoted above and the story that went with it:

> Tradition reporteth, that this *Uter-Pendragon* had a design, to fortifie the Castle of *Pen-Dragon* in this County. In order whereunto, with much *art* and *industry*, he *invited* and *tempted* the River of *Eden*, to forsake his old chanell, and all to no purpose.

The proverb, Fuller adds, 'is appliable to such who *offer a rape* to Nature, indeavouring what is cross and contrary thereunto'.

The story and the rhyme were added to Camden's *Britannia* by Gibson (1695), and the rhyme itself found its way into eighteenth-century collections of proverbs. The legend seems to have survived and gone its own way in oral tradition, as in 1902 it was said locally that Uther Pendragon, father of King Arthur, had died in the castle while fighting the Saxons, who, failing to take it, poisoned the well. In fact the 'Uther' of the rhyme seems to have been Robert de Clifford, one of Edward I's 'Great Captains', who in 1309 was granted a licence to crenellate his castles of Brougham (NY 5329) and 'Pendragon' – hitherto known in records as Mallerstang. The Plantagenet kings had, to suit themselves, recast King Arthur as an English hero, and Robert probably crenellated the castle, strengthened it with the ditches that gave rise to the rhyme, and renamed it Pendragon when the Arthurian cult was at its height at Edward's court. Robert had family reasons for identifying himself with the cult – the Cliffords were a Welsh-Norman family connected by marriage with the dynasty of Llewellyn the Great, who had worn the crown of Arthur, taken by Edward among his spoils after the defeat of the Welsh in 1282 (see **Sarn Helen**, p.355).

It is likely that Robert – celebrated as one of the great soldiers of his age in *The Song of Caerlaverock*, written in Northern French after the siege of that castle in July 1300, possibly by his own herald – also had a strong personal interest in 'chivalry'. He may even have assumed the name 'Uther Pendragon' at the sort of feast and joust combined known in the Middle Ages as a 'Round Table'.

'Nothing left unto it unconsumed by time':
Pendragon Castle, Mallerstang, Cumbria

They are recorded as having taken place in Britain on eight occasions between 1242 and 1345, the last, held at Windsor, the consequence of a vow made by Edward III in 1344 to found an order of 300 knights in imitation of the Knights of the Round Table. Although popes and other churchmen fulminated against these events as expensive, dangerous and licentious, not even the threat of excommunication could prevent people risking life and limb to act out their fantasies. At Round Tables – which also spread to the wealthy bourgeoisie – combatants took the names of Arthur's knights, sometimes wearing their devices and trying to emulate their deeds. Elaborate scenarios were constructed: in 1446, at Saumur in France, King René of Anjou built a 'Joyous Garde' of wood, and lions, tigers and unicorns (!) from his menagerie took part in the display. Occasionally the Round Table was virtually the dramatic performance of a well-known romance: the marriage celebrations of Edward I in 1299 included the entrance during a feast (in true Arthurian style) of the Loathly Lady (see **High Hesket**, p.375), actually a squire made up to look hideous with a long nose and goitre.

It is tempting to think that Robert may himself have held a

Round Table at the prehistoric earthwork south of Penrith (NY 523284) which, says the King's antiquary Leland in 1538, 'is of sum caullid the Round Table and of sum, Arture's Castel'. Could this be the origin of the country sports that were held there in the eighteenth century? In 1724 Stukeley tells us that the country folk still gathered there for games and 'military exercises' such as shooting with the bow, while in 1773 the Cumberland historian Hutchinson says he was told by villagers that it was an ancient tilting yard where jousts had once been held.

Brougham Castle and Arthur's Round Table: AM. Admission to the Round Table any reasonable time. The actual Round Table preserved in Castle Hall, Westgate, Winchester, may be the one Edward III proposed to build when he was planning to revive the Arthurian fellowship, though its decoration is thought to belong to the reign of Henry VIII. What remains of Pendragon Castle stands on an artificial mound with a few trees on it between the river and the B6259 running south from Kirkby Stephen over Mallerstang Common to join the A684 near Garsdale Head. Brougham Castle and Arthur's Round Table, Sheet 90.

ST BEES, CUMBRIA   Sheet 89
(formerly CUMBERLAND)   NX 9711

St Bees takes its name from an ancient Irish princess who, when her father said she should marry a Norwegian chieftain, fled across the Irish Sea and settled 'in a wooded region' in Cumbria as a recluse.

This much we know from the twelfth-century *Life and Miracles of St Bega the Virgin*. But the legend of Bega or Bee, as she was later known, came to include the tradition that she was shipwrecked off the Cumberland coast and there founded a nunnery. Among her miracles, Camden (trans. Holland, 1610) says were 'the taming of a wild bul, & the procuring of a mighty deepe snow, which in the longest Summer day, by her praiers, fell, and lay thicke upon the valleies and tops of hilles'. Edmund Sandford, writing of the antiquities and great families of Cumberland in about 1675, gives us the full story. A 'pious religious Lady Abbess' and some of her nuns were driven by a storm into Whitehaven, where the ship foundered. The wife of the Lord of Egremont Castle (NY 010105) asked him to help the nuns and he sarcastically promised to give them as much land as snow fell on next morning – namely none, 'being midsumerday'. But when next day he rose and looked out of his window, he saw the ground white with snow from Egremont to the sea, and chastened by this he built St Bees Priory 'and gave the land was snowen unto it', including the site of Whitehaven (NX 9718), which takes its name from these events.

This pretty story is an embroidery on an account in the *Life* of how, to settle a boundary dispute between the local Meschines family and the Priory, Bega showed them exactly how the land lay by covering the Meschines properties with snow while those of the Priory stayed bare. The 'Snow in Summer' story was also told at **Wroxall Abbey** (p.286), where a nun called Alice Croft was promised by the Virgin Mary that she would show her the site on which to build a Lady Chapel. Next morning when Alice went out, having already confidently hired her workmen, she found 'a certayne ground covered with snow although it was harvest time'. The very same tale was told of the foundation of Santa Maria Maggiore on the Esquiline Hill in Rome. It was probably drawn into the legend of St Bee because of the name 'Whitehaven'.

Although there is nothing impossible in the account of Bega's origins given in her *Life* – there were indeed colonies of Norsemen in Ireland by the ninth century with whom such a marriage might be arranged – some scholars have cast doubt on her existence. In the early thirteenth century, we hear several times of the bracelet of St Bega, kept at the Priory Church, on which oaths were sworn, as in pagan Scandinavia they were sworn on holy arm-rings kept in the temples. The custom may well have survived in Cumberland, also settled by the Norse, and some think that Bega's name in fact comes from OE *beag*, 'a ring', and that a holy ring, not a person, lay behind her cult. This is by no means unlikely. 'But', as Fuller would say, 'this *Nut* (perchance) deserves not the *Cracking*'.

SMITHILLS HALL, BOLTON, GTR MANCHESTER (formerly LANCASHIRE)

Sheet 109
SD 6911

On the threshold of one of the doors of —— Hall there is a bloody footstep impressed into the doorstep, and ruddy as if the bloody foot had just trodden there, and it is averred that, on a certain night of the year, and at a certain hour of the night, if you go and look at that doorstep, you will see the mark wet with fresh blood.

This is Nathaniel Hawthorne, who once stayed at Smithills Hall, recounting its 'Bloody Footstep' legend in *Septimius* (1872). For the purposes of his novel, he gives a romantic explanation of the print, but it is traditionally said to be that of George Marsh, one of three Lancashire Protestant martyrs in Queen Mary's reign. He was interrogated at Smithills Hall by its owner, Mr Barton, a magistrate, before being burnt at the stake at Boughton, Cheshire, in 1555. During the questioning, Marsh stamped on the floor, praying that there might remain on the spot a permanent memorial of the injustice of his enemies. A cavity in a stone flag in the passage outside the dining-room was in the nineteenth century shown as his footprint. About the beginning of the eighteenth century, so it was said, two or three young men of the Barton family took up this flag and threw it in a clough, but the house was so disturbed that night they were obliged to go and bring it back (cf. 'Screaming Skull' legends, under **Burton Agnes Hall**, p.401). It was also claimed that, in 1732, a guest sleeping in the 'Green Chamber' saw Marsh's ghost with a book in its hand disappearing through the doorway.

Marsh left his own account of what took place at Smithills Hall, and naturally mentions no footprint. Its first appearance seems to be in a tract printed at Bolton and dated 1787. The truth of 'Popery' was likewise proved by a footprint stamped into the church wall by a priest (or some said the Devil) at Brindle (SD 5924).

Bolton Metropolitan Borough. Parts of the Hall, in Smithills Dean Road, date from the early fifteenth century, making it one of the oldest manor houses in Lancashire. Open to the public – for times, see *HHC&G*.

SOUTHER FELL, CUMBRIA
Sheet 90
(formerly CUMBERLAND)
NY 3529

East of Skiddaw and Blencathra is a mountain called Souther

(pronounced Souter) Fell, where in the early eighteenth century, a phantom army was seen. In the *Gentleman's Magazine* in 1747, only a decade after the appearances, was published an account by someone who had questioned the witnesses:

> On Midsummer-eve, 1735, Wm. Lancaster's servant related that he saw the east side of Souter-fell, towards the top, covered with a regular marching army for above an hour together; he said they consisted of distinct bodies of troops, which appeared to proceed from an eminence in the north end, and marched over a nitch in the top, but, as no other person in the neighbourhood had seen the like, he was discredited and laughed at. Two years after, on Midsummer-eve also, betwixt the hours of eight and nine, Wm. Lancaster himself imagined that several gentlemen were following their horses at a distance, as if they had been hunting, and, taking them for such, pay'd no regard to it till about ten minutes after; again turning his head towards the place, they appeared to be mounted, and a vast army following, five in rank, crowding over at the same place, where the servant said he saw them two years before. He then called his family, who all agreed in the same opinion, and, what was most extraordinary, he frequently observed that some one of the five would quit rank and seem to stand in a fronting posture, as if he was observing and regulating the order of their march, or taking account of the numbers, and after some time appeared to return full gallop to the station he had left, which they never failed to do as often as they quitted their lines, and the figure that did so was generally one of the middlemost men in the rank. As it grew later, they seemed more regardless of discipline, and rather had the appearance of people riding from a market than an army, though they continued crowding on and marching off as long as they had light to see them.

The 'phænomenon' was not seen again until the Midsummer Eve preceding the Scottish Rebellion of 1745. Those who had previously observed it summoned other families, so that in all about twenty-six people witnessed the apparition, some of them so convinced that what they had seen was real, that they next morning climbed the mountain-side looking for hoofprints, though not a vestige of one was found.

William Lancaster, who lived at 'Blake hills' (Blake Hills Farm, NY 365282), said that, as for himself, he never thought it was a real army because of the difficulty of the terrain, and because the number of troops was incredible, 'for they filled lengthways near half a mile, and continued so in a swift march for above an hour, and much longer he thinks if night had kept off'. But the villagers, with hindsight, believed the apparition to be a presentiment of the coming Rebellion.

Commentators explained it rather as an optical illusion – indeed, the editor of the *Lonsdale Magazine* (No. xx, August 1821) stated categorically (though so far as one can see without evidence) that it had been 'rebels exercising on the western coast of Scotland, whose movements had been reflected by some fine transparent vapour similar to the *Fata Morgana*'. Possibly. The Fata Morgana was a mirage seen during the summer months by fishermen near ancient Rhegium, modern Reggio, in southern Italy, and taking the form of a spectral city. For the same sort of mirage, caused by reflection, in the Lake District, one has only to read Wordsworth's *Guide Through the District of the Lakes* (5th edition, 1835).

But while such an explanation might cover, for example, the Green Isles of the Sea (see **Milford Haven**, p.352), it is inadequate wholly to account for the Souther Fell army. Souther Fell is not the only place where spectral armies have been seen – they also appeared on *Brodwels Downe* in Somerset in 1580, in Leicestershire in 1707, and at **Edge Hill** (p.266) and **Flower's Barrow** (p.62). Their beginnings may lie in illusion, but their interpretation by witnesses as armies on the march or engaged in manœuvres is something else again. They are undoubtedly the same order of apparition as the Wild Host (see **Peterborough**, p.187), not to be explained piecemeal as tricks of the light, but collectively as the end product of a long tradition.

WADDOW HALL, NR BRUNGERLEY, LANCASHIRE

Sheet 103

SD 7342

Stepping-stones across the river Ribble at Brungerley (SD 738428) near Clitheroe had of old an evil reputation. Locally it was said that every seven years a life was required to appease the anger of the river spirit. Harland and Wilkinson in their *Lancashire*

*'Peg O'Nelly's Well', showing the broken statue known as Peg O'Nell,
from Roby's* Traditions of Lancashire, Second Series, II *(1831)*

Folklore (1867) suggest that the tradition may have been attached
to the stepping-stones because it was here that Henry VI was
treacherously betrayed.

Maybe so, but belief in an indwelling spirit of the river may go
back to the Celtic cult of deities of rivers and springs. The Romans
when they came saw fit to propitiate these local gods and goddesses,
among them the water-spirit Coventina, in whose well near Carraw-
burgh were found coins and offerings from pre-Roman times to
the fourth century A.D., and the goddess Verbeia, the spirit of the
Wharfe, whose altar, dedicated to her by Roman legionaries from
eastern Gaul, can still be seen in the parish church of Ilkley in
Yorkshire. The Ribble itself is thought to have been sacred in
Roman times to the Celtic goddess Belisama, whom the Romans
equated with Minerva as goddess of battle, and it may be that the

'one life in seven years' tradition attached to Brungerley is a garbled memory of her rites.

One cannot press the point, however. Though it is often said that mothers in later ages exploited these traditions of water-spirits, transforming them into evil hags, to keep their children away from water, they could have invented them from the same impulse of fear that led the Celts to propitiate the rivers. But wherever they came from, the nineteenth century had Peg Powler of the Tees, and in the rivers of Lancashire, the stagnant, weed-covered pools of Cheshire, and at Ellesmere, Shropshire, Jenny Greenteeth, an old woman with long green fangs who lurked under the weeds to catch unwary children. Reminiscent of the Russian Rusalkas with their green teeth and green hair, she seems to be a personification of water-weed – particularly duckweed – who developed into a bogey or witch. Marjorie Rowling reports in her *Folklore of the Lake District* (1976) being terrified as a child, in about 1908, of 'Jinny Greenteeth', whom the maid who took her and her sister for walks had told them lived in the Back Lane at Kirkby Lonsdale. Her original home had been in a pool in the beck that once flowed under the lane and this had dried up, but 'the witch', said the maid, still lurked in Lunefield Wood, and would rush out and gobble them up if they misbehaved.

Ancient goddess or personification, the Ribble had its own bogey. From Roby (1831) comes the tale that at the Brungerley stepping-stones, people attributed the frequent drownings to Peggy, the evil spirit of Peggy's Well, not far from the river, in a field below Waddow Hall (SD 736426). A headless stone figure known as 'Peggy of the Well' stood by the spring, and was said to have been turned out of the Hall to allay the fears of the servants, who held her responsible for every ill that befell the house.

Roby also knew her as a ghost – Peggy O'Nell or Peggy O'Nelly, a servant at Waddow Hall 'drowned i' the well by one of the men for concubinage', and it is as Peg O'Nell that she appears in a story recounted by William Dobson in his *Rambles by the Ribble* (1864). There was once a servant at Waddow Hall whose name was Peg O'Nell, who one frosty night was sent to the well to fetch water. She had a quarrel with the master or mistress of Waddow, who had wished that she might break her neck and this angry malediction was now fulfilled. Peg's pattens slipped on the icy stones, she fell and broke her neck, and ever since that night has haunted Waddow Hall. Indeed, she became the tormentor of the whole neighbourhood, where no chicken was stolen, no cow died, no sheep strayed, no child was ill, no youth 'took bad ways' but Peggy was behind it. Part-ghost, part-boggart, something still remained of the ancient water-spirit: it was said that every seventh year, on a certain night, the Ribble would claim a victim. 'It was consequently the custom on "Peg's night" to drown a bird, or a cat, or a dog in the river, and a life being thus given, Peggy was appeased for another seven years.'

Peggy's Well is marked on the OS 1:25 000 map, though regrettably only by the symbol 'W'.

WHINFELL PARK, CUMBRIA   Sheet 90
(formerly WESTMORLAND)   NY 5528

On the boundary of Whinfell Park once stood a great oak tree locally known as the Hartshorn Tree. Its story is told by Gibson, in his additions to Camden's *Britannia* (1695):

> ... so all along by the side of *Whinfeld-Park* to Harthorn-tree, which may seem to give name to *Hornby-hall*, the seat of the *Birkbecks*, and to have borrow'd its own from a *Stag* which was cours'd by a single Grey-hound to the *Red Kirk* in Scotland, and back again to this place, where, being both of them spent, the Stag leapt the pales, but dy'd on the other side; and the Grey-hound attempting to leap, fell, and dy'd on this side. Whence they nail'd up their heads upon the tree; and (the dog's name being *Hercules*) they made this rhyme upon them:
>
> > *Hercules kill'd Hart-a-greese,*
> > *And Hart-a-greese kill'd Hercules.*

The same story of the stag and the greyhound had been told a little earlier by Aubrey in his *Remaines* (1686–7). The rhyme, he tells us, was engraved on 'a plate of lead' (one supposes he thought it was fixed to the tree) and the details are less sensational – the chase is merely 'a matter of xxx miles' and there is no dramatic leaping of the pales. His version seems to represent a sort of halfway house between fact and fiction, because luckily we know what this story was all about from the memoirs (1658) of Lady Anne Clifford:

> This summer, by some few mischievous people secretly in the night, was there broken off and taken downe from thatt Tree near the Paile of Whinfeld Parke (which, for that cause was called the *Hart's Horne Tree*) one of those old Hartes Hornes which (as is mentioned in the Summerie of my Ancestors, Robert Lord Clifford's Life,) was sett upp in the year 1333, att a generall huntinge when Edward Ballioll, then King of Scottes . . . lay for a while in the said Robert, Lord Clifford's castle in Westmoreland, where the said King hunted a greate Stagg which was killed nere the sayd Oake Tree. In memory whereof the Hornes were nayled upp in it, growing as it were naturally in the Tree, and have remayned there ever since, till thatt in the year 1648, one of those Hornes was broken downe by some of the Army, and the other was broken downe (as aforesaid) this year. So, as now, there is no part thereof remayneing, the Tree itselfe being now so decayed, and the Barke of it so peeled off that it cannot last long.

This family tradition connected with the royal visit evidently did not satisfy local craving for the sensational, and a more dramatic version of events took shape.

Despite Lady Anne's forebodings, the Hartshorn Tree was still there twelve years later, when on 14 October 1670, she again passed that way between her castles of Brougham and Appleby and stopped her coach to look at it. We do not know its condition in 1731, when Sir John Clerk, a Scottish baronet, visited the district, for in his journal he does not speak of seeing the tree, though he reports: 'In the hall of the lodge I was shown a pair of large stag horns which had been got in the hart of an oak tree, together with two clasps of iron by which they had been fixed.'

Some have assumed from Lady Anne's remark 'there is no part thereof remayneing' that these were not the original horns, but she may simply have meant 'no part remaining on the tree'. The lodge of which Sir John speaks was Lord Thanet's hunting lodge, and possibly the horns had been recovered and hung up on its walls.

Part of the trunk of the tree itself survived to 1790, and its roots remained in place to 1807. Although the name 'Whinfeld-park' is a little changed, 'Hornby-hall' is much the same (NY 5629). As for 'Hart-a-greese', his name means 'hart of grease', evidently a hunting term for a fat buck, though Sir John knew him by the altogether prettier one of Hart of Grace.

11
North-east

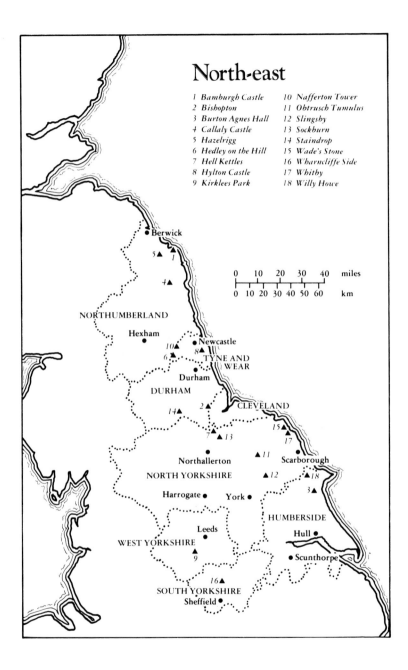

North-east

1 Bamburgh Castle
2 Bishopton
3 Burton Agnes Hall
4 Callaly Castle
5 Hazelrigg
6 Hedley on the Hill
7 Hell Kettles
8 Hylton Castle
9 Kirklees Park
10 Nafferton Tower
11 Obtrusch Tumulus
12 Slingsby
13 Sockburn
14 Staindrop
15 Wade's Stone
16 Wharncliffe Side
17 Whitby
18 Willy Howe

0 10 20 30 40 miles
0 10 20 30 40 50 60 km

● Berwick
5 ▲ ▲ 1
4 ▲

NORTHUMBERLAND
● Hexham
10 ▲ ● Newcastle
6 ▲ 8 ▲ TYNE AND
● WEAR
● Durham
DURHAM
14 ▲ 2 ▲ CLEVELAND
7 ▲ ▲ 13 15 ▲
17
● ▲ 11
Northallerton Scarborough
NORTH YORKSHIRE ▲ 12
Harrogate ● ● York ● ▲ 18
3 ▲
HUMBERSIDE
● Leeds Hull ●
WEST YORKSHIRE ▲ ● Scunthorpe
9
16 ▲
SOUTH YORKSHIRE
Sheffield ●

In Hutchinson's *View of Northumberland* (1778) was printed a ballad called 'The Laidley Worm of Spindlestone Heugh', purporting to be 'A Song 500 years old, made by the old Mountain Bard, Duncan Frasier, living on Cheviot AD 1270'. The ballad came from the Rev. Robert Lambert of Norham, who claimed to have got it from 'an ancient manuscript', but this is certainly moonshine. The ballad is evidently his own work, although parts of it seem to be based on genuine traditional ballads and perhaps local folklore.

It tells how a king brings home to Bamburgh a new wife who is jealous of her stepdaughter Margaret and turns her into a 'Laidley Worm', a loathly serpent or dragon. The milk of seven cows is served to her daily in a trough at the foot of Spindlestone Heugh where she makes her lair, but though her diet is mild, the countryside is blasted by her venomous breath. News of the devastation reaches 'Childy Wynd', the heir of Bamburgh, far beyond the sea, and he and his men set sail for Northumbria. Despite the wicked queen's attempts to keep them from landing, they come safely ashore at 'Budle-sands' (NU 1536) and the Childe, drawn sword in hand, advances on the Worm. She cries out to him to disenchant her by giving her kisses three, which he does and discovers his sister. They confront the wicked queen and by turning her own spell back on her, change her into a hideous toad.

And there she still is, in a cave under Bamburgh – or at least there she still was in the 1870s when the local girls were afraid she would vent her malice by spitting at them. The tradition was that she would sit there as big as a 'clockin hen' until someone passed the invisible door that only opened once in seven years and released her from the spell with three kisses – a garbling of 'The Laidley Worm' with the 'sleeping hero' tale as told at Sewingshields (NY 8090) and at Richmond Castle, North Yorkshire (see under **Eildon Hills**, p.452). 'The Laidley Worm' itself is a localized version of the ballad 'Kemp Owyne', telling of a girl whose stepmother throws her over a crag into the sea, at the same time turning her into a monster. She can only be 'borrowed' (disenchanted) by kisses three from the hero Kemp Owyne, Knight Owain, who gave his name to Childy *Wynd*.

This story in turn reminds us of a tale in *The Travels of Sir John Mandeville* (fourteenth century) in which 'the Lady of the Land', the daughter of the physician Hippocrates living on the island of Cos, is transformed by Diana into a dragon, an enchantment from which she cannot escape until kissed by a knight. A champion of Rhodes flees on seeing her and the spell is only broken by a shepherd knighted for the task.

Bamburgh Castle, restored 1894–1905, is open to the public – for times, see *HHC&G*. A painting by R. J. S. Bertram illustrating the legend of the Laidley Worm is displayed on an easel in the Museum. Also in the Museum are Bamburgh's other 'monsters' – the ferocious little beast found in other Anglo-Saxon works of art of the seventh century and at Bamburgh engraved on a small gold plaque discovered during excavations in 1971, and intertwined 'gripping' beasts on a pair of ninth-century bronze and silver strap-ends whose decoration is so minute that it is best viewed on the enlarged X-ray photograph displayed alongside. Coincidentally, no doubt, these creatures are not unlike the twining monster, her hair wound thrice about the tree, who was disenchanted by Kemp Owyne, and was the forerunner of the Laidley Worm. Spindlestone Heughs (NZ 1533) are marked on the OS 1:25 000 map, as is 'Laidley Worm's Trough' (NZ 156339), but the Laidley Worm's Cave is gone – it had been quarried away already by the end of the nineteenth century.

BISHOPTON, DURHAM   Sheet 93
                                               NZ 3621

In the nineteenth century, the motte on Castle Hill (NZ 3621), raised in the twelfth century by Roger Conyers, was known as the Fairy Hill. The story goes that the people were once carting it away when a mysterious voice was heard to ask:

'Is all well?'

'Yes,' came the reply.

'Then keep well when you *are* well, and leave the Fairy Hill alone.'

The warning was ignored, however, and presently the workmen came on a large black chest, so heavy that it took several of them to carry it away to the blacksmith to break it open. They thought it would hold treasure, but it was full of iron nails. The chest long remained in the blacksmith's shop, where the aunt of the woman who told this tale to William Brockie (*Legends and Superstitions of*

'The Fairy Hill': Castle Hill, Bishopton, County Durham

Durham, 1886) had often seen it.

Burial mounds, especially round barrows, were also commonly held to be fairy dwellings – an example is Beedon Barrow or Hill in Berkshire – and it was dangerous to interfere with them. Robert Kirk tells us that the Highlanders of his time (1691) refused to move earth or timber from a fairy knoll, and in Ireland as late as 1909 engineers making a new road in Ballinrobe, Co. Mayo, were forced to find another route after the local people had protested against their cutting through a 'fairy fort'.

BURTON AGNES HALL, HUMBERSIDE   Sheet 101
(formerly YORKSHIRE, EAST RIDING)   TA 1063

There is no want of foundation for the statement that three sisters built the Hall in the reign of Queen Elizabeth, and were most impatient to see the work completed – especially so was the youngest of the three. One day, when wandering alone in the park, Miss Ann was murderously attacked and robbed by an outlaw, who seriously wounded her. This brought on a fever of which she died. Before her death she

'Owd Nance': detail from 'The Three Miss Griffiths' by Marc Gheeraerts (1620), Burton Agnes Hall, Humberside

grieved incessantly that she would never see the grand structure complete, and made her sisters promise to remove her head to the new grand Hall, where it was to be placed on a table. This they agreed to do, but after her death they buried her without fulfilling the compact. Nothing happened until they took up their abode at Burton Agnes. Then strange moanings and weird sounds made the sisters' lives a burden to them. No servants would stay; so at last after two years they caused the body to be dug up and decapitated, and placed the now fleshless head upon the table. For many years it was left there uncovered, until one day a certain maid professing to ridicule the story, took it up and threw it on a loaded waggon standing near. The horses plunged and reared, the house shook, pictures fell, until it was once more restored to the place of honour. It used to be a belief that so long as the skull was left undisturbed nothing serious would happen to any of the Boyntons, and woe betide the moving of it. To avoid calamity, it has now been placed in a niche of the wall, especially prepared for it, and hidden from view.

The author of this account of Britain's most famous 'Screaming

Skull', quoted by Mrs Gutch in her *Folk-Lore of the East Riding* (1912), adds that implicit belief in the skull was 'a second religion' with the Boyntons, then owners of the Hall. 'Miss Ann' herself was Anne Griffith, to whose family Burton Agnes had belonged since the reign of Edward I. Later, through her sister Frances, and following the death of the last Griffith heir, her brother Henry, in 1654, it passed by marriage to the Boyntons, who still live there today. The red-brick Hall was in fact built not for Anne and her sisters but for their father, Sir Henry Griffith, by Robert Smithson, the architect of Hardwick Hall.

Never mind – 'Owd Nance', as she was called, lived on for years in local tradition as a ghost. One reason for this may have been the portrait at Burton Agnes (in the Inner Hall) of 'The Three Miss Griffiths', painted by Marc Gheeraerts in the year of Anne's death, 1620. Anne is on the right, the only one in black – cause enough, perhaps, for her becoming a ghost (cf. Lady Hoby at **Bisham Abbey**, p.51).

Burton Agnes Hall is open to the public – for times see *HHC&G*. The room said to be haunted by Anne's ghost is the Queen's State Bedroom. The Norman manor house (TA 103633) which preceded the Hall can also be visited: AM (any reasonable time).

CALLALY CASTLE, NORTHUMBERLAND

Sheet 81
NU 0509

At Callaly, the seat of the Claverings, tradition reports that while the workmen were engaged in erecting the castle upon a hill, a little distance from the site of the present edifice, they were surprised every morning to find their former day's work destroyed, and the whole impeded by supernatural obstacles, which causing them to watch, they heard a voice saying:

> 'Callaly castle stands on a height,
> It's up in the day, and down at night:
> Build it down on the Shepherd's Shaw,
> There it will stand and never fa'.'

Upon which the building was transferred to the place mentioned, where it now stands.

This tradition, recorded in John Bell's *Rhymes of Northern Bards* (1812), might like many church-siting legends be based on observation. The hill in the story is Callaly Castle Hill on which was an old earthwork whose inner rampart had at some later date been strengthened with mortar-laid ashlar, suggestive of castle walls. But in this case the tale is likely to preserve a local or family-memory, for when the site was excavated in the 1890s, the remains of a medieval building were found, probably 'the Castle of Old Callaly', mentioned in a list of fortified places in the Borders drawn up in 1415. The 'New Callaly' implied by this would be the peel tower built at the foot of the hill in the thirteenth century, to which in the seventeenth was joined the present mansion.

Callaly Castle is open to the public – for times, see *HHC&G*.

HAZELRIGG (OLD), NORTHUMBERLAND   Sheet 75
                                                    NU 0533

People in the neighbourhood of Hazelrigg used to be tormented by the Hazelrigg Dunny, the ghost of a reiver who frequented a cave on the side of Cockenheugh, near Hazelrigg, known as 'Cuddie's Cave' (NU 0535). According to tradition, he had lost a great treasure which he had buried hereabouts, and used to lament as follows:

> 'In Collier heugh there's gear eneugh,
> In Cocken heugh there's mair,
> But I've lost the keys of Bowden doors,
> I'm ruined for evermair.'

'Collier heugh', like Cockenheugh, was a tract of moorland and the Bowden Doors a craggy mass of rock near Lyham (NU 0632–0732). According to the *Denham Tracts* (1846–59), in which this story is preserved, the Dunny was so-called because he sometimes took the form of a dun-coloured horse, cutting the same sort of capers as the Hedley Kow (see next entry).

Cuddie's Cave is on the map marked as 'St Cuthbert's Cave', 'Cuddie' being the familiar Northumbrian name for the saint, cf. Cuddy's or St Cuthbert's Well at Bellingham, also Northumberland. It is said to have been one of the resting places for St Cuthbert's body on its journey from Lindisfarne to Durham. NT, access by foot only from the car park by Holburn Grange Cottages.

HEDLEY ON THE HILL, NORTHUMBERLAND   Sheet 88
NZ 0759

About sixty years ago, the country people in the neighbourhood of Hedley, a small village in the south of Northumberland, not far from Ebchester . . . were frequently annoyed by the pranks of a bogle called the *Hedley Kow*. His appearance was never terrific, and . . . he usually ended his frolics with a horse-laugh at the fear or astonishment of those on whom he had played a trick. To an old woman gathering sticks by the hedge-side, he would sometimes appear like a *fad*, or truss of straw, lying in the road. This the old dame was generally tempted to take possession of; but, in carrying it home, her load would become so heavy, that she would be obliged to lay it down. The straw would then appear as if *quick*; would rise upright, and shuffle away before her . . . every now and then setting up a laugh, or giving a shout . . . and at last wholly vanishing from her sight.

Such is the account of the Hedley Kow given by 'Stephen Oliver' (W. A. Chatto) in his *Rambles in Northumberland* (1835), and a lively story embroidering on this theme was given by the collector Mrs Balfour to Joseph Jacobs for *More English Fairy Tales* (1894). Mrs Balfour had got it from a 'Mrs M' of south Northumberland, whose mother told the tale as having happened to someone she had known when young. She herself had seen the Hedley Kow twice, once as a donkey, once as a wisp of straw.

According to Chatto, he had been known to appear as a favourite cow which led the milkmaid a dance round the meadow, and he would also get into the farmhouse, where he would plague the servant-girls, overturning the kail-pot, setting the cat to the cream, unravelling the knitting and jamming the spinning-wheel. But he was at his most plaguey when a child was about to be born, and so torment the horse of the man going for the midwife that he and the 'howdy' were tumbled in the road.

In his *Folk-Lore of the Northern Counties* (1879), Henderson tells how a farmer named Forster, who lived near Hedley, went out one morning into the field and caught, as he believed, his own grey horse. But after he had hitched him to the cart and was about to drive off, the creature slipped from the traces like a knotless thread, and with a nicker kicked up his heels and scoured away. Then there was the time when two young men from Newlands (NZ 0955) went out one evening to meet their sweethearts, thought they saw the girls, and followed them for the best part of three miles, quite unable to overtake them, until they found themselves in a bog. The 'sweethearts' vanished with a loud 'Ha! ha!', and once clear of the bog, the young men ran for home as fast as they could, the bogey at their heels hooting and mocking them all the way.

As in these tales, the Hedley Kow always took himself off after playing his pranks with a nicker or 'Ha! ha!' and is related to those other shape-changing and horse-laughing bogies, the Picktree Brag, from County Durham, and the **Creech Hill** (p.18), bullbeggar. Such bogeys belong to the same family as Ben Jonson's Robin Goodfellow, who declares:

> 'Sometimes I meete them like a man,
>   Sometimes an ox, sometimes a hound,
> And to a horse I turn me can,
>   To trip and trot them round.

> 'But if to ride
> My back they stride,
> More swift than wind away I go:
>   O'er hedge and lands,
>   Through pools and ponds,
> I whirry laughing, Ho! ho! ho!'

The bogey in the form of a horse has a long history: such are the 'grants' mentioned by Gervase of Tilbury (*ca.* 1212) – 'like foals of a year old' – such, too, the spirit known in Lincolnshire as the 'shag-foal', of whose Northamptonshire equivalent the poet John Clare (*The Village Minstrel*, 1821) writes:

It's a common tradition in villages that the devil often appears in the form of a shagg'd foal; and a man in our parish firmly believes that he saw him in that character one morning early in harvest.

The Hedley Kow's name is a little misleading. 'In Northern English and Lowland Scots the word "kow" has the meaning of "goblin" or "spirit",' writes Lewis Spence (*Minor Traditions of British Mythology*, 1948), and we see from Chatto that he only sometimes appeared as a *cow*. He undoubtedly belongs with the shag-foals, but whatever his character as a manifestation, he goes back to at least the eighteenth century. When the antiquary George Allan was cataloguing some books sold in 1748, he noted among them a transcript of inquisitions and the like in the County Palatine of Durham:

> At the end of this vol. there is a declaration made and signed by one Thomas Stevenson, of Framwellgate, in Durham, before Justice Burdus, and by him witnessed at the bottom, that on 7 Aug., 1729, between eight and nine at night, the said Stevenson, returning from Hedley, in Northumberland, saw an apparition that looked sometimes in the shape of a foal, sometimes of a man, which took the bridle from off his horse and beat him until he was sore, and misled him on foot three miles to Coalburne. And that . . . it vanished not till daybreak, and then though he touched not the bridle, after it was taken from his horse . . . he found it bound about his waist. His horse he found where he first saw the apparition, by the Green bank top, and saith it was commonly reported by the neighbourhood, that a spirit called HEDLEY KOW did haunt that place.

HELL KETTLES, DARLINGTON, DURHAM

Sheet 93
NZ 2810

The Hell Kettles, three small circular ponds about seventeen feet (5.2 m) deep, between Darlington and Croft, have long been regarded with superstitious awe. 'What the foolish people dreame of the hell Kettles, it is not worthy the rehersall', said William Harrison in 1577, in the 'Description of the Islande of Britayne' preceding Holinshed's *Chronicle*:

> ... yet ... I will say thus much ... Ther are certeine pittes
> or rather three litle poles a myle from Darlington, and a
> quarter of a myle distant from the These [Tees] bankes, which
> yᵉ people call the Kettles of hell, or the deuils Ketteles, as if he
> shoulde seethe soules of sinfull men and women in them: they
> adde also that the spirites haue oft beene harde to crye and
> yell about them ...

Harrison adds that 'the water is nowe and then warme', and
Camden had heard the same – 'the common peple tearme them
Hel-Kettles, because the water in them by the *Antiperistasis* or
reverberation of the cold aire striking thereupon, waxeth hote'.

But had Harrison or Camden tested the water or had they
simply heard the pits described in much the same terms as were
used in 1634 by 'a captain, a lieutenant, and an ancient' of the
Military Company in Norwich, who were engaged on a survey
and said in their report: 'The three admired deepe pitts, called Hell
Kettles, we left boyling by Darlington'? This might refer to heat or
motion – the kettles contain vigorous springs – and the water was
certainly not hot in the nineteenth century, nor indeed at the turn
of the seventeenth.

For Camden had said that the 'pittes' were of 'wonderful depth',
and this was put to the test by 'a very ingenious Gentleman' (Dr
Jabez Kay) on behalf of Camden's second translator, Gibson
(1695):

> SIR,
>   According to the promise which I made you, I went to
> sound the depth of *Hell-Kettles* near *Darlington*. The name of
> the bottomleβ pits made me provide my self with a line above
> a hundred fathoms long ... but much smaller preparations
> would have serv'd: for the deepest of them took but fifteen
> fathoms, or thirty yards of our line. I cannot imagine ...
> upon what grounds the people of the Country have suppos'd
> them to be bottomleβ ...

As to Camden's theory of Antiperistasis – 'They are full of water
(*cold*, not *hot*, as Mr Camden has been misinform'd) ...'

That more persons than one must have known that the Kettles
were not very deep did nothing to dampen the belief that they
were bottomless, and in the forepart of the nineteenth century they

were proverbial – 'As Deep as Hell Kettles'. Regarding their origin, Daniel Defoe was scathing – ''Tis evident they are nothing but coal pits filled with water' – but here Camden was probably nearer the mark when he reported the belief of the 'wiser sort' that they came 'by the sinking downe of the ground swallowed up in some earth-quake'. This might have been the one described in Brompton's *Chronicle*, *ca.* 1328:

> 1179 [i.e. 1178] About Christmas, a wonderful and unheard of event fell out at Oxenhale, viz., that . . . the ground rose up on high with such vehemence, that it was equal to the highest tops of the mountains, and towered above the lofty pinnacles of the churches; and at that height remained from the ninth hour of the day even to sunset. But at sunset it fell with so horrible a crash, that it terrified all who saw that heap, and heard the noise of its fall, whence many died from that fear; for the earth swallowed it up, and caused in the same place a very deep pit.

'Oxenhale', also known as Oxenhall, Oxen-le-Field and Oxeney-field, was the part of the township of Darlington, south of the town, where the Hell Kettles lay. Whether or not they were created thus in 1178, a tradition of an earthquake (or perhaps an acquaintance with Camden) seems to lie behind a tale told here in the nineteenth century. According to the version in the *Denham Tracts* (1846–59), the farmer who centuries ago owned the land was about to cart his hay on St Barnabas's Day (11 June), and when reproved for this act of impiety replied:

> 'Barnaby yea, Barnaby nay,
> A cart-load of hay, whether God will or nay.'

Instantly he, his carts and his horses were swallowed up in the pools, where they can still be seen, said a correspondent of the *Durham Advertiser* quoted by W. Hylton Dyer Longstaffe in 1854, on a fine day and clear water 'floating midway, many fathoms deep'.

HYLTON CASTLE, SUNDERLAND, TYNE &   Sheet 88
WEAR   NZ 3558
(formerly NORTHUMBERLAND)

The fifteenth-century tower-house of Hylton Castle was once the haunt of a spirit known as the Cauld Lad of Hilton. The servants who slept in the great hall would hear him every night at work in the kitchen, tidying what was untidy, but turning what was neat topsy-turvy. They determined to get rid of him – and perhaps he read the signs, for he would be heard singing in a melancholy tone:

> 'Wae's me! Wae's me!
> The acorn is not yet
> Fallen from the tree,
> That's to grow the wood,
> That's to make the cradle,
> That's to rock the bairn,
> That's to grow to a man,
> That's to lay me.'

Eventually they left a green cloak and hood for him by the kitchen fire and hid themselves to watch. They saw the Cauld Lad come in, gaze at the clothes, try them on, and in great delight jump and frisk about the kitchen until cock-crow, when he vanished with the cry:

> 'Here's a cloak, and here's a hood,
> The Cauld Lad of Hilton will do no more good.'

Now, giving him a gift of clothes is the traditional way of banishing a Brownie. The Brownie, King James tells us (1597), 'appeared like a rough man' – i.e. was hairy – and used to do 'necessarie turnes' about the house. Those who may have known better than the King what those 'turnes' would be specify grinding corn, malt and mustard, chopping kindling and sweeping floors. But, says Reginald Scot (1584):

> ... he would chafe exceedingly, if the maid or goodwife of the house, having compassion of his nakednes, laid anie clothes for him, besides his messe of white bread and milke, which was his standing fee. For in that case he saith; What haue we

here? Hemton, hamten,* here will I neuer more tread nor stampen.

Much the same story was later in Yorkshire told of the Hobs of Hart Hall, Glaisdale, Sturfit Hall, near Reeth, and Close House, Skipton-in-Craven, and the tradition must have already been well-known in the fourteenth century when the Dominican preacher John of Bromyard told it of a *diabolus* who, on being rewarded for his labours at the quern with clothes, at once stopped work, '*dicens Anglice, "Modo habeo capam et capuciam, amplius bonum non faciam"*' ('saying in English, "Now I have a cape and a hood, I will do no more good"') – virtually the rhyme in which the Cauld Lad expressed his disgust.

But the loss of a Brownie was almost always looked upon as a disaster – most people were only too glad of the help of the 'drudging goblin' and believed his presence made their house, as King James put it, 'all the sonsier'. So the Cauld Lad, who the servants are eager to see the back of, is not quite the traditional Brownie, but much more like the Silky of Black Heddon (NZ 0776), half-bogle and half-ghost, who likewise tidied what was untidy, and untidied what was left straight. Moreover, the Cauld Lad's doleful 'Wae's me! Wae's me!' suggests that he longs to go – he *wants* to be exorcised, like many a miserable ghost. And indeed most of the stories attached to him are ghost stories. Richardson, who tells us about him in his *Table Book* (1846), says there was a room in Hylton Castle long known as the Cauld Lad's Room, which was never used unless the castle was otherwise full. Within the last century many reliable persons had heard the wailing of the lad, 'who some maintained was the spirit of a servant whom one of the barons of Hilton had killed unintentionally in a fit of passion'.

Surtees in his *History and Antiquities of Durham* (1820) tells the amplified version of this: the baron of Hilton had called for his horse and when it did not appear went to the stables, where he

---

* Hempton, hamten – from early times the Brownie has been connected with *hempen* garments. In his *Terrors of the Night* (1594) Thomas Nashe tells us: 'The Robbin-good-fellowes, Elfes, Fairies, Hobgoblins of our latter age . . . did most of their merry prankes in the Night. Then ground they malt, and had hempen shirts for their labours . . .', from which it would appear that a hempen smock was their customary reward. But Scot's Brownie takes the same view as the Hart Hall Hob who complains at being given *only* such a garment – a 'hardin hamp', rough and coarse ('hardin') like sacking.

found the stable-lad loitering. Taking up a pitchfork he struck and killed him, and having hidden the corpse under the straw until night, threw it into a pond, 'where the skeleton of a boy was . . . discovered in the last Baron's time'. Surtees suggests that the story is based on fact, a free pardon for the manslaughter of one Roger Skelton by Robert Hilton of Hilton with 'a Syth' appearing on the Durham episcopal rolls for 6 September 1609.

Whether or no, one suspects that the tale of the Cauld Lad took shape in the eighteenth century, when the castle itself was remodelled. In the early part of the century, the fortified tower-house was enlarged with wings with 'Gothick' detail, giving it the romantic appearance it has in the drawing by J. M. W. Turner. A fondness for embellishing family seats with appropriate 'legends' at about this time is illustrated by the 'Luck' of **Edenhall** (p.372) and the 'Radiant Boy' of **Knebworth** (p.138).

The Cauld Lad's name – the Cold Lad, as most interpret it – suggests a connection with another ghost, the Cauld Lad of

Haunt of the Cauld Lad:
Hylton Castle, Tyne & Wear, drawn by J. M. W. Turner

Gilsland on the Cumberland–Northumberland border (NY 6346). Henderson (*Folklore of the Northern Counties*, 1879) was told a story that had been current there earlier in the century of a boy who had died of cold at the contrivance of a cruel uncle or stepmother, and ever after haunted the family. Now when William Howitt visited Hylton Castle at some time before the publication of his *Visits to Remarkable Places*, Second Series (1842), he was told what was perhaps the germ of a similar story:

> The woman who shewed me the house, on arriving at a certain chamber, pointed to a cupboard over the door, and said, 'that is the place where they used to put the Cold Lad.' I replied, 'to which he used to retreat, you mean.' 'No, no,' reiterated she pertinaciously, 'where they used to put him.' In her story it was a boy, that on some account had been treated cruelly, and kept in confinement in this cupboard, where, no doubt, in the winter, he acquired the unenviable epithet of The Cold Lad.

From the Gilsland story we can perhaps see why at Hylton Castle 'Cold Lad' and Brownie traditions have run together: the Gilsland Cauld Lad is not just a ghost but a household or family spirit. When anyone in the family was about to fall sick, he would appear shivering at their bedside, his teeth chattering loudly and, if the illness were fatal, lay an icy hand on the presumed seat of the sickness, crying:

> 'Cauld, cauld, ay cauld,
> An' ye'se be cauld for evermair!'

Hylton Castle AM. Exterior only. The eighteenth-century wings seen in Turner's picture of the castle were demolished in the 1860s, giving it the appearance it has today.

KIRKLEES PARK, WEST YORKSHIRE   Sheet 104
(formerly YORKSHIRE, WEST RIDING)   SE 1721

'Here,' says Camden (trans. Holland, 1610), 'is the tomb of *Robin Hood* that right good and honest robber . . .' Robin Hood's Grave (SE 174215) is marked by a stone on which there was an inscription

– according to the antiquary Thoresby, copied by Dr Gale, Dean of York from 1697 to 1702 – which read:

> Here undernead dis latil stean
> Laiz Robert Earl of Huntington
> Nea arcir ver az hie sa geud
> An pipl kauld im Robin Heud
> Sick utlaz az hi an iz men
> Vil England nivr si agen
>   Obit 24 Kal. Dekemris 1247.

Whatever this is, it isn't ancient. For the rest, see **Sherwood Forest** (p.251).

NAFFERTON TOWER, HORSLEY, NORTHUMBERLAND

Sheet 88
NZ 0765

Immediately north of the road from Newcastle to Carlisle, among the trees along the banks of the Whittle Burn, are the remains (NZ 072657) of a peel tower that was never finished. The Royal Forester for Northumberland in the reign of King John, Philip de Ulecote, started to build it, but the work was brought to a halt in 1217 as 'adulterine' – i.e. he had no licence to fortify.

The tower fell into ruin and in local tradition became a place of sinister reputation. Variously known as Nafferton Tower and Nafferton or Whittle Dene Castle, it is also marked on some maps as 'Lonkin's Hall', because it was said to be the lair of Long Lonkin. According to legend, he murdered a woman and child at Welton Hall (NZ 0667), a ruined fifteenth-century peel tower, built of stone from the Roman Wall, to which is attached a manor house, built mostly in 1614.

The story localized here is told in a ballad that survives in several versions. The Northumbrian 'Long Lonkin', communicated to Bishop Percy in 1775, is probably the oldest, but has to be pieced out from the more complete Scottish versions. The most powerful of these, known simply as 'Lamkin' (an ironic name for a nursery terror), gives us the crime's motivation:

> It's Lamkin was a mason good
>   as ever built wi' stane;

He built Lord Wearie's castle,
    but payment got he nane.

'O pay me, Lord Wearie,
    come, pay me my fee':
'I canna pay you, Lamkin,
    for I maun gang oer the sea' . . .

'O gin ye winna pay me,
    I here sall make a vow,
Before that ye come hame again,
    ye sall hae cause to rue.'

Lord Wearie sails off, charging his lady to keep the castle close, but the treacherous nurse lets Lamkin in at 'a little shot-window'. With a long knife he stabs Lord Wearie's son:

Then Lamkin he rocked,
    and the fause nourice sang,
Till fra ilke bore o the cradle
    the red blood out sprang.

The lady asks from the stairs why the child cries so, and the nurse entices her down until she comes face to face with Lamkin:

'O sall I kill her, nourice,
    or sall I lat her be?'
'O kill her, kill her, Lamkin,
    for she neer was good to me.'

The deed is done, but when three months are up, Lord Wearie returns and sees the bloodstains on the floor. Justice follows: Lamkin is condemned to die, and the casually vindictive nurse is burnt at the stake.

Although the Scottish and Northumbrian ballads seem to tell pretty much the same tale, in local tradition, still alive in the 1840s, it was said that Long Lonkin's motive for the murders was revenge on the lady of Nafferton who had rejected him. It was also reported that Lonkin had hidden from pursuit in a tree overhanging a pool in the Whittle Burn, and when discovered had plunged headlong in and drowned. In 1844 it was still known as Long Lonkin's Pool

and declared to be bottomless, but Long Lonkin's Tree in which
he hid had been felled some thirty or forty years previously.
According to another tradition, he had thrown his victims' bodies
into the pool, perhaps the deep one by the little waterfall known as
the Whirl Dub, where he was likewise reputed to have concealed a
treasure wrapped in a bull-hide. Certainly Long Lonkin's ghost
was believed to haunt Whittle Dene through which the stream
runs, and as late as 1891 children were told to be home before dark
or Lonkin would get them.

Nafferton Tower is shown as Lonkin's Hall on the OS 1:25 000 map.
Welton Hall, Sheet 87.

OBTRUSCH TUMULUS, FARNDALE WEST,   Sheet 94
NORTH YORKSHIRE   SE 6694
(formerly YORKSHIRE, NORTH RIDING)

The mound marked on the map as Obtrusch tumulus was in the
nineteenth century known as 'Obtrush Rook' or 'Roque' – the
home of a Hobthrush. While in Yorkshire tradition the names
'Hob' and 'Hobthrush' are generally interchangeable, the Hob
may once have been a domestic spirit like a Brownie, whereas the
Hobthrush lived in the wild.

The name 'Hobthrush', known from 1590, is explained by
Francis Grose in his *Provincial Glossary* (1787) as 'HOBTHRUST or
rather HOB O T'HURST. A spirit supposed to haunt woods only.' But
the OED, following Jacob Grimm, gives its derivation as being
from 'Hob' plus 'Thurse', in English and Norse tradition a sort of
giant. Either derivation would fit the Hobtrush Hob, who haunted
a cave in Mulgrave Woods, also connected with the giant Wade
(see **Wade's Stone**, p.421). The Hobtrush Hob was a frightening
bogle who used to be addressed and to reply as follows:

> 'Hob-trust Hob! Where is thou?'
> 'Ah's tying on mah left-fuit shoe;
> An' Ah'll be wiv thee . . . Noo!'

There was a hint of ogre, too, about the Hobthrush at East Halton,
Humberside (TA 1319), who could be made to 'walk' by stirring

the contents of an iron pot in the cellar supposed to contain 'children's thumb-bones'. But the Hobthrush who gave his name to Hobthrush Rock, though a pest, was less alarming – more like a boggart. He used to visit one of the Farndale farms and so vexed the farmer that he decided to move. Very early in the morning, as he was trudging on his way with all his household goods in a cart, he was accosted by a neighbour with 'I see you're flitting'. Before the farmer could reply, a voice said from the churn, 'Ay, we're flutting'. On which the farmer, seeing well that a change of house would not rid him of the Hobthrush, turned his horse's head for home.

This is the story as told by John Phillips in *The Rivers, Mountains, and Sea-Coast of Yorkshire* (1853). One very similar was included in Roby's *Traditions of Lancashire* (1829) and by implication attached to **Boggart Hole Clough** (p.367) though it seems not to have been a local tale. It was, however, traditional at West Land Ends farm in Northumberland (NY 83262), in the 1870s remembered as the haunt of a bogle called Jesse. In Holderness it was told of the spirit Robin Round-cap, and it was familiar in Lincolnshire, where it was heard by Alfred, Lord Tennyson, and retold in 'Walking to the Mail' (1842). In Scandinavia, where it was related of the malicious Nis, he uses much the same expression – '*i dag flytter vi*' ('today we're moving').

From 'Ay, we're flitting', as this story is known, the boggart, Hob or Hobthrush, seems to have been a sort of domestic bogle, much like a poltergeist,

> a jolly ghost, that shook
> The curtains, whined in lobbies, tapt at doors,
> And rummaged like a rat

as Tennyson put it. Like banshees and some ghosts, he was attached not to places but families.

West Land Ends farm, Sheet 87; East Halton, 107.

SLINGSBY, NORTH YORKSHIRE   Sheet 100
(formerly YORKSHIRE, NORTH RIDING)   SE 6974

Observing that the road from Hovingham to Malton, instead of going in a straight line as it passed through Slingsby, for no apparent reason bent to the right, the antiquary Roger Dodsworth asked the local inhabitants why this was and received a singular explanation:

> The tradition is that betwixt Malton and this towne ther was sometymes a serpent that lyved upon pray of passengers, which this Wyvill and dogg did kill wher he received his deathe's wound. Ther is a great hole half a myle from the towne, round within and 3 yerdes broad and more, wher this serpent lay, in which tyme the street was turned a myle on the South side, which doth still show itt self, if any take payns to search it.

This was written after a visit in the period 1619–31; in the 1870s the villagers still pointed out the serpent's (i.e. dragon's) lair, and showed, in the parish church, the effigy of 'this Wyvill' and his dog, who both perished in the fight or soon after, and were here commemorated in stone.

Similar tales were told in the nineteenth century at Kellington (SE 5524), at Handale (NZ 7215, now Cleveland) and at Nunnington (SE 6679). They are probably all connected, especially those of Slingsby and Nunnington, where Peter Loschy and his dog also died after killing a dragon, from breathing its venom. But whereas Loschy seems to be an invented hero who has taken his name from a local place-name, 'this Wyvill' may belong to a group of local landowners immortalized as dragon-slayers (as at **Brent Pelham**, p.128), for the Wyvills of Osgodby were living at Slingsby Manor by 1215–16, and continued there to the mid fourteenth century.

The effigy in Slingsby church to which the story is attached is the mutilated figure in the south chapel of an unidentified knight wearing armour of the late thirteenth century. This is too early, alas, to be the actual tomb of the Wyvill who, by 'Dragon of Wantley' standards (see **Wharncliffe Side**, p.426), is the most suitable candidate. This was William Wyvill, who in 1318 with his men assaulted a creditor suing him for debt. They took away the man's greyhound, and when he fled to the church, imprisoned him there until his neighbours raised the siege. Wyvill was never punished for this, we know not why, but may well have been remembered as a roaring boy.

Handale, Sheet 94; Kellington, 105.

SOCKBURN, DURHAM

Sheet 93
NZ 3407

In 1396 died Sir John Conyers, lord of the manor of Sockburn, which he held by the feudal service of presenting a falchion or short-bladed sword to the Bishop of Durham on his first entry into the County Palatine. In the days of Sir Edward Blackett, who owned Sockburn in the closing years of the eighteenth century and into the nineteenth, the Bishop came into the diocese by crossing the Tees either at Croft Bridge (NZ 2809) or the ford at Neasham (NZ 3210). Sir Edward or his representative would then ride on to the bridge or into the river, the falchion drawn in his hand, and present it to the Bishop whilst speaking an ancient form of words. The Bishop would take the falchion and look at it, then give it back again, wishing the lord of the manor health and the enjoyment of his estates.

There were once many such nominal services. Manors might be held by the annual presentation of a sword, a horn, an axe, a pair of tongs, or by 'flower rents' of a garland or a single red rose. These curious tenures, when their origins were lost, were often explained by legends. The Sockburn service was said to have been won by Sir John Conyers slaying a dragon, as a note in British Library Harley MS 2118, of the reign of Charles I, tells us:

S^r Jo: Conyers de Sockburn Kn^t who slew ye monstrous venomd & poisond wiverne Ask or worme which overthrew & devourd many people in fight, for the scent of the poyson was soe strong, that noe p[er]son was able to abide it, yet hee by the providence of god overthrew it, & lyes buryed at Sockburn before the Conquest, but before hee did enterprise it (hauing but one child), he went to the church in compleate armour & offerd vp his sonne to the holy ghost, which monum^t is yet to see, & the place where the serpent lay is called Graystone[.]

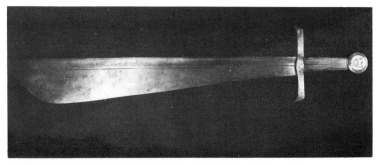

*The Sockburn Falchion, formerly presented to the Bishop of Durham
as feudal service for the manor of Sockburn,
and now in Durham Cathedral Treasury*

The ceremony of the falchion is claimed to date from the reign of Richard I, but the first mention we have of it comes from the inquisition *post mortem* of Sir John. It was performed for the last time in 1826, and the falchion deposited in Durham Cathedral Treasury, where it may still be seen. As for the story, it was known to Camden's third translator, Gough (1789), though apparently not to Camden himself (1586) nor to Gibson (1695). Gough tells us that the falchion was painted in a window of Sockburn church and also cut on the tomb of Sir John, who was shown with both a dog and a monstrous serpent lying at his feet.

A similar tradition was attached to the Pollard family of Bishop Auckland (NZ 2029), whose presentation of a falchion was also said to commemorate the slaying of a monster. This is now generally said to be a boar, the Pollard Brawn, but in the form of words used at the tenure ceremony in 1771 it was 'a great and venomous serpent'.

Durham Cathedral Treasury: for times of opening see *M&G*.

STAINDROP, DURHAM

Sheet 92
NZ 1220

A farmer from Staindrop was one night crossing a bridge when a cat jumped out, stood before him and looking him full in the face said:

'Johnny Reed! Johnny Reed!
Tell Madam Momfort
That Mally Dixon's dead.'

The farmer returned home and related this to his wife, whereupon up started their black cat, crying: 'Is she?' and vanished, never to return. It was supposed that she was a fairy in disguise who went to attend a sister's funeral.

This story was current in the 1840s; according to another version that appeared in *Notes & Queries* in 1852, Joaney or Johnny Reed was the parish clerk of a village near Newcastle, to whom the message was passed, 'Joaney Reed, Joaney Reed, tell Dan Ratcliffe that Peg Powson is dead.' Later, in 1886 William Brockie gave the same tale in his *Legends and Superstitions of Durham* as attached to John Bonner, the farmer at Beggar-Bush, between Easington (NZ 4143) and Castle Eden (NZ 4238). He was to tell his own cat 'Catherine Curly's deed', whereupon she leapt up crying 'Aw mun awa''. Brockie was told the story by the daughter of the farmer who followed John Bonner at Beggar-Bush.

The selfsame tale was told in Denmark of a philandering troll disguised as a cat, who was able to go home to the troll-mound once he heard that Knurre-Murre (the troll-husband) was dead. In Britain the story sometimes ends – 'What, is so-and-so dead? Then I'm the King of the Cats!'

WADE'S STONE, BARNBY, NORTH YORKSHIRE (formerly YORKSHIRE, NORTH RIDING)

Sheet 94
NZ 8313

South of the road from Whitby to Loftus (A174) is a standing-stone (NZ 831130) whose name takes us to the remote past of the English people. According to the Rev. George Young in his *History of Whitby* (1817), it had once had another near it and the pair of them were said to mark the grave of a giant called Wade. Two smaller stones near Goldsborough, about a hundred feet (30.5 m) apart, bore the same reputation – one of these survives (NZ 830144).

Although it is uncertain to which of the two sites it applied, the giant's grave tradition had been heard more than two centuries

Wade's Castle: Mulgrave Castle, from J. W. Ord's
History and Antiquities of Cleveland *(1846)*.
'Mougreve' is the ruin in the centre of the picture

earlier by the antiquary Leland, who writes that 'the north hille on the toppe of it hath certen stones communely caullid Waddes Grave, whom the people there say to have bene a gigant and owner of Mougreve'. 'Mougreve' is Mulgrave Castle – the old castle in Mulgrave Woods (NZ 840117), set on a ridge between two deep gullies. Camden also (trans. Holland, 1610) knew this to be Wade's Castle, though he believed Wade was a Saxon duke called Wada, who after his defeat by King Ardulph of Northumbria had fled and 'by a languishing sicknesse ended his life':

> . . . and heere within the hill betweene two entire and solid stones about seven foote high lieth entombed: which stones because they stand eleven foote asunder, the people doubt not to affirme, that here was a mighty Giant.

Curiously enough, though Camden was undoubtedly right in saying that the giant's grave tradition sprang from the distance between the stones (cf. **Weston**, p.168), there *was* a grave here at the Barnby stone, at whose base archaeologists found an unburnt Anglian burial, probably that of a warrior.

Whatever Camden thought, later folklore brooks no question but that Wade was a giant. The Rev. Young tells us he was thought to have built Mulgrave and Pickering Castles with the help of his wife, whose name was Bell. They built a castle apiece, but having only one hammer between them used to throw it back and forth, giving a shout each time to warn the other it was coming (cf. **Putney**, p.151). The Roman road supposed to communicate between the two castles, actually built to link the Roman camps with Malton, the garrison town, was known as 'Wade's causey' – Wade's Causeway. It had been built in a trice, with Wade paving and his wife carrying the stones, though once or twice her apron-strings broke, leaving a great heap of stones on the spot as mute witness to the truth of the tale.

According to one version of the story, the Causeway was built by Wade for his wife so that she could cross the moors to milk her cow, which was likewise gigantic – 'above 100 years ago', the Rev. Young tells us, someone had the idea of passing off as the rib of Bell Wade's Cow the jawbone of a young whale (cf. **Guy's Cliffe**, p.269, and **Stanion**, p.254). The relic was long shown under this name at the old Mulgrave Castle, dismantled in 1647, but in Young's own time lay neglected in the joiner's shop by the present castle. It was four feet (1.2 m) long and three or four inches (7.6–10.2 cm) round, and was covered with the initials of those who had come to see it.

These traditions are chiefly interesting for the parallel between Wade's Causeway and earthworks built by giants or gods such as **Wansdyke** (p.83), and between Bell Wade's Cow and the fairy cow belonging to the giant of **Mitchell's Fold** (p.314). Chaucer knew something a bit more lively – 'He song; she pleyde; he tolde the tale of Wade', he says in *Troilus and Criseyde*, and would that we could have eavesdropped on Pandarus's story, for Chaucer expected his audience to know what it was, and does not give details. Coming from Pandarus, it was probably pretty salacious, and we get the same idea from the 'Merchant's Tale', where 'old wedwes' apparently knew all about 'Wades boot' ('boat' in Chaucer's East Midlands). We get tantalizingly near this boat and then shear off again with Speght, an early editor of Chaucer, who in 1598 remarks: 'Concerning Wade and his bote Guingelot, as also his strange exploits in the same, because the matter is long and

Wade's Causeway:
Roman road on Wheeldale Moor, North Yorkshire

fabulous, I passe it over.'

But all is not lost. In the twelfth century, the gossipy Walter
Map tells the story of a knight called Gado – and Gado probably
equals Wade (cf. guarantee and warranty). He was the son of the
Vandal king but had left his native land to fight the world's
monsters. He was extraordinarily wise, spoke the language wherever he went, and succeeded in all he did, 'as if everything that
lived and moved obeyed his wish'. After helping the Indians out of
their difficulties, he arrived in England just in time to join forces
with King Offa (see **Offa's Dyke**, p.316) at Colchester against the
Romans. He is a superhuman figure, and Map had evidently heard
that he was a giant, because he goes out of his way to deny it.
Gado was 'not a monster himself like Alcides, in gigantic height,
nor, like Achilles, by fairy descent'. Nevertheless, he could not

quite resist the tug of tradition, and goes on to describe Gado as 'a huge man with a sprinkling of grey hairs', accompanied by knights 'conspicuous for great stature'.

So who was this middle-aged giant who owned a wonderful boat and whose works rivalled those of the dyke-builders Offa and Woden? The earliest mention of his name comes from the Old English poem *Widsith* (perhaps seventh century), but not until medieval times do we learn from the German poem *Kudrun* that he is a great warrior, like Gado grizzled and wise, who plays the well-known folktale role of supernatural helper. We hear more about him and, if not his, then *a* boat, in the *Saga of Thidrek*, the story of the Ostrogoth king Theodoric of Verona, written in Norway in the thirteenth century. This says that Wade was the son of a sea-woman who rose out of the waves and caught his father's ship by the prow to tell him she was bearing his child. Wade himself was the father of Weland (see **Wayland's Smithy**, p.278), whom he took to the dwarves to educate, agreeing that they should kill the boy if he did not return within two years. Wade was himself killed in the meantime, but Weland made his escape, and coming to a great river built a wonderful boat which carried him to the sea.

Whether the wonderful boat originally belonged to Wade or Weland, their family in these tales is persistently connected with water. In another German poem we hear how Weland's son Widia was fleeing for his life when a 'sea-woman', his ancestress Wachilt – presumed to be the mother of Wade – carried both him and his horse to safety at the bottom of the sea. From such snippets of legend, scholars conclude that Wade was originally a sea-giant from somewhere in the Baltic region, of whom tales were carried to these shores by the early Anglo-Saxon settlers. In England he was remembered as a giant-builder and his name linked with stone ruins and Roman roads, whereas in Denmark and North Germany he remained connected with the sea. His name means exactly what it says – it comes from the Germanic word 'to wade' – and it is told of him in the *Saga of Thidrek* that he once waded the Groenasund, a deep strait between two of the Danish islands, Christopher-like, carrying his little son Weland on his shoulder.

Wade's Causeway is in parts one of the best-preserved Roman roads in

Britain. It runs north-east from the Roman camps at Cawthorn to the Esk
near Grosmont, and a section about a mile (1.6 km) long has been
uncovered on Wheeldale Moor, near Goathland (SE 802970–812988):
AM (any reasonable time). Wade's Stone, Mulgrave Castle and Wade's
Causeway all lie within the North York Moors National Park. For Wade's
Causeway in particular, use the OS 1:25 000 Outdoor Leisure Map 27,
North York Moors (East Sheet).

WHARNCLIFFE SIDE, SOUTH YORKSHIRE   Sheet 110
(formerly YORKSHIRE, WEST RIDING)   SK 2994

'The present favourite pantomime at Covent Garden Theatre,'
wrote a correspondent to the *Gentleman's Magazine* in 1824, 'is
founded on the old song of "The Dragon of Wantley".' As a
subject for theatre it had already been going strong for almost a
century, since the highly popular burlesque opera *The Dragon of
Wantley* by Henry Carey (1737), like the pantomime taking its
story from a ballad so far as we know first printed in 1699 in *Wit*

*The Dragon of Wantley
slain by More of More
Hall, Wharncliffe Side,
South Yorkshire. Ballad
illustration*

and Mirth: Or, Pills to Purge Melancholy. The somewhat indelicate title of this gives an idea of the ballad, a broadly humorous spoof on dragon-slaying *à la* Lambton Worm. It is minutely localized:

> In Yorkshire, near fair Rotherham,
>   The place I know it well;
> Some two or three miles, or thereabouts,
>   I vow I cannot tell;
> But there is a hedge, just on the hill's edge,
>   And Matthew's house hard by it;
> There and then was this dragon's den,
>   You could not chuse but spy it.

Nearby lived More of More Hall, a 'furious knight', who could 'kick, cuff and huff', and swing a horse by its tail till it died. To him came the local inhabitants as supplicants:

> 'O save us all, More of More Hall,
>   Thou peerless knight of these woods;
> Do but slay this dragon, who won't leave us a rag on,
>   We'll give thee all our goods.'

> 'Tut, tut,' quoth he, 'no goods I want;
>   But I want, I want, in sooth,
> A fair maid of sixteen, that's brisk and keen,
>   With smiles about the mouth;
> Hair black as sloe, skin white as snow,
>   With blushes her cheeks adorning;
> To anoint me o'er night, e'er I go to fight,
>   And to dress me in the morning.'

This achieved, he goes off to Sheffield for a suit of armour set with spikes and like a 'strange outlandish hedgehog' sallies forth. The people climb trees and chimneys to view the fight, while More, his courage up with a quart of *aqua vitae* and six pots of ale, hides in the well where the dragon comes to drink. As the dragon stoops, up pops our hero crying 'Boh!' and clouts him on the muzzle. We will draw a veil over the dragon's reaction and pass on to the end of the fight, when More kicks him in the vent, Rosa Kleb-style, with the spiked toe of his boot.

'Murder, murder!' the dragon cried,
   'Alack, alack for grief!
Had you but missed that place, you could
   Have done me no mischief.'
Then his head he shaked, trembled and quaked,
   And down he laid and cried;
First on one knee, then on back tumbled he,
   So groaned, kicked, shat, and died.

The ballad with a bizarre logic takes all the improbabilities of the traditional dragon-tale and makes us look at them again – yes, the spiked armour would have looked ridiculous, and really what better place to stab a highly armoured dragon apart from the conventional throat – the toothy end – if you are a hero of More's calibre. As for More himself, the colourless landowners and knights of the average dragon-tale can't hold a candle to him: foul-mouthed, irascible, drunken, immensely strong and fiendishly canny – note that he takes his reward in advance, and expects (rightly) that the odd maiden, who in another sort of tale would have been sacrificed to the dragon, will not be too much to ask.

'Coarse country fare' as the cook book says – no wonder it was popular. But what was it all about? There are no church monuments or questions of land-ownership to be explained as in other Northern dragon-tales (see **Slingsby**, p.418, and **Sockburn**, p.419). After Bishop Percy had printed the ballad in his *Reliques* (1765), a local informant told him that it had been composed as a satire on a lawsuit over tithes in the reign of James I. The dragon was Sir Francis Wortley of Wortley Hall (SK 312996) and More the attorney who conducted the lawsuit against him on behalf of some of the neighbouring gentry. Percy's correspondent was the descendant of one of these, so the tradition, evidently handed down in his family, may well be correct. But a slightly different account is given by Joseph Hunter in his *Hallamshire* (1819), 'as it was committed to writing by a Yorkshire clergyman, Mr Oliver Heywood, of Coley, near Halifax, a hundred and fifty years ago', and relating to Sir Thomas, not Sir Francis, Wortley, who beggared some freeholders on his estates with costly lawsuits, then pulled their houses down to make a deer park. Retribution overtook him in the end, for 'it came to pass that before he dyed he belled like a deer and was distracted.'

More himself is said by some to have been based on one of the Mores of Lancashire, perhaps Sir William de la More, who distinguished himself at Poitiers (1356) and was famous for gallantry. Hunter, however, remarks that the marriage in 1460 of John More of More-hall to Margaret, sister of Sir Thomas Wortley, may have a bearing on the tale. As for the setting of the story, in footnotes to later editions of the *Reliques*, Bishop Percy gives an extract from a letter from an unnamed correspondent in about 1769:

> In Yorkshire, six miles above Rotherham, is a village called Wortley, the seat of the late Wortley Montague Esq. About a mile from this village is a lodge, named Warncliffe Lodge, but vulgarly called Wantley: here lies the scene of the song. I was there above forty years ago; and it being a wooded rocky place, my friend made me clamber over rocks and stones, not telling me to what end, until I came to a sort of cave; then . . . pointing to one end says, Here lay the dragon killed by More of More Hall; here lay his head; here lay his tail; and the stones we came over on the hill, are those he could not crack; and yon white house you see half a mile off, is More Hall. I had dined at the Lodge, and knew that the man's name was Matthew, who was a keeper to Mr Wortley, and, as he endeavoured to persuade me, was the same Matthew mentioned in the song; in the house is a picture of the dragon and More of More Hall; and near it a well, which, he says, is the well described in the ballad.

The 'sort of cave' was in Hunter's time still known as 'the Dragon's Den'.

Wharncliffe Lodge (SK 305997). The 'wooded rocky place' sounds like Wharncliffe Crags (SK 297975). The ballad of 'The Dragon of Wantley' can be found in Jacqueline Simpson's *British Dragons* (1980), the book to which I am indebted for most of my dragon-tales. So can the rather more celebrated story of the Lambton Worm, attached to Lambton Castle, County Durham.

WHITBY ABBEY, WHITBY, NORTH YORKSHIRE
(formerly YORKSHIRE, NORTH RIDING)

Impossible that the traditions of Whitby should not be dominated by the Abbess Hild, founder of Whitby Abbey in 651 A.D. A member of the Northumbrian royal family, she ruled the double monastery (both monks and nuns) for the rest of her life, and her authority is reflected in the tale that she rid Eskdale of serpents by driving them off a cliff into the sea. The proof of this was plain to behold. Says Camden (1610):

> Here are found certaine stones faschioned like serpents folded and wrapped round as in a wreathe ... A man would thinke verily they had beene sometime serpents, which, a coate or crust of stone had now covered all over. But people to [sic.] credulous ascribe this to the Praiers of Saint *Hilda*, as if shee had transformed and changed them ...

This is why fossil ammonites appear as the device of St Hilda's College, Oxford, and also in the arms of St Hilda's, Durham. It accounts likewise for the arms of Whitby Urban District Council: 'Barry wavy of ten argent and azure, three serpents coiled proper'.

A legend of the same sort referred to in Sir Walter Scott's *Marmion* (1808) is that crinoid debris littering the beaches of Lindisfarne were rosary beads forged by St Cuthbert on dark and stormy nights.

St Hilda's abbey was destroyed by the Danes in about 870 A.D. It was refounded as a Benedictine house towards the end of the eleventh century, and this is the Whitby Abbey whose ruins (NZ 904115) we see today. AM.

WILLY HOWE, THWING, HUMBERSIDE
(formerly YORKSHIRE, EAST RIDING)

Not far from Wold Newton, in the valley of the Gypsey Race, is a gigantic round barrow known as Willy Howe (TA 061724). Like the other barrows along the course of this stream, it may have been set there, perhaps in the Late Neolithic, because the place was numinous. The Gypsey Race (hard *g*), one of several streams that in wet seasons spring intermittently from the Wolds, must always have been a thing of wonder, coming and going as it did, and sometimes vanishing for two or three years at a time. In the twelfth century, as in Michael Drayton's day (1612), its appearance was said to presage death, and later it was held to prophesy all manner of disaster (cf. **Oundle**, p.248). It is perhaps not surprising that to Willy Howe, next to this mysterious stream, there should be attached one of the earliest English fairytales.

It is told by the twelfth-century chronicler William of Newburgh, a native of these parts:

> In the province of the Deiri . . . not far from the place of my nativity [East Newton], an extraordinary event occurred, which I have known from my childhood. There is a village some miles distant from the Eastern Ocean, near which those famous waters, commonly called Gipse, spring from the ground . . . A certain rustic belonging to the village, going to see his friend, who resided in the neighbouring hamlet, was returning, a little intoxicated, late at night; when, behold, he heard, as it were, the voice of singing and revelling on an adjacent hillock, which I have often seen, and which is distant from the village only a few furlongs. Wondering who could be thus disturbing the silence of midnight with noisy mirth, he was anxious to investigate the matter more closely; and perceiving in the side of the hill an open door, he approached, and, looking in, he beheld the house, spacious and lighted up, filled with men and women, who were seated, as it were, at a solemn banquet. One of the attendants, perceiving him stand-ing at the door, offered him a cup: accepting it, he wisely forbore to drink; but, pouring out the contents, and retaining the vessel, he quickly departed. A tumult arose among the company, on account of the stolen cup, and the guests pursued him; but he escaped by the fleetness of his steed, and reached the village with his extraordinary prize. It was a vessel of unknown material, unusual colour, and strange form . . .

William goes on to tell us that the cup was given 'as a great present' to Henry I, and by him handed on to his wife's brother, King David of Scotland, in whose treasury for many years it remained. Then 'a few years since', as William had learnt from sources he felt he could trust, it was passed back by William of Scotland to Henry II, who had expressed a wish to see it.

William's story ends here and the rest is silence. What became of the cup is unknown. Was it perhaps the same fairy cup that Gervase of Tilbury says was presented to Henry I by Robert, Earl of Gloucester (see **Rillaton Barrow**, p.29)? Gervase may well have taken his tale from William's pages. It is interesting that William himself heard it told in an area of Danish settlement, for similar legends are found in North Germany and Denmark, where several churches owned chalices said to be of fairy origin. But also from England comes a medieval Latin account of a fairy cup that came to the notice of Henry de Sanford, Bishop of Rochester (1227–35).

Just as smugglers seem to have put out ghost stories to keep people well away from their customary hidey-holes, so illicit barrow-breakers may have 'explained' their finds as gifts of the fairies (not that the Earl of Gloucester was taken in). At the same time, we cannot doubt but that the story contains some very ancient traditions. One strand in the complex web of fairy origin seems to have been the cult of the dead in their burial mounds – for such mounds are commonly connected with fairies, both in Ireland where the *Tuatha de Danann* inhabit the *sidh*, the fairy hill, and in Britain, where round barrows in particular were long believed to be fairy dwellings (see **Bishopton**, p.400).

The Willy Howe story connects even more closely with Scandinavian notions of the dead continuing some sort of after-life inside certain mountains. The fairy feast inside the howe (and this barrow is hill-sized) reminds one of nothing so much as a tale in the Icelandic *Eyrbyggja saga* (or in William Morris's phrase, 'The Tale of the Ere-Dwellers'), written in the mid thirteenth century. Þórólfr Mostrarskegg, a follower of Thor, greatly reverenced a mountain near his house and 'believed that thither would he go when he died, and all his kindred.' After Þórólfr's death, his son Þorsteinn Þorskabítr inherited the estate, and not long afterwards, when he was out fishing, he and all his crew were drowned. Before the news reached his home, his shepherd, out on the fells, chanced to look up at Helgafell, Þórólfr's 'Holy Mountain', and as he looked it seemed to him that the side of the mountain stood open, and sounds of merriment and feasting came from within. He caught

Fairies dancing outside the fairy hill,
from an early English chapbook

faint strains of speech, and managed to make out that Þorsteinn
and his men were being welcomed into the fell.

Barrows are traditionally, for obvious reasons, linked with
treasure, and folklore continued to harp on the note sounded so
early by William's tale of the fairy cup. In a story printed in
Hone's *Table Book* (1827) we are told that a person once dug into
the top of Willy Howe in search of a large chest of gold supposed
to be buried there. On finding the chest, he had a long train of
horses, extending upwards of a quarter of a mile, hitched to it by
strong iron traces, and was on the point of getting it out when he
exclaimed:

> 'Hop Perry, prow Mark,
> Whether God's will or not, we'll have this ark.'

No sooner had he uttered this blasphemy than the traces broke
and the chest sank still deeper into the hill, where it yet remains.
Similar stories are told elsewhere of treasure and also bells (cf.
Marden, p.312).

In another story, one of the fairies who lived in Willy Howe once told a man she was particularly fond of, that if he went to the top of the howe every morning he would find a guinea, provided he told no one whence it came. For some time he obeyed the injunction, but it proved too much for him at last and he told his secret. More – he took another person to the hill. Not only did he lose his luck, but 'met with a severe punishment' (one supposes a drubbing) from the fairies in revenge. A man who lived at **Stow-market** (p.193) also lost his fairy gift in this way, and indeed Aubrey in his *Remaines of Gentilisme* tells much the same story:

> Not far from Sr Bennet Hoskyns, there was a labouring-man, that rose up early every day to goe to worke; who for a good while many dayes together found a ninepence in the way that he went. His wife wondering how he came by so much money, was afraid he gott it not honestlye; at last he told her, and afterwards he never found any more.

The taboo on speaking of gifts from the fairies was one of the many fairy traditions Shakespeare knew: 'This is fairy gold, boy, and 'twill prove so . . . We are lucky, boy; and to be so still requires nothing but secrecy' (*Winter's Tale*, iii.iii.121–4).

12
Scottish Lowlands

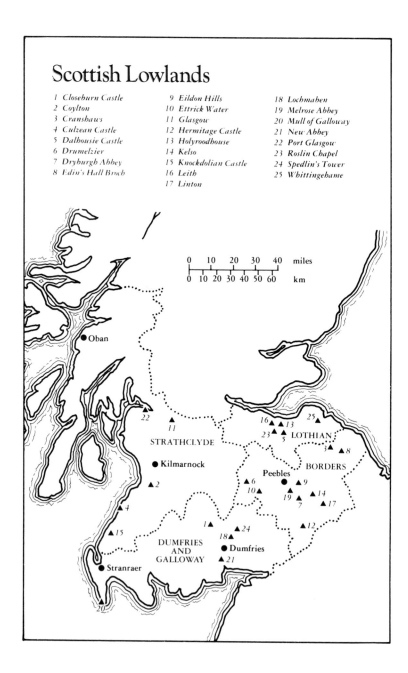

Scottish Lowlands

1 Closeburn Castle
2 Coylton
3 Cranshaws
4 Culzean Castle
5 Dalhousie Castle
6 Drumelzier
7 Dryburgh Abbey
8 Edin's Hall Broch

9 Eildon Hills
10 Ettrick Water
11 Glasgow
12 Hermitage Castle
13 Holyroodhouse
14 Kelso
15 Knockdolian Castle
16 Leith
17 Linton

18 Lochmaben
19 Melrose Abbey
20 Mull of Galloway
21 New Abbey
22 Port Glasgow
23 Roslin Chapel
24 Spedlin's Tower
25 Whittingehame

0   10   20   30   40   miles

0 10 20 30 40 50 60 km

● Oban

22 ▲   ▲
          11

STRATHCLYDE

● Kilmarnock

▲ 2

▲ 4

▲ 15

● Stranraer

16 ▲ ▲ 13   25 ▲
  23 ▲ ▲   LOTHIAN
       5   ▲ 3 ▲ 8

                BORDERS

Peebles
▲ 6   ●   ▲ 9
10 ▲   ▲ 14
       19   ▲ 17
        7

1 ▲   ▲ 24   ▲ 12
  18 ▲
DUMFRIES
  AND   ● Dumfries
GALLOWAY ▲ 21

20 ▲

CLOSEBURN CASTLE, DUMFRIES & GALLOWAY
(formerly DUMFRIES)

According to a mid nineteenth-century tradition, whenever one of the Kirkpatricks of the fourteenth-century tower-house of Close-burn Castle was about to die, a swan would appear on the loch surrounding the castle, coming from and departing none knew where.

It is said that, in days gone by, the grounds of the castle were the haunt every summer of a pair of swans, whose arrival happened twice to coincide with the sudden recovery from serious illness of members of the house, so that they came to be regarded as harbingers of good fortune.

For a century and a half they came yearly, until Robert Kirkpatrick, the heir, when not quite thirteen, went to Edinburgh, where he saw *The Merchant of Venice*. Much taken with the lines 'Make a swan-like end/Fading in music', he determined to test the truth of the old tale of swan-song and killed one with his crossbow. Frightened at what he had done, he buried the bird and said nothing, and when the swans failed next year to return, people assumed that they had died abroad. Then one day on the loch appeared a single swan with a blood-red stain on its breast. In less than a week after that, the head of the family died, and henceforth the swan always came as a harbinger of death.

This is one of the saddest of many death-omens in the form of a bird – for the superstition as attached particularly to *white* birds, see **Zeal Monachorum** (p.41). As to the age of the tradition, though Closeburn and its loch are described in some detail by Grose in his *Antiquities of Scotland* (1789), and though he dearly loved a tale to 'enliven the dullness of antiquarian disquisition', he does not mention the swans.

COYLTON, STRATHCLYDE
(formerly AYRSHIRE)

Of the village of Coylton, which lies on the Water of Coyle, the *Old Statistical Account of Scotland* for 1798 says 'it is believed, very ill-founded, that Coylton derives its name from a King Coilus who was killed in battle in the neighbourhood and buried in the church of Coylton'. Fergus Loch, to the west of the church (NS 3918), 'is supposed by some to take its name from King Fergus, who defeated Coel King of the Britons in the adjacent field'. Others laid the scene of the battle in the parish of Tarbolton, in the grounds of Coilsfield House, where stood a group of stones crowning a burial mound known as 'King Coil's tomb'.

These traditions go back to at least the sixteenth century, to the historian Hector Boece, who in 1526 compiled a Latin *Chronicle of Scotland*, a blend of fact and fancy which especially in its Scots translation (1535) was to prove highly popular. According to Boece, the Scots, who were descended from a daughter of Pharaoh called Scota, settled in Ireland first, then later colonized the west coast of Scotland from Ayrshire to Argyll. Not long after this, a fleet of Picts arrived from Scythia, whom the Scots allowed to settle their borders and to whom they gave Scottish wives, on condition they would always choose their rulers from the female line.

In those days the southern part of Albion was still in the hands of 'the belleall* British' and, says Boece:

> Ane king thai had wes callit Coilus
> Doggit and dour, mad and malicious . . .

who set the Picts and Scots at loggerheads, so that the Scots were forced to send to Ireland for reinforcements. More Scots from Ireland shortly arrived, led by King Fergus, who soon discovered that Coilus was at the bottom of the trouble and made a new alliance against him with the Picts.

From his capital at York, King Coilus launched a massive raid on Ayrshire and Galloway, camping overnight before the Scots citadel and intending to strike at dawn. But forewarned by scouts, King Fergus led a night-attack on the British encampment, taking them by surprise, so that they were routed. Some found safety in flight; others, not knowing the land, were either hunted down and captured or else swallowed up by the bogs. Coilus was of this number, abandoned by his bodyguard and sucked down into the morass, leaving only his name as a perpetual memorial. According to tradition, it is preserved not only in 'Coylton' but in the district-

---

* belleall = treacherous

name of Kyle, in 1153 recorded as 'Cul'.

Boece sets these events in about 330 B.C. – when the Scots had not yet arrived, for they did not settle in Britain before about 400 A.D. But though at first his story looks like fantasy, there may be a substratum of fact, for the Scots did indeed come from Ireland, and in southern Scotland there really was in about 420 a British king called Coil.

Or rather Coel, a leader of the Men of the North, as the Welsh called them, the British princedoms on either side of Hadrian's Wall in the two centuries after the departure of the Romans. The Men of the North were remembered in early Welsh poetry, where we hear of the 'sons of Coel', and in Welsh genealogies no fewer than eight out of the thirteen princely families who traced their descent from the Men of the North claimed as ancestor someone called *Coel Hen Guotepauc*, Old Cole the Splendid. By the late sixth century, the whole of the old Roman frontier zone from Edinburgh to Lancashire was in the hands of the 'sons of Coel', suggesting that he himself may have ruled the whole territory undivided.

Some have wondered if this early fifth-century king may not in fact have been the last of the *Duces Britanniarum* or commanders of the Roman troops stationed in Britain, whose headquarters were actually at York. However this may be, it is clear that Coel was a power to be reckoned with, for the Scots founded no settlements south of the Clyde estuary until centuries after his death.

As for why he should be especially remembered in Ayrshire – by the early 600s the British princedoms in the North had gone, fallen to the Anglo-Saxons, except for that of Strathclyde, centred on the rock of Dumbarton, and that held out right up to 1018, when it was absorbed into the Scottish kingdom. The British language itself survived in this part of the country to the fourteenth century, the vehicle no doubt for ancient tales of the Men of the North and particularly of Coel. Whether he died as Boece says, at the Water of Doon (NS 3317), or at Coylton, or Coilsford, he lived in tradition – not least perhaps in rhyme. For although the old nursery rhyme 'Old King Cole', known from the eighteenth century, is usually explained as referring to the eponymous founder of Colchester (see **Cymbeline's Castle**, p.132 and **Sarn Helen**, p.355) some of the earliest versions of it seem to be specifically Scottish – this one, for instance:

> Our auld King Coul was a jolly auld soul
>   And a jolly auld soul was he
> Our auld King Coul fill'd a jolly brown bowl
>   And he called for his fiddlers three
> Fidell didell, fidell didell quo' the fiddlers
>   There's no lass in a' Scotland
> Like our sweet Marjorie.

This was contributed to the *Scots Musical Museum* (1797) by Robert Burns, who said, 'I have met with many different sets of the words and music.' Where he heard it he does not say, but he was an Ayrshire man who spent much of his life in Kyle.

'King Coil's tomb' is probably the cairn marked on the map near Coilsfield Mains at NS 447263. 'Old Cole the Splendid' is discussed in detail by Charles Kightly in *Folk Heroes of Britain* (London, 1982).

CRANSHAWS, BORDERS   Sheet 67
(formerly BERWICKSHIRE)   NT 6961

From George Henderson's *Popular Rhymes of Berwickshire* (1856) comes the tale of the Brownie of Cranshaws, who for years threshed the corn at Cranshaws farm until at length after one harvest someone thoughtlessly remarked that it was not well mowed, i.e. piled up in a 'mow' in the barn. The next night the noise of great activity was heard coming from the barn and the Brownie's voice muttering:

> 'It's no weel mowed! It's no weel mowed!
> Then it's ne'er be mowed by me again;
> I'll scatter it oure the Raven stane,
> And they'll hae some wark e'er it's mowed again.'

The 'Raven stane' or Raven Crag was a great rock above the burn about two miles from Cranshaws and the furious Brownie stumped back and forth all night until he had tipped all the corn into the stream. Needless to say, he was not seen at Cranshaws again.

  If it wasn't one thing, it was another with a Brownie – were they more trouble than they were worth? Compare the shenanigans caused by Hobs, Hobthrushes, Cauld Lads, Boggarts and the like south of the Border.

Long since abandoned by its Brownie: Cranshaws Tower, Borders

'Cranshaws farm' I take to refer to Cranshaws Tower (NT 683618), a fine Border peel, once a Douglas stronghold, standing near the remains of the church.

CULZEAN CASTLE, MAYBOLE, STRATHCLYDE (formerly AYRSHIRE)

Sheet 70
NS 2310

In the olden days, the owners of Culzean Castle (ancestors of the Marquess of Ailsa) were known by the title of Lairds o' Co', a name given to Culzean, perched on the coast of Carrick on a rock eighty feet (24 m) above the sea, because of the three 'co's' or caves beneath it, 'well known', says Francis Grose (1791), 'for the legendary tales related of them' (and he refers us to Burns's 'Halloween').

An Ayrshire tale tells us that one day a tiny boy with a little wooden can in his hand accosted the Laird o' Co' near his castle gate, begging a little ale for his sick mother. The Laird sent him up to the house to the butler, to get his pannikin filled, and the butler began to draw the ale from a barrel that was about half full. To his surprise the barrel ran out before the can was filled, and not wanting to broach another, he went to consult the Laird. The Laird told him to fill the pannikin even if it took every drop of ale that was in the cellar, so the butler broached another cask. But scarcely a drop had he drawn when the wooden can was full and the little boy departed with many expressions of thanks.

Some years later, the Laird was at the wars in Flanders, and was taken prisoner and condemned to die. The night before his execution, the doors of his dungeon flew wide and the little boy appeared and said:

> 'Laird o' Co'
> Rise an' go.'

Outside the prison, the boy bade the Laird get up upon his shoulders, and in a trice had set him down at his own gate, on the spot where they first met, saying:

> 'Ae gude turn deserves anither . . .
> Tak ye that for being sae kin' to my auld mither'

and with that vanished, being of course a fairy.

This story, from Chambers's *Popular Rhymes* (1842), was taken by him from the Liverpool periodical *Kaleidoscope*, where it had appeared 'some years ago'. Though the verse would not have shamed MacGonagall, the story of fairy gratitude is a kindly one, related to several tales of people spirited away by the fairies on the whirlwind (see **Duffus Castle**, p.495).

Perhaps the closest parallel is the tale of Sir Godfrey MacCuloch recorded by Sir Walter Scott (1802). Once, when riding near his own house in Galloway, he was accosted by a little old man dressed in green (the fairies' colour) and riding a white palfrey. The old man gave Sir Godfrey to understand that he lived under his house, and that one of Sir Godfrey's drains emptied into his best room (cf. **Lochmaben**, p.472). Sir Godfrey promised to change its direction, and this indeed he did. Years later, he had the

'Laird o' Co, rise and go!': Culzean Castle, Strathclyde

misfortune to kill someone in an affray and was condemned to lose his head on Edinburgh's Castle Hill. But hardly had he reached the scaffold when the little man came riding through the crowd and bade Sir Godfrey jump up behind him. He spurred his palfrey down the steep bank, and neither he nor Sir Godfrey was ever seen again.

Culzean Castle is a late-eighteenth-century mansion built round the medieval tower-house of the Kennedys, and one of the finest Adam houses in Scotland. NTS. Times of opening also in *HHC&G*.

DALHOUSIE CASTLE, LOTHIAN   Sheet 66
(formerly MIDLOTHIAN)   NT 3263

Dalhousie Castle, dating from the fifteenth century and formerly the seat of the Ramsays, was in the eighteenth century and perhaps earlier possessed of a traditional death-warning. In his *Poems* (1721), the Scottish poet Allan Ramsay speaks of the Edgewell Tree, 'an oak tree which grows on the side of a fine spring, nigh the castle of Dalhousie, very much observed by the country people, who give out, that before any of the family died, a branch fell from the Edgewell Tree. The old tree, some few years ago, fell altogether, but another sprung from the same root, which is now tall and flourishing . . .'

The same superstition attached to the Prophet Elm which gave warning to the Eckleys of Credenhall Court, Shropshire, and to one of the lime trees at **Cuckfield Park** (p.104); and for a similar and ancient omen, see **Brereton Hall** (p.298).

DRUMELZIER, BORDERS   Sheet 72
(formerly PEEBLESHIRE)   NT 1334

'There is one thing remarkable here,' wrote Alexander Pennecuik in *A Geographical, Historical Description of Tweeddale* (1715), 'which is. The Burn called *Pausayl*, runs by the Eastside of this Church-yeard into *Tweed*, at the side of which Burn, a little below the Church-yeard, the famous Prophet *Merlin* is said to be buried. The particular place of his Grave, at the Root of a Thorn-Tree, was shewn me many years ago, by the Old and Reverend Minister of the place Mr. *Richard Brown*, and here was the old Prophecy fulfilled, delivered in *Scots* Ryme to this purpose.

> *When* Tweed *and* Pausayl, *meet at Merlin's Grave,*
> Scotland and England, *shall one Monarch have.*'

For, says Pennecuik, in 1603, on the day when James VI of Scotland became England's James I, the Tweed indeed overflowed and met the Powsail at this place. But, as Robert Chambers sceptically remarks, 'there is nothing in the local circumstances to make the meeting of the two waters at that spot in the least wonderful, as Merlin's grave is in the *haugh* or meadow close to the Tweed, which the river must of course cover whenever it is in flood.'

As for how Merlin came to be buried at Drumelzier – the story of his triple death in the Tweed is told in 'Lailoken and Kentigern' (for which see **Glasgow**, p.459). This is not, however, Merlin's only resting place – he is also supposed to be sleeping near Carmarthen.

In his *Popular Rhymes of Scotland* (1826), Chambers includes some lines of verse which, he says in a later edition, he first heard in the deep voice of Sir Walter Scott:

> Tweed said to Till,
> 'What gars ye rin sae still?'
> Till said to Tweed,
> 'Though ye rin wi' speed,
>   And I rin slaw,
> Yet where ye droun ae man,
> I droun twa!'

Like other traditions of life-demanding rivers (cf. **Conon House**, p.493, and **Waddow Hall**, p.391), this seems to reach back to Celtic times and an ancient belief in the indwelling spirits of rivers and their need to be appeased. Though the spirit of the Tweed with its broad and shallow bed was evidently not so hungry for sacrifice as that of the deep and narrow Till, it was still a force to be reckoned with – or so the Baron of Drumelzier was led to believe. To his castle of Drumelzier, at the west of the Tweeddale chain of Border fortresses, he returned from the Crusades to find his wife nursing a child he could not account for, considering the years he had been away. When he asked her how she had come by it, she explained that she had been walking one day by the Tweed when the spirit of the river had come up and ravished her. For reasons best known to himself, the Baron accepted her story and the child eventually became Baron of Drumelzier after him and the chief of the clan.

This is the tale as Sir Walter Scott tells it in a note to *The Lay of the Last Minstrel* (1805). In his *Picture of Scotland* (1827), Chambers adds that the story was still current in the countryside in his day and was popularly held to account for the family name of 'Tweedie', for as such had the child been commonly known – a rustic joke by which the Baron was doubtless not amused. But he was not alone in his predicament, for a similar tale was told in France of the birth of Merovée or Merowig, first of the Merovingian kings.

The supposed site of Merlin's Grave is marked on the OS 1:25 000 map at NT 134345. Close by is Merlindale (NT 127342). The Powsail burn is marked as Drumelzier Burn. In Wales, Merlin lies imprisoned by the spells of the nymph Vivien or Nimue in a cave on the lower slopes of Bryn Myrddin, 'Merlin's Hill' (Sheet 159, SN 4120), up the valley of the Towy (Tywi) from Carmarthen. According to local tradition, if you stand at the right spot, you can hear him groaning underground. Edmund Spenser mentions the cave and its noises in his *Faerie Queene* (1590–1609), but places it further up the Tywi in the grounds of Dynevor Castle (SN 6122).

DRYBURGH ABBEY, MERTOUN, BORDERS (formerly BERWICKSHIRE)

Sheet 74
NT 5931

In *Minstrelsy of the Scottish Border* (1802), Sir Walter Scott tells the tale of a female vagrant who about fifty years before had taken up residence in a vault among the ruins of Dryburgh Abbey, whence she emerged only by night. Then, after dark, she would sally forth to beg at the neighbouring houses of Newmains and Shielfield, at twelve o'clock every night lighting a candle and returning to her vault. She told her neighbours that in her absence her home was tended by a sprite whom she called Fatlips and described as a little man wearing heavy iron shoes, with which he would trample the clay floor to dispel the damp. Because of her claims about this spirit, the well-informed thought her mad, while the uneducated went in fear of her.

She would never explain why she had taken up this way of life, but it was generally believed to be the result of a vow that, while her lover was absent, she would not look upon the sun. But he never returned, having fallen in the 'Fortyfive', and never in her life would she look on the light of day again.

The vault where she lived and died, says Sir Walter, still in his day went by her name and few of the neighbouring peasants dared enter it by night. The sad and crazed old vagrant gave him the idea for the nun in Drybergh bower who never looked on day in his romantic ballad 'The Eve of St John', set at Smailholm and first published in 'Monk' Lewis's *Tales of Wonder* (1801).

But if the old lady was cracked, her eccentricity ran on traditional lines – for iron shoes were characteristic of the Border Redcaps (see **Hermitage Castle**, p.462).

AM. The ruins of Dryburgh Abbey, founded by Hugh de Moreville in

1150 as a house of Premonstratensian canons, are picturesquely sited in a
bend of the Tweed, and it is not surprising that Sir Walter Scott should
have wanted to be buried here, quite apart from the fact that he was the
last representative of the Haliburtons of Newmains, whose property the
abbey became in 1700. The 'vault' referred to by Sir Walter is the run of
three vaulted cellars entered through a doorway in the north-west corner
of the cloister walk. They were built after the Reformation. The familiar
spirit's name of Fatlips may be connected with that of Fatlips Castle,
Minto (NT 5820), as indeed this must be with Fatlips Castle, *Tinto*, in
Strathclyde (NS 968457). 'What the origin or meaning of the name may
be, seems quite inexplicable,' writes Robert Chambers in *The Picture of
Scotland* (1827), 'but some ingenious antiquary may perhaps be able to
deduce it from, or connect it with, a custom which has from time
immemorial obtained among parties of pleasure visiting the top of Minto –
that every gentleman, by indefeasible privilege, kisses one of the ladies
on entering the ruin'. Fatlips Castle, Minto, is marked as such on the
OS 1:50 000 (Sheet 73). Fatlips Castle, Tinto, is shown by name only at
the larger scale.

EDIN'S HALL BROCH, DUNS, BORDERS   Sheet 67
(formerly BERWICKSHIRE)   NT 7760

> There was ance twa widows that lived ilk ane on a small bit o'
> ground, which they rented from a farmer. Ane of them had
> two sons, and the other had ane; and by and by it was time
> for the wife that had twa sons to send them away to spouss
> their fortune.

And so begins one of Scotland's oldest fairytales, the story of 'The
Red Etin' as told by Chambers in his *Popular Rhymes* (1842). The
widow with the two sons tells the eldest to bring water in a can
from the well to make a cake, but by the time he has fetched it
home most of the water has run out of a hole and so the cake is
small. His mother asks him if he will take half the cake with her
blessing or the whole cake with her curse, and seeing that the cake
is small he takes the whole with her 'malison'. Before he leaves, he
takes his brother aside and gives him his knife, to keep until he
returns, telling him to look at it every morning. If it is clear and
bright, he is safe; if dim and rusty, then ill has befallen him.

Off he sets to 'spouss' his fortune, and on the third day he meets
up with an ancient shepherd tending his flock of sheep. When he
asks who the sheep belong to, the ancient man replies:

'The Red-Etin of Ireland
  Ance lived in Bellygan,
And stole King Malcolm's daughter,
  The King of fair Scotland,
He beats her, he binds her,
  He lays her on a band;
And every day he dings her
  With a bright silver wand.
Like Julian the Roman,
He's one that fears no man.

'It's said there's ane predestinate
  To be his mortal foe;
But that man is yet unborn,
  And lang may it be so.'

The widow's son goes on with his journey, and he has not gone far
when he meets another old man, a swineherd, with whom he
exchanges the same question and same reply. On a bit further and
he comes to an old man herding goats, and again the same question

The castle of the Red Etin:
Edin's Hall broch and hill-fort, Borders

and answer, but this time the goatherd adds that he must beware of the next beasts he meets as they will be different from any he has yet seen.

Sure enough, by and by the lad encounters a multitude of dreadful beasts each with two heads and on every head four horns. He runs away as fast as his legs will carry him and comes to a castle on a hill whose door stands open. Inside he finds an old woman sitting by the fire and asks her for shelter. She says indeed he may stay the night but it is a bad place to be, as the castle belongs to the Red Etin, a three-headed ogre, who spares no man on whom he can lay his hand. The lad asks the old woman to hide him, so she does, but presently in comes the Red Etin and cries:

> 'Snouk butt, and snouk ben,
> I find the smell of an earthly man;
> Be he living or be he dead,
> His heart this night shall kitchen my bread.'

The Red Etin soon finds the lad in his hidey-hole and pulls him out, and asks him three riddles on which depend his life. But these the lad cannot answer, so the Red Etin knocks him on the head with his great mallet and turns him into a pillar of stone.

The morning after this happens, the widow's second son takes out his brother's knife and looks at it, and lo! it has rust on the blade. He tells his mother it is time for him to leave also, and she sends him to the well. All happens as before – he chooses to take the whole cake with his mother's malison, and ends up in the Red Etin's castle as a pillar of stone.

When the other widow's son hears what has happened, he determines to set out to help his friends and his mother gives him a can to go to the well in his turn. As he is coming home, a raven overhead cries out to him to look to his can, and he sees it is holed. He patches the holes with clay, and so brings home enough water to make a large cake, and when his mother asks which will he have, the whole cake or the half, he takes the half with her blessing. After he has travelled a fair way, he meets an old woman who begs a piece of his cake, and though he has but the half he gives it her gladly. In return she gives him a magic wand and tells him the answers to the Red Etin's riddles. Then she vanishes – for she is a fairy (and probably the raven as well).

The lad goes on his way until he, like his neighbours, meets the ancient shepherd tending his flock of sheep, but this time when he asks whose sheep they are, the old man answers:

> 'The Red-Etin of Ireland
>   Ance lived in Bellygan,
> And stole King Malcolm's daughter,
>   The King of fair Scotland.
> He beats her, he binds her,
>   He lays her on a band;
> And every day he dings her
>   With a bright silver wand.
> Like Julian the Roman,
> He's one that fears no man.
>
> 'But now I fear his end is near,
>   And destiny at hand;
> And you're to be, I plainly see,
>   The heir to all his land.'

The swineherd and the goatherd say exactly the same; and when the lad comes to the place of the beasts with two heads he does not run away but strides bravely through them, and the first that comes up to devour him, he strikes with his wand and lays dead at his feet.

When he reaches the Red Etin's castle, the old woman sitting by the fire warns him of what has happened to his two neighbours, but he does not care for that, for he has made up his mind to help them. Soon the Red Etin comes in, saying:

> 'Snouk butt, and snouk ben,
> I find the smell of an earthly man;
> Be he living, or be he dead,
> His heart shall be kitchen to my bread.'

He soon spies the young man and, bidding him come out, asks him the three riddles. But because the fairy woman has told him the answers, the lad guesses the riddles aright, and the Red Etin's power is broken. Then the lad takes up an axe and chops off his three heads.

After that the old woman leads him upstairs, where there are many doors, and out of every door comes a beautiful lady who had been a prisoner, among them the princess, the king's daughter of Scotland. The old woman also leads him down into a low room where are two stone pillars, and he touches them with his wand and immediately his two neighbours are restored to life. Next day they all set out for the king of Scotland's court and the king gives the lad his daughter, and nobles' daughters to his two friends, so they live happily ever after.

The tale of the Red Etin – though whether precisely *this* tale we do not know – goes back at least to the sixteenth century, when it is mentioned in the *Complaynt of Scotland* (1548). It was also one of the nursery tales with which the poet David Lyndsay (*ca.* 1486–1555) in his *Dreme* claims to have amused the infant James V. When Chambers was first writing his *Popular Rhymes* in 1826, the Red Etin was still a well-known character in Scotland, 'supposed to go searching about for what he may devour, and constantly exclaiming:

> Snouk butt, snouk ben,
> I find the smell of earthly men.'

'Snouk,' says Chambers, 'signifies, to search for with the nose like a dog . . .', and the Red Etin is clearly a traditional ogre, able to sniff out the flesh of man – how like his rhyme is to 'Fee, fi, fo, fum', the one which Shakespeare knew (*King Lear*, iii.iv.180–1).

He also resembles a giant described by Hesiod and Vergil, the three-headed Geryon of the isle of Gades (Cadiz) who was destroyed by Hercules. Geryon, too, kept numerous flocks. Direct influence from classical legend is entirely possible, but Lewis Spence (*Minor Traditions of British Mythology*, 1948) believed that the Red Etin was identical with the Celtic *Gruagach*, in Scottish and Irish tales a protector of cattle, sometimes a giant, and frequently described as wearing a gorgeous red mantle.

The riddles set by the Red Etin on which the lad's life depends (and to which we never hear the answers) have parallels in other old tales (cf. **High Hesket**, p.375), as does the life-token – the object which tells whether its absent owner is alive or dead. Indeed charms serving as life-tokens were used in real life in days when communications were poor to keep those left at home in some sort of touch with those away. The life-token was always something the absent person had owned or which had been part of him, and had to be capable of changing its appearance. Knives were often used, as in the tale, but a favourite token was the absent person's urine, kept in a bottle tightly corked: if the liquid was clear, he was well; if cloudy, in danger or ill. If it dried up altogether, he was assumed to be dead.

This old fairytale, with its web of traditional lore, has because of some fancied resemblance of name become attached (though not by Chambers) to Edin's Hall Broch, on the north-eastern slope of Cockburn Law. One of only ten Iron Age brochs known in Lowland Scotland, it is exceptional among them for its size, and was originally defended by a series of outworks. Its massive appearance as well as its name probably helped attract to it the belief that it was the castle of the monstrous Red Etin – one of the great etens or ettins that used to stride our fells, descendants of the Old English *eoten* or giant.

AM (any reasonable time). Signposted from the A6112 to Duns, and reached by footpath off the Oldhamstocks road (NT 792609).

EILDON HILLS, BORDERS   Sheet 73
(formerly ROXBURGHSHIRE)   NT 5532

According to a tradition recorded in 1822 by James Hogg, the Ettrick Shepherd, the Eildon Hills formed one large peak until the wizard Michael Scot set one of his devils the task of splitting it into three. Geologically speaking, Eildon is one hill with three peaks dominating Tweeddale. Eildon Hill North (NT 5532), commanding important valley routes and a naturally defensive position, was the site of a hill-fort, the largest in Scotland, some of whose remains can still be seen, and was later used by the Romans as a signal station. Down below, to the east of Newstead (NT 5634), in *ca.* 81 A.D. Agricola founded the major stronghold of Trimontium or 'Three Hills', kingpin of the network of forts built for the occupation of Scotland.

It was not far from Trimontium and below these dominating hills that, according to a fifteenth-century romance, Thomas the

Rhymer – Thomas of Erceldoune – first met the Fairy Queen. As well as the romance, we have a ballad on the same theme, the oldest version of which goes back to the first half of the eighteenth century. The ballad undoubtedly sprang from the romance and for the most part – it stops short of the denouement – tells the same story. Thomas of Erceldoune, says the romance, was lying on Huntlie Bank when he saw a lady of unearthly beauty riding by. Thinking that she was the Queen of Heaven, he ran down to meet her at the Eildon Tree, and saluted her. She was not the Queen of Heaven, she said, but came from another country. Evidently emboldened by this, Thomas begged her to lie with him and at length she agreed, though she said it would ruin her beauty. As indeed it did – the act of love transformed her into a hag, but it also gave her power over Thomas and she compelled him to go with her. She led him under Eildon, where for three days and nights in utter darkness he waded through water over the knees – a journey transformed in the sinister imagination of the ballad-maker:

> For forty days and forty nights
>   He wade through red blood to the knee,
> And he saw neither sun nor moon,
>   But heard the roaring of the sea.

At length he cried out that he was dying of hunger, and she led him out into the light, and to a fair garden where all kinds of fruits were growing – but he might touch none of these, for the curse of Hell was on the fruit of that country. But now she told him to lay his head in her lap and she would show him five marvels: a mountain path leading to Heaven, a valley road to Paradise, a road to Purgatory across a plain, one plunging downwards into the fires of Hell, and on a hill a shining castle where the King and Queen of fairies lived. And this the ballad has seized and dramatized into a simple choice between the good, the bad and the ambiguous moral territory of the fairies:

> O see not ye yon narrow road,
>   So thick beset wi thorns and briers?
> That is the path of righteousness,
>   Tho after it but few enquires.

> And se not ye that braid braid road,
>   That lies across yon lillie leven?
> That is the path of wickedness,
>   Tho some call it the road to heaven.
>
> And se not ye that bonny road,
>   Which winds about the fernie brae?
> That is the road to fair Elfland,
>   Whe[re] you and I this night maun gae.

Returning to the romance, when Thomas looks again at the Fairy Queen he sees that she has recovered her beauty. They are now at the threshold of Fairyland, and she warns him not to speak to anyone but herself the whole time he is there. She blows her horn, the gates open and they enter a place that is filled with music, dancing and revelry, where Thomas lives for what seems like three days but which he later learns has been three years. Then the teind or tribute to Hell falls due, and fearing that the choice will fall on him, the Queen takes Thomas back into Middle Earth and leaves him under the Eildon Tree. At parting she gives him the gift of a tongue that cannot lie and from her he learns many prophecies.

The story of Thomas of Erceldoune is made up of many motifs which appear in the earliest British fairytales, and clearly go back to very ancient lore: green as the colour worn by fairies (in the ballad 'Her skirt was of the grass-green silk') or sometimes assumed by them (**Woolpit**, p.210); the loss or gain of beauty with sex (**High Hesket**, p.375): fairyland inside a hill (**Willy Howe**, p.430); the underground passage or cavern leading to a fair country (**Peak Cavern**, p.249, and **Vale of Neath**, p.363); the taboo on fairy food (**Dagworth**, p.180); the supernatural lapse of time in fairyland (**Hereford**, p.306). The Eildon Tree itself has a peculiar significance: it is a commonplace of the early medieval Breton *lais*, which embody Celtic legend, that those who sleep or even lie down under certain trees place themselves in the power of the fairies. The ritual silence to be observed when dealing with fairies is a theme that occurs over and over again in folk tradition (cf. **New Abbey**, p.478), and the fairies' tribute to Hell appears also in the ballad of 'Tam Lin', expressing the theological view of the origin of fairies as Fallen Angels (see **Church Stowe**, p.224).

When precisely this rich mix was first attached to 'True Thomas' is unknown, but the fifteenth-century romance is thought to go back to an earlier original. It may have been told of him not long after his death, for Thomas of Erceldoune was an historical person, who lived in the latter part of the thirteenth century and was the owner of land at Earlston in Berwickshire, from which he took his name. He was known as a poet and prophet already in the early fourteenth century, and it may be that he did actually compose some of the fifty-odd surviving prophecies attributed to him. In the fourteenth century he was held to have prophesied the reign of a great king, which some took to be Robert the Bruce, others Edward II of England. A traditional rhyme current in the early nineteenth century and ascribed to Thomas runs on the same theme:

> When is seen the nest of the ringle-tailed gled,*
> The lands of the north sall a' be free,
> And ae king rule owre kingdoms three.

Through some confusion of ideas, Thomas the prophet came himself to be the prophesied leader. The 'sleeping hero' legend is told of him at Dumbuck, near Dumbarton, at Tom-na-hurich, near Inverness, as well as here at Eildon. In all three places, Thomas still lives in the fairy hill but comes out from time to time to buy horses of a special colour or kind for his host of warriors. When he has them all, the great battle will be fought and the king come into his own. The man who sells him the horses usually gets paid when he comes to the hill, inside which he sees the warriors sleeping.

This story was current by the seventeenth century, when it was told in 'An excellent discourse of the Nature and substance of Devils and Spirits' added by an anonymous author to the third edition of Reginald Scot's *Discovery of Witchcraft* (1665). Sir Walter Scott, who intended himself to write a novel based on the legend, in the 1829 edition of *Waverley* tells it as it was current in the Borders in his time. A horse-coper called 'Canobie Dick' (from Canonbie, Dumfriesshire) who one moonlight night was riding over Bowden Moor (NT 5231) with a pair of horses he had been unable to sell, met an aged man in antique costume who bought them both, paying for them in ancient golden coins. He asked the coper to bring more horses to that spot, which Dick did more than

* gled = kite

once, the last time hinting to the old man that there was no luck in
a dry bargain. The old man thereupon led him up a narrow path to
a little hill between the southernmost and central peaks of Eildon
known from its shape as the Lucken Hare*. Dick was startled to
see the old man enter at the foot of the hill by a passage or cavern
he had never noticed, though he knew the Lucken Hare well.
Inside they came to stables filled with coal-black horses, and by
each horse a sleeping knight in coal-black armour. At the far end
of the great hall stood a table on which were lying a sword and a
horn. The old man, who now revealed himself as the prophet
Thomas of Erceldoune, told Dick that he who drew the sword and
sounded the horn would be king of all Britain – but that everything
hung on which he took up first. The coper seized the horn and
blew a blast, and the thunderous peal it made woke the knights.
Seeing them coming at him, he dropped the horn and tried to raise
the sword, but heard a great voice proclaim:

> 'Woe to the coward that ever he was born,
> Who did not draw the sword before he blew the horn.'

A whirlwind then carried Dick off and cast him down the bank,
where he was found next morning by shepherds, living just long
enough to tell his tale.

A version of this story in which the sleeping warriors in the hill
are King Arthur and his knights seems to have been current at
much the same time, and was recorded by John Leyden in his
poem *Scenes of Infancy* (1803). This is the form the story also took
at Sewingshields Castle in Northumberland in the Rev. John
Hodgson's day (1840). Much the same tale was told of Brinkburn
Priory, Northumberland, and Richmond Castle, North Yorkshire,
and certainly underlies the legend of 'Guy the Seeker' at Dunstanburgh Castle, popularized (at the least) by 'Monk' Lewis
(1775–1818). The 'sleeping hero' tradition was likewise attached to
'Freebro's huge mount, immortal Arthur's tomb' as John Hall
Stevenson called it in *A Cleveland Prospect* (1736) – Freeburgh or
Freebrough Hill, south of Castleton, North Yorkshire. It has been
pointed out that the concentration of 'sleep sites' in northern
England and just into Scotland lends strength to the identification
of Roman Camboglanna (Birdoswald in Cumbria) as the site of

---

* Lucken = lying, i.e. crouched

Camlann, Arthur's last battle. Sewingshields in particular and two other locations where Arthur is supposed to lie, the Sneep, near Allansford, not far from Consett, in County Durham, and Threl-keld Fell near Keswick in Cumbria, are feasible places to which a stricken king might have been borne and where he might still be sleeping (see **Cadbury Castle, Somerset**, p. 6). A similar tradition attached to several places in Wales, notably Craig-y-Ddinas, Mid-Glamorgan, although some say that the sleeping hero is not Arthur but the outlaw hero Owen Lawgoch, 'Owen of the Red Hand'.

As for the scene of True Thomas's original encounter with the Fairy Queen, Sir Walter Scott used to show visitors to Abbotsford Huntlie Bank and the Rhymer's Glen (NT 5232) conveniently located on his own property. But apropos of Scott's visit to Rokeby in 1812, J. B. S. Morritt noted that he 'was but half satisfied with the most beautiful scenery when he could not connect it with some local legend, and when I was forced sometimes to confess . . . "Story! God bless you! I have none to tell, sir" – he would laugh, and say, "then let us make one – nothing so easy as to make a tradition."' There is no doubt that Scott transported the legend. The Huntlie Bank of the romance was within sight of the Eildon Tree, and the Eildon Stone, traditionally supposed to mark the tree's site, is on the slope of the easternmost of the peaks of Eildon, near the Bogle Burn.

But before we castigate the Laird of Abbotsford for feeling free to appropriate someone else's heritage, let it be said that True Thomas's encounter with the Fairy Queen is, barring the proph-ecies, precisely that of Ogier the Dane with Morgan le Fay, related in the French medieval romance *Ogier le Danois*. Moreover, Ogier, one of Charlemagne's paladins, under his Danish name of Holger Danske, is a 'sleeping hero' lying underneath Kronborg Castle (Shakespeare's Elsinore) awaiting Denmark's darkest hour, when he will come forth to save her. In both cases there is no doubt that we are dealing with Celtic fairy traditions transmitted through French romance probably by way of Brittany. It is too late now to ask where such stories were first located – to be anything but thankful that when people heard a good tale, they made it their own, attaching it to men and places they knew.

For the stouthearted (and stoutly shod) the best way of seeing the sites is to follow the Eildon Way, a circular route of about four miles (6.4 km) beginning and ending at Melrose. The first signpost is in Dingleton Road, off Market Square, and the route leads more or less direct to Eildon Hill North. Those who feel up to it can climb the hill to the hill-fort and Roman signal-station on the summit, but the marked route mercifully follows the line of the 200 m contour east along a hedge to the Eildontree Plantation (NT 562334), before descending to the Melrose–Newtown Road. The Eildon Stone (NT 563336), formerly marking the site of the Eildon Tree and also the approximate site of the Roman customs post, is up the road a step towards Newtown. Erected by the Melrose Literary Society in 1929, it was moved to its present site on the opposite side of the road in 1970. If you rejoin the Eildon Way, it will lead you across the road and through the back of Newstead to the site of Trimontium (various stages, NT 539337, 563331, 567336, 569336, 572343). The finds from the site are in the National Museum, Edinburgh. From Newstead the route leads back into Melrose along Prior's Walk. The Lucken Hare can be seen from the B6359 opposite Bowdenmoor (NT 5331). It is also known as the Little Hill and the Devil's Spadeful, from the tradition that it was dropped by one of the familiars of Michael Scot (see under **Melrose Abbey**, p.475). Eildontree Plantation, but not the Eildon Stone, is shown by name on the OS 1:25 000 map. Brinkburn Priory, Dunstanburgh Castle and Richmond Castle: AM.

ETTRICK WATER, BORDERS (formerly SELKIRKSHIRE)

Sheet 79
NT 3018

In the introduction to his *Minstrelsy of the Scottish Border* (1802), Sir Walter Scott speaks of '*Shellycoat*, a spirit who resides in the waters, and has given his name to many a rock and stone upon the Scotish coast'. He says that Shellycoat belonged to the class of bogles, and got his name from the fact that he was decked out in shells whose clattering announced his approach. In a later edition, Sir Walter suggests that Shellycoat may be identical with the North of England Brag, whose frolics usually ended with a horse-laugh (see **Hedley on the Hill**, p.405), and certainly he seems closer to the essentially harmless earthbound English Brag than the malignant Scottish water kelpie.

One of his haunts was a great rock on the site of the present docks at Leith, round which children would run shouting:

> 'Shellycoat, Shellycoat, gang awa' hame,
> I cry na yer mercy, I fear na yer name.'

It was said that after he had performed any particularly hard task he would take off his coat of shells and hide it under a rock, and was then, like selkies and swan-maidens, powerless.

In the Border country Shellycoat was believed to especially haunt the old tower-house of Gorrenberry (NY 469971) on Hermitage Water in Liddesdale, although he might be met with, too, along Ettrick Water, where, in the words of Sir Walter Scott, 'One of his pranks is thus narrated':

> Two men, in a very dark night, approaching the banks of the Ettrick, heard a doleful voice from its waves repeatedly exclaim – 'Lost! Lost!' – They followed the sound, which seemed to be the voice of a drowning person, and to their infinite astonishment, they found that it ascended the river. Still they continued, during a long and tempestuous night, to follow the cry of the malicious sprite; and arriving, before morning's dawn, at the very sources of the river, the voice was now heard descending the opposite side of the mountain in which they arise. The fatigued and deluded travellers now relinquished the pursuit; and had no sooner done so than they heard *Shellycoat* applauding, in loud bursts of laughter, his successful roguery.

GLASGOW, STRATHCLYDE   Sheet 64
(formerly LANARKSHIRE)   NS 5965

On a seal of the thirteenth-century bishopric of Glasgow is portrayed one of the miracles of St Kentigern (St Mungo), its founder and patron saint. It shows a man with a sword, a woman holding a ring, and between them the saint. Around the seal an inscription reads: REX FURIT, HAEC PLORAT, PATET AURUM, DUM SACER ORAT, 'The king rages, she weeps, the gold appears, while the saint prays.'

The story as told in the *Acta Sanctorum* (1643) is that a certain king had given his wife a ring which she had then parted with to a handsome soldier. The king was made aware of the fact, and when, out hunting, he found the soldier asleep on the riverbank, drew the ring from his finger and cast it into the Clyde. He then demanded the ring of the queen, who sent to the soldier, and when he could not produce it, in despair appealed to St Kentigern. The saint promptly found the missing ring in the stomach of a salmon taken from the river and returned it to the queen. The king, on seeing it, thought she had been falsely accused and rounded on her calumniators. In memory of this event, the arms of the City of Glasgow still include a salmon with a ring in its mouth.

Glasgow cathedral is traditionally held to stand on a site which has been a holy place since the sixth century, when Kentigern built the first church here. But was Kentigern a real person? Some scholars have thought not, for though the sources for his life go back to the eleventh and twelfth centuries, they are packed with even older legendary themes. Should we, for instance, believe that he was the illegitimate son of Owen of Rheged, son of the great Urien, by a princess of Lothian, and that his mother was cast adrift in a boat, much like the mother of Perseus? Perhaps not – but out of the miasma of legend there emerges a little ground that we may trust to as solid. Kentigern may well have been royal – St Columba was – and if he were illegitimate, all the more reason for encouraging him to become a monk and eschew dynastic ambitions. It may also be true that he was educated by the shadowy St Serf, the apostle of western Fife, at Culross, and himself became a monk in the austere Irish tradition; that he was made bishop of Strathclyde, but during the political upheavals of the period exiled to Cumbria (where traditions of him are strong); that he later returned to Strathclyde, to Hoddom in Dumfries and then Glasgow, where he died. Certainly Glasgow claimed his relics.

Kentigern indeed seems to share the half-real, half-legendary world inhabited by Myrddin or Merlin, generally believed to be the same as the wild man Lailoken of Scottish tradition, said to have lived in the woods in Lowland Scotland towards the end of the sixth century. In the twelfth-century *Life of St Kentigern* by the monk Joscelin of Furness is included a prophecy made by Lailoken after Kentigern's death and while Lailoken himself was living at the court of 'Rederech' – in Welsh literature Rhydderch Hael, Rydderch the Generous, king of Dumbarton, at that time still in British hands.

More dramatically, from a fifteenth-century manuscript in the British Museum comes the tale of 'Lailoken and Kentigern', in which Kentigern in a deserted place meets the naked and hairy Lailoken, who declares he has run mad because of a vision during the Battle of Arfderydd (identified with the parish of Arthuret in Cumbria, below the confluence of the Liddel and the Esk). During the battle, of which he confesses himself the cause, the heavens opened and a voice accused him of his crime and condemned him to live in the woods with the beasts of the forest to the end of his days. Then he saw in the sky, amid intolerable brightness, countless troops of warriors brandishing their fiery lances at him (cf. **Souther Fell**, p.389). Crazed with guilt and fear he had fled, as now he suddenly fled again from Kentigern's presence. Later he reappeared, and begged the saint to give him the Sacrament, as he was about to die a triple death. Kentigern granted his request, and the same day the shepherds of King Meldred waylaid Lailoken and beat him with cudgels and stones, then cast him into the Tweed, where his body was pierced by a stake – beating, drowning and transfixing.

In another story, Lailoken is murdered at the instigation of Meldred's queen, whom he has accused of adultery – reminding us of the way in which the king rounds on the queen's accusers in the tale of the missing ring. And perhaps this theme was what originally led to the ring-story being attached to St Kentigern, for it is peculiar neither to him nor indeed to Scotland. It is, for example, told in Brand's *History of Newcastle* (1789) as occurring there in about 1559, when a man named Anderson – some said Sir Francis Anderson – dropped his ring into the Tyne and recovered it from the stomach of a fish brought by his servant from Newcastle market. A similar tale was told in the twelfth century of another saint, the Saxon St Egwin of Evesham Abbey.

Such stories are related to the classical tale 'The Ring of Polycrates', told by Herodotus in his *Histories*. Polycrates, the tyrant of Samos, famous for his success, was warned by the King of Egypt to guard himself against the nemesis which would surely one day overtake him, for luck such as his was too good to last. He advised Polycrates by way of precaution to throw away the most precious thing he possessed, and he accordingly put out to sea and threw overboard a valuable ring. But there is no struggling against destiny – a few days later a fisherman caught a fish he deemed fit for a king and presented it to Polycrates. When Polycrates' servants cut it open, there lay the ring.

Glasgow cathedral: AM.

HERMITAGE CASTLE, CASTLETON,   Sheet 79
BORDERS   NY 4996
(formerly ROXBURGHSHIRE)

On the north bank of Hermitage Water and once protected by a
moat formed by the river and two small streams, Castle Sike and
Lady Sike, stands Hermitage Castle, built in the thirteenth century
to guard the western approach into Scotland. The Castle took its
name from the nearby hermitage chapel, built by a recluse in the
1170s, but it sadly belies its reputation.

'The castle of Hermitage', wrote John Leyden in Scott's *Border
Minstrelsy* (1802), 'unable to support the load of iniquity which
had been long accumulating within its walls, is supposed to have
partly sunk beneath the ground; and its ruins are still regarded by
the peasants with peculiar aversion and terror.' Certainly the walls
seem to have subsided and certainly deeds of ill fame have been
perpetrated here – including the starving to death of Sir Alexander
Ramsay by Sir William Douglas in 1342.

But the evil reputation which clung to the castle centred mainly
on one of its early owners, the infamous 'Lord Soulis' – William,
Lord Soulis, who had royal blood in his veins. Warden of the
Scottish Marches in the days of Robert the Bruce, he forfeited his
great possessions and died a prisoner in Dumbarton Castle for his
part in a conspiracy designed, according to Barbour (*ca.* 1370), to
make him king. In legend he combined prodigious physical strength
with cruelty and treachery, harassing the neighbouring barons and
fortifying his castle against the king by the help of demons. He
also used his vassals as beasts of burden – Leyden, in a note to his
Poems and Ballads (1858), says it was a tradition in Liddesdale that
Lord Soulis put *bores* (holes, perforations) in their shoulders, the
better to yoke them to the sledges on which they dragged the
materials for building the castle.

He had a familiar called Redcap, a category of spirit which
haunted old Border castles and peels, and was elsewhere known as
Red-comb or Bloodycap. In his *Folk-Lore of the Northern Counties*
(1879), Henderson tells us that he was generally described as 'a
short thickset old man, with long prominent teeth, skinny fingers,
armed with talons like eagles, large eyes of a fiery red colour, grisly
hair streaming down his shoulders, iron boots, a pikestaff in his
left hand and a red cap on his head.' He would torment night-

bound travellers, sometimes butchering them and catching their blood in his cap, hence Redcap. But the pronouncement of the Holy Name would send him off in a 'flaucht' of fire, though he always left behind him one of his teeth.

In the eighteenth century, Redcap was still believed to haunt the castle. In the *Border Minstrelsy* Leyden writes:

> The door of the chamber, where Lord SOULIS is said to have held his conferences with the evil spirits, is supposed to be opened once in seven years, by that dæmon, to which, when he left the castle, never to return, he committed the keys, by throwing them over his left shoulder, and desiring it to keep them till his return. Into this chamber, which is really the dungeon of the castle, the peasant is afraid to look; for such is the active malignity of its inmate, that a willow, inserted at the chinks of the door, is found peeled, or stripped of its bark, when drawn back.

In Leyden's ballad of 'Lord Soulis', which was included in the *Border Minstrelsy* along with his account of the legend, Redcap becomes rather less of a peasant bogey and more of an elemental.

Home of the diabolist Lord Soulis: Hermitage Castle, Borders

As long as he remains Lord Soulis's familiar, Soulis bears a charmed life, to be killed neither by 'forged steel, nor hempen band' (i.e. the sword and the gallows). If danger threatens, he has no more to do than knock thrice an old chest with rusty padlocks and Redcap will appear – but on condition that when the lid rises Lord Soulis never looks. At the last he *does* look, the contract is broken, and the end is swiftly at hand.

Complaints had so often been made of Lord Soulis by his neighbours to the King that at last he said in exasperation, 'Boil him, if you please but let me hear no more of him!' They hastened to comply, and spurring to Hermitage seized Lord Soulis and bore him to Nine Stane Rig, where was an ancient stone circle:

> On a circle of stones they placed the pot,
>   On a circle of stones but barely nine;
> They heated it red and fiery hot,
>   Till the burnished brass did glimmer and shine.
>
> They rolled him up in a sheet of lead,
>   A sheet of lead for a funeral pall;
> They plunged him in the cauldron red,
>   And melted him, lead, and bones, and all.

The Nine Stane Rig (now Ninestone Rig) where this dreadful scene took place is a declivity leading down to Hermitage Water from the hills between Liddesdale and Teviotdale. It took its name from the stone circle (NY 518973) 'nine of which', Leyden says, 'remained to a late period' (but see **Nine Ladies Stone Circle**, p.244). Two of the remaining five were in his day pointed out as those which supported the iron bar from which hung the pot. The cauldron itself was said long to have been preserved at Skelfhill, a hamlet between Hawick and the Hermitage (NY 4504), but by the time Chambers wrote *A Picture of Scotland* (1827) it had been bequeathed by the farmer 'to his relative Mr Pott, of Pencryst, where it now is'. Leyden in 1858 reported the cauldron to be, not medieval, but 'an old kail-pot of no very extraordinary size, which was purchased of some of the followers of the rebel army in 1715'.

Sir Walter Scott himself tells us in a note to this ghoulish tale that it has a parallel in the real history of Scotland. Melville of Glenbervie, sheriff of the Mearns, was so harsh in the execution of his duties that he was much complained of to James I (or, say others, to the Duke of Albany). In an unguarded moment, the King exclaimed: 'Sorrow gin the Sheriff were soddin, and supped in broo'!' Shortly after this, the lairds of Arbuthnot, Mather, Laurieston and Pittaraw decoyed Melville to the top of the hill of Garvock, above Laurencekirk (Grampian), on the pretext of a hunt, where had been prepared a fire and a boiling cauldron. Into this the sheriff was plunged, and after he was 'soddin' (seethed) for a sufficient time, they fulfilled the King's mandate by partaking of the broo'.

The King's unguarded exclamation, so like that of Henry II which led to the execution of Becket, may or may not be historically true – though boiling was used as a judicial punishment in the Middle Ages. Whether or no, this incident almost certainly lies behind the tale of Lord Soulis. One wonders if there were ever a version in which it did not appear, for it is unnecessary. The use of a sheet of lead and the pot is dictated by the terms of Lord Soulis's compact with Redcap – that ropes will not bind him nor steel weapons touch.

Scott in a later edition of the *Border Minstrelsy* adds the footnote that, in the autumn of 1806, the Earl of Dalkeith ordered the rubbish cleared away from the door of the dungeon at Hermitage and a little way from it was found a rusty iron key. It was generally agreed among the country people that Redcap had finally given up his charge and resigned the key to the Earl, who was heir-apparent. A large iron ladle was also found, 'somewhat resembling that used by plumbers', and was evidently assumed to be the one with which the lairds did their supping.

AM. Times of opening also in *HHC&G*. The castle was extensively restored in the early nineteenth century, but the oldest work is thought to date from the fourteenth. Ninestane (or Ninestone) Rig is to the east of the castle, beyond the Whitterhope Burn. The Ninestones stone circle (NY 518973) is in the parish of Castleton.

HOLYROODHOUSE, EDINBURGH, LOTHIAN (formerly MIDLOTHIAN)

Sheet 66
NT 2573

On 9 March 1566, David Rizzio, the Italian secretary and friend of

Mary, Queen of Scots, was murdered at the Palace of Holyrood by certain Protestant noblemen at her court with the connivance of her husband Darnley. The hapless Rizzio, whose only crime seems to have been that he was wittier than the half-baked Darnley, was torn from the Queen's side as she sat at supper and dragged through her apartments to the outer door, while the Queen herself, though pregnant, was held at point of knife by the Earl of Ruthven, who declared himself to be ready to cut her 'into collops' if she lifted a hand.

Rizzio's corpse was left all night on the floor in the doorway – and a bloody corpse it was too, stabbed fifty-six times, like Caesar bearing a rent for each conspirator so that all might share the guilt. No wonder that, from at least 1722, a dark stain on the floor at the outer door of the Queen's apartments was shown to visitors as Rizzio's blood.

Numerous stories are still told of bloodstains that cannot be removed, however often they are washed or scrubbed, for blood has in folklore a peculiar sanctity and deeds of violence always leave their mark (cf. **Smithills Hall**, p.388). It was the over-use of the indelible bloodstain by the 'Gothick' school, perhaps, that provoked Sir Walter Scott, normally one to give legends more than their due, into levity on the subject. In his *Chronicles of the Canongate* (1827–8), a Cockney traveller in patent cleaner demonstrates his wares on the Holyrood stain – an idea brought to full beauty in another setting in Oscar Wilde's 'The Canterville Ghost'.

But if ever an 'indelible bloodstain' was likely to be real, it was, from the circumstances of the murder, the one at Holyroodhouse. It is all the more a shame that the hygienists have had their way and that there is now nothing more sinister than a brass tablet to mark the fatal spot.

AM. Times of opening also in *HHC&G*.

KELSO, BORDERS (formerly ROXBURGHSHIRE)

Sheet 74
NT 7233

In Roxburgh Street, Kelso, the outline of a horseshoe is said to mark the spot where Prince Charles Edward's horse cast a shoe as he was riding through the town on his way to Carlisle in 1745. He is also said to have planted a white rosebush in his host's garden, and descendants of 'Prince Charlie's White Rose' are believed still to flourish in Kelso.

Prince Charles Edward Stuart did indeed spend a day in the town on his road south in November 1745, and the tradition of the horseshoe expresses the strength of Scottish devotion to 'Bonnie Prince Charlie', for it is the ancient one of the divine visitor who leaves behind the footprint of himself or his horse (cf. **Corngafallt**, p.336).

The horseshoe is embedded in a granite sett in the middle of the road outside the Selkirk and Kelso Society Co-op.

KNOCKDOLIAN (KNOCKDOLION) CASTLE, COLMONELL, STRATHCLYDE (formerly AYRSHIRE)

Sheet 76
NX 1285

'The old house of Knockdolion stood near the water of Girvan, with a black stone at the end of it', Robert Chambers writes in his *Popular Rhymes of Scotland* (1870). A mermaid used to come from the water at night, and taking her seat upon the stone, would sing for hours, at the same time combing her long yellow hair. But the lady of Knockdolion found that the singing wakened her baby, so had the servants break up the stone, and when the mermaid came next night and found that her favourite seat had gone, she sang:

'Ye may think on your cradle – I'll think on my stane;
And there'll never be an heir to Knockdolion again.'

Soon after that, the cradle was found overturned and the baby dead beneath it. The family thereafter became extinct, and, says Chambers, 'One can see a moral in such a tale – the selfishness of the lady calling for some punishment.'

A similar tale is given by Cromek in *Remains of Nithsdale & Galloway Song* (1810) of the Mermaid of Galloway, who haunted a deep and beautiful pool formed in the mouth of Dalbeattie Burn by the eddy of Orr (now Urr) Water (NX 8260). There of a moonlight night she would sit on a block of granite combing her golden hair and giving the people of the neighbourhood the benefit of her medical advice (cf. the mermaid of **Port Glasgow**, p.480). But a woman living nearby, in a fit of religious zeal, Bible in hand, pushed the mermaid's 'chair' into the pool. Next morning her only child lay dead in its cradle and thereafter at dusk the mermaid's voice would often be heard from the pool, saying:

> 'Ye may look i' yere toom* cradle,
> And I'll look to my stane;
> And meikle we'll think, and meikle we'll look,
> But words we'll ne'er hae nane!'

Weeds and filth were gathered together and thrown into the pool, until it was so polluted that the mermaid was forced to depart, leaving the curse of barrenness on the house, 'which all the neighbours for several miles around, are ready to certify'.

This is one of many familiar tales that are now ambiguous. Did its original audience hear it simply as a dire warning against interference with numinous sites (as in several tales of disaster attached to ancient monuments), or did they hear it as Chambers did and as we do today as a plea for neighbourly toleration?

LEITH, LOTHIAN   Sheet 66
(formerly MIDLOTHIAN)   NT 2676

From Richard Bovet's *Pandaemonium, or The Devil's Cloyster* (1684) comes an account given him by a Captain George Burton of the Fairy Boy of Leith. This was a child of ten or eleven, possessed of 'a cunning much above his years', who claimed to be a drummer to the fairies:

> He seemed to make a motion like drumming upon the Table with his Fingers, upon which I asked him, whether he could beat a drum? To which he replied, yes Sir, as well as any man in *Scotland*; for every *Thursday* Night I beat all points to a sort of people that use to meet under yonder Hill (pointing to a great Hill between *Edenborough* and *Leith* . . .

---

* toom = empty. Although Chambers speaks of 'Knockdolion' near Girvan Water, he must, I think, have meant Knockdolian Castle on the River Stinchar (NX 122853). Dalbeattie Burn is named on the OS 1:25 000 map; the confluence with Urr Water is at NX 831603. (Sheet 84.)

The boy managed to slip away on just such a trysting night despite Burton's efforts to detain him, to join the company under Calton Hill:

> I demanded of him, how he got under the Hill? To which he replied, that there were a great pair of gates that opened to them, though they were invisible to others, and that within there were brave large rooms as well accomodated as most in *Scotland*.

Within the hill would be a great gathering of men and women, with all sorts of music beside the drum, and an abundance of food and wine. Sometimes the whole company would be carried to Holland or France and back the same night – for what purpose he does not say, but perhaps to revel in the king's cellars (see **Duffus Castle**, p.495).

The fairy dwelling under the hill is an old and persistent tradition (see **Willy Howe**, p.430), and the description of the fairies' gathering with 'al maner menstracie' and fine viands comes straight from court scenes in medieval romance. Being caught up by the fairies in magical flight is also a very old theme. In the anonymous 'Discourse on Devils and Spirits' appended to the 1665 edition of Reginald Scot's *Discoverie of Witchcraft*, we read:

> And many such have been taken away by the sayd Spirits, for a fortnight or month together, being carryed by them in chariots through the Air, over Hills, and dales, Rocks and Precipices, till at last they have been found lying in some Meddow or Mountain bereaved of their sences, and commonly one of their Members to boot.

This tradition lasted long, especially in Scotland, and Sir Walter Scott tells us in 1802 of 'The Poor Man of Peatlaw', who late in the previous century fell asleep in a fairy ring and found himself being whisked through the air at a rate of knots so that before he knew where he was he had landed in Glasgow. His coat had been left behind on Peatlaw in Selkirkshire, and his blue bonnet was later found sticking on the kirk steeple of Lanark. By good fortune he happened to meet a carter who knew him and conveyed him to Selkirk again – though if anyone believed his story, history does not say.

Often the fairies caught people up in a whirlwind – exactly as the Devil did the old woman of **Leverington** (p.184) and the magicians Jack o' Kent and Michael Scot were accredited with similar magical flight (see **Grosmont**, p.341, and **Melrose Abbey**, p.475). In Scotland, as one can see from the witchcraft trials, the boundaries between fairies and practitioners of Black Magic were by the seventeenth century not clear – hence perhaps the smack of sulphur that clings about the Fairy Boy. This preternaturally clever child was clearly not thought himself to be a fairy, but to consort with fairies like a witch – and perhaps something more, for was it not a *drum* that he played, like the notorious Demon Drummer of Tedworth, the celebrated 'racketing ghost' (i.e. poltergeist) of South Tidworth in Hampshire in the seventeenth century?

LINTON, BORDERS   Sheet 74
(formerly ROXBURGHSHIRE)   NT 7726

> The wode laird of Lariestoun
> Slew the wode worm of Wormistoune,
> And wan all Linton paroschine.

It was Sir Walter Scott who recorded this local rhyme in his *Minstrelsy of the Scottish Border* (1802). It was supposed to be the wording of the inscription, already in Scott's time defaced, that accompanied a piece of sculpture over the south door of the old parish church. This represented a knight with a falcon on his arm, encountering two monsters, one of whom he attacked with his lance. The sculpture was popularly explained as the 'wode' (angry) Laird of Lariston slaying a serpent or 'worm' on a green hillock, in Scott's time still known as Wormeston in memory of the deed. The proof of the tale was still visible, for in its agony the serpent contracted its folds, leaving the impression of its coils on the hill.

In a later edition of the *Border Minstrelsy*, Sir Walter was able to include an account of this dragon-slaying from a genealogical MS in the Advocates Library, written in about 1680 and concerning the Somervilles:

> In the parochen of Lintoun, within the sheriffdom of Rox-
> burgh, there happened to breed a monster, in form of a
> serpent, or worme; in length, three Scots yards, and somewhat

bigger than an ordinary man's leg ... It had its den in a hollow piece of ground, a mile south-east from Lintoun church; it destroyed both men and beast that came in its way. Several attempts were made to destroy it, by shooting of arrows, and throwing of darts, none daring to approach so near as to make use of a sword or lance. John Somerville undertakes to kill it, and being well mounted, and attended with a stoute servant, he cam, before the sun-rising, before the dragon's den, having prepared some long, small, and hard peats (bog-turf dried for fuel), bedabbed with pitch, rosett, and brimstone, fixed with small wyre upon a wheel, at the point of his lance: these, being touched with fire, would instantly break out into flames; and ... about the sun-rising, the serpent, dragoune, or worme, so called by tradition, appeared with her head, and some part of her body, without the den; whereupon his servant set fire to the peats upon the wheel, at the top of the lance, and John Somerville, advancing with a full gallop, thrust the same with the wheel, and a great part of the lance, directly into the serpent's mouthe, which wente down its throat into the belly, and was left there, the lance breaking by the rebounding of the horse, and giving a deadly wound to the dragoun; for which action he was knighted by King William; and his effigies was cut in stone in the posture he performed this actione, and placed above the principal church door of Lintoun, where it is yet to be seen, with his name and sirname: and the place, where this monster was killed, is at this day called, by the common people ... the Wormes Glen. And further to perpetuate this actione, the barons of Lintoun, Cowthally, and Drum, did always carry for crest, a wheel, and theron a dragon.

This tale which sets out to explain so much – the carving over the door, the crest of the Somervilles, the indentations on a certain hill – was probably primarily a charter-myth, i.e. a story intended to justify a family's claim to certain lands. (cf. **Bisterne**, p.53). Many such were manufactured, especially in the fifteenth century, in the absence of written records, but whether they were ever believed by the families concerned is highly doubtful – they were perhaps simply an aspect of heraldry. What the local peasantry made of such traditions is another question.

The Advocates MS tells us that John Somerville was the son of Roger de Somerville, baron of Whichenever in Staffordshire, and that he was made chief falconer by William the Lion (hence, we are to suppose, the falcon on the knight's arm). In fact the Somerville who first acquired the barony of Linton from the king was William de Somerville, grandson of an earlier William who was descended from the Whichenever Somervilles and came to Scotland in the reign of David I. Moreover, the tympanum known as the Somerville Stone, built into the comparatively modern parish church now standing on the site of the old, may have been intended to represent St Michael overcoming the Devil. Apart from the two monsters (it is uncertain what these are, though the Devil normally appears as a dragon) the picture includes what seems to be the Agnus Dei, so the whole may have reference to Revelation 12:11, 'And they overcame him by the blood of the Lamb'. That this might have given rise to a dragon-slaying even without help from the Somerville crest is shown by the case of Brinsop in Herefordshire, where a twelfth-century tympanum of St George slaying the dragon has led to the tradition that the deed was done on this spot – that the dragon lived inside Dragon's Well in a meadow to the south of the church and the battle took place in a field called Lower Stanks.

However this may be, if you look from Linton church towards 'Wormiston' (Linton Hill, NT 7827) you *can* see the marks of the dragon's coils.

LOCHMABEN, DUMFRIES & GALLOWAY (formerly DUMFRIES)

Sheet 78
NY 0882

> A woman, who lived in the ancient Burgh of Lochmaben, was returning late one evening to her home from a gossiping. A little, lovely boy, dressed in green, came to her, saying . . . '*Coupe yere dish-water farther frae yere doorstep, it pits out our fire!*' This request was complied with, and plenty abode in the good woman's house all her days.

This little tale from Cromek's *Remains of Nithsdale & Galloway Song* (1810) is a politer version of one also told in Wales. In 1882, the folklorist Sir John Rhys heard from a local smith the tale of a farmer who had lived a short time before at Deunant, near Aberdaron. This farmer, said the smith, used to go outside his front door last thing at night to relieve himself before he went to bed. One night as he stood there, a stranger appeared and said he had no idea how he was annoying him. The farmer asked how so, to which the stranger replied that his house was below where they stood. If the farmer would stand on his foot, he would see that it was true. So the farmer placed his foot on the stranger's, and at once he could see plain that the slops from his house went down the other's chimney. On the fairy's advice he walled up the door and made another at the back, and ever after that he and his cattle prospered.

Such 'Good Neighbours' stories, in which a fairy complains that a householder's slops are putting out his fire, reflect a belief that fairies might live in subterranean dwellings beneath the houses of humans. In *Clan Traditions and Popular Tales of the Western Highlands* (1895), J. G. Campbell tells how the wife of a tenant farmer in a remote part of Lewis, who was often alone in the house, when she was spinning one day saw a little woman 'of reddish appearance' come in through the door with two dogs. She asked the woman of the house for the loan of a small cauldron, and when this was granted, the dogs bore it away. Five days later it was returned, the little woman remarking to the wife that she could hear her singing songs above her dwelling. Sad to say, the good neighbourliness was put a stop to by the woman's husband, who told the minister what had passed, and on his advice pulled down his house, burning every scrap of the old thatch and pouring nine cogfuls of charmed sea-water on the rafters.

Sometimes the fairy dwellings are under the threshold of the human house, as in the Lochmaben story, but sometimes under the hearth, the hearthstone serving as the door. Walter Gill in *A Second Manx Scrapbook* (1932) quotes a story from the *Celtic Review* about a house at Airlie in Angus (now Tayside), supposed to be haunted by fairies because cakes baking at the fire sometimes disappeared. Finally the house was pulled down, and the hearth-stone discovered to be the roofstone of an underground dwelling. A number of mouldy cakes were found, which were thought to have slipped through the crack. Perhaps they had – perhaps there *were* no fairies: but in a Shetland tale of the same kind the hearthstone is raised and a hand comes up to snatch a cake.

Such stories were very likely inspired by souterrains, in Cornwall

*A 'Pecht house'? A good example of an earth-house or souterrain:
Culsh Earth-House, Grampian*

called 'fogous', stone-built galleries with a slab roof below ground
level, dating from the last centuries B.C. They are likely to have
been storage cellars, but in eastern Scotland were known as Pictish
houses – and all over Scotland the 'Pechs' were much confused
with fairies, if indeed the last remnants of this people did not
contribute to fairy belief.

Though tales of the 'borrowing fairies' were once held to reflect
the contact of such a people with those of a higher culture – the
things borrowed are often made of iron, and kettles or cauldrons
are favourites – in the stories as we have them the borrowing
works both ways. 'The Dumb Woman from the Land of the Dead
took my kettle', complains an old fairy man in a Gaelic rhyme of
the housewife who lived above his dwelling in the world of mortal

men (and was silent because it was dangerous to speak to fairies). At **Frensham** (p.106), too, one went to the fairies for the famous Frensham Cauldron, before they were supplanted by a witch.

Standing on the fairy's foot to see his dwelling echoes a report received by the antiquary Aubrey concerning those 'who had the Second sight, That if at any time when they see those strange Sights they set their Foot upon the foot of another who hath not the Second-sight, that other will for that time see what they are seeing . . .' (*Miscellanies*, 1696). A good souterrain to visit in connection with 'Good Neighbours' stories is that of Culsh in the parish of Tarland, Grampian (NJ 504054), which still has its roof. AM. Remember to take a torch.

MELROSE ABBEY, BORDERS (formerly ROXBURGHSHIRE)

Sheet 73
NT 5434

Still shown at Melrose Abbey is the grave of Michael Scot, the Scottish wizard. When and where he was born is unknown, but in the nineteenth century traditions were current that his birthplace was Balwearie Castle in Fife, that he lived at Oakwood Tower on Ettrick Water (NT 420260), and that he was buried at the Cistercian abbey of Melrose.

Although Oxford is claimed as his university, the details of his education are unknown, except that, since he is referred to as 'Master Michael Scot', he had presumably taken his master's degree, and he was of course a cleric – later, in 1223, he declined the offer of the archbishopric of Cashel in Ireland. He may have taught Latin grammar early in his career, and around 1217 was living in Toledo as a translator. Described by a contemporary as proficient in Latin, Hebrew and Arabic, he it was who among other things introduced the work of the Arab scholars Averroes and Avicenna to the West. He also lived at the splendid imperial court of the Holy Roman Emperor Frederick II at Palermo, where he was employed as physician, philosopher and astrologer.

Although Scot was widely read in books of magic, which he did not distinguish from astrology, there is nothing to suggest that he ever practised it – indeed, he condemns it in his own writings. But as perhaps the leading scholar of Western Europe in the early thirteenth century, his works were very well known, and his interest in 'science' and astrology noted. Men have been thought wizards for much less (cf. Sir Francis Drake under **Combe Sydenham Hall**, p.16, and Jack o' Kent under **Grosmont**, p.341). At all events, by the time Dante placed him in the *Inferno*, Scot's reputation as a wizard had spread.

In later folklore, one of his magic arts, like St Aldhelm of **Malmesbury Abbey** (p.70), was that of magical flight. In his *Superstitions of the Highlands & Islands of Scotland* (1900), John Gregorson Campbell recounts the tale that once when Michael Scot wanted to visit Rome, he took a fairy horse fleeter than the wind, and the Pope was amazed to see snow still on his bonnet. He was also a great builder, usually on the scale of giant-builders such as Wade (see **Wade's Stone**, p.421). Sir Walter Scott mentions him in *The Lay of the Last Minstrel* (1805) as having 'cleft Eildon hills in three, And bridled the Tweed with a curb of stone', while in Northumberland, where he was known as Mitchell Scott, he was said with the Devil's help to have built Hadrian's Wall. Like Wade he also made roads – in the *History of Rutherglen* (1793), David Ure writes: 'Watling Street in many places of England is called Mitchell Scott's Causeway, and it is believed by the credulous vulgar there that the devil and his friend Mitchell made it in one night.'

From Northumberland in the nineteenth century comes the tale that Michael Scot would have made the river Wansbeck navigable between Morpeth and the sea were it not for some native son's want of courage. After repeating certain cantrips, he commanded the man to run from the Wansbeck's mouth at Cambois to Morpeth, without once looking back. But the runner heard the roaring of the waters behind him, and so his courage failed and he looked behind, whereupon the tide stopped flowing after him and Morpeth lost its chance. (No such faltering ruined a similar scheme of Francis Drake's, when by magic he brought water to Plymouth.)

The story of Michael Scot commanding the waters was much earlier told in Cumberland, where, says Edmund Sandford in his *Antiquities* (*ca.* 1675), mounted on a devil's horse the magician was bidden ride towards Carlisle without looking back, but, terrified by the noise of waters, turned in the saddle, 'and there, the sea Stopt at Boostat hill, 8 miles from Carleile'.

Michael Scot's connection with Cumberland did not end here – a latish tradition says that he built Bolton Old Church in the upper

Ellen valley north of Bassenthwaite, and another claims that in old age he retired to Holm Cultram Abbey, whose abbots, according to Camden in the *Britannia* of 1610, built Wolsty Castle to house their records, 'wherein the secret works, they say, of Michael the Scot lie in conflict with mothes'. In 1629 another topographer, Satchells, visiting Burgh under Bowness, saw 'one of Sir Michael's Histories hanging on an iron pin in the castle', which no one had dared to read, and he also states that he was shown Sir Michael's tomb in the church.

But there is no evidence that Michael Scot ever returned from abroad to these shores, and the claims that he was buried at Burgh under Bowness, or, another contender, Glenluce, or at Melrose, all have about as much chance as one another of being true.

AM. Times of opening also in *HHC&G*. The traditional grave of Michael Scot is the one with a cross on it, level with the ground, next to the double piscina in the South Transept chapel nearest the Presbytery. The 'curb of stone' with which he bridled the Tweed is said to be the barrier in the river near Maxton.

MULL OF GALLOWAY, DUMFRIES & GALLOWAY (formerly WIGTOWNSHIRE)

Sheet 82
NX 1530

The lonely coasts of the Mull of Galloway are said to be the last home of the Picts, the 'Pechs' as they were known in Scotland. Of all the traditions about them, certainly the most poignant is the story of heather ale.

The Pechs were a great people for ale, which they brewed from heather, a secret known only to themselves and handed down father to son with strict injunctions never to tell anyone else. But the Pechs had great wars and soon they had come to be a mere handful of people. It came at last to a great battle between them and the Scots, and all were killed save two, father and son. These were brought to the King of the Scots, who wanted to learn the secret of heather ale. When he threatened them with torture, the father said he saw it was useless to resist and would tell him on one condition. When the King asked what it was, the Pech replied:

> 'My son ye maun kill,
>   Before I will you tell
> How we brew the yill
>   Frae the heather bell!'

The King immediately had the son put to death, but as soon as the old Pech saw the lad was dead, he cried that the King might do with him as he wished – for though he might have forced the secret from his son, who was but a weak youth, he'd never hear it from his lips:

> 'And though you may me kill,
>   I will not tell,
> How we brew the yill
>   Frae the heather bell.'

And so the secret of heather ale died with the last of the Pechs.

  This sad little story, recorded by Chambers in his *Popular Rhymes of Scotland* (1870), was popularized by Robert Louis Stevenson in a ballad, 'Heather Ale', which may in its turn have affected oral tradition – Ernest Marwick (*The Folklore of Orkney and Shetland*, 1975) tells us that versions of the story current in Orkney and Shetland have 'a suspiciously "bookish" quality'. Marwick also reports that a recipe for making heather ale seems to have been remembered up to recent times: an old woman had frequently told him that she used to be sent out as a child at four o'clock in the morning in summer to gather the green heather tops for brewing. Unfortunately for us, though she knew there was some special reason for gathering the tops at that hour, she could no longer remember what it was.

NEW ABBEY, DUMFRIES & GALLOWAY   Sheet 184
(formerly KIRKCUDBRIGHTSHIRE)   NX 9666

Alexander Harg, a cottar in the parish of New Abbey, had married a pretty girl whom the fairies had long attempted to entice away. A few nights after the wedding, he was standing with his net, awaiting the incoming tide, not far from two old wrecks visible at mid-water mark which were reckoned to be occasionally visited by fairies when crossing the mouth of the Nith. From one of these wrecks came the noise as of carpenters at work, and a hollow voice cried from the other: 'Ho, what'rye doing!' To which came the reply: 'I'm making a wyfe to Sandy Harg!'

Terrified, he threw down his net and hastened home, shut up all the windows and doors, and folded his wife in his arms. At midnight, someone rapped gently thrice at the door, but in silence he kept his wife from answering. A footstep was heard to depart and the cattle started bellowing, and ramping as if pulling at their stakes. Though the wife entreated, the silent husband still held her fast – and faster still when the horses neighed and pranced, and snorted as if the stable were on fire. Still in utter silence he held her, but as soon as dawn came he hurried outside. There he saw, reared against his garden dyke, the effigy of his wife made of moss oak. This devilish object he burnt.

In this story from Cromek's *Remains of Nithsdale & Galloway Song* (1810), the ritual silence to be observed in dealings with the fairies and the clasping of the person to be won from them are traditional themes (cf. **Eildon Hills**, p.452, and **Menstrie**, p.510; and the old ballad of 'Tam Lin'). So too is the notion that, if not prevented, the fairies would have stolen the wife and left a stock. It was a current belief in the Middle Ages that a changeling might take the form of a stock or log of wood in the likeness of the abducted person – Walter Map, writing in the twelfth century, tells the tale of women abducted at the moment of death by demons who left images to be buried in their place, whilst the women themselves were later seen and spoken with. Similarly in a medieval Icelandic tale, a waxen image is left by a pair of magicians in the place of an abducted queen.

Some authorities, among them Lewis Spence (*Fairy Tradition in Britain*, 1948), believed that the idea of a fairy stock is a lingering relic of fetishism – the belief that inanimate objects may be the dwelling place of spirits, especially if they have been made expressly for that purpose. In the Society Islands, Captain Cook noticed that the wooden images at the burial grounds were not thought of simply as memorials, but as the abodes of the souls of the dead, and it may be that the fairy stock leads us back – as do their dwellings underground and the offerings made to them until quite recent times in certain cup-marked rocks – to the conviction that belief in fairies had at least part of its origin in a cult of the dead.

But though fetishism may provide the *background* for the notion of the fairy stock, something else may also be at work. In Walter Map's tale, the image is a substitute for a corpse, but Robert Kirk in his *Secret Common-wealth* (1691) speaks of 'a Woman taken out of her Childbed, and having a Lingering Image of her substituted in her room, which resemblance Decay'd, dy'd, and was buri'd . . .', implying that there was a period of some sort of animation. Just as belief in infant changelings – always wizened little creatures – seems to have its roots in rejection of babies who were not quite normal, notably mongols, so the idea of the stock replacing adults stolen by the fairies may have something to do with the notion of 'blockishness'. Grimm long ago pointed out that the German word *Hampelmann* was employed alike for 'goblin', 'puppet' and 'mannikin', and in Elizabethan English 'puppet' was often used to mean a fairy – 'You demi-puppets that/By moonshine do the green sour ringlets make', as Shakespeare adjures them. This might only allude to size; but it might also belong to the same habit of mind that has transformed the Old English word *ælf* into both 'elf' and 'oaf', in earlier use not a boor but an idiot.

PORT GLASGOW, STRATHCLYDE Sheet 63
(formerly RENFREWSHIRE)   NS 3274

A mermaid who had her home in the Firth of Clyde above Port Glasgow, as the funeral procession of a girl who had died of consumption was passing by, raised her head above the water and cried:

> 'If they wad drink nettles in March,
>   And eat muggons in May,
>   Sae mony braw maidens
>   Wadna gang to the clay.'

This tradition, recorded by Chambers in *Popular Rhymes* (1842), is paralleled by one printed by Cromek (1810) of a Galloway mermaid who, on hearing a lover lament his dying sweetheart, sang:

> 'Wad ye let the bonnie May die i'yere hand,
>   An' the mugwort flowering i' the land?'

The young man straightway gathered the flowers of the mugwort and gave the girl the juice to drink, whereupon she recovered.

Chambers writes, 'As may be readily surmised, muggons or mugwort (also called southernwood), and a decoction of nettles, form a favourite prescription for consumption amongst the common people.' Mugwort, probably because it is or was one of the most abundant, was one of the commonest herbs in daily use, especially in magic. It is the leader in the Anglo-Saxon 'Nine Herbs Charm', which begins:

> Gemyne ðu, mucgwyrt, hwæt þu ameldodest,
> hwaet þu renadest æt Regenmelde.
> Una þu hattest yldost wyrta . . .

'Remember, Mugwort, what you made known,/What you arranged at the Great Proclamation./You were called Una, the oldest of herbs . . .'

Anciently it was worn to prevent tiredness, but from the medicinal point of view, ever since the time of Hippocrates, it has been the sovereign cure for 'women's troubles'. Its botanical name, *Artemisia vulgaris*, links it with the Greek goddess Artemis, because its powers are identical with hers. Identified by the Greeks with the moon goddess Selene, Artemis was not worshipped simply as a virgin huntress, but was in some places honoured as a goddess of birth – as at Ephesus, where her celebrated statue was covered all over with breasts to symbolize her connection with childbirth. Mugwort itself was thought to aid menstrual cycles, governed by the moon ('menstrual' means 'monthly', and 'month' literally meant the interval from new moon to new moon). It is indeed still used for painful menstruation and the difficulties attendant on the menopause. Southernwood, too, although despite Chambers *not* the same as mugwort, being *Artemisia abrotanum*, is used to govern the menstrual flow. Out of this by association perhaps grew the belief that it prevented consumption (also witnessed by a loss of blood).

It must be more than coincidence that in some parts of Greece Artemis was conceived of as a freshwater mermaid in whose care were lakes, marshes, rivers and streams. As Arethusa, she was the deity of a spring on the island of Ortygia, near Syracuse, and in Arcadia she was represented as a fish from the waist down. But quite how the connection between moon, mugwort and mermaid has been handed down from classical times into modern folklore is another question.

ROSLIN CHAPEL, ROSLIN, LOTHIAN (formerly MIDLOTHIAN)

Sheet 66
NT 2763

According to the *Gentleman's Magazine* for September 1817, visitors to the fifteenth-century Roslin Chapel used to be shown round by an old crone named Annie Wilson, who was wont to deliver you 'a sort of cottage version' of its legends.

Mrs Wilson's strong point was the *Apprentice's* Pillar. 'There

The work of art that cost a lad his life:
the Prentice Pillar, Roslin Chapel, Lothian

ye see it, gentlemen, with the lace bands winding sae beautifully roond aboot it. The maister had gane awa to Rome to get
a plan for it, and while he was awa his 'prentice made a plan
himself and finished it. And when the maister cam back and
fand the pillar finished, he was sae enraged that he took a
hammer and killed the 'prentice. There you see the 'prentice's
face – up there in ae corner, wi' a red gash in the brow, and
his mother greeting for him in the corner opposite. And there,
in another corner, is the maister, as he lookit just before he
was hanged; it's him wi' a kind o' ruff roond his face,' with a
good deal more of the like twaddle, which Annie had told for
fifty years without ever hearing a word of it doubted, and
never once doubting it herself.

And why would she? Her little *spiel* was of more interest to
visitors no doubt than the mere fact that the pillar, a fluted column
wreathed with foliage and flowers, is a fine specimen of Gothic
tracery. But the antiquary Francis Grose, who also tells the tale in
The Antiquities of Scotland (1789) and who from the way he speaks
of a 'cicceroni' had evidently heard of, if not himself heard, Annie
Wilson, was not a believer: 'Most certainly this is all fiction', he
says, pointing out that the head supposed to be that of the
apprentice, its wound 'marked with red oker', was that of a bearded
old man.

It matters not. Like 'Shakespeare on a Deer' at **Charlecote Park**
(p.264), the heads supporting brackets on the wall and said to be
'the heads of the parties' were no more than bonuses on a good
tale and people cheerfully turned a blind eye to such discrepancies.

For the tale *is* a good one – well enough loved to be told not
only at Roslin, but in Somerset, at Huish Episcopi, and of windows
at Melrose, Rouen and **Lincoln** (p.239). At Rouen the rose window
in the north transept is, like the Prentice Pillar, said to have been
made by an apprentice whose jealous master took a hammer to his
head. At Lincoln Cathedral, however, where the tale involves not
one but two rose windows, The Bishop's Eye and The Dean's Eye,
when the master saw that The Bishop's Eye, made by the apprentice, was the finer, he threw himself off the scaffolding in rage.

SPEDLIN'S TOWER, LOCHMABEN, DUMFRIES & GALLOWAY (formerly DUMFRIES)

Sheet 78

NY 0987

Spedlin's Tower (NY 097876) or Spedlin's Castle, as it was known to Francis Grose writing *The Antiquities of Scotland* in 1789, is a border fortalice a little to the north of Lochmaben on the western bank of the river Annan, and anciently the property of the Jardines of Applegarth.

But this building is chiefly famous for being haunted by a Bogle, or Ghost. As the relation will enliven the dullness of antiquarian disquisition, I will here relate it, as it was told me by an honest woman who resides on the spot, and who, I will be sworn from her manner, believed every syllable of it. In the time of the late Sir John's grandfather, a person, named Porteus, living in the parish of Applegarth, was taken up on suspicion of setting fire to a mill, and confined in the Lord's prison, the pit, or dungeon, at this castle. The Lord being suddenly called to Edinburgh . . . in his hurry forgot to leave the key of the pit, which he always held in his own custody. Before he discovered his mistake, and could send back the key . . . the man was starved to death, having first, through the extremity of hunger, gnawed off one of his hands. Ever after that time the castle was terribly haunted, till a Chaplain of the family exorcised and confined the Bogle to the pit, whence it could never come out, so long as a large Bible, which he had used on that business, remained in the castle. It is said that the Chaplain did not long survive this operation. The Ghost, however, kept quietly within the bounds of his prison till a long time after, when the Bible, which was used by the whole family, required a new binding: for which purpose it was sent to Edinburgh. The Ghost, taking advantage of its absence, was extremely boisterous in the pit, seeming as if it would break through the iron door, and making a noise like that of a large bird fluttering its wings. The Bible being returned, and the pit filled up, every thing has since remained perfectly quiet. But the good woman declared, that should it again be taken off the premises, no consideration whatsoever would induce her to remain there a single night.

The death of Porteus is said to have taken place in the days of Sir Alexander Jardine, during the reign of Charles II. When, in about 1770, the family moved to their new house of Jardine Hall (NY 0987), they left the Bible at Spedlin's Tower. According to Chambers's *Picture of Scotland* (1827) it was after this move that the Bible was dispatched to Edinburgh, 'but the ghost, getting out of the dungeon and crossing the river, made such a disturbance in the new house . . . that the Bible was recalled before it reached the capital, and placed in its former situation . . . But the charm seems to be now broken, or the ghost must have become either quiet or disregarded; for the Bible is at present kept in the house of Jardine-Hall.' However, the same superstition seems to have remained attached to it, for though the Hall was sold in 1884, the Bible was still there when Beard wrote his *Lucks and Talismans* (1934), kept in a brass-bound box made of beams from Spedlin's Tower. The Bible, printed by Robert Baker at London in 1634, may well always have been the focus of the legend and gives some sort of date for its inception.

Bogle-haunted Spedlin's Tower, Dumfries & Galloway:
engraving of 'Spedlin's Castle', published by S. Hopper, 1790–1,
from Grose's Antiquities of Scotland *(1797)*

Chambers tells us that after the ghost had been confined to the pit, he continued to cry, 'Let me out, let me out; I'm deean' o' hunger!' and never failed to strip the bark off twigs thrust through the keyhole – a favourite trick also of the bogey Redcap of **Hermitage Castle** (p.462).

WHITTINGEHAME, LOTHIAN (formerly EAST LOTHIAN)

Sheet 67
NT 6073

When Chambers was writing his *Popular Rhymes of Scotland* (1826), it was supposed to be little more than half a century since the people of the village of Whittingehame had got rid of their ghost.

This was the restless spirit of an unbaptized child whom its unnatural mother had murdered at a large tree not far from the village. Afterwards the child was often seen on dark nights running distractedly between the tree and the churchyard (NT 603737), and occasionally heard to 'greet' because it was unable to get a proper footing in the next world on account of having no name. No one dared to speak to the miserable little ghost for fear of dying, and it looked as if Whittingehame would be haunted to the end of time.

At length by good fortune a drunkard came reeling home one night and with the bonhomie born of liquor hailed the ghost: 'How's a' wi' ye this morning, Short-hoggers?' At which the little ghost at once ran off, joyfully exclaiming:

> 'O weel's me noo, I've gotten a name;
> They ca' me Short-hoggers o' Whittinghame!'

And since that time it has never been heard or seen. The name the drunkard gave it indicates that it wore 'short-hoggers' or short stockings without feet – not unlikely considering the years that it had 'walked'. Chambers got the story from someone who had himself heard it from the lips of an old woman of Whittingehame who had actually *seen* the ghost.

The idea that one may die after speaking to a ghost is connected on the one hand with the belief that it was death to meet Black Dogs (**Bungay**, p.176) or the Wild Hunt (**Clun Forest**. p.300), and on the other with the taboo on speaking to fairies (see **New Abbey**, p.478). Falstaff holds similar beliefs in *The Merry Wives of Windsor* (v.v.48–9):

> They are fairies; he that speaks to them shall die.
> I'll wink and couch: no man their works must eye.

Indeed, 'Short-hoggers' is more of a fairy than a ghost – precisely the same tale is told of the Brownie of Clochfoldich farm (NN 895530), near Pitlochry, Tayside, who used to splash about in the Altmor Burn until a drunk called out 'Well, Puddlefoot, how is it with you the night?' and crying 'Oh! no! I've gotten a name! 'Tis Puddlefoot they call me!' he vanished. The dismissal by naming belongs to a traditional belief in the power of names over fairies – the pivot of the Suffolk fairytale 'Tom Tit Tot' (the English Rumpelstiltskin) – and the parallel idea that it is dangerous to use their real names. Just as it was safer for the Greeks to call the Furies the Eumenides, or 'Kindly Ones', so we hear in a Scottish rhyme current in the early nineteenth century:

> Gin ye ca' me imp or elf,
> I rede* ye look weel to yourself;
> Gin ye ca' me fairy,
> I'll work ye muckle tarrie;†
> Gin gude neebor ye ca' me,
> Then gude neebor I will be;
> But gin ye ca' me seelie wicht,‡
> I'll be your freend baith day and nicht.

The village of Whittingehame (formerly spelt Whittinghame) used to be south-west of the parish church, but, already decaying, it was pulled down in 1817, when James Balfour of Balbirnie bought the estate and built the mansion of Whittingehame House. South-west of the house is Whittingehame Castle or Tower, built in the fifteenth and sixteenth centuries, and now restored. Either in this tower or under an ancient yew tree in the grounds, Darnley's murder is said to have been plotted. Clochfoldich farm, Sheet 52.

* rede = counsel
† tarrie = trouble
‡ seelie wicht = blessed spirit

13
Highlands and Islands

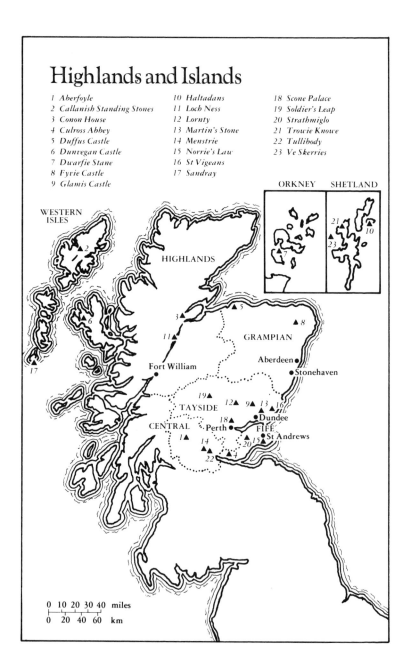

Highlands and Islands

1 Aberfoyle
2 Callanish Standing Stones
3 Conon House
4 Culross Abbey
5 Duffus Castle
6 Dunvegan Castle
7 Dwarfie Stane
8 Fyrie Castle
9 Glamis Castle
10 Haltadans
11 Loch Ness
12 Lornty
13 Martin's Stone
14 Menstrie
15 Norrie's Law
16 St Vigeans
17 Sandray
18 Scone Palace
19 Soldier's Leap
20 Strathmiglo
21 Trowie Knowe
22 Tullibody
23 Ve Skerries

ORKNEY   SHETLAND

WESTERN
ISLES

HIGHLANDS

GRAMPIAN

Aberdeen

Stonehaven

Fort William

TAYSIDE

CENTRAL   Perth   Dundee

FIFE

St Andrews

0 10 20 30 40 miles
0   20 40 60   km

The most scientific account of fairies in the seventeenth century
was that of Robert Kirk, the Presbyterian minister of Aberfoyle,
entitled *The Secret Common-wealth*. Probably written in 1690 or
1691, it is a level-headed look at fairies as a natural phenomenon,
free of the bigotry that led most of his Puritan contemporaries to
confuse fairies with witches. But though Kirk was a serious scholar
and a sensible man he was not moving among sensible people. He
was evidently regarded by the country folk amongst whom he
pursued his research as meddling in things he had much better
have left alone and when he was found unconscious one morning
by Aberfoyle's Fairy Knowe, word soon got about that what had
been brought home was a fairy stock (see **New Abbey**, p.478).
Kirk himself, they said, had been abducted by the fairies and was
in the Fairy Hill.

   In his *Letters on Demonology and Witchcraft* (1830), Sir Walter
Scott tells the tale of how, shortly after his funeral and following
the birth of his posthumous child, Kirk's apparition was supposed
to have appeared to a relation, asking him to go to their mutual
cousin, Graham of Duchray. 'Say . . . that I am not dead, but a
captive in Fairy Land; and only one chance remains for my
liberation.' When his new-born child was christened, he would
appear in the room, and if Duchray were to throw over his head
the dirk he held in his hand, Kirk would be freed from his
enchantment – 'but if this opportunity is neglected, I am lost
forever.' Duchray was told, and held his dirk ready, but when the
spectre appeared he was too afraid to throw it, so Kirk remains in
the Fairy Hill.

   According to a tradition recorded in 1943, if a child were born
and christened at the Manse, and during the christening someone
stuck a knife in Kirk's old chair, he would be freed from Fairyland.
In both Scott's account and this one, the role of the dirk is to
break the enchantment with cold iron – a thing the fairies could
not abide. For the old belief in the Fairy Hill, see **Willy Howe**
(p.430).

   Kirk has been transformed from a student of the fairies into
their victim by much the same mechanism as that which earlier

transformed Michael Scot from a scholar of astrology into a wizard (see **Melrose Abbey**, p.475).

CALLANISH STANDING-STONES, UIG, LEWIS, WESTERN ISLES (formerly ROSS-SHIRE)

Sheet 8
NB 2133

West of Stornoway on a desolate moorland is one of the most remote of all the sites of antiquity in Britain. Callanish is a cruciform setting with an avenue of nineteen standing-stones, 27 feet (8.2 m) wide and 270 feet (82.3 m) long, leading into a circle of thirteen stones. On either side of this is a cross-row of four stones and beyond is a short avenue 12 feet (3.7 m) wide consisting of six stones. Two cairns, one within the circle and one just touching it, complete the site, probably laid out *ca.* 2000–5000 B.C. in stages – there are other stone circles nearby.

It stands aloof and mysterious on a promontory extending into Loch Roag, and mysterious are its legends. Until recently it was believed that at sunrise on Midsummer Day the 'Shining One'

The False Men: Callanish standing-stones, Lewis, Western Isles

walked along the avenue, his coming heralded by the call of the cuckoo, the bird of Tir-nan-Og, the Celtic Land of Youth. Another tradition is that of a priest-king who came to the island bringing with him not only the stones but black men to raise them. He was attended by other priests and the whole company wore robes of bird-skins and feathers. These tales smack a little of Druidism, but genuine folk tradition seems to lie behind the Gaelic name for the stones, *Fir Chreig*, or the 'False men'. They are said to be the old giant inhabitants, who would not build a church, nor let themselves be baptized by St Kieran when he came to preach to them, so he turned them into stone.

Whatever their origin, the stones of Callanish were long held in awe by the local people, who used to visit them especially at Midsummer and on May Day. Though the visits were condemned by the Kirk, they continued to be made in secret, 'for it would not do to neglect the stones'.

AM (any reasonable time).

CONON (CONAN) HOUSE, HIGHLAND   Sheet 26
(formerly ROSS-SHIRE)   NH 5353

The river Conon or Conan is one of several which are the haunts of malignant spirits, last vestiges, perhaps, of the river-deities honoured and propitiated by the ancient Celts (see **Dartmeet**, p. 19, **Drumelzier**, p.444, and **Waddow Hall**, p.391). Belief in the indwelling spirits of rivers seems to have lingered late in certain districts. It was of something more than a personification of the river that a Derbyshire woman spoke in 1904 when she told a folklore collector of a stranger who had been drowned in the Derwent: 'He didna know Darrant. He said it were naught but a brook. But Darrant got 'im. They never saw his head. He threw his arms up, but Darrant wouldna let him go. Aye, it's a sad pity, seven children! But he shouldna ha' made so light of Darrant. He knows now.'

The Conon itself, notoriously dangerous in flood, was haunted by a spirit which, says the geologist Hugh Miller in *My Schools and Schoolmasters* (1862), used to appear 'as a tall woman dressed in green ... distinguished chiefly by her ... countenance, ever distorted by a malignant scowl'. She would leap out of the stream at the side of travellers and point a skinny finger at them or beckon them to follow. Once she caught a poor Highlander who had passed the banks of the river after nightfall, and though he clung to a tree, helped by the lad who was with him, he was dragged into the current and drowned.

There was hardly a stretch of the Conon from Contin to the sea that did not have a legend of the waterwraith or else the kelpie. One such place was in the woods of Conon House and this is how W. W. Gibbings in *Folklore and Legends of Scotland* (1889) sets the scene: 'There are thick mirk-woods on ilka side; the river, dark an' awesome, an' whirling round an' round in mossy eddies, sweeps away behind it; an' there is an auld burying-ground, wi' the broken ruins o' an auld papist kirk, on the tap. Ane can see amang the rougher stanes the rose-wrought mullions of an arched window, an' the trough that ance held the holy water. About twa hunder years ago . . . the building was entire; an' a spot near it, whar the wood now grows thickest, was laid out in a cornfield. The marks o' the furrows may still be seen amang the trees.'

A party of Highlanders were cutting the corn one day in harvest in that field, and just about at noon, they heard a voice exclaim, 'The hour is come but not the man.' Looking round they saw the kelpie standing in what was called the false ford, just in front of the church. 'There is a deep black pool baith aboon an' below, but i' the ford there's a bonny ripple, that shows as ane might think, but little depth o' water; an just i' the middle o' that, in a place where a horse might swim, stood the kelpie.' It repeated its baleful words, then flashing through the water like a drake, disappeared into the lower pool. Even as they stood there wondering, they saw a man come spurring down the hill to the ford. Four of the strongest leapt out of the cornfield to stop him and told him what the kelpie had said, but he would not listen. Determined to save him whether he would or no, the Highlanders pulled him from his horse and carried him into the old kirk, where they locked him until the hour of danger was passed. When they came back and called him, there was no answer, and going into the church they found him face down in the water in that very stone trough that was to be seen among the ruins. He had had a fit and drowned in the trough as he was destined to do, for his hour had come as the kelpie had foretold.

This is a very old story, a version of which was told by Gervase of Tilbury in his *Otia Imperialia, ca.* 1212, of a deep pool in the Rhône near Arles.

CULROSS ABBEY, FIFE

It was said in the nineteenth century that an underground passage ran beneath Culross Abbey (NS 989862) in which a man was seated in a golden chair, ready to give valuable treasures to any who succeeded in finding him. A blind piper and his dog once entered the vaults at the head of the Newgate, and the sound of his pipes was heard as far as the West Kirk, a distance of three-quarters of a mile. But though the dog at last emerged into the upper air, the piper himself never reappeared, having been seized, it was thought, by subterranean demons.

Similar legends of underground passages, with and without treasure, are told the length and breadth of Britain, in England the piper's role usually being played by a fiddler, as at Binham Priory, Norfolk, though it was a drummer boy who thus disappeared at Richmond Castle, North Yorkshire.

AM. Of the Cistercian Abbey founded in 1217, only the south wall of the nave is early-thirteenth-century, the rest dating mostly from around 1300. The choir is still used as the parish church and applications to visit should be made at the Manse.

DUFFUS CASTLE, GRAMPIAN
(formerly MORAY)

Aubrey in his *Miscellanies* includes a letter dated 25 March 1695 'from a Learned Friend' in Scotland, whom he had asked about 'Transportation by an Invisible Power'. This was the answer:

As soon as I read your Letter of *May* 24 I called to mind, a Story which I heard long ago, concerning one of the Lord *Duffus* (in the Shire of *Murray*) his Predecessors, of whom it is reported, That upon a time, when he was walking abroad in the Fields near to his own House, he was suddenly carried away, and found the next Day at *Paris* in the *French* King's Cellar with a Silver Cup in his Hand; that being brought into the King's Presence and Question'd by him, Who he was? And how he came thither? He told his name, his Country, and the place of his Residence, and that on such a Day of the Month (which proved to be the Day immediately preceeding) being in the Fields, he heard the noise of a Whirlwind, and of voices crying Horse and Hattock (this is the Word which the Fairies are said to use when they remove from any Place) whereupon he cried (Horse and Hattock) also, and was immediately caught up, and transported through the Air, by the Fairies to that place where after he had Drunk heartily he fell a-sleep, and before he awoke, the rest of the Company were gone, and left him in the posture wherein he was found. It's said, the King gave him the Cup which was found in his Hand, and dismiss'd him.

Aubrey's Learned Friend enquired through a tutor to the family the present Lord Duffus's opinion of the tale and learned 'That there has been, and is such a Tradition, but that he thinks it Fabulous.' He himself had had the tale from his father, and he from his father before him, and there was in his possession an old silver cup known as the Fairy Cup, though it was marked by nothing more than the family arms.

That Lord Duffus saw fit to mention he thought the tale 'Fabulous' reminds us that he lived in an age of belief, and indeed the tutor who had acted as go-between told Aubrey's Learned Friend a case of much the same thing which he himself had witnessed:

He reports, that when he was a Boy at School in the Town of *Forres*, yet not so Young, but that he had Years and Capacity, both to observe and remember that which fell out; he and his School-fellows were upon a time whipping their Tops in the Church-yard before the Door of the Church; though the Day was calm, they heard a noise of a Wind, and at some distance saw the small Dust begin to arise and turn round, which motion continued, advancing till it came to the place where they were; whereupon they began to Bless themselves: But one of their number (being it seems a little more bold and

confident than his Companions) said, Horse and Hattock with
my Top, and immediately they all saw the top lifted up from
the Ground; but could not see what way it was carried, by
reason of a Cloud of Dust which was raised at the same time:
They sought for the Top all about the place where it was
taken up, but in vain; and it was found afterwards in the
Church-yard, on the other side of the Church.

A whirlwind, you will say, and perhaps you may be right. But the
boys believed it was the *oiteag sluaigh*, 'the people's puff of wind'
or fairy eddy. The Rev. John Gregorson Campbell, minister of
Tiree 1861–91, tells us in *Superstitions of the Highlands & Islands
of Scotland* (1900) that the way to make the fairies drop whatever
they were taking away – men, women, children or animals – was
to throw one's left shoe at it. The same results could be got by
throwing one's bonnet, saying 'this is yours, that's mine', or earth
from a molehill, or else a naked knife (cf. the proceedings at
Aberfoyle, p.491).

The fairy eddy story could be told in simple form as in the tale
of the Poor Man of Peatlaw (see **Leith**, p.468) or else combined as
here with the drinking bout in the King's cellar. To this variation
could be further added an ending also found in quite a different
tale, 'The Return for Good Deeds' (see **Culzean Castle**, p.441).
This threefold pattern is used in stories from nineteenth-century
Cornwall set at Porthallow, Talland, and on Tregarden Down.
Here a man heard the fairies cry 'Ho! and away for Par Beach!'
and by repeating it found himself on the sands at Par. Next the cry
was 'Ho! and away for Squire Tremaine's cellar!' and there he got
so drunk that he never heard the fairies leave with 'Ho! and away
for Par Beach!' again. When he was found in the cellar, his story
was not believed, and he was sentenced to death. As he stood
awaiting execution, a little lady pushed through the crowd to the
scaffold and cried 'Ho! and away for France!' whereupon he took
up the cry and both vanished. At Duffus, the fairy eddy story was
probably originally used to account for the Fairy Cup – names
often came first and legends after. This was very likely a family
talisman much like the Fairy Flag of **Dunvegan Castle** (see next
entry) and was perhaps at first a simple fairy gift or perhaps a theft
from the fairies as in medieval fairy cup stories (on the subject of
which see **Rillaton Barrow**, p.29).

The ruined fourteenth-century castle of Duffus (NJ 188672) is the finest example in the north of Scotland of a motte and bailey castle. AM (any reasonable time).

DUNVEGAN CASTLE, SKYE, HIGHLAND   Sheet 23
(formerly INVERNESS-SHIRE)   NG 2449

Dunvegan Castle on Skye, the stronghold of the Macleods since the thirteenth century, is the home of the famous Fairy Flag. This silken banner is nowadays usually said to have been given to an ancestral Macleod by his fairy wife at parting, but the earliest account of it we have, in Thomas Pennant's description of his second tour of the Islands, gives a slightly different tale.

Pennant visited Dunvegan on 18 July 1772, and in *A Tour in Scotland* we read:

> Here is preserved the *Braolauch shi*, or fairy-flag of the family, bestowed on it by *Titania* the *Ben-shi*, or wife to *Oberon* king of the fairies. She blessed it at the same time with powers of the first importance, which were to be exerted on only three occasions: but on the last, after the end was obtained, an invisible Being is to arrive and carry off standard and standard-bearer, never more to be seen. A family of *Clan y Faitter* had this dangerous office, and held by it, three lands in *Bracadale*.
>
> The flag has been produced thrice. The first time in an unequal engagement against the *Clan-Ronald*, to whose sight the *Macleods* were multiplied ten-fold. The second, preserved the heir of the family, being then produced [to] save the longings of the lady of the family: and the third time, to save my own; but it was so tattered, that *Titania* did not seem to think it worth sending for.

It is usually said that it was produced at the Battle of Glendale in 1490 and again in 1580 at Trumpan, both times conferring victory. As Pennant points out, the victory-producing flag or banner is a Norse tradition, both in fact and in fiction. According to the Anglo-Saxon Chronicle, the English captured a banner called *Hræfn* ('Raven') from the Danes in 878 A.D., which the *Annals of St Neots* later say was woven by the daughters of the great Viking hero Ragnar Lódbrók. The raven on it fluttered for victory and drooped for defeat, 'and this has often been proved'. But the Fairy Flag of Dunvegan was a talisman in a wider sense than this. Alexander Smith, writing in about 1865 in *A Summer in Skye*, records that the Macleod was once asked by the peasantry to wave it at the time of the potato famine, but he refused to do so. Whether by association with the flag or in his own person, the lord of Dunvegan himself was also thought to influence fertility – from Dr Johnson's *Journey to the Western Islands of Scotland* (1775) we learn that his return to Dunvegan after a long absence was supposed always to result in an unusually good catch of herring.

Although Pennant implies that the flag was kept shut away, it was certainly got out for Sir Walter Scott when he visited Dunvegan in the August of 1814. The castle was in process of being altered by the twenty-fourth chief, John Norman MacLeod of MacLeod, to include romantic mock turrets and battlements, and Scott was invited to sleep in the Haunted Chamber, of which he was told many tales. 'It certainly was [the] finest scene I ever saw for a ghost . . .', he wrote in 1828 in a letter to Miss Anne Wagner, but alas, 'I felt nothing but that I had had a busy day had eaten a good dinner had drunk a bottle of excellent claret and was much disposed to sleep – And so to my eternal shame without troubling myself about the ghost . . . I went to bed, and slept quietly . . .' So much for romance.

Dunvegan Castle is open to the public – for times, see *HHC&G*. The Fairy Flag, thought to be from the island of Rhodes and to date from the seventh century, is displayed in the drawing-room.

DWARFIE STANE, HOY AND GRAMSAY, ORKNEY

Sheet 7
HY 2400

The Dwarfie Stane on the island of Hoy (HY 244005) is a huge block of sandstone into which, probably *ca.* 2000–1600 B.C., has been cut a burial chamber. No other tomb of this type is known in the British Isles, but it resembles the rock-cut chamber tombs common in the Mediterranean and along the Atlantic seaboard.

In his *Description of the Western Islands of Scotland* (1703), Martin Martin writes:

The retreat of a giant and his wife: the Dwarfie Stane, rock-cut burial chamber, ca. 2000–1600 B.C., Hoy and Gramsay, Orkney

> At one of the ends within this stone there is cut out a bed and pillow capable of two persons to lie in, at the other opposite end there is a void space cut out resembling a bed, and above both these there is a large hole which is supposed was a vent for smoke.

Eighteenth- and nineteenth-century antiquaries thought it was something to do with the Druids, but the 'folk' had other ideas. 'The common tradition', says Martin, 'is that a giant and his wife made this their place of retreat.'

Martin visited the Islands in about 1695, but much the same tradition seems to have been current already *ca.* 1590, except that the hole in the roof was then supposed to have been gnawed by a giant attempting to escape when another giant had blocked him in.

Sir Walter Scott is thought to have visited the Dwarfie Stane in August 1814, and in *The Pirate* he tells us that 'the misshapen form of the necromantic owner may sometimes still be seen sitting by the Dwarfie Stone.' He numbers this owner among the trolls, and certainly a dwarf or 'trow' would be an easier fit in the stone than a giant. And his instinct as usual is sure – very little is said in Orkney folk tradition about dwarves but a great deal about the trows.

AM (any reasonable time).

FYVIE CASTLE, GRAMPIAN (formerly ABERDEENSHIRE)

Sheet 29
NJ 7639

A tradition current in Aberdeenshire when Robert Chambers wrote his *Popular Rhymes of Scotland* (1842) was that the walls of Fyvie Castle had stood seven years and a day *wall-wide* in expectation of Thomas the Rhymer (see **Eildon Hills**, p.452). At length he appeared in a thunderstorm so violent that it stripped the leaves off the trees and blew the castle gates shut, though there was not breath enough of air to stir the grass round the place he was standing. Finding himself shut out, he angrily pronounced the following malison on the castle:

> 'Fyvie, Fyvie, thou's never thrive,
> As lang's there's in thee stanes three:
> There's ane intill the highest tower,
> There's ane intill the ladye's bower,
> There's ane aneath the water-yett,
> And thir three stanes ye'se never get.'

It was usually said that two of these stones had been found, but the one beneath the water-gate to the Ythan had never been brought to light.

Another version of the rhyme given by the Rev. Walter Gregor in *The Folklore of the North-East of Scotland* (1881) implies that, to lift the curse, the stones must be incorporated into rather than removed from the castle:

> 'Fyvyns riggs and towers,
> Hapless shall your mesdames be,
> Till ye shall hae within your methes*
> Frae harryit kirk's land stanes three – '

* methes = boundaries

and so on. This is said to be explained by the fact that, when Fyvie Castle, originally a thirteenth-century peel-tower, came into the hands of Henry de Preston in the fifteenth century and he added the Preston Tower, he took the stones for the building from a neighbouring religious house which he had demolished – 'harryit kirk's land'. During the work, three of the stones, possibly having, it is suggested, some talismanic power, fell into the river Ythan and were lost.

Oddly enough, Thomas the Rhymer's prophecy about Fyvie has more or less been fulfilled, in that time after time the male succession has failed. Henry de Preston's heir was his daughter, and since his day the castle has several times passed out of the owner's family altogether or descended through the female line.

'Fyvie's lands lie broad and wide, and O but they lie bonny,' says the Scottish ballad 'Mill o'Tifty's Annie', and indeed its wooded park, threaded by the river Ythan, is a fine setting for this beautiful castle. The earliest parts of the fabric date from the fifteenth and sixteenth centuries, but considerable additions were made in the seventeenth. Its four old towers, one of which comes into the story, are named after their builders: Gordon, Meldrum, Preston and Seton. NTS (scheduled to be opened to the public, May 1986).

GLAMIS CASTLE, TAYSIDE
(formerly ANGUS)

Sheet 54
NO 3846

In Glamis Castle is said to be a secret room which though it has a window has never been identified. In the nineteenth century it was rumoured that the only people who knew where it was were Lord Strathmore and his heir, and the factor, and they were all three bound to reveal it to none save their successors.

Several different legends about the room were offered. In the *Picture of Scotland* (1827), Robert Chambers gives the tale of Alexander, Earl of Crawford, popularly known as 'Earl Beardie', notorious in Scottish history for his rebellion against James II and in legend 'invested with all the terrible attributes understood by the term "a wicked laird"'. It was the tradition at Glamis that Earl Beardie was playing cards in the castle when, being warned to desist, as he was losing heavily, he swore in a transport of rage that

Behind which window lurks the secret of Glamis? From an original
watercolour by James Moore, now at Glamis Castle, Tayside

he would 'play until the day of judgment'. At that the Devil
appeared in their midst and they – Earl Beardie, his cronies, the
room, and all – promptly vanished. No one knew where the
invisible room was located, but it was well enough understood that
if it were ever discovered, Earl Beardie and his friends would be
found still playing cards and would do so until the end of time.
Some said, indeed, that on windy nights the gamblers could be
heard stamping their feet at one another and cursing.

Another tradition was that during one of the many feuds between
the Lindsays and the Ogilvies, a number of the Ogilvies came to
Glamis seeking refuge and the owner took them in. Pretending to
help them, he hid them in the secret room, but then left them to
starve. The sight of their mouldering bones so horrified one of the
Lords Strathmore that he had the room walled up.

But the favourite explanation was that of the monstrous child
born two or three hundred years ago and concealed in a secret
room constructed within the thickness of the walls. As each heir to
the earldom came of age at twenty-one, he was told the terrible
secret and shown the rightful earl, who is supposed to have lived

until the 1920s. The age of these traditions is doubtful. In the summer of 1793, Sir Walter Scott passed a night at Glamis, and in his *Letters on Demonology and Witchcraft* (1830) records his impressions. He refers to the secret room without, alas, telling its secret. Andrew Lang suggested that, as he did not mention the Ogilvie legend, it perhaps did not exist before the time of the visit, but we cannot place too much reliance on this. Whatever Sir Walter heard had its effect, or perhaps the claret was not so good as at **Dunvegan Castle** (p.498), for he writes:

> I was conducted to my apartment in a distant corner of the building. I must own, that as I heard door after door shut, after my conductor had retired, I began to consider myself too far from the living, and somewhat too near to the dead.

The tradition of the secret room at Glamis also took hold of the Victorian imagination. In a journal entry apparently written during a visit there on 6 October 1879, Augustus Hare writes:

> As we drove up to the haunted castle at night, its many turrets looked most eerie and weird against the moonlit sky, and its windows blazed with red light ... Lord Strathmore himself has an ever sad look. The Bishop of Brechin, who was a great friend of the house, felt this strange sadness so deeply that he went to Lord Strathmore and ... said how, having heard of the strange secret that oppressed him, he could not help entreating him to make use of his services as an ecclesiastic, if he could in any way, by any means, be of use to him. Lord Strathmore was deeply moved, though he said that he thanked him, but that in his unfortunate position *no one* could ever help him.

Hare adds that Lord Strathmore had built a new wing for the servants and children to sleep in, as the servants would not sleep in the main house and he would not allow the children to do so.

One tradition seems to have attracted another – there are several ghosts at Glamis, including Macbeth, who according to local lore, if not to Shakespeare and the chronicles, murdered Duncan here. Historical ghosts you might expect, but Hare had also heard (in 1902) as having happened at Glamis 'a story which I have often heard without definition of place'. According to this, a visitor looked out at night and saw a carriage driving up and down. For a moment it paused, and its driver looked up, showing 'a marked and terrible face' in the moonlight. When he asked about this, Lord Strathmore told him that no one had arrived at that hour of night. Some time later, in an hotel in Paris, he saw the same face in a lift. Taken aback, he did not enter, and at that moment the lift fell down, killing all its occupants.

On such stories as these throve after-dinner conversation in Augustus Hare's circle, and one cannot tell if it was anything more than the impulse of the moment that attached the tale to Glamis. Though the castle received its present appearance in the seventeenth century, it is in parts much older, and like other old houses has had a chequered history with many dark passages. For example, in 1537, the mother of the then Lord of Glamis, Janet Dalrymple, was found guilty of making an attempt on the life of James V by witchcraft. She was burned at the stake on Castle Hill in Edinburgh, and only afterwards did it come to light that her two principal accusers, one of them her son, the other a rejected suitor, had committed perjury. Such dark deeds in real life were bound to create a climate in which legends flourished.

Glamis Castle is open to the public – for times, see *HHC&G*.

HALTADANS, FETLAR, SHETLAND

The Haltadans at Gravins in the parish of Fetlar (HU 622923) is a circle of low stones with two further stones at its centre. Local legend as reported in this century says that the stones are trows, who were wont to dance there by the light of the moon. Once and once only they made the mistake of dancing until the dawn, and were turned to stone as a punishment. The two stones at the centre are supposed to be the trowie fiddler and his wife, and three small cairns with retaining circles to the north-west (HU 618927), known as the Fiddlers' Crus, 'the fiddlers' enclosures', were probably also part of the story.

The tale is a reminder of the Norse colonization of these islands – the troll overtaken by sunrise is very much a figure of Northern tradition. The 'punishment' element may have crept in from the tale we in Britain more often hear – the medieval legend of dancers turned to stone for dancing on a Sunday. The classic version of this is the one told of the stone circles of Stanton Drew in Somerset, already by 1644 known as 'the Wedding'. William Stukeley, who visited Stanton Drew in July 1723, later wrote:

> This noble monument is vulgarly call'd the *Weddings*; and they say, 'tis a company who assisted a nuptial solemnity, thus petrify'd. In an orchard near the church is a cove consisting of three stones ... this they call the parson, the bride, and bridegroom. Other circles are said to be the company dancing: and a separate parcel of stones standing a little from the rest, are call'd the fidlers, or the band of musick.

Dancing on a Sunday was also punished by petrifaction at the Merry Maidens, St Buryan, and several other megalithic monuments in Cornwall. There are petrified brides and grooms in Norway and Germany, whole weddings also in northern France. The tradition may be traceable to a medieval exemplum – a subject for sermons – that was very popular in the Middle Ages, generally known as 'The Dancers of Colbeck'. As William of Malmesbury (*ca.* 1090–1143) tells it, some people in North Germany dancing in a churchyard during the Christmas festival were doomed by their parish priest to dance a whole year without stopping, and literally danced themselves into the ground, sinking lower and lower until they were buried up to the hips.

Though the fiddler story may have been borrowed from such legends of Sabbath-breakers, it is particularly appropriate to Halta-dans. The sort of troll called a hill-trow shared several character-istics with the fairies (see **Trowie Knowe**, p.523), the most pleasant of which was a love of music. The trows would lure a fiddler away to their home in the hill where he would remain a year and a day, unconscious of the passing of time (cf. King Herla at **Hereford**, p.306). But he would be well rewarded for his efforts – John Scott, the fiddler of Easting, was told by trows that he would never lack money, and that proved to be the case, for whenever he put his hand into his pocket the coins were always there. But when he was drunk one time he told the secret, and that was the last of his good luck, for the trowie money never came again (cf. **Stowmarket**, p.193).

But if trowie money did not last, trowie music did. Certain traditional Shetland tunes are supposed to have been learnt from trows or heard in the trow-hill, the most famous being the Trowie Reel, learned by an old fiddler known to John Spence (*Shetland Folk-Lore*, 1899), as he rested outside the hill of Gulla Hammar. The tune the trowies danced to here at Haltadans is the one still known by that name, 'Haltadans', 'the limping dance' – perhaps a reference to the traditional ungainliness of trolls. It goes back at least to 1642, and so possibly may the legend.

Haltadans and the Fiddlers' Crus are marked by name on the OS 1:25 000 map (listed under HU 67, not 69 as you might expect).

LOCH NESS, HIGHLAND   Sheet 26
(formerly INVERNESS-SHIRE)   NH 5023

In former times some would tell that Loch Ness got its name from an Irish hero called Nysus, who was the first to sail the lake, or from the daughter of a giantess who was drowned in it. Others would say that it came from the remark of a woman who went one day to the well to fetch water. She found the spring flowing so fast that she was afraid and ran away. She never stopped to draw breath until she got to the top of a high hill, when she turned and saw the glen filled with water. 'Aha!' said she. 'Tha Loch ann a nis!' – 'There is a lake in it now!' – and so it was called Loch Ness.

Though this story was only recorded in the nineteenth century, by J. F. Campbell in his *Popular Tales of the West Highlands* (1860), the tale of the overflowing well is a very old Celtic pattern – it was also told of Llyn Lech Owen in Dyfed and seems to underlie the legend of **Cardigan Bay** (p.332).

As for the Loch Ness Monster – he's been there a long time. In Adomnan's *Life of Columba* (seventh century), we are told that St Columba saw a man who had been seized and bitten by a 'water beast' in the river Ness being buried on the bank by the other inhabitants. Notwithstanding this, the saint ordered that one of his companions should swim to the opposite bank and bring back a boat that was moored there. Lugne mocu-Min immediately plunged into the water, whereupon the beast, who had been lurking in the depths, was disturbed by his swimming and darted up at him. The monster came open-mouthed and roaring, and everyone was terror-struck except for Columba, who made the sign of the cross and sternly bade it return to its lair. At his command, it fled and was never seen again.

Well, hardly ever.

LORNTY, TAYSIDE (formerly PERTHSHIRE)

In his *Popular Rhymes of Scotland* (1826), Robert Chambers tells us that the young Laird of Lorntie was one evening returning home from a hunting excursion past a lonely lake about three miles from Lorntie, in those days surrounded by woods, when suddenly he heard a woman shrieking. Spurring his horse to the lakeside, he saw a beautiful woman in the process of drowning. Dismounting, he waded in and was about to grasp her by her long yellow hair when his manservant pulled him back. 'Bide, Lorntie – bide a blink!' he cried, as the Laird was about to cast him off. 'That wauling madam was none other, God sauf us! than the mermaid.' Believing him, the Laird made to remount his horse, whereat the mermaid rose from the water and in a fiendish voice exclaimed:

> 'Lorntie, Lorntie,
> 　Were n't na your man,
> I had gart your heart's blude
> 　Skirl in my pan.'

Chambers's 'Lorntie in Angus-shire' is modern Lornty, Tayside, and the lake to which he refers is evidently Loch Benachally (NO 0750) out of which flows Lornty Burn. The ferocious mermaid in this tale is more akin to the malevolent water kelpie of **Conon House** (p.493) than to the kindly mermaids of Renfrewshire and Galloway (see **Port Glasgow**, p.480), even though, like them, she lives in fresh water.

MARTIN'S STONE, TEALING, TAYSIDE (formerly ANGUS)

Long ago, when Scotland was still infested with beasts of prey, there was a peasant lived at Pittempton, about three miles from Dundee, who had nine beautiful daughters. One day he sent the eldest to fetch a pitcher of water from the well a short distance from the house. When she did not return, he sent the next eldest to look for her, and after her the next. It was not until the fourth, fifth, sixth, seventh, eighth and ninth daughters had all gone to the well and none returned, though night was falling, that their father became alarmed, and catching up his fish-spear ran to the well. There to his horror he found a dragon lying besmeared with blood, seemingly having devoured all nine of the maidens. Unable to deal with the monster by himself, the peasant gathered several hundred of his neighbours and returned. The dragon tried to flee, but the villagers gave chase, foremost a young man called Martin, the lover of one of the nine girls. The dragon veered north, but was presently hard beset at a place called Baldragon, now drained but then a moss, where he was wetted (Scots *draiglit*). Away again to the north and he was surrounded, and Martin struck him with his club. As he was about to retaliate, the onlookers cried out, 'Strike, Martin!', and Martin gave him another blow, which was almost the end of him. He crawled heavily away, until half a mile further on he was again hemmed in, and finished off by the heroic Martin.

A stone bearing the outline of a serpent, says Chambers in his *Popular Rhymes* (1826), 'still marks the spot, and is always called Martin's Stane', while the well went by the name of 'The Nine Maidens' Well'. On Martin's Stone, 'in very rude and ancient characters', was supposed to be the following rhyme, evidently the dragon's last words:

> I was tempted at Pittempton,
> Draiglit at Baldragon,
> Stricken at Strike-Martin,
> And killed at Martin's Stane.

The story was evidently inspired by the place-name Baldragon and the carvings of outlandish beasts on Martin's Stone, a boulder in a field at Balkello (NO 374375), believed to be a Pictish cross-slab.

Other place-names were then drawn in and 'explained' – Strike-Martin being said to represent local pronunciation of Strathmartine.

The dragon who guards a well against all-comers is a very old motif found also at Longwitton in Northumberland, where three magic healing wells were taken over by a dragon who would no longer allow pilgrims to drink. A dragon such as this one was also slain in Greece by Cadmus at the Spring of Ares on the site of Thebes. These stories may hark back to very ancient myths indeed, current among all the Indo-European peoples, for the Hindu *Rig Veda* (*ca.* 1200 B.C.) contains a hymn that had probably been in use for many centuries in honour of Indra, celebrating his feat of slaying the dragon Vṛtra and releasing the waters. This motif was not understood by the writer of *The Old Statistical Account of Scotland* (1793) who gives us another – that the nine maidens went to the well on a Sunday, i.e. were punished for breaking the Sabbath.

Martin's Stone, an upright broken cross-slab 4' h × 2'3" w (1.2 × 0.69 m), sculpted in relief on one side, is now enclosed by an iron fence. For other Pictish sculptured stones in the area, visit Aberlemno – a cross-slab in the kirkyard (NO 522555) and three stones beside the B9134 (NO 522559) – and St Vigeans Museum (NO 6342). There are others at Meigle Museum (NO 2844). All AM (Aberlemno stones, any reasonable time). While in Tealing parish, visit the Tealing Earth House (NO 411380): AM. See **Lochmaben** (p.472). Meigle, Sheet 53.

MENSTRIE, CENTRAL   Sheet 58
(formerly CLACKMANNANSHIRE)   NS 8496

An honest miller once dwelt in Menstrie. He had a very bonnie wife, and the fairies takin' a notion o' her, carried her awa'. The puir man was much cast doon at the loss o' his wife, mair especially as he heard her every morning, chanting aboon his head (but he could na see her):

> 'O! Alva woods are bonnie,
>   Tillicoultry hills are fair:
> But when I think on the braes o' Menstrie
>   It makes my heart aye sair.'

Riddlin caff [chaff] ae day at the mooth o' his mill door, he chanced to stand upon ae fit, as the hens do in rainy weather – the enchantment which bound his wife was immediately broken, and lo! she stood beside him.

This version of the tale of the Miller of Menstrie comes from *The Scottish Journal of Topography* for 1848. Robert Chambers, who had told it earlier, in his *Popular Rhymes of Scotland* (1826), speaks of the miller's 'magical posture' but does not tell us what it was.

Menstrie seems to have been a particular haunt of fairies – we hear in Ferguson's *Ochil Fairy Tales* (1911) the story of the Black Laird of Dunblane, who returning late one night from Alloa, fell in with the fairies in Menstrie Glen. They invited him to go with them and mounted bundles of 'windlestrae', he a plough-beam left in a furrow. Crying 'Brechan to the Bridal' they flew thither through the air, now it appeared mounted on white horses. They entered a mansion where a banquet was prepared, and ate and drank, invisible to the guests. Then crying 'Cruinan to the dance!' they passed through the keyhole and flew in the same way to Cruinan. But at length the Laird could not help but exclaim, 'Weel dune, Watson's auld plough-beam!' and at once found himself alone, astride the plough in the furrow whence he had started.

He had, of course, broken the taboo on speaking to the fairies (see **Eildon Hills**, p.452, and **New Abbey**, p. 478). The story is a variation on the well-known tale of 'Horse and Hattock!' (see **Duffus Castle**, p.495) and belongs to the same area of belief as tales of the fairy whirlwind (see **Leith**, p.468).

Not far from Menstrie is a Fairy Knowe (Sheet 57, NS 796983). 'Windle-strae' or windlestraw is a very old dialectal word meaning a long, thin, dry piece of grass – possibly one suitable for plaiting, as OE *windel* means 'basket' and comes from the verb 'to wind'.

NORRIE'S LAW, LARGO, FIFE

Sheet 59
NO 4007

At the turn of the century, it was said that Norrie's Law, a cairn on the northern coast of the Firth of Forth, near Largo (NO 409073), was made by the demons who served Michael Scot, the great wizard supposed to have lived at Balwearie Castle (see **Melrose Abbey**, p.475). Were these demons perhaps the familiars

Prig, Prim and Pricker, whom Robert Chambers reports in *The Picture of Scotland* (1827) to have been such a nuisance that Michael Scot was obliged to keep them constantly busy, and when they had cleft the Eildon Hills and bridled the Tweed with a curb of stone set them to twisting ropes of sand? Whoever they were, he commanded them to level Largo Law (NO 4205), but they had only thrown from the top one shovelful when they were summoned away – the shovelful landed and so was formed Norrie's Law.

Earlier, in *Popular Rhymes of Scotland* (1826), Chambers had told the following tale. It was supposed by the people of the neighbourhood that under Largo Law was a rich mine of gold – so rich, indeed, that when sheep lay on it their fleeces turned yellow. A great many years ago, a ghost appeared on the spot and was accosted by a shepherd, who asked why it had come. It requested a meeting on a particular night at precisely eight o'clock, when, it said:

> 'If Auchindownie cock disna craw,
> And Balmain horn disna blaw,
> I'll tell ye where the gowd mine is in Largo Law.'

The shepherd took the measures necessary to prevent these things happening and spoiling his chances. Not a cock was left alive at Auchindownie (NO 4205), and at Balmain (NO 4105) they were warned not to blow the horn to call the cattle. The hour was come, and the ghost had appeared, when Tammie Norrie, the Balmain cowherd, from forgetfulness or obstinacy, blew the horn.

> 'Woe to the man that blew the horn,
> For out of the spot he shall ne'er be borne!'

exclaimed the ghost and vanished. Tammie Norrie was struck dead on the spot, and when it was found impossible to move him, a cairn was raised over his corpse, which became known as Norrie's Law and was still in Chambers's time regarded as uncanny.

In the 1870 edition of *Popular Rhymes*, Chambers added that this tale, 'taken down from tradition in 1825', had since proved to have 'a basis in fact' in that, in about 1819, a man quarrying Norrie's Law for sand had found in it a cist containing a silver hoard. From the *Book of Days* (1864), we hear that a man living near Largo was observed to have money to spend, at about the same time that a silversmith in Cupar was offered an antique silver hoard, and it was noticed that the cairn had been broken into. The owner of the land, General Durham, set enquiries afoot which brought to light the fact that the man had excavated the mound. Influenced, some said, by conscience, others by superstition, he had not removed all he found, but left some of the silver *in situ*. General Durham had the mound explored again, and the remains of silver armaments were found, including what were thought to be scales from a silver coat of mail.

Now in the *Book of Days* is also recorded a tradition that does not appear in *Popular Rhymes* – that a warrior in silver armour was supposed to be buried in the mound. The finding of the very mailcoat afforded 'indisputable evidence', Chambers says, 'of the very long perseverance ... which may characterize popular tradition'. Of course it proves no such thing. With nothing to show that the tale of silver armour existed *before* the opening of the mound, this can only be reckoned a post-excavation tradition, such as one suspects at **Mold** (p.353), and **Rillaton Barrow** (p.29). When Chambers speaks of the legend as having 'a basis in fact', he is being woolly-minded: the gold mine and treasure-guardian in the story belong to *Largo* Law. It is easy to see how one legend may have led to another under the influence of the find.

Norrie's Law, about eighty-five yards (80 m) south-west of Norrieslaw Cottage, is reached by the track to Bonnyton from the New Gilston road (NO 409077). Whether by excavation, quarrying for sand or agriculture, it is much worn away.

ST VIGEANS, TAYSIDE
(formerly ANGUS)

One of Scotland's many kelpie stories concerns the ancient kirk of St Vigeans, not far from Arbroath, where between 1699 and 1736 the sacrament had never been administered:

A tradition had long prevailed here, that the water-kelpy ... carried the stones for building the church; that the foundation of it was supported upon large bars of iron; and that under the fabric there was a lake of great depth. As the administration of the sacrament had been so long delayed, the people had brought themselves to believe, that the first time the ordinance should be dispensed, the church would sink, and the whole people would be carried down and drowned in the lake. The belief of this had taken such hold of the people's minds, that on the day the sacrament was administered, some hundreds of the parishioners sat on an eminence about 100 yards from the church, expecting the dreaded catastrophe.

This curious incident, reported in *The Old Statistical Account of Scotland* ·in 1794, embodies a well-known tradition about the kelpie. Though he might appear as a grey old man, or a handsome young one come a-courting but eventually betrayed by the rushes in his hair, he most often took the form of a horse. In this shape he might be captured, the procedure being to throw over his head a bridle over which the sign of the cross had been made. Once in harness he could be forced to labour. Chambers (1826) gives a traditional rhyme from the Mearns voicing the protest of the kelpie said by some to haunt the 'Ponnage', or Pontage Pool in the north Esk. The laird who built the castle at Morphie (NO 7164) had thrown a pair of branks over his head and compelled him to carry prodigious loads of stones. When he was finally released, before he disappeared, he turned and pronounced this retribution:

> 'Sair back and sair banes,
> Drivin' the laird o' Morphie's stanes!
> The laird o' Morphie'll never thrive
> As lang's the kelpy is alive!'

And indeed the line of the Grahams of Morphie, once powerful, sank in fortune until it became extinct.

The St Vigeans legend combines this trait of the kelpie with a curious piece of lore concerning 'Sunken Churches': 'The 18th instant, being Saturday,' wrote Abraham de la Pryme, the Yorkshire diarist, in July 1696, 'I went to see a place, between Sanclif and Conisby, called the Sunken Church, the tradition concerning which says that there was a church there formerly, but that it sunk in the ground with all the people in it, in the times of popery. But I found it to be only a fable, for that they shew to be the walls therof, yet standing, is most manifestly nothing but a natural rock

. . .' The Sunken Church at Sancliff was still known by that name in the mid nineteenth century, when the legend ran that the church and the whole congregation had been swallowed up by the earth, but one day each year, on the anniversary of the event, if you went there early in the morning you would hear the bells ringing for Mass.

Similar stories are found elsewhere in Britain and Germany, and explain the name of, for example, the Sunkenkirk stone circle on Swinside Fell, Cumbria. They also account for the names of 'Sunken Kirk', marking the site of a stone circle on Tofthills farm (NJ 552266) in the parish of Clatt, and of 'Chapel o' Sink', on the farm of Westerton (NJ 710186), near Fetternear. Of this at the turn of the century it was said that attempts had been made to build a chapel in the circle but every night the walls sank out of sight until the builders despaired and abandoned the project.

The old church of St Vigeans, founded in the eleventh century, has been much restored. See under **Martin's Stone** (p.509) for St Vigeans Museum. While 'Chapel o' Sink' seems to be the stone circle marked on the OS map at NJ 706159, the location of 'Sunken Kirk' is in doubt. L. V. Grinsell, *Folklore of Prehistoric Sites in Britain* (1976), suggests by his map reference that it is the stone circle south-west of Ardlair, NJ 552279. But James Ritchie in 'Folklore of the Aberdeenshire Stone Circles and Standing-Stones', *Proceedings of the Society of Antiquaries of Scotland*, vol. LX, 5th series, vol. XII (1927), p.306, says that 'not a stone remains and the absence is accounted for by the story that the spirits have caused the circle to sink underground'. 'Sunken Kirk', Sheet 37; 'Chapel o' Sink', 38; Morphie, 45.

SANDRAY, WESTERN ISLES (formerly INVERNESS-SHIRE)

Sheet 31
NL 6491

The uninhabited island of Sandray south of Barra is the scene of the Gaelic tale of 'Sanntraigh' collected in Barra in 1859 and printed by J. F. Campbell in *Popular Tales of the West Highlands* (1860). There was a herd's wife on the island of Sanntraigh who had a kettle, and a woman of peace (a fairy) would come every day to borrow the kettle. She would not say a word when she came but would catch hold of the kettle, and the woman of the house would say:

> 'A smith is able to make
> Cold iron hot with coal.
> The due of a kettle is bones,
> And to bring it back again whole.'

And the woman of peace would come back every day with the kettle with flesh and bones left in it.

One day the housewife wanted to go over by ferry to Baile a Chaisteil and she said to her husband, 'If you will say to the woman of peace as I say, I will go to Baile Castle.' 'Oh, I will say it,' he said. But when he saw the woman of peace coming and a shadow from her feet, he was afraid and shut the door against her. The woman of peace went to the hole in the roof and the kettle gave two jumps, and at the third it went out through the hole. Night came and the kettle came not. When the housewife returned, she asked: 'Where is the kettle?' And the man told her what he had done. 'She will come tomorrow with it.' 'She will not come.'

The housewife went to the fairy hill, and it was after dinner and no one was there but one old man. She saw the kettle and took it up, heavy though it was with remnants they had left in it. When the old man saw her take it, he said:

> 'Silent wife, silent wife,
> That came on us from the land of chase,
> Thou man on the surface of the "Bruth",
> Loose the Black, and slip the Fierce.'

Two dogs were let loose, and soon she heard them coming behind her. She put her hand in the kettle and threw them a quarter of what was in it. That stopped them for a while, but then they closed on her again and she threw them another piece. When she came near the farm she turned the pot upside down and left them all that was in it. The dogs of the town started to bark when they saw the dogs of peace stopping. But the woman of peace never came again to seek the kettle.

This tale is one of many of the 'borrowing fairies', from which some scholars have supposed that fairy origins lay in contact between the wild and shy Neolithic people – who did not work metal – with the men of the Iron Age. The woman's rhyme that binds the woman of peace to return the kettle with the price of its hire mentions cold iron – which is what fairies traditionally feared (cf. **Aberfoyle**, p.491). The kettle or cauldron, the basic cooking vessel, is the thing most often lent, as at **Frensham** (p.106), though there the borrowing is in reverse.

The human woman is called the 'silent wife' because she keeps the ritual silence thought necessary in dealing with the fairies. The most interesting thing about this tale is that to the old fairy man in the 'bruth' – the fairy hill – the silent woman is as uncanny as to her husband had been the woman of peace.

The same story, located on Bac Fhionnlaidh ('Finlay's Sandbank') on the farm of Ballevulin, Tiree, was heard 'several years before he saw Mr Campbell's book' by his namesake J. G. Campbell (*Superstitions of the Highlands & Islands of Scotland*, 1900).

Although now uninhabited, Sandray was once, for example when Sir Donald Munro visited it in 1549, 'inhabit and manurit, guid for corne and fishing'. Baile a Chaisteil in the story is Bagh a Chaisteil, Castlebay (NL 6698) on Barra.

SCONE PALACE, TAYSIDE (formerly PERTHSHIRE)

Sheet 58
NO 1126

According to the chronicler Robert of Gloucester (fl. 1230–1300), an ancestress of the Scots (see **Coylton**, p.437),

> . . . broghte into Scotland a whyte marble ston,
> Þat was ordeyned for hure kyng, whan he coroned wer.
> And for a grete Jewyll long hit was yholde ther . . .

This was the Stone of Scone, the Stone of Destiny, said originally to have come from Spain, whence it was carried into Ireland by the Scots and later brought by King Fergus to Scotland. Its first home there was traditionally said to be Dunstaffnage Castle, the seat of the early Dalriadic kings. 'Here for a long time', writes Francis Grose (1789), 'was preserved the famous stone, the Palladium of Scotland, brought as the legend has it, from Spain. It was afterwards removed by Kenneth II to Scone . . .' In the abbey church at Scone it remained for something like four hundred years until 1296, when it was captured by Edward I. He took it to Westminster Abbey and set it in a chair, the Coronation Chair since that time used by the English kings. Scottish Nationalists took it back to Scotland in 1950, but in 1951 surrendered it again on the High Altar of Arbroath Abbey. Some say it was never returned to Westminster and that the real Stone of Scone remains in Scotland.

Why any Scot should need to think this is beyond comprehension. Despite the change of site the stone is still fulfilling its function, as Weever recognized in his *Ancient Funerall Monuments* (1631), perhaps written when the first of the Stuarts was on the throne:

> Vpon the Chaire wherein the stone is inclosed, this famous propheticall Distichon is inscribed.
>
> > Ni fallat vatum Scoti hunc quocunque locatum
> > Invenient lapidem, regnare tenentur ibidem.
>
> > If Fates goe right where ere this stone is pight,
> > The Regall race of Scots shall rule that place.
>
> Which, by whomsoever it was written, we, who now live, finde it happily accomplished.

But why such a fuss about a stone? Why did Edward I take it to England? Not merely to cock a snook at the defeated Scots, but because he was a superstitious man who fully believed in the power of the *Fatale Marmor*, as Hector Boece (1526) calls it, the Stone of Fate. For the stone was invested with mana – it may not have been Jacob's Pillow in the Bible, as some versions of the legend claim, but it very likely *did* come from Ireland with the Scots, and once it was at Scone thirty-four successive Scottish kings were enthroned upon it, as the custom had been among their Irish ancestors.

In Ireland there were several such stones of inauguration – one of the most famous being that of the O'Neills, which stood at Tullaghage, the medieval capital of Tyrone. It was a chair formed of three great slabs and the last time it was used was at the inauguration of Hugh O'Neill, who became Earl of Tyrone in 1597. In 1602 it was destroyed, but a stone that can still be seen is St Columba's Stone, near Londonderry, which has two depressions like the marks of feet. The chiefs of the O'Dohertys are said to have stood on this stone with bare feet at their inaugurations. The custom is thought to have originally had to do with the cult of the

The Stone of Destiny: the Coronation Chair with beneath it the Stone of Scone, Westminster Abbey, London

ancestors, whose spirits perhaps dwelt in the stone, so that the newly invested king received the 'luck' or mana of his predecessors by contact with it. A similar idea seems to lie behind the practice of 'howe-sitting' in ancient Norway, where kings were evidently enthroned on the burial mounds of their forebears.

At this point it must be said that, despite what the guidebooks claim, the Stone of Scone is the one and only genuine coronation stone to be seen in this country. The so-called 'Coronation Stone' of Kingston-Upon-Thames is totally bogus. Though you will read time and again that the Anglo-Saxon kings were crowned on it and that this is how Kingston got its name, this is a myth. In the eleventh century, Kingston's name was *Cyningestūn*, 'the King's *tūn*', because it was a royal manor. Certainly half-a-dozen Anglo-Saxon kings are believed to have been inaugurated there in the tenth century. But Edgar the Peaceful, the first Anglo-Saxon king to have a coronation in the medieval and modern sense, chose to hold it, in 973 A.D., at Bath, while in the eleventh century kings who were not quite certain of their hold – Cnut (1017), Harold (1066) and William (1066) – selected London, the merchant capital, because they needed its support. If there was no one place for coronations, then no particular sanctity attached to Kingston, which was chosen because it was a royal *tūn* – and in those days the kings lived off the produce of their manors – conveniently close to both London and Canterbury, with whose archbishops the tenth-century kings of the Wessex dynasty had an old alliance.

We know little of the inauguration of Anglo-Saxon kings, but that the coronation ritual used for Edgar was in the main devised out of Frankish rites suggests that there was no time-hallowed ceremonial. Certainly there is no mention of a stone.

Just when the Kingston stone was first declared to be a 'coronation stone' is doubtful: it is said to have been preserved from ancient times in the chapel of St Mary, which fell down in 1730, but it is mentioned neither by Leland in his *Itinerary* (*ca.* 1535–43) nor Camden (1586). Says Leland, 'The tounisch men have certen knowlege of a few kinges crounid there afore the Conqueste; and contende that 2. or 3. kinges were buried yn their paroche chirch; but they can not bring no profe nor likelihod of it.' Was the stone, whatever it was, drawn into the picture to supply the lacking 'profe' of Kingston's royal connection? I note that the stone was still being used as a mounting-block outside the town-hall to 1850, in which year the mayor, a local antiquary, placed it on its present base and unveiled it with suitable ceremony on a public holiday.

But if the Kingston stone is dubious, not so the Stone of Scone, apart from Stonehenge perhaps the most powerfully evocative object in these islands.

Although the Stone of Destiny is no longer at Scone, do not miss this historic palace, the third to stand on the site. Its 'Gothic' appearance, acquired in the early nineteenth century, is no guide to the antiquity of the place, whose associations go back to the Dark Ages and the Picts. For times of opening, see *HHC&G*.

THE SOLDIER'S LEAP, PASS OF KILLIECRANKIE, TAYSIDE (formerly PERTHSHIRE)

The name 'The Soldier's Leap' refers to a couple of rocks twenty feet (6.5 m) or more apart on either side of the river Garry where it cuts through a chasm. It is said to have arisen from an incident that took place after the Battle of Killiecrankie on 27 July 1689, when Graham of Claverhouse ('Bonnie Dundee') at the head of 3000 Highlanders loyal to James II defeated the troops of William III under General Mackay. One of Mackay's soldiers, a certain Donald MacBean, who had been stationed as a sentry at the head of the Pass, after the battle tried to make his escape, but was hotly pursued by the Highlanders to the edge of the chasm. Seeing no help for it, he leapt; and though wounded in the shoulder in the attempt, got safely over. He is said later to have served under

The desperate feat: The Soldier's Leap,
Pass of Killiecrankie, Tayside

General Wade, famous as a road-builder (any relation of the *giant* Wade? – see **Wade's Stone**, p.421) and to have frequently shown his scars as proof of the tale.

This story is often told in local history books as if it were factually true, but there is no reason why it should be. It is one of many 'prodigious leaps' in British tradition – examples are **Byard's Leap** in Leicestershire (p.218), Bodrugan's Leap, near Mevagissey, Cornwall, The Huntsman's Leap, near St Govan's Head, Dyfed, and The Tinker's Loup, on the Water of Deugh in Galloway. The first and third stories are frankly fabulous, and precisely the same sort of tradition is found elsewhere in Europe and in North America, leaving not much room for doubt that what we are dealing in is fantasy.

NTS.

STRATHMIGLO, FIFE   Sheet 58
                                                   NO 2110

In his *History of Fife* (1840), John Leighton relates the tale of a Brownie who lived at Strathmiglo castle (NO 221103) and used every day to cross the river Meglo by stepping-stones to get to the tower of Cash. There he would labour cheerfully, both in barn and in byre, threshing the corn and milking the cows for his master's poor neighbours. Though he himself was invisible, people could see the work going on, and all he asked in recompense was to help himself to any food he chose that had not been put aside specially for him.

One morning, after heavy rains, the river was swollen and the stepping-stones covered, and the servants said to themselves that he would not come to Cash that day. There was no bridge nearer than the west end of the town, and they could not think that he'd go the long way round. But they discovered that they were mistaken, when one of the serving maids, who was eating her cogful of porridge and had only taken a spoonful or two, found it disappearing without her assistance. Brownie was immediately asked how he had got there, and explained he had gone 'roun by the brig' – whence has arisen a local proverb for going the long way, 'gone roun' by the brig, as Brownie did'.

This amiable Brownie makes a pleasant change from the touchy creatures in the Lowlands (e.g. **Cranshaws**, p.440).

Strathmiglo consists of one principal street on the north side of the river Eden with several wynds (lanes) running off it north and south. On the south side of the river are two wynds once known as Cash Feus, which housed the tradesmen of the village. The castle stood at a short distance to the east of the town, but was removed in 1734. The only candidate for the 'tower of Cash' today is the tower marked on the OS 1:25 000 map at NO 207098, but this does not seem to fit the circumstances of the story, in which the west end of Strathmiglo is 'the long way round'. Note that just north of Strathmiglo is Brownie's Chair (NO 208122).

TROWIE KNOWE, NORTHMAVINE, SHETLAND

Sheets 1 and 2
HU 3685

The Norse settlers of Shetland brought with them not only their own tongue but their mythology and folklore, including traditions of the trolls. They were commemorated in place-names – for example Trolla Stack (HU 3782) and Trolladale Water (HU 3273) – and everyday Shetland speech contained expressions which tell us about them: *trollmolet* meant 'troll-mouthed', i.e. surly, and *trollet*, 'misshapen', while a *trollamog* was a small mischievous person, a *trollaplukk* a slow-moving clod.

Like giants, the trolls or trows, as they came to be known, were grotesquely ugly, and came out only at night. If overtaken by daylight, they were liable to be turned to stone (see **Haltadans**, p.505). They were usually dressed in grey (like the stones that they became), and in some respects resembled not giants but fairies. Because they were ugly, trows, like the fairies, would frequently try to exchange their wizened puling infants for human babies. They likewise stole human girls to be their wives, and also women in childbed, leaving in their place a stock (cf. **New Abbey**, p.478). Like fairies, too, they loved music, and several famous Shetland tunes, including 'Haltadans', are said to have come from them.

The sort of troll called a hill-trow was a good deal smaller than a man and inhabited a hill or tumulus (cf. **Willy Howe**, p.430). Such a place was the Trowie Knowe, the 'troll-mound', a chambered cairn in Northmavine parish, Loch of Housetter, Mainland (HU

362855). It seems to have no particular legend, but evidently in the past the trows were thought to live there, and perhaps their music was heard from the mound.

Trolladale Water, Sheet 3.

TULLIBODY, CENTRAL
(formerly CLACKMANNANSHIRE)
Sheet 58
NS 8695

There was a poor woman of Tullibody who was afflicted with a good-for-nothing husband, a salt-man known far and wide as 'the drucken [drunken] Sautman o' Tullibody'. She was continually railing on him for his misconduct but everything she said 'fell like rain on desert'. At the end of her tether, she called on the fairies to take her away. 'The fairies took hold of her in a twinklin', and up the lum [chimney] they flew singin' –

> 'Deedle linkum dodie,
> We're aff wi' drucken Davie's wife,
> The *Sautman* o' Tullibody.'

They carried her to Cauldhame, the palace of the fairies, and there she lived like a queen. But after a while she began to yearn after drunken Davie, so the fairies carried her home again. But before they left her, one of them gave her a little stick, saying that as long as she kept it, Davie would nevermore be the worse for drink.

This nice little story, from the *Scottish Journal of Topography* (1848), shows the fairies as abductors in rather a better light than most such tales (cf. the story of Sandy Harg's wife, under **New Abbey**, p.478). But has it been adapted? In Chambers's *Popular Rhymes* (1826), where it is told of the *smith* of Tullibody, the wife is not returned.

VE SKERRIES, SHETLAND
Sheet 3
HU 1065

The Ve Skerries, north-west of Papa Stour, were once thought to be the haunt of 'sea-trows'. Dr Samuel Hibbert, in *A Description of the Shetland Isles* (1822), records the beliefs of the Shetlanders concerning them in his time.

They resembled human beings, and were subject to death, but were of surpassing beauty and had limited supernatural powers. They lived far below the region of the fish in the depths of the ocean, where there was an atmosphere adapted to their respiratory organs. They would not be able to rise through the sea, and up to the world above, were it not for their ability to put on the skin of some amphibious animal. Once on land they would take off the skin and resume their natural shape, but if they lost the skin, they were unable to return to the sea and must remain for ever on land. As to their origins:

> These inhabitants of a submarine world were, in later periods of Christianity, regarded as fallen angels who were compelled to take refuge in the sea: they had, therefore, the name of Sea-Trows given to them, as belonging to the dominion of the Prince of Darkness.

One of the sea-trows' particular haunts on land were the Ve Skerries, where they would revel by moonlight, protected from the gaze of men by the raging surf that beat around them. Here is set a tale told by Keightley in his *Fairy Mythology* (1850) of a sea-trow who lost his skin and what became of him. Fishermen from Papa Stour had landed on a skerry frequented by seals, stunned several and skinned them, and left the beasts senseless on the rocks. Then they gathered up the skins and prepared to depart, but a tremendous swell suddenly arose, and in the rush to get to the boat and get away, one man was left behind. His companions tried to rescue him but after several attempts were finally obliged to abandon him to his fate.

After a while, some seals that had been scared from the rock by the fishermen returned, and stripping off their skins revealed themselves as sea-trows. They hastened to revive the stunned seals and these too resumed their proper form, bitterly lamenting the loss of their skins, without which they could not return home. Now Gioga, the mother of Ollavitinus, promised the fisherman that she would carry him back to Papa Stour, if he would bring her the seal-skin belonging to her son. This he agreed to do, and she bore him to Akers Geo (HU 149619). From there he went to Skeo at Hamma Voe (HU 1659), where the skins had been taken, and gave Gioga that of her son, enabling him to return to his undersea home.

Sources

Desperate diseases require desperate remedies
– Guy Fawkes, 1570–1606, who cribbed the line from:
– William Shakespeare, 1564–1616, who lifted it from:
– Michel de Montaigne, 1533–1616, who updated it from:
– Geoffrey Chaucer, 1340–1400, who translated it from:
– Hippocrates, 460–357 B.C., and I can't trace his source.*

And that, essentially, is what this book is about. I cannot tell you where a tradition begins, only cite the earliest authorities, so far as I know, to refer to the tale. Often it has seemed pedantic to do more than mention them by name, so what they wrote is explained below – or in the case of anonymous works of literature, what they are.

ANEIRIN (sixth century A.D.)
Late sixth-century poet to whom is attributed the Welsh elegy *Y Goddodin*, a lament for the Men of the North, surviving from the thirteenth century, but containing material which dates to the ninth and tenth. I have used the translation by K. H. Jackson, *The Gododdin* (Edinburgh, 1969).

THE ANGLO-SAXON CHRONICLE
A chronicle of events in England from the coming of Christianity to the reign of King Stephen in the mid twelfth century. Perhaps begun at Winchester in the ninth century under the inspiration of Alfred the Great, this is not a single work but a set of different versions of the same chronicle kept up at various monasteries, including Abingdon, Canterbury, Peterborough and Worcester. It

---

* But I know mine: Carl Duerr, *Management Kinetics*, Pan Management Series (London, 1973), p.243.

is the first history of a West European country to be written in its own language, and quotations are taken from *The Anglo-Saxon Chronicle, A Revised Translation* ed. Dorothy Whitelock, with David C. Douglas and Susie I. Tucker (London, 1961).

ASSER (d. 908 or 909)

Welshman brought up and ordained at St David's and possibly its bishop when first summoned by Alfred of Wessex to his court, probably in 885 A.D. He became Alfred's teacher and helper in his programme of translating Latin works into Old English for the benefit of his clergy and in 893 wrote his Latin *Life of King Alfred*, the earliest known biography of an Anglo-Saxon king. Dividing his time between St David's and the kingdom of Wessex, Asser became Bishop of Sherborne some time between 892 and 900, and died in 908 or 909. I have used the translation of Asser by Simon Keynes and Michael Lapidge in the Penguin Classics *Alfred the Great* (Harmondsworth, 1983); but the rhyme comes from J. A. Giles, *Six Old English Chronicles* (London, 1843).

JOHN AUBREY (1626-97)

According to his contemporary Anthony Wood, 'a shiftless person, roving, magotie-headed and sometimes little better than crased.' An antiquary from his early days as an undergraduate at Oxford, Aubrey in his lifetime amassed a wonderful ragbag collection of folklore contained in several works, of which only the *Miscellanies* were published in his lifetime. Of his writings, I draw on: *Brief Lives* (1669–96), ed. Andrew Clark, 2 vols (Oxford, 1898); *Miscellanies* (London, 1696); 'Perambulation of Half the County of Surrey', published as *The Natural History and Antiquities of the County of Surrey*, ed. Richard Rawlinson, 5 vols (London, 1718–19); *Remains of Gentilisme and Judaisme* (1686–7), ed. James Britten, Publications of the Folk-Lore Society IV (London, 1881); and the Wiltshire collections published as *The Natural History of Wiltshire* (1656–91), ed. John Britton, Wiltshire Topographical Society (London, 1847) and *Wiltshire: The Topographical Collections* (1659–70), corrected and enlarged J. E. Jackson, Wiltshire Archaeology and Natural Society (Devizes, 1862).

JOHN BALE (1495–1563)

East Anglian priest who became an ardent and vocal supporter of the Reformation in England. His splenetic anti-Catholic writings earned him the nickname 'Bilious Bale' from **Thomas Fuller**. The work here quoted is *'English Votaries'*, i.e. *Englysh Votaryes* (London, 1551).

BEDE (*ca.* 673–735)

The Venerable Bede, an Anglo-Saxon monk who spent most of his life at the monastery of Jarrow in Northumberland. The foremost European scholar of his age, he is known as 'the father of English history' for his greatest work, *Historia Ecclesiastica Gentis Anglorum*, completed 731 A.D. Like all learned works of its time, the *Historia* is written in Latin: extracts are taken from the Penguin Classics translation by Leo Sherley-Price, *A History of the English Church and People* (Harmondsworth, 1955).

THE BLACK BOOK OF CARMARTHEN

A Welsh MS of *ca.* 1200 now in the National Library of Wales, Aberystwyth. The Black Book, so-called from the colour of its binding, is a collection of poems by Welsh bards of the sixth and seventh centuries. Amongst other things, it includes *Verses on the Graves of the Heroes* (or 'Stanzas of the Graves'), which refer to the mystery of Arthur's burial place. For material from the Black Book, I am indebted to K. H. Jackson, 'Arthur in Early Welsh Verse', *Arthurian Literature in the Middle Ages*, ed. Roger Sherman Loomis (Oxford, 1959).

THOMAS BLOUNT (1618–79)

English antiquary best known for his *'Ancient Tenures'*, i.e. *Fragmenta Antiquitatis. Antient Tenures of Land, And Jocular Customs Of some Mannors* (1679). I have used the edition by W. Carew Hazlitt, *Tenures of Land and Customs of Manors* (London, 1874).

THE HON. JOHN BYNG (1742–1813)

English traveller who for the last fortnight of his life was the fifth Viscount Torrington, hence the title given to the journals of his tours on horseback between 1781 and 1794, *The Torrington Diaries*, ed. C. Bruyn Andrews, 4 vols (London, 1934–8). It is impossible not to be captivated by Byng, a man of great good sense, as he describes the countryside of England and Wales forty years before Cobbett.

WILLIAM CAMDEN (1551–1623)

English antiquary and historian, sometime Clarenceux King of Arms, whose *Britannia* (London, 1586) is probably the best-known of all British topographical works. It became a source book for poets seeking legends, both in its original Latin form, which had run to six editions by 1607, and in Philemon Holland's translation, *Britain, or A Chorographical description of the most flourishing kingdomes, England, Scotland, and Ireland, and the Ilands adioyning* (London, 1610). This is the version of the *Britannia* that I most frequently cite, but you will also find occasional references to the translations of Edmund Gibson (London, 1695) and Richard Gough (London, 1789), both of which contain additional material.

RICHARD CAREW (1555–1620)

Cornish topographer. *The Survey of Cornwall* (London, 1602), probably written in the 1580s and inspired by Lambard's *Perambulation of Kent*, was published by Carew only tardily in response to pressure from friends.

SIR WILLIAM DUGDALE (1605–86)

English antiquary and historian, Garter King of Arms. He is perhaps the most famous of the great county historians, *The Antiquities of Warwickshire* (London, 1656) marking an advance in scholarship in the use of original records.

CELIA FIENNES (1662–1741)

Lady traveller. Her journeys on horseback through England, accompanied by her maid, cover the period *ca.* 1685–*ca.* 1703. Her journal of these tours was intended only for her large family and was not published. Although known in MS to nineteenth-century historians, no complete text of it appeared until *The Journeys of Celia Fiennes*, ed. Christopher Morris (London, 1947).

THOMAS FULLER (1608–61)

Anglican preacher, best known for 'Fuller's *Worthies*', i.e. *The*

History of the Worthies of England (London, 1662). Published a year after his death, this is not simply the set of biographies that the title suggests, but a topographical survey of England compiled from material gathered on Fuller's journeys.

GEOFFREY OF MONMOUTH (*ca.* 1100–1154)
Monk and 'historian', or so Geoffrey himself would have us believe. In fact his *Historia Regum Britanniae* ('History of the Kings of Britain'), written *ca.* 1136, and the *Vita Merlini* ('Life of Merlin'), a little over a decade later, are undoubtedly in part the products of his own imagination. The *History* was immediately popular, circulating in MS both in its original Latin form and soon after its first appearance also in Norman-French. During the thirteenth century it was translated into English and Welsh, and is the source of most of our major traditions concerning King Arthur. The translation I have used is *The British History . . . of Jeffrey of Monmouth* by Aaron Thompson (London, 1718).

GERALD OF WALES (*ca.* 1145–1223)
Churchman and Latin author otherwise known as Giraldus Cambrensis, Archdeacon of Brecon. He wrote Latin accounts of travels in Wales undertaken in the course of his duties: *Itinerarium Kambriae* (completed 1191) and *Descriptio Kambriae* (first version 1193 or 1194, second version 1215). A contemporary and friend of **Walter Map**, he shared his interest in the supernatural, especially the fairy realm. I have used the Penguin Classics translation by Lewis Thorpe, *Gerald of Wales: The Journey through Wales and The Description of Wales* (Harmondsworth, 1978). This also contains extracts from Gerald's *De principis instructione* (1193–9) and *Speculum Ecclesiae* (*ca.* 1216) concerning the finding of Arthur's grave at Glastonbury.

GERVASE OF TILBURY (*ca.* 1150–*ca.* 1220)
Churchman and Latin author. A native of Tilbury, Essex, who was educated in Rome and subsequently became a teacher of law at Bologna, Gervase later in his career entered the service of the Holy Roman Emperor Otto IV, who made him Marshal of the kingdom of Arles. He was a travelled man who collected a good deal of folklore from various sources, and set it down in Book III of his

Otia Imperialia, a compendium of odds and ends of natural history, politics, and superstition, written for Otto's amusement in about 1212. One of Gervase's friends was **Ralph of Coggeshall**, to whom he communicated several pieces of lore, as Ralph himself exchanged material with **William of Newburgh**. Like Ralph and William, he records some of our earliest fairy traditions. I have used *Otia Imperialia, Book III*, ed. F. Liebrecht (Hanover, 1856), and C. C. Oman's 'The English Folklore of Gervase of Tilbury', *Folklore* LV, March 1944, No. 1 (pp.1–15).

GILDAS (*ca*. 500–70 A.D.)
Saint and historian, born in Strathclyde, subsequently moving to Wales, where he became a monk. His Latin history *De Excidio et Conquestu Britanniae* ('Concerning the Ruin and Conquest of Britain'), written probably between 516 A.D. and 547 A.D., covers the period from the coming of the Romans up to his own time. Gildas exaggerates the evils of his day, making his work unreliable as history, but he is valuable none the less for the glimpse he gives of an historical Arthur. I have used the translations of *De Excidio* and the *Vita Gildae* ('Life of Gildas') by Caradoc of Llancarfan in *Gildas: The Ruin of Britain*, ed. Hugh Williams, Cymmrodorion Record Series, No. 3, Pt 2 (London, 1901).

JOSEPH HALL (1574–1656)
Seventeenth-century divine, sometime Bishop of Exeter, later of Norwich, and a writer (in Latin) of satires and devotional literature. Bishop Hall is mentioned several times in these pages, notably in connection with his prose satire *Mundus Alter et Idem* (Frankfurt, 1605), translated into English by John Healey as *The Discovery of a New World* (London, 1609).

GERVASE HOLLES (1607–75)
English antiquary, MP for Grimsby (1640, 1641) and also its mayor. Holles fought on the side of Charles I during the Civil War, and when his house at Grimsby was plundered by Parliamentarians a great part of his collections was lost. He was never able to continue the history of Lincolnshire he had planned, but many of his notes survive in the British Library as Harley MS 6829.

JAMES I OF ENGLAND, VI OF SCOTLAND

An extraordinary mixture of scholar, pedant and dunderhead, James I is important in the realms of folklore for his *Daemonologie, in forme of a dialogue* (Edinburgh, 1597), a refutation of **Reginald Scot**.

JOHN LELAND (?1506–52)

Appointed 'King's antiquary' in 1533 by Henry VIII. Between 1535 and 1543, Leland travelled widely in England and Wales, noting antiquities of all kinds, with the intention of writing a work on ancient Britain. He became insane in 1550, before this scheme could be fulfilled, and his *Itinerary*, a fragmentary record of his travels, remained in MS long after his death. Several generations of writers, among them Camden, made use of it in this form until it was finally published at Oxford, 1710–12. I have used the standard edition by Lucy Toulmin Smith, *The Itinerary of John Leland*, 5 vols (London, 1906–7).

THE MABINOGION

A selection of eleven stories from three Welsh MSS, the White Book of Rhydderch (*ca.* 1300–25), the **Red Book of Hergest** and the sixteenth-century *Hanes Taliesin*, translated by Lady Charlotte Guest (1838–49). She entitled her collection *The Mabinogion* believing this to be the plural of *mabinogi*, 'tales of youth', a name that properly applies only to the stories of Pwyll, Branwen, Manawydan and Math, which she found in the Red Book of Hergest. However, Lady Guest made the title so famous that translators have continued to use it, and I have followed suit, indicating the approximate date of a particular tale. Bear in mind that, though the MSS Lady Guest drew on are comparatively late, the stories in them seem to represent the stock-in-trade of the Welsh bards, handed down by word of mouth from generation to generation, and are undoubtedly much older than the texts in which they survive. The translation I have used is that of Gwyn Jones and Thomas Jones, *The Mabinogion*, Everyman's Library 97 (London and New York, 1949).

WALTER MAP (*ca.* 1140–1209)
Cleric of Anglo-Norman parentage, probably from Herefordshire, Archdeacon of Oxford (1197). Map was clerk to Henry II, who made him an itinerant judge, and it was perhaps on journeys in this capacity that he heard some of the stories he set down in *De Nugis Curialium* ('Courtier's Trifles'), written in about 1190. This is a commonplace book, filled with Map's observations on his life and times, and containing a number of tales of the supernatural – an interest he shared with his friend **Gerald of Wales**. Appropriately, it has been translated out of its original Latin by the master of the ghost story, M. R. James: *Walter Map's 'De Nugis Curialium'*, trans. M. R. James, notes by J. C. Lloyd, ed. E. S. Hartland, Cymmrodorion Record Series, No. 9 (London, 1923).

NENNIUS (fl. 796 A.D.)
A Welsh cleric, living on the borders of Mercia. Nennius is traditionally said to be the author of the *Historia Britonum* ('The History of the Britons'), assembled in about 800 A.D. from old British sources. Although **Camden** for one did not think much of him as an historian, for students of Arthur he is full of interest. The Latin *Historia* has been translated, as *Nennius's 'History of the Britons'*, by A. W. Wade-Evans, Church Historical Society (London, 1938).

THOMAS PERCY (1729–1811)
Antiquary, poet and churchman. Bishop of Dromore in Ireland (1782), and hence known as Bishop Percy, he is celebrated for 'Percy's *Reliques*', i.e. *Reliques of Ancient English Poetry*, 4 vols (London, 1765). This is a collection of 176 ballads, 45 of which were taken from a folio MS of the seventeenth century which had come into his hands. Comparison with the Percy Folio shows that Bishop Percy a good deal 'improved' the ballads selected for his *Reliques*, but the notes accompanying them are still very valuable.

ABRAHAM DE LA PRYME (1671–1704)
Yorkshire clergyman and antiquary. As an undergraduate at Cambridge, he seems to have devoted much time to investigating natural history, chemistry and magic, going on to become a Fellow of the Royal Society at only thirty. His interests are reflected in his diary,

which includes accounts of local antiquities and old traditions. Quotations are from *The Diary of Abraham de la Pryme*, ed. Charles Jackson, Surtees Society, Vol. LIV (Durham, London and Edinburgh, 1870), dated as entry.

RALPH OF COGGESHALL (fl. 1207)

A native of Cambridgeshire and Abbot of the Cistercian monastery of Coggeshall, Essex (1207–18). Ralph seems to have had a special interest in supernatural occurrences, and to have exchanged stories on this theme with **William of Newburgh**. Another friend of his who gave him information on traditional lore was **Gervase of Tilbury**. Ralph's Latin chronicle, written *ca.* 1210, contains some of our earliest fairytales. I have used the edition by J. Stevenson, *Chronicon Anglicanum* (London, 1875).

THE RED BOOK OF HERGEST

A late-fourteenth-century Welsh MS, so-called from Hergest Court in Herefordshire, and now at Jesus College, Oxford. Besides chronicles and poems, it contains the four *mabinogi* of Pwyll, Branwan, Manawydan and Math which give their name to *The Mabinogion*.

REGINALD SCOT (*ca.* 1538–99)

A Kentishman, MP for New Romney, 1588. Author of the celebrated '*Discovery of Witchcraft*' i.e. *The Discouerie of Witchcraft* (London, 1584). Intended as an exposure ('discovery') of those who took it upon themselves 'to pursue the poor, to accuse the simple, and to kill the innocent', it attempted to demonstrate the fallacies on which witchcraft beliefs were founded. This prompted **James I** (James VI of Scotland as he then was) to refute it with his own *Daemonologie*, and, when he came to the English throne, he went so far as to have it burnt by the public hangman. This was not the end of his career, however, and to a third edition (1665) was anonymously added 'An excellent discourse of the Nature and substance of Devils and Spirits'. For students of folklore Scot is full of interest: he tells us of Brownies and gives a famous list of the supernatural beings of his boyhood, including bullbeggars.

SIR WALTER SCOTT (1771–1832)

Inspired as a boy by **Percy's** *Reliques*, Scott's interest in the oral literature of the peasantry led to a collection of traditional Border ballads, which, augmented with imitations by himself and friends, was published in two volumes in 1802 as *The Minstrelsy of the Scottish Border*, commonly known as the *Border Minstrelsy*. A third volume followed in 1803. Border traditions were again brought together in *The Border Antiquities of England and Scotland*, 2 vols (Edinburgh, London, 1814–17). My many references to Sir Walter's poems and novels are testimony to the wide use he made of legendary material: as well as specific legends, he preserved a great deal of incidental matter, not least in his introduction to the ballad of 'Tamlane' in Volume II of the *Border Minstrelsy*, which takes the form of an essay 'On the Fairies of Popular Superstition', and in his *Letters on Demonology and Witchcraft* (London, 1830). Note that in quoting Scott, I have used the 1839 edition of the *Border Minstrelsy*, and that correspondence concerning Dunvegan Castle and Knebworth House is quoted from Coleman O. Parson's *Witchcraft and Demonology in Scott's Fiction* (Edinburgh and London, 1964).

THE OLD STATISTICAL ACCOUNT OF SCOTLAND

In 1791 under the editorship of Sir John Sinclair began the compilation of what is now known as *The Old Statistical Account of Scotland* (a *New Statistical Account* was produced by the Church of Scotland in 1845). The *Old Statistical Account*, in twenty-one volumes, completed in 1799, consisted of reports by various ministers on their parishes, in which some of them also recorded local beliefs.

WILLIAM STUKELEY (1687–1765)

One of the leading antiquaries of his age, and the man who more than any other is responsible for the totally unfounded belief that megalithic monuments were connected with Druids. His *Itinerarium Curiosum*, first published in 1724, is an account of the antiquities observed in his travels through Britain. Among his other remains are the records of his fieldwork at Stonehenge and Avebury, in particular *Stonehenge: a Temple Restor'd to the British Druids* (London, 1740) and *Abury, a temple of the British Druids* (London, 1743).

THE *TRIADS*

The *Triads* are an ancient Welsh literary device – short lists of three persons, objects or events celebrated in legendary history. They survive in MSS of the thirteenth century and later, but the oldest collections of them appear to include very early traditions. They are thought originally to have been drawn up in bardic schools as mnemonic aids for students mastering the once vast body of bardic lore. As the oral tradition faded, the *Triads* were written down, probably in the eleventh and twelfth centuries, in an attempt to preserve this lore, but too often all that remains is a bare list of names.

JOHN WEEVER (1576–1632)

Lancashire-born poet and antiquary most celebrated for his '*Ancient Funerall Monuments*'; i.e. *Ancient Funerall Monvments within the vnited monarchie of Great Britaine, Ireland, and the Islands adiacent* (London, 1631). Weever's great work is more than the catalogue of tombs and their occupants that this title might suggest, illustrated as it is with 'Historicall obseruations' and notes extracted from old records, charters and manuscripts. Very often he stops to record legendary histories and a great many antiquarian traditions.

WILLIAM OF NEWBURGH (b. 1135 or 1136)

Monk and chronicler of the Augustinian priory of Newburgh in Yorkshire. His Latin history of England covers the period 1066–1198, but mainly the reigns of Stephen and Henry II. He records several supernatural occurrences and seems to have been a friend of **Ralph of Coggeshall**, from whom he probably heard the story of the Green Children. I have used J. Stevenson's translation, *The History of William of Newburgh, The Church Historians of England*, Vol. IV, Pt 2 (London, 1856).

Bibliography

ALLIES, JABEZ. *Observations on Certain Curious Indentations in the Old Red Sandstone of Worcestershire and Herefordshire.* London, Worcester [1835].

On the Ignis Fatuus, or Will-o'-the-Wisp, and the Fairies. London, Worcester, 1846. An expanded version of this was added to *On the British, Roman, and Saxon Antiquities of Worcestershire* (1840), and the whole published as *On the Ancient British, Roman, and Saxon Antiquities and Folk-lore of Worcestershire.* London, Worcester, 1852.

Beowulf. Edited by Fr. Klaeber. 3rd edn with first and second supplement. Boston, 1950.

BLOMEFIELD, FRANCIS. *Essay towards a Topographical History of the County of Norfolk.* 5 vols (with continuation by the Rev. Charles Parkin). Fersfield, Lynn, 1739–45.

BOECE, HECTOR. *The Chronicle of Scotland.* Compiled by Hector Boece (1526). Translated into Scots by John Bellenden, 1531. Edited by R. W. Chambers, E. C. Batho and H. W. Husbands. 2 vols. Publications of the Scottish Text Society, Third Series, X, XV. Edinburgh and London, 1938–41.

BRAY, MRS A. E. *Traditions, Legends, Superstitions and Sketches of Devonshire on the Borders of the Tamar and Tavy.* 3 vols. London, 1838. (Letters addressed to the poet Southey.)

BURNE, MISS CHARLOTTE. *Shropshire Folk-Lore: A Sheaf of Gleanings.* Edited by Charlotte Sophia Burne, from the collection of Georgina Jackson. London, Shrewsbury, Chester, 1883.

CAMPBELL, J. F. *Popular Tales of the West Highlands.* 4 vols. Edinburgh, 1860–2.

CARRINGTON, JOHN. '*Memorandoms for . . .*' *The Diary between 1798 and 1810 of John Carrington.* Edited by W. Branch Johnson. London and Chichester, 1973.

CHAMBERS, ROBERT. *The Popular Rhymes of Scotland*. Edinburgh, London, 1826.

Popular Rhymes, Fireside Stories, and Amusements, of Scotland. Edinburgh, London, 1842 (3rd edn of above).

Popular Rhymes of Scotland. New edition. London and Edinburgh, 1870 (4th edn).

The Picture of Scotland. Edinburgh, 1827.

The Book of Days. 2 vols. London and Edinburgh, 1863–4.

CHAUCER, GEOFFREY. *The Complete Works of Geoffrey Chaucer*. Edited by F. N. Robinson. 2nd edn, rev. Boston, 1957.

CLIFFORD, LADY ANNE. *The Diary of Lady Anne Clifford*. With an introduction by V. Sackville-West. London, 1923.

CUSSANS, JOHN EDWIN. *History of Hertfordshire*. London, Hertford, 1870–81. (Vol. I, 1870–3; vol. II, 1874–8; vol. III, 1879–81.)

DEFOE, DANIEL. *A Tour thro' the Whole Island of Great Britain*. 3 vols. London 1724–7 [6].

DELONEY, THOMAS. *Thomas of Reading, Or, The sixe worthy yeomen of the West*. 4th edn, corrected and enlarged. London, 1612.

Other works: *The Works of Thomas Deloney*. Edited by F. O. Mann. Oxford, 1912.

DENHAM, MICHAEL AISLABIE. *The Denham Tracts*. A collection of Folk-Lore by M. A. Denham and reprinted from the original tracts and pamphlets printed by Mr Denham between 1846 and 1859. Edited by James Hardy. 2 vols. Publications of the Folk-Lore Society, XXIX, XXXV. London, 1892–5.

DODSWORTH, ROGER. *Yorkshire Church Notes, 1619–1631*. Edited by J. W. Clay. Yorkshire Archaeological Society Record Series, XXXIV. 1904.

DRAYTON, MICHAEL. *Poly-olbion*. Pt 1 (Songs 1–18). London, 1612.

Englands Heroicall Epistles. Newly enlarged. London, 1598.

DUNCUMB, JOHN. *Collections towards the History and Antiquities of the County of Hereford*. 2 vols. Hereford, 1804–12.

FLORENCE OF WORCESTER. See STEVENSON, J.

Sir Gawain and the Green Knight. Edited by J. R. R. Tolkien and C. V. Gordon. Repr. with corrections. Oxford, 1963.

GROSE, FRANCIS. *The Antiquities of England and Wales*. 4 + 2 vols. London, 1773–87.

The Antiquities of Scotland. 2 vols. London, 1789–91.

A Provincial Glossary. London, 1787.

HARE, AUGUSTUS. *In My Solitary Life*. Edited by Malcolm Barnes. London, 1953. (Dated as journal entry.)

HARLAND, JOHN and WILKINSON, T. T. *Lancashire Folk-Lore*. London, New York, 1867.

    Lancashire Legends, Traditions, Pageants, Sports &c. London, Manchester, 1873.

HARRISON, WILLIAM. *An historicall description of the Islande of Britayne*. In R. Holinshed, *The First volume of the Chronicles of England*. London, 1577.

HASTED, EDWARD. *The History and Topographical Survey of the County of Kent*. 4 vols. Canterbury, 1778–99.

HEARNE, THOMAS. *Gulielmi Neubrigensis Historia, sive Chronica Rerum Anglicarum*. Edited by T. Hearne, 3 vols. Oxford, 1719.

    A Collection of Curious Discourses written by Eminent Antiquaries. Oxford, 1720.

HIGDEN, RANULPH. *Polychronicon*, translated by John Trevisa (1387). Vol. VIII (Rosamond). Edited by J. R. Lumby. Rolls Series. London, 1882.

HONE, WILLIAM. *The Every-Day Book*. 2 vols. London, 1826–7.

    The Table Book. 2 vols in 1. London, 1827–8.

HUTCHINS, JOHN. *The History and Antiquities of the County of Dorset*. 2 vols. London, 1774.

HUTCHINSON, WILLIAM. *An excursion to the Lakes, In Westmoreland and Cumberland, August 1773*. London 1774.

    The History of the County of Cumberland. 2 vols. Carlisle, 1794.

KILVERT, REV. FRANCIS. *Kilvert's Diary*, edited by William Plomer. 3 vols. London, 1938–40.

KIRK, ROBERT. *The Secret Common-wealth, or, A Treatise Displaying the Chief Curiosities among the People of Scotland as they are in Use to this Day* (written 1690 or 1691). Edited by Stewart Sanderson. Folklore Society, Mistletoe Series. Cambridge and Totowa, NJ, 1976.

LAMBARD, WILLIAM. *A Perambulation of Kent ... Collected and written (for the most part) in the yeare 1570*. London, 1576.

LATHAM, MRS CHARLOTTE. 'Some West Sussex superstitions lingering in 1868'. *Folk-Lore Record* I. London [1878].

LAYAMON. *Brut*. Edited by G. F. Brooke and R. F. Leslie. 2 vols. Early English Text Society. London, 1963–78.

LIPSCOMB, GEORGE. *The history and antiquities of the County of Buckingham.* 4 vols. London, 1847.

LONGSTAFFE, W. HYLTON DYER. *Richmondshire, Its Ancient Lords and Edifices.* London 1853.
  The History and Antiquities of the Parish of Darlington. Darlington and London, 1854.

LUPTON, THOMAS. *A Thousand Notable things, of sundrie sortes.* London [1579].

LYSONS, DANIEL and SAMUEL. *Magna Britannia.* 6 vols. London, 1814. (First vol., covering Bedfordshire, Berkshire and Buckinghamshire, first pub. in 1806.)

MANNYNG OF BRUNNE (MANNING OF BOURNE), ROBERT. *The Story of England by Robert Mannyng ... AD 1338.* Edited by F. J. Furnivall. 2 pts. Rolls Series. London, 1887.

MORE, SIR THOMAS. *A Dialogue concerning Heresies* (1529). Edited by Thomas Lawter, Germain Marc' Hadour and Richard Marvis. In *The Complete Works of St Thomas More,* Vol. VI, pts 1 and 2. Yale, New Haven and London, 1981.

MUNRO, SIR DONALD. *A Description of the Western Isles of Scotland* (visited 1549). Included in *A Description of the Western Islands of Scotland. Circa 1695,* by Martin Martin. Edited by Donald J. Macleod. Stirling, 1934. (But Martin himself is quoted from the first edn of his *Description of the Western Islands,* London, 1703.)

MURRAY'S HANDBOOKS. *Handbook for Essex, Suffolk, Norfolk and Cambridgeshire.* (By Richard J. King.) London, 1870.
  Handbook for Travellers in Berks, Bucks, and Oxfordshire. London, 1860.

NICHOLS, REV. JOHN. *The History and Antiquities of the County of Leicester.* London, 1795–1811.

NORDEN, JOHN. *Speculi Britanniae Pars. A Topographical and Historical description of Cornwall* (written 1584). London, 1728.

PECK, FRANCIS. *The Survey and Antiquitie of the Towne of Stanford,* 1646. Continued to 1660 and enlarged in *Academia tertia Anglicana; or, the Antiquarian Annals of Stanford.* London, 1727.

PINNOCK, WILLIAM. *Pinnock's County Histories,* Vol. III: *The History and Topography of Huntingdonshire.* London, 1822.

RICHARDSON, M. A. *The Local Historian's Table Book, of Remarkable Occurrences, Historical Facts, Traditions ... &c., Connected with the Counties of Newcastle-upon-Tyne, Northumberland and Durham.* Legendary Division, 3 vols. London, Newcastle-upon-Tyne, 1843–6.

RISDON, TRISTRAM. *The Chorographical Description, or Survey, of the County of Devon* (1605–30). 2 pts. London, 1714.

ROBERT OF GLOUCESTER. *The Metrical Chronicle of Robert of Glouces-ter* (from Brutus to 1270). Edited by W. A. Wright. 2 vols. Rolls Series. London, 1887.

ROBY, JOHN. *Traditions of Lancashire*, First Series, 2 vols. London, 1829, Second Series, 2 vols. London, 1831.

ROGER OF WENDOVER. *Flores historiarum.* Translated by J. A. Giles as *Roger of Wendover's Flowers of History, AD 447–1235.* 2 vols. Bohn's Library. London, 1849.

SALMON, NATHANIEL. *The History of Hertfordshire.* London, 1728. *The History and Antiquities of Essex.* London, 1740.

SANDFORD, EDMUND. *A Cursory Relation of all the Antiquities and Familyes in Cumberland. by E. Sandford, circa 1675.* Edited by Chancellor Ferguson, Cumberland and Westmorland Anti-quarian and Archaeological Society Tract Series 4. London, Kendal, 1890.

SKINNER, REV. JOHN. *Ten Day's Tour through the Isle of Anglesea, December, 1802.* BL Add. MSS 33, 636.

STEVENSON, JOSEPH. *The Church Historians of England*, 5 vols in 8. London, 1853–8. Translations of: Vol. II. Pt 1, Florence of Worcester; Vol. III, Pt 1, William of Malmesbury; and see under WILLIAM OF NEWBURGH, Sources, p.537.

SYMONDS, RICHARD. 'Church notes concerning Oxfordshire, Worces-tershire and Berkshire, 1644.' BL Harley MS 965.

WARKWORTH, JOHN. *A Chronicle of the first thirteen years of the reign of King Edward the Fourth* (1461–74). Edited by James O. Halliwell. Camden Society, First Series, Vol. X. London, 1839.

WARTON, THOMAS. *The Poetical Works of ... T. W.* Fifth edition corrected and enlarged by R. Mant. 2 vols. Oxford, 1802.

WESTCOTE, THOMAS. *A view of Devonshire 1630, with a pedigree of its gentry.* Edited by George Oliver and Pitman Jones. Exeter, 1845.

WILLIAM OF MALMESBURY. See STEVENSON, J.

WOOD, JOHN. *Choir Gaure*. Oxford, 1747.

    An Essay towards a Description of Bath. 2nd edn corrected and enlarged. London, 1749.

YONGE (YOUNG), JAMES. *The Journal of James Yonge [1647–1721], Plymouth Surgeon*. Edited by F. N. L. Poynter. London, 1963.

I quote Shakespeare from the current Arden editions, published by Methuen & Co.; traditional ballads from F. J. Child, *The English and Scottish Popular Ballads*, 5 vols (Boston, 1882–98); and Old English spells from G. Storms, *Anglo-Saxon Magic* (The Hague, 1948). Place-name evidence is taken from *The Concise Oxford Dictionary of English Place-Names* by Eilert Ekwall, 4th edn (Oxford, 1960), and individual volumes in the County Place-Names series; and map references for Ancient Monuments from the *List of Ancient Monuments in England*, 3 vols (HMSO, 1977), and its equivalents for Wales (1975) and Scotland (1976).

Photo Credits

Cadbury Castle, Somerset. *Cambridge University Collection*

The Tristan Stone. *Janet and Colin Bord*

'Screaming Skull', Chilton Cantelo. *Robert Estall*

Glastonbury Tor. *Janet and Colin Bord*

The Hurlers, Bodmin Moor. *Janet and Colin Bord*

Wistman's Wood. *Robert Estall*

The Oxenham Omen, Zeal Monachorum. *British Library*

One of the Aldworth Giants. *British Library*

The Cerne Giant. *Cambridge University Collection*

Flower's Barrow Camp. *Cambridge University Collection*

The Giants' Dance: Stonehenge. *Janet and Colin Bord*

Wansdyke. *Cambridge University Collection*

Herne's Oak, the Home Park, Windsor. *British Library*

The lime avenue, Cuckfield Park. *Paul Spencer*

The tomb of Catigern: Kit's Coty House. *Mansell Collection*

The Long Man of Wilmington. *Crown copyright reserved*

The Knucker Hole. *Paul Spencer*

Tomb of Sir Robert de Shurland. *Paul Spencer*

The Bartlow Hills. *Photo: John Freeman & Co.*

Gogmagog and Corineus. *Guildhall Library*

Dick Whittington? *Gloucester City Museum and Art Gallery*

Tomb of Lady Anne Grimston. *Robert Estall*

Romano-British cult head. *Newport Museum and Art Gallery*

The Jerusalem Chamber, Westminster Abbey. *Jarrold*

Claw-marks of the Black Dog. *Janet and Colin Bord*

Bench-end, Hadleigh church. *National Monuments Record*

Bench-end, Swaffham. *National Monuments Record*

Seventeenth-century pargeting, Saffron Walden. *National Trust*

Wandlebury Camp. *Crown copyright reserved*

Boston Stump. *Janet and Colin Bord*

Parish church, Church Stowe. *Janet and Colin Bord*

Black Annis? *Janet and Colin Bord*

Grim, Havelok and Goldborough. *Great Grimsby Borough Council*

The Nine Stones of Harthill Moor. *Janet and Colin Bord*

Peak Cavern. *Mansell Collection*

Sir Thomas Holte. *Birmingham Museums and Art Gallery*

Guy's Cliffe. *Photo: Fiona French*

Earl Guy. *National Monuments Record*

Wayland in his smithy. *British Museum*

Effigy on the Bargates Almshouses. *Hereford and Worcester County Libraries*

Black Vaughan and Gethin the Terrible. *National Monuments Record*

North Capital, Holy Trinity Church. *National Monuments Record*

The notorious Drida cast adrift. *British Library*

Castell Dinas Bran. *Janet and Colin Bord*

Harold's Stones. *Janet and Colin Bord*

Llangorse Lake. *Janet and Colin Bord*

Moll Walbee's Stone. *Janet and Colin Bord.*

'A coat of gold.' *British Museum*

Boggart Hole Clough. *Manchester Public Library*

Thirteenth-century Syrian glass beaker. *Victoria and Albert Museum*

The Devil's Bridge. *National Monuments Record*

Pendragon Castle. *National Monuments Record*

'Peg O'Nelly's Well.' *British Library*

Castle Hill, Bishopton. *Janet and Colin Bord*

'Owd Nance.' *Jarrold*

Hylton Castle. *Society of Antiquaries*

The Sockburn Falchion. *Dean and Chapter of Durham*

Wade's Castle. *Photo: John Freeman & Co.*

Wade's Causeway. *Janet and Colin Bord*

The Dragon of Wantley. *Fortean Picture Library*

Fairies dancing. *Fortean Picture Library*

Cranshaws Tower. *Crown copyright: Royal Commission on Ancient Monuments, Scotland*

Culzean Castle. *National Trust for Scotland*

Edin's Hall. *Crown copyright: Royal Commission on Ancient Monuments, Scotland*

Hermitage Castle. *Crown copyright: Royal Commission on Ancient Monuments, Scotland*

Culsh Earth-house. *Janet and Colin Bord*

The Prentice Pillar. *Scottish Tourist Board*

Spedlin's Tower. *Photo: John Freeman & Co.*

Callanish standing-stones. *Gerald Ponting and Janet and Colin Bord*

The Dwarfie Stane. *Crown copyright: Royal Commission on Ancient Monuments, Scotland*

Glamis Castle. *Crown copyright: Royal Commission on Ancient Monuments, Scotland*

The Stone of Scone. *Jarrold*

The Soldier's Leap. *National Trust for Scotland*

Index of Places and Themes